INTERNATIONAL LAW

INTERNATIONAL LAW

by

MALCOLM N. SHAW, LL.M., Ph.D.

of Gray's Inn, Barrister

Ironsides Ray & Vials Professor of Law
University of Leicester

THIRD EDITION

CAMBRIDGE
GROTIUS PUBLICATIONS LIMITED
1991

SALES & GROTIUS PUBLICATIONS LTD.
ADMINISTRATION PO BOX 115, CAMBRIDGE CB3 9BP
     ENGLAND
FAX   0233 311032 (from abroad: 44+223+311032)

British Library Cataloguing in Publication Data

Shaw, Malcolm N. (Malcolm Nathan), 1947-
 International Law — 3rd ed.
 I. Title
 341

ISBN 0-949009-95-4

Typset by Afal, Cardiff

Printed in Great Britain by
Gomer Press, Llandysul, Dyfed

Cover: From a painting of the International Court of Justice by Prudence Lovell

TO MY WIFE, JUDITH
AND TO MY MOTHER, PAULETTE
AND IN MEMORY OF MY FATHER, BEN SHAW CBE
AND OF MY MOTHER-IN-LAW, DENISE AXELROD

TABLE OF CONTENTS

PREFACE

This is now the third edition of a work first published in 1977. It has been thoroughly revised since the last edition appeared in 1986 to take account of the accelerating pace of change within the international community, which is inevitably finding its reflection in international law. A new Chapter on International Environmental Law has been added as concerns over pollution and threats to the fragile structure of the earth begin to produce significant international institutional and legal responses. I have also been able to add significantly to certain areas, for example human rights law, jurisdictional immunities and the use of force. Additionally, a table of treaties now forms part of this work for the first time.

The rapidly changing nature of international relations noted above was underlined as this book was emerging from the presses by the failed coup in the USSR and the consequential reaction against the existing political structure of that state. Whether the Soviet Union will survive as a unitary state or dissolve into a series of independent units, or continue in some modified form of arrangement, is as yet unclear. What is certain is that the effects of these changes currently under way upon international relations generally and international law in particular are likely to be significant.

I would like to reiterate the gratitude expressed to Grotius Publications in the Preface to the second edition. It continues to be a pleasure to work with them and to be able to benefit from their expertise, enthusiasm and style. I am especially grateful to Mr Robin Pirrie for all his assistance and kindness, while I readily acknowledge the invaluable help of Mr John Adlam in the trying task of copy-editing and proof-reading. A particular debt is owed to Mr Eli Lauterpacht CBE, QC, Director of the Research Centre for International Law at the University of Cambridge, for his encouragement and assistance in the publication and development of this work.

Many of my colleagues, too numerous to acknowledge individually, have helped in the preparation of this edition by proffering their advice and suggestions. I remain very grateful for this, while happy to reassure them that all responsibility for the end product rests squarely with me. I am also pleased to acknowledge the receipt of a grant from the Research Board of the University of Leicester.

The Index and preliminary materials have been prepared by my wife Judith with her usual care and dedication. To Judith and my children, Talia, Ilan and Daniella, I owe much. They have borne the brunt of my travails and endured the inevitable pressures and done so in a caring and loving manner. Their support remains the indispensable foundation of this work.

Malcolm N. Shaw

Faculty of Law
University of Leicester
Summer 1991

TABLE OF CASES

TABLE OF TREATIES AND AGREEMENTS

TABLE OF ABBREVIATIONS

AC	Law Reports, Appeal Cases
AFDI	Annuaire Français de Droit International
AJIL	American Journal of International Law
All ER	All England Law Reports
ALR	Argus Law Reports
Annuaire	Annuaire de l'Institut de Droit International
BFSP	British and Foreign State Papers
Burr.	Burrow's Reports
BYIL	British Yearbook of International Law
Cal	California Reports
Cd., Cmd. or Cmnd.	UK Command Papers
CERD	Committee on the Elimination of Racial Discrimination
Ch.	Law Reports, Chancery Division
Cl. Ct.	US Court of Claims Reports
CLR	Commonwealth Law Reports
COMECON	Council for Mutual Economic Assistance
Cranch	Cranch Reports, United States Supreme Court
C.Rob.	C.Robinson's Admiralty Reports
Dall.	Dallas, Pennsylvania and United States Reports
DLR	Dominion Law Reports
Dod.	Dodson's Admiralty Reports
DUSPIL	Digest of US Practice in International Law
EC	European Communities
ECHR	European Convention on Human Rights
ECOSOC	Economic and Social Council
ECR	European Court Reports
ECSC	European Coal and Steel Community
EEC	European Economic Community
Encyclopedia	Encyclopedia of Public International Law
ER	English Reports
Euratom	European Atomic Energy Community
Ex.D.	Law Reports, Exchequer Division
Fam.	Law Reports, Family Division
FAO	Food and Agriculture Organisation
FCO	Foreign and Commonwealth Office
F.(J.)	Faculty of Advocates
F.Supp.	Federal Supplement
F.2d	Federal Reporter (Second Series)
GAOR	General Assembly Official Records
GDR	German Democratic Republic
HC Deb.	House of Commons Debates

HLC	House of Lords Reports (Clark)
HL Deb.	House of Lords Debates
HMSO	Her Majesty's Stationery Office
HR	Hague Academy of International Law, Recueil des Cours
HRJ	Human Rights Journal
HRLJ	Human Rights Law Journal
HRQ	Human Rights Quarterly
ICAO	International Civil Aviation Organisation
ICJ	International Court of Justice
ICLQ	International and Comparative Law Quarterly
ICRC	International Committee of the Red Cross
ILA	International Law Association
ILC	International Law Commission
ILM	International Legal Materials
ILO	International Labour Organisation
ILR	International Law Reports (incorporating the Annual Digest and Reports of Public International Law Cases)
Iran-US CTR	Iran-United States Claims Tribunal Reports
ITU	International Telecommunications Union
KB	Law Reports, King's Bench Division
LL. R	Lloyd's Law Reports
LNOJ	League of Nations Official Journal
LNTS	League of Nations Treaty Series
LQR	Law Quarterly Review
MLR	Modern Law Review
NATO	North Atlantic Treaty Organisation
NE	Northeastern Reporter
NILR	Netherlands International Law Review
NLM	National Liberation Movement
NQHR	Netherlands Quarterly of Human Rights
NY	New York Reports
NYS	New York Supplement
OAS	Organisation of American States
OAU	Organisation of African Unity
OECD	Organisation for Economic Co-operation and Development
OECS	Organisation of Eastern Caribbean States
P.	Law Reports, Probate, Divorce and Admiralty Division, 1891-
PAIGC	Partido Africano da Independencia da Guine e Cabo Verde

PASIL	Proceedings of the American Society of International Law
PCA	Permanent Court of Arbitration
PCIJ	Permanent Court of International Justice
PD	Law Reports, Probate, Divorce and Admiralty Division, 1875-90
Pet.	Peter's United States Supreme Court Reports
PLO	Palestine Liberation Organisation
QB	Law Reports, Queen's Bench Division
RIAA	United Nations Reports of International Arbitral Awards
SADR	Saharan Arab Democratic Republic
SC	Supreme Court
SCOR	Security Council Official Records
S. Ct.	Supreme Court Reporter
Stat.	United States Statutes at Large
TFSC	Turkish Federated State of Cyprus
UKMIL	United Kingdom Materials in International Law
UNCIO	United Nations Conference of International Organisation
UNESCO	United Nations Educational, Scientific and Cultural Organisation
UNJYB	United Nations Juridical Yearbook
UNTS	United Nations Treaty Series
US	United States Reports (Supreme Court)
USC	United States Code
USLW	United States Law Weekly
Va JIL	Virginia Journal of International Law
Ves. Jun.	Vesey Junior's Chancery Reports
Wheat	Wheaton, United States Supreme Court Reports
WHO	World Health Organisation
WLR	Weekly Law Reports
YBWA	Yearbook of World Affairs
ZaöRV	Zeitschrift für ausländisches öffentliches Recht und Völkerrecht

CHAPTER ONE

The Nature and Development of International Law

In the long march of mankind from the cave to the computer a central role has always been played by the idea of law – the idea that order is necessary and chaos inimical to a just and stable existence. Every society whether it be large or small, powerful or weak, has created for itself a framework of principles within which to develop. What can be done, what cannot be done, permissible acts, forbidden acts have all been spelt out within the consciousness of that community. Progress, with its inexplicable leaps and bounds, has always been based upon the group as men and women combine to pursue commonly accepted goals whether these be hunting animals, growing food or simply making money.

Law is that element which binds the members of the community together in their adherence to recognised values and standards. It is both permissive in allowing individuals to establish their own legal relations with rights and duties, as in the creation of contracts, and coercive, as it punishes those who infringe its regulations. Law consists of a series of rules regulating behaviour, and reflecting, to some extent, the ideas and preoccupations of the society within which it functions.

And so it is with what is termed international law, with the important difference that the principal subjects of international law are nation-states, not individual citizens. There are many contrasts between the law within a country (municipal law) and the law that operates outside and between states, international organisations and so on.

International law itself is divided into conflict of laws (or private international law as it is sometimes called) and public international law (usually just termed international law). The former deals with those cases, *within* particular legal systems, in which foreign elements obtrude raising questions as to the application of foreign law or the role of foreign courts.[1] For example, if two Englishmen make a contract in France to sell goods situated in Paris, an English court

---

[1] See e.g. Cheshire and North, *Private International Law*, 11th ed., 1987, and Morris and North, *Cases and Materials on Private International Law*, 1984.

would apply French law as regards the validity of that contract. By contrast, public international law is not simply an adjunct of a legal order, but a separate system altogether, and it is this field that shall be considered in this book.

It covers relations between states in all their myriad forms, from war to satellites, and regulates the operations of the many international institutions.

It may be universal or general, in which case the stipulated rules bind all the states (or practically all depending upon the nature of the rule) or regional, whereby a group of states linked geographically or ideologically may recognise special rules applying only to them, for example, the practice of diplomatic asylum that has developed to its greatest extent in Latin America.[2]

The rules of international law must be distinguished from what is called international comity, or practices such as saluting the flags of foreign warships at sea, which are implemented solely through courtesy and are not regarded as legally binding.[3] Similarly, the mistake of confusing international law with international morality must be avoided. While they may meet at certain points, the former discipline is a legal one both as regards its content and its form, while the concept of international morality is a branch of ethics. This does not mean, however, that international law can be divorced from its values.

In this chapter and the next, the characteristics of the international legal system and the historical and theoretical background necessary to a proper appreciation of the part to be played by the law in international law will be examined.

LAW AND POLITICS IN THE WORLD COMMUNITY

Probably the first reaction upon an introduction to international law is to question its legal quality. It is recalled that in practically every international dispute both sides proclaim their adherence to the principles of the system and declare that they are acting in accordance with its provisions. It is alleged, for example, that the other side has committed unprovoked aggression and the only suitable reaction is to follow the dictates of the rules governing

---

[2] See further *infra*, p.78.
[3] *North Sea Continental Shelf* cases, ICJ Reports, 1969, p.44; 41 *ILR*, p.29. See also Akehurst, "Custom as a Source of International Law", 47 *BYIL*, 1974-5, p.1.

self-defence or perhaps the principles of self-determination have been ignored and the values of international law must be upheld.

Again a state may have taken over certain foreign-owned enterprises and counter criticism by pleading national sovereignty and non-intervention in domestic affairs. The tendency is to become cynical because above all there is no independent institution able to determine the issue and give a final decision.

Virtually everybody who starts reading about international law does so having learned or absorbed something about the principal characteristics of ordinary or domestic law. What are those identifying marks? A recognised body to legislate or create laws, a hierarchy of courts with compulsory jurisdiction to settle disputes over such laws and an accepted system of enforcing those laws. Without a legislature, judiciary and executive, one cannot talk about a legal order.[4] How can one accept a universal system of international law therefore if this is the case?

International law has no legislature. True there is the General Assembly of the United Nations comprising delegates from all the member-states, but its resolutions are not legally binding on anybody save for certain of the organs of the United Nations for certain purposes.[5] There is no system of courts. The International Court of Justice does exist at The Hague but it can only decide cases when both sides agree[6] and it cannot ensure that its decisions are complied with. It is important but it is only peripheral to the international community. Above all there is no executive or governing entity. The Security Council of the United Nations, which was intended to have such a role in a sense, has been effectively constrained by the veto power of the five permanent members (USA, USSR, China, France and the United Kingdom).[7] Thus, if there is no identifiable institution either to establish rules, or clarify them or see that those who break them are punished, how can what is called international law be law?

It will, of course, be realised that the basis for this line of argument is the comparison of domestic law with international law, and the

---

[4] See generally, Dias, *Jurisprudence*, 4th ed., 1979; Hart, *The Concept of Law*, 1961 and Stein and Shand, *Legal Values in Western Society*, 1974.
[5] See article 17(1) of the United Nations Charter. See also Johnson, "The Effect of Resolutions of the General Assembly of the United Nations", 32 *BYIL*, 1955-6, p.97 and *infra*, Chapter 19.
[6] See article 36 of the Statute of the International Court of Justice and *infra*, Chapter 17.
[7] See Bowett, *The Law of International Institutions*, 4th ed., 1984 and *infra*, Chapter 19.

assumption of an analogy between the national system and the international order. And this is at the heart of all discussions about the nature of international law.

The English philosopher John Austin elaborated at the turn of the nineteenth century a theory of law based upon the notion of a sovereign issuing a command backed by a sanction or punishment. Since international law did not fit within that definition it was relegated to the category of 'positive morality'.[8] This concept has been criticised for oversimplifying and even confusing the true nature of law within a society and for over-emphasising the role of the sanction within the system by linking it to every rule.[9] This is not the place for a comprehensive summary of Austin's theory but the idea of coercion as an integral part of any legal order is a vital one that needs looking at in the context of international law.

THE ROLE OF FORCE

There is no unified system of sanctions[10] in international law in the sense that there is in municipal law, but there are circumstances in which the use of force is regarded as justified and legal. Within the United Nations system, sanctions may be imposed by the Security Council upon the determination of a threat to the peace, breach of the peace or act of aggression.[11] Such sanctions may be economic, for example those proclaimed in 1966 against Rhodesia,[12] or even military as in the Korean war in 1950,[13] or indeed both, as in 1990 against Iraq.[14]

[8] See Austin, *The Province of Jurisprudence Determined* (ed. Hart), 1954, pp.134-42.

[9] See e.g. Hart, *op. cit.*, Chapter X.

[10] See e.g. Reisman, "Sanctions and Enforcement" in *The Future of the International Legal Order* (eds. Black and Falk), 1971, p.273; Brierly, "Sanctions", 17 *Transactions of the Grotius Society*, 1932, p.68; Hart, *op. cit.*, pp.211-21; D'Amato, "The Neo-Positivist Concept of International Law", 59 *AJIL*, 1965, p.321; Fitzmaurice, "The Foundations of the Authority of International Law and the Problem of Enforcement", 19 *MLR*, 1956, p.1 and *The Effectiveness of International Decisions* (ed. Schwebel), 1971. See also *infra*, Chapter 2.

[11] Chapter VII of the United Nations Charter. See also Harris, *Cases and Materials on International Law*, 3rd ed., 1983, pp.680-81, and *infra* Chapter 18.

[12] Security Council resolution 221 (1966). Note also Security Council resolution 418 (1977) imposing a mandatory arms embargo on South Africa.

[13] Security Council resolutions of June 25, June 27 and July 7, 1950. See Bowett, *United Nations Forces*, 1964.

[14] Security Council resolutions 661 and 678 (1990). See *The Kuwait Crisis: Basic Documents* (eds. Lauterpacht, Greenwood, Weller and Bethlehem), 1991, pp.88 and 98. See also *infra*, Chapter 18.

Coercive action within the framework of the UN is rare because it requires co-ordination amongst the five permanent members of the Security Council and this obviously needs an issue not regarded by any of the great powers as a threat to their vital interests.

Korea was an exception and joint action could only be undertaken because of the fortuitous absence of the USSR from the Council as a protest at the seating of the Nationalist Chinese representatives.[15]

Apart from such institutional sanctions, one may note the bundle of rights to take violent action known as self-help.[16] This procedure to resort to force to defend certain rights is characteristic of primitive systems of law with blood-feuds, but in the domestic legal order such procedures and methods are now within the exclusive control of the established authority. States may use force in self-defence, if the object of aggression, and may take action in response to the illegal acts of other states. In such cases the states themselves decide whether to take action, and if so, the extent of their measures, and there is no supreme body to rule on their legality or otherwise, in the absence of an examination by the International Court of Justice, acceptable to both parties, although international law does lay down relevant rules.[17]

Accordingly those writers who put the element of force to the forefront of their theories face many difficulties in describing the nature, or rather the legal nature of international law with its lack of a coherent, recognised and comprehensive framework of sanctions. To see the sanctions of international law in the states' rights of self-defence and reprisals,[18] is to misunderstand the role of sanctions within a system because they are at the disposal of the states, not the system itself. Neither must it be forgotten that the current trend in international law is to restrict the use of force as far as possible, thus leading to the absurd result that the more force is controlled in international society, the less legal international law becomes.

Since one cannot discover the nature of international law by reference to a definition of law predicated upon sanctions, the

---

[15] See Luard, *A History of the United Nations*, Vol.I, The Years of Western Domination 1945-55, 1982, pp.229-74 and *infra*, Chapter 18.

[16] See Bowett, *Self-Defence in International Law*, 1958 and Brownlie, *International law and the Use of Force by States*, 1963.

[17] *Infra*, Chapter 18. See also Larkin, *Law Without Sanctions*, 1967.

[18] See e.g. Kelsen, *General Theory of Law and State*, 1946, p.328 *et seq*.

character of the international legal order has to be examined in order to seek to discover whether in fact states feel obliged to obey the rules of international law and if so, why. If, indeed, the answer to the first question is negative, that states do not feel the necessity to act in accordance with such rules, then there does not exist any system of international law worthy of the name.

THE INTERNATIONAL SYSTEM [19]

It has already been hinted that the key to the search lies within the unique attributes of the international system. While the legal structure within all but the most primitive societies is hierarchical and authority is vertical, rather like a pyramid with the sovereign person or unit in a position of supremacy on top, the international system is horizontal consisting of 160 or so independent states, all equal in legal theory (in that they all possess the characteristics of sovereignty) and recognising no one in authority over them. The law is above individuals in domestic systems, but international law only exists as between the states. Individuals only have the choice as to whether to obey the law or not. They do not create the law. That is done by specific institutions. In international law, on the other hand, it is the states themselves that create the law and obey or disobey it.[20] This, of course, has profound repercussions as regards the sources of law as well as the means for enforcing accepted legal rules.

International law, as will be shown in succeeding chapters, is primarily formulated by international agreements, which create rules binding upon the signatories, and customary rules, which are basically state practices recognised by the community at large as laying down patterns of conduct that have to be complied with.

However, it may be argued that since states themselves sign treaties and indulge in courses of action that they may or may not regard as legally obligatory, international law would appear to consist of a series of rules displayed as if on a market stall for states

---

[19] See Henkin, *How Nations Behave*, 2nd ed., 1979; Kaplan and Katzenbach, *The Political Foundations of International Law*, 1961; Jenks, *The Common Law of Mankind*, 1958; Friedmann, *The Changing Structure of International Law*, 1964, and Sheikh, *International Law and National Behaviour*, 1974.

[20] This leads Rosenne to refer to international law as a law of co-ordination, rather than, as in internal law, a law of subordination; *Practice and Methods of International Law*, 1984, p.2.

to pick and choose from. And if this is so, how can one identify international law with domestic law? Is it not merely an illusion behind which lurks the real regulator of world affairs – brute force?

Contrary to popular belief, states do observe international law, and violations are comparatively rare. However, such violations (like armed attacks and racial oppression) are well-publicised and strike at the heart of the system, the creation and preservation of international peace and justice. But just as incidents of murder, robbery and rape do occur within national legal orders without bringing down the whole edifice or stimulating citizens to deny that law exists, so analogously assaults upon international legal rules point up the weaknesses of the system without denigrating their validity or their necessity. Thus, despite the occasional gross violation the vast majority of the provisions of international law are followed.[21]

In the daily routine of international life, tens of thousands of agreements are observed and many customs are adhered to. The need is felt in the hectic interplay of world affairs for some kind of regulatory framework, for some kind of rules network within which the game can be played, and international law fulfils that requirement. States feel this necessity because it imports an element of stability and predictability into the situation.

Where countries are involved in a disagreement or a dispute, it is handy to have recourse to the rules of international law even if there are conflicting interpretations since at least there is a common frame of reference and one state will be aware of how the other state will develop its argument. They will both be talking a common language and this factor of communication is vital since misunderstandings occur so easily and often with tragic consequences. Where the antagonists dispute the understanding of a particular rule and adopt opposing stands as regards its implementation they are at least on the same wavelength and communicate by means of the same phrases. That is something. It is not everything, for it is a mistake as well as inaccurate to claim for international law more than it can possibly deliver. It can constitute a mutually understandable vocabulary book and suggest possible solutions which follow from

---

[21] See Morgenthau, *Politics Among Nations,* 5th ed., 1973, pp.290-1; Henkin, *op. cit.,* pp.46-49; Brierly, *The Outlook for International Law,* 1944, p.5 and Jessup, *A Modern Law of Nations,* 1948, pp.6-8.

a study of its principles. What it cannot do is solve every problem no matter how dangerous or complex merely by being there. International law has not yet been developed, if it ever will, to that particular stage and one should not exaggerate its capabilities while pointing to its positive features.

But what is to stop a state from simply ignoring international law when proceeding upon its chosen policy? Can a legal rule against aggression, for example, of itself prevail over political temptations? There is no international police force to prevent such an action, but there are a series of other considerations closely bound up with the character of international law which might well cause a potential aggressor to forbear.

There is the element of reciprocity at work and a powerful weapon it can be. States quite often do not pursue one particular course of action which might bring them short term gains, because it could disrupt the mesh of reciprocal tolerance which could very well bring long-term disadvantages. For example, states everywhere protect the immunity of foreign diplomats for not to do so would place their own officials abroad at risk.[22] Thus, it usually is, though of course it need not be, an inducement to states to act reasonably and moderate demands in the expectation that this will similarly encourage other states to act reasonably and so avoid confrontations. Because the rules can ultimately be changed by states altering their patterns of behaviour and causing one custom to supersede another, or by mutual agreement, a certain definite reference to political life is retained. But the point must be made that a state, after weighing up all possible alternatives, might very well feel that the only method to protect its vital interests would involve a violation of international law and that responsibility would just have to be taken. Where survival is involved international law may take second place.

Another significant factor is the advantages, or "rewards", that may occur in certain situations from an observance of international law. It may encourage friendly or neutral states to side with one country involved in a conflict rather than its opponent, and even take a more active role than might otherwise have been the case. In many ways, it is an appeal to public opinion for support and all states employ this tactic.

---

[22] See *Case Concerning United States Diplomatic and Consular Staff in Teheran*, ICJ Reports, 1980, p.3; 61 *ILR*, p.502.

In many ways, it reflects the esteem that law is held in. The Soviets made considerable use of legal arguments in their effort to establish their non-liability to contribute towards the peace-keeping operations of the United Nations[23] and the Americans too, justified their activities with regard to Cuba[24] and Vietnam[25] by reference to international law. In some cases it may work and bring considerable support in its wake, in many cases it will not, but in any event the very fact that all states do it is a constructive sign.

A further element worth mentioning in this context is the constant formulation of international business in characteristically legal terms. Points of view and disputes, in particular, are framed legally with references to precedent, international agreements and even the opinions of juristic authors. Claims are pursued with regard to the rules of international law and not in terms of, for example, morality or ethics.[26] This has brought into being a class of officials throughout governmental departments, in addition to those working in international institutions, versed in international law and carrying on the everyday functions of government in a law-orientated way. Many writers have, in fact, emphasised the role of officials in the actual functioning of law and the influence they have upon the legal process.[27]

Having come to the conclusion that states do observe international law and will usually only violate it on an issue regarded as vital to their interests, the question arises as to the basis of this sense of obligation. The nineteenth century with its business-orientated philosophy stressed the importance of the contract, as the legal basis of an agreement freely entered into by both (or all) sides, and this influenced the theory of consent in international law.[28] States were independent, and free agents, and accordingly they could only be bound with their own consent. There was no authority in existence able theoretically or practically to impose rules upon the various nation-states. This approach found its extreme expression in the

[23] See *Certain Expenses of the United Nations*, ICJ Reports, 1962, p.151; 34 *ILR*, p.281 and Higgins, *United Nations Peace-Keeping; Documents and Commentary*, 4 vols., 1969-81.

[24] See e.g. Chayes, *The Cuban Missile Crisis*, 1974, and Henkin, *op. cit.*, pp.279-302.

[25] See e.g. *The Vietnam War and International Law* (ed. Falk), 4 vols., 1968-76; Moore, *Law and the Indo-China War*, 1972 and Henkin, *op. cit.*, pp.303-12.

[26] See Hart, *op. cit.*, p.223.

[27] See e.g. McDougal, Lasswell and Reisman, "The World Constitutive Process of Authoritative Decision" in *International Law Essays* (eds. McDougal and Reisman), 1981, p.191.

[28] See Friedmann, *Legal Theory*, 5th ed., 1967, pp.573-76.

theory of auto-limitation, or self-limitation, which declared that states could only be obliged to comply with international legal rules if they had first agreed to be so obliged.[29]

Nevertheless, this theory is most unsatisfactory as an account of why international law is regarded as binding or even as an explanation of the international legal system.[30] To give one example, there are about 100 states that have come into existence since the end of the Second World War and by no stretch of the imagination can it be said that such states have consented to all the rules of international law formed prior to their establishment. It could be argued that by 'accepting independence', states consent to all existing rules, but to take this view relegates consent to the role of a mere fiction.[31]

This theory also fails as an adequate explanation of the international legal system, because it does not take into account the tremendous growth in international institutions and the network of rules and regulations that have emerged from them within the last generation.

To accept consent as the basis for obligation in international law begs the question as to what happens when consent is withdrawn. The state's reversal of its agreement to a rule does not render that rule optional or remove from it its aura of legality. It merely places that state in breach of its obligations under international law if that state proceeds to act upon its decision. Indeed, the principle that agreements are binding (*pacta sunt servanda*) upon which all treaty law must be based cannot itself be based upon consent.[32]

One current approach to this problem is to refer to the doctrine of consensus.[33] This reflects the influence of the majority in creating new norms of international law and the acceptance by other states of such new rules. It attempts to put into focus the change of emphasis that is beginning to take place from exclusive concentration upon the nation-state to a consideration of the developing forms of international co-operation where such concepts as consent and sanction are inadequate to explain what is happening.

[29] E.g. Jellinek, *Allgemeine Rechtslehre*, 1905.
[30] See also Hart, *op. cit.*, pp.219-20.
[31] See further *infra*, p.78.
[32] See *infra*, Chapter 3.
[33] See e.g. D'Amato, "On Consensus", 8 *Canadian Year Book of International Law*, 1970, p.104. Note also the "gentleman's agreement on consensus" in the Third UN Conference on the Law of the Sea: see Sohn, "Voting Procedures in United Nations Conferences for the Codification of International Law", 69 *AJIL*, 1975, p.318 and UN Doc.A/Conf.62/WP.2.

THE FUNCTION OF POLITICS

It is clear that there can never be a complete separation between law and policy. No matter what theory of law or political philosophy is professed, the inextricable bonds linking law and politics must be recognised.

Within developed societies a distinction is made between the formulation of policy and the method of its enforcement. In the United Kingdom, Parliament legislates while the courts adjudicate and a similar division is maintained in the United States between the Congress and the courts system. The purpose of such divisions, of course, is to prevent a concentration of too much power within one branch of government. Nevertheless, it is the political branch which makes laws and in the first place creates the legal system. Even within the hierarchy of courts, the judges have leeway in interpreting the law and in the last resort make decisions from amongst a number of alternatives.[34] This position, however, should not be exaggerated because a number of factors operate to conceal and lessen the impact of politics upon the legal process. Foremost amongst these is the psychological element of tradition and the development of the so-called 'law-habit'.[35] A particular legal atmosphere has been created, which is buttressed by the political system and recognises the independent existence of law institutions and methods of operation characterised as 'just' or 'legal'. In most countries overt interference with the juridical process would be regarded as an attack upon basic principles and hotly contested. The use of legal language and accepted procedures together with the pride of the legal profession reinforce the system and emphasise the degree of distance maintained between the legislative-executive organs and the judicial structure.[36]

However, when one looks at the international legal scene the situation changes. The arbiters of the world order are, in the last resort, the states and they both make the rules (ignoring for the moment the secondary, if growing, field of international organisations) and interpret and enforce them.

[34] See e.g. Dworkin, *Taking Rights Seriously*, 1977.
[35] See e.g. Llewellyn, *The Common Law Tradition*, 1960, and generally Lloyd, *Introduction to Jurisprudence*, 4th ed., 1979.
[36] See Stein and Shand, *op. cit.*

While it is possible to discern an 'international legal habit' amongst governmental and international officials, the machinery necessary to enshrine this does not exist.

Politics is much closer to the heart of the system than is perceived within national legal orders, and power much more in evidence.[37] The interplay of law and politics in world affairs is much more complex and difficult to unravel, and signals a return to the earlier discussion as to why states comply with international rules. Power politics stresses competition, conflict and supremacy and adopts as its core the struggle for survival and influence.[38] International law aims for harmony and the regulation of disputes. It attempts to create a framework, no matter how rudimentary, which can act as a kind of shock-absorber clarifying and moderating claims and endeavouring to balance interests. In addition, it sets out a series of principles declaring how states should behave. Just as any domestic community must have a background of ideas and hopes to aim at even if few can be or are ever attained, so the international community, too, must bear in mind its ultimate values.

International law cannot be a source of instant solutions to problems of conflict and confrontation because of its own inherent weaknesses in structure and content. To fail to recognise this encourages a utopian approach which when faced with reality will fail. On the other hand, the cynical attitude with its obsession with brute power is equally inaccurate, if more depressing.

It is the medium road, recognising the strength and weakness of international law and pointing out what it can achieve and what it cannot, which offers the best hope. Man seeks order, welfare and justice not only within the state in which he lives, but also within the international system in which he lives.

HISTORICAL DEVELOPMENT[39]

The foundations of international law (or the law of nations) as it is understood today lie firmly in the development of western culture and political organisation.

[37] See generally Henkin, *op. cit.*

[38] See Schwarzenberger, *Power Politics*, 3rd ed., 1964 and *International Law*, vol.1, 3rd ed., 1957; Morgenthau, *Politics Among Nations*, 4th ed., 1967.

[39] See in particular Nussbaum, *A Concise History of the Law of Nations*, 1962; *Encyclopedia of Public International Law*, vol.7, 1984, pp.127-273 and Verzijl, *International Law in Historical Perspective*, 10 vols., 1968-79. See also Cassese, *International Law in a Divided World*, 1986.

The growth of European notions of sovereignty and the independent nation-state required an acceptable method whereby inter-state relations could be conducted in accordance with commonly accepted standards of behaviour, and international law filled the gap. But although the law of nations took root and flowered with the sophistication of Renaissance Europe, the seeds of this particular hybrid plant are of far older lineage. They reach far back into history.

Early Origins

While the modern international system can be traced back some four hundred years, certain of the basic concepts of international law can be discerned in political relationships thousands of years ago. Around 2100 BC, for instance, a solemn treaty was signed between the rulers of Lagash and Umma, the city-states situated in the area known to historians as Mesopotamia. It was inscribed on a stone block and concerned the establishment of a defined boundary to be respected by both sides under pain of alienating a number of Sumerian gods.[40] The next major instance known of an important, binding, international treaty is that concluded over a thousand years later between Rameses II of Egypt and the king of the Hittites for the establishment of eternal peace and brotherhood.[41] Other points covered in that agreement signed, it would seem, at Kadesh, north of Damascus, included respect for each other's territorial integrity, the termination of a state of aggression and the setting up of a form of defensive alliance.

Since that date many agreements between the rival Middle Eastern powers were concluded, usually aimed at embodying in a ritual form a state of subservience between the parties or attempting to create a political alliance to contain the influence of an over-powerful empire.[42]

The role of ancient Israel must also be noted. A universal ethical stance coupled with rules relating to warfare were handed down to other peoples and religions and the demand for justice and a fair

---

[40] Nussbaum, *op. cit.,* pp.1-2.

[41] *Ibid.* See also *Encyclopedia of Public International Law,* vol.7, 1984, p.133.

[42] Preiser emphasises that the era between the 17th and 15th centuries BC witnessed something of a competing state system involving five independent (at various times) states: *ibid.,* pp.133-34.

system of law founded upon strict morality permeated the thought and conduct of subsequent generations.[43]

For example, the Prophet Isaiah declared that sworn agreements, even where made with the enemy, must be performed.[44] Peace and social justice were the keys to man's existence, not power.

After much neglect, there is now more consideration of the cultures and standards evolved, before the birth of Christ, in the Far East, in the Indian[45] and Chinese[46] civilisations. Many of the Hindu rules displayed a growing sense of morality and generosity and the Chinese empire devoted much thought to harmonious relations between its constituent parts. Regulations controlling violence and the behaviour of varying factions with regard to innocent civilians were introduced and ethical values instilled in the education of the ruling classes. In times of Chinese dominance, a regional tributary-states system operated which fragmented somewhat in times of weakness, but this remained culturally alive for many centuries.

However, the predominant approach of ancient civilisations was geographically and culturally restricted.

There was no conception of an international community of states co-existing within a defined framework. The scope for any "international law" of states was extremely limited and all that one can point to is the existence of certain ideals, such as the sanctity of treaties, which have continued to this day as important elements in society. But the notion of a universal community with its ideal of world order was not in evidence.

The era of classical Greece, from about the sixth century BC and

---

[43] See Weil, "Le Judaisme et le Développement du Droit International", 151 *HR*, p.253 and Rosenne, "The Influence of Judaism on International Law", *Nederlands Tijdschrift voor Internationaal Recht*, 1958, p.119.

[44] See Nussbaum, *op. cit.*, p.3.

[45] *Ibid.* See also Alexandrowicz, *An Introduction to the History of the Law of Nations in the East Indies*, 1967 and "The Afro-Asian World and the Law of Nations (Historical Aspects)", 123 *HR*, p.117; Chatterjee, *International Law and Inter-State Relations in Ancient India*, 1958 and Nagendra Singh, "The Distinguishing Characteristics of the Concept of the Law of Nations as it Developed in Ancient India", *Liber Amicorum for Lord Wilberforce* (eds. Bos and Brownlie), 1987, p.91.

[46] Nussbaum, *op. cit.*, p.4. See also Gong, *The Standard of 'Civilisation' in International Society*, 1984, pp.130-63 and *ibid.*, pp.164-200 with regard to Japan and *ibid.*, pp.201-37 with regard to Siam; Hsu, *China's Entrance into the Family of Nations*, 1960, and Iriye, "The Principles of International law in the Light of Confucian Doctrine", 120 *HR*, p.1.

onwards for a couple of hundred years, has, one must note, been of overwhelming significance for European thought.

Its critical and rational turn of mind, its constant questioning and analysis of man and nature and its love of argument and debate were spread throughout Europe and the Mediterranean world by the Roman empire which adopted Hellenic culture wholesale, and penetrated western consciousness with the Renaissance. However, Greek awareness was limited to their own competitive city-states and colonies. Those of different origin were barbarians not deemed worthy of association.

The value of Greece in a study of international law lies partly in the philosophical, scientific and political analyses bequeathed to mankind and partly in the fascinating state of inter-relationship built up within the Hellenistic world.[47]

Numerous treaties linked the city-states together in a network of commercial and political associations.

Rights were often granted to the citizens of the states in each other's territories and rules regarding the sanctity and protection of diplomatic envoys developed. Certain practices were essential before the declaration of war and the horrors of war were somewhat ameliorated by the exercise, for example, of religious customs regarding sanctuaries. But no overall moral approach similar to those emerging from Jewish and Hindu thought, particularly, evolved. No sense of a world community can be traced to Greek ideology in spite of the growth of Greek colonies throughout the Mediterranean area. This was left to the able administrators of the Roman Empire.[48]

The Romans had a profound respect for organisation and the law.[49] The law knitted together their empire and constituted a vital source of reference for every inhabitant of the far flung domain. The early Roman law (the *jus civile*) applied only to Roman citizens. It was formalistic and hard and reflected the status of a small, unsophisticated society rooted in the soil.

It was totally unable to provide a relevant background for an expanding, developing nation. This need was served by the creation and progressive augmentation of the *jus gentium*. This provided

[47] Nussbaum, *op. cit.*, pp.5-9. See also Ténékidès, "Droit International et Communautés Fédérales dans la Grèce des Cités", 90 *HR*, p.469, and *Encyclopaedia of Public International Law*, vol. 7, 1984, pp.154-56.

[48] *Ibid.*, pp.136-39 and Nussbaum, *op. cit.*, pp.10-16.

[49] See e.g. Jolowicz, *Historical Introduction to Roman Law*, 3rd ed., 1972.

simplified rules to govern the relations between foreigners, and between foreigners and citizens. The instrument through which this particular system evolved was the official known as the Praetor Peregrinus, whose function it was to oversee all legal relationships including bureaucratic and commercial matters, within the empire.

The progressive rules of the *jus gentium* gradually overrode the narrow *jus civile* until the latter system ceased to exist. Thus, the *jus gentium* became the common law of the Roman Empire and was deemed to be of universal application.

It is this all-embracing factor which so strongly distinguishes the Roman from the Greek experience, although, of course, there was no question of the acceptance of other nations on a basis of equality and the *jus gentium* remained a "national law" for the Roman Empire.

One of the most influential of Greek concepts taken up by the Romans was the idea of Natural Law.[50] This was formulated by the Stoic philosophers of the third century BC and their theory was that it constituted a body of rules of universal relevance. Such rules were rational and logical and because the ideas and precepts of the "law of nature" were rooted in human intelligence, it followed that such rules could not be restricted to any nation or any group but were of world-wide relevance. This element of universality is basic to modern doctrines of international law and the Stoic elevation of human powers of logical deduction to the supreme pinnacle of "discovering" the law foreshadows the rational philosophies of the west. As well as being a fundamental concept in legal theory, Natural Law is vital to an understanding of international law, as well as being an indispensible precursor to contemporary concern with human rights.

Certain Roman philosophers incorporated those Greek ideas of Natural Law into their own legal theories, often as a kind of ultimate justification of the *jus gentium*, which was deemed to enshrine rational principles common to all civilised nations.

However, the law of nature was held to have an existence over and above that of the *jus gentium*.

This led to much confusion over the exact relationship between the two ideas and different Roman lawyers came to different conclusions as to their identity and characteristics. The important

---

[50] See e.g. Lloyd, *op. cit.*, pp.79-169.

factors though that need to be noted are the theories of the universality of law and the rational origins of legal rules that were founded, theoretically at least, not on superior force but on superior reason.

The classical rules of Roman law were collated in the *Corpus Juris Civilis*, a compilation of legal material by a series of Byzantine philosophers completed in 534 AD.[51] Such a collection was to be invaluable when the darkness of the early Middle Ages, following the Roman collapse, began gradually to evaporate. For here was a body of developed laws ready made and awaiting transference to an awakening Europe.

At this stage reference must be made to the growth of Islam.[52] Its approach to international relations and law was predicated upon a state of hostility towards the non-Moslem world and the concept of unity, Dar al-Islam, as between Moslem countries. Generally speaking, humane rules of warfare were developed and the "peoples of the book" (Jews and Christians) were treated better than non-believers, although in an inferior position to Moslems. Once the period of conquest was over and power was consolidated, norms governing conduct with non-Moslem states began to develop. The law dealing with diplomats was founded upon notions of hospitality and safety (*aman*), while rules governing international agreements grew out of the concept of respecting promises made.[53]

The Middle Ages and the Renaissance

The Middle Ages were characterised by the authority of the organised Church and the comprehensive structure of power that it commanded.[54] All Europe was of one religion, and the ecclesiastical law applied to all, notwithstanding tribal or regional affiliations. For much of the period, there were struggles between the religious authorities and the rulers of the Holy Roman Empire.

---

[51] See generally with regard to Byzantium, De Taube, "L'Apport de Byzance au Développement du Droit International Occidental", 67 *HR*, p.233 and Verosta, "International Law in Europe & Western Asia between 100-650 AD", 113 *HR*, p.489.

[52] See e.g. Draz, "Le Droit International Public et l'Islam", 5 *Revue Egyptienne de Droit International*, p.17; Khadduri, "Islam and the Modern Law of Nations", 50 *AJIL*, p.358 and *War and Peace in the Law of Islam*, 2nd ed., 1962; and Mahmassani, "The Principles of International Law in the Light of Islamic Doctrine", 117 *HR*, p.205.

[53] See *Encyclopedia, op. cit.*, pp.141-42, and Nussbaum, *op. cit.*, pp.51-54.

[54] *Ibid.*, pp.17-23 and *Encyclopedia, op. cit.*, pp.143-49.

These conflicts were eventually resolved in favour of the Papacy, but the victory over secularism proved of relatively short duration. Religion and a common legacy derived from the Roman Empire were strongly unifying influences, while political and regional rivalries were not. But before a recognised system of international law could be created, social changes were essential.

Of particular importance during this era was the authority of the Holy Roman Empire and the supranational character of canon law.[55] Nevertheless, commercial and maritime law developed apace. English law established the *Law Merchant*, a code of rules covering foreign traders and this was declared to be of universal application.[56]

Throughout Europe, mercantile courts were set up to settle disputes between tradesmen at the various fairs, and while it is not possible to state that a Continental *Law Merchant* came into being, a network of common regulations and practices weaved its way across the commercial fabric of Europe and constituted an embryonic international trade law.[57]

Similarly, maritime customs began to be accepted throughout the Continent. Founded upon the Rhodian Sea Law, a Byzantine work, many of whose rules were enshrined in the Rolls of Oleron in the twelfth century, and other maritime textbooks, a series of commonly applied customs relating to the sea permeated the naval powers of the Atlantic and Mediterranean coasts.[58]

Such commercial and maritime codes while at this stage merely expressions of national legal systems were amongst the forerunners of international law because they were created and nurtured upon a backcloth of cross-national contacts and reflected the need for rules that would cover international situations.

Such rules, growing out of the early Middle Ages, constituted the seeds of international law, but before they could flourish, European thought had first to be developed by that intellectual explosion known as the Renaissance.

[55] Note in particular the influence of the Church on the rules governing warfare and the binding nature of agreements: see Nussbaum, *op. cit.*, pp.17-18 and *Encyclopedia, op. cit.*, pp.146-47.

[56] See Holdsworth, *A History of English Law*, vol.5, 1924, pp.60-63.

[57] *Ibid.*, pp.63-129.

[58] Nussbaum, *op. cit.*, pp.29-31. Note also the influence of the Consolato del Mare, composed in Barcelona in the mid-fourteenth century and the Maritime Code of Wisby (approx. 1407) followed by the Hanseatic League.

This complex of ideas changed the face of European society and ushered in the modern era of scientific humanistic and individualistic thought.[59]

The collapse of the Byzantine Empire centred on Constantinople before the Turkish armies in 1453 drove many Greek scholars to seek sanctuary in Italy and enliven Europe's cultural life. The introduction of printing during the fifteenth century provided the means to disseminate knowledge, and the undermining of feudalism in the wake of economic growth and the rise of the merchant classes provided the background to the new inquiring attitudes taking shape.

Europe's developing self-confidence manifested itself in a sustained drive overseas for wealth and luxury items. By the end of the fifteenth century, the Arabs had been ousted from the Iberian peninsula and the Americas reached.

The rise of the nation-states of England, France and Spain in particular characterised the process of the creation of territorially consolidated independent units, in theory and doctrine, as well as in fact. This led to a higher degree of interaction between sovereign entities and thus the need to regulate such activities in a generally acceptable fashion. The pursuit of political power and supremacy became overt and recognised, as Machiavelli's *The Prince* (1513) demonstrated.

The city-states of Italy struggled for supremacy and the Papacy too, became a secular power. From these hectic struggles emerged many of the staples of modern international life; diplomacy, statesmanship, the theory of the balance of power and the idea of a community of states.[60]

Notions such as these are immediately appreciable and one can identify with the various manoeuvres for political supremacy. Alliances, betrayals, manipulations of state institutions and the drive for power are not unknown to us. We recognise the roots of our society.

It was the evolution of the concept of an international community of separate, sovereign, if competing states, that marks the beginning of what is understood by international law. The Renaissance bequeathed the prerequisites of independent, critical thought and

[59] See e.g. Friedmann, *op. cit.*, footnote 19, pp.114-16.
[60] See e.g. Mattingley, *Renaissance Diplomacy*, 1955.

a humanistic, secular approach to life as well as the political framework for the future. But it is the latter factor which is vital to the subsequent growth of international law. The Reformation and the European religious wars that followed emphasised this, as did the growing power of the nations. In many ways these wars marked the decline of a continental system founded on religion and the birth of a continental system founded on the supremacy of the state.

Throughout these countries the necessity was felt for a new conception of human as well as state relationships. This search was precipitated, as has been intimated, by the decline of the Church and the rise of what might be termed "free-thinking". The theory of international law was naturally deeply involved in this reappraisal of political life and it was tremendously influenced by the rediscovery of Greco-Roman ideas. The Renaissance stimulated a rebirth of Hellenic studies and ideas of Natural Law, in particular, became popular.

Thus, a distinct value-system to underpin international relations was brought into being and the law of nations was heralded as part of the universal law of nature.

With the rise of the modern state and the emancipation of international relations, the doctrine of sovereignty emerged. This concept, first analysed systematically in 1576 in the *Six Livres de la République* by Jean Bodin, was intended to deal with the structure of authority within the modern state. Bodin, who based his study upon his perception of the politics of Europe rather than on a theoretical discussion of absolute principles, emphasised the necessity for a sovereign power within the state that would make the laws. While such a sovereign could not be bound by the laws he himself instituted, he was subject to the laws of God and of nature.[61]

The idea of the sovereign as supreme legislator was in the course of time transmuted into the principle which gave the state supreme power vis-à-vis other states. The state was regarded as being above the law. Such notions as these formed the intellectual basis of the line of thought known as positivism which will be discussed later.[62]

The early theorists of international law were deeply involved with the ideas of Natural Law and used them as the basis of their

---

[61] See Gardot, "Jean Bodin — Sa Place Parmi les Fondateurs du Droit International", 50 *HR*, p.549.
[62] *Infra*, p.23.

philosophies. Included within that complex of Natural Law principles from which they constructed their theories was the significant merging of Christian and Natural Law ideas that occurred in the philosophy of St. Thomas Aquinas.[63] He maintained that Natural Law formed part of the law of God, and was the participation by rational creatures in the Eternal Law. It complemented that part of the Eternal Law which had been divinely revealed. Reason, declared Aquinas, was the essence of man and thus must be involved in the ordering of life according to the divine will. Natural Law was the fount of moral behaviour as well as of social and political institutions and it led to a theory of conditional acceptance of authority with unjust laws being unacceptable. Aquinas' views of the late thirteenth century can be regarded as basic to an understanding of present Catholic attitudes, but should not be confused with the later interpretation of Natural Law which stressed the concepts of natural rights.

It is with such an intellectual background that Renaissance scholars approached the question of the basis and justification of a system of international law. Maine, a British historical lawyer, wrote that the birth of modern international law was the grandest function of the law of nature and while that is arguable, the point must be taken.[64] International law began to emerge as a separate topic to be studied within itself, although derived from the principles of Natural Law.

The Founders of Modern International Law

The essence of the new approach to international law can be traced back to the Spanish philosophers of that country's Golden Age.[65] The leading figure of this school was *Francisco Vitoria,* Professor of Theology at the University of Salamanca, (1480-1546). His lectures were preserved by his students and published posthumously. He demonstrated a remarkably progressive attitude for his time towards the Spanish conquest of the South American Indians and contrary to the views prevalent until then, maintained that the Indian peoples

---

[63] *Summa Theologia*, English ed., 1927.

[64] *Ancient Law*, 1861, pp.56 and 64-66.

[65] Note Preiser's view that "[t]here was hardly a single important problem of international law until the middle of the 17th century which was not principally a problem of Spain and the allied Habsburg countries": *Encyclopedia, op. cit.,* p.150. See also Nussbaum, *op. cit.,* pp.79-93.

should be regarded as nations with their own legitimate interests. War against them could only be justified on the grounds of a just cause. International law was founded on the universal law of nature and this meant that non-Europeans must be included within its ambit.

However, Vitoria by no means advocated the recognition of the Indian nations as equal to the Christian states of Europe. For him, opposing the work of the missionaries in the territories was a just reason for war, and he adopted a rather extensive view as to the rights of the Spaniards in South America. Vitoria was no liberal and indeed acted on behalf of the Spanish Inquisition, but his lectures did mark a step forward in the right direction.[66]

Suarez, (1548-1617), was a Jesuit and Professor of Theology and deeply immersed in medieval culture. He noted that the obligatory character of international law was based upon Natural Law, while its substance derived from the Natural Law rule of carrying out agreements entered into.[67]

From a totally different background but equally, if not more, influential was *Alberico Gentili*, (1552-1608). He was born in Northern Italy and fled to England to avoid persecution, having converted to Protestantism. In 1598 his *De Jure Belli* was published.[68] It is a comprehensive discussion of the law of war and contains a valuable section on the law of treaties. Gentili, who became a professor at Oxford, has been called the originator of the secular school of thought in international law and he minimised the hitherto significant theological theses.

It is, however, *Hugo Grotius*, a Dutch scholar, who towers over this period and has been celebrated, if a little exaggeratedly, as the father of international law. He was born in 1583 and was the supreme Renaissance man. A scholar of tremendous learning, he mastered history, theology, mathematics and the law.[69]

His primary work was the *De Jure Belli ac Pacis*, written during

---

[66] *Ibid.*, pp.79-84 and *Encyclopedia*, pp.151-52. See also Vitoria, *De Indis et de Jure Belli Relectiones*, Classics of International Law, 1917 and Scott, *The Spanish Origin of International Law, Francisco de Vitoria and his Law of Nations*, 1934.

[67] Nussbaum, *op. cit.*, pp.84-91. See also *ibid.*, pp.92-93 regarding the work of Ayala (1548-84).

[68] *Ibid.*, pp.94-101. See also Van der Molen, *Alberico Gentili and the Development of International Law*, 2nd ed., 1968.

[69] Nussbaum, *op. cit.*, pp.102-14. See also Knight, *The Life and Works of Hugo Grotius*, 1925 and *Commemoration of the Fourth Century of the Birth of Grotius* (various articles), 182 *HR*, pp.371-470.

1623 and 1624. It is an extensive work and includes rather more devotion to the exposition of private law notions than would seem appropriate today. He refers both to Vitoria and Gentili and the latter was of special influence with regard to many matters, particularly organisation of material.

Grotius finally excised theology from international law and emphasised the irrelevance in such a study of any conception of a divine law. He remarked that the law of nature would be valid even if there were no God. A statement which, although suitably clothed in religious protestation, was extremely daring. The law of nature now reverted to being founded exclusively on reason. Justice was part of man's social make-up and thus not only useful but essential. Grotius conceived of a comprehensive system of international law and his work rapidly became a university textbook. However, in many spheres he followed well-trodden paths. He retained the theological distinction between a just and an unjust war, a notion that was soon to disappear from treatises on international law, but which in some way underpins modern approaches to aggression, self-defence and liberation.

One of his most enduring opinions consists in his proclamation of the freedom of the seas. The Dutch scholar opposed the "closed seas" concept of the Portuguese that was later elucidated by the English writer John Selden[70] and emphasised instead the principle that the nations could not appropriate to themselves the high seas. They belonged to all. It must, of course, be mentioned, parenthetically, that this theory happened to accord rather nicely with prevailing Dutch ideas as to free trade and the needs of an expanding commercial empire.

However, this merely points up what must not be disregarded, namely that concepts of law as of politics and other disciplines are firmly rooted in the world of reality, and reflect contemporary preoccupations. No theory develops in a vacuum, but is conceived and brought to fruition in a definite cultural and social environment. To ignore this is to distort the theory itself.

Positivism and Naturalism

Following Grotius, but by no means divorced from the thought of previous scholars, a split can be detected and two different

---

[70] In *Mare Clausum Sive de Dominio Maris,* 1635.

schools identified. On the one hand the "naturalist" school, exemplified by *Samuel Pufendorf*, (1632-1694),[71] who attempted to identify international law completely with the law of nature and on the other hand the exponents of "positivism", who distinguished between international law and Natural Law and emphasised practical problems and current state practices. Pufendorf regarded Natural Law as a moralistic system, and misunderstood the direction of modern international law by denying the validity of the rules about custom. He also refused to acknowledge treaties as in any way relevant to a discussion of the basis of international law. Other "naturalists" echoed those sentiments in minimising or ignoring the actual practices of states in favour of a theoretical construction of absolute values that seemed slowly to drift away from the complexities of political reality.

One of the principal initiators of the positivist school was Richard Zouche, (1590-1660), who lived at the same time as Pufendorf, but in England.[72] While completely dismissing Natural Law he paid scant regard to the traditional doctrines. His concern was with specific situations and his book contains many examples from the recent past. He elevated the law of peace above a systematic consideration of the law of war and eschewed theoretical expositions.

In similar style Bynkershoek, (1673-1743), stressed the importance of modern practice, and virtually ignored Natural Law. He made great contributions to the developing theories of the rights and duties of neutrals in war, and after careful studies of the relevant facts decided in favour of the freedom of the seas.[73]

The positivist approach, like much of modern thought, was derived from the empirical method adopted by the Renaissance. It was concerned not with an edifice of theory structured upon deductions from absolute principles, but rather with viewing events as they occurred and discussing actual problems that had arisen. Empiricism as formulated by Locke and Hume[74] denied the existence of innate principles and postulated that ideas were derived from experience. The scientific method of experiment and verification of hypotheses emphasised this approach.

From this philosophical attitude, it was a short step to

---

[71] *On the Law of Nature and of Nations*, 1672. See also Nussbaum, *op. cit.*, pp.147-50.
[72] *Ibid.*, pp.165-67.
[73] *Ibid.*, pp.167-72.
[74] See Friedmann, *op. cit.* footnote 28, pp.253-55.

reinterpreting international law in terms not of concepts derived from reason but rather in terms of what actually happened between the competing states. What states actually do was the key, not what states ought to do given basic rules of the law of nature. Agreements and customs recognised by the states were the essence of the law of nations.

Positivism developed as the modern nation-state system emerged, after the Peace of Westphalia in 1648, from the religious wars. It coincided, too, with theories of sovereignty such as those propounded by Bodin and Hobbes,[75] which underlined the supreme power of the sovereign and led to notions of the sovereignty of states.

Elements of both positivism and naturalism appear in the works of *Vattel*, (1714-67), a Swiss lawyer of the eighteenth century. His *Droit des Gens* was based on Natural Law principles yet practically orientated. He introduced the doctrine of the equality of states into international law, declaring that a small republic was no less of a sovereign than the most powerful kingdom just as a dwarf was as much a man as a giant. By distinguishing between laws of conscience and laws of action and stating that only the latter were of practical concern, he minimised the importance of Natural Law.[76]

Ironically, at the same time that positivist thought appeared to demolish the philosophical basis of the law of nature and relegate that theory to history, it re-emerged in a modern guise replete with significance for the future. Natural Law gave way to the concept of natural rights.[77]

It was an individualistic assertion of political supremacy. The idea of the social contract, that an agreement between individuals pre-dated and justified civil society, emphasised the central role of the individual, and whether such a theory was interpreted pessimistically to demand an absolute sovereign as Hobbes declared, or optimistically to mean a conditional acceptance of authority as Locke maintained, it could not fail to be a revolutionary doctrine. The rights of man constitute the heart of the American and French Revolutions and the essence of modern democratic society.

Yet, on the other hand, the doctrine of Natural Law has been employed to preserve the absoluteness of sovereignty and the

[75] *Leviathan*, 1651.

[76] See Nussbaum, *op. cit.*, pp.156-64.

[77] See e.g. Finnis, *Natural Law and Natural Rights*, 1980 and Tuck, *Natural Rights Theories*, 1979.

sanctity of private possessions. The theory has a reactionary aspect because it could be argued that what was, ought to be, since it evolved from the social contract or was divinely ordained, depending upon how secular one construed the law of nature to be.

The Nineteenth Century

The eighteenth century was a ferment of intellectual ideas and rationalist philosophies that contributed to the evolution of the doctrine of international law. The nineteenth century by contrast was a practical, expansionist and positivist era. The Congress of Vienna, which marked the conclusion of the Napoleonic wars, enshrined the new international order which was to be based upon the European balance of power. International law became Euro-centric, the preserve of the civilised, Christian states, into which overseas and foreign nations could enter only with the consent of and on the conditions laid down by the western powers. Paradoxically, whilst international law became geographically internationalised through the expansion of the European empires, it became less universalist in conception and more, theoretically as well as practically, a reflection of European values.[78]

There are many other features that mark the nineteenth century. Democracy and nationalism, both spurred on by the wars of the French revolution and empire, spread throughout the Continent and changed the essence of international relations.[79] No longer the exclusive concern of aristocratic élites, foreign policy characterised both the positive and negative faces of nationalism. Self-determination emerged to threaten the multi-national empires of central and eastern Europe, while nationalism reached its peak in the unifications of Germany and Italy and began to exhibit features such as expansionism and doctrines of racial superiority. Democracy brought to the individual political influence and a say in government. It also brought home the realities of responsibility, for wars became the concern of all.

Conscription was introduced throughout the Continent and large national armies replaced the small professional forces.[80] The

---

[78] See Nussbaum, *op. cit.*, pp.186-250 and, e.g., Alexandrowicz, *The European-African Confrontation*, 1973.

[79] See especially Cobban, *The Nation State and National Self-Determination*, 1969.

[80] Best, *Humanity in Warfare*, 1980 and Bailey, *Prohibitions and Restraints in War*, 1972.

Industrial Revolution mechanised Europe, created the economic dichotomy of capital and labour and propelled western influence throughout the world. All these factors created an enormous increase in the number and variety of both public and private international institutions, and international law grew rapidly to accommodate them.[81]

European conferences proliferated and contributed greatly to the development of rules governing the waging of war. The International Committee of the Red Cross, founded in 1863, helped promote the series of Geneva Conventions beginning in 1864 dealing with the "humanisation" of conflict, and the Hague Conferences of 1899 and 1907 established the Permanent Court of Arbitration and dealt with the treatment of prisoners and the control of warfare.[82] Numerous other conferences, conventions and congresses emphasised the expansion of the rules of international law and the close network of international relations.

Positivist theories dominate this century. The proliferation of the powers of states and the increasing sophistication of municipal legislation gave force to the idea that laws were basically commands issuing from a sovereign person or body. Any question of ethics or morality was irrelevant to a discussion of the validity of man-made laws. The approach was transferred onto the international scene and immediately came face to face with the reality of a lack of supreme authority.

Since law was ultimately dependent upon the will of the sovereign in national systems, it seemed to follow that international law depended upon the will of the sovereign states.

This implied a confusion of the supreme legislator within a state with the state itself and thus positivism had to accept the metaphysical identity of the state. The state had a life and will of its own and so was able to dominate international law. This stress on the abstract nature of the state did not appear in all positivist theories and was a late development.[83]

It was the German thinker Hegel who first analysed and proposed the doctrine of the will of the state. The individual was subordinate to the state, because the latter enshrined the "wills" of all citizens

---

[81] See e.g. Bowett, *op. cit.* footnote 7 and *The Evolution of International Organisations* (ed. Luard), 1966.

[82] See further *infra*, Chapter 18.

[83] See *infra*, Chapter 2.

and had evolved into a higher will, and on the external scene the state was sovereign and supreme.[84] Such philosophies led to disturbing results in the twentieth century and provoked a re-awakening of the law of nature, dormant throughout the nineteenth century.

The growth of international agreements, customs and regulations induced positivist theorists to tackle this problem of international law and the state; and as a result two schools of thought emerged.

The monists claimed that there was one fundamental principle which underlay both national and international law. This was variously posited as "right" or social solidarity or the rule that agreements must be carried out (*pacta sunt servanda*). The dualists, more numerous and in a more truly positivist frame of mind, emphasised the element of consent.

For Triepel, another German theorist, international law and domestic (or municipal) law existed on separate planes, the former governing international relations, the latter relations between individuals and between the individual and the state. International law was based upon agreements between states (and such agreements included according to Triepel both treaties and customs) and because it was dictated by the "common will" of the states it could not be unilaterally altered.[85]

This led to a paradox. Could this common will bind individual states and if so, why? It would appear to lead to the conclusion that the will of the sovereign state could give birth to a rule over which it had no control. The state will was not, therefore, supreme but inferior to a collection of states' wills. Triepel did not discuss these points, but left them open as depending upon legal matters. Thus did positivist theories weaken their own positivist outlook by regarding the essence of law as beyond juridical description. The nineteenth century also saw the publication of numerous works on international law, which emphasised state practice and the importance of the behaviour of countries to the development of rules of international law.[86]

---

[84] See e.g. Avineri, *Hegel's Theory of the Modern State*, 1972, and Friedmann, *op. cit.* footnote 28, pp.164-76.

[85] *Ibid.*, pp.576-77. See also *infra*, Chapter 4.

[86] See e.g. Wheaton, *Elements of International Law*, 1836; Hall, *A Treatise on International Law*, 1880; Von Martens, *Völkerrecht*, 2 vols., 1883-6; Pradier-Fodéré, *Traité de Droit International Public*, 8 vols., 1855-1906; and Fiore, *Il Diritto Internazionale Codificato e la Sua Sanzione Giuridica*, 1890.

The Twentieth Century

The First World War marked the close of a dynamic and optimistic century. European empires ruled the world and European ideologies reigned supreme, but the 1914-18 Great War undermined the foundations of European civilisation. Self-confidence faded, if slowly, the edifice weakened and the universally accepted assumptions of progress were increasingly doubted. Self-questioning was the order of the day and law as well as art reflected this.

The most important legacy of the 1919 Peace Treaty from the point of view of international relations was the creation of the League of Nations.[87] The old anarchic system had failed and it was felt that new institutions to preserve and secure peace were necessary. The League consisted of an Assembly and an executive Council, but was crippled from the start by the absence of the United States and the Soviet Union for most of its life and remained a basically European organisation.

While it did have certain minor successes with regard to the maintenance of international order, it failed when confronted with determined aggressors. Japan invaded China in 1931 and two years later withdrew from the League. Italy attacked Ethiopia and Germany embarked unhindered upon a series of internal and external aggressions. The Soviet Union, in a final forlorn gesture, was expelled from the organisation in 1939 following its invasion of Finland.

Nevertheless much useful groundwork was achieved by the League in its short existence and this helped to consolidate the United Nations later on.[88]

The Permanent Court of International Justice was set up in 1921 at The Hague to be succeeded in 1946 by the International Court of Justice, the International Labour Organisation was established soon after the end of the First World War and it still exists today, and many other international institutions were inaugurated or increased their work during this period.[89]

Other ideas of international law that first appeared between the wars included the system of mandates, by which colonies of the defeated powers were administered by the Allies for the benefit of

[87] See Nussbaum, *op. cit.*, pp.251-90 and *infra*, Chapter 19.
[88] See also Scott, *The Rise and Fall of the League of Nations*, 1973.
[89] *Infra*, Chapter 19.

their inhabitants rather than being annexed outright, and the attempt made to provide a form of minority protection guaranteed by the League. This latter creation was not a great success but it paved the way for later concern to secure human rights.[90]

After the trauma of the Second World War the League was succeeded in 1946 by the United Nations Organisation, which tried to remedy many of the defects of its predecessor. It established its site at New York, reflecting the realities of the shift of power away from Europe, and determined to become a truly universal institution. The advent of decolonisation fulfilled this expectation and the General Assembly of the United Nations today has 160 member-states.

Many of the trends which first came into prominence in the nineteenth century have continued to this day. The vast increase in the number of international agreements and customs, the strengthening of the system of arbitration and the development of international organisations have established the essence of international law as it exists today.

Communist Approaches to International Law

Classic Marxist theory described law and politics as the means whereby the ruling classes maintained their domination of society. The essence of economic life was the ownership of the means of production, and all power flowed from this control. Capital and labour were the opposing theses and their mutual antagonism would eventually lead to a revolution out of which a new, non-exploitive form of society would emerge.[91] National states were dominated by the capitalist class and would have to disappear in the re-organising process. Indeed, the theory was that law and the state would wither away once a new basis for society had been established[92] and because classical international law was founded upon the state, it followed that it too would go.

However, the reality of power and the existence of the USSR surrounded by capitalist nations led to a modification in this approach. The international system of states could not be changed

---

[90] *Infra*, Chapter 6.
[91] See Lloyd, *op. cit.*, Chapter 10 and Friedmann, *op. cit.* footnote 28, Chapter 29.
[92] Engels, *Anti-Duhring*, quoted in Lloyd, *op. cit.*, pp.773-74.

overnight into a socialist order, so a period of transition was inevitable. Nevertheless basic changes were seen as having been wrought.

Professor Tunkin, for example, emphasises that the Russian October revolution produced a new series of international legal ideas. These, it is noted, can be divided into three basic, inter-connected groups: (a) principles of socialist internationalism in relations between socialist states, (b) principles of equality and self-determination of nations and peoples, primarily aimed against colonialism, and (c) principles of peaceful co-existence aimed at relations between states with different social systems.[93]

We shall briefly look at these concepts in this section, but first an historical overview is necessary.

During the immediate post-revolution period, it was postulated that a transitional phase had commenced. During this time, international law as a method of exploitation would be criticised by the socialist state, but it would still be recognised as a valid system. The two Soviet theorists Korovin and Pashukanis were the dominant influences in this phase. The transitional period demanded compromises, in that until the universal victory of the revolution some forms of economic and technical co-operation would be required since they were fundamental for the existence of the international social order.[94] Pashukanis expressed the view that international law was an interclass law within which two antagonistic class systems would seek accommodation until the victory of the socialist system. Socialism and the Soviet Union could still use the legal institutions developed by and reflective of the capitalist system.[95] However, with the rise of Stalinism and the "socialism in one country" call, the position hardened. Pashukanis altered his line and recanted. International law was not a form of temporary compromise between capitalist states and the USSR but rather a means of conducting the class war. The Soviet Union was bound only by those rules of international law which accorded with its purposes.[96]

The new approach in the late 1930s was reflected politically in

[93] *Theory of International Law*, 1974, p.4. See also Grzybowski, *Soviet Public International Law*, 1970, especially Chapter I, and generally Baade, *The Soviet Impact on International Law*, 1964 and Friedmann, *op. cit.* footnote 19, pp.327-40.

[94] Tunkin, *op. cit.*, p.5.

[95] *Ibid.*, pp.5-6. See also Babb and Hazard, *Soviet Legal Philosophy*, 1951.

[96] Grzybowski, *op. cit.*, pp.6-9.

Russia's successful attempt to join the League of Nations and its policy of wooing the western powers, and legally by the ideas of Vyshinski. He adopted a more legalistic view of international law and emphasised the Soviet acceptance of such principles as national self-determination, state sovereignty and the equality of states, but not others. The role of international law did not constitute a single international legal system binding all states. The Soviet Union would act in pursuance of Leninist-Stalinist foreign policy ideals and would not be bound by the rules to which it had not given express consent.[97]

The years that followed the Second World War saw a tightening up of Soviet doctrine as the Cold War gathered pace, but with the death of Stalin and the succession of Kruschev a thaw set in. In theoretical terms the law of the transitional stage was replaced by the international law of peaceful co-existence. War was no longer regarded as inevitable between capitalist and socialist countries and a period of mutual tolerance and co-operation was inaugurated.[98]

Tunkin recognised that there is a single system of international law of universal scope rather than different branches covering socialist and capitalist countries, and that international law is founded upon agreements between states which are binding upon them. He has defined contemporary general international law as:

> the aggregate of norms which are created by agreement between states of different social systems, reflect the concordant wills of states and have a generally democratic character, regulate relations between them in the process of struggle and co-operation in the direction of ensuring peace and peaceful co-existence and freedom and independence of peoples, and are secured when necessary by coercion effectuated by states individually or collectively.[99]

It is interesting to note the basic elements here, such as the stress on state sovereignty, the recognition of different social systems and the aim of peaceful co-existence. The role of sanctions in law is emphasised and reflects much of the positivist influence upon Soviet thought. Such preoccupations are also reflected in the

[97] *Ibid.,* p.9.

[98] *Ibid.,* pp.16-22. See also Higgins, *Conflict of Interests,* 1964, Part III.

[99] *Op. cit.,* p.251. See also Tunkin, "Co-existence and International Law", 95 *HR,* pp.1, 51 *et seq.* and McWhinney, "Contemporary Soviet General Theory of International Law: Reflections on the Tunkin Era", 25 *Canadian Yearbook of International Law,* 1989, p.187.

definition of international law contained in the leading Soviet textbook by Professor Kozhevnikov where it was stated that:

> international law can be defined as the aggregate of rules governing relations between states in the process of their conflict and co-operation, designed to safeguard their peaceful co-existence, expressing the will of the ruling classes of these states and defended in case of need by coercion applied by states individually or collectively.[100]

Originally, treaties alone were regarded as proper sources of international law but custom is now also accepted as a kind of tacit or implied agreement with great stress laid upon *opinio juris* or the legally binding element of custom. While state practice need not be general to create a custom, its recognition as a legal form must be.[101]

Peaceful co-existence itself rests upon certain basic concepts, for example non-intervention in the internal affairs of other states and the sovereignty of states. Any idea of a world authority is condemned as a violation of the latter principle. The doctrine of peaceful co-existence is also held to include such ideas as good neighbourliness, international co-operation and the observance in good faith of international obligations.

The concept is regarded as based on specific trends of laws of societal development and as a specific form of class struggle between socialism and capitalism, one in which armed conflict is precluded.[102] It is an attempt, in essence, to reiterate the basic concepts of international law in a way that is taken to reflect an ideological trend. But it must be emphasised that the principles themselves have long been accepted by the international community.

While Tunkin at first attacked the development of regional systems of international law, he later came around to accepting a socialist law which reflected the special relationship between communist countries. The Soviet interventions in eastern Europe,

---

[100] *International Law*, 1961.

[101] *Theory of International Law, op. cit.*, p.118. See also Tunkin, "The Contemporary Soviet Theory of International Law", *Current Legal Problems*, 1978, p.177.

[102] *Ibid.*, pp.35-48. See also Vallat, "International Law — A Forward Look", 18 *YBWA*, 1964, p.251; Hazard, "Codifying Peaceful Co-existence", 55 *AJIL*, 1961, pp.111-12; McWhinney, *Peaceful Co-existence and Soviet-Western International Law*, 1964 and Grzybowski, "Soviet Theory of International Law for the Seventies", 77 *AJIL*, 1983, p.862.

[103] See Grzybowski, *op. cit.* footnote 93, pp.16-22.

particularly in Czechoslovakia in 1968, played a large part in augmenting such views.[103] In the Soviet view relations between socialist (communist) states represented a new, higher type of international relations and a socialist international law. Common socio-economic factors and a political community created an objective basis for lasting friendly relations whereas, by contrast, international capitalism involved the exploitation of the weak by the strong. The principles of socialist or proletarian internationalism constituted a unified system of international legal principles between countries of the socialist bloc arising by way of custom and treaty. Although the basic principles of respect for state sovereignty, non-interference in internal affairs and equality of states and peoples existed in general international law, the same principles in socialist international law were made more positive by the lack of economic rivalry and exploitation and by increased co-operation. Accordingly, these principles incorporated not only material obligations not to violate each other's rights, but also the duty to assist each other in enjoying and defending such rights against capitalist threats.[104]

The Soviet emphasis on territorial integrity and sovereignty, while designed in practice to protect the socialist states in a predominantly capitalist environment, proved of great attraction to the developing nations of the Third World, anxious too to establish their own national identities and counteract western financial and cultural influences.

With the decline of the Cold War and the onset of *perestroika* (restructuring) in the Soviet Union, a process of re-evaluation in the field of international legal theory has been taking place.[105] The concept of peaceful co-existence has been modified and the notion of class warfare virtually eliminated from the Soviet political lexicon. Global interdependence and the necessity for international co-operation are now emphasised, as it is accepted that the tension between capitalism and socialism is no longer the major conflict in the contemporary world and that beneath the former dogmas lie many common interests.[106] The essence of new Soviet thinking has

---

[104] Tunkin, *op. cit.,* pp.431-43.

[105] See, for example, *Perestroika and International Law* (eds. Carty and Danilenko), 1990; Mullerson, "Sources of International Law: New Tendencies in Soviet Thinking", 83 *AJIL,* 1989, p.494; Vereshchetin & Mullerson, "International Law in an Interdependent World", 28 *Columbia Journal of Transnational Law,* 1990, p.291 and Quigley, "*Perestroika* and International Law", 82 *AJIL,* 1988, p.788.

[106] Vereschetin & Mullerson, *op. cit.,* p.292.

been stated to lie in the priority of universal human values and the resolution of global problems, which is directly linked to the growing importance of international law in the world community. It has also been pointed out that international law has to be universal and not artificially divided into capitalist, socialist and Third World "international law" systems.[107]

Soviet writers and political leaders have accepted that past activities such as the interventions in Czechoslovakia in 1968 and Afghanistan in 1979 were contrary to international law, while the attempt to create a state based on the rule of law is seen as requiring the strengthening of the international legal system and the rule of law in international relations. In particular, a renewed emphasis upon the role of the United Nations is now evident in Soviet policy.[108]

While relatively little has previously been known of Chinese attitudes a few points can be made. Western concepts are regarded primarily as aimed at preserving the dominance of the bourgeois class on the international scene. Soviet views were partially accepted but since the late 1950s and the growing estrangement between the two major communist powers, the Chinese concluded that the Russians were interested chiefly in maintaining the *status quo* and Soviet-American superpower supremacy. The Soviet concept of peaceful co-existence as the mainstay of contemporary international law was treated with particular suspicion and disdain.[109]

The Chinese conception of law was, for historical and cultural reasons, very different from that developed in the west. "Law" never attained the important place in Chinese society that it did in European civilisation.[110] A sophisticated bureaucracy laboured to attain harmony and equilibrium and a system of legal rights to protect the individual in the western sense did not really develop. It was believed that society would be best served by example and established morality, rather than by rules and sanctions. This Confucian philosophy was, however, swept aside after the successful

[107] *Ibid.*

[108] See Quigley, *op. cit.*, p.794.

[109] See Chiu, "Communist China's Attitude towards International Law", 60 *AJIL*, 1966, p.245; Fairbank, *The Chinese World Order*, 1968; Cohen, *China's Practice of International Law*, 1972; Anglo-Chinese Educational Trust, *China's World View*, 1979; Cohen and Chiu, *People's China and International Law*, 2 vols., 1974, and Kim, "The People's Republic of China and the Charter-based International Legal Order", 72 *AJIL*, 1978, p.317.

[110] See Lloyd, *op. cit.*, pp.760-63; Van der Sprenkel, *Legal Institutions in Northern China*, 1962 and Unger, *Law in Modern Society*, 1976, pp.86-109.

communist revolution, to be replaced by strict Marxism-Leninism, with its emphasis on class warfare.[111]

The Chinese seem to have recognised several systems of international law, for example, western, socialist, and revisionist (Soviet Union) and to have implied that only with the ultimate spread of socialism would a universal system be possible.[112] International agreements are regarded as the primary source of international law and China has entered into many treaties and conventions and carried them out as well as other nations.[113] One exception, of course, is China's disavowal of the so-called "unequal treaties" whereby Chinese territory was annexed by other powers, in particular the Tsarist Empire, in the nineteenth century.[114]

On the whole, international law has been treated as part of international politics and subject to considerations of power and expediency, as well as ideology. Where international rules conform with Chinese policies and interests, then they will be observed. Where they do not, they will be ignored.

However, now that the isolationist phase of its history appears to be over, relations with other nations established and its entry into the United Nations secured, Communist China appears to be adopting a more cautious approach in international relations. This appears to have led to a legalisation of its view of international law as has occurred with the Soviet Union, and as China seeks in a multi-power world to increase its influence and power.

The Third World

In the evolution of international affairs since the Second World War one of the most decisive events has been the disintegration of the colonial empires and the birth of scores of new states in the so-called Third World. This has thrust onto the scene states which carry with them a legacy of bitterness over their past status as well as a host of problems relating to their social, economic and political

[111] Lloyd, *op. cit.*, and Li, "The Role of Law in Communist China", *China Quarterly*, 1970, p.66 cited in Lloyd, *op. cit.*, pp.801-8.

[112] See e.g. Cohen and Chiu, *op. cit.*, pp.62-64.

[113] *Ibid.*, pp.77-82, and Part VIII generally.

[114] See e.g. Detter, "The Problem of Unequal Treaties", 15 *ICLQ* 1966, p.1069; Nozari, *Unequal Treaties in International Law*, 1971; Chiu, *op. cit.*, pp.239-67 and Chen, *State Succession Relating to Unequal Treaties*, 1974.

development.[115] In such circumstances it was only natural that the structure and doctrines of international law would come under attack. The nineteenth century development of the law of nations founded upon Eurocentrism and imbued with the values of Christian, urbanised and expanding Europe[116] did not, understandably enough, reflect the needs and interests of the newly independent states of the mid- and late twentieth century. It was felt that such rules had encouraged and then reflected their subjugation, and that changes were required.[117]

It is basically those ideas of international law that came to fruition in the last century that have been so clearly rejected, that is, those principles that enshrined the power and domination of the west.[118] The underlying concepts of international law have not been discarded. On the contrary. The new nations have eagerly embraced the ideas of the sovereignty and equality of states and the principles of non-aggression and non-intervention, in their search for security within the bounds of a commonly accepted legal framework.

While this new internationalisation of international law that has occurred in the last twenty years has destroyed its European-based homogeneity, it has emphasised its universalist scope.[119] The composition of, for example, both the International Court of Justice and the Security Council of the United Nations mirrors such developments. Article 9 of the Statute of the International Court of Justice points out that the main forms of civilisation and the principal legal systems of the world must be represented within the Court, and there is an arrangement that of the ten non-permanent seats in the Security Council five should go to Afro-Asian states and

[115] See e.g. Anand, "Attitude of the Afro-Asian States Towards Certain Problems of International Law", 15 *ICLQ*, 1966, p.35; Elias, *New Horizons in International Law*, 1980 and Higgins, *op. cit.*, Part II. See also Hague Academy of International Law, Colloque, *The Future of International Law in a Multicultural World*, especially pp.117-42 and Henkin, *How Nations Behave*, 2nd ed., 1979, pp.121-27.

[116] See e.g. Verzijl, *International Law in Historical Perspective*, vol.1, 1968, pp.435-36. See also Roling, *International Law in an Expanded World*, 1960, p.10.

[117] The converse of this has been the view of some writers that the universalisation of international law has led to a dilution of its content, see e.g. Friedmann, *op. cit.* footnote 19, p.6; Stone, *Quest for Survival: The Role of Law and Foreign Policy*, 1961, p.88 and Brierly, *The Law of Nations*, 6th ed., 1963, p.43.

[118] See e.g. Alexandrowicz, *The European-African Confrontation*, 1973.

[119] See Okoye, *International Law and the New African States*, 1972; Elias, *Africa and the Development of International Law*, 1972 and *Encyclopedia of Public International Law*, vol. 7, 1984, pp.205-51.

two to Latin American states (the others going to Europe and other states). The composition of the International Law Commission has also recently been increased and structured upon geographic lines.[120]

The influence of the new states has been felt most of all within the General Assembly, where they constitute a majority of the 160 member-states.[121] The content and scope of the various resolutions and declarations emanating from the Assembly are proof of their impact and contain a record of their fears, hopes and concerns.

The Declaration on the Granting of Independence to Colonial Countries and Peoples of 1960, for example, enshrined the right of colonies to obtain their sovereignty with the least possible delay and called for the recognition of the principle of self-determination. This principle, which is discussed elsewhere in this book,[122] is regarded by most authorities as a settled rule of international law although with undetermined borders. Nevertheless, it symbolises the rise of the post-colonial states and the effect they are having upon the development of international law.

Their concern for the recognition of the sovereignty of states is complemented by their support of the United Nations and its Charter and supplemented by their desire for "economic self-determination" or the right of permanent sovereignty over natural resources.[123] This expansion of international law into the field of economics is a major development of this century and is evidenced in myriad ways, for example, by the creation of the General Agreement on Tariffs and Trade, the United Nations Conferences on Trade and Development, and the establishment of the International Monetary Fund and World Bank.

The interests of the new states of the non-western, non-communist Third World are often in conflict with those of the industrialised nations, witness disputes over nationalisations. But it has to be emphasised that, contrary to many fears expressed in the early years of the decolonisation saga, international law has not been discarded nor altered beyond recognition. Its framework has been retained as the new states, too, wish to obtain the benefits of rules

---

[120] By General Assembly resolution 36/39, 21 of the 34 members are to be nationals of Afro-Asian-Latin American States.

[121] As of autumn 1990.

[122] See *infra*, Chapter 5.

[123] See *infra*, Chapter 13.

such as those governing diplomatic relations and the controlled use of force, while campaigning against rules which run counter to their perceived interests.

While the new countries share a common history of foreign dominance and underdevelopment, compounded by an awakening of national identity, it has to be recognised that they are not a homogenous group. Widely differing cultural, social and economic attitudes and stages of development characterise them and the rubric of the "Third World" masks diverse political affiliations. On many issues the interests of the new states conflict with each other and this is reflected in the different positions adopted. The states possessing oil and other valuable natural resources are separated from those with few or none and the states bordering on oceans are to be distinguished from land-locked states. The list of diversity is endless and variety governs the make-up of the southern hemisphere to a far greater degree than in the north.

It is possible that in legal terms tangible differences in approach may emerge in the future as the passions of decolonisation die down and the western supremacy over international law is further eroded. This trend will also permit a greater understanding of, and greater recourse to, historical traditions and conceptions that pre-date colonisation and an increasing awareness of their validity for the future development of international law.[124]

In the medium term, however, it has to be recognised that with the end of the Cold War and the rapid development of Soviet-American co-operation, the axis of dispute is turning from East-West to North-South. This is beginning to manifest itself in a variety of issues ranging from economic law to the law of the sea and human rights.

[124] See e.g. Sarin, "The Asian-African States and the Development of International Law", in Hague Academy Colloque, *op. cit.*, p.117 and *Encyclopedia of Public International Law*, vol.7, 1984, pp.205-51. See also Jenks, *The Common Law of Mankind*, 1958, p.169 and Cassese, *op. cit.*, p.64 *et seq.*

CHAPTER TWO

International Law Today

THE EXPANDING LEGAL SCOPE OF INTERNATIONAL CONCERN

International law in the second half of the twentieth century has been developing in many directions, as the complexities of life in the modern era have multiplied. For, as already emphasised, law reflects the conditions and cultural traditions of the society within which it operates. The community evolves a certain specific set of values, social, economic and political, and this stamps its mark on the legal framework which orders life in that environment. Similarly, international law is a product of its environment. It has developed in accordance with the prevailing notions of international relations and to survive it must be in harmony with the realities of the age.

Nevertheless, there is a continuing tension between those rules already established and the constantly evolving forces that seek changes within the system. One of the major problems of international law is to determine when and how to incorporate new standards of behaviour and new realities of life into the already existing framework, so that, on the one hand the law remains relevant and on the other, the system itself is not too vigorously disrupted.

Changes that occur within the international community can be momentous and reverberate throughout the system. One example that comes to mind is the advent of nuclear arms, creating a status quo in Europe and a balance of terror throughout the world, and constituting a factor of unease as other states seek to acquire nuclear technology.[1] Another example is the technological capacity to mine the oceans and the consequent questions as to the nature and beneficiaries of exploitation.[2] There are several instances of how modern developments demand a constant reappraisal of the structure of international law and its rules.

The scope of international law today is immense. From the regulation of space expeditions to the question of the division of the ocean floor and from the protection of human rights to the

---

[1] See *infra*, Chapter 18.
[2] See *infra*, Chapter 10.

management of the international financial system, its involvement has spread out from the primary concern with the preservation of peace, to embrace all the interests of contemporary international life.

But the *raison d'être* of international law and the determining factor in its composition remains the needs and characteristics of the international political system. Where more than one entity exists within a system, there has to be some conception as to how to deal with other such entities, whether it be on the basis of co-existence or hostility. International law as it has developed since the seventeenth century has adopted the same approach and has in general (though with notable exceptions) eschewed the idea of permanent hostility and enmity. Because the state, while internally supreme, wishes to maintain its sovereignty externally and needs to cultivate other states in an increasingly interdependent world, so it must acknowledge the rights of others. This acceptance of rights possessed by all states, something unavoidable in a world where none can stand alone, leads inevitably on to a system to regulate and define such rights and, of course, obligations.

And so one arrives at some form of international legal order, no matter how unsophisticated and how occasionally positively disorderly.[3] The current system developed in the context of European civilisation as it progressed, but this is changing. The rise of the United States and the Soviet Union mirrored the decline of Europe, while the process of decolonisation is also making a considerable impact.

This means that international law, faced with radical changes in the world structure of power, has had to come to terms with new ideas that could no longer be ignored.

The Eurocentric character of international law has been gravely weakened in the last sixty years or so and the opinions, hopes and needs of other cultures and civilisations are beginning to play an increasing role in the evolution of world juridical thought.

International law reflects first and foremost the basic state-oriented character of world politics. Units of formal independence benefiting from equal sovereignty in law and equal possession of

---

[3] For views as to the precise definition and characteristics of the international order or system or community, see Schwarzenberger and Brown, *A Manual of International Law*, 6th ed., 1976, pp.9-12; Yalem, "The Concept of World Order", 29 *YBWA*, 1975, p.320 and Pogany, "The Legal Foundations of World Order", *ibid.*, 1983, p.277.

the basic attributes of statehood[4] have succeeded in creating a system enshrining such values. Examples that could be noted here include non-intervention in internal affairs, territorial integrity, non-use of force and equality of voting in the United Nations General Assembly. In addition to this, many factors cut across state borders and create a tension in world politics, such as inadequate economic relationships, international concern for human rights and the rise in new technological forces.[5] State policies and balances of power, both international and regional, are a necessary framework within which international law operates, as indeed are domestic political conditions and tensions. Law mirrors the concern of forces within states and between states.

It is also important to realise that states need law in order to seek and attain certain goals, whether these be economic well-being, survival and security or ideological advancement. The system therefore has to be certain enough for such goals to be ascertainable, and flexible enough to permit change when this becomes necessary due to the confluence of forces demanding it.[6]

International law, however, has not just expanded horizontally to embrace the new states which have been established relatively recently; it has extended itself to include individuals, groups and international organisations within its scope. It has also moved into new fields covering such issues as international trade, problems of environmental protection and outer space exploration.

The growth of positivism in the nineteenth century had the effect of focusing the concerns of international law upon sovereign states. They alone were the "subjects" of international law and were to be contrasted with the status of non-independent states and individuals as "objects" of international law. But the gradual sophistication of positivist doctrine, combined with the advent of new approaches to the whole system of international relations, has broken down this exclusive emphasis and extended the roles played by non-state entities, such as individuals, multi-national firms and international institutions.[7] It was, of course, long recognised that

---

[4] See *infra*, Chapter 5.

[5] For examples of this in the context of the law relating to territory, see Shaw, *Title to Territory in Africa*, 1986, pp.1-11.

[6] See Hoffman, "International Systems and International Law", 14 *World Politics*, 1961-2, p.205.

[7] See further *infra*, Chapter 5.

individuals were entitled to the benefits of international law, but it is only recently that they have been able to act directly rather than rely upon their national states.

The Nuremberg and Tokyo Tribunals set up by the victorious Allies after the close of the Second World War were a vital part of this process. Many of those accused were found guilty of crimes against humanity and against peace and were punished accordingly. It was a recognition of individual responsibility under international law without the usual interposition of the state. Similarly the 1948 Genocide Convention provided for the punishment of offenders after conviction by national courts or by an international criminal tribunal.[8] The developing concern with human rights is another aspect of this move towards increasing the role of the individual in international law. The Universal Declaration of Human Rights adopted by the United Nations in 1948 lists a series of political and social rights, although it is only a guideline and not legally binding as such. The European Convention for the Protection of Human Rights and Fundamental Freedoms signed in 1950 and the International Covenants on Human Rights of 1966 are of a different nature and binding upon the signatories. In an effort to function satisfactorily various bodies of a supervisory and implementational nature were established. Within the European Economic Community (the Common Market), individuals and corporations have certain rights of direct appeal to the Court of Justice of the EEC against decisions of the various Community institutions. In addition, individuals may appear before certain international tribunals. Nevertheless, the whole subject has been highly controversial, with some writers (for example Soviet theorists prior to *perestroika*) denying that individuals may have rights as distinct from duties under international law, but it is indicative of the trend away from the exclusivity of the state.[9]

International organisations have now been accepted as possessing rights and duties of their own and a distinctive legal personality. The International Court of Justice in 1949 delivered an Advisory Opinion[10] in which it stated that the United Nations was a subject of international law and could enforce its rights by bringing

[8] *Ibid.*

[9] See further *infra*, Chapter 6.

[10] *Reparation for Injuries Suffered in the Service of the United Nations,* ICJ Reports, 1949, p.174; 16 *ILR*, p.318.

international claims, in this case against Israel following the assassination of Count Bernadotte, a United Nations official. Such a ruling can be applied to embrace other international institutions, like the International Labour Organisation and the Food and Agriculture Organisation, which all have a judicial character of their own. Thus, while states remain the primary subjects of international law, they are now joined by other non-state entities, whose importance is likely to grow in the future. The growth of regional organisations should also be noted at this stage. Many of those were created for reasons of military security, for example NATO and the opposing Warsaw Pact organisations, others as an expression of regional and cultural identity such as the Organisation of African Unity and the Organisation of American States. In a class of its own is the European Common Market which has gone far down the road of economic co-ordination and standardisation and has a range of common institutions serviced by a growing bureaucracy stationed primarily at Brussels.

Such regional organisations have added to the developing sophistication of international law by the insertion of "regional-international law sub-systems" within the universal framework and the consequent evolution of rules that bind only member-states.[11]

The range of topics covered by international law has expanded hand in hand with the upsurge in difficulties faced and the proliferation in the number of participants within the system. It is no longer exclusively concerned with issues relating to the territory or jurisdiction of states narrowly understood, but is beginning to take into account the specialised problems of contemporary society. Many of these have already been referred to, such as the vital field of human rights, the growth of an international economic law covering financial and development matters, concern with environmental despoliation, the space exploration effort and the exploitation of the resources of the oceans and deep sea-bed. One can mention also provisions relating to the bureaucracy of inter-national institutions (international administrative law), international labour standards, health regulations and communications controls.

---

[11] See further *infra*, Chapter 19.

MODERN THEORIES AND INTERPRETATIONS

At this point some modern theories as to the nature and role of international law will be briefly noted, in addition to the Soviet and Chinese approaches surveyed in the last Chapter.

Positive Law and Natural Law

Throughout the history of thought there has been a complex relationship between idealism and realism, between the way things ought to be and the way things are, and the debate as to whether legal philosophy should incorporate ethical standards or confine itself to an analysis of the law as it stands is a vital one that continues today.[12]

The positivist school, which developed so rapidly in the pragmatic, optimistic world of the nineteenth century, declared that law as it exists should be analysed empirically shorn of all ethical elements. Moral aspirations were all well and good but had no part in legal science. Man-made law must be examined as such and the metaphysical speculations of Natural Law rejected because what counted were the practical realities, not general principles which were imprecise and vague, not to say ambiguous.[13]

This kind of approach to law in society reached its climax with Kelsen's "Pure Theory of Law". Kelsen defined law solely in terms of itself and eschewed any element of justice, which was rather to be considered within the discipline of political science. Politics, sociology and history were all excised from the pure theory which sought to construct a logical unified structure based on a formal appraisal.[14]

Law was to be regarded as a normative science, that is, consisting of rules which lay down patterns of behaviour. Such rules, or norms, depend for their legal validity on a prior norm and this process continues until one reaches what is termed the basic norm of the

[12] See e.g. Lyons, *Ethics and the Rule of Law*, 1984; Dworkin, *Taking Rights Seriously*, 1977; Hart, *The Concept of Law*, 1961 and Stein and Shand, *Legal Values in Western Society*, 1974. See also Lloyd, *op. cit.* and Dias, *Jurisprudence*, 4th ed., 1976.

[13] See Hart, *op. cit.* and "Positivism and the Separation of Law and Morals", 71 *Harvard Law Review*, 1958, p.593. Cf. Fuller, "Positivism and Fidelity to Law — A Reply to Professor Hart", *ibid.*, p.630.

[14] "The Pure Theory of Law", 50 *LQR*, 1934, pp.474, 477-85 and 51 *LQR*, 1935, pp.517-22.

whole system. This basic norm is the foundation of the legal edifice, because rules which can be related back to it therefore become *legal* rules. To give a simple example, a court order empowering an official to enforce a fine is valid if the court had that power which depends upon an Act of Parliament establishing the court. A rule becomes a legal rule if it is in accordance with a previous (and higher) legal rule and so on. Layer builds upon layer and the foundation of it all is the basic norm.[15]

The weakness of Kelsen's "pure" system lies primarily in the concept of the basic norm for it relies for its existence upon non-legal issues. In fact, it is a political concept, and in the United Kingdom it would probably be the principle of the supremacy of Parliament.[16]

This logical, structured system of validity founded upon an extra-legal concept encounters difficulties when related to international law. For Kelsen international law is a primitive legal order because of its lack of strong legislative, judicial and enforcement organs and its consequent resemblance to a pre-state society. It is accordingly characterised by the use of self-help.[17] The principles of international law are valid if they can be traced back to the basic norm of the system, which is hierarchical in the same sense as a national legal system. For Kelsen, the basic norm is the rule that identifies custom as the source of law, or stipulates that, as he wrote, "the states ought to behave as they customarily behaved".[18] One of the prime rules of this category is *pacta sunt servanda* declaring that agreements must be carried out in good faith and upon that rule is founded the second stage within the international legal order. This second stage consists of the network of norms created by international treaties and conventions and leads on to the third stage which includes those rules established by organs which have been set up by international treaties, for instance, decisions of the International Court of Justice.[19]

The problem with Kelsen's formulation of the basic norm of international law is that it appears to be tautological: it merely

[15] *Ibid.* See also Lloyd, *op. cit.,* Chapter 5.

[16] *Ibid.,* pp.291-96. See also Stone, "Mystery and Mystique in the Basic Norm", 26 *MLR,* 1963, p.34 and Raz, *Practical Reason and Norms,* 1975, pp.129-31.

[17] *General Theory of Law and State,* 1946, pp.328 *et seq.* See also Lador-Lederer, "Some Observations on the 'Vienna School' in International Law", 17 *NILR,* 1970, p.126.

[18] *Op. cit.,* pp.369-70.

[19] *Ibid.*

repeats that states which obey rules ought to obey those rules.[20] It seems to leave no room for the progressive development of international law by new practices accepted as law for that involves states behaving differently from the way they have been behaving. Above all, it fails to answer the question as to why custom is binding.

Nevertheless, it is a model of great logical consistency which helps explain, particularly with regard to national legal systems, the proliferation of rules and the importance of validity which gives as it were a mystical seal of approval to the whole structured process. It helps illustrate how rule leads to rule as stage succeeds stage in a progression of norms forming a legal order.

Another important element in Kelsen's interpretation of law is his extreme "monist" stance. International law and municipal law are not two separate systems but one interlocking structure and the former is supreme. Municipal law finds its ultimate justification in the rules of international law by a process of delegation within one universal normative system.[21]

Kelsen's pure theory seemed to mark the end of that particular road, and positivism was analysed in more sociological terms by Hart in his book *The Concept of Law*, 1961.

Hart comprehends law as a system of rules, based upon the interaction of primary and secondary rules. The former, basically, specify standards of behaviour while the latter provide the means for identifying and developing them and thus specify the constitutional procedures for change. Primitive societies would possess only the primary rules and so would be characterised by uncertainty, inefficiency and stagnation, but with increasing sophistication the secondary rules would develop and identify authority and enable the rules to be adapted to changing circumstances in a regular and accepted manner.[22]

The international legal order is a prime example of a simple form of social structure which consists only of the primary rules, because of its lack of a centralised legislature, network of recognised courts with compulsory jurisdiction and organised means of enforcement. Accordingly, it has no need of, or rather has not yet evolved, a basic norm or in Hart's terminology a rule of recognition, by reference

---

[20] Hart terms this "mere useless reduplication": *The Concept of Law*, 1961, p.230.

[21] *General Theory of Law and State*, pp.366-68. See further *infra*, Chapter 4.

[22] *The Concept of Law*, 1961, Chapter 5. See also e.g. Dworkin, *op. cit.*; Raz, *The Concept of a Legal System*, 1970 and MacCormick, *Legal Reasoning and Legal Theory*, 1978.

to which the validity of all the rules may be tested. Following this train of thought, Hart concludes that the rules of international law do not as yet constitute a "system" but are merely a "set of rules". Of course, future developments may see one particular principle, such as *pacta sunt servanda*, elevated to the state of a validating norm but in the present situation this has not yet occurred.[23]

This approach can be criticised for its over-concentration upon rules to the exclusion of other important elements in a legal system such as principles and policies,[24] and more especially as regards international law, for failing to recognise the sophistication or vitality of the system. In particular, the distinction between a system and a set of rules in the context of international law is a complex issue and one difficult to delineate.

The strength of the positivist movement has waned this century as the old certainties disintegrated and social unrest grew. Law, as always, began to reflect the dominant pressures of the age, and new theories as to the role of law in society developed. Writers started examining the effects of sociological phenomena upon the legal order and the nature of the legal process itself, with analyses of judicial behaviour and the means whereby rules were applied in actual practice. This was typified by Roscoe Pound's view of the law as a form of social engineering, balancing the various interests within the society in the most efficacious way.[25] Law was regarded as a method of social control and conceptual approaches were rejected in favour of functional analyses. What actually happened within the legal system, what claims were being brought and how they were satisfied: these were the watchwords of the sociological school.[26]

It was in one sense a move away from the ivory tower and into the court room. Empirical investigations proliferated, particularly in the United States, and the sciences of psychology and anthropology as well as sociology became allied to jurisprudence. Such concern with the wider social context led on to the theories of Realism, which treated law as an institution functioning within a particular community with a series of jobs to do. A study of legal

[23] *The Concept of Law, op. cit.*, pp.228-31.
[24] See Dworkin, *op. cit.*
[25] See e.g. *Philosophy of Law*, 1954, pp.42-47. See also Freeman, *The Legal Structure*, 1974, Chapter 4.
[26] *Outlines of Jurisprudence*, 5th ed., 1943, pp.116-19.

norms within a closed logical system in the Kelsenite vein was regarded as unable to reveal very much of the actual operation of law in society. For this an understanding of the behaviour of courts and the various legal officials was required. Historical and ethical factors were relegated to a minor role within the Realist-Sociological tradition, with its concentration upon field studies and "technical" dissections. Legal rules were no longer to be accepted as the heart of the legal system.[27]

Before one looks at contemporary developments of this approach and how they have affected interpretations of international law, the rival of Natural Law this century has first to be considered.

In the search for meaning in life and an ethical basis to law, Natural Law has adopted a variety of different approaches. One of them has been a refurbishment of the principles enumerated by Aquinas and adopted by the Catholic Church, emphasising the dignity of man and the supremacy of reason together with an affirmation of the immorality (though not necessarily the invalidity) of law contrary to right reason and the eternal law of God.[28] A more formalistic and logic-orientated trend has been exemplified by writers such as Stammler, who tried to erect a logical structure of law with an inbuilt concept of "Natural Law with a changing content".

This involved contrasting the *concept* of law, which was intended to be an abstract, formal definition universally applicable, with the *idea* of law, which embodies the purposes and direction of the system. This latter precept varied, of necessity, in different social and cultural contexts.[29]

As distinct from this formal idealist school, there has arisen a sociologically inspired approach to the theme of Natural Law represented by Gény and Duguit. This particular trend rejected the emphasis upon form, and concentrated instead upon the definition of Natural Law in terms of universal factors, physical, psychological, social and historical, which dominate the framework of society within which the law operated.[30]

---

[27] See e.g. Llewellyn, *The Common Law Tradition*, 1960 and *Jurisprudence*, 1962. See also Twining, *Karl Llewellyn and the Realist Movement*, 1973 and Loevinger, "*Jurimetrics* — The Next Step Forward", 33 *Minnesota Law Review*, 1949, p.455.

[28] See e.g, Maritain, *Man and the State*, 1951 and Dabin, *General Theory of Law*, 2nd ed., 1950.

[29] See e.g. Stammler, *Theory of Justice* and Del Vecchio, *Formal Bases of Law*, 1921.

[30] See e.g. Gény, *Méthode d'Interprétation et Sources en Droit Privé Positif*, 1899 and Duguit, *Law in the Modern State*, 1919 and "Objective Law", 20 *Columbia Law Review*, 1920, p.817.

The discussion of Natural Law increased and gained in importance following the Nazi experience. It stimulated a German philosopher, Radbruch, to formulate a theory whereby unjust laws had to be opposed by virtue of a higher, Natural Law.[31]

As far as international law is concerned, the revival of Natural Law came at a time of increasing concern with international justice and the formation of international institutions. Many of the ideas and principles of international law today are rooted in the notion of Natural Law and the relevance of ethical standards to the legal order, such as the principles of non-aggression and human rights.[32]

New Approaches

Traditionally, international law has been understood in a historical manner and studied chronologically. This approach was especially marked in the nineteenth century as international relations multiplied and international conferences and agreements came with an increasing profusion. Between the World Wars, the opening of government archives released a wealth of material and further stimulated a study of diplomatic history, while the creation of such international institutions as the League of Nations and the Permanent Court of International Justice encouraged an appreciation of institutional processes.

However, after the Second World War a growing trend appeared intent upon the analysis of power politics and the comprehension of international relations in terms of the capacity to influence and dominate. The approach was a little more sophisticated than might appear at first glance for it involved a consideration of social and economic as well as political data that had a bearing upon a state's ability to withstand as well as direct pressures.[33]

Nevertheless, it was a pessimistic interpretation because of its centring upon power and its uses as the motive force of inter-state activity.

[31] *Introduction to Legal Philosophy*, 1947. See also Hart, *op. cit.* footnote 13 and Fuller, *op. cit.* footnote 13 and "The Legal Philosophy of Gustav Radbruch", 6 *Journal of Legal Education*, 1954, p.481.

[32] See Lauterpacht, *International Law and Human Rights*, 1950. Note more generally the approach of Rawls, *A Theory of Justice*, 1971, and D'Amato, "International Law and Rawls' Theory of Justice", 5 *Denver Journal of International Law and Policy*, 1975, p.525.

[33] See e.g. Morgenthau, *Politics Among Nations*, 4th ed., 1967 and Thompson, *Political Realism and the Crisis of World Politics: An American Approach to Foreign Policy*, 1960.

The next "wave of advance", as it has been called, witnessed the successes of the behaviouralist movement. This particular train of thought introduced elements of psychology, anthropology and sociology into the study of international relations and paralleled similar developments within the Realist School. It reflected the altering emphasis from analyses in terms of idealistic or cynical ("realistic") conceptions of the world political order, to a mechanistic discussion of the system as it operates today, by means of field studies and other tools of the social sciences. Indeed, it is more a method of approach to law and society than a theory in the traditional sense.[34]

One can trace the roots of this school of thought to the changing conceptions of the role of government in society. The nineteenth century ethic of individualism and the restriction of state intervention to the very minimum has changed radically in the last three generations. The emphasis is now more upon the responsibility of the government towards its citizens and the phenomenal growth in welfare legislation illustrates this. Rules and regulations controlling wide fields of human activity, something that would have been unheard of in the mid-nineteenth century, have proliferated throughout the nations of the developed world and theory has had to try and keep up with such re-orientations.

Since the law now plays a much deeper role in society with the increase in governmental intervention, impetus has been given to legal theories that reflect this growing involvement. Law, particularly in the United States, is seen as a tool to effect changes in society and Realist doctrine underlines this. It emphasises that it is community values and policy decisions that determine the nature of the law and accordingly the role of the judge is that much more important. He is no longer an interpreter of a body of formal legal rules, but should be seen more as an active element in making decisions of public policy.

This means that to understand the operation of law, one has to consider the character of the particular society, its needs and values. Law thus becomes a dynamic process and has to be studied in the context of society and not merely as a collection of legal rules capable of being comprehended on their own. The social sciences

[34] See e.g. *Contending Approaches to International Politics* (eds. Knorr and Rosenau), 1969, and Gould and Barkun, *International Law and the Social Sciences*, 1970.

have led the way in this re-interpretation of society and their influence has been very marked on the behavioural method of looking at the law, not only in terms of general outlook but also in providing the necessary tools to dissect society and discover the way it operates and the direction in which it is heading. The interdisciplinary nature of the studies in question was emphasised, utilising all the social sciences, including politics, economics and philosophy.[35] In particular the use of the scientific method, such as obtaining data and quantitive analysis, has been very much in evidence.

Behaviouralism has divided the field of international relations into basically two studies, the first being a consideration of foreign policy techniques and the reasons whereby one particular course of action is preferred to another, and the second constituting the international systems analysis approach.[36] This emphasises the interaction of the various players on the international stage and the effects of such mutual pressures upon both the system and the participants. More than that, it examines the various international orders that have existed throughout history in an attempt to show how the dynamics of each particular system have created their own rules and how they can be used as an explanation of both political activity and the nature of international law. In other words, the nature of the international system can be examined by the use of particular variables in order to explain and to predict the role of international law.

For example, the period between 1848 and 1914 can be treated as the era of the "balance of power" system. This system depended upon a number of factors, such as a minimum number of participants (accepted as five), who would engage in a series of temporary alliances in an attempt to bolster the weak and restrict the strong, for example the coalitions Britain entered into to overawe France. It was basic to this system that no nation wished totally to destroy

[35] Note Barkun's comment that "the past theoretical approaches of the legal profession have involved logical manipulations of a legal corpus more often than the empirical study of patterns of human behaviour", *Law Without Sanctions*, 1968, p.3. See also Falk, "New Approaches to the Study of International Law", in *New Approaches to International Relations* (ed. Kaplan), 1968, pp.357-80, and Frankel, *Contemporary International Theory and the Behaviour of States*, 1973, pp.21-22.

[36] See e.g. McClelland, *Theory and International Systems*, 1966; Kaplan, *System and Process in International Politics*, 1964; Kaplan and Katzenbach, *The Political Foundations of International Law*, 1961, and Falk and Black, *The Future of International Legal Order*, 1969.

any other state, but merely to humble and weaken, and this contributed to the stability of the order.[37]

This system nurtured its own concepts of international law, especially that of sovereignty which was basic to the idea of free-floating alliances and the ability of states to leave the side of the strong to strengthen the weak. The balance of power collapsed with the First World War and after a period of confusion a discernible, loose "bipolar" system emerged in the years following the Second World War.

This was predicated upon the polarisation of capitalism and communism and the consequent rigid alliances that were created. It included the existence of a Third World of basically non-aligned states, the objects of rivalry and of competition while not in themselves powerful enough to upset the bipolar system. This kind of order facilitated "frontier" conflicts where the two powers collided, such as Korea, Berlin and Vietnam, as well as modifying the nature of sovereignty within the two alliances thus allowing such organisations as NATO and the Common Market on the one hand, and the Warsaw Pact and COMECON on the other, to develop. The dark side of this coin has been the freedom felt by the superpowers to control wavering states within their respective spheres of influence, for example, the Russian actions in Poland, Hungary and Czechoslovakia and those of the USA particularly within Latin America.[38]

Behaviouralism has been enriched by the use of such techniques as games theory.[39] This is a mathematical method of studying decision-making in conflict situations where the parties react rationally in the struggle for benefits. It can be contrasted with the fight situation where the essence is the actual defeat of the opponent (for example, the Israel-Arab conflict) and with the debate situation, which is an effort to convince the participants of the rightness of one's cause. Other factors which are taken into account include communications, integration, environment and capabilities. Thus

[37] See Frankel, *International Relations in a Changing World,* 1979, pp.152-57, and Kaplan and Katzenbach, *op. cit.,* pp.62-70.

[38] *Ibid.,* pp.50-55. As far as the systems approach is concerned see also Hoffman, "International Systems and International Law" in *The International System* (eds. Knorr and Verba), 1961, p.205; Clark and Sohn, *World Peace Through World Law,* 3rd ed., 1966, and *The Strategy of World Order,* (eds. Falk and Mendlovitz), 4 vols., 1966.

[39] See e.g. Lieber, *Theory and World Politics,* 1972, Chapter 2; *Game Theory and Related Approaches to Social Behaviour* (ed. Shubik), 1964, and Mackenzie, *Politics and Social Sciences,*

the range and complexity of this approach far exceeds that of prior theories.

All this highlights the switch in emphasis that has taken place in the consideration of law in the world community. The traditional view was generally that international law constituted a series of rules restricting the actions of independent states and forming exceptions to state sovereignty. The new theories tend to look at the situation differently, more from the perspective of the international order expanding its horizons than the nation-state agreeing to accept certain defined limitations upon its behaviour.

The rise of quantitative research has facilitated the collation and ordering of vast quantities of data. It is primarily a methodological approach utilising political, economic and social data and statistics, and converting facts and information into a form suitable for scientific investigation.

Such methods with their behavioural and quantitative aspects are beginning to impinge upon the field of international law. They enable a greater depth of knowledge and comprehension to be achieved and a wider appreciation of all the various processes at work.[40]

The behavioural approach to international relations has been translated into international law theory by a number of writers, in particular Professor McDougal, with some important modifications. This "policy-orientated" movement regards law as a comprehensive process of decision-making rather than as a defined set of rules and obligations. It is an active all-embracing approach seeing international law as a dynamic system operating within a particular type of world order.[41] It therefore minimises the role played by rules, for such a traditional conception of international law "quite obviously offers but the faintest glimpse of the structures, procedures and types of decision that take place in the contemporary world community".[42]

---

[40] Note also the functionalist approach to international law. This orientation emphasises the practical benefits to states of co-operation in matters of mutual interest: see e.g. Friedmann, *An Introduction to World Politics*, 5th ed., 1965, p.57; Haas, *Beyond the Nation State*, 1964; Mitrany, *A Working Peace System*, 1946; Jenks, *Law, Freedom and Welfare*, 1964 and Stone, *Legal Controls of International Conflict*, 1959. See also Johnston, "Functionalism in the Theory of International Law", 25 *Canadian Yearbook of International Law*, 1988, p.3.

[41] See e.g. McDougal, "International Law, Power and Policy", 82 *HR*, p.133; McDougal, Lasswell and Reisman, "Theories about International Law: Prologue to a Configurative Jurisprudence", 8 *Va JIL*, 1968, p.188; McDougal, "International Law and the Future", 50 *Mississippi Law Journal*, 1979, p.259 and Falk, *op. cit.* footnote 35.

[42] McDougal and Reisman, *International Law in Contemporary Perspective*, 1980, p.5.

It has been emphasised that the law is a constantly evolving process of decision-making and the way that it evolves will depend on the knowledge and insight of the decision-maker.[43] In other words, it is the social process of constant human interaction that is seen as critical and in this process, claims are continually being made in an attempt to maximise values at the disposal of the participants. Eight value-institution categories have been developed to analyse this process: power, wealth, enlightenment, skill, wellbeing, affection, respect and rectitude. This list may be further developed. It is not exhaustive. Law is to be regarded as a product of such social processes.[44] International law is the whole process of authoritative decision-making involving crucially the concepts of authority and control. The former is defined in terms of the structure of expectation concerning the identity and competence of the decision-maker, whilst the latter refers to the actual effectiveness of a decision, whether or not authorised.[45]

McDougal's work and that of his followers emphasises the long list of values, interests and considerations that have to be taken into account within the international system by the persons actually faced with the decisions to make. This stress upon the so-called 'authoritative decision-maker', whether he be in the United States Department of State, in the British Foreign Office or "anyone whose choice about an event can have some international significance",[46] as the person who in effect has to choose between different options respecting international legal principles, emphasises the practical world of power and authority.

Such a decision-maker is subject to a whole series of pressures and influences, such as the values of the community in which he operates, and the interests of the particular nation-state he serves. He will also have to consider the basic values of the world order, for instance human dignity.

[43] "The Policy-Oriented Approach to Law", 40 *Virginia Quarterly Review*, 1964, p.626. See also Suzuki, "The New Haven School of International Law: An Invitation to a Policy-Oriented Jurisprudence", 1 *Yale Studies in World Public Order*, 1974, p.1.

[44] Suzuki, *op. cit.*, pp.22-23. See also McDougal, "Some Basic Theoretical Concepts about International Law: A Policy-Oriented Framework of Inquiry", 4 *Journal of Conflict Resolution*, 1960, pp.337-54.

[45] McDougal and Lasswell, "The Identification and Appraisal of Diverse Systems of Public Order", 53 *AJIL*, 1959, pp.1, 9.

[46] McDougal and Reisman, *op. cit.*, p.2.

This approach involves a complex dissection of a wide-ranging series of factors and firmly fixes international law within the ambit of the social sciences, both with respect to the procedures adopted and the tools of analysis. International law is seen in the following terms, as

> a comprehensive process of authoritative decision in which rules are continuously made and remade; that the function of the rules of international law is to communicate the perspectives (demands, identifications and expectations) of the peoples of the world about this comprehensive process of decision; and that the national application of these rules in particular instances requires their interpretation, like that of any other communication, in terms of who is using them, with respect to whom, for what purposes (major and minor), and in what context.[47]

Legal rules articulate and seek to achieve certain goals and this value factor must not be ignored. The values emphasised by this school are basically those of human dignity, familiar from the concepts of western democratic society.[48]

The policy-oriented movement has been greatly criticised by traditional international lawyers as unduly minimising the legal content of the subject and for ignoring the fact that nations generally accept international law as it is and obey its dictates.[49] States rarely indulge in a vast behavioural analysis, studiously considering every relevant element in a particular case and having regard to fundamental objectives like human dignity and welfare. Indeed, so to do may weaken international law, it has been argued.[50]

Other writers, such as Professor Falk, accept the basic comprehensive approach of the McDougal school, but point to its inconsistencies and overfulsome cataloguing of innumerable interests. They tend to adopt a global outlook based upon a deep

---

[47] McDougal, "A footnote", 57 *AJIL*, 1963, p.383.

[48] See McDougal, Lasswell and Chen, *Human Rights and World Public Order*, 1980. For a discussion of the tasks required for a realistic inquiry in the light of defined goals, see McDougal, "International Law and the Future", *op. cit.*, pp.259, 267.

[49] See in particular Allott, "Language, Method and the Nature of International Law", 45 *BYIL*, p.79. Higgins has vividly drawn attention to the differences in approach to international law adopted by American and British writers: "Policy Considerations and the International Judicial Process", 17 *ICLQ*, 1968, p.58.

[50] Allott, *op. cit.*, p.128 *et seq.*

concern for human welfare and morality, but with an emphasis upon the importance of legal rules and structure.[51]

What, however, is clear is that international law functions in a particular, concrete world system, involving a range of actors from states to international organisations, companies and individuals, and as such is responsive to the needs and aspirations of such participants. Law is not the only way in which issues transcending borders are negotiated and settled or indeed fought over. It is one of a number of methods for dealing with an existing complex and shifting system, but it is a way of some prestige and influence for it is of its very nature in the form of mutually accepted obligations. Law and politics cannot be divorced. They are engaged in a crucial symbiotic relationship. It does neither discipline a service to minimise the significance of the other.[52]

---

[51] See e.g. Falk, *The Status of Law in International Society*, 1970 and *Human Rights and State Sovereignty*, 1980. But note the approach of, e.g., Watson, "A Realistic Jurisprudence of International Law", 34 *YBWA*, 1980, p.265 and Lane, "Demanding Human Rights: A Change in the World Legal Order", 6 *Hofstra Law Review*, 1978, p.269.

[52] See also, for recent discussions of the role of international law, *inter alia*, Carty, *The Decay of International Law*, 1986; De Lupis, *The Concept of International Law*, 1987; *The Structure and Process of International Law* (eds. Macdonald and Johnston), 1983; Kennedy, *International Legal Structures*, 1987; Kaskenniemi, *The Structure of International Legal Arguments*, 1989 and Allott, *Eunomia*, 1990.

CHAPTER THREE

Sources [1]

When the law on any given point in, for example, the English legal
system is sought, it is not usually too difficult a process. One looks
to see whether the matter is covered by an Act of Parliament and,
if it is, the law reports are consulted as to how it has been interpreted
by the courts. If the particular point is not specifically referred to
in a statute, court cases will be examined to elicit the required
information. In other words, there is a definite method of discovering
what the law is. In addition to verifying the contents of the rules,
this method also demonstrates how the law is created, namely, by
parliamentary legislation or judicial case-law. This gives a degree
of certainty to the legal process because one is able to tell when a
proposition has become law and the necessary mechanism to resolve
any disputes about the law is evident. It reflects the hierarchical
character of a national legal order with its gradations of authority
imparting to the law a large measure of stability and predictability.

The contrast is very striking when one considers the situation in
international law. The lack of a legislature, executive and structure
of courts within international law has been noted and the effects
of this will become clearer as one proceeds. There is no single
body able to create laws on the world scene binding upon everyone,
nor a proper system of courts with compulsory jurisdiction to
interpret and extend the law. One is therefore faced with the
problem of discovering where the law is to be found and how one
can tell whether a particular proposition amounts to a legal rule.
This perplexity is reinforced because of the anarchic nature of
world affairs and the clash of competing sovereignties. Nevertheless,
international law does exist and is ascertainable. There are "sources"
available from which the rules may be extracted and tested.

By "sources" one means those provisions operating within the legal

---

[1] See generally Parry, *The Sources and Evidences of International Law*, 1965; Sørensen, *Les
Sources de Droit International*, 1946; Tunkin, *Theory of International Law*, 1974, pp.89-203;
Verzijl, *International Law in Historical Perspective*, vol.1, 1968, p.1; Lauterpacht, *International
Law: Collected Papers*, vol.1, 1970, p.58 and Virally, "The Sources of International Law" in *Manual
of Public International Law* (ed. Sørensen), 1968, p.116. See also *Change and Stability in
International Law-Making* (eds. Cassese and Weiler), 1988 and Bos, *A Methodology of International
Law*, 1984.

system on a technical level, and such ultimate sources as reason or morality are excluded, as are more functional sources such as libraries and journals. What is intended is a survey of the process whereby rules of international law emerge.[2]

Article 38(1) of the Statute of the International Court of Justice is widely recognised as the most authoritative statement as to the sources of international law.[3] It provides that:

the Court, whose function is to decide in accordance with international law such disputes as are submitted to it, shall apply:

(a) international conventions, whether general or particular, establishing rules expressly recognised by the contesting states; (b) international custom, as evidence of a general practice accepted as law; (c) the general principles of law recognised by civilised nations; (d) subject to the provisions of Article 59, judicial decisions and the teachings of the most highly qualified publicists of the various nations, as subsidiary means for the determination of rules of law.

Some writers have sought to categorise the distinctions in this provision, so that international conventions, custom and the general principles of law are described as the three exclusive law-creating processes while judicial decisions and academic writings are regarded as law-determining agencies, dealing with the verification of alleged rules.[4] But in reality it is not always possible to make hard and fast divisions. The different functions overlap to a great extent so that in many cases treaties (or conventions) merely reiterate accepted rules of customary law, and judgments of the International Court of Justice may actually create law in the same way that municipal judges formulate new law in the process of interpreting existing law.[5]

A distinction has sometimes been made between formal and material sources.[6] The former, it is claimed, confer upon the rules an obligatory character, while the latter comprise the actual content of the rules. Thus the formal sources appear to embody the constitutional mechanism for identifying law while the material

[2] See also, e.g., McDougal and Reisman, "The Prescribing Function: How International Law is Made", 6 *Yale Studies in World Public Order*, 1980, p.249.

[3] See e.g. Brownlie, *Principles of Public International Law*, 4th ed., 1990, p.3 and Hudson, *The Permanent Court of International Justice*, 1934, p.601 *et seq.*

[4] See e.g. Schwarzenberger, *International Law*, 3rd ed., vol.1, 1957, pp.26-27.

[5] There are a number of examples of this: see *infra*, Chapter 4, p.106.

[6] See e.g. Brownlie, *op. cit.*, p.1.

sources incorporate the heart or matter of the regulations. This division has been criticised particularly in view of the peculiar constitutional set-up of international law and it tends to distract attention from some of the more important problems by its attempt to establish a clear separation of substantive and procedural elements, something difficult to maintain in international law.

CUSTOM [7]

Introduction

In any primitive society certain rules of behaviour emerge and prescribe what is permitted and what is not. Such rules develop almost subconsciously within the group and are maintained by the members of the group by social pressures and with the aid of various other more tangible implements. They are not, at least in the early stages, written down or codified, and survive ultimately because of what can be called an aura of historical legitimacy.[8] As the community develops it will modernise its code of behaviour by the creation of legal machinery, such as courts and legislature. Custom, for this is how the original process can be described, remains and may also continue to evolve.[9] It is regarded as an authentic expression of the needs and values of the community at any given time.

Custom within contemporary legal systems, particularly in the developed world, is relatively cumbersome and unimportant and often of only nostalgic value.[10] In international law on the other hand

---

[7] See generally, D'Amato, *The Concept of Custom in International Law*, 1971; Akehurst, "Custom as a Source of International Law", 47 *BYIL*, 1974-5, p.1; Bin Cheng, "Custom: The Future of General State Practice in a Divided World" in *The Structure and Process of International Law* (eds. Macdonald and Johnston), 1983, p.513; Thirlway, *International Customary Law and Codification*, 1972; Wolfke, *Custom in Present International Law*, 1964; Kopelmanas, "Custom as a Means of the Creation of International Law", 18 *BYIL*, 1937, p.127; Lauterpacht, *The Development of International Law by the International Court*, 1958, pp.368-93; Kunz, "The Nature of Customary International Law", 47 *AJIL*, 1953, p.662 and Carty, *The Decay of International Law*, 1986, Chapter 3.

[8] See e.g. Unger, *Law in Modern Society*, 1976, who notes that customary law can be regarded as "any recurring mode of interaction among individuals and groups, together with the more or less explicit acknowledgement by these groups and individuals that such patterns of interaction produce reciprocal expectations of conduct that ought to be satisfied", p.49. See also Dias, *Jurisprudence*, 4th ed., 1976, Chapter 8 and Hart, *The Concept of Law*, 1961.

[9] See e.g. Lloyd, *Introduction to Jurisprudence*, 4th ed., 1979, p.649 and Maine, *Ancient Law*, 1861.

[10] See e.g. Dias, *op. cit.*

it is a dynamic source of law in the light of the nature of the international system, and its lack of centralised government organs.

The existence of customary rules can be deduced from the practice and behaviour of states and this is where the problems begin. How can one tell when a particular line of action adopted by a state reflects a legal rule or is merely prompted by, for example, courtesy? Indeed, how can one discover what precisely a state is doing or why, since there is no living "state" but rather thousands of officials in scores of departments exercising governmental functions? Other issues concern the speed of creation of new rules and the effect of protests.

There are disagreements as to the value of a customary system in international law. Some writers deny that custom can be significant today as a source of law, noting that it is too clumsy and slow-moving to accommodate the evolution of international law any more,[11] while others declare that it is a dynamic process of law creation and more important than treaties since it is of universal application.[12] Another view recognises that custom is of value since it is activated by spontaneous behaviour and thus mirrors the contemporary concerns of society. However, since international law now has to contend with a massive increase in the pace and variety of state activities as well as having to come to terms with many different cultural and political traditions, the role of custom is stated to be much diminished.[13]

There are elements of truth in each of these approaches. Amidst a wide variety of conflicting behaviour, it is not easy to isolate the emergence of a new rule of customary law and there are immense problems involved in collating all the necessary information.

It is not always the best instrument available for the regulation of complex issues that arise in world affairs, but in particular situations it may meet the contingencies of modern life. As will be seen, it is possible to point to something called "instant" customary law in certain circumstances that can prescribe valid rules without having to undergo a long period of gestation, and custom can and often does dovetail neatly within the complicated mechanisms now

---

[11] See e.g. Friedmann, *The Changing Structure of International Law*, 1964, pp.121-23. See also De Lupis, *The Concept of International Law*, 1987, pp.112-16.

[12] E.g. D'Amato, *op. cit.*, p.12.

[13] De Visscher, *Theory and Reality in Public International Law*, 3rd ed., 1960, pp.161-62.

operating for the identification and progressive development of the principles of international law.

More than that, custom does mirror the characteristics of the decentralised international system. It is democratic in that all states may share in the formulation of new rules, though the precept that some are more equal than others in this process is not without its grain of truth. If the international community is unhappy with a particular law it can be changed relatively quickly without the necessity of convening and successfully completing a world conference. It reflects the consensus approach to decision-making with the ability of the majority to create new law binding upon all, while the very participation of states encourages their compliance with customary rules. Its imprecision means flexibility as well as ambiguity. Indeed, the creation of the concept of the exclusive economic zone in the law of the sea may be cited as an example of this process. This is discussed further in Chapter 10.

The essence of custom according to article 38 is that it should constitute "evidence of a general practice accepted as law". Thus, it is possible to detect two basic elements in the make-up of a custom. These are the material facts, that is, the actual behaviour of states, and the psychological or subjective belief that such behaviour is "law".

It is understandable why the first requirement is mentioned, since customary law is founded upon the performance of state activities and the convergence of practices, in other words, what states actually do. It is the psychological factor that needs some explanation.

If one left the definition of custom as state practice then one would be faced with the problem of how to separate international law from principles of morality or social usage. This is because states do not restrict their behaviour to what is legally required. They may pursue a line of conduct purely through a feeling of goodwill and in the hope of reciprocal benefits. States do not have to allow tourists in or launch satellites. There is no law imposing upon them the strict duty to distribute economic aid to developing nations. The bare fact that such things are done does not mean that they have to be done.

The issue therefore is how to distinguish behaviour undertaken because of a law from behaviour undertaken because of a whole range of other reasons ranging from goodwill to pique, and from ideological support to political bribery. And if customary law is restricted to the overt acts of states, one cannot solve this problem.

Accordingly, the second element in the definition of custom has been elaborated. This is the psychological factor, the belief by a state that behaved in a certain way that it was under a legal obligation to act that way. It is known in legal terminology as *opinio juris* and was first formulated by the French writer François Gény as an attempt to differentiate legal custom from mere social usage.[14]

However, the relative importance of the two factors, the overt action and the subjective conviction, is disputed by various writers.

Positivists, with their emphasis upon state sovereignty, stress the paramount importance of the psychological element. States are only bound by what they have consented to, so therefore the material element is minimised to the greater value of *opinio juris*. If states believe that a course of action is legal and perform it, even if only once, then it is to be inferred that they have tacitly consented to the rule involved. Following on from this line of analysis, various positivist thinkers have tended to minimise many of the requirements of the overt manifestation, for example, with regard to repetition and duration.[15] Other writers have taken precisely the opposite line and maintain that *opinio juris* is impossible to prove and therefore of no tremendous consequence. Kelsen, for one, has written that it is the courts that have the discretion to decide whether any set of usages is such as to create a custom and that the subjective perception of the particular state or states is not called upon to give the final verdict as to its legality or not.[16]

The Material Fact

The actual practice indulged in by states constitutes the initial factor. There are a number of points to be considered concerning its nature, including the duration, consistency, repetition and generality of a particular practice by states. As far as the duration

---

[14] *Méthode d'Interprétation et Sources en Droit Privé Positif*, 1899, para.110.

[15] See e.g. Anzilotti, *Corso di Diritto Internazionale*, 3rd ed., 1928, pp.73-76; Strupp, "Les Règles Générales du Droit de la Paix", 47 *HR*, p.263; Tunkin, *op. cit.*, pp.113-33 and "Remarks on the Juridical Nature of Customary Norms of International Law", 49 *California Law Review*, 1961, pp.419-21, and Cheng, "United Nations Resolutions on Outer Space: 'Instant' International Customary Law?", 5 *Indian Journal of International Law*, 1965, p.23.

[16] "Théorie du Droit International Coutumier", 1 *Revue International de la Théorie du Droit*, 1939, pp.253, 264-66. See also Guggenheim, *Traité de Droit International Public*, 1953, pp.46-48; Gihl, "The Legal Character of Sources of International Law", 1 *Scandinavian Studies in Law*, 1957, pp.53, 84, and Oppenheim, *International Law*, vol.1, 8th ed., 1955, pp.25-27.

is concerned, most countries specify a recognised time-scale for the acceptance of a practice as a customary rule within their municipal systems. This can vary from "time immemorial" in the English Common Law dating back to 1189, to figures from thirty or forty years on the Continent.

In international law there is no rigid time element and it will depend upon the circumstances of the case and the nature of the usage in question. In certain fields, such as air and space law, the rules have developed quickly; in others, the process is much slower. Duration is thus not the most important of the components of state practice.[17] The essence of custom is to be sought elsewhere.

The basic rule as regards continuity and repetition was laid down in the *Asylum* case by the International Court of Justice (ICJ), decided in 1950.[18] The Court declared that a customary rule must be "in accordance with a constant and uniform usage practised by the States in question".[19] The case concerned one Haya de la Torre, a Peruvian, who was sought by his government after an unsuccessful revolt. He was granted asylum by Colombia in its embassy in Lima, but Peru refused to issue a safe conduct to permit Torre to leave the country. Colombia brought the matter before the International Court of Justice and requested a decision recognising that it (Colombia) was competent to define Torre's offence, as to whether it was criminal as Peru maintained, or political, in which case asylum and a safe conduct could be allowed.

The Court, in characterising the nature of a customary rule, held that it had to constitute the expression of a right appertaining to one state (Colombia) and a duty incumbent upon another (Peru). However, the Court felt that in the *Asylum* litigation, state practices had been so uncertain and contradictory as not to amount to a "constant and uniform usage" regarding the unilateral qualification of the offence in question.[20] The issue involved here dealt with a regional custom pertaining only to Latin America and it may be argued that the same approach need not necessarily be

---

[17] See D'Amato, *op. cit.*, pp.56-58 and Akehurst, *op. cit.*, pp.15-16. Judge Negulesco in an unfortunate phrase emphasised that custom required immemorial usage: *European Commission of the Danube*, PCIJ, Series B, no.14, 1927, p.105. See also Brownlie, *op. cit.*, p.6 and the *North Sea Continental Shelf* cases, ICJ Reports, 1969, pp.3, 43; 41 *ILR*, pp.29, 72.

[18] ICJ Reports, 1950, p.266; 17 *ILR*, p.280.

[19] *Ibid.*, pp.276-77; 17 *ILR*, p.284.

[20] *Ibid.*

followed where a general custom is alleged and that in the latter instance a lower standard of proof would be upheld.[21]

The ICJ emphasised its view that some degree of uniformity amongst state practices was essential before a custom could come into existence in the *Anglo-Norwegian Fisheries* case.[22] The United Kingdom, in its arguments against the Norwegian method of measuring the breadth of the territorial sea, referred to an alleged rule of custom whereby a straight line may be drawn across bays of less than ten miles from one projection to the other, which could then be regarded as the baseline for the measurement of the territorial sea. The Court dismissed this by pointing out that the actual practice of states did not justify the creation of any such custom. In other words, there had been insufficient uniformity of behaviour.

In the *North Sea Continental Shelf* cases,[23] which involved a dispute between Germany on the one hand and Holland and Denmark on the other over the delimitation of the continental shelf, the ICJ remarked that state practice had to be "both extensive and virtually uniform in the sense of the provision invoked". This was held to be indispensable to the formation of a new rule of customary international law.[24] However, the Court emphasised in the *Nicaragua v. United States* case[25] that it was not necessary that the practice in question had to be "in absolutely rigorous conformity" with the purported customary rule. The Court continued:

> In order to deduce the existence of customary rules, the Court deems it sufficient that the conduct of states should, in general, be consistent with such rules, and that instances of state conduct inconsistent with a given rule should generally have been treated as breaches of that rule, not as indications of the recognition of a new rule.[26]

The threshold that needs to be attained before a legally binding custom can be created will depend both upon the nature of the alleged rule and the opposition it arouses. This partly relates to the

---

[21] See further, *infra*, p.78.

[22] ICJ Reports, 1951, pp.116, 131 and 138; 18 *ILR*, p.86.

[23] ICJ Reports, 1969, p.3; 41 *ILR*, p.29.

[24] *Ibid.*, p.43; 41 *ILR*, p.72. Note that the Court was dealing with the creation of a custom on the basis of what had been purely a treaty rule. See Akehurst, *op. cit.*, p.21, especially footnote 5. See also the *Paquete Habana* case, 175 US 677 (1900) and the *Lotus* case, PCIJ, Series A, no.10, 1927, p.18; 4 *ILR*, p.153.

[25] ICJ Reports, 1986, p.14; 76 *ILR*, p.349.

[26] *Ibid.*, p.98; 76 *ILR*, p.432.

problem of ambiguity where it is not possible to point to the alleged custom with any degree of clarity, as in the *Asylum* case where a variety of conflicting and contradictory evidence had been brought forward.

On the other hand, an unsubstantiated claim by a state cannot be accepted because it would amount to unilateral law-making and compromise a reasonably impartial system of international law. If a proposition meets with a great deal of opposition then it would be an undesirable fiction to ignore this and talk of an established rule.

Another relevant factor is the strength of the prior rule which is purportedly overthrown.[27] For example, the customary law relating to a state's sovereignty over its airspace developed very quickly in the years immediately before and during the First World War. Similarly, the principle of non-sovereignty over the space route followed by artificial satellites came into being soon after the launching of the first Sputniks. Bin Cheng has argued that in such circumstances repetition is not at all necessary provided the *opinio juris* could be clearly established. Thus, "instant" customary law is possible.[28]

This contention that single acts may create custom has been criticised, particularly in view of the difficulties of proving customary rules any other way but through a series of usages. Nevertheless, the conclusion must be that it is the international context which plays the vital part in the creation of custom. In a society constantly faced with new situations because of the dynamics of progress, there is a clear need for a reasonably speedy method of responding to such changes by a system of prompt rule-formation. In new areas of law, customs can be quickly established by state practices by virtue of the newness of the situations involved, the lack of contrary rules to be surmounted and the overwhelming necessity to preserve a sense of regulation in international relations.

One particular analogy that has been used to illustrate the general nature of customary law was considered by de Visscher. He likened the growth of custom to the gradual formation of a road across vacant land. After an initial uncertainty as to direction, the majority of users begin to follow the same line which becomes a single path. Not long

---

[27] See D'Amato, *op. cit.*, pp.60-61 and Akehurst, *op. cit.*, p.19. See also Judge Alvarez, the *Anglo-Norwegian Fisheries* case, ICJ Reports, 1951, pp.116, 152; 18 *ILR*, pp.86, 105 and Judge Loder, the *Lotus* case, PCIJ, Series A, no.10, 1927, pp.18, 34.

[28] *Op. cit.* footnote 15.

elapses before that path is transformed into a road accepted as the only regular way, even though it is not possible to state at which precise moment this latter change occurs.

And so it is with the formation of a custom. De Visscher develops this idea by reflecting that just as some make heavier footprints than others due to their greater weight, the more influential states of the world mark the way with more vigour and tend to become the guarantors and defenders of the way forward.[29]

The reasons why a particular state acts in a certain way are varied but are closely allied to how it perceives its interests. This in turn depends upon the power and role of the state and its international standing. Accordingly, custom should to some extent mirror the perceptions of the majority of states, since it is based upon usages which are practised by nations as they express their power and their hopes and fears. But it is inescapable that some states are more influential and powerful than others and that their activities should be regarded as of greater significance. This is reflected in international law so that custom may be created by a few states, provided those states are intimately connected with the issue at hand, whether because of their wealth and power or because of their special relationship with the subject-matter of the practice, as for example maritime nations and sea law. Law cannot be divorced from politics or power and this is one instance of that proposition.[30]

The influence of the United Kingdom, for example, on the development of the law of the sea and prize law in the nineteenth century when it was at the height of its power, was predominant. A number of propositions later accepted as part of international customary law appeared this way. Among many instances of this, one can point to navigation procedures. Similarly, the impact of the Soviet Union and the United States on space law has been paramount.[31]

One can conclude by stating that for a custom to be accepted and recognised it must have the concurrence of the major powers in that particular field. A regulation regarding the breadth of the

[29] *Op. cit.*, p.149. See also Lauterpacht, *op. cit.*, p.368; Cobbett, *Leading Cases on International Law*, 4th ed., 1922, p.5 and Akehurst, *op. cit.*, pp.22-23.

[30] See e.g. the *North Sea Continental Shelf* cases, ICJ Reports, 1969, pp.3, 42-43; 41 *ILR*, pp.29, 71-73.

[31] See e.g. Bin Cheng, *op. cit.* footnote 15 and Christol, *The Modern International Law of Outer Space*, 1982.

territorial sea is unlikely to be treated as law if the great maritime nations do not agree to or acquiesce in it, no matter how many land-locked states demand it. Other countries may propose ideas and institute pressure, but without the concurrence of those most interested, it cannot amount to a rule of customary law. This follows from the nature of the international system where all may participate but the views of those with greater power carry greater weight.

Accordingly, the duration and generality of a practice may take second place to the relative importance of the states precipitating the formation of a new customary rule in any given field. Universality is not required, but some correlation with power is. Some degree of continuity must be maintained but this again depends upon the context of operation and the nature of the usage.

Those elements reflect the external manifestations of a practice and establish that it is in existence and exhibited as such. That does not mean that it is law and this factor will be considered in the next sub-section. But it does mean that all states who take the trouble can discover its existence. This factor of conspicuousness emphasises both the importance of the context within which the usage operates and the more significant elements of the overt act which affirms the existence of a custom.

The question is raised at this stage of how significant a failure to act is. Just how important is it when a state, or more particularly a major state, does not participate in a practice? Can it be construed as acquiescence in the performance of the usage? Or, on the other hand, does it denote indifference implying the inability of the practice to become a custom until a decision one way or the other has been made?

Failures to act are in themselves just as much evidence of a state's attitudes as are actions. They similarly reflect the way in which a nation approaches its environment. Britain consistently fails to attack France, while Chad consistently fails to send a man to the moon. But does this mean that Britain recognises a rule not to attack its neighbour and that Chad accepts a custom not to launch rockets to the moon? Of course, the answer is in the first instance yes, and in the second example no. Thus, a failure to act can arise from either a legal obligation not to act, or an incapacity or unwillingness in the particular circumstances to act.

Indeed, it has been maintained that the continued habit of not taking actions in certain situations may lead to the formation of a legal rule.[32]

The danger of saying that a failure to act over a long period creates a negative custom, that is a rule actually not to do it, can be shown by remarking the absurdity of the proposition that a continual failure to act until the late 1950s is evidence of a legal rule not to send artificial satellites or rockets into space. On the other hand, where a particular rule of behaviour is established it can be argued that abstention from protest by states may amount to agreement with that rule.

In the particular circumstances of the *Lotus* case[33] the Permanent Court of International Justice, the predecessor of the International Court of Justice, laid down a high standard by declaring that abstention could only give rise to the recognition of a custom if it was based on a conscious duty to abstain. In other words, states had actually to be aware that they were not acting a particular way because they were under a definite obligation not to act that way. The decision has been criticised and would appear to cover categories of non-acts based on legal obligations, but not to refer to instances where, by simply not acting as against a particular rule in existence, they are tacitly accepting the legality and relevance of that rule.

It should be mentioned, however, that acquiescence must be based upon full knowledge of the rule invoked. Where a failure to take a course of action is in some way connected or influenced or accompanied by a lack of knowledge of all the relevant circumstances, then it cannot be interpreted as acquiescence.

What is State Practice?

Some of the ingredients of state activities have been surveyed and attempts made to place them in some kind of relevant context. But what is state practice? Does it cover every kind of behaviour initiated by the state, or is it limited to actual, positive actions? To put it more simply, does it include such things as speeches, informal documents and governmental statements or is it restricted to what states actually do?

---

[32] See e.g. Tunkin, *op. cit.* footnote 1, pp.116-17. But cf. D'Amato, *op. cit.*, pp.61-63 and 88-89.

[33] PCIJ, Series A, no.10, 1927, p.18; 4 *ILR*, p.153.

It is how states behave in practice that forms the basis of customary law, but evidence of what a state does can be obtained from numerous sources. A state is not a living entity, but consists of governmental departments and thousands of officials, and state activity is spread throughout a whole range of national organs. There are the state's legal officers, legislative institutions, courts, diplomatic agents and political leaders. Each of these engages in activity which relates to the international field and therefore one has to examine all such material sources and more in order to discover evidence of what states do.[34]

The obvious way to find out how countries are behaving is to read the newspapers, consult historical records, listen to what governmental authorities are saying and peruse the many official publications. There are also memoirs of various past leaders, official manuals on legal questions, diplomatic interchanges and the opinions of national legal advisors. All these methods are valuable in seeking to determine actual state practice.

In addition, one may note resolutions in the General Assembly, comments made by governments on drafts produced by the International Law Commission, decisions of the international judicial institutions, decisions of national courts, treaties and the general practice of international organisations.[35]

International organisations in fact may be instrumental in the creation of customary law. For example, the Advisory Opinion of the International Court of Justice declaring that the United Nations possessed international personality was partly based on the actual behaviour of the UN.[36] The International Law Commission has pointed out that "records of the cumulative

---

[34] See e.g. *Yearbook of the ILC*, 1950, vol.II, pp.368-72. Note also Brierly's comment that not all contentions put forward on behalf of a state represent that state's settled or impartial opinion, *The Law of Nations*, 6th ed., 1963, p.60. See also Brownlie, *op. cit.*, p.5 and Akehurst, *op. cit.*, p.2.

[35] The United States has produced an extensive series of publications covering its practice in international law. See the Digests of International Law produced by Wharton (1887), Moore (1906) and Whiteman (1963-70). Since 1973, an annual *Digest of US Practice in International Law* has been produced. See also Smith, *Great Britain and the Law of Nations*, 2 vols., 1932-5; McNair, *International Law Opinions*, 3 vols., 1956; Parry, *British Digest of International Law*, 1965, and E. Lauterpacht, *British Practice in International Law*, 1963-7. Several yearbooks now produce sections devoted to national practice, e.g. *British Yearbook of International Law* and *Annuaire Français de Droit International*.

[36] The *Reparation* case, ICJ Reports, 1949, p.174; 16 *ILR*, p.318. See also the *Reservations to the Genocide Convention* case, ICJ Reports, 1951, pp.15, 25; 18 *ILR*, p.364.

practice of international organisations may be regarded as evidence of customary international law with reference to states' relations to the organisations".[37]

States' municipal laws may in certain circumstances form the basis of customary rules. In the *Scotia* case decided by the US Supreme Court in 1871,[38] a British ship had sunk an American vessel on the high seas. The Court held that British navigational procedures established by an Act of Parliament formed the basis of the relevant international custom since other states had legislated in virtually identical terms. Accordingly, the American vessel, in not displaying the correct lights, was at fault. The view has also been expressed that mere claims as distinct from actual physical acts cannot constitute state practice. This is based on the precept that "until it [a state] takes enforcement action, the claim has little value as a prediction of what the state will actually do".[39] But as has been demonstrated this is decidedly a minority view.[40] Claims and conventions of states in various contexts have been adduced as evidence of state practice and it is logical that this should be so,[41] though the weight to be attached to such claims, may, of course, vary according to the circumstances. This approach is clearly the correct one since the process of claims and counterclaims is one recognised method by which states communicate to each other their perceptions of the status of international rules and norms. In this sense they operate in the same way as physical acts. Whether *in abstracto* or with regard to a particular situation, they constitute the raw material out of which may be fashioned rules of international law.[42] It is suggested that the formulation that "state practice covers any act or statements by a state from which views about customary law may be inferred",[43] is substantially correct.

[37] *Yearbook of the ILC,* 1950, vol.II, pp.368-72. See also Akehurst, *op. cit.,* p.12.

[38] 14 Wallace 170 (1871). See also the *Nottebohm* case, ICJ Reports, 1955, pp.4, 22; 22 *ILR,* p.349 and the *Paquete Habana* case, 175 US 677 (1900).

[39] D'Amato, *op. cit.,* p.88 and pp.50-51. See also Judge Read (dissenting), the *Anglo-Norwegian Fisheries* case, ICJ Reports, 1951, pp.116, 191; 18 *ILR,* pp.86, 132.

[40] Akehurst, *op. cit.,* pp.2-3. See also Thirlway, *op. cit.,* p.58.

[41] E.g. the *Asylum* case, ICJ Reports, 1950, pp.266, 277; 17 *ILR,* p.280; the *Rights of US Nationals in Morocco* case, ICJ Reports, 1952, pp.176, 200, 209; 19 *ILR,* p.255, and the *North Sea Continental Shelf* cases, ICJ Reports, 1969, pp.3, 32-33, 47 and 53; 41 *ILR,* p.29. See also the *Fisheries Jurisdiction* cases, ICJ Reports, 1974, pp.3, 47, 56-58, 81-88, 119-20, 135 and 161; 55 *ILR,* p.238.

[42] But see Thirlway, *op. cit.,* pp.58-59.

[43] Akehurst, *op. cit.,* p.10. This would also include omissions and silence by states: *ibid.*

Opinio Juris [44]

Once one has established the existence of a specified usage, it becomes necessary to consider how the state views its own behaviour. Is it to be regarded as a moral or political or legal act or statement? The *opinio juris*, or belief that a state activity is legally obligatory, is the factor which turns the usage into a custom and renders it part of the rules of international law. To put it slightly differently, states will behave a certain way because they are convinced it is binding upon them to do so.

The Permanent Court of International Justice expressed this point of view when it dealt with the *Lotus* case.[45] The issue at hand concerned a collision on the high seas (where international law applies) between the *Lotus*, a French ship, and the *Boz-Kourt*, a Turkish ship. Several people aboard the latter ship were drowned and Turkey alleged negligence by the French officer of the watch. When the *Lotus* reached Istanbul, the French officer was arrested on a charge of manslaughter and the case turned on whether Turkey had jurisdiction to try him. Among the various arguments adduced, the French maintained that there existed a rule of customary law to the effect that the flag state of the accused (France) had exclusive jurisdiction in such cases and that accordingly the national state of the victim (Turkey) was barred from trying him. To justify this, France referred to the absence of previous criminal prosecutions by such states in similar situations and from this deduced tacit consent in the practice which therefore became a legal custom.

The Court rejected this and declared that even if such a practice of abstention from instituting criminal proceedings could be proved in fact, it would not amount to a custom. It held that "only if such abstention were based on their [the states] being conscious of a duty to abstain would it be possible to speak of an international custom".[46] Thus the essential ingredient of obligation was lacking and the practice remained a practice, nothing more.

A similar approach occurred in the *North Sea Continental Shelf* cases.[47] In the general process of delimiting the continental shelf

---

44 *Ibid.*, pp.31-42 and D'Amato, *op. cit.*, pp.66-72. See also Bos, *op. cit.*, p.236 *et seq.*
45 PCIJ, Series A, no.10, 1927, p.18; 4 *ILR*, p.153.
46 *Ibid.*, p.28; 4 *ILR*, p.159.
47 ICJ Reports, 1969, p.3; 41 *ILR*, p.29.

of the North Sea in pursuance of oil and gas exploration, lines were drawn dividing the whole area into national spheres. However, West Germany could not agree with either Holland or Denmark over the respective boundary lines and the matter came before the International Court of Justice.

Article 6 of the Geneva Convention on the Continental Shelf of 1958 provided that where agreement could not be reached, and unless special circumstances justified a different approach, the boundary line was to be determined in accordance with the principle of equidistance from the nearest points of the baselines from which the breadth of the territorial sea of each state is measured. This would mean a series of lines drawn at the point where Germany met Holland on the one side and Denmark on the other and projected outwards into the North Sea. However, because Germany's coastline is concave, such equidistant lines would converge and enclose a relatively small triangle of the North Sea. The Federal Republic had signed but not ratified the 1958 Geneva Convention and was therefore not bound by its terms. The question thus was whether a case could be made out that the "equidistance – special circumstances principle" had been absorbed into customary law and was accordingly binding upon Germany.

The Court concluded in the negative and held that the provision in the Geneva Convention did not reflect an already existing custom. It was emphasised that when the International Law Commission had considered this point in the draft treaty which formed the basis of discussion at Geneva, the principle of equidistance had been proposed with considerable hesitation, somewhat on an experimental basis and not at all as an emerging rule of customary international law.[48] The issue then turned on whether practice subsequent to the Convention had created a customary rule. The Court answered in the negative and declared that although time was not of itself a decisive factor (only three years had elapsed before the proceedings were brought):

> an indispensable requirement would be that within the period in question, short though it might be, state practice, including that of states whose interests are specially affected, should have been both extensive and virtually uniform in the sense of the provision invoked, and should

[48] *Ibid.*, pp.32-41.

moreover have occurred in such a way as to show a general recognition that a rule of law or legal obligation is involved.[49]

This approach was maintained by the Court in the *Nicaragua* case[50] and express reference made to the *North Sea Continental Shelf* cases. The Court noted that:

> for a new customary rule to be formed, not only must the acts concerned "amount to a settled practice", but they must be accompanied by the *opinio juris sive necessitatis*. Either the States taking such action or other States in a position to react to it, must have behaved so that their conduct is "evidence of a belief that this practice is rendered obligatory by the existence of a rule of law requiring it. The need for such a belief, i.e. the existence of a subjective element, is implicit in the very notion of the *opinio juris sive necessitatis*." [51]

It is thus clear that the Court has adopted and maintained a high threshold with regard to the overt proving of the subjective constituent of customary law formation.

The great problem connected with the *opinio juris* is that if it calls for behaviour in accordance with law, how can new customary rules be created since that obviously requires action different from or contrary to what until then is regarded as law? If a country claims a three mile territorial sea in the belief that this is legal, how can the rule be changed in customary law to allow claims of, for example, twelve miles since that cannot also be in accordance with prevailing law?[52]

Obviously if one takes a restricted view of the psychological aspects, then logically the law will become stultified and this demonstrably has not happened.

Thus, one has to treat the matter in terms of a process whereby states behave in a certain way in the belief that such behaviour is law or is becoming law. It will then depend upon how other states react as to whether this process of legislation is accepted or rejected. It follows that rigid definitions as to legality have to be modified to

---

[49] *Ibid.*, p.43. See also e.g. the *Asylum* case, ICJ Reports, 1950, pp.266, 277; 17 *ILR*, p.280 and the *Right of Passage* case, ICJ Reports, 1960, pp.6, 42-43; 31 *ILR*, pp.23, 55.

[50] ICJ Reports, 1986, p.14; 76 *ILR*, p.349.

[51] *Ibid.*, pp.108-9; 76 *ILR*, pp.442-43, citing ICJ Reports, 1969, p.44; 41 *ILR*, p.73.

[52] See Akehurst, *op. cit.*, pp.32-34 for attempts made to deny or minimise the need for *opinio juris*.

see whether the legitimating stamp of state activity can be provided or not. If a state proclaims a twelve mile limit to its territorial sea in the belief that although the three mile limit has been accepted law, the circumstances are so altering that a twelve mile limit might now be treated as becoming law, it is vindicated if other states follow suit and a new rule of customary law is established. If other states reject the proposition, then the projected rule withers away and the original rule stands, reinforced by state practice and commonly accepted. As the Court itself noted in the *Nicaragua* case,[53] "[r]eliance by a State on a novel right or an unprecedented exception to the principle might, if shared in principle by other States, tend towards a modification of customary international law". The difficulty in this kind of approach is that it is sometimes hard to pinpoint exactly when one rule supersedes another, but that is a complication inherent in the nature of custom. Change is rarely smooth but rather spasmodic.

This means taking a more flexible view of the *opinio juris* and tying it more firmly with the overt manifestations of a custom into the context of national and international behaviour. This should be done to accommodate the idea of an action which, while contrary to law, contains the germ of a new law and relates to the difficulty of actually proving that a state, in behaving a certain way, does so in the belief that it is in accordance with the law. An extreme expression of this approach is to infer or deduce the *opinio juris* from the material acts. Judge Tanaka, in his dissenting opinion in the *North Sea Continental Shelf* cases, remarked that there was:

> no other way than to ascertain the existence of *opinio juris* from the fact of the external existence of a certain custom and its necessity felt in the international community, rather than to seek evidence as to the subjective motives for each example of State practice.[54]

However, states must be made aware that when one state takes a course of action, it does so because it regards it as within the confines of international law, and not as, for example, purely a political or moral gesture. There has to be an aspect of legality about

[53] ICJ Reports, 1986, pp.14, 109; 76 *ILR*, pp.349, 443.

[54] ICJ Reports, 1969, pp.3, 176; 41 *ILR*, pp.29, 171. Lauterpacht wrote that one should regard all uniform conduct of governments as evidencing the *opinio juris*, except where the conduct in question was not accompanied by such intention: *op. cit.* footnote 7, p.580; but cf. Cheng, *op. cit.* footnotes 7, p.36 and 15, pp.530-32.

the behaviour and the acting state will have to confirm that this is so, so that the international community can easily distinguish legal from non-legal practices. This is essential to the development and presentation of a legal framework amongst the states.[55]

Protest, Acquiescence and Change in Customary Law [56]

Some writers have maintained that abstention can amount to consent to a customary rule and that the absence of protest implies agreement. In other words where a state or states take action which they declare to be legal, the silence of other states can be used as an expression of *opinio juris* or concurrence in the new legal rule. This means that actual protests are called for to break the legitimising process.[57]

In the *Lotus* case, the Court held that "only if such abstention were based on their [the states] being conscious of having a duty to abstain would it be possible to speak of an international custom".[58] Thus, one cannot infer a rule prohibiting certain action merely because states do not indulge in that activity. But the question of not reacting when a state behaves a certain way is a slightly different one. It would seem that where a new rule is created in new fields of international law, for example space law, acquiescence by other states is to be regarded as reinforcing the rule whether it stems from actual agreement or lack of interest depending always upon the particular circumstances of the case. Acquiescence in a new rule which deviates from an established custom is more problematic.

The decision in the *Anglo-Norwegian Fisheries* case[59] may appear

---

[55] Note D'Amato's view that to become a custom, a practice has to be preceded or accompanied by the "articulation" of a rule, which will put states on notice than an action etc. will have legal implications, *op. cit.*, p.75. Cf. Akehurst, *op. cit.*, pp.35-36, who also puts forward his view that "the practice of states needs to be accompanied by *statements* that something is already law before it can become law": such statements need not be beliefs as to the truths of the given situation, *ibid.*, p.37. Akehurst also draws a distinction between permissive rules, which do not require express statements as to *opinio juris* and duty-imposing rules, which do; *ibid.*, pp.37-38.

[56] See Lauterpacht, "Sovereignty over Submarine Areas", 27 *BYIL*, 1950, p.376; MacGibbon, "Some Observations on the Part of Protest in International Law", 29 *BYIL*, 1953, p.293 and "Customary International Law and Acquiescence", 33 *BYIL*, 1957, p.115 and Wolfke, *op. cit.*, pp.157-65.

[57] See e.g. MacGibbon, "Customary International Law and Acquiescence", *op. cit.*, p.131 and McDougal *et al.*, *Studies in World Public Order*, 1960, pp.763-72.

[58] *Supra*, footnote 46.

[59] ICJ Reports, 1951, p.116; 18 *ILR*, p.86.

to suggest that where a state acts contrary to an established customary rule and other states acquiesce in this, then that state is to be treated as not bound by the original rule. The Court noted that "in any event the . . . rule would appear to be inapplicable as against Norway inasmuch as she had always opposed any attempt to apply it to the Norwegian coast".[60] In other words, a state opposing the existence of a custom from its inception would not be bound by it, but the problem of one or more states seeking to dissent from recognised customs by adverse behaviour coupled with the acquiescence or non-reaction of other states remains unsettled.

States fail to protest for very many reasons. A state might not wish to give offence gratuitously or it might wish to reinforce political ties or other diplomatic and political considerations may be relevant. It could be that to protest over every single act with which a state does not agree would be an excessive requirement. It is, therefore, unrealistic to expect every state to react to every single act of every other state. If one accepted that a failure to protest validated a derogation from an established custom in every case then scores of special relationships would emerge between different states depending upon acquiescence and protest. In many cases a protest might be purely formal or part of diplomatic manoeuvring designed to exert pressure in a totally different field and thus not intended to alter legal relationships.

Where a new rule which contradicts a prior rule is maintained by a large number of states, the protests of a few states would not overrule it, and the abstention from reaction by other countries would merely reinforce it. Constant protest on the part of a particular state when reinforced by the acquiescence of other states might create a recognised exception to the rule, but it will depend to a great extent on the facts of the situation and the views of the international community. Behaviour contrary to a custom contains within itself the seeds of a new rule and if it is endorsed by other nations, the previous law will disappear and be replaced, or alternatively there could be a period of time during which the two customs co-exist until one of them is generally accepted,[61] as was the position for many

---

[60] *Ibid.*, p.131; 18 *ILR*, p.93. See also the *North Sea Continental Shelf* cases, ICJ Reports, 1969, pp.3, 26-27; 41 *ILR*, pp.29, 55-56 and the *Asylum* case, ICJ Reports, 1950, pp.266, 277-78; 17 *ILR*, pp.280, 285.

[61] See also protests generally: Akehurst, *op. cit.*, pp.38-42.

until one of them is generally accepted,[61] as was the position for many years with regard to the limits of the territorial sea.[62] It follows from the above, therefore, that customary rules are binding upon all states except for such states as have dissented from the start of that custom.[63] This raises the question of new states and custom, for the logic of the traditional approach would be for such states to be bound by all existing customs as at the date of independence. The opposite view, based upon the consent theory of law, would permit such states to choose which customs to adhere to at that stage, irrespective of the attitude of other states.[64] However, since such an approach could prove highly disruptive, the proviso is often made that by entering into relations without reservation with other states, new states signify their acceptance of the totality of international law.[65]

Local Custom [66]

It is possible for rules to develop which will bind only a set group of states, or indeed just two states.

In the *Asylum* case,[67] the International Court of Justice discussed the Colombian claim of a regional or local custom peculiar to the Latin American states, which would validate its position over the granting of asylum. The Court declared that the "party which relies on a custom of this kind must prove that this custom is established in such a manner that it has become binding on the other party".[68] It found that such a custom could not be proved because of uncertain and contradictory evidence.

In such cases, the standard of proof required, especially as regards the obligation accepted by the party against whom the local custom is maintained, is higher than in cases where an ordinary or general custom is alleged.

In the *Right of Passage over Indian Territory* case,[69] Portugal claimed

---

[62] See *infra*, Chapter 10, p.348.

[63] See e.g. the *North Sea Continental Shelf* cases, ICJ Reports, 1969, pp.3, 38, 130; 41 *ILR*, pp.29, 67, 137.

[64] See e.g. Tunkin, *op. cit.*, p.129.

[65] *Ibid.*

[66] See Akehurst, op. cit., pp.29-31; D'Amato, *op. cit.*, Chapter 8; and Wolfke, *op. cit.*, pp.86-92. Sometimes referred to as regional or special custom.

[67] ICJ Reports, 1950, p.266; 17 *ILR*, p.280.

[68] *Ibid.*, p.276; 17 *ILR*, p.284.

[69] ICJ Reports, 1960, p.6; 31 *ILR*, p.23.

the Portuguese enclaves, and this was upheld by the International Court of Justice over India's objections that no local custom could be established between only two states. The Court declared that it was satisfied that there had in the past existed a constant and uniform practice allowing free passage and that the "practice was accepted as law by the parties and has given rise to a right and a correlative obligation".[70]

Such local customs therefore depend upon a particular activity by one state being accepted by the other state (or states) as an expression of a legal obligation or right. While in the case of a general customary rule the process of consensus is at work so that a majority or a substantial minority of interested states can be sufficient to create a new custom, a local custom needs the positive acceptance of both (or all) parties to the rule.[71] This is because local customs are an exception to the general nature of customary law, which involves a fairly flexible approach to law-making by all states, and instead constitutes a reminder of the former theory of consent whereby states are bound only by what they assent to. Exceptions may prove the rule, but they need greater proof than the rule to establish themselves.

TREATIES [72]

In contrast with the process of creating law through custom, treaties (or international conventions) are a more modern and more deliberate method.[73] Article 38 refers to "international conventions, whether general or particular, establishing rules expressly recognised by the contracting states". Treaties will be considered in more detail in Chapter 15 but in this survey of the sources of international law reference must be made to the role of international conventions.

Treaties are known by a variety of differing names, ranging from Conventions, International Agreements, Pacts, General Acts, Charters, through to Statutes, Declarations and Covenants. All these terms refer to a similar transaction, the creation of written agreements whereby the states participating bind themselves legally to act in a particular way or to set up particular relations between

---

[70] Ibid., p.40; 31 ILR, p.53. See Wolfke, op. cit., p.90.

[71] See Cohen-Jonathan, "La Coutume Locale", 7 AFDI, 1961, p.119.

[72] See generally McNair, The Law of Treaties, 1961. See further infra, Chapter 15.

[73] Oppenheim emphasises that "custom is the original source of international law, treaties are a source the power of which derives from custom", op. cit., p.28.

themselves. A series of conditions and arrangements are laid out which the parties oblige themselves to carry out.

It is possible to divide treaties into "law-making" treaties, which are intended to have universal or general relevance, and "treaty-contracts", which apply only as between two, or a small number of states. Such a distinction is intended to reflect the general or local applicability of a particular treaty and the range of obligations imposed. It cannot be regarded as hard and fast and there are many grey areas of overlap and uncertainty.[74]

Treaties are express agreements and are a form of substitute legislation undertaken by states. They bear a close resemblance to contracts in a superficial sense in that the parties create binding obligations for themselves, but they have a nature of their own which reflects the character of the international system. The number of treaties entered into has expanded over the last century, witness the growing number of volumes of the United Nations Treaty Series or the United Kingdom Treaty Series. They fulfil a vital role in international relations.

As governmental controls increase and the technological and communications revolutions affect international life, the number of issues which require some form of inter-state regulation multiplies.

For Soviet writers, as for many others, treaties are the most important sources of international law as they require the express consent of the contracting parties, and are to be regarded as superior to custom, which is regarded in any event as a form of tacit agreement.[75]

As examples of important treaties one may mention the Charter of the United Nations, the Geneva Conventions on the treatment of prisoners and the protection of civilians and the Vienna Conventions on Diplomatic Relations. All kinds of agreements exist ranging from the regulation of outer space exploration to the control of drugs and the creation of international financial and development institutions. It would be impossible to telephone abroad or post a letter overseas or take an aeroplane to other countries without the various international agreements that have laid down the necessary, recognised conditions of operation.

---

[74] See Virally, *op. cit.*, p.126; Sørensen, *op. cit.*, p.58 *et seq.* and Tunkin, *op. cit.*, pp.93-95.

[75] *Ibid.*, pp.91-113. See also Mullerson, "Sources of International Law: New Tendencies in Soviet Thinking", 83 *AJIL*, 1989, pp.494, 501-9 and Danilenko, "The Theory of International Customary Law", 31 *German Yearbook of International Law*, 1988, p.9.

It follows from the essence of an international treaty that, like a contract, it sets down a series of propositions which are then regarded as binding upon the parties. How then is it possible to treat conventions as sources of international law, over and above the obligations imposed upon the contracting parties? It is in this context that one can understand the term "law-making treaties". They are intended to have an effect *generally*, not restrictively, and they are to be contrasted with those treaties which merely regulate limited issues between a few states. Law-making treaties are those agreements whereby states elaborate their perception of international law upon any given topic or establish new rules which are to guide them for the future in their international conduct. Such law-making treaties, of necessity, require the participation of a large number of states to emphasise this effect, and may produce rules that will bind all.[76] They constitute normative treaties, agreements that prescribe rules of conduct to be followed. Examples of such treaties would include, in addition to some of those already mentioned, the Antarctica Treaty and the Genocide Convention. There are also many agreements which declare the existing law or codify existing customary rules, such as the Vienna Convention on Diplomatic Relations of 1961.[77]

Parties that do not sign and ratify the particular treaty in question are not bound by its terms. This is a general rule and was illustrated in the *North Sea Continental Shelf* cases[78] where West Germany had not ratified the relevant Convention and was therefore under no obligation to heed its terms. However, where treaties reflect customary law then non-parties are bound, not because it is a treaty provision but because it reaffirms a rule or rules of customary international law. Similarly, non-parties may come to accept that provisions in a particular treaty can generate customary law, depending always upon the nature of the agreement, the number of participants and other relevant factors.

The possibility that a provision in a treaty may constitute the basis of a rule which, when coupled with the *opinio juris*, can lead to the creation of a binding custom governing all states, not just those party

[76] See Brownlie, *op. cit.*, pp.12-13 and Baxter, "Treaties and Custom", 129 *HR*, p.27. See also Schachter, "Entangled Treaty and Custom" in *International Law at a Time of Perplexity* (ed. Dinstein), 1989, p.717.

[77] Brownlie, *op. cit.*, Chapter 1.

[78] ICJ Reports, 1969, pp.3, 25; 41 *ILR*, pp.29, 54.

to the original treaty, was considered by the International Court of
Justice in the *North Sea Continental Shelf* cases[79] and regarded as one
of the recognised methods of formulating new rules of customary
international law. The Court, however, declared that the particular
provision had to be "of a fundamentally norm-creating character",[80]
that is, capable of forming the basis of a general rule of law. What
exactly this amounts to will probably vary according to the time and
place, but it does confirm that treaty provisions may lead to custom
providing other states, parties and non-parties to the treaty fulfil
the necessary conditions of compatible behaviour and *opinio juris*.
It has been argued that this possibility may be extended so that
generalisable treaty provisions may of themselves, without the
requirement to demonstrate the *opinio juris* and with little passage
of time, generate *ipso facto* customary rules.[81] This, while
recognising the importance of treaties, particularly in the human
rights field, containing potential norm-creating provisions, is clearly
going too far. The danger would be of a small number of states
legislating for all, unless dissenting states actually entered into
contrary treaties.[82] This would constitute too radical a departure
for the current process of law-formation within the international
community.

It is now established that even where a treaty rule comes into being
covering the same ground as a customary rule, the latter will not
be simply absorbed within the former but will maintain its separate
existence. The Court in the *Nicaragua* case[83] did not accept the
argument of the US that the norms of customary international law
concerned with self-defence had been "subsumed" and "supervened"
by article 51 of the United Nations Charter. It was emphasised that
"even if a treaty norm and a customary norm relevant to the present
dispute were to have exactly the same content, this would not be a
reason for the Court to take the view that the operation of the treaty

[79] *Ibid.*, p.41; 41 *ILR*, p.71. The Court stressed that this method of creating new customs
was not to be lightly regarded as having been attained, *ibid.*

[80] But see the minority opinions, *ibid.*, pp.56, 156-58, 163, 169, 172-80, 197-200, 221-32
and 241-47; 41 *ILR*, p.85. See also the *Gulf of Maine* case, ICJ Reports, 1984, pp.246, 295; 71
ILR, pp.74, 122 and the *Libya-Malta Continental Shelf* case, ICJ Reports, 1985, pp.13, 29-34;
81 *ILR*, pp.239, 261-66.

[81] See D'Amato, *op. cit.*, p.104 and "The Concept of Human Rights in International
Law", 82 *Columbia Law Review*, 1982, pp.1110, 1129-47. See also Akehurst, *op. cit.*, pp.42-52.

[82] D'Amato, "The Concept of Human Rights", *op. cit.*, p.1146.

[83] ICJ Reports, 1986, p.14; 76 *ILR*, p.349.

reason for the Court to take the view that the operation of the treaty process must necessarily deprive the customary norm of its separate applicability".[84] The effect of this in the instant case was that the Court was able to examine the rule as established under customary law, whereas due to an American reservation, it was unable to analyse the treaty-based obligation.

Of course, two rules with the same content may be subject to different principles with regard to their interpretation and application; thus the approach of the Court as well as being theoretically correct is of practical value also. In many cases, such dual source of existence of a rule may well suggest that the two versions are not in fact identical, as in the case of self-defence under customary law and article 51 of the Charter, but it will always depend upon the particular circumstances.[85]

Certain treaties attempt to establish a "regime" which will, of necessity, also extend to non-parties.[86] The United Nations Charter, for example, in its creation of a definitive framework for the preservation of international peace and security, declares in article 2(6) that "the organisation shall ensure that states which are not members of the United Nations act in accordance with these Principles [listed in article 2] so far as may be necessary for the maintenance of international peace and security". One can also point to the 1947 General Agreement on Tariffs and Trade (GATT) which sets up a common code of conduct in international trade and has an important effect on non-party states as well.

On the same theme, treaties may be constitutive in that they create international institutions and act as constitutions for them, outlining their proposed powers and duties.

"Treaty-contracts" on the other hand are not law-making instruments in themselves since they are between only small numbers of states and on a limited topic, but may provide evidence of customary rules. For example, a series of bilateral treaties containing a similar rule may be evidence of the existence of that rule in

---

[84] *Ibid.*, pp.93-97; 76 *ILR*, pp.427-31. See also Czaplinski, "Sources of International Law in the *Nicaragua* case", 38 *ICLQ*, 1989, p.151.
[85] See further Chapter 18.
[86] See further *infra*, Chapter 15.

GENERAL PRINCIPLES OF LAW [87]

In any system of law, a situation may very well arise where the court in considering a case before it realises that there is no law covering exactly that point, neither parliamentary statute nor judicial precedent. In such instances the judge will proceed to deduce a rule that will be relevant, by analogy from already existing rules or directly from the general principles that guide the legal system, whether they be referred to as emanating from justice, equity or considerations of public policy. Such a situation is perhaps even more likely to arise in international law because of the relative underdevelopment of the system in relation to the needs with which it is faced.

There are fewer decided cases in international law than in a municipal system and no method of legislating to provide rules to govern new situations. It is for such a reason that the provision of "the general principles of law recognised by civilised nations" was inserted into article 38 as a source of law, to close the gap that might be uncovered in international law and solve this problem which is known legally as *non liquet*.[88]

There are various opinions as to what the general principles of law concept is intended to refer. Some writers regard it as an affirmation of Natural Law concepts, which are deemed to underlie the system of international law and constitute the method for testing the validity of the positive (i.e. man-made) rules.[89] Other writers, particularly positivists, treat it as a sub-heading under treaty and customary law and incapable of adding anything new to international law unless it reflects the consent of states. Soviet writers like Tunkin subscribe to this approach and regard the "general principles of law" as reiterating the fundamental precepts

[87] See e.g. Cheng, *General Principles of Law as Applied by International Courts and Tribunals*, 1953; McNair, "The General Principles of Law Recognised by Civilised Nations", 33 *BYIL*, 1957, p.1; Lauterpacht, *Private Law Sources and Analogies of International Law*, 1927 and Waldock, "General Course on Public International Law", 106 *HR*, p.54.

[88] See e.g. Stone, *Of Law and Nations*, 1974, Chapter III. See also Lauterpacht, "Some Observations on the Prohibition of Non Liquet and the Completeness of the Legal Order", *Symbolae Verzijl*, 1958, p.196.

[89] See e.g. Lauterpacht, *op. cit.* footnote 87. See also Waldock, *op. cit.*, p.54; Jenks, *The Common Law of Mankind*, 1958, p.169 and Judge Tanaka (dissenting), *South West Africa* case, (Second Phase), ICJ Reports, 1966, pp.6, 294-99; 37 *ILR*, pp.243, 455-59.

of international law, for example, the law of peaceful coexistence, which have already been set out in treaty and custom law.[90]

Between these two approaches, most writers are prepared to accept that the general principles do constitute a separate source of law but of fairly limited scope, and this is reflected in the decisions of the Permanent Court of International Justice and the International Court of Justice. It is not clear, however, in all cases, whether what is involved is a general principle of law appearing in municipal systems or a general principle of international law. But perhaps this is not a terribly serious problem since both municipal legal concepts and those derived from existing international practice can be defined as falling within the recognised catchment area.[91]

While the reservoir from which one can draw contains the legal operations of 160 or so states, it does not follow that judges have to be experts in every legal system. There are certain common themes that run through the many different orders. Anglo-American Common Law has influenced a number of states throughout the world, as have the French and Germanic systems. There are many common elements in the law in Latin America, and most Afro-Asian states have borrowed heavily from the European experience in their efforts to modernise the structure administering the state and westernise economic and other enterprises.[92]

Reference will now be made to some of the leading cases in this field to illustrate how this is working out in practice.

In the _Chorzów Factory_ case in 1928,[93] which followed the seizure of a nitrate factory in Upper Silesia by Poland, the Permanent Court of International Justice declared that "it is a general conception of law that every violation of an engagement involves an obligation to make reparation". The Court also regarded it as:

a principle of international law that the reparation of a wrong may consist in an indemnity corresponding to the damage which the nationals of the injured state have suffered as a result of the act which is contrary to international law.

The most fertile fields, however, for the implementation of municipal law analogies have been those of procedure, evidence

---

[90] _Op. cit._, Chapter 7.
[91] See Brownlie, _op. cit._, pp.15-17 and Virally, _op. cit._, pp.144-48.
[92] See generally, David and Brierley, _Major Legal Systems in the World Today_, 2nd ed., 1978.
[93] PCIJ, Series A, no.17, 1928, p.29; 4 _ILR_, p.258.

and the machinery of the judicial process. The International Court of Justice in the *Corfu Channel* case,[94] when referring to circumstantial evidence, pointed out that "this indirect evidence is admitted in all systems of law and its use is recognised by international decisions". Five years later, in the *Administrative Tribunal* case,[95] the Court dealt with the problem of the dismissal of members of the United Nations Secretariat staff and whether the General Assembly had the right to refuse to give effect to awards to them made by the relevant Tribunal.

In giving its negative reply, the Court emphasised that:

> according to a well-established and generally recognised principle of law, a judgment rendered by such a judicial body is *res judicata* and has binding force between the parties to the dispute.[96]

The Court has also considered the principle of estoppel which provides that a party that has acquiesced in a particular situation cannot then proceed to challenge it. In the *Temple* case[97] the International Court of Justice applied the doctrine, but in the *Serbian Loans* case[98] in 1929, in which French bondholders were demanding payment in gold francs as against paper money upon a series of Serbian loans, the Court declared the principle inapplicable.

Thus it follows that it is the court which has the discretion as to which principles of law to apply in the circumstances of the particular case under consideration, and it will do this upon the basis of the inability of customary and treaty law to provide the required solution.

In this context, one must consider the *Barcelona Traction* case[99] between Belgium and Spain. The International Court of Justice relied heavily upon the municipal law concept of the limited liability company and emphasised that if

> the Court were to decide the case in disregard of the relevant institutions of municipal law it would, without justification, invite serious legal

---

[94] ICJ Reports, 1949, pp.4, 18; 16 *ILR*, pp.155, 157.

[95] ICJ Reports, 1954, p.47; 21 *ILR*, p.310.

[96] Ibid., p.53; 21 *ILR*, p.314. See also *AMCO* v. *Republic of Indonesia*, 27 *ILM*, 1988, pp.1281, 1290.

[97] ICJ Reports, 1962, pp.6, 23, 31 and 32; 33 *ILR*, pp.48, 62, 69-70. See also the *Eastern Greenland* case, PCIJ, Series A/B, no.53, p.52 *et seq.*; 6 *ILR*, pp.95, 100-102.

[98] PCIJ, Series A, no.20; 5 *ILR*, p.466.

[99] ICJ Reports, 1970, p.3; 46 *ILR*, p.178.

difficulties. It would lose touch with reality, for there are no corresponding institutions of international law to which the Court could resort.[100]

However, international law did not refer to the municipal law of a particular state, but rather to the rules generally accepted by municipal legal systems which, in this case, recognise the idea of the limited company.

Equity and International Law [101]

Apart from the recourse to the procedures and institutions of municipal legal systems to reinforce international law, it is also possible to see in a number of cases references to equity as a set of principles constituting the values of the system. The most famous decision on these lines was that of Judge Hudson in the *Diversion of Water from the Meuse* case[102] in 1937 regarding a dispute between Holland and Belgium. Hudson pointed out that what are regarded as principles of equity have long been treated as part of international law and applied by the courts. "Under article 38 of the Statute", he declared, "if not independently of that article, the Court has some freedom to consider principles of equity as part of the international law which it must apply." However, one must be very cautious in interpreting this.

The concept of equity has been referred to in several cases. In the *Rann of Kutch Arbitration* between India and Pakistan in 1968[103] the Tribunal agreed that equity formed part of international law and that accordingly the parties could rely on such principles in

---

[100] *Ibid.*, p.37; 46 *ILR*, p.211. See also generally the *Abu Dhabi* arbitration, 1 *ICLQ*, 1952, p.247; 18 *ILR*, p.44 and *Texaco* v. *Libya*, 53 *ILR*, p.389.

[101] See Akehurst, "Equity and General Principles of Law", 25 *ICLQ*, 1976, p.801; Cheng, "Justice and Equity in International Law", 8 *Current Legal Problems*, 1955, p.185; Degan, *L'Équité et le Droit International*, 1970; E. Lauterpacht, "Equity, Evasion, Equivocation and Evolution in International Law", *Proceedings of the American Branch of the ILA*, 1977-8, p.33 and *Aspects of the Administration of International Justice*, 1991, pp.117-52, and Chattopadhyay, "Equity in International Law: Its Growth and Development", 5 *Georgia Journal of International and Comparative Law*, 1975, p.381. Equity generally may be understood in the contexts of adapting law to particular areas, filling gaps in the law and as a reason for not applying unjust laws: see Akehurst, *loc. cit.* See also *infra*, Chapter 16 for the extensive use of equity in the context of state succession.

[102] PCIJ, Series A/B, no.70, pp.73, 77; 8 *ILR*, pp.444, 450.

[103] 50 *ILR*, p.2.

the presentation of their cases.[104] The International Court of Justice in the *North Sea Continental Shelf* cases directed a final delimitation between the parties, West Germany, Holland and Denmark, "in accordance with equitable principles"[105] and discussed the relevance to equity in its consideration of the *Barcelona Traction* case.[106] Judge Tanaka, however, has argued for a wider interpretation in his dissenting opinion in the Second Phase of the *South West Africa* cases[107] and has treated the broad concept as a source of human rights ideas.

However, what is really in question here is the use of equitable principles in the context of a rule requiring such an approach. The relevant courts are not applying principles of abstract justice to the cases,[108] but rather deriving equitable principles and solutions from the applicable law.[109] Equity has been used by the courts as a way of mitigating certain inequities, not as a method of refashioning nature to the detriment of legal rules.[110] Its existence, therefore, as a separate and distinct source of law is at best highly controversial.

The use of equitable principles, however, has been marked in the 1982 Law of the Sea Convention. Article 59, for example, provides that conflicts between coastal and other states regarding the exclusive economic zone are to be resolved "on the basis of equity", while by article 74 delimitation of the zone between states with opposite or adjacent coasts, is to be effected by agreement on the basis of international law in order to achieve an equitable solution. A similar provision applies by article 83 to the delimitation of the continental

---

[104] *Ibid.*, p.18. In deciding the course of the boundary in two deep inlets, the Tribunal had recourse to the concept of equity: *ibid.*, p.520.

[105] ICJ Reports, 1969, pp.3, 53; 41 *ILR*, pp.29, 83. Equity was used in the case in order to exclude the use of the equidistance method in the particular circumstances: *ibid.*, pp.48-50; 41 *ILR*, pp.78-80.

[106] ICJ Reports, 1970, p.3; 46 *ILR*, p.178. See also the *Burkina Faso* v. *Mali* case, ICJ Reports, 1986, pp.554, 631-33; 80 *ILR*, pp.459, 532-35.

[107] ICJ Reports, 1966, pp.6, 294-99; 37 *ILR*, pp.243, 455-59. See also the *Corfu Channel* case, ICJ Reports, 1949, pp.4, 22; 16 *ILR*, p.155.

[108] The International Court of Justice may under article 38(2) of its Statute decide a case "*ex aequo et bono*" if the parties agree, but it has never done so.

[109] See the *North Sea Continental Shelf* cases, ICJ Reports, 1969, pp.3, 47; 41 *ILR*, pp.29, 76, and the *Fisheries Jurisdiction* cases, ICJ Reports, 1974, pp.3, 33; 55 *ILR*, pp.238, 268.

[110] See the *North Sea Continental Shelf* cases, ICJ Reports, 1969, pp.3, 49-50; 41 *ILR*, pp.29, 78-80, and the *Anglo-French Continental Shelf* case, Cmnd. 7438, 1978, pp.116-17; 54 *ILR*, pp.6, 123-24. See also the *Tunisia-Libya Continental Shelf* case, ICJ Reports, 1982, pp.18, 60; 67 *ILR*, pp.4, 53, and the *Gulf of Maine* case, ICJ Reports, 1984, pp.246, 313-14 and 325-30; 71 *ILR*, pp.74, 140-41 and 152-57.

shelf.[111] These provisions possess flexibility, which is important, but are also very uncertain. Precisely how any particular dispute may be resolved, and the way in which that is likely to happen and the principles to be used are far from clear and an unfortunate element of unpredictability has been introduced.

JUDICIAL DECISIONS [112]

Although these are, in the words of article 38, to be utilised as a subsidiary means for the determination of rules of law rather than as an actual source of law, judicial decisions can be of immense importance. While by virtue of article 59 of the Statute of the International Court of Justice the decisions of the Court have no binding force except as between the parties and in respect of the case under consideration, the Court has striven to follow its previous judgments and insert a measure of certainty within the process: so that while the doctrine of precedent as it is known in the Common Law, whereby the rulings of certain courts must be followed by other courts, does not exist in international law, one still finds that states in disputes and textbook writers quote judgments of the Permanent Court and the International Court of Justice as authoritative decisions.

The International Court of Justice itself will closely examine its previous decisions and will carefully distinguish those cases which it feels should not be applied to the problem being studied. But just as English judges, for example, create law in the process of interpreting it, so the judges of the International Court of Justice sometimes do a little more than merely "determine" it. One of the most outstanding instances of this occurred in the *Anglo-Norwegian Fisheries* case,[113] with its statement of the criteria for the recognition of baselines from which to measure the territorial sea, which was later enshrined in the 1958 Geneva Convention on the Territorial Sea and Contiguous Zone.

Other examples include the *Reparation* case,[114] which recognised

---

[111] See also article 140 providing for the equitable sharing of financial and other benefits derived from activities in the deep sea-bed area.

[112] See e.g. Lauterpacht, *op. cit.* footnote 7; Waldock, *op. cit.*, and Schwarzenberger, *op. cit.*, p.30 *et seq.*

[113] ICJ Reports, 1951, p.116; 18 *ILR*, p.86. See further *infra*, Chapter 10.

[114] ICJ Reports, 1949, p.174; 16 *ILR*, p.318. See further *infra*, Chapter 19.

the legal personality of international institutions in certain cases, the *Genocide* case,[115] which dealt with reservations to treaties and the *Nottebohm* case,[116] which considered the role and characteristics of nationality.

Of course, it does not follow that a decision of the Court will be invariably accepted in later discussions and formulations of the law. One example of this is part of the decision in the *Lotus* case,[117] which was criticised and later abandoned in the Geneva Conventions on the Law of the Sea. But this is comparatively rare and the degree of respect accorded to the Court and its decisions renders its opinions vital to the growth and exposition of international law.

In addition to the Permanent Court and the International Court of Justice, the phrase "judicial decisions" also encompasses international arbitral awards and the rulings of national courts. There have been many international arbitral tribunals such as the Permanent Court of Arbitration created by the Hague Conferences of 1899 and 1907 and the various mixed-claims tribunals, including the Iran-US Claims Tribunal, and, although they differ from the international courts in some ways, many of their decisions have been extremely significant in the development of international law.

This can be seen in the existence and number of the Reports of International Arbitral Awards published since 1948 by the United Nations.

One case that should be mentioned is the *Alabama Claims* arbitration,[118] which marked the opening of a new era in the peaceful settlement of international disputes, in which increasing use was made of judicial and arbitration methods in resolving conflicts. This case involved a vessel built in Liverpool to the specifications of the Confederate States, which succeeded in capturing some 70 Federal ships during the American Civil War. The United States sought compensation after the war for the depredations of the *Alabama* and other ships and this was accepted by the Tribunal. Britain had infringed the rules of neutrality and was accordingly obliged to pay damages to the United States.

Another illustration of the impact of such arbitral awards is the

[115] ICJ Reports, 1951, p.15; 18 *ILR*, p.364.
[116] ICJ Reports, 1955, p.4; 22 *ILR*, p.349.
[117] PCIJ, Series A, no.10, 1927, p.18; 4 *ILR*, p.5. See *infra*, p.372.
[118] Moore, *International Arbitrations*, vol.1, p.653.

Island of Palmas case[119] which has proved of immense significance in the subject of territorial sovereignty and will be discussed later.

As has already been seen, the decisions of municipal courts[120] may provide evidence of the existence of a customary rule. They may also constitute evidence of the actual practice of states which, while not a description of the law as it has been held to apply, nevertheless affords examples of how states actually behave, in other words the essence of the material act which is so necessary in establishing a rule of customary law. British and American writers, in particular, tend to refer fairly extensively to decisions of national courts.

One may, finally, also point to decisions by the highest courts of federal states, like Switzerland and the United States, in their resolution of conflicts between the component units of such countries, as relevant to the development of international law rules in such fields as boundary disputes. A boundary disagreement between two US states which is settled by the Supreme Court is in many ways analogous to the International Court of Justice considering a frontier dispute between two independent states, and as such provides valuable material for international law.[121]

WRITERS [122]

Article 38 includes as a subsidiary means for the determination of rules of law, "the teachings of the most highly qualified publicists of the various nations".

Historically, of course, the influence of academic writers on the development of international law has been marked. In the heyday of Natural Law it was analyses and juristic opinions that were crucial, while the role of state practice and court decisions was of less value. Writers such as Gentilis, Grotius, Pufendorf, Bynkershoek and Vattel were the supreme authorities of the sixteenth to eighteenth

[119] 2 *RIAA*, p.829; 4 *ILR*, p.3. See also the *Beagle Channel* award, HMSO, 1977; 52 *ILR*, p.93 and the *Anglo-French Continental Shelf* case, Cmnd. 7438, 1978; 54 *ILR*, p.6.

[120] See e.g. *Thirty Hogsheads of Sugar, Bentzon* v. *Boyle*, 9 Cranch 191 (1815); the *Paquete Habana*, 175 US 677 (1900) and the *Scotia*, 14 Wallace 170 (1871). See also the *Lotus* case, PCIJ, Series A, no.10, 1927, p.18; 4 *ILR*, p.153. For further examples in the fields of state and diplomatic immunities particularly, see *infra*, Chapter 12.

[121] See e.g. *Vermont* v. *New Hampshire*, 289 US 593 (1933) and *Iowa* v. *Illinois*, 147 US 1 (1893).

[122] See e.g. Parry, *op. cit.*, pp.103-5 and Lauterpacht, *op. cit.* footnote 7, pp.23-25.

centuries and determined the scope, form and content of international law.[123]

With the rise of positivism and the consequent emphasis upon state sovereignty, treaties and custom assumed the dominant position in the exposition of the rules of the international system, and the importance of legalistic writings began to decline. Thus, one finds that textbooks are used as a method of discovering what the law is on any particular point rather than as the fount or source of actual rules. There are still some writers who have had a formative impact upon the evolution of particular laws, for example Gidel on the law of the sea,[124] and others whose general works on international law tend to be referred to virtually as classics, for example Oppenheim and Rousseau, but the general influence of textbook writers has somewhat declined this century.

Nevertheless, books are important as a way of arranging and putting into focus the structure and form of international law and of elucidating the nature, history and practice of the rules of law. Academic writings have also a useful role to play in stimulating thought about the values and aims of international law as well as pointing out the defects that exist within the system, and making suggestions as to the future.

Because of the lack of supreme authorities and institutions in the international legal order, the responsibility is all the greater upon the publicists of the various nations to inject an element of coherence and order into the subject as well as to question the direction and purposes of the rules.

States in their presentation of claims, national law officials in their opinions to their governments, the various international judicial and arbitral bodies in considering their decisions, and the judges of municipal courts when the need arises, all consult and quote the writings of the leading juristic authorities.[125]

Of course, the claim can be made, and often is, that textbook writers merely reflect and reinforce national prejudices,[126] but it is an allegation which has been exaggerated. It should not lead us to

---

[123] See *supra*, Chapter 1.

[124] *Droit International Public de la Mer*, 3 vols., 1932-4.

[125] See Brownlie, *op. cit.*, pp.25-26.

[126] See e.g. Huber in the *Spanish Zone of Morocco* case, 2 *RIAA*, pp.615, 640; 2 *ILR*, pp.157, 164 (note). See also Carty, *The Decay of International Law?*, 1986, pp.128-31.

dismiss the value of writers, but rather to assess correctly the writer within his particular environment.

OTHER POSSIBLE SOURCES OF INTERNATIONAL LAW

In the discussion of the various sources of law prescribed by the Statute of the International Court of Justice, it might have been noted that there is a distinction between, on the one hand, actual sources of rules, that is those devices capable of instituting new rules such as law-making treaties, customary law, and many decisions of the International Court of Justice since they cannot be confined to the category of merely determining or elucidating the law, and on the other hand those practices and devices which afford evidence of the existence of rules, such as juristic writings, many treaty-contracts and some judicial decisions both at the international and municipal level. In fact, each source is capable, to some extent, of both developing new law and identifying existing law. This results partly from the disorganised state of international law and partly from the terms of article 38 itself.

A similar confusion between law-making, law-determining and law-evidencing can be discerned in the discussion of the various other methods of developing law that have emerged since the conclusion of the Second World War. Foremost among the issues that have arisen and one that reflects the growth in the importance of the Third World states and the gradual de-Europeanisation of the world order is the question of the standing of the resolutions and declarations of the General Assembly of the United Nations.[127]

Certain resolutions of the Assembly[128] are binding upon the organs and member-states of the United Nations. Other resolutions, however, are not legally binding and are merely recommendatory, putting forward opinions on various issues with varying degrees of majority support. This is the classic position and reflects the intention

---

[127] See e.g. Asamoah, *The Legal Significance of the Declarations of the General Assembly of the United Nations*, 1966; Johnson, "The Effect of Resolutions of the General Assembly of the United Nations", 32 *BYIL*, 1955-6, p.97; Castañeda, *Legal Effects of United Nations Resolutions*, 1969 and Falk, "On the Quasi-Legislative Competence of the General Assembly", 60 *AJIL*, 1966, p.782. See also Cassese, *International Law in a Divided World*, 1986, pp.192-95; Sloan, "General Assembly Resolutions Revisited (40 Years After)", 58 *BYIL*, 1987, p.39 and Schwebel, "United Nations Resolutions, Recent Arbitral Awards and Customary International Law" in *Realism in Law-Making* (eds. Bos and Siblesz), 1986, p.203.

[128] See e.g. article 17 of the UN Charter.

that the Assembly was to be basically a parliamentary advisory body with the binding decisions to be taken by the Security Council.

Nowadays, the situation is somewhat more complex. The Assembly has produced a great number of highly important resolutions and declarations and it was inevitable that these should have some impact upon the direction adopted by modern international law. The way states vote in the General Assembly and the explanations given upon such occasions constitute evidence of state practice and state understanding as to the law. Where a particular country has consistently voted in favour of, for example, the abolition of apartheid, it could not afterwards deny the existence of a usage condemning racial discrimination and it may even be that that usage is for that state converted into a binding custom.

The Court in the *Nicaragua* case tentatively expressed the view that the *opinio juris* requirement could be derived from the circumstances surrounding the adoption and application of a General Assembly resolution. It noted that the relevant

> *opinio juris* may, though with all due caution, be deduced from, *inter alia*, the attitude of the Parties [i.e. the US and Nicaragua] and the attitude of States towards certain General Assembly resolutions, and particularly resolution 2625 (XXV) entitled "Declaration on Principles of International Law concerning Friendly Relations and Co-operation among States in accordance with the Charter of the United Nations".[129]

The effect of consent to resolutions such as this one "may be understood as acceptance of the validity of the rule or set of rules declared by the resolution by themselves".[130] This comment, however, may well have referred solely to the situation where the resolution in question defines or elucidates an existing treaty (i.e. Charter) commitment.

Where the vast majority of states consistently vote for resolutions and declarations on a topic, that amounts to a state practice and a binding rule may very well emerge. For example, the 1960 Declaration on the Granting of Independence to Colonial Countries and Peoples, which was adopted with no opposition and only nine

---

[129] ICJ Reports, 1986, pp.14, 99-100; 76 *ILR*, pp.349, 433-34.
[130] *Ibid.*, p.100; 76 *ILR*, p.434.

abstentions and followed a series of resolutions in general and specific terms attacking colonialism and calling for the self-determination of the remaining colonies, has, it would seem, marked the transmutation of the concept of self-determination from a political and moral principle to a legal right and consequent obligation, particularly taken in conjunction with the 1970 Declaration on Principles of International Law.[131]

Declarations such as that on the Legal Principles Governing Activities of States in the Exploration and Use of Outer Space (1963) can also be regarded as examples of state practices which are leading to, or have led to, a binding rule of customary law. Apart from that, they can be understood as authoritative interpretations by the Assembly of the various principles of the United Nations Charter.[132]

Accordingly, such resolutions are able to speed up the process of the legalisation of a state practice and thus enable a speedier adaptation of customary law to the conditions of modern life. The presence of representatives of virtually all of the states of the world in the General Assembly enormously enhances the value of that organ in general political terms and in terms of the generation of state practice that may or may not lead to binding custom.

Nevertheless, one must be alive to the dangers in ascribing legal value to everything that emanates from the Assembly. Resolutions are often the results of political compromises and arrangements and comprehended in that sense, never intended to constitute binding norms. Great care must be taken in moving from a plethora of practice to the identification of legal norms.

As far as the practice of other international organisations is concerned,[133] the same approach, but necessarily tempered with a little more caution, may be adopted. Resolutions may evidence an existing custom or constitute usage that may lead to the creation

---

[131] See further *infra*, Chapter 5.

[132] See e.g. Schachter, "Interpretation of the Charter in the Political Organs of the United Nations" in *Law, States and International Order*, 1964, p.269; Higgins, *The Development of International Law Through the Political Organs of the United Nations*, 1963 and Shaw, *Title to Territory in Africa*, 1986, Chapter 2.

[133] See generally as to other international organisations in this context, Tammes, "Decisions of International Organs as a Source of International Law", 94 *HR*, p.265; Virally, "La Valeur Juridique des Recommendations des Organisations Internationales", *AFDI*, 1956, p.66 and Thierry, "Les Résolutions des Organes Internationaux dans la Jurisprudence de la Cour Internationale de Justice", 167 *HR*, p.385.

of a custom and the *opinio juris* requirement may similarly emerge from the surrounding circumstances, although care must be exercised here.[134]

The International Law Commission

The International Law Commission was established by the General Assembly in 1947 with the declared object of promoting the progressive development of international law and its codification. It consists of thirty-four members from Africa, Asia, America and Europe, who remain in office for five years each and who are appointed from lists submitted by national governments. The Commission is aided in its deliberations by consultations with various outside bodies including the Asian-African Legal Consultative Committee, the European Commission on Legal Co-operation and the Inter-American Council of Jurists.[135]

Many of the most important international conventions have grown out of the Commission's work. Having decided upon a topic, the International Law Commission will prepare a draft. This is submitted to the various states for their comments and is usually followed by an international conference convened by the United Nations. Eventually a treaty will emerge. This procedure was followed in such international conventions as those on the Law of the Sea in 1958, Diplomatic Relations in 1961, Consular Relations in 1963, Special Missions in 1969 and the Law of Treaties in 1969. Of course, this smooth operation does not invariably occur, witness the many conferences at Caracas in 1974, and Geneva and New York from 1975 to 1982 necessary to produce a new Convention on the Law of the Sea.

Apart from preparing such drafts, the International Law Commission also issues reports and studies, and has formulated such documents as the Draft Declaration on Rights and Duties of States of 1949 and the Principles of International Law recognised in the Charter of the Nuremberg Tribunal and in the Judgment of the

---

[134] See the *Nicaragua* case, ICJ Reports, 1986, pp.14, 100-2; 76 *ILR*, pp.349, 434-36.

[135] See articles 2, 3 and 8 of the Statute of the ILC. See also e.g. Ramcharan, *The International Law Commission*, 1977; Rosenne, "The International Law Commission 1949-59", 36 *BYIL*, 1960, p.104 and "Relations Between Governments and the International Law Commission", 19 *YBWA*, 1965, p.183, and Dhokalia, *The Codification of Public International Law*, 1970.

Tribunal of 1950. The Commission is at present considering the problems of jurisdictional immunities and state responsibility, amongst others.

Thus, one can see that the International Law Commission is involved in at least two of the major sources of law. Its drafts form the bases of international treaties which bind those states which have signed and ratified them and which may continue to form part of general international law, and its work is part of the whole range of state practice which can lead to new rules of customary law. Its drafts, indeed, may constitute evidence of custom as well as contribute to the corpus of usages which may create new law. In addition, it is not to be overlooked that the International Law Commission is a body composed of eminently qualified publicists including many governmental legal advisers whose reports and studies may be used as a method of determining what the law actually is, in much the same way as books.

Other Bodies

Although the International Law Commission is by far the most important of the organs for the study and development of the law, there do exist certain other bodies which are involved in the same mission. The United Nations Commission on International Trade Law (UNCITRAL) and the United Nations Conference on Trade and Development (UNCTAD) for example, are actively increasing the range of international law in the fields of economic, financial and development activities, while temporary organs such as the Committee on the Principles of International Law have been engaged in producing various declarations and statements. Nor can one overlook the tremendous work of the many specialised agencies like the International Labour Organisation and the United Nations Educational, Scientific and Cultural Organisation (UNESCO), which are constantly developing international law in their respective spheres.

There are also some independent bodies which are actively involved in the field. The International Law Association and the Institut de Droit International are the best known of such organisations which study and stimulate the law of the world community, while the various Harvard Research drafts produced before the Second World War are still of value today.

Unilateral Acts

In certain situations, the unilateral acts of states may give rise to international legal obligations.[136] For this, the intention of the state making the declaration in question to be bound is crucial as will be the element of publicity.[137] The intention here may be ascertained by interpretation of the act, and the question is clearly based upon the principle of good faith. The International Court has stressed that where states make statements by which their freedom of action is limited, a restrictive interpretation is required.[138] Recognition will be important here in so far as third states are concerned, in order for such an act or statement to be opposable to them.

HIERARCHY OF SOURCES AND *JUS COGENS*[139]

Judicial decisions and writings clearly have a subordinate function within the hierarchy in view of article 38(1), while the role of general principles of law as a way of complementing custom and treaty law places that category fairly firmly in third place. The question of priority as between custom and treaty law is more complex. As a general rule, the later in time will have priority. Treaties are usually formulated to replace or codify existing custom, while treaties in turn may themselves fall out of use and be replaced by new customary rules.

Article 53 of the Convention on the Law of Treaties, 1969, provides that a treaty will be void "if, at the time of its conclusion, it conflicts with a peremptory norm of general international law". This rule (*jus cogens*) will also apply in the context of customary rules so that no derogation would be permitted to such norms by way of local or special custom.

Such a peremptory norm is defined by the Convention as one

---

[136] See Virally, *op. cit.* footnote 1, pp.154-56; Brownlie, *op. cit.*, pp.637-40 and Garner, "The International Binding Force of Unilateral Oral Declarations", 27 *AJIL*, 1933, p.493.

[137] The *Nuclear Tests* cases, ICJ Reports, 1974, pp.253, 267; 57 *ILR*, pp.398, 412.

[138] *Ibid.* See also the *Nicaragua* case, ICJ Reports, 1986, pp.14, 132; 76 *ILR*, pp.349, 466 and the *Burkina Faso* v. *Mali* case, ICJ Reports, 1986, pp.554, 573-74; 80 *ILR*, pp.459, 477-78.

[139] See Akehurst, "The Hierarchy of the Sources of International Law", 47 *BYIL*, 1974- 5, p.273, and Virally, *op. cit.* footnote 1, pp.165-66. See also to this effect *Restatement (Third) of Foreign Relations Law of the United States*, 1987, vol.1, pp.27-28. See Dalton, "International Agreements in the Revised Restatement", 25 *Va JIL*, 1984, pp.153, 157-58, cf. Mosler, *The International Society as a Legal Community*, 1980, pp.84-86.

"accepted and recognised by the international community of states as a whole as a norm from which no derogation is permitted and which can be modified only by a subsequent norm of general international law having the same character". The concept of *jus cogens* is based upon an acceptance of fundamental and superior values within the system and in some respects is akin to the notion of public order or public policy in domestic legal orders.[140] It also reflects the influence of natural law thinking. Various examples of the content of *jus cogens* have been provided, particularly during the discussions on the topic in the International Law Commission, such as an unlawful use of force, genocide, slave trading and piracy.[141] However, no clear agreement has been manifested regarding other areas, and even the examples given are by no means uncontroverted. More important, perhaps, is the identification of the mechanism by which rules of *jus cogens* may be created, since once created no derogation is permitted.

A two stage approach is here involved in the light of article 53: first, the establishment of the proposition as a rule of general international law and secondly the acceptance of that rule as a peremptory norm by the international law community of states as a whole. It will be seen therefore that a stringent process is involved, and rightly so, for the establishment of a higher level of binding rules has serious implications for the international law community. The situation to be avoided is that of foisting peremptory norms upon a political or ideological minority, for that in the long run would devalue the concept. The appropriate test would thus require universal acceptance of the proposition as a legal rule by states and recognition of it as a rule of *jus cogens* by an overwhelming majority of states, crossing ideological and political divides.[142] It is also clear that only rules based on custom or treaties may form the foundation of *jus cogens* norms. This is particularly so in view of the hostile attitude of many states to general principles as an independent source of

---

[140] See e.g. Sztucki, *Jus Cogens and the Vienna Convention on the Law of Treaties*, 1974; Sinclair, *The Vienna Convention on the Law of Treaties*, 2nd ed., 1984, p.203; Virally, "Réflexions sur le *jus cogens*", 12 *AFDI*, 1966, p.1; Rozakis, *The Concept of Jus Cogens in the Law of Treaties*, 1976; Gomez Robledo, "Le *jus cogens* international", 172 *HR*, p.17; Gaja, "*Jus Cogens* beyond the Vienna Conventions", *ibid.*, p.279 and Hannikainen, *Peremptory Norms (Jus Cogens) in International Law*, 1988. See also *infra*, Chapter 15.

[141] *Yearbook of the ILC*, 1966, vol.II, p.248.

[142] See e.g. Sinclair, *op. cit.*, pp.218-24 and Akehurst, *loc. cit.* footnote 139.

international law and the universality requirement of *jus cogens* formation. The dangers of not being sufficiently stringent are visible in the ILC's draft on State Responsibility, article 18(2) of which provides that an unlawful act may be rendered lawful if such an act has subsequently become compulsory as a result of a rule of *jus cogens*. This apparently retroactive provision may be the cause of problems in the future.[143]

As article 53 of the Vienna Convention notes, a treaty that is contrary to an existing rule of *jus cogens* is void *ab initio*,[144] whereas by virtue of article 64 an existing treaty that conflicts with an emergent rule of *jus cogens* terminates from the date of the emergence of the rule. It is not void *ab initio*, nor by article 71 is any right, obligation or legal situation created by the treaty prior to its termination affected, provided that its maintenance is not in itself contrary to the new peremptory norm.

---

[143] See *Yearbook of the ILC*, vol.II, pp.91-92.
[144] See also article 71.

CHAPTER FOUR

International Law and Municipal Law [1]

The role of the state in the modern world is a complex one. According to legal theory, each state is sovereign and equal. In reality, with the phenomenal growth in communications and consciousness, and with the constant reminder of global rivalries, not even the most powerful of states can be entirely sovereign. Interdependence and the close-knit character of contemporary international commercial and political society ensures that virtually any action of a state could well have profound repercussions upon the system as a whole and the decisions under consideration by other states.

Thus, reality circumscribes the concept of sovereignty in operation and increases the necessity for world-wide coordination of matters as different as copper prices, exchange rates and the policies adopted to combat economic problems.

With the rise and extension of international law, questions begin to arise paralleling the role played by the state within the international system and concerned with the relationship between the internal legal order of a particular country and the rules and principles governing the international community as a whole. Municipal law governs the domestic aspects of government and deals with issues between individuals, and between individuals and the administrative apparatus, while international law focuses primarily upon the relations between states. Nevertheless, there are many instances where problems can emerge and lead to difficulties between the two systems. In a case before a municipal court a rule of international law may be brought forward as a defence to a charge. For example, a vessel may be prosecuted for being in what, in domestic terms, is regarded as territorial waters but in international law would be treated as part of the high seas.

There may also be questions as to the precise status of a municipal legal rule before an international tribunal. It is questions such as

---

[1] See generally, Kelsen, *Principles of International Law,* 2nd ed., 1966, pp.290-94 and 551-88; Brownlie, *Principles of Public International Law,* 4th ed., 1990, Chapter II; Lauterpacht, *International Law: Collected Papers,* vol.1, 1970, pp.151-77; Morgenstern, "Judicial Practice and the Supremacy of International Law", 27 *BYIL,* 1950, p.42; Starke, "Monism and Dualism in the Theory of International Law considered from the standpoint of the Rule of Law", 92 *HR,* pp.5, 70-80.

these that will be looked at in this chapter. But first some of the various ideas put forward as to the required frames of reference will be considered.

THE THEORIES [2]

Positivism stresses the overwhelming importance of the state and tends to regard international law as founded upon the consent of states. It is actual practice, illustrated by custom and by treaty, that formulates the role of international law, and not formalistic structures, theoretical deductions or moral stipulations. Accordingly, when positivists such as Triepel[3] and Strupp[4] consider the relationship of international law to municipal law, they do so upon the basis of the supremacy of the state, and the existence of wide differences between the two functioning orders. This theory is known as *dualism* (or sometimes as *pluralism*) and stresses that the rules of the systems of international law and municipal law exist separately and cannot purport to have an effect on, or overrule, the other.

This is because of the fundamentally different nature of inter-state and intra-state relations and the different legal structure employed on the one hand by the state and on the other hand as between states. Where municipal legislation permits the exercise of international law rules, this is on sufferance as it were and is an example of the supreme authority of the state within its own domestic jurisdiction, rather than of any influence maintained by international law within the internal sphere.[5]

Those writers who disagree with this theory and who adopt the *monist* approach tend to fall into two distinct categories: those who, like Lauterpacht, uphold a strong ethical position with a deep concern for human rights, and others, like Kelsen, who maintain a monist position on formalistic logical grounds. The monists are united in accepting a unitary view of law as a whole and are opposed to the strict division posited by the positivists.

The "naturalist" strand represented in England by Lauterpacht's works sees the primary function of all law as concerned with the

[2] See *supra*, Chapters 1 and 2.

[3] *Völkerrecht und Landesrecht*, 1899.

[4] 47 *HR*, p.389. See also Anzilotti, *Corso di Diritto Internazionale*, 3rd ed., 1928, vol.1, p.43 *et seq*.

[5] See Oppenheim, *International Law*, vol.1, 8th ed., 1955, p.37.

well-being of individuals, and advocates the supremacy of international law as the best method available of attaining this. It is an approach characterised by deep suspicion of an international system based upon the sovereignty and absolute independence of states, and illuminated by faith in the capacity of the rules of international law to imbue the international order with a sense of moral purpose and justice founded upon respect for human rights and the welfare of individuals.[6]

The method by which Kelsen elucidates his theory of monism is markedly different and utilises the philosophy of Kant as its basis. Law is regarded as constituting an order which lays down patterns of behaviour that ought to be followed, coupled with provision for sanctions which are employed once an illegal act or course of conduct has occurred or been embarked upon. Since the same definition appertains both within the internal sphere and the international sphere, a logical unity is forged, and because states owe their legal relationship to one another to the rules of international law, such as the one positing equality, since states cannot be equal before the law without a rule to that effect, it follows that international law is superior to or more basic than municipal law.[7]

Reference has already been made to Kelsen's hierarchical system whereby the legality of a particular rule is affirmed once it conforms to an anterior rule. This process of referring back to previous or higher rules ends with the so-called basic norm of the legal order. However, this basic norm is basic only in a relative sense, since the legal character of states, such as their jurisdiction, sovereignty and equality, is fixed by international law. Thus, Kelsen emphasises the unity of the entire legal order upon the basis of the predominance of international law by declaring that it is the basic norm of the international legal order which is the ultimate reason of validity of the national legal orders too.[8]

A third approach, being somewhat a modification of the dualist position and formulated by Fitzmaurice and Rousseau amongst others, attempts to establish a recognised theoretical framework tied to reality. This approach begins by denying that any common field

---

[6] *Op. cit.* See also *International Law and Human Rights,* 1950.
[7] *Op. cit.,* pp.557-59. See also *General Theory of Law and State,* 1945, pp.363-80.
[8] See further, *supra,* Chapter 2, p.45.

of operation exists as between international law and municipal law by which one system is superior or inferior to the other. Each order is supreme in its own sphere, much as French law and English law are in France and England. And just as one cannot talk in terms of the supremacy of French law over English law, but only of two distinct legal systems each operating within its own field, so it is possible to treat international law and municipal law in the same way. They are both the legal element contained within the domestic and international systems respectively, and they exist within different juridical orders.

What may, and often does, happen is what is termed a conflict of obligations, that is the state within its own domestic sphere does not act in accordance with its obligations as laid down by international law. In such a case, the domestic position is unaffected (and is not overruled by the contrary rule of international law) but rather the state as it operates internationally has broken a rule of international law and the remedy will lie in the international field, whether by means of diplomatic protest or judicial action.

This method of solving the problem does not delve deeply into theoretical considerations, but aims at being practical and in accord with the majority of state practice and international judicial decisions.[9]

THE ROLE OF MUNICIPAL RULES IN INTERNATIONAL LAW [10]

The general rule with regard to the position of municipal law within the international sphere is that a state which has broken a stipulation of international law cannot justify itself by referring to its domestic legal situation. It is no defence to a breach of an international obligation to argue that the state acted in such a manner because it was following the dictates of its own municipal laws. The reasons for this inability to put forward internal rules as an excuse to evade international responsibility are obvious. Any other

[9] Fitzmaurice, *op. cit.*, pp.70-80. See also Rousseau, *Droit International Public*, 1979, pp.4-16; Borchard, "The Relations between International Law and Municipal Law", 27 *Virginia Law Review*, 1940, p.137; McDougal, "The Impact of International Law upon National Law: A Policy-Orientated Perspective" in McDougal *et al.*, *Studies in World Public Order*, 1960, p.157.

[10] See e.g. Jenks, *The Prospects of International Adjudication*, 1964, Chapter 9; Lauterpacht, *The Development of International Law by the International Court*, 1958 and Morgenstern, *op. cit.*, p.43 *et seq.*

situation would permit international law to be evaded by the simple method of domestic legislation.

Accordingly, state practice and decided cases have established this provision and thereby prevented countries involved in international litigation from pleading municipal law as a method of circumventing international law. Article 27 of the Vienna Convention on the Law of Treaties 1969 lays down that in so far as treaties are concerned, a party may not invoke the provisions of its internal law as justification for its failure to carry out an international agreement.[11] And this provision is reflected in the rules governing international litigation.

In the *Alabama Claims* arbitration of 1872, the United States objected strenuously when Britain allowed a Confederate ship to sail from Liverpool to prey upon American shipping. It was held that the absence of British legislation necessary to prevent the construction or departure of the vessel could not be brought forward as a defence, and Britain was accordingly liable to pay damages for the depredations caused by the warship in question.[12]

However, such expressions of the supremacy of international law over municipal law in international tribunals do not mean that the provisions of domestic legislation are either irrelevant or unnecessary.[13] On the contrary, the role of internal legal rules is vital to the workings of the international legal machine. One of the ways that it is possible to understand and discover a state's legal position on a variety of topics important to international law is by examining municipal laws.[14] A country will express its opinion on such vital international matters as the extent of its territorial sea, or the jurisdiction it claims or the conditions for the acquisition of nationality through the medium of its domestic law-making. Thus,

[11] Note also article 13 of the Draft Declaration on the Rights and Duties of States, 1949, which provides that every state "has the duty to carry out in good faith its obligations arising from treaties and other sources of international law, and it may not invoke provisions in its constitution or its laws as an excuse for failure to perform this duty", *Yearbook of the ILC*, 1949, pp.286, 289.

[12] Moore, *International Arbitrations*, vol.1, pp.495, 653. See also e.g. the *Free Zones* case, PCIJ, Series A/B, no.46, 1932, p.167; 6 *ILR*, p.362; the *Greco-Bulgarian Communities* case, PCIJ, Series B, no.17, 1930, p.32; 5 *ILR*, p.4 and the *Nottebohm* case, ICJ Reports, 1955, pp.4, 20-21; 22 *ILR*, pp.349, 357-58.

[13] See e.g. Jenks, *op. cit.*, pp.547-603 and Marek, *Droit International et Droit Interne*, 1961. See also Brownlie, *op. cit.*, pp.39-43.

[14] See e.g. the *Anglo-Iranian Oil Co.* case, ICJ Reports, 1952, p.93; 19 *ILR*, p.507.

it is quite often that in the course of deciding a case before it, an international court will feel the necessity to make a study of relevant pieces of municipal legislation. Indeed, there have been instances, such as the *Serbian Loans* case of 1929,[15] when the crucial issues turned upon the interpretation of internal law, and the rules of international law in a strict sense were not at issue.

In addition to the role of municipal law as revealing the legal position of the state on topics of international importance, the rules of municipal law can be utilised as evidence of compliance or non-compliance with international obligations. This was emphasised in the *Certain German Interests in Polish Upper Silesia* case,[16] where the Permanent Court of International Justice declared that:

> the Court is certainly not called upon to interpret the Polish law as such; but there is nothing to prevent the Court's giving judgment on the question whether or not, in applying that law, Poland is acting in conformity with its obligations towards Germany under the Geneva Convention.[17]

Nevertheless, and despite the many functions that municipal law rules perform within the sphere of international law, the point must be emphasised that the presence or absence of a particular provision within the internal legal structure of a state, including its constitution if there is one, cannot be applied to evade an international obligation. Any other solution would render the operations of international law rather precarious.

INTERNATIONAL LAW BEFORE MUNICIPAL COURTS [18]

The problem of the role of international law within the municipal law system is, however, rather more complicated than the position discussed above, and there have been a number of different approaches to it. We shall look first at the attitudes adopted by the British courts, and then proceed to note the views taken by the United States and other countries.

---

[15] PCIJ, Series A, no.20; 5 *ILR*, p.466. See also the *Brazilian Loans* case, *ibid.*, no.21.

[16] PCIJ, Series A, no.7, p.19.

[17] For criticism of the view that municipal law provisions are regarded as "mere facts", see Brownlie, *op. cit.*, pp.42-43.

[18] See e.g. Morgenstern, *op. cit.*, pp.48-66.

The United Kingdom [19]

As regards the applicability of international law rules to the domestic scene, various theories have been put forward. These attempt to explain the precise nature of the relationship and provide a guide for the courts faced with an international element in a case before it.

One expression of the positivist-dualist position has been the doctrine of *transformation*. This is based upon the perception of two quite distinct systems of law, operating separately, and maintains that before any rule or principle of international law can have any effect within the domestic jurisdiction, it must be expressly and specifically "transformed" into municipal law by the use of the appropriate constitutional machinery, such as an Act of Parliament. This doctrine grew from the procedure whereby international agreements are rendered operative in municipal law by the device of ratification by the sovereign and the idea has developed from this that any rule of international law must be transformed, or specifically adopted, to be valid within the internal legal order.

Another approach, known as the doctrine of *incorporation*, holds that international law is part of the municipal law automatically without the necessity for the interposition of a constitutional ratification procedure. The best known exponent of this theory is the eighteenth century lawyer Blackstone, who declared in his Commentaries that:

> the law of nations, wherever any question arises which is properly the object of its jurisdiction, is here adopted in its full extent by the common law, and it is held to be a part of the law of the land.[20]

This doctrine refers to customary international law and different rules apply to treaties.

---

[19] See e.g. Morgenstern, *op. cit.*; Lauterpacht, "Is International Law A Part of the Law of England?", 25 *Transactions of the Grotius Society*, 1939, p.51; Fawcett, *The British Commonwealth in International Law*, 1963, Chapter 2; Oppenheim, *op. cit.*, pp.39-41 and Holdsworth, *Essays in Law and History*, 1946, p.260. See also Collier, "Is International Law Really Part of the Law of England?", 38 *ICLQ*, 1989, p.924.

[20] *Commentaries*, IV, Chapter 5.

(a) *Customary International Law*

It is in this sphere that the doctrine of incorporation has become the main British approach. It is an old established theory dating back to the eighteenth century, owing its prominence at that stage to the considerable discussion then taking place as to the precise extent of diplomatic immunity. In the case of *Buvot* v. *Barbuit*,[21] Lord Talbot declared unambiguously that "the law of nations in its full extent was part of the law of England", so that a Prussian commercial agent could not be rendered liable for failing to perform a decree. This was followed 27 years later by *Triquet* v. *Bath*,[22] where Lord Mansfield, discussing the issue as to whether a domestic servant of the Bavarian Minister to Britain could claim diplomatic immunity, upheld the earlier case and specifically referred to Talbot's statement.

This acceptance of customary international rules as part and parcel of the common law of England so vigorously stated in a series of eighteenth century cases, was subject to the priority granted to Acts of Parliament and tempered by the principle of *stare decisis* or precedent, maintained by the British courts and ensuring that the judgments of the higher courts are binding upon the lower courts of the hierarchical system. Accordingly, a rule of international law would not be implemented if it ran counter to a statute or decision by a higher court.[23]

In the nineteenth century, a series of cases occurred which led many writers to dispute the validity of the hitherto accepted incorporation doctrine and replace it with the theory of trans-formation, according to which the rules of customary international law only form part of English law if they have been specifically adopted, either by legislation or case-law. The turning point in this saga is marked by the case of *R* v. *Keyn*[24] which concerned a German ship, the *Franconia*, which collided with and sank a British vessel in the English Channel within three miles of the English coast. The German captain was indicted for manslaughter following the death of a passenger from the British ship, and the question that

[21] (1737) Cases t. Talbot 281.
[22] (1764) 3 Burr. 1478.
[23] But see now *Trendtex Trading Corporation* v. *Central Bank of Nigeria*, [1977] 2 WLR 356; 64 *ILR*, p.111, *infra*, p.111.
[24] (1876) 2 Ex.D. 63.

came before the Court for Crown Cases Reserved was whether an English court did indeed have jurisdiction to try the offence in such circumstances.

The Court came to the conclusion that no British legislation existed which provided for jurisdiction over the three mile territorial sea around the coasts. It was true that such a rule might be said to exist in international law, but it was one thing to say that the state had the right to legislate over a part of what had previously been the high seas, and quite another to conclude that the state's laws operate at once there, independently of any legislation. One thing did not follow from another, and it was imperative to keep distinct on the one hand the power of Parliament to make laws, and on the other the authority of the courts, without appropriate legislation, to apply the criminal law where it could not have been applied before. The question, as Lord Cockburn emphasised, was whether, acting judicially, the Court could treat the power of Parliament to legislate as making up for the absence of actual legislation. The answer came in the negative and the German captain was released.

This case was seen by some as marking a change to a trans-formation approach,[25] but the judgment was in many respects ambiguous, dealing primarily with the existence or not of any right of jurisdiction over the territorial sea.[26] It must also be pointed out that in many respects the differences between the incorporation and transformation theories as interpreted in modern times lie more in a shift in presumption than any comprehensive theoretical revolution.[27] In any event, any doubts as to the outcome of any further *Franconia* situations were put to rest by the Territorial Waters Jurisdiction Act, 1878, which expressed British jurisdiction rights in similar circumstances.

The opinions put forward in the *West Rand Gold Mining Co.* case[28] showed a further blurring of the distinction between the incorporation and transformation theories. Lord Alverstone declared that whatever had received the common consent of civilised nations, must also have received the assent of Great Britain and as such would be applied by the municipal tribunals. However, he went on to

[25] See e.g. Holdsworth, *op. cit.*, pp.263-66 and Halsbury, *Laws of England*, 3rd ed., vol. VII, p.264.
[26] See e.g. Lauterpacht, *op. cit.* footnote 19, pp.60-61.
[27] See e.g. Brownlie, *op. cit.*, p.47.
[28] [1905] 2 KB 391.

modify the impact of this by noting that any proposed rule of international law would have to be proved by satisfactory evidence to have been "recognised and acted upon by our own country" or else be of such a nature that it could hardly be supposed any civilised state would repudiate it. Lord Mansfield's view in *Triquet's* case could not be so interpreted as to include within the common law rules of international law which appear in the opinions of text book writers and as to which there is no evidence that Britain ever assented.[29] This emphasis on assent, it must be noted, bears a close resemblance to the views put forward by the Court in *R* v. *Keyn* as to the necessity for conclusive evidence regarding the existence and scope of any particular rule of customary law. Indeed, the problem is often one of the uncertainty of existence and scope of customary law.

Not long after the *West Rand* case, another important dispute came before the courts. In *Mortensen* v. *Peters*,[30] a Danish captain was convicted by a Scottish court for contravening a fishing by-law regarding the Moray Firth. His ship had been operating within the Moray Firth and was within the area covered by the relevant by-law, but it was beyond the three mile limit recognised by international law. The issue came to the Scottish Court of Justiciary, where Lord Dunedin, in discussing the captain's appeal, concentrated upon the correct construction to be made of the relevant legislation. He noted that an Act of Parliament duly passed and assented to was supreme and the Court had no option but to give effect to its provisions. In other words, statutes had predominance over customary law, and a British court would have to heed the terms of an Act of Parliament even if it involved the breach of a rule of international law. This is so even though there is a presumption in British law that the legislation is to be so construed as to avoid a conflict with international law. Where such a conflict does occur, the statute has priority and the state itself will have to deal with the problem of the breach of a customary rule.[31]

This modified incorporation doctrine was clearly defined by Lord Atkin in *Chung Chi Cheung* v. *R.*[32] He noted that:

[29] *Ibid.*, pp.407-8.

[30] (1906) 8 F.(J.) 93.

[31] See also 170 HC Deb., col.472, 4 March 1907 and the Trawling in Prohibited Areas Prevention Act, 1909.

[32] [1939] AC 160; 9 *ILR*, p.264. See also *Commercial and Estates Co. of Egypt* v. *Board of Trade*, [1925] 1 KB 271, 295; 2 *ILR*, p.423.

international law has no validity except in so far as its principles are accepted and adopted by our own domestic law . . . The courts acknowledge the existence of a body of rules which nations accept among themselves. On any judicial issue they seek to ascertain what the relevant rule is, and having found it they will treat it as incorporated into the domestic law, so far as it is not inconsistent with rules enacted by statutes or finally declared by their tribunals.

It goes without saying, of course, that any alleged rule of customary law must be proved to be a valid rule of international law, and not merely an unsupported proposition.

One effect of the doctrines as enunciated by the courts in practice is that international law is not treated as a foreign law but in an evidential manner as part of the law of the land. This means that whereas any rule of foreign law has to be proved as a fact by evidence, as occurs with other facts, the courts take judicial notice of any rule of international law and may refer, for example, to text books rather than require the presence and testimony of expert opinion.

In ascertaining the existence and nature of any particular rule, the courts may have recourse to a wider range of authoritative material than would normally be the case, such as "international treaties and conventions, authoritative textbooks, practice and judicial decisions" of the courts of other countries.[33]

The case of *Trendtex Trading Corporation* v. *Central Bank of Nigeria*[34] raised anew many of these issues. The case concerned a claim for sovereign or state immunity by the Central Bank of Nigeria.[35] In *Trendtex* all three judges of the Court of Appeal accepted the incorporation doctrine as the correct one. Lord Denning, reversing his opinion in an earlier case,[36] stressed that otherwise the courts could not recognise changes in the norms of international law.[37] Stephenson LJ emphasised in an important statement that:

[33] Per Lord MacMillan, *The Cristina*, [1938] AC 485, 497; 9 *ILR*, p.250. See *Re Piracy Jure Gentium*, [1934] AC 586, 588; 7 *ILR*, p.213 and Stephenson LJ, *Trendtex Trading Corporation* v. *Central Bank of Nigeria*, [1977] 2 WLR 356, 379; 64 *ILR*, pp.111, 135. But see also Lauterpacht, *op. cit.* footnote 19, p.87, note m.

[34] [1977] 2 WLR 356; 64 *ILR*, p.111.

[35] See further *infra*, Chapter 12.

[36] *R* v. *Secretary of State for the Home Department, ex p. Thakrar*, [1974] 2 WLR 593, 597; 59 *ILR*, p.450.

[37] [1977] 2 WLR 356, 365; 64 *ILR*, pp.111, 128. See also Shaw LJ, *ibid.*, 386 and Stephenson LJ, *ibid.*, 378-81.

it is the nature of international law and the specific problems of ascertaining it which create the difficulty in the way of adopting or incorporating or recognising as already incorporated a new rule of international law.[38]

The issue of *stare decisis,* or precedent, and customary international law was also discussed in this case. It had previously been accepted that the doctrine of *stare decisis* would apply in cases involving customary international law principles as in all other cases before the courts, irrespective of any changes in the meantime in such law.[39] This approach was reaffirmed in *Thai-Europe Tapioca Service Ltd* v. *Government of Pakistan.*[40] However, in *Trendtex,* Lord Denning and Shaw LJ emphasised that international law did not know a rule of *stare decisis.*[41] Where international law had changed, the court could implement that change "without waiting for the House of Lords to do it".[42] The true principle, noted Shaw LJ, was that "the English courts must at any given time discover what the prevailing international rule is and apply that rule".[43] This marked a significant approach and one that in the future may have some interesting consequences, for example, in the human rights field.

The dominant incorporationist approach was clearly reaffirmed by the Court of Appeal in *Maclaine Watson* v. *Department of Trade and Industry.*[44] This case concerned the consequences of the demise of the International Tin Council and the attempts *inter alia* to render states that were members of the ITC liable for the debts incurred by that unfortunate organisation. Nourse LJ emphasised that the *Trendtex* case had resolved the rivalry between the incorporation and transformation doctrines in favour of the former.[45] One of the major points at issue in the *Tin Council* litigation was whether a rule existed in international law stipulating that the

---

[38] *Ibid.,* p.379.
[39] See e.g. Brownlie, *op. cit.,* pp.45-46 and *Chung Chi Cheung* v. *R,* [1939] AC 160, 169; 9 *ILR,* p.214. But see Morgenstern, *op. cit.,* pp.80-82.
[40] [1975] 3 All ER 961, 967, 969-70; 64 *ILR,* p.81.
[41] [1977] 2 WLR 356, 365; 64 *ILR,* pp.111, 128.
[42] Per Lord Denning, *ibid.,* 366.
[43] *Ibid.,* 388; 64 *ILR,* p.152. But cf. Stephenson LJ, *ibid.,* 381. See also e.g. Goff J., *Iº Congreso del Partido,* [1977] 3 WLR 778, 795; 64 *ILR,* p.154.
[44] [1988] 3 WLR 1033; 80 *ILR,* p.49.
[45] *Ibid.,* p.1116; 80 *ILR,* p.132.

states members of an international organisation with separate personality could be rendered liable for the latter's debts.

If such a rule did exist, the question would then arise as to how that would be accepted or manifested in the context of municipal law. This, of course, would depend upon the precise content of such a claimed international rule and, as Kerr LJ noted, no such rule did exist in international law permitting action against member-states "in any national court".[46] It was also not possible for an English court to remedy the gap in international law by itself creating such a rule.[47] Nourse LJ, however, took a different position on this point, stating that "where it is necessary for an English court to decide such a question [i.e. an uncertain question of international law], and whatever the doubts and difficulties, it can and must do so".[48] This, with respect, is not and cannot be the case, not least because it strikes at the heart of the community-based system of international law creation.

Lord Oliver in the House of Lords judgment[49] clearly and correctly emphasised that

> It is certainly not for a domestic tribunal in effect to legislate a rule into existence for the purposes of domestic law and on the basis of material that is wholly indeterminate.[50]

(b) *Treaties* [51]

As far as treaties are concerned, different rules apply as to their application within the domestic jurisdiction for very good historical and political reasons. While customary law develops through the evolution of state practice, international conventions are in the form of contracts binding upon the signatories. For a custom to emerge it is usual, though not always necessary, for several states to act in a certain manner believing it to be in conformity with the law. Therefore, in normal circumstances the influence of one particular

---

[46] *Ibid.*, p.1095; 80 *ILR*, p.109.
[47] *Ibid.*
[48] *Ibid.*, p.1118; 80 *ILR*, p.135.
[49] [1989] 3 All ER 523; 81 *ILR*, p.671.
[50] *Ibid.*, at 554; 81 *ILR*, p.715.
[51] See generally McNair, *The Law of Treaties*, 1961, pp.81-97 and Mann, "The Enforcement of Treaties by English Courts", 44 *Transactions of the Grotius Society*, 1958-9, p.29.

state is not usually decisive. In the case of treaties, the states involved may create new law that would be binding upon them irrespective of previous practice or contemporary practice. In other words, the influence of the executive is generally of greater impact where treaty law is concerned than is the case with customary law.

It follows from this that were treaties to be rendered applicable directly within the state without any intermediate stage after signature and ratification and before domestic operation, the executive would be able to legislate without the legislature. Because of this, any incorporation theory approach to treaty law has been rejected. Indeed, as far as this topic is concerned, it seems to turn more upon the particular relationship between the executive and legislative branches of government than upon any pre-conceived notions of international law.

One of the principal cases in English law illustrating this situation is the case of the *Parlement Belge*.[52] This involved a collision between this ship and a British tug, and the claim for damages brought by the latter vessel before the Probate, Divorce and Admiralty division of the High Court. The *Parlement Belge* belonged to the King of the Belgians and was used as a cargo boat. During the case, the Attorney-General intervened to state that the Court had no jurisdiction over the vessel as it was the property of the Belgian monarch and that further by a political agreement of 1876 between Britain and Belgium, the same immunity from foreign legal process as applied to warships should apply also to this packet boat. In discussing the case, the Court concluded that only public ships of war were entitled to such immunity and that such immunity could not be extended to other categories by a treaty without parliamentary consent. Indeed, it was stated that this would be "a use of the treaty-making prerogative of the Crown . . . without precedent, and in principle contrary to the law of the constitution".[53]

Thus it is that treaties cannot operate of themselves within the state, but require the passing of an enabling statute. The Crown in Britain retains the right to sign and ratify international agreements, but is unable to legislate directly. Before a treaty can become part of English law, an Act of Parliament is essential. This fundamental

[52] (1879) 4 PD 129.
[53] *Ibid.*, p.154.

proposition was clearly spelt out by Lord Oliver in the House of Lords decision in *Maclaine Watson* v. *Department of Trade and Industry*.[54] He noted that:

> as a matter of the constitutional law of the United Kingdom, the royal prerogative, whilst it embraces the making of treaties, does not extend to altering the law or conferring rights on individuals or depriving individuals of rights which they enjoy in domestic law without the intervention of Parliament. Treaties, as it is sometimes expressed, are not self-executing. Quite simply, a treaty is not part of English law unless and until it has been incorporated into the law by legislation.[55]

It therefore followed that as far as individuals were concerned such treaties were *res inter alia acta* from which they cannot derive rights and by which they cannot be deprived of rights or subjected to obligations.[56] Such sentiments were also expressed by Lord Templeman[57] and thus constitute a major restatement of the English law position.

However, this rule does not apply to all treaties. Those relating to the conduct of war or cession of territory do not need an intervening act of legislation before they can be made binding upon the citizens of the country.[58] A similar situation exists also with regard to relatively unimportant administrative agreements which do not require ratification, providing of course they do not purport to alter municipal law. Such exceptions occur because it is felt that, having in mind the historical compromises upon which the British constitutional structure is founded, no significant legislative powers are being lost by Parliament. In all other cases where the rights and duties of British subjects are affected, an Act of Parliament is

---

[54] [1989] 3 All ER 523, 531; 81 *ILR*, pp.671, 684.

[55] *Ibid.*, at pp.544-45; 81 *ILR*, p.701.

[56] *Ibid.*

[57] *Ibid.*, at p.526; 81 *ILR*, p.676.

[58] See e.g. Brownlie, *op. cit.*, p.48; de Smith and Brazier, *Constitutional and Administrative Law*, 6th ed., 1989, pp.140-42 and Wade and Phillips, *Constitutional and Administrative Law*, 9th ed., 1977, pp.303-6. See also *Attorney-General for Canada* v. *Attorney-General for Ontario*, [1937] AC 326, 347; 8 *ILR*, p.41; *Walker* v. *Baird*, [1892] AC 491; *Republic of Italy* v. *Hambro's Bank*, [1950] 1 All ER 430; *Cheney* v. *Conn*, [1968] 1 WLR 242; 41 *ILR*, p.421; *Porter* v. *Freudenberg*, [1915] 1 KB 857, 874-80 and McNair, *op. cit.*, pp.89-91.

necessary to render the provisions of the particular treaty operative within Britain.[59]

There is in English law a presumption that legislation is to be so construed as to avoid a conflict with international law. This operates particularly where the Act of Parliament which is intended to bring the treaty into effect is itself ambiguous. Accordingly, where the provisions of a statute implementing a treaty are capable of more than one meaning, and one interpretation is compatible with the terms of the treaty while others are not, it is the former approach that will be adopted. For, as Lord Diplock pointed out:

> Parliament does not intend to act in breach of international law, including therein specific treaty obligations.[60]

However, where the words of a statute are unambiguous the courts have no choice but to apply them irrespective of any conflict with international agreements.[61] Attempts have been made to consider treaties in the context of domestic legislation not directly enacting them, or as indications of public policy, particularly with regard to human rights treaties,[62] and it seems that account may be taken of them in seeking to interpret ambiguous provisions.[63]

---

[59] By virtue of the "Ponsonby rule" Parliament is informed of the terms of treaties to be ratified 21 days before ratification, 171 HC Deb., col.2001, 1 April 1924. This is regarded not as a binding rule, but as a constitutional usage: see Wade and Phillips, *op. cit.*, p.304.

[60] *Salomon* v. *Commissioners of Customs and Excise*, [1967] 2 QB 116, 143; *Post Office* v. *Estuary Radio Ltd*, [1968] 2 QB 740 and *Brown* v. *Whimster*, [1976] QB 297. See also *National Smokeless Fuels Ltd* v. *IRC, The Times*, 23 April 1986, p.36 and Lord Oliver in *Maclaine Watson* v. *Department of Trade and Industry*, [1989] 3 All ER 523, 545; 81 *ILR*, pp.671, 702.

[61] *Ellerman Lines* v. *Murray*, [1931] AC 126 and *IRC* v. *Collco Dealings Ltd*, [1962] AC 1. See Sinclair, "The Principles of Treaty Interpretation and their Application by the English Courts", 12 *ICLQ*, 1963, p.508 and Schreuer, "The Interpretation of Treaties by Domestic Courts", 45 *BYIL*, 1971, p.255. See also Mann, *Foreign Affairs in English Courts*, 1986, pp.97-114.

[62] See e.g. *Blathwayt* v. *Baron Cawley*, [1976] AC 397.

[63] See e.g. in the context of the European Convention on Human Rights, *R* v. *Secretary of State for the Home Department, ex p. Bhajan Singh*, [1975] 2 All ER 1081; 61 *ILR*, p.260; *R* v. *Chief Immigration Officer, Heathrow Airport, ex p. Salamat Bibi*, [1976] 3 All ER 843; 61 *ILR*, p.267; *R* v. *Secretary of State for the Home Department, ex p. Phansopkar*, [1976] QB 606; 61 *ILR*, p.390; *Waddington* v. *Miah*, [1974] 1 WLR 683; 57 *ILR*, p.175; *Cassell* v. *Broome*, [1972] AC 1027; *Malone* v. *MPC*, [1979] Ch.344; 74 *ILR*, p.304; *R* v. *Secretary of State for the Home Department, ex p. Anderson*, [1984] 1 All ER 920 and *Trawnik* v. *Ministry of Defence*, [1984] 2 All ER 791. In *R* v. *Secretary of State for the Home Department, ex p. Brind*, [1990] 1 All ER, it was held that subordinate legislation and executive discretion did not fall into this category.

However, ministers are under no obligation to do this in reaching decisions.[64]

In the interpretation of international treaties incorporated by statute, the English courts have adopted a broader approach than is customary in statutory interpretation. In particular, recourse to the relevant *travaux préparatoires* may be possible.[65]

Lord Oliver in *Maclaine Watson* v. *Department of Trade and Industry*[66] has also emphasised that the conclusion of an international treaty is a question of fact and that while a treaty may be referred to as part of the factual background against which a particular issue arises, the legal results that flow from such a treaty in international law are not such questions of fact and are thus not justiciable before the English courts.

There are many reasons why certain issues may be non-justiciable before the English courts,[67] ranging from judicial propriety to act of state and state immunity situations, but whether the doctrine can or should be expressed quite so baldly may be questioned. There may indeed be situations where legal consequences will be deemed to flow from the existence and nature of particular unincorporated treaties.[68]

Reference should also be made to the growing importance of entry into the European Communities in this context. The case-law of the Communities demonstrates that fundamental rights are an integral part of the general principles of law, the observance of which the European Court of Justice seeks to ensure. The system provides that Community law prevails over national law and that the decisions of the European Court are to be applied by the domestic courts of the member-states. The potential for change through this route is, therefore, significant.[69]

---

[64] See e.g. *R* v. *Secretary of State for the Home Department, ex p. Fernandes*, [1984] 2 All ER 390.

[65] See *Buchanan* v. *Babco*, [1978] AC 141 and *Fothergill* v. *Monarch Airlines*, [1981] AC 251; 74 *ILR*, p.648. Compare in the latter case the restrictive approach of Lord Wilberforce, *ibid.*, p.278; 74 *ILR*, p.656 with that of Lord Diplock, *ibid.*, p.283; 74 *ILR*, pp.661-62. See also *Goldman* v. *Thai Airways International Ltd*, [1983] 3 All ER 693.

[66] [1989] 3 All ER 523, 545; 81 *ILR*, pp.671, 702.

[67] See further *infra*, p.128.

[68] See Kerr LJ, *Maclaine Watson* v. *Department of Trade and Industry*, [1988] 3 WLR 1033, 1075-76; 80 *ILR*, pp.49, 86-88.

[69] See e.g. *Nold* v. *EC Commission*, [1974] ECR 491, 508 and *Rutili* v. *Ministry of Interior of French Republic*, [1975] ECR 1219.

The United States [70]

As far as the American position on the relationship between municipal law and customary international law is concerned, it appears to be very similar to the English practice, apart from the need to take the Constitution into account. An early acceptance of the incorporation doctrine was later modified as in the UK. It was stated in the *Paquete Habana* case[71] that:

> international law is part of our law and must be ascertained and administered by the courts of justice of appropriate jurisdiction as often as questions of right depending upon it are duly presented for their determination.[72]

Similarly, the early pure incorporation cases gave way to a more cautious approach.[73]

The current accepted position is that customary international law in the US is federal law and that its determination by the federal courts is binding on the state courts.[74]

The similarity of approach with the UK is not surprising in view of common historical and cultural traditions, and parallel restraints upon the theories are visible. American courts are bound by the doctrine of precedent and the necessity to proceed according to previously decided cases, and they too must apply statute as against any rules of customary international law that do not accord with it.[75] The Court of Appeals recently reaffirmed this position in the *Committee of United States Citizens Living in Nicaragua* v. *Reagan*[76] case, where it was noted that "no enactment of Congress can be challenged

---

[70] See e.g. Morgenstern, *op. cit.*; Seidl-Hohenveldern, "Transformation or Adoption of International Law into Municipal Law", 12 *ICLQ*, 1963, p.88; Oppenheim, *op. cit.*, p.41 *et seq.*; Dickinson, "The Law of Nations as part of the National Law of the United States", 101 *University of Pennsylvania Law Review*, 1953, p.793; Falk, *The Role of Domestic Courts in the International Legal Order*, 1964 and Lillich, "Domestic Institutions" in *The Future of the International Legal Order*, (eds. Black and Falk), vol.4, 1972, p.384.

[71] 175 US 677 (1900). See also *Respublica* v. *De Longchamps*, 1 Dall. 111.

[72] *Ibid.*, p.700. See *Hilton* v. *Guyot*, 159 US 113 and *United States* v. *Melekh*, 190 F.Supp. 67 (1960), cf. *Pauling* v. *McElroy*, 164 F.Supp. 390 (1958).

[73] See e.g. *Cook* v. *United States*, 288 US 102 (1933); 6 *ILR*, p.3 and *United States* v. *Claus*, 63 F.Supp. 433 (1944).

[74] See *US* v. *Belmont*, 301 US 324, 331, 57 S. Ct. 758, 761 (1937); 8 *ILR*, p.34 and *Restatement (Third) of Foreign Relations Law of the United States*, 1987, Vol.1, pp.48-52.

[75] See e.g. *Schroeder* v. *Bissell*, 5 F.2d 838, 842 (1925).

[76] 859 F.2d 929 (1988).

on the ground that it violates customary international law".[77] It has been noted that the political and judicial organs of the United States have the power to ignore international law, where this occurs pursuant to a statute or "controlling executive act". This has occasioned much controversy,[78] as has the general relationship between custom and inconsistent pre-existing statutes.[79] However, it is now accepted that statutes supersede earlier treaties or customary rules of international law.[80] There does exist, as in English law, a presumption that legislation is not assumed to run counter to international law and as it was stated by the Court in *Schroeder* v. *Bissell*:[81]

> unless it unmistakably appears that a congressional act was intended to be in disregard of a principle of international comity, the presumption is that it was intended to be in conformity with it.[82]

The relationship between US law and customary law has been the subject of recent re-examination in the context of certain human rights situations. In *Filartiga* v. *Pena-Irala*,[83] the US Court of Appeals for the Second Circuit dealt with an action brought by Paraguayans against a Paraguayan for the torture and death of the son of the plaintiff. The claim was based on the Alien Tort Claims Act of 1789 which provides that "[t]he district courts shall have original jurisdiction of any civil action by an alien for a tort only, committed in violation of the law of nations". The Court of Appeals held that torture constituted a violation of international customary law and was thus actionable. The Court accordingly held against

---

[77] *Ibid.*, at 939. See also *Tag* v. *Rogers*, 267 F.2d 664, 666 (1959); 28 *ILR*, p.467.

[78] See *Brown* v. *United States*, 12 US (8 Cranch) 110, 128 (1814) and *Whitney* v. *Robertson*, 124 US 190, 194 (1888). See also Henkin, "International Law as Law in the United States", 82 *Michigan Law Review*, 1984, p.1555. See also *Rodriguez-Fernandez* v. *Wilkinson*, 654 F.2d 1382 (1981); 505 F.Supp. 787 (1980); *US* v. *PLO*, 695 F.Supp. 1456 (1988) and *Klinghoffer* v. *SNC Achille Lauro*, 739 F.Supp. 854 (1990).

[79] See *Restatement (Third) of Foreign Relations Law of the United States*, 1987, Vol.1, pp.63-69 (§115); the *Reagan* case, 859 F.2d 929 and Goldklang, "Back on Board the *Paquete Habana*", 25 *Va JIL*, 1984, p.143.

[80] See previous footnote.

[81] 5 F.2d 838 (1925).

[82] *Ibid.*, p.842. See also *Macleod* v. *United States*, 229 US 416 (1913) and *Littlejohn & Co.* v. *United States*, 270 US 215 (1926); 3 *ILR*, p.483.

[83] 630 F.2d 876 (1980); 77 *ILR*, p.169. See e.g. Lillich, *Invoking Human Rights Law in Domestic Courts*, 1985 and Comment, "Torture as a Tort in Violation of International Law", 33 *Stanford Law Review*, 1981, p.353.

the defendant despite the fact that both parties were alien and all the operative acts occurred in Paraguay. Other cases came before the courts in which the incorporation of international customary law provisions concerning human rights issues was argued with mixed success.[84] An attempt to obtain a judgment in the US against the Republic of Argentina for torturing its own citizens, however, ultimately foundered upon the doctrine of sovereign immunity,[85] while it has recently been held that acts of "international terrorism" are not actionable under the Alien Tort Claims Act.[86]

The relative convergence of practice between Britain and the United States with respect to the assimilation of customary law is not reflected as regards the treatment of international treaties. In the United Kingdom, it is the executive branch which negotiates, signs and ratifies international agreements, with the proviso that parliamentary action is required prior to the provisions of the agreement being accepted as part of English Law. In the United States, on the other hand, Article VI Section 2 of the Constitution provides that:

> . . . all Treaties made or which shall be made with the authority of the United States, shall be the supreme law of the land and the Judges in every state shall be bound thereby, anything in the Constitution or Laws of any state to the contrary notwithstanding.[87]

There is also a difference in the method of approval of treaties, for Article II of the Constitution notes that while the President has the power to make international agreements, he may only ratify them if at least two-thirds of the Senate approve.

There is an exception and this is the institution of the executive agreements. These are usually made by the President on his own authority, but still constitute valid treaties within the framework of

[84] See e.g. *Fernandez* v. *Wilkinson*, 505 F.Supp. 787 (1980) and *In re Alien Children Education Litigation*, 501 F.Supp. 544 (1980).

[85] *Siderman* v. *Republic of Argentina*, no. CV 82-1772-RMT (MCx) and *International Practitioner's Notebook*, July 1985, p.1. See also *infra*, Chapter 12.

[86] *Tel-Oren* v. *Libyan Arab Republic*, 517 F.Supp. 542 (1981), *aff'd per curiam*, 726 F.2d 774 (1984), *cert. denied* 53 U.S.L.W. 3612 (1985); 77 *ILR*, p.192. See e.g. D'Amato, "What Does Tel-Oren Tell Lawyers?", 79 *AJIL*, 1985, p.92.

[87] See e.g. *Ware* v. *Hylton*, 3 US (3 Dall.) 199 (1796) and *Foster* v. *Nielson*, 27 US (2 Pet.) 253 (1829). See also on treaty powers and the "reserved powers" of the states the tenth amendment, *Missouri* v. *Holland*, 252 US 416 (1920); 1 *ILR*, p.4 and *United States* v. *Curtiss-Wright Export Corporation*, 299 US 304 (1936); 8 *ILR*, p.48.

international law. As distinct from ordinary treaties, the creation of executive agreements is not expressly covered by the Constitution, but rather implied from its terms and subsequent practice, and they have been extensively used. The Supreme Court, in cases following the 1933 Litvinov Agreement, which established American recognition of the Soviet government and provided for the assignment to the US of particular debts owing to the USSR, emphasised that such executive agreements possessed the same status and dignity as treaties made by the President with the advice and consent of the Senate under Article II of the Constitution.[88]

American doctrines as to the understanding of treaty law are founded upon the distinction between "self-executing" and "non-self-executing" treaties. The former are able to operate automatically within the domestic sphere, without the need for any municipal legislation, while the latter require enabling acts before they can function inside the country and bind the American courts. Self-executing treaties apply directly within the United States as part of the supreme law of the land, whereas those conventions deemed not self-executing are obliged to undergo a legislative transformation and until they do so they cannot be regarded as legally enforceable against American citizens or institutions.

But how does one know when an international agreement falls into one category or the other? This matter has absorbed the courts of the United States for many years, and the distinction appears to have been made upon the basis of political content. In other words, where a treaty involves political questions of definition or exposition, then the issue should be left to the legislative organs of the nation, rather than automatic operation.[89] Examples of this would include the acquisition or loss of territory and financial arrangements. The Supreme Court in *Edye* v. *Robertson*[90] declared that treaties which

contain provisions which are capable of enforcement as between private parties in the courts of the country . . . [are] in the same category as other laws of Congress.

---

[88] See e.g. *United States* v. *Pink*, 315 US 203 (1942); 10 *ILR,* p.48. See, as regards the President's power to settle claims and create new rules of law applicable to pending legislation, *Dames & Moore* v. *Regan*, 101 SC 2972 (1981); 72 *ILR*, p.270.

[89] See Chief Justice Marshall, *Foster* v. *Neilson*, 27 US (2 Pet.) 253, 314 (1829).

[90] 112 US 580 (1884).

This would seem to mean that an international convention would become a law of the land, where its terms determine the rights and duties of private citizens, and contrasts with the position where a political issue is involved and the treaty thereby treated as non-self-executing.

Of course such generalisations as these are bound to lead to considerable ambiguity and doubt in the case of very many treaties; and the whole matter was examined again in 1952 before the Supreme Court of California in *Sei Fujii* v. *California*.[91] The plaintiff was a Japanese citizen who had purchased some land in 1948 in California. By legislation enacted in that state, aliens had no right to acquire land. To prevent the property from going to the state, the plaintiff argued that, amongst other things, such legislation was not consistent with the Charter of the United Nations, an international treaty which called for the promotion of human rights without racial distinction.

The issue raised was whether the UN Charter was a self-executing treaty and, by virtue of such, part of the law of the land, which would supersede inconsistent local statutes. The Court declared that in making a decision as to whether a treaty was self-executing or not, it would have to consult the treaty itself to try to deduce the intentions of the signatories and examine all relevant circumstances. Following *Edye's* case it would have to see whether the provisions of the treaty laid down rules that were to be enforceable of themselves in the municipal courts.

The Court concluded after a comprehensive survey that the relevant provisions of the UN Charter were not intended to be self-executing. They laid down various principles and objectives of the United Nations Organisation, but "do not purport to impose legal obligations on the individual member nations or to create rights in private persons". The Court held that it was obvious that further legislative action by the signatories would be called for to turn the principles of the UN into domestic laws binding upon the individual citizens of states.[92] Accordingly, they could not be regarded as part of the law of the land and could not operate to deflect the Californian legislation in question.

[91] 38 Cal (2d) 718 (1952).
[92] *Ibid.*, p.721.

The case was decided in favour of the plaintiff, but on other grounds altogether.[93]

As is the case with the UK system, it is possible for the American legislature to take action which not only takes no account of international law rules but may be positively contrary to them, and in such an instance the legislation would be supreme within the American jurisdiction.

In *Diggs* v. *Schultz*,[94] the Court had to consider the effect of the Byrd Amendment which legalised the importation into the USA of strategic materials, such as chrome from Rhodesia, a course of action which was expressly forbidden by a United Nations Security Council resolution which in the circumstances was binding. The Court noted that the Byrd Amendment was "in blatant disregard of our treaty undertakings" but concluded that:

> under our constitutional scheme, Congress can denounce treaties if it sees fit to do so, and there is nothing the other branches of government can do about it.

Although in municipal terms the Amendment was unchallengeable, the United States was, of course, internationally liable for the breach of an international legal rule.

Other Countries

In other countries where the English common law was adopted, such as the majority of Commonwealth states and, for example, Israel,[95] it is possible to say that in general the same principles apply. Customary law is regarded on the whole as part of the law of the land. Municipal laws are presumed not to be inconsistent with rules of international law, but in cases of conflict the former have precedence.

---

[93] See e.g. *People of Saipan ex rel. Guerrero* v. *United States Department of Interior*, 502 F.2d 90 (1974); 61 *ILR*, p.113. See also *Camacho* v. *Rogers*, 199 F.Supp. 155 (1961) and *Diggs* v. *Dent*, 14 *ILM*, 1975, p.797. Note also Schachter, "The Charter and the Constitution", 4 *Vanderbilt Law Review*, 1951, p.643.

[94] 470 F.2d 461, 466-67 (1972); 60 *ILR*, pp.393, 397.

[95] See the *Eichmann* case, 36 *ILR*, p.5, and Lapidoth, *Les Rapports entre le Droit International Public et le Droit Interne en Israel*, 1959. See also the *Affo* case before the Israeli Supreme Court, 29 *ICM*, 1990, pp.139, 156-57.

As far as treaties are concerned, Lord Atkin expressed the general position in *Attorney-General for Canada* v. *Attorney-General for Ontario*,[96] which was a case dealing with the respective legislative competences of the Dominion Parliament and the Provincial legislatures. He noted that within the then British Empire it was well enshrined that the making of a treaty was an executive act, while the performance of its obligations, if they involved alteration of the existing domestic law, required legislative action. "The question", remarked Lord Atkin,

> is not how is the obligation formed, that is the function of the executive, but how is the obligation to be performed, and that depends upon the authority of the competent legislature or legislatures.[97]

Although this constitutes the approach adopted by the majority of common law states, complications have arisen where the country in question has a written constitution, whether or not specific reference is made therein to the treatment of international agreements. An example of the latter is India, whose constitution refers only in the vaguest of terms to the provisions of international law,[98] whereas by contrast the Irish constitution clearly states that the country will not be bound by any treaty involving a charge upon public funds unless the terms of the agreement have been approved by the Dáil.[99] In such cases where there is a written constitution, serious questions of constitutional law may be involved, and one would have to consider the situation as it arises and within its own political context. But in general common law states tend to veer towards the aforementioned approaches which have characterised the British attitudes.

The practice of those states which posses the civil law system, based originally on Roman law, shows certain differences.

The Basic Law of the Federal Republic of Germany, for example, specifically states in article 25 that "the general rules of public international law are an integral part of federal law. They shall take precedence over the laws and shall directly create rights and duties

---

[96] [1937] AC 326; 8 *ILR*, p.41.

[97] *Ibid.*, pp.347-48; 8 *ILR*, pp.43-44.

[98] See e.g. Basu, *Commentaries on the Constitution of India*, vol.II, 1962, and *Constitutions of the World* (ed. Peaslee), 3rd ed., 1968, vol.II, p.308.

[99] Peaslee, *op. cit.* vol.III, p.463 (article 29(5)2).

for the inhabitants of the federal territory." This provision, which not only treats international law as part of municipal law but regards it as superior to municipal legislation, has been the subject of a great deal of controversy as writers and lawyers have tried to establish whether international legal rules would invalidate any inconsistent municipal legislation and, indeed, whether international rules could override the constitution. Similarly, the phrase "general rules of public international law" has led to problems over interpretation as it may refer to all aspects of international law, including customary and treaty rules, or merely general principles common to all, or perhaps only certain nations.[100]

As far as treaties are concerned, the German federal courts will regard these as superior to domestic legislation, though they will not be allowed to operate so as to affect the constitution. Article 59 of the Basic Law declares that treaties which regulate the political relations of the federation or relate to matters of federal legislation shall require the consent or participation, in the form of a federal law, of the bodies competent in any specific case for such federal legislation.

Holland has approached the whole topic in much more of a monist frame of mind. The constitution provides that treaties have precedence over domestic laws and that any municipal legislation, whether enacted prior to or subsequent to an international agreement, is invalid if its provisions prove incompatible with those of the agreement.[101]

The French Constitution of 1958 declares that treaties duly ratified and published shall operate as laws within the domestic system. However, the constitution provides that on an extensive range of international agreements, ratification can only take place by means of legislation. Example include commercial treaties which entail some form of financial outlay. Once the relevant legislation has been passed, the agreement is promulgated and becomes binding upon the courts. The provisions of the particular treaty will be superior to those of domestic laws, but only if this situation

---

[100] See e.g. O'Connell, *International Law*, 2nd ed., 1970, vol.1, pp.71-76, and sources therein cited. See also generally Drzemczewski, *The European Human Rights Convention in Domestic Law*, 1983, and Peaslee, *op. cit.*, vol.III, p.361.

[101] See e.g. Alkema, "Fundamental Human Rights and the Legal Order of the Netherlands", in *International Law in the Netherlands* (ed. Van Panhuys *et al.*), vol.3, 1980, p.109, and Peaslee, *op. cit.* vol.III, p.652.

applies also as regards the other party or parties to the treaty.[102] It
is also now accepted that the French courts may declare a statute
inapplicable for conflicting with an earlier treaty.[103]

This survey of the attitudes adopted by various countries of the
common law or civil law persuasions leads to a few concluding
remarks. The first of these is that a strict adherence to either the
monist or dualist position will not enable one to get to grips with
the situation as it actually exists. Most countries accept the operation
of customary rules within their own jurisdictions, providing there
is no conflict with existing laws, and some even will allow international
law to prevail over municipal provisions. One can regard this as a
significant element in extending the principles and protection of
international law, whether or not it is held that the particular
provision permitting this, whether by constitutional enactment or
by case law, illustrates the superiority of municipal law in so acting.

The situation as regards treaties is much more complex, as
different attitudes are maintained by different states. In some
countries, certain treaties will operate internally by themselves (self-
executing) while others must undergo a process of domestic
legalisation. There are countries where legislation is needed for
virtually all international agreements, for example, Belgium. It is
by no means settled as a general principle whether treaties prevail
over domestic rules. Some countries allow treaties to supersede all
municipal laws, whether made earlier or later than the agreement.
Others, such as Norway, adopt the opposite stance. Where there are
written constitutions, an additional complicating factor is introduced
and some reasonably stable hierarchy incorporating ordinary laws,
constitutional provisions and international law has to be maintained.
It will be up to the individual country to adopt its own list of
preferences.[104]

---

[102] See e.g. O'Connell, *op. cit.*, pp.65-68; Rousseau, *Droit International Public,* 1979, and
Peaslee, *op. cit.* vol.III, p.312.

[103] See the *Cafés Jacques Vabre* case, 16 *Common Market Law Review,* 1975, p.336 and *In
re Nicolo,* 84 *AJIL,* 1990, p.765.

[104] See Drzemczewski, *op. cit.,* and Peaslee, *op. cit.* vol.III, pp.76 and 689. See also as
regards Soviet practice, Grzybowski, *Soviet Public International Law,* 1970, pp.30-32, and
as regards Australian practice, e.g. *Koowarta* v. *Bjelke-Petersen,* High Court of Australia, 39
ALR 417 (11 May 1982); 68 *ILR,* p.181; *Tabag* v. *Minister for Immigration and Ethnic Affairs,*
Federal Court of Australia, 45 ALR 705 (23 December 1982) and *Commonwealth of Australia*
v. *State of Tasmania,* High Court of Australia, 46 ALR 625, (1 July 1983); 68 *ILR,* p.266.

Of course, such diverse attitudes can lead to confusion and by no means assist in explaining what international law is and how it operates. But in the light of the present state of international law, it is inevitable that its enforcement and sphere of activity will become entangled with the ideas and practices of municipal law. Indeed, it is precisely because of the inadequate enforcement facilities that lie at the disposal of international law that one must consider the relationship with municipal law as of more than marginal importance. This is because the extent to which domestic courts apply the rules of international law may well determine the effectiveness of international legislation and judicial decision making.

However, to declare that international legal rules therefore prevail over all relevant domestic legislation is incorrect in the vast majority of cases and would be to overlook the real in the face of the ideal. States jealously guard their prerogatives, and few are more meaningful than the ability to legislate free from outside control; and, of course, there are democratic implications. The consequent supremacy of municipal legal systems over international law in the domestic sphere is not exclusive, but it does exist as an undeniable general principle.

It is pertinent to refer here briefly to the effect of the European Communities upon their member-states.[105] In addition to the treaties creating the EC, there is a great deal of secondary legislation issuing forth from its institutions, which can apply to the member-states. This takes the form of regulations, decisions or directives. Of these, the first two are directly applicable and enforceable within each of the countries concerned without the need for enabling legislation. While it is true that the legislation for this type of activity has been passed by, for example section 2(1) of the European Communities Act, 1972, in the UK, which permits in advance this form of indirect law-making, and is thus assimilated into municipal law, the fact remains that the member-states have accepted an extraterritorial source of law, binding in certain circumstances upon them. In this context, it is worth noting the acceptance by the House of Lords

---

[105] See e.g. Lasok and Bridge, *Introduction to the Law and Institutions of the European Communities*, 4th ed., 1987; Collins, *European Community Law in the United Kingdom*, 3rd ed., 1984 and Kovar, "The Relationship between Community Law and National Law" in *Thirty Years of Community Law* (Commission of the European Communities), 1981, p.109. See also *supra*, p.117.

in *Factortame Ltd.* v. *Secretary of State for Transport*[106] that one of the consequences of UK entry into the European Communities and the European Communities Act 1972 was that an interim injunction could be granted, the effect of which would be to suspend the operation of a statute on the grounds that the legislation in question allegedly infringed Community law. This is one illustration of the major effect joining the Community has had in terms of the English legal system and previously accepted legal principles. The mistake, however, should not be made of generalising from this specific relationship to the sphere of international law as a whole.

JUSTICIABILITY, ACT OF STATE AND RELATED DOCTRINES

An issue is justiciable basically if it can be tried according to law.[107] It would, therefore, follow that matters that fall within the competence of the executive branch of government are not justiciable before the courts. Accordingly, the test as to whether a matter is or is not justiciable involves an illumination of that grey area where the spheres of executive and judiciary merge and overlap. One important aspect of justiciability is the doctrine of act of state. An act of state generally relates to the activities of the executive in relations with other states,[108] but in the context of international law and municipal courts it refers particularly to the doctrine that no state can exercise jurisdiction over another state.[109] As such it is based upon the principles of the sovereignty and equality of states.

The concept of non-justiciability applies with regard to both domestic and foreign executive acts. In the former case,[110] the courts will refuse to adjudicate upon an exercise of sovereign power,

---

[106] See *The Times*, 12 October 1990, p.31. See also *R* v. *Secretary of State for Transport, ex parte Factortame*, European Court of Justice case C-213/89, *The Times*, 20 June 1990, p.31.

[107] See Mann, *op. cit.*, Chapter 4.

[108] See e.g. Wade and Phillips, *op. cit.*, pp.299-303; Moore, *Acts of State in English Law*, 1906; Mann, *op. cit.*, Chapter 9: Singer, "The Act of State Doctrine of the UK", 75 *AJIL*, 1981, p.283; Akehurst, "Jurisdiction in International Law", 46 *BYIL*, 1972-3, pp.145, 240 and Zander, "The Act of State Doctrine", 53 *AJIL*, 1959, p.826.

[109] See Lord Pearson, *Nissan* v. *Attorney-General*, [1970] AC 179, 239; 44 *ILR*, pp.359, 390.

[110] See *Nissan* v. *Attorney-General*, [1970] AC 179 and *Buron* v. *Denman*, (1848) 145 ER 450. See also de Smith and Brazier, *Constitutional and Administrative Law*, 6th ed., 1989, pp.145-51 and Mann, *op. cit.*, Chapter 10.

such as making war and peace, making international treaties or ceding territory.[111] As far as the latter instance is concerned, Lord Wilberforce declared in *Buttes Gas and Oil Co.* v. *Hammer (No.3)*[112]

> there exists in English law a general principle that the courts will not adjudicate upon the transactions of foreign sovereign states . . . it seems desirable to consider this principle . . . not as a variety of "act of state" but one for judicial restraint or abstention.[113]

Such a principle was not one of discretion, but inherent in the nature of the judicial process. Although that case concerned litigation in the areas of libel and conspiracy, the House of Lords felt that a determination of the issue would have involved the court in reviewing the transactions of four sovereign states and having to find that part of those transactions were contrary to international law. Quite apart from the possibility of embarrassment to the foreign relations of the executive, there were no judicial or manageable standards by which to judge such issues.[114]

It has been held, for example, that judicial review would not be appropriate in a matter which would have serious international repercussions and which was more properly the sphere of diplomacy.[115]

Legislation can, of course, impinge upon the question as to whether an issue is or is not justiciable, and sovereign, or state, immunity is particularly relevant here, especially as it too is founded upon the principles of the sovereignty and equality of states. The UK State Immunity Act 1978, for example, removed sovereign immunity for commercial transactions.[116] One of the questions that the Court of Appeal addressed in *Maclaine Watson* v. *International Tin Council*[117] was whether in such circumstances the doctrine of non-justiciability survived. It was emphasised that the two concepts

[111] See also *Council for Civil Service Unions* v. *Minister for the Civil Service*, [1984] 3 All ER 935, 956.

[112] [1982] AC 888; 64 *ILR*, p.331.

[113] *Ibid.*, p.931; 64 *ILR*, p.344. See also *Duke of Brunswick* v. *King of Hanover*, (1848) 1 HLC 1.

[114] *Ibid.*, p.938; 64 *ILR*, p.351.

[115] See e.g. *R* v. *Secretary of State for Foreign and Commonwealth Affairs, ex parte Pirbai*, *The Times*, 17 October, 1985, p.4 (Court of Appeal).

[116] See *Empresa Exportadora de Azucar* v. *Industria Azucarera Nacional S.A.*, [1983] 2 Ll.R 171, 194-95; 64 *ILR*, p.368. See further Chapter 12.

[117] [1988] 3 WLR 1169; 80 *ILR*, p.191

of immunity and non-justiciability had to be kept separate and concern was expressed that the *Buttes* non-justiciability principle could be used to prevent proceedings being brought against states in commercial matters, contrary to the Act.[118]

This warning should be heeded. Non-justiciability acts, in essence, as an evidential bar, since an issue cannot be raised or proved, whereas the immunity doctrine provides that the courts cannot exercise jurisdiction with regard to the matter in question, although it is open to the state concerned to waive its immunity and thus remove the jurisdictional bar. Indeed, whereas non-justiciability in the above sense relates to a clear inter-state relationship or situation which is impleaded in a seemingly private action, immunity issues will invariably arise out of a state-private party relationship that will not relate to inter-state activities as such.[119] Nevertheless, in practice, it is often difficult to disentangle the different conceptual threads, although the end result in terms of the inability of the plaintiff to surmount the sovereign hurdle may often be the same.

The issue of justiciability was discussed in *Maclaine Watson* v. *Department of Trade and Industry* both by the Court of Appeal[120] and the House of Lords[121] in the context of the creation of the collapsed International Tin Council by a group of states by a treaty which was unincorporated into English law. Kerr LJ emphasised that the doctrine in this context rested upon the principles that unincorporated treaties do not form part of the law of England and that such international agreements were not contracts which the courts could enforce.[122] However, this did not prevent reference to an unincorporated treaty where it was necessary or convenient, for example in order to assess the legal nature of the International Tin Council.[123]

Lord Oliver in the House of Lords decision reaffirmed the essence of the doctrine of justiciability. He noted that it was

---

[118] *Ibid.*, p.1188 *per* Kerr LJ; 80 *ILR*, p.209.,
[119] See e.g. *Amalgamated Metal Trading* v. *Department of Trade and Industry, The Times*, 21 March 1989, p.40.
[120] [1988] 3 WLR 1033; 80 *ILR*, p.49.
[121] [1989] 3 All ER 523; 81 *ILR*, p.671.
[122] [1988] 3 WLR 1033, 1075; 80 *ILR*, pp.49, 86.
[123] *Ibid.*, 1075-76. See also Nourse LJ, *ibid.*, p.1130; 80 *ILR*, p.148.

axiomatic that municipal courts have not and cannot have the competence to adjudicate upon or to enforce the rights arising out of transactions entered into by independent sovereign states between themselves on the plane of international law.[124]

However, this did not mean that the court must never look at or construe a treaty. A treaty could be examined as a part of the factual background against which a particular issue has arisen.[125] It was pointed out that the creation of the Council by a group of states was a sovereign act and that the adjudication of the rights and obligations between the member-states of the Council and the Council itself could only be undertaken on the international plane.[126] In other words, the situation appeared to involve not only the *Buttes* form of act of state non-justiciability, but also non-justiciability on the basis of an unincorporated treaty.

The principle of non-justiciability, which includes but goes beyond the concept of act of state, must exist in an international system founded upon sovereign and formally equal states. Having said that, there is no doubt that the extent of the doctrine is open to question. While the courts would not inquire into the validity of acts done in a sovereign capacity, such as the constitutionality of foreign laws as such,[127] they may not feel constrained from investigating in a dispute involving private rights the legal validity of an act done by a citizen purporting to act on behalf of the sovereign or sovereign state.[128]

The US courts have similarly recognised the existence of areas of non-justiciability for sensitive political reasons. This is usually referred to as the political question doctrine and operates to prevent the courts from considering issues of political delicacy in the field of foreign affairs.[129] In the *Greenham Women against Cruise Missiles* v. *Reagan case*,[130] for example, the Court held that a suit to prevent the US deployment of cruise missiles at an air force base in the UK

---

[124] [1989] 3 All ER 523, 544; 81 *ILR*, pp.671, 700.

[125] *Ibid.*, p.545; 81 *ILR*, p.701.

[126] *Ibid.*, p.559; 81 *ILR*, p.722. See also Ralph Gibson LJ in the Court of Appeal judgment, [1988] 3 WLR 1033, 1143-44; 80 *ILR*, pp.49, 163.

[127] See *Buck* v. *Attorney-General*, [1965] I Ch. 745; 42 *ILR*, p.11.

[128] See e.g. *Dubai Bank* v. *Galadari*, *The Times*, 14 July 1990.

[129] See e.g. *Underhill* v. *Hernandez*, 168 US 250 (1897) and Henkin, "Is There a 'Political Question' Doctrine?", 85 *Yale Law Journal*, 1976, p.597.

[130] 591 F.Supp. 1332 (1984). See also *Baker* v. *Carr*, 369 US 181 (1962).

constitutes a non-justiciable political question, not appropriate for judicial resolution.

In *Banco Nacional de Cuba* v. *Sabbatino*,[131] the US Supreme Court held that the act of state concept was not a rule of public international law, but related instead to internal constitutional balances.[132] The Court declared that the judicial branch would not examine the validity of a taking of property within its own territory by a foreign sovereign government,[133] irrespective of the legality in international law of that action.[134] This basic approach was supported in a subsequent case,[135] whereas in *Alfred Dunhill of London Inc.* v. *Republic of Cuba*[136] the Supreme Court employed sovereign immunity concepts as the reason for not recognising the repudiation of the commercial obligations of a state instrumentality as an act of state. However, it now appears that there is an exception to the strict act of state doctrine where a relevant treaty provision between the parties specifies the standard of compensation to be payable and thus provides "controlling legal principles".[137]

In an important recent case, the Supreme Court examined anew the extent of the act of state doctrine. *Kirkpatrick* v. *Environmental Tectonics*[138] concerned a claim brought by an unsuccessful bidder on a Nigerian government contract in circumstances where the successful rival had bribed Nigerian officials. The Court unanimously held that the act of state doctrine did not apply since the validity of no foreign sovereign act was at issue. While the doctrine clearly

[131] 376 US 398 (1964); 35 *ILR*, p.2.

[132] *Ibid.*, pp.427-8; 35 *ILR*, p.37.

[133] *Ibid.*

[134] This approach was reversed by Congress in the Hickenlooper Amendment to the Foreign Assistance Act of 1964, Pub L No 86-663, para.301(d)(4), 78 Stat.1013 (1964), 79 Stat. 653, 659, as amended 22 USC, para.23470(e)(2), (1982). Note that in *Williams & Humbert Ltd* v. *W & H Trade Marks (Jersey) Ltd*, [1986] 1 All ER 129; 75 *ILR*, p.312, the House of Lords held that an English court would recognise a foreign law effecting compulsory acquisition and any change of title to property which came under the control of the foreign state as a result and would accept and enforce the consequences of that compulsory acquisition without considering its merits.

[135] *First National City Bank* v. *Banco Nacional de Cuba*, 406 US 759 (1972); 66 *ILR*, p.102.

[136] 96 Sup.Ct.1854 (1976); 66 *ILR*, p.212. See also Halberstam, "Sabbatino Resurrected", 79 *AJIL*, 1985, p.68.

[137] See *Kalamazoo Spice Extraction Co* v. *Provisional Military Government of Socialist Ethiopia*, 729 F.2d 422 (1984). See also *AIG* v. *Iran*, 493 F.Supp. 522 (1980) and Justice Harlan in the *Sabbatino* case, 376 US 398, 428 (1964); 35 *ILR*, pp.25, 37.

[138] 29 *ILM*, 1990, p.182.

meant that a US court had to accept that the acts of foreign sovereigns taken within their jurisdictions were to be deemed valid, this did not extend to cases and controversies that may embarrass foreign governments in situations falling outside this. Act of state was not to be extended.[139]

EXECUTIVE CERTIFICATES

There is an established practice adopted by the British courts of applying to the executive branch of government for the conclusive ascertainment of certain facts. Examples include the status of a foreign state or government, questions as to whether a state of war is in operation as regards a particular country or as between two foreign states and whether or not a particular person is entitled to diplomatic status. This means that in such matters of state the courts will consult the government and regard the executive certificate (or Foreign Office certificate as it is sometimes called), which is issued following the request, as conclusive, irrespective of any relevant rules of international law.[140] This was firmly acknowledged in *Duff Development Co Ltd* v. *Kelantan*,[141] which concerned the status of the State of Kelantan in the Malay Peninsula and whether it was able to claim immunity in the English courts. The government declared it was regarded as an independent state and the House of Lords noted that "where such a statement is forthcoming, no other evidence is admissible or needed," and that:

it was not the business of the Court to inquire whether the Colonial Office rightly concluded that the Sultan [of Kelantin] was entitled to be recognised as a sovereign by international law.[142]

---

[139] See also *Restatement (Third) of Foreign Relations Law of the United States*, 1987, vol.1, pp.366-89, and *Bandes* v. *Harlow & Jones*, 82 *AJIL*, 1988, p.820, where the Court of Appeals held that the act of state doctrine was inapplicable to takings by a foreign state of property located outside its territory.

[140] See e.g. Oppenheim, *op. cit.*, pp.765-68.

[141] [1924] AC 797; 2 *ILR*, p.124. See also *The Fagernes*, [1927] P.311; 3 *ILR*, p.126 and *Post Office* v. *Estuary Radio Ltd*, [1968] 2 QB 740; 43 *ILR*, p.114. But cf. *Hesperides Hotels* v. *Aegean Turkish Holidays*, [1978] 1 All ER 277; 73 *ILR*, p.9.

[142] Note that under s.7, Diplomatic Privileges Act, 1964 and s.21, State Immunity Act, 1978, such certificates are "conclusive evidence" as to issues of diplomatic and state immunity. See further *infra*, Chapter 12.

This basic position was reaffirmed in *R* v. *Secretary of State for Foreign and Commonwealth Affairs, ex p. Trawnik*,[143] in which it was held that certificates under section 40(3) of the Crown Proceedings Act, 1947 and section 21 of the State Immunity Act, 1978 were reviewable in the courts only if they constituted a nullity in that they were not genuine certificates or if on their face they had been issued outside the scope of the relevant statutory power. The contents of such certificates were conclusive of the matters contained therein and in so far as they related to recognition of foreign states were matters within the realm of the royal prerogative and not subject to judicial review.

Problems may very well arise in the context of the decision of the UK announced in 1980 not to accord recognition to governments, but rather to treat the question of an unconstitutional change of regimes as one relating to diplomatic relations.[144] It is unclear whether the courts will continue to request certificates from the executive in such cases and if so what the nature of the response will be. The executive may not wish to issue certificates or may not provide a conclusive statement as to the status of the new regime. If certificates are provided which include no "recognition" element, it will be interesting to see whether the courts will take it upon themselves to determine the status of the new government and what facts will be considered in the process.

The United States State Department similarly offers "suggestions" on such matters, although they tend to be more extensive than their British counterparts, and include comments upon the issues and occasionally the views of the executive.[145]

---

[143] *The Times*, 18 April, 1985, p.4. See also Warbrick, "Executive Certificates in Foreign Affairs: Prospects for Review and Control", 35 *ICLQ*, 1986, p.138 and Wilmshurst, "Executive Certificates in Foreign Affairs: The United Kingdom", *ibid*., p.157.

[144] See further *infra*, Chapter 7, p.253.

[145] O'Connell, *op. cit.*, pp.119-22. See *The Pisaro*, 255 US 216 (1921); *Anderson* v. *N.V. Transandine Handelmaatschappij*, 289 NY 9 (1942); 10 *ILR*, p.10; *Mexico* v. *Hoffman*, 324 US 30 (1945); 12 *ILR*, p.143 and the *Navemar*, 303 US 68 (1938); 9 *ILR*, p.176.

CHAPTER FIVE

The Subjects of International Law [1]

LEGAL PERSONALITY — INTRODUCTION

In any legal system, certain entities, whether they be individuals or companies, will be regarded as possessing rights and duties enforceable at law. Thus an individual may prosecute or be prosecuted for assault and a company can sue for breach of contract. They are able to do this because the law recognises them as "legal persons" possessing the capacity to have and to maintain certain rights, and being subject to perform specific duties. Just which persons will be entitled to what rights in what circumstances will depend upon the scope and character of the law. But it is the function of the law to apportion such rights and duties to such entities as it sees fit.[2] Legal personality is crucial. Without it institutions and groups cannot operate, for they need to be able to maintain and enforce claims. In municipal law individuals, limited companies and public corporations are recognised as each possessing a distinct legal personality, the terms of which are circumscribed by the relevant legislation.[3] It is the law which is the foundation of legal personality for it will determine the scope and nature of personality. There are things that an individual can do which an organisation cannot do, for example commit an act of physical assault, and vice versa. So that being accepted as a subject of the law does not mean the

---

[1] See e.g. Brownlie, *Principles of Public International Law*, 4th ed., 1990, Part II; Crawford, *The Creation of Statehood in International Law*, 1979; O'Connell, *International Law*, 2nd ed., 1970, vol.I; Verzijl, *International Law in Historical Perspective*, vol.II, 1969; Lissitzyn, "Territorial Entities other than Independent States in the Law of Treaties", 125 *HR*, p.5; Berezowski, *Mélanges Offerts à Juraj Andrassy* (ed. Ibler), 1968, p.31; Lauterpacht, *International Law: Collected Papers*, vol.II, 1975, p.487; Rousseau, *Droit International Public*, vol.II, 1974; Mugerwa, "Subjects of International Law", *Manual of Public International Law* (ed. Sørensen), 1968, p.247; Schwarzenberger, *International Law*, 3rd ed., vol.I, 1957, p.89, and Cassese, *International Law in a Divided World*, 1986, Chapter 4.

[2] See Dias, *Jurisprudence*, 4th ed., 1976, Chapter 11.

[3] *Ibid.*, pp.338, 341 and 344.

same thing in all cases. Different subjects will have different rights and duties in different ways.[4]

Personality involves the examination of certain concepts within the law such as status, capacity, competence as well as the nature and extent of particular rights and duties. The status of a particular entity may well be determinative of certain powers and obligations, while capacity will link together the status of a person with particular rights and duties. The whole process operates within the confines of the relevant legal system, which circumscribes personality, its nature and definition. This is especially true in international law. A particular view adopted of the system will invariably reflect upon the question of the identity and nature of international legal persons.[5]

Personality in international law necessitates the consideration of the interrelationship between rights and duties afforded under the international system and capacity to enforce claims. One needs to have close regard to the rules of international law in order to determine the precise nature of the capacity of the entity in question. Certain preliminary issues need to be faced. Does the personality of a particular claimant, for instance, depend upon its possession of the capacity to enforce rights? Indeed, is there any test of the nature of enforcement, or can even the most restrictive form of operation on the international scene be sufficient? One view suggests, for example, that while the quality of responsibility for violation of a rule usually co-exists with the quality of being able to enforce a complaint against a breach in any legal person, it would be useful to consider those possessing one of these qualities as indeed having juridical personality.[6] Other writers, on the other hand, emphasise the crucial role played by the element of enforceability of rights within the international system.[7]

However, a range of factors needs to be carefully examined before it can be determined whether an entity has international personality and, if so, what rights, duties and competences apply

---

[4] *Ibid.*, pp.338-58. See the *Reparation for Injuries* case, ICJ Reports, 1949, pp.174, 178; 16 *ILR*, pp.318, 321. See further, *infra*, p.182.

[5] See, for example, the Soviet view, Tunkin, *Theory of International Law*, 1974.

[6] See e.g. Sørensen, "Principes de Droit International Public", 101 *HR*, pp.5, 127. For a wider definition, see Mosler, *The International Society As a Legal Community*, 1980, p.32.

[7] See e.g. Verzijl, *op. cit.*, p.3.

in the particular case. Personality is a relative phenomenon varying with the circumstances. It will always involve a test of judgment and perception of the situation at hand and the overall context of the current nature and requirements of the international community at large.

One of the distinguishing characteristics of contemporary international law has been the wide range of participants performing on the international scene. These include states, international organisations, regional organisations, non-government organisations, public companies, private companies and individuals. Not all such entities will constitute legal persons, although they may act with some degree of influence upon the international plane. International personality is participation plus some form of community acceptance. The latter element will be dependent upon many different factors, including the type of personality under question. It may be manifested in many forms and may in certain cases be inferred from practice. It will also reflect a need. Particular branches of international law here are playing a crucial role. Human rights law, the law relating to armed conflicts and international economic law are specially important in generating and reflecting increased participation and personality in international law.

STATES

As Lauterpacht observes:

> the orthodox positivist doctrine has been explicit in the affirmation that only states are subjects of international law.[8]

However, it is less clear that in practice this position was maintained. The Holy See (particularly from 1871-1929), insurgents and belligerents, international organisations, chartered companies and various territorial entities such as the League of Cities were all at one time or another treated as possessing the capacity to become international persons.[9]

---

[8] *Op. cit.*, p.489.
[9] See e.g. Verzijl, *op. cit.*, pp.17-43 and Lauterpacht, *op. cit.*, pp.494-500. See also the *Western Sahara* case, ICJ Reports, 1975 pp.12, 39; 59 *ILR*, pp.30, 56 and *Survey of International Law in Relation to the work of Codification of the International Law Commission*, Memorandum of the Secretary General, 1949, A/CN.4/1/Rev.1 p.24.

Creation of Statehood [10]

The relationship in this area between factual and legal criteria is a crucial shifting one. Whether the birth of a new state is primarily a question of fact or law and how the interaction between the criteria of effectiveness and other relevant legal principles may be reconciled are questions of considerable complexity and significance. Since *terrae nullius* are no longer apparent,[11] the creation of new states in the future, once the decolonisation process is at an end, can only be accomplished as a result of the diminution or disappearance of existing states, and the need for careful regulation thus arises. In addition, the decolonisation movement has stimulated a re-examination of the traditional criteria. Article 1 of the Montevideo Convention on Rights and Duties of States 1933[12] lays down the most widely accepted formulation of the criteria of statehood in international law. It notes that the state as an international person should possess the following qualifications:

(a) a permanent population; (b) a defined territory; (c) government; and (d) capacity to enter into relations with other states.

This provision is not exhaustive, nor is it immutable. As will be seen below, other factors may be relevant, including self-determination and recognition. What is clear is that the essence of the framework revolves around territorial effectiveness.

The existence of a permanent population is naturally required and there is no specification of a minimum number of inhabitants, as examples such as Nauru and Tuvalu demonstrate. However, one of the issues raised by the Falkland Islands conflict does relate to the question of an acceptable minimum with regard to self-determination issues,[13] and it may be that the matter needs further clarification as there exists a number of small islands awaiting

[10] See in particular Crawford, *op. cit.*; Higgins, *The Development of International Law through the Political Organs of the United Nations*, 1963, pp.11-57; Marek, *Identity and Continuity of States in Public International Law*, 2nd ed., 1968, and Whiteman, *Digest of International Law*, vol.I, 1963, pp.221-33, 283-476.

[11] See as regards Antarctica, O'Connell, *op. cit.*, p.451. See also *infra*, p.309.

[12] 165 LNTS 19. International law does not require the structure of a state to follow any particular pattern: *Western Sahara* case, ICJ Reports, 1975, pp.12, 43-44; 59 *ILR*, pp.30, 60-61.

[13] *Infra*, Chapter 8, p.305.

decolonisation. The need for a defined territory focuses upon the requirement for a particular territorial base upon which to operate.

However, there is no necessity in international law for defined and settled boundaries. A state may be recognised as a legal person even though it is involved in a dispute with its neighbours as to the precise demarcation of its frontiers, so long as there is a consistent band of territory which is undeniably controlled by the government of the alleged state. For this reason at least, therefore, the "State of Palestine" declared in November 1988 at a conference in Algiers cannot be regarded as a valid state. The Palestinian organisations do not control any part of the territory they claim.[14]

Albania prior to the First World War was recognised by many countries even though its borders were in dispute. More recently, Israel has been accepted by the majority of nations as well as the United Nations as a valid state despite the fact that its frontiers have not to this day been finally settled and despite its involvement in hostilities with its Arab neighbours over its existence and territorial delineation.[15] What matters is the presence of a stable community within a certain area, even though its frontiers may be uncertain. Indeed it is possible for the territory of the state to be split into distinct parts, for example Pakistan, prior to the Bangladesh secession of 1971.

For a political society to function reasonably effectively it needs some form of government or central control. However, this is not a pre-condition for recognition as an independent country.[16] It should be regarded more as an indication of some sort of coherent political structure and society, than the necessity for a sophisticated apparatus of executive and legislative organs. The requirement relates to the nineteenth century concern with "civilisation" as an essential of independent statehood and ignores the modern tendency

[14] See *Keesing's Record of World Events*, p.36438 (1989).

[15] Brownlie, *op. cit.*, p.73. In fact most of the new states emerging after the First World War were recognised *de facto* or *de jure* before their frontiers were determined by treaty: Lauterpacht, *Recognition in International Law*, 1948, p.30. See *Deutsche Continental Gas-Gesellschaft* v. *Polish State* (1929), 5 *ILR*, pp.11, 15. See also Jessup speaking on behalf of the US regarding Israel's admission to the UN, SCOR, 3rd year, 383rd meeting, p.41. The general rule is reaffirmed in the *North Sea Continental Shelf* cases, ICJ Reports 1969, pp.3, 32; 41 *ILR*, pp.29, 62.

[16] See e.g. The Congo Case, Higgins, *op. cit.*, pp.162-64 and Hoskyns, *The Congo Since Independence*, 1965.

to regard sovereignty for non-independent peoples as the paramount consideration, irrespective of administrative conditions.

As an example of the former tendency one may note the *Aaland Islands* case of 1920. The report of the International Committee of Jurists appointed to investigate the status of the islands remarked with regard to the establishment of the Finnish Republic in the disordered days following the Russian revolution that it was extremely difficult to name the date that Finland became a sovereign state. It was noted that:

> [t]his certainly did not take place until a stable political organisation had been created, and until the public authorities had become strong enough to assert themselves throughout the territories of the state without the assistance of the foreign troops.[17]

The capacity to enter into relations with other states is an aspect of the existence of the entity in question as well as an indication of the importance attached to recognition by other countries. It is a capacity not limited to sovereign nations, since both international organisations and non-independent states can enter into legal relations with other entities under the rules of international law. But it is essential for a sovereign state to be able to create such legal relations with other units as it sees fit. Where this is not present, the entity cannot be an independent state. One is not talking here of political pressure by one country over another which may cause it to adopt, or reject, a particular course of action, something which is constantly occurring throughout the spectrum of the international community, but rather the total incapacity to enter into legal relations. For example, Eire may be heavily influenced by either Britain or the United States, but not the exclusion of all independent action in the international sphere. On the other hand, the City of Liverpool is not able to establish diplomatic relations with Brazil. The difference is the presence or absence of legal capacity, not the degree of persuasion or influence that may affect decisions.

The essence of such capacity is independence. This is crucial to statehood and amounts to a conclusion of law in the light of particular circumstances. It is a formal statement that the state is

---

[17] LNOJ Sp.Supp.no.4 (1920), pp.8-9. But cf. the view of the Commission of Rapporteurs in this case, LN Council Doc. B7 21/68/106 (1921), p.22.

subject to no other sovereignty and is unaffected either by factual dependence upon other states or submission to the rules of international law.[18] It is arguable that a degree of actual as well as formal independence may also be necessary. This question has been raised in relation to the grant of independence by South Africa to its Bantustans. In the case of the Transkei, for example, a considerable proportion, perhaps 90%, of its budget is contributed by South Africa, while Bophuthatswana is split into a series of areas divided by South African territory.[19] Both the Organisation of African Unity and the United Nations have declared such "independence" invalid and called upon all states not to recognise the new entities. These entities are, apart from South Africa, totally unrecognised. However, many states are as dependent upon aid from other states and economic success would not alter the attitude of the international community. Since South Africa is able to alienate parts of its own territory under international law, these entities would appear to be formally independent. It is suggested that the answer as to their status lies elsewhere than in an elucidation of this category of the criteria of statehood.[20]

An example of the complexities that may attend such a process is provided by the unilateral declaration of independence by Lithuania, one of the Baltic states unlawfully annexed by the Soviet Union in 1940, on 11 March 1990.[21] The 1940 annexation was never recognised *de jure* by the Western states and thus the control exercised by the USSR was accepted only upon a *de facto* basis. The 1990 declaration of independence was politically very sensitive, coming at a time of increasing disintegration within the Soviet Union, but went unrecognised by any state. In view of the continuing constitutional crisis within the USSR and the possibility of a new confederal association freely accepted by the fifteen Soviet republics, it is premature to talk of Lithuania as an independent state. It

[18] See *Austro-German Customs Union* case, (1931) PCIJ, Series A/B no.41, pp.41 (Court's Opinion) and 57-58 (Separate Opinion of Judge Anzilotti); 6 *ILR*, pp.26, 28, and *infra*, p.132. See also Marek, *op. cit.*, pp.166-80; Crawford, *op. cit.*, pp.48-52 and Rousseau, *Droit International Public*, vol.II, 1974, pp.53, 93.

[19] This was cited as one of the reasons for UK non-recognition, by the Minister of State, FCO, see UKMIL, 57 *BYIL*, 1986, pp.507-8.

[20] See Shaw, *Title to Territory in Africa*, 1985, pp.161-62. See also OAU Resolution, CM.Res.493 (XXVII), General Assembly resolution, 31/61A and Security Council statements on 21 September 1979 and 15 December 1981.

[21] See *Keesing's Record of World Events*, p.37299 (1990).

should, of course, be noted that the Soviet authorities maintain substantial control within that territory and thus the required independence criterion is lacking. It is unclear how the situation will develop.[22]

Self-determination and the Criteria of Statehood

It is the criterion of government which, as suggested above, has been most affected by the development of the legal right to self-determination. The traditional exposition of the criterion concentrated upon the stability and effectiveness needed for this factor to be satisfied,[23] while the representative and democratic nature of the government has also been put forward as a requirement. The evolution of self-determination has affected the standard necessary as far as the actual exercise of authority is concerned, so that it appears a lower level of effectiveness, at least in decolonisation situations, has been accepted. This can be illustrated by reference to a couple of cases.

The former Belgian Congo became independent on 30 June 1960 in the midst of widespread tribal fighting which had spread to the capital. Within a few weeks the Force Publique had mutinied, Belgian troops had intervened and the province of Katanga announced its secession. Notwithstanding the virtual breakdown of government, the Congo was recognised by a large number of states after independence and was admitted to the UN as a member-state without opposition. Indeed, at the time of the relevant General Assembly resolution in September 1960, two different factions of the Congo government sought to be accepted by the UN as the legitimate representatives of the state. In the event, the delegation authorised by the Head of State was accepted and that of the Prime Minister rejected.[24] A rather different episode occurred with regard to the Portuguese colony of Guinea-Bissau. In 1972, a UN Special Mission was dispatched to the "liberated areas" of the territory and concluded that the colonial power had lost effective administrative control of large areas of the territory. Foreign observers appeared

---

[22] See the view of the UK government, 166 HC Deb., col.697, Written Answers, 5 February 1990.

[23] See Lauterpacht, *op. cit.* footnote 15, p.28.

[24] *Keesings Contemporary Archives*, pp.17594-95 and 17639-40 and Hoskyns, *op. cit.*, pp.96-99.

to accept the claim of the PAIGC, the local liberation movement, to control between two-thirds and three-quarters of the area. The inhabitants of these areas, reported the Mission, supported the PAIGC which was exercising effective *de facto* administrative control.[25] On 24 September 1973, the PAIGC proclaimed the Republic of Guinea-Bissau an independent state. The issue of the "illegal occupation by Portuguese military forces of certain sections of the Republic of Guinea-Bissau" came before the General Assembly and a number of states affirmed the validity of the independence of the new state in international law. Western states denied that the criteria of statehood had been fulfilled. However, 93 states voted in favour of Assembly resolution 3061 (XXVIII) which mentioned "the recent accession to independence of the people of Guinea-Bissau thereby creating the sovereign state of the Republic of Guinea-Bissau". Many states argued in favour of this approach on the basis that a large proportion of the territory was being effectively controlled by the PAIGC, though neither a majority of the population nor the major towns.[26]

In addition to modifying the traditional principle with regard to the effectiveness of government in certain circumstances, the principle of self-determination may also be relevant as an additional criterion of statehood. In the case of Rhodesia, UN resolutions denied the legal validity of the unilateral declaration of independence on 11 November 1965 and called upon member-states not to recognise it.[27] No state did recognise Rhodesia and a civil war ultimately resulted in its transformation into the recognised state of Zimbabwe. Rhodesia might have been regarded as a state by virtue of its satisfaction of the factual requirements of statehood but this is a dubious proposition. The evidence of complete non-recognition, the strenuous denunciations of its purported independence by the international community and the developing civil war militate strongly against this. It could be argued on the other hand that, in

[25] *Yearbook of the UN,* 1971, pp.566-67 and A/AC.109/L 804, p.19. See also A/8723/Rev.1 and Assembly resolution 2918 (XXVII).

[26] See GAOR, 28th Session, General Committee, 213rd meeting, pp.25-26, 28, 30 and 31, GAOR, 28th session, plenary, 2156th meeting, pp.8, 12 and 16 and 2157th meeting, pp.22-25 and 65-67. See also *Yearbook of the UN,* 1973, pp.143-47 and CDDH/SR.4., pp.33-37. See also the Western Sahara situation, *infra,* p.164.

[27] E.g. General Assembly resolutions 2024 (XX) and 2151 (XXI) and Security Council resolutions 216 (1965) and 217 (1966). See Higgins, *The World Today,* 1967, p.94 and Crawford, *op. cit.,* pp.103-6. See also Shaw, *op. cit.*

the absence of recognition, no entity could become a state but this constitutive theory of recognition is not acceptable.[28] The best approach is to accept the development of self-determination as an additional criterion of statehood, denial of which would obviate statehood. This can only be acknowledged in relation to self-determination situations and would not operate in cases, for example, of secessions from existing states. In other words, in the case of an entity seeking to become a state and accepted by the international community as being entitled to exercise the right of self-determination, it may well be necessary to demonstrate that the internal requirements of the principle have not been offended. One cannot define this condition too rigorously in view of state practice to date, but it would appear to be a sound proposition that systematic and institutionalised discrimination might invalidate a claim to statehood.

Recognition

Recognition is a method of accepting certain factual situations and endowing them with legal significance, but this relationship is a complicated one. In the context of the creation of statehood, recognition may be viewed as constitutive or declaratory, as will be noted in more detail in Chapter 7. The former theory maintains that it is only through recognition that a state comes into being under international law, whereas the latter approach maintains that once the factual criteria of statehood have been satisfied, a new state exists as an international person, recognition becoming merely a political and not a legal act in this context. Various modifications have been made to these theories, but the role of recognition, at the least in providing strong evidential demonstration of satisfaction of the relevant criteria, must be acknowledged.

Extinction of Statehood

While it is not unusual for governments to disappear, it is rather rarer for states to become extinct. This will not happen in international law as a result of the illegal use of force, as the Kuwait crisis of August 1990 and the consequent United Nations response

[28] *Infra,* Chapter 7, p.243.

clearly demonstrates,[29] but it may occur by consent. Two examples illustrated this during 1990. On 22 May North and South Yemen united to form one state, the Republic of Yemen,[30] while on 3 October, the two German states reunified as a result of a constitutional accession of the *Länder* of the German Democratic Republic to the Federal Republic of Germany.[31]

The Fundamental Rights of States

The fundamental rights of states exist by virtue of the international legal order, which is able, as in the case of other legal orders, to define the characteristics of its subjects.

(a) *Independence*

Perhaps the outstanding characteristic of a state is its independence. This was defined in the Draft Declaration on the Rights and Duties of States prepared in 1949 by the International Law Commission, as the capacity of a state to provide for its own well-being and development free from the domination of other states, providing it does not impair or violate their legitimate rights.[32] By independence, one is referring to a legal concept and it is no deviation from independence to be subject to the rules of international law. Any political or economic dependence that may in reality exist does not affect the legal independence of the state, unless that state is formally compelled to submit to the demands of a superior state, in which case dependent status is concerned.

A discussion on the meaning and nature of independence took place in the *Austro-German Customs Union* case before the Permanent Court of International Justice in 1931.[33] It concerned a proposal to create a free trade customs union between the two German-speaking states and whether this was incompatible with the 1919 Peace Treaties (coupled with a subsequent protocol of 1922)

---

[29] See further Chapter 18, *infra*.

[30] See *Keesing's Record of World Events*, p.37470 (1990).

[31] See *infra* p.160.

[32] *Yearbook of the ILC*, 1949, p.286. Judge Huber noted in the *Island of Palmas* case that "independence in regard to a portion of the globe is the right to exercise therein, to the exclusion of any other state, the functions of a state," (1928) 2 RIAA, pp.829, 838; 4 *ILR*, p.3.

[33] PCIJ Series A/B, no.41, 1931; 6 *ILR*, p.26.

pledging Austria to take no action to compromise its independence. In the event, and in the circumstances of the case, the Court held that the proposed union would adversely affect Austria's sovereignty. Speaking generally, however, Judge Anzilotti noted that restrictions upon a state's liberty, whether arising out of customary law or treaty obligations, do not as such affect its independence. As long as such restrictions do not place the state under the legal authority of another state, the former maintains its status as an independent country. As it was declared in this important but dissenting opinion:

> restrictions on its liberty of action which a state may agree to do not affect its independence, provided that the state does not thereby deprive itself of its organic powers.[34]

The notion of independence in international law implies a number of rights and duties: for example, the right of a state to exercise jurisdiction over its territory and permanent population, or the right to engage upon an act of self-defence in certain situations. It implies also the duty not to intervene in the internal affairs of other sovereign states.

Precisely what constitutes the internal affairs of a state is open to dispute and is in any event a constantly changing standard. It was maintained by the western powers for many years that any discussion or action by the United Nations[35] with regard to their colonial possessions was contrary to international law.

However, this argument by the European colonial powers did not succeed and the United Nations examined many colonial situations.[36] It has been suggested that issues related to human rights and racial oppression do not fall within this closed category of domestic

---

[34] *Ibid.*, p.77; 6 *ILR*, p.30. See also the *North Atlantic Coast Fisheries* case, (1910), Scott, *Hague Court Reports*, p.141 at p.170 and the *Wimbledon* case, PCIJ, Series A, no.1, 1923, p.25; 2 *ILR*, p.99.

[35] Article 2(7) of the UN Charter provides that "nothing in the present Charter shall authorise the United Nations to intervene in matters which are essentially within the domestic jurisdiction of any state". On the relationship between this article and the general international law provision, see Brownlie, *op. cit.*, p.293.

[36] See Higgins, *op. cit.*, pp.58-130; Brownlie, *op. cit.*, pp.291-92; Rajan, *United Nations and Domestic Jurisdiction*, 2nd ed., 1961 and Kelsen, *Principles of International Law*, 2nd ed., 1966.

jurisdiction, or internal affairs, at all and that international law permits outside scrutiny. In fact, the position is rather more ambiguous than this.

This duty not to intervene in matters within the domestic jurisdiction of any state was included in the Declaration on Principles of International Law Concerning Friendly Relations and Co-operation among States adopted in October 1970 by the United Nations General Assembly. It was emphasised that

> [n]o state or group of states has the right to intervene, directly or indirectly, for any reason whatever, in the internal or external affairs of any other state. Consequently, armed intervention and all other forms of interference or attempted threats against the personality of the state or against its political, economic and cultural elements, are in violation of international law.

The prohibition also covers any assistance or aid to subversive elements aiming at the violent overthrow of the government of a state. In particular, the use of force to deprive peoples of their national identity amounts to a violation of this principle of non-intervention.[37]

The principles surrounding sovereignty, such as non-intervention, are essential in the maintenance of a reasonably stable system of competing states. By setting limits on the powers of states vis-à-vis other states, it contributes to some extent to a degree of stability within the legal order. As the International Court of Justice pointed out in the *Corfu Channel* case in 1949, "between independent states, respect for territorial sovereignty is an essential foundation of international relations".[38]

By a similar token a state cannot purport to enforce its laws in the territory of another state, nor may it dispatch policemen or other governmental officials to arrest alleged criminals residing abroad without the consent of the state concerned.

However, international law would seem to permit the state to continue to exercise its jurisdiction, notwithstanding the illegality of the apprehension.[39]

---

[37] See also the use of force, *infra,* Chapter 18.
[38] ICJ Reports, 1949, pp.4, 35; 16 *ILR,* pp.155, 167. See *infra,* p.355.
[39] See e.g. the *Eichmann* case, 36 *ILR,* p.5. See further *infra,* p.413.

(b) *Equality*

One other crucial principle is the legal equality of states. It is a concept of law and should not be confused with political equality. What is referred to here is equality of legal rights and duties. Malta is a sovereign state as is the United States. It has the same juridical capacities and functions, and is likewise entitled to one vote in the United Nations General Assembly. In many ways, the doctrine of the legal equality of states is an umbrella category for it includes within its scope the recognised rights and obligations which fall upon all states.

This was recognised in the 1970 Declaration on Principles of International Law. This provides that:

All states enjoy sovereign equality. They have equal rights and duties and are equal members of the international community, notwithstanding differences of an economic, social, political or other nature.

In particular, sovereign equality includes the following elements:

(a) States are juridically equal;

(b) Each state enjoys the rights inherent in full sovereignty;

(c) Each state has the duty to respect the personality of other states;

(d) The territorial integrity and political independence of the state are inviolable;

(e) Each state has the right freely to choose and develop its political, social, economic and cultural systems;

(f) Each state has the duty to comply fully and in good faith with its international obligations and to live in peace with other states.[40]

In many respects this doctrine owes its origins to Natural Law thinking. Just as equality was regarded as the essence of man and thus contributed philosophically to the foundation of the state, so naturalist scholars treated equality as the natural condition of states. With the rise in positivism, the emphasis altered and rather than postulating a general rule applicable to all and from which a series of rights and duties may be deduced, international lawyers concentrated upon the sovereignty of each and every state, and the

---

[40] See also Final Act of the Conference on Security and Co-operation in Europe, Helsinki, 1975, Cmnd. 6198, pp.2-3. See also O'Connell, *op. cit.*, pp.322-24; Kooijmans, *The Doctrine of the Legal Equality of States*, 1964 and Marshall CJ, *The Antelope*, 10 Wheat, pp.66, 122.

necessity that international law be founded upon the consent of states.

The notion of equality before the law is accepted by states in the sense of equality of legal personality and capacity. However, it would not be strictly accurate to talk in terms of the equality of states in creating law. The major powers will always have an influence commensurate with their status, if only because their concerns are much wider and their interests much deeper, not ignoring the unassailable truth that their capacity to uphold their views is far greater than that of smaller nations.

Within the General Assembly of the United Nations, the doctrine is maintained by the rule of one state, one vote, irrespective of the realities of power. It is a situation that has elicited much criticism, especially from the west as the preponderance of the Third World Afro-Asian-Arab bloc has become clearer as the universality of membership is extended.[41] However, one should not overlook the existence of the veto possessed by the USA, USSR, China, France and the United Kingdom in the Security Council.

(c) *Peaceful Co-existence*

One concept falling within the province of the basic rights and obligations of states that has been developing over the last twenty or so years is the idea of peaceful co-existence. It has been formulated in different ways and with different views as to its legal nature by the USSR, China and the Third World. The theory was elaborated in 1954 as the Five Principles of Peaceful Co-existence by India and China, which concerned the mutual respect for each other's territorial integrity and sovereignty, mutual non-aggression, non-interference in each other's affairs and the principle of equality.[42]

The idea was expanded in a number of international documents such as the final communiqué of the Bandung Conference in 1955 and in various resolutions of the United Nations.[43] Its recognised constituents also appear in the list of Principles of the Charter of

---

[41] See e.g. Sohn, *Cases on UN Law*, 2nd ed., 1967, pp.232-90 and Clark and Sohn, *World Peace Through World Law*, 3rd ed., 1966, pp.399-402.

[42] See e.g. Tunkin, *Theory of International Law*, 1974, pp.69-75. See also Ramondo, *Peaceful Co-existence*, 1967 and Higgins, *Conflict of Interests*, 1965, pp.99-170.

[43] See e.g. General Assembly resolutions 1236 (XII) and 1301 (XIII). See also *Yearbook of the UN*, 1957, pp.105-9; *ibid.* 1961, p.524 and *ibid.* 1962, p.488.

the Organisation of African Unity. Among the points enumerated are the concepts of sovereign equality, non-interference in the international affairs of states, respect for the sovereignty and territorial integrity of states as well as a condemnation of subversive activities carried out from one state and aimed against another. Other concepts that have been included in this category comprise such principles as non-aggression and the execution of international obligations in good faith. The view of the Soviet Union appears to be that peaceful co-existence constitutes the guiding principle in contemporary international law.[44]

The exposition of such a theory involves in effect the elaboration of the basic rights and duties of states. Peaceful co-existence in its fundamental form merely connotes an alternate classification of principles already known and accepted as rules of international law. Its existence and evident popularity as a separate category relate to political developments and the recognition of a world system emerging gradually from a bi-polar Soviet-American shape into a rather less secure multi-polar situation with a number of power centres.[45]

Protectorates and Protected States [46]

A distinction is sometimes made between a protectorate and a protected state. In the former case, in general, the entity concerned enters into an arrangement with a state under which, while separate legal personality may be involved, separate statehood is not. In the case of a protected state, the entity concerned retains its status as a separate state but enters into a valid treaty relationship with another state affording the latter certain extensive functions possibly internally and externally. However, precisely which type of arrangement is made and the nature of the status, rights and duties in question will depend upon the circumstances and in particular

[44] Tunkin, *op. cit.*, pp.35-48.
[45] See also as regards the fundamental rights of states, Kiss, *Répertoire de la Pratique Française en Matière de Droit International Public*, vol.II, 1966, pp.21-50 and *Survey of International Law*, prepared by the UN Secretary-General, A/CN.4/245.
[46] See Crawford, *op. cit.*, pp.187-208, O'Connell, *op. cit.*, pp.341-44, and Verzijl, *op. cit.*, pp.412-27. Note also the special institution of the colonial protectorate, Shaw, *op. cit.*, Chapter 1.

the terms of the relevant agreement and third party attitudes.[47] In the case of Morocco, the Treaty of Fez of 1912 with France gave the latter the power to exercise certain sovereign powers on behalf of the former, including all of its international relations. Nevertheless, the ICJ emphasised that Morocco had in the circumstances of the case remained a sovereign state.[48]

The extent of powers delegated to the protecting state in such circumstances may vary, as may the manner of the termination of the arrangement. In these cases, formal sovereignty remains unaffected and the entity in question retains its status as a state, and may act as such in the various international fora, regard being had of course to the terms of the arrangement. The obligation may be merely to take note of the advice of the protecting state, or it may extend to a form of diplomatic delegation subject to instruction, as in the case of Liechtenstein. Liechtenstein was refused admission to the League of Nations since it was held unable to discharge all the international obligations imposed by the Covenant in the light of its delegation of sovereign powers such as diplomatic representation, administration of Post, Telegraph and Telephone services and final decisions in certain judicial cases.[49] Liechtenstein, however, has been a party to the Statute of the International Court of Justice and was a party to the *Nottebohm*[50] case before the Court, a facility only open to states. In autumn 1990, Liechtenstein joined the United Nations.

Federal States [51]

There are various forms of federation or confederation, according to the relative distribution of power between the central and local organs. In some states, the residue of power lies with the central

[47] See the *Tunis and Morocco Nationality Decrees* case, (1923) PCIJ, Series B no.4, p.27; 2 *ILR*, p.349. See also the question of the Ionian Islands, Lindley, *The Acquisition and Government of Backward Territory in International Law*, 1926, pp.181-82.

[48] *Rights of Nationals of the United States of America in Morocco*, ICJ Reports, 1952, pp.176, 188; 19 *ILR*, pp.255, 263.

[49] See Crawford, *op. cit.*, p.190; Report of the 5th Committee of the League, 6 December 1920, Hackworth, *Digest of International Law*, vol.I, 1940, pp.48-49; Higgins, *op. cit.*, p.34, note 30.

[50] ICJ Reports, 1955, p.4; 22 *ILR*, p.349.

[51] See Bernier, *International Legal Aspects of Federalism*, 1973 and Okeke, *op. cit.*, pp.35-62.

government, in others with the local or provincial bodies. A confederation implies a more flexible arrangement, leaving a considerable degree of authority and competence with the component units to the detriment of the central organ.

The division of powers inherent in such arrangements often raises important questions for international law, particularly in the areas of personality, responsibility and immunity. Whether the <u>federation dissolves into two or more states also brings into</u> focus <u>the doctrine of self-determination in the form of secession.</u> Such a dissolution may be the result of an amicable and constitutional agreement or may occur pursuant to a forceful exercise of secession. In the latter case, international legal rules may be pleaded in aid, but the position would seem to be that (apart from recognised colonial situations) there is no right of self-determination applicable to independent states that would justify the resort to secession. There is, of course, no international legal duty to refrain from secession attempts: the situation remains subject to the domestic law. However, should such a secession prove successful in fact, then the concepts of recognition and the appropriate criteria of statehood would prove relevant and determinative as to the new situation.[52]

The federal state will itself, of course, have personality, but the question of the personality and capability of the component units of the federation on the international plane can really only be determined in the light of the constitution of the state concerned and state practice. For instance, the Soviet Republics of Byelorussia and the Ukraine were admitted as members of the United Nations in 1945 and to that extent possess international personality.[53] Component states of a federation that have been provided with a certain restricted international competence may thus be accepted as having a degree of international personality. The issue has arisen especially with regard to treaties. Lauterpacht, in his Report on the Law of Treaties, for example, noted that treaties concluded by component units of federal states "are treaties in the meaning of international law",[54] although Fitzmaurice adopted a different approach in his Report on the Law of Treaties by stating that such

---

[52] *Infra*, p.172.
[53] See e.g. Bernier, *op. cit.*, pp.64-66. These entities were also members of a number of international organisations and have signed treaties.
[54] *Yearbook of the ILC*, 1953, vol.II, p.139.

units act as agents for the federation which alone possesses international personality and which is the entity bound by the treaty and responsible for its implementation.[55] Article 5(2) of the International Law Commission's Draft Articles on the Law of Treaties provided that

> [s]tates members of a federal union may possess a capacity to conclude treaties if such capacity is admitted by the federal constitution and within the limits there laid down

but this was ultimately rejected at the Vienna Conference on the Law of Treaties,[56] partly on the grounds that the rule was beyond the scope of the convention itself. The major reasons for the rejection, however, were that the provision would enable third states to intervene in the internal affairs of federal states by seeking to interpret the constitutions of the latter and that, from another perspective, it would unduly enhance the power of domestic law to determine questions of international personality to the detriment of international law. This perhaps would indeed have swung the balance too far away from the international sphere of operation.

Different federations have evolved different systems with regard to the allocation of treaty-making powers. In some cases, component units may enter into such arrangements subject to varying conditions. The constitution of Switzerland, for example, enables the cantons to conclude treaties with foreign states on issues concerning public economy, frontier relations and the police, subject to the provision that the Federal Council acts as the intermediary.[57] In the case of the United States, responsibility for the conduct of foreign relations rests exclusively with the Federal Government,[58] although American states have entered into certain compacts with foreign states or component units (such as Manitoba and Quebec provinces of Canada) dealing with the construction and maintenance of highways and international bridges, following upon consultations with the

---

[55] *Yearbook of the ILC,* 1958, vol.II, p.24. Cf. Waldock, *ibid.,* 1962, vol.II, p.36.

[56] A/CONF.39/SR.8, 28 April 1969.

[57] See e.g. Looper, "The Treaty Power in Switzerland", 7 *American Journal of Comparative Law,* 1958, p.178.

[58] See e.g. Article I, Section 10 of the US Constitution; *US* v. *Curtiss-Wright Export Corp.,* 299 US 304 (1936); 8 *ILR,* p.48 and *Zachevning* v. *Miller,* 389 US 429 (1968). See also generally, Brownlie, *op. cit.,* pp.62-63; Whiteman, *Digest of International Law,* vol.14, pp.13-17 and Rousseau, *Droit International Public,* vol.II, 1974, pp.138-213 and 264-68.

foreign state conducted by the federal authorities. In any event, it is clear that the internal constitutional structure is crucial in endowing the unit concerned with capacity. What, however, turns this into international capacity is recognition.

An issue recently the subject of concern and discussion has been the question of the domestic implementation of treaty obligations in the case of federations, especially in the light of the fact that component units may possess legislative power relating to the subject-matter of the treaty concerned. Although this issue lies primarily within the field of domestic constitutional law, there are important implications for international law. In the US, for example, the approach adopted has been to insert "federal" reservations to treaties in cases where the states of the Union have exercised jurisdiction over the subject-matter in question, providing that the Federal Government would take appropriate steps to enable the competent authorities of the component units to take appropriate measures to fulfil the obligations concerned.[59] In general, however, there have been few restrictions on entry into international agreements.[60]

The question as to divided competence in federations and international treaties has arisen in the past particularly with regard to conventions of the International Labour Organisation, which typically encompass areas subject to the law-making competence of federal component units. In Canada, for example, early attempts by the central government to ratify ILO conventions were defeated by the decisions of the courts on constitutional grounds, supporting the views of the provinces,[61] while the US has a poor record of ratification of ILO conventions on similar grounds of local competence and federal treaty-making.[62] The issue that arises therefore is the position of a state that either refuses to ratify or sign a treaty on grounds of component unit competence in the area in question or alternatively the problem of implementation and thus responsibility where ratification does take place. In Australia, for

---

[59] See e.g. the proposed reservations to four human rights treaties in 1978, *US Ratification of the Human Rights Treaties* (ed. Lillich), 1981, pp.83-103.

[60] See e.g. *Missouri* v. *Holland*, 252 US 416 (1920); 1 *ILR*, p.4.

[61] See especially, *Attorney-General for Canada* v. *Attorney-General for Ontario*, [1937] AC 326; 8 *ILR*, p.41.

[62] Bernier, *op. cit.*, pp.162-63, and Looper, "Federal State Clauses in Multilateral Instruments", 32 *BYIL*, 1955-6, p.162.

instance, the issue has turned on the interpretation of the constitutional grant of federal power to make laws "with respect to . . . external affairs".[63] Two recent cases have analysed this, in the light particularly of the established principle that the Federal Government could under this provision legislate on matters, not otherwise explicitly assigned to it, which possessed an intrinsic international aspect.[64] In *Koowarta* v. *Bjelke-Petersen*[65] in 1982, the Australian High Court in dealing with an action against the Premier of Queensland for breach of the Racial Discrimination Act 1975 (which incorporated parts of the International Convention on the Elimination of All Forms of Racial Discrimination adopted in 1965) held that the relevant legislation was valid with respect to the "external affairs" provision under section 51(29) of the Constitution. In other words, the "external affairs" power extended to permit the implementation of an international agreement, despite the fact that the subject-matter concerned was otherwise outside federal power. It was felt that if Australia accepted a treaty obligation with respect to an aspect of its own internal legal order, the subject of the obligation thus became an "external affair" and legislation dealing with this fell within section 51(29), and was thereby valid constitutionally.[66] It was not necessary that a treaty obligation be assumed: the fact that the norm of non-discrimination was established in customary international law was itself sufficient in the view of Stephen J to treat the issue of racial discrimination as part of external affairs.[67]

In *Commonwealth of Australia* v. *Tasmania*,[68] the issue concerned the construction of a dam in an area placed on the World Heritage List established under the 1972 UNESCO Convention for the Protection of the World Cultural and Natural Heritage, to which Australia was a party. The Federal Government in 1983 wished to stop the scheme by reference *inter alia* to the "external affairs" power as interpreted in *Koowarta*, since it possessed no specific

---

[63] See e.g. Zines, *The High Court and the Constitution*, 1981 and Byrnes and Charlesworth, "Federalism and the International Legal Order: Recent Developments in Australia", 79 *AJIL*, 1985, p.622.

[64] *R* v. *Burgess, ex p. Henry*, 55 CLR 608 (1936); 8 *ILR*, p.54.

[65] 68 *ILR*, p.181.

[66] *Ibid.*, pp.223-24 (Stephen J); p.235 (Mason J) and p.255 (Brennan J).

[67] *Ibid.*, pp.223-24.

[68] *Ibid.*, p.266. The case similarly came before the High Court.

legislative power over the environment. The majority of the Court
held that the "external affairs" power extended to the implementation of treaty obligations. It was now necessary that the subject-matter
of the treaty be inherently international.

The effect of these cases seen, of course, in the context of the
Australian Constitution, is to reduce the problems faced by federal
states of implementing international obligations in the face of local
jurisdiction. From the point of view of international law it is a
heartening trend in that it minimises the power of component
units to prevent the implementation of international duties. It
remains to be seen how far other federal states will manifest this
trend.

Federal practice in regulating disputes between component units
is often of considerable value in international law. This operates
particularly in cases of boundary problems, where similar issues
arise.[69] Conversely, international practice may often be relevant in
the resolution of conflicts between component units. Questions
relating to responsibility and immunities also arise in respect of
federal states and these are referred to in the appropriate chapters.[70]

SUI GENERIS TERRITORIAL ENTITIES

Mandated and Trust Territories [71]

After the end of the First World War and the collapse of the Axis
and Russian empires, the Allies established a system for dealing with
the colonies of the defeated powers that did not involve annexation.
These territories would be governed according to the principle that
"the well-being and development of such peoples form a sacred trust
of civilisation". The way in which this principle would be put into
effect would be to entrust the tutelage of such people to "advanced
nations who by reason of their resources, their experience or their

---

[69] See e.g. E. Lauterpacht, "River Boundaries: Legal Aspects of the Shatt-Al-Arab
Frontier", 9 *ICLQ*, 1960, pp.208, 216 and Cukwurah, *The Settlement of Boundary Disputes
in International Law*, 1967.

[70] See *infra*, Chapters 12 and 13.

[71] See generally Duncan Hall, *Mandates, Dependencies and Trusteeships*, 1948; Whiteman,
op. cit. vol.1, pp.598-911 and vol.XIII, p.679 *et seq.*; Toussaint, *The Trusteeship System of the
United Nations*; Verzijl, *op. cit.*, vol.II, pp.545-73; Wright, *Mandates Under the League of Nations*,
1930; Dugard, *The South West Africa/Namibia Dispute*, 1973 and Slonim, *South West Africa
and the United Nations*, 1973.

geographical position" could undertake the responsibility. The arrangement would be exercised by them as mandatories on behalf of the League.[72] Upon the conclusion of the Second World War and the demise of the League, the mandate system was transmuted into the United Nations trusteeship system under Chapters XII and XIII of the UN Charter. The strategic trust territory of the Pacific, taken from Japan, the mandatory power, was placed in a special category subject to Security Council rather than Trusteeship Council supervision for security reasons,[73] while South Africa refused to place its mandated territory under the system. Quite who held sovereignty in such territories was the subject of extensive debates over many decades.[74]

As far as the trust territory of the Pacific was concerned, the US signed a Covenant with the Commonwealth of the Northern Mariana Islands and Compacts of Free Association with the Federated States of Micronesia and with the Republic of the Marshall Islands. Upon their entry into force in autumn 1986, it was determined that the trusteeship had been terminated. This procedure providing for political union with the US was accepted by the Trusteeship Council as a legitimate exercise of self-determination. However, the proposed Compact of Free Association with the Republic of Palau (the final part of the former trust territory) did not enter into force as a result of disagreement over the transit of nuclear-powered or armed vessels and aircraft through Palauan waters and airspace and, therefore, the US continued to act as administering authority under the trusteeship agreement.[75]

South West Africa was administered after the end of the First World War as a mandate by South Africa, which refused after the Second World War to place the territory under the trusteeship system. Following this, the International Court of Justice in 1950 in its Advisory Opinion on the *International Status of South West Africa*[76] stated

---

[72] See article 22 of the Covenant of the League of Nations.

[73] See McHenry, *Micronesia: Trust Betrayed*, 1975; Whiteman, *op. cit.* vol.I, pp.769-839; de Smith, *Micro-States and Micronesia*, 1970; *DUSPIL*, 1973, pp.59-67; *ibid.*, 1974, pp.54-64; *ibid.*, 1975, pp.94-104; *ibid.*, 1976, pp.56-61; *ibid.*, 1977, pp.71-98 and *ibid.*, 1978, pp.204-31.

[74] See in particular Judge McNair, *International Status of South West Africa*, ICJ Reports, 1950, pp.128, 150 and the Court's view, *ibid.*, p.132; 17 *ILR*, pp.47, 49.

[75] See *Contemporary Practice of the United States Relating to International Law*, 81 *AJIL*, 1987, pp.405-8. See also *Bank of Hawaii* v. *Balos*, 701 F.Supp. 744 (1988).

[76] ICJ Reports, 1950, pp.128, 143-44; 17 *ILR*, pp.47, 57-60.

that while there was no legal obligation imposed by the United Nations Charter to transfer a mandated territory into a trust territory, South Africa was still bound by the terms of the mandate agreement and the Covenant of the League of Nations, and the obligations that it had assumed at that time. The Court emphasised that South Africa alone did not have the capacity to modify the international status of the territory. This competence rested with South Africa acting with the consent of the United Nations, as successor to the League of Nations. Logically flowing from this decision was the ability of the United Nations to hear petitioners from the territory in consequence of South Africa's refusal to heed United Nations decisions and in pursuance of League of Nations practices.[77]

In 1962 the ICJ heard the case brought by Ethiopia and Liberia, the two African members of the League, that South Africa was in breach of the terms of the mandate and had thus violated international law. The Court initially affirmed that it had jurisdiction to hear the merits of the dispute.[78] However, by the Second Phase of the case, the Court (its composition having slightly altered in the meanwhile) decided that Ethiopia and Liberia did not have any legal interest in the subject-matter of the claim (the existence and supervision of the mandate over South West Africa) and accordingly their contentions were rejected.[79] Having thus declared on the lack of standing of the two African appellants, the Court did not discuss any of the substantive questions which stood before it.

This judgment aroused a great deal of feeling particularly in the Third World and occasioned a shift in emphasis in dealing with the problem of the territory in question.[80]

The General Assembly began to take a more active part and in October 1966 resolved that since South Africa had failed to fulfil its obligations, the mandate was therefore terminated. South West Africa (or Namibia as it was to be called) was to come under the direct responsibility of the United Nations,[81] The Security Council in a number of resolutions upheld the action of the Assembly and called upon South Africa to withdraw its administration from the

[77] ICJ Reports, 1955, p.68; 22 *ILR*, p.651 and *ibid.*, 1956, p.23; 23 *ILR*, p.38.
[78] ICJ Reports, pp.141 and 143.
[79] ICJ Reports, 1966, p.6; 37 *ILR*, p.243.
[80] See e.g. Dugard, *op. cit.*, p.378.
[81] Resolution 2145 (XXI). A Council was established to oversee the territory, see General Assembly resolutions 2145 (XXI) and 2248 (XXII).

territory. It also requested other States to refrain from dealing with the South African Government in so far as Namibia was concerned.[82]

The Security Council ultimately turned to the International Court and requested an Advisory Opinion as to the *Legal Consequences for States of the Continued Presence of South Africa in Namibia*.[83] The Court concluded that South Africa's presence in Namibia was indeed illegal in view of the series of events culminating in the United Nations resolutions on the grounds of a material breach of a treaty (the mandate agreement) by South Africa, and further that "a binding determination made by a competent organ of the United Nations to the effect that a situation is illegal cannot remain without consequence". South Africa was obligated to withdraw its administration from the territory, and other states members of the United Nations were obliged to recognise the illegality and the invalidity of its acts with regard to that territory and aid the United Nations in its efforts concerning the problem.[84]

The opinion was approved by the Security Council in resolution 301 (1971), which also reaffirmed the national unity and territorial integrity of Namibia. In 1978 South Africa announced its acceptance of proposals negotiated by the five western contact powers (UK, USA, France, Canada and West Germany) for Namibian independence involving a UN supervised electing and peace-keeping force.[85] However, negotiations continued with a variety of problems arising, including, for example, the issue of linkage with the withdrawal of Cuban forces from Angola. In April 1981, the Security Council failed to adopt four draft resolutions which would have imposed comprehensive and mandatory sanctions against South Africa because of the Namibian situation as a result of the negative votes cast by the UK, USA and France.[86] However, Namibia finally obtained its independence on 23 April 1990.[87]

---

[82] See e.g. Security Council resolutions 263 (1969), 269 (1969) and 276 (1970).
[83] ICJ Reports, 1971, p.16; 49 *ILR*, p.3.
[84] *Ibid.*, pp.52-58.
[85] 17 *ILM*, May 1978, pp.762-69 and *DUSPIL*, 1978, pp.38-54. See Security Council resolution 435 (1978). See also *Africa Research Bulletin*, April 1978, p.4829 and July 1978, p.4935.
[86] See S/14459; S/14460/Rev.1; S/14461 and S/14462.
[87] See 28 *ILM*, 1989, p.944.

Germany 1945

With the defeat of Germany on 5 June 1945, the Allied Powers assumed "supreme authority" with respect to that country, while expressly disclaiming any intention of annexation.[88] Germany was divided into four occupation zones with four-power control over Berlin. The Control Council established by the Allies acted on behalf of Germany and in such capacity entered into binding legal arrangements. The state of Germany continued, however, and the situation, as has been observed, was akin to legal representation or agency of necessity.[89] Under the 1952 Treaty between the three western powers and the Federal Republic of Germany, full sovereign powers were granted to the latter subject to retained powers concerning the making of a peace treaty and in 1972 the Federal Republic of Germany and the German Democratic Republic, established in 1954 by the Soviet Union in its zone, recognised each other as sovereign states.[90]

However, following a series of dramatic events during 1989 in Central and Eastern Europe deriving in essence from the withdrawal of Soviet control, the drive for a reunified Germany in 1990 became unstoppable. A State Treaty on German Economic, Monetary and Social Union was signed by the Finance Ministers of the two German states on 18 May and this took effect on 1 July.[91] A State Treaty on Unification was signed on 31 August, providing for unification on 3 October by the accession of the German Democratic Republic under article 23 of the Basic Law of the Federal Republic, with Berlin as the capital.[92] The external obstacle to unity was removed by the signing on 12 September of a treaty between the two German states and the four wartime allies (UK, USA, USSR and France). Under this treaty, a reunified Germany agreed to accept the current Oder-Neisse border with Poland and to limit its armed forces to 370,000 persons, while pledging not to acquire atomic, chemical or biological

---

[88] See Whiteman, *op. cit.* vol.I, pp.325-26.

[89] Brownlie, *op. cit.*, p.109. See also Whiteman, *op. cit.*, p.333.

[90] 12 *ILR*, p.16. Both states became members of the UN the following year. See also Crawford, *op. cit.*, pp.273-81 and Mann, *Studies in International Law*, 1973, pp.634-59 and 660-706.

[91] See *Keesing's Record of World Events*, p.37466 (1990).

[92] *Ibid.*, p.37661.

weapons.[93] It was also agreed that on the day preceding reunification day, representatives of the four allied powers occupying Berlin would sign over their control to Germany.[94]

Condominium

In this instance two or more states equally exercise sovereignty with respect to a territory and its inhabitants. There are arguments as to the relationship between the states concerned, the identity of the sovereign for the purposes of the territory and the nature of the competences involved.[95] In the case of the New Hebrides, a series of Anglo-French agreements established a region of joint influence with each power retaining sovereignty over its nationals and neither exercising separate authority over the area.[96] A Protocol listed the functions of the condominial government and vested the power to issue joint regulations respecting them in a British and French High Commissioner. This power was delegated to resident commissioners who dealt with their respective nationals. Three governmental systems accordingly co-existed with something of a legal vacuum with regard to land tenure and the civil transactions of the indigenous population.[97] The process leading to the independence of the territory also reflected its unique status as a condominium.[98] It was noted that the usual independence Bill would not have been appropriate, since the New Hebrides was not a British colony. Its legal status as an Anglo-French condominium had been established by international agreement and could only be terminated in the same fashion. The nature of the condominium was such that it assumed that the two metropolitan powers would always act together and unilateral action was not provided for in the basic constitutional documents.[99] The territory became

[93] See *The Economist,* 15 September 1990, p.63.

[94] *Ibid.,* 29 September 1990, p.52.

[95] Brownlie, *op. cit.,* pp.116-17; see also O'Connell, *op. cit.,* pp.327-28 and Coret, *Le Condominium,* 1960.

[96] See e.g., 99 *BFSP,* p.229 and 114 *BFSP,* p.212.

[97] O'Connell, *op. cit.,* p.328.

[98] Lord Trefgarne, the government spokesman, moving the second reading of the New Hebrides Bill in the House of Lords, 404 HL Deb., cols. 1091-92, 4 Feb.1980.

[99] See Mr Luce, Foreign Office Minister, 980 HC Deb., col. 682, 8 March 1980 and 985 HC Deb., col. 1250, 3 June 1980. See also O'Connell, "The Condominium of the New Hebrides", 43 *BYIL,* p.71.

independent on 30 July 1980 as the state of Vanuatu. The entity involved prior to independence grew out of an international treaty and established an administrative entity arguably distinct from its metropolitan governments but more likely operating on the basis of a form of joint agency with a range of delegated powers.[100]

International Territories

In such cases a particular territory is placed under a form of international regime, but the conditions under which this has been done have varied widely, from autonomous areas within states to relatively independent entities.[101] Attempts were made to create such a regime for Jerusalem under the General Assembly partition resolution for Palestine in 1947 as a "*corpus separatum* under a special international regime ... administered by the United Nations", but this never materialised for a number of reasons.[102] The term "international territory" has no legal meaning as such and the nature and capacity of the entity created will depend upon all the relevant circumstances. In some instances a separate legal person will here be established, in others not. In any event, such institutions have not on the whole worked successfully and the device is unlikely to be used frequently in the future.

Taiwan [103]

This territory was ceded by China to Japan in 1895 and remained in the latter's hands until 1945. Japan undertook on surrender not to retain sovereignty over Taiwan and this was reaffirmed under the

[100] See also the joint Saudi Arabian-Kuwaiti administered Neutral Zone based on the treaty of 2 December 1922, 133 *BFSP*, 1930 Part II, pp.726-27. See e.g. *The Middle East* (ed. Mansfield), 4th ed., 1973, p.187. Both states enjoyed an equal right of undivided sovereignty over the whole area. However, on 7 July 1965, both states signed an agreement to partition the neutral zone, although the territory apparently retained its condominium status for exploration of resources purposes; see Albaharna, *The Legal Status of the Arabian Gulf States*, 1968, pp.264-77.

[101] See Ydit, *International Territories*, 1961; Crawford, *op. cit.*, pp.160-69; Brownlie, *op. cit.*, pp.62-63 and Rousseau, *op. cit.* vol.II, pp.413-48.

[102] Resolution 18(II). See e.g. E. Lauterpacht, *Jerusalem and the Holy Places*, 1968 and Ydit, *op. cit.*, pp.273-314.

[103] See e.g. *China and the Question of Taiwan* (ed. Chen) Reisman, "Who Owns Taiwan?", 81 *Yale Law Journal*, p.599 and Morello, *The International Legal Status of Formosa*, 1966.

Peace Treaty between the Allied Powers (but not the USSR and China) and Japan, under which all rights to the island were renounced without specifying any recipient. After the Chinese Civil War, the Communist forces took over the mainland while the Nationalist regime installed itself on Taiwan (Formosa) and the Pescadores. The key point affecting status has been that both governments have claimed to represent the whole of China. No claim of separate statehood for Taiwan has been made and in such a case it is difficult to maintain that such an unsought status exists.[104] Total lack of recognition merely reinforces this point. Accordingly, Taiwan would appear to be a non-state territorial entity which is *de jure* part of China but under separate administration. It is interesting to note that when in early 1990 Taiwan sought accession to the General Agreement on Tariffs and Trade (GATT), it did so by requesting entry for the "customs territory" of "Taiwan, Penghu, Kinmen and Matsu," thus avoiding an assertion of statehood.[105]

The Turkish Federated State of Cyprus [106]

In 1974, following a coup in Cyprus backed by the military regime in Greece, Turkish forces invaded the island. The Security Council in resolution 353 (1974) called upon all states to respect the sovereignty, independence and territorial integrity of Cyprus and demanded an immediate end to foreign military intervention in the island that was contrary to such respect. On 13 February 1975 the Turkish Federated State of Cyprus was proclaimed in the area occupied by Turkish forces. A resolution adopted at the same meeting of the Council of Ministers and the Legislative Assembly of the Autonomous Turkish Cypriot Administration at which the proclamation was made, emphasised the determination "to oppose resolutely all attempts against the independence of Cyprus and its

---

[104] See Crawford, *op. cit.*, p.145. Note that the 1972 USA-China communiqué accepted that Taiwan was part of China, 11 *ILM*, pp.443, 445. In 1979 the USA withdrew its recognition of Taiwan as the government of China; see 73 *AJIL*, p.227. See also 833 HC Deb., col. 32, 13 March 1972, and *Reel* v. *Holder*, [1981] 1 WLR 1226.

[105] See *Keesing's Record of World Events*, p.37671 (1990). This failed, however, to prevent a vigorous protest by China; *ibid.* As to Rhodesia (1965-79) and the Bantustans, see *supra*, pp.141 and 143.

[106] See Nadjatigil, *The Cyprus Conflict: A Lawyer's View*, 3rd ed., 1983; White, *The World Today*, April 1981, p.135 and Crawford, *op. cit.*, p.118.

partition or union with any other state" and resolved to establish a separate administration until such time as the 1960 Cyprus constitution was amended to provide for a federal republic.[107]

On 15 November 1983, the Turkish Cypriots proclaimed their independence.[108] This was declared illegal by the Security Council in resolution 541 (1983) and its withdrawal called for. All states were requested not to recognise the "purported state" or assist it in any way. This was reiterated in Security Council resolution 550 (1984). In the light of this and the very heavy dependence of the territory upon Turkey, it cannot be regarded as a sovereign state, but remains as a *de facto* administered entity within the recognised confines of the Republic of Cyprus and dependent upon Turkish assistance.[109]

The Saharan Arab Democratic Republic [110]

In February 1976, the Polisario liberation movement conducting a war to free the Western Saharan territory from Moroccan control declared the independent sovereign Saharan Arab Democratic Republic.[111] Over the succeeding years, many states recognised the new entity, including a majority of OAU members. In February 1982, the OAU Secretary-General sought to seat a delegation from SADR on that basis, but this provoked a boycott by some 19 states and a major crisis. However, in November 1984 the Assembly of Heads of State and Government of the OAU did agree to seat a delegation from SADR, despite Morocco's threat of withdrawal from the organisation.[112] This, therefore, can be taken as OAU recognition of statehood and as such of major evidential significance. Indeed, in view of the reduced importance of the effectiveness of control criterion in such self-determination situations, a strong argument can now be made regarding SADR's statehood, although the issue is still controversial, particularly in view of the continuing hostilities.

---

[107] Resolution no.2 in Supplement IV, Official Gazette of the TFSC, cited in Nadjatigil, *op. cit.*, p.123.

[108] See *The Times*, 16 November 1983, p.12 and 21(4) *UN Chronicle*, 1984, p.17.

[109] See also Foreign Affairs Committee, Third Report, Session 1986-7, Cyprus: HCP 23 (1986-7).

[110] See Shaw, *op. cit.*, Chapter Three.

[111] *Africa Research Bulletin,* June 1976, p.4047 and July 1976, pp.4078 and 4081.

[112] See *Keesings Contemporary Archives,* pp.33324-45.

Associations of States

There are a number of ways in which states have become formally associated with one another. Such associations do not constitute states but have a certain effect upon international law. Confederations, for example, are probably the closest form of co-operation and they generally involve several countries acting together by virtue of an international agreement, with some kind of central institutions with limited functions. This is to be contrasted with the situation as it exists with regard to federations. A federal unit is a state with strong centralised organs and usually a fairly widespread bureaucracy with extensive powers over the citizens of the state, even though the powers of the state are divided between the different units.[113]

There are in addition certain "associated states" which by virtue of their smallness and lack of development have a close relationship with another state. One instance is the connection between the Cook Islands and New Zealand, where internal self-government is allied to external dependence.[114] Another example was the group of islands which constituted the Associated States of the West Indies. These were tied to the United Kingdom by the terms of the West Indies Act, 1967, which provided for the latter to exercise control with regard to foreign and defence issues. Nevertheless, such states were able to and did attain their independence.[115]

The status of such entities in an association relationship with a state will depend upon the constitutional nature of the arrangement and may in certain circumstances involve international personality distinct from the metropolitan state depending also upon international acceptance. It must, however, be noted that such status is one of the methods accepted by the UN of exercising the right to self-determination.[116] Provided that an acceptable level of powers, including those dealing with domestic affairs, remain with the associated state, and that the latter may without undue difficulty revoke the arrangement, some degree of personality would appear desirable and acceptable.

---

[113] See Crawford, *op. cit.*, p.291 and *supra*, p.151. See also with regard to the proposed arrangement between Gambia and Senegal, 21 *ILM*, 1982, pp.44-47.

[114] Crawford, *op. cit.*, pp.372-74. See also as regards Puerto Rico and Niue, *ibid.*

[115] See e.g. Fawcett, *Annual Survey of Commonwealth Law*, 1967, pp.709-11.

[116] See with regard to the successors of the trust territory of the Pacific, *supra*, p.157.

The Commonwealth of Nations (the former British Commonwealth) is perhaps the most well-known of the loose associations which group together sovereign states on the basis usually of common interests and historical ties. Its members are all fully independent states who co-operate through the assistance of the Commonwealth Secretariat and periodic conferences of Heads of Government. Regular meetings of particular ministers also take place. The Commonwealth does not constitute a legally binding relationship, but operates as a useful forum for discussions. It would appear unlikely in the circumstances that it possesses separate international personality.[117]

Conclusions

Whether or not the entities discussed above constitute international persons or indeed states or merely part of some other international person is a matter for careful consideration in the light of the circumstances of the case, in particular the claims made by the entity in question, the facts on the ground especially with regard to third party control and the degree of administrative effectiveness manifested and the reaction of other international persons. The importance here of recognition, acquiescence and estoppel is self-evident. Acceptance of some international personality need not be objective so as to bind non-consenting states nor unlimited as to time and content factors. These elements will be considered below. It should, however, be noted here that the international community itself also has needs and interests that bear upon this question as to international status. This is particularly so with regard to matters of responsibility and the protection of persons via the rules governing the recourse to and conduct of armed conflicts.[118]

---

[117] See Fawcett, *The British Commonwealth in International Law*, 1963; O'Connell, *op. cit.*, pp.346-56; Whiteman, *op. cit.* vol.I, pp.476-544; Rousseau, *op. cit.* vol.II, pp.214-64 and Sale, *The Modern Commonwealth*, 1983. See also as regards the French Community, Whiteman, *op. cit.*, pp.544-82 and O'Connell, *op. cit.*, pp.356-59.
[118] As to the specific regime established in the Antarctica Treaty 1959, see *infra*, p.308. See also *infra*, p.388, with regard to the International Seabed Authority under the Law of the Sea Convention, 1982.

· SPECIAL CASES

The Sovereign Order of Malta

This Order, established during the Crusades as a military and medical association, ruled Rhodes from 1309-1522 and was given Malta by treaty with Charles V in 1530 as a fief of the Kingdom of Sicily. This sovereignty was lost in 1798 and in 1834 the Order established its headquarters in Rome as a humanitarian organisation.[119] The Order already had international personality at the time of its taking control of Malta and even when it had to leave the island it continued to exchange diplomatic legations with most European countries. The Italian Court of Cassation in 1935 recognised the international personality of the Order, noting that "the modern theory of the subjects of international law recognises a number of collective units whose composition is independent of the nationality of their constituent members and whose scope transcends by virtue of their universal character the territorial confines of any single state".[120] This is predicated upon the functional needs of the entity as accepted by third parties. It is to be noted, for example, that the Order maintains diplomatic relations with over 40 states.

The Holy See and the Vatican City [121]

In 1870, the conquest of the Papal states by Italian forces ended their existence as sovereign states. The question therefore arose as to the status in international law of the Holy See, deprived, as it then was, of normal territorial sovereignty. In 1929 the Lateran Treaty was signed with Italy which recognised the state of the Vatican City and "the sovereignty of the Holy See in the field of international relations as an attribute that pertains to the very nature of the Holy See, in conformity with its traditions and with the demands of its

---

[119] O'Connell, *op. cit.*, pp.85-86 and Whiteman, *op. cit.* vol.I, pp.584-87.

[120] *Nanni v. Pace and the Sovereign Order of Malta*, 8 *ILR*, p.2. See also *Scarfo v. Sovereign Order of Malta*, 24 *ILR*, p.1 and *Sovereign Order of Malta v. Soc. An. Commerciale*, 22 *ILR*, p.1.

[121] See Crawford, *op. cit.*, pp.152-60; Rousseau, *op. cit.* vol.II, pp.353-77, and Graham, *Vatican Diplomacy: A Study of Church and State on the International Plane*, 1959.

mission in the world".[122] The question thus interrelates with the problem of the status today of the Vatican City. The latter has no permanent population apart from Church functionaries and exists only to support the work of the Holy See. Italy carries out a substantial number of administrative functions with regard to the City. Some writers accordingly have concluded that it cannot be regarded as a state.[123] Nevertheless, it is a party to many international treaties and a member of the Universal Postal Union and the International Telecommunications Union. It would appear that by virtue of recognition and acquiescence in the context of its claims, it does exist as a state.

As far as the Holy See is concerned, it continued after 1870 to engage in diplomatic relations and enter into international agreements and concordats. Accordingly its status as an international person was accepted by such partners. Whether its personality is objective or qualified is open to question, however.[124]

Insurgents and Belligerents

International law has recognised that such entities may in certain circumstances, primarily dependent upon the *de facto* administration of specific territory, enter into valid arrangements.[125] In addition they will be bound by the rules of international law with respect to the conduct of hostilities and may in due course be recognised as governments. The traditional law is in process of modification as a result of the right to self-determination, and other legal principles such as territorial integrity, sovereign equality and non-intervention in addition to recognition will need to be taken into account.[126]

National Liberation Movements (NLMs)

The question of whether or not NLMs constitute subjects of international law and if so, to what extent, is bound up with the

[122] 130 *BFSP*, p.791. See also O'Connell, *op. cit.*, p.289.

[123] See Crawford, *op. cit.*, p.154 and Mendelson, "The Diminutive States in the United Nations", 21 *ICLQ*, p.609. See also Brownlie, *op. cit.*, p.65.

[124] See Crawford, *op. cit.*, pp.154-56 and 159-60; Brownlie, *op. cit.*, pp.65-66 and Fitzmaurice, *Yearbook of the ILC*, 1956, vol.II, pp.107, 118.

[125] See Lauterpacht, *op. cit.*, pp.494-95; Brownlie, *op. cit.*, pp.64-65 and Chen, *Recognition*, 1951. See also Cassese, *op. cit.*, p.81.

[126] *Infra*, p.172.

development of the law relating to non-self-governing territories and the principle of self-determination. The trusteeship system permitted the hearing of individual petitioners and this was extended to all colonial territories. In 1977, the General Assembly Fourth Committee voted to permit representatives of certain NLMs from Portugal's African territories to participate in its work dealing with such territories.[127] The General Assembly endorsed the concept of observer status for liberation movements recognised by the Organisation of African Unity in resolution 2918 (XVII). In resolution 3247 (XXIX), the Assembly accepted that NLMs recognised by the OAU or the Arab League could participate in Assembly sessions, in conferences arranged under the auspices of the Assembly and in meetings of the UN specialised agencies and the various Assembly organs.[128]

The inclusion of the regional recognition requirement was intended both to require a minimum level of effectiveness with regard to the organisation concerned before UN acceptance and to exclude in practice secessionist movements. The Economic and Social Committee of the UN has also adopted a similar approach and under its procedural rules it may invite any NLM recognised by or in accordance with General Assembly resolutions to take part in relevant debates without a vote.[129]

The UN Security Council has also permitted the Palestine Liberation Organisation (PLO) to participate in its debates with the same rights of participation as conferred upon a member-state not a member of the Security Council, although this did raise serious constitutional questions.[130] Thus the possibility of observer status in the UN and related organs for NLMs appears to have been

---

[127] See Shaw, "The International Status of National Liberation Movements", 5 *Liverpool Law Review*, 1983, p.19. See also Cassese, *op. cit.*, p.90 and Wilson, *International Law and the Use of Force by National Liberation Movements*, 1988.

[128] While the leader of the PAGC was not permitted to speak at the Assembly in 1973, the leader of the PLO was able to address the body in 1974; see A/C.4/SR.1978 p.23 and resolution 3237 (XXIX).

[129] ECOSOC resolution 1949 (LVII), 8 May 1975, rule 73. See also as regards the Human Rights Commission, CHR/Res.19 (XXIX). The General Assembly and ECOSOC have also called upon the specialised agencies and other UN related organisations to assist the peoples and NLMs of colonial territories, see e.g. Assembly resolutions 33/41 and 35/29.

[130] See *Yearbook of the UN*, 1972, p.70 and 1978, p.297; S/PV 1859 (1975); S/PV 1870 (1976); *UN Chronicle*, April 1982, p.16 and *DUSPIL*, 1975, pp.73-75. See also Shaw, *op. cit.* footnote 127.

affirmatively settled in international practice. The question of international personality, however, is more complex and more significant, and recourse must be made to state practice.[131] Whether extensive state recognition of a liberation movement is of itself sufficient to confer such status is still a controversial issue.

As far as Namibia was concerned, the territory was regarded as having an international status[132] and had an NLM recognised as the authentic representative of the people[133] but it was, theoretically, administered by the UN Council for Namibia. This body was established in 1967 by the General Assembly in order to administer the territory and to prepare it for independence; it was disbanded in 1990. There were 31 UN member-states on the Council, which was responsible to the General Assembly.[134] The Council sought to represent Namibian interests in international organisations and in conferences, and issued travel and identity documents to Namibians which were recognised by most states.[135] In 1974, the Council issued Decree No. 1 which sought to forbid the exploitation under South African auspices of the territory's resources, but little was in practice achieved by this Decree, which was not drafted in the clearest possible manner.[136] The status of the Council was unclear, but it was clearly recognised as having a role within the UN context and may thus have possessed some form of qualified personality.

International Public Companies

This type of entity, which may be known by a variety of names, for example, multinational public enterprises or international bodies corporate, is characterised in general by an international agreement providing for co-operation between governmental and private enterprises.[137] One writer, for example, defined such entities as corporations which "have not been constituted by the exclusive

---

[131] See the *UN Headquarters Agreement* case, ICJ Reports, 1988, p.12; 82 *ILR,* p.225.

[132] The *Namibia* case, ICJ Reports, 1971, p.16; 49 *ILR,* p.3.

[133] Assembly resolution 3295 (XXIX).

[134] The UK did not recognise the Council; see 408 HL Deb., col.758, 23 April 1980.

[135] See e.g. Engers, "The UN Travel and Identity Documents for Namibia", 65 *AJIL,* p.571.

[136] See *Decolonisation,* no.9, December 1977.

[137] See e.g. Fligler, *Multinational Public Enterprises,* 1967; Brownlie, *op. cit.,* pp.67-69 and Ijalaye, *The Extension of Corporate Personality in International Law,* 1978, pp.57-146.

application of one national law; whose members and directors represent several national sovereignties; whose legal personality is not based, or at any rate not entirely, on the decision of a national authority or the application of a national law; whose operations, finally, are governed, at least partially, by rules that do not stem from a single or even from several national laws".[138] Such enterprises may vary widely in constitutional nature and in competences. Examples of such companies would include INTELSAT, established in 1973 as an intergovernmental structure for a global commercial telecommunications satellite system; Eurofima, established in 1955 by fourteen European states in order to lease equipment to the railway administrations of those states and the Bank of International Settlement, created in 1930 by virtue of a treaty between five states and the host country Switzerland. The personality question will depend upon the differences between municipal and international personality. If the entity is given a range of powers and is distanced sufficiently from municipal law, an international person may be involved, but it will require careful consideration of the circumstances.

Transnational Corporations

Another possible candidate for international personality is the transnational or multi-national enterprise. Various definitions exist of this important phenomenon in international relations.[139] They in essence constitute private business organisations comprising several legal entities linked together by parent corporations and are distinguished by size and multi-national spread. In the years following the *Barcelona Traction* case,[140] an increasing amount of practice has been evident on the international plane dealing with such corporations. What has been sought is a set of guidelines governing the major elements of the international conduct of these entities.[141]

---

[138] Cited in Ijalaye, *op. cit.*, p.69.
[139] See e.g. Jenks, *Transnational Law in a Changing Society* (eds. Friedman, Henkin and Lissitzyn), 1972, p.70; Baade, *Legal Problems of a Code of Conduct for Multinational Enterprises* (ed. Horn), 1980.
[140] ICJ Reports, 1970, pp.3, 46-47; 46 *ILR*, pp.178, 220-21.
[141] See e.g. OECD Guidelines for Multinational Enterprises, 75 *US Dept. State Bull.*, p.83 (1976) and ILO Tripartite Declaration of Principles concerning Multinational Enterprises and Social Policy, 17 *ILM*, pp.423-30. See also Baade, *op. cit.*, pp.416-40.

However, progress has been slow and several crucial issues remain to be resolved, ranging from the legal effect, if any, of such a Code to the applicable tests for nationalisation and compensation.[142] Should such a Code come into effect containing duties directly imposed upon transnational corporations, as well as rights ascribed to them as against the host state, it would be possible to regard them as international persons. This, however, has not yet occurred.[143]

THE RIGHT OF ALL PEOPLES TO SELF-DETERMINATION [144]

The Establishment of the Legal Right

This principle, which traces its origin to the concepts of nationality and democracy as evolved primarily in Europe, first appeared in major form after the First World War. Despite President Wilson's efforts, it was not included in the League of Nations Covenant and it was clearly not regarded as a legal principle.[145] However, its influence can be detected in the various provisions for minority protection[146] and in the establishment of the mandates system based as it was upon the sacred trust concept. In the ten years before the Second World War, there was relatively little practice regarding self-determination in international law. A number of treaties concluded by the USSR in this period noted the principle,[147] but in the *Aaland Islands* case it was clearly accepted by both the

---

[142] See the Draft Code of Conduct produced by the UN Commission on Transnational Corporations, 22 *ILM*, pp.177-206. See also Draft Code, 23 *ILM*, p.627 and *ibid.*, p.602 (Secretariat report on outstanding issues).

[143] The *Restatement (Third) of Foreign Relations Law of the United States*, 1987, p.126 notes that the transnational corporation, while an established feature of international life, "has not yet achieved independent status in international law".

[144] See in general e.g. Umourike, *Self-Determination in International Law*, 1972; Rigo-Sureda, *The Evolution of the Right of Self-Determination*, 1973; Shukri, *The Concept of Self-Determination in the United Nations*, 1967; Pomerance, *Self-Determination in Law and Practice*, 1982; Shaw, *op. cit.*, pp.59-144; Crawford, *op. cit.*, pp.84-105; Rousseau, *op. cit.* vol.II, pp.17-35 and Tunkin, *op. cit.*, pp.60-69. See also Wilson, *op. cit.*

[145] See Cobban, *The Nation-State and National Self-Determination*, 1969; Miller, *The Drafting of the Covenant*, vol.II, 1928, pp.12-13; Wambaugh, *Plebiscites since the World War*, vol.I, 1933, p.42 and Pomerance, *op. cit.*

[146] See e.g. Claude, *National Minorities*, 1955 and Lador-Lederer, *International Group Protection*, 1968.

[147] See e.g. The Baltic States' treaties, Martens, *Recueil Général de Traités*, 3rd Series, XI, pp.864, 877 and 888 and Cobban, *op. cit.*, pp.187-218. See also Whiteman, *op. cit.* vol.4, p.56.

International Commission of Jurists and the Committee of Rapporteurs dealing with the situation that the principle of self-determination was not a legal rule of international law, but purely a political concept.[148] The situation, which concerned the Swedish inhabitants of an island alleged to be part of Finland, was resolved by the League's recognition of Finnish sovereignty coupled with minority guarantees.

The Second World War stimulated further consideration of the idea and the principle was included in the UN Charter. Article 1(2) noted as one of the organisation's purposes the development of friendly relations among nations based upon respect for the principle of equal rights and self-determination and article 55 reiterated the phraseology. It is disputed whether the reference to the principle in these very general terms was sufficient to entail its recognition as a binding right, but the majority view is against this. Not every statement of a political aim in the Charter can be regarded as automatically creative of legal obligations. On the other hand, its inclusion in the Charter, particularly within the context of the statement of purposes of the UN, provided the opportunity for the subsequent interpretation of the principle both in terms of its legal effect and consequences and with regard to its definition. It is also to be noted that Chapters XI and XII of the Charter deal with non-self-governing and trust territories and may be seen as relevant within the context of the development and definition of the right to self-determination, although the term is not expressly used.[149]

Practice since 1945 within the UN, both generally as regards the elucidation and standing of the principle and more particularly as regards its perceived application in specific instances, can be seen as having ultimately established the legal standing of the right in international law. This may be achieved either by treaty or by custom or indeed, more controversially, by virtue of constituting a general principle of law. All these routes are relevant, as will be seen. The UN Charter is a multilateral treaty which can be interpreted by

---

[148] LNOJ Supp. no.3, 1920, pp.5-6 and Doc. B7/21/68/106[VII] pp.22-23. See also Barros, *The Aaland Islands Question,* 1968 and Verzijl, *op. cit.,* pp.328-32.

[149] See e.g. O'Connell, *op. cit.,* p.312; Bentwich and Martin, *Commentary on the Charter of the UN,* 1950, p.7; Nincic, *The Problem of Sovereignty in the Charter and the Practice of States,* 1970, p.221; Kelsen, *Law of the United Nations,* 1950, pp.51-53 and Lauterpacht, *International Law and Human Rights,* 1950, pp.147-49. See also Judge Tanaka, *South West Africa* cases, ICJ Reports, 1966, pp.288-89; 37 *ILR,* pp.243, 451-52.

subsequent practice, while the range of state and organisation practice evident within the UN system can lead to the formation of customary law. The amount of material dealing with self-determination in the UN testifies to the importance of the concept and some of the more significant of this material will be briefly noted.

Resolution 1514 (XV), the Declaration on the Granting of Independence to Colonial Countries and Peoples, adopted in 1960 by 89 votes to none, with 9 abstentions, stressed that:

> all peoples have the right to self-determination; by virtue of that right they freely determine their political status and fully pursue their economic, social and cultural development.

Inadequacy of political, social, economic or educational preparedness was not to serve as a protest for delaying independence, while attempts aimed at the partial or total disruption of the national unity and territorial integrity of a country was deemed incompatible with the UN Charter. This Colonial Declaration set the terms for the self-determination debate in its emphasis upon the colonial context and its opposition to secession, and has been regarded by some as constituting a binding interpretation of the Charter.[150] The Declaration was reinforced by the establishment of a Special Committee on Decolonisation, which now deals with all dependent territories and has proved extremely active, and by the fact that virtually all UN resolutions dealing with self-determination expressly refer to it. Indeed, the International Court has specifically referred to the Colonial Declaration as an "important stage" in the development of international law regarding non-self-governing territories and as the "basis for the process of decolonisation".[151]

In 1966, the General Assembly adopted the International Covenants on Human Rights. Both these Covenants have an identical first article, declaring *inter alia* that "[a]ll peoples have the right to self-determination. By virtue of that right they freely determine their political status," while states parties to the instruments "shall promote the realisation of the right of self-determination and shall respect that right in conformity with the

---

[150] See e.g. Brownlie, *op. cit.*, p.595 and Asamoah, *The Legal Significance of the Declarations of the General Assembly of the United Nations*, 1966, pp.177-85. See also Shaw, *op. cit.*, Chapter 2.

[151] The *Western Sahara* case, ICJ Reports, 1975, pp.12, 31 and 32; 59 *ILR*, pp.14, 49.

provisions of the Charter of the United Nations". The Covenants came into force in 1976 and thus constitute binding provisions as between the parties, but in addition they also may be regarded as authoritative interpretations of several human rights provisions in the Charter, including self-determination. The 1970 Declaration on Principles of International Law Concerning Friendly Relations can be regarded as constituting an authoritative interpretation of the seven Charter provisions it expounds. The Declaration states *inter alia* that "by virtue of the principle of equal rights and self-determination of peoples enshrined in the Charter of the United Nations, all people have the right freely to determine ... their political status" while all states are under the duty to respect this right in accordance with the Charter. The Declaration was specifically intended to act as an elucidation of certain important Charter provisions and was indeed adopted without opposition by the General Assembly.[152]

In addition to this general, abstract approach, the UN organs have dealt with self-determination in a series of specific resolutions with regard to particular situations and this practice may be adduced as reinforcing the conclusions that the principle has become a right in international law by virtue of a process of Charter interpretation. Numerous resolutions have been adopted in the General Assembly and also the Security Council.[153] It is also possible that a rule of customary law has been created since practice in the UN system is still state practice, but the identification of the *opinio juris* element is not easy and will depend upon careful assessment and judgment.

Judicial discussion of the principle of self-determination has been relatively rare and centres on the *Namibia*[154] and *Western Sahara*[155] advisory opinions by the International Court. In the former case, the Court emphasised that "the subsequent development of international law in regard to non-self-governing territories as enshrined in the Charter of the United Nations made

---

[152] Adopted in resolution 2625 (XXV) without a vote. See e.g. Rosenstock, "The Declaration of Principles of International Law Concerning Friendly Resolutions", 65 *AJIL*, 1971, pp.16, 111 and 115.

[153] See e.g. Assembly resolutions 1755 (XVII); 2138 (XXI); 2151 (XXI); 2379 (XXIII); 2383 (XXIII) and Security Council Resolutions 183 (1963); 301 (1971); 377 (1975) and 384 (1975).

[154] ICJ Reports, 1971, p.16; 49 *ILR*, p.3.

[155] ICJ Reports, 1975, p.12; 59 *ILR*, p.30. See also Shaw, "The Western Sahara Case", 49 *BYIL*, p.119.

the principle of self-determination applicable to all of them".[156] The *Western Sahara* case reaffirmed this point.[157] This case arose out of the decolonisation of that territory, controlled by Spain as the colonial power but subject to irredentist claims by Morocco and Mauritania. The Court was asked for an opinion with regard to the legal ties between the territory at that time and Morocco and the Mauritanian entity. The Court stressed that the request for an opinion arose out of the consideration by the General Assembly of the decolonisation of Western Sahara and that the right of the people of the territory to self-determination constituted a basic assumption of the questions put to the Court.[158] After analysing the Charter provisions and Assembly resolutions noted above, the Court concluded that the ties which had existed between the claimants and the territory during the relevant period of the 1880s were not such as to affect the application of resolution 1514 (XV), the Colonial Declaration, in the decolonisation of the territory and in particular the right to self-determination. In other words, it is clear that the Court regarded the principle of self-determination as a legal one in the context of such territories.

The Definition of Self-determination

If the principle exists as a legal one, and it is believed that such is the case, the question arises then of its scope and application. As noted above, UN formulations of the principle from the 1960 Colonial Declaration to the 1970 Declaration on Principles of International Law and the 1966 International Covenants on Human Rights stress that it is the right of "all peoples". If this is so, then all peoples would become thereby to some extent subjects of international law as the direct repositories of international rights, and if the definition of "people" used was the normal political-sociological one,[159] a major re-arrangement of international law

---

[156] ICJ Reports, 1971, pp.16, 31; 49 *ILR*, pp.3, 21.

[157] ICJ Reports, 1975, pp.12, 31; 59 *ILR*, pp.30, 48.

[158] *Ibid.*, p.68; 59 *ILR*, p.85. See in particular the views of Judge Dillard that "a norm of international law has emerged applicable to the decolonisation of those non-self-governing territories which are under the aegis of the United Nations", *ibid.*, pp.121-22; 59 *ILR*, p.138. See also Judge Petren, *ibid.*, p.110; 59 *ILR*, p.127.

[159] See e.g. Cobban, *op. cit.*, p.107, and Deutsche, *Nationalism and Social Communications*, 1952. See also the *Greco-Bulgarian Communities* case, PCIJ, Series B, no.17; 5 *ILR*, p.4.

perceptions would have been created. In fact, that has not occurred and an international law concept of what constitutes a people for these purposes has been evolved, so that the "self" in question must be determined within the accepted colonial territorial framework. Attempts to broaden this have not been successful and the UN has always strenuously opposed any attempt at the partial or total disruption of the national unity and territorial integrity of a country.[160] The UN has based its policy on the proposition that "the territory of a colony or other non-self-governing territory has under the Charter a status separate and distinct from the territory of the state administering it" and that such status was to exist until the people of that territory had exercised the right to self-determination.[161] Self-determination has also been used in conjunction with the principle of territorial integrity so as to protect the territorial framework of the colonial period in the decolonisation process and to prevent a rule permitting secession from independent states from arising. Self-determination as a concept is capable of developing further so as to apply to sovereign states in various ways including secession, but that has not as yet happened.[162] It clearly applies within the context, however, of decolonisation of the European empires and thus provides the peoples of such territories with a degree of international personality.

The principle of self-determination provides that the people of the colonially defined territorial unit in question may freely determine their own political status. Such determination may result in independence, integration with a neighbouring state, free association with an independent state or any other political status freely decided upon by the people concerned.[163] Self-determination also has a role within the context of creation of statehood, preserving the sovereignty and independence of states, in providing criteria

---

[160] See e.g. the Colonial Declaration 1960; the 1970 Declaration on Principles and Article III [3] of the OAU Charter.

[161] 1970 Declaration on Principles of International Law. Note also that resolution 1541 (XV) declared that there is an obligation to transmit information regarding a territory "which is geographically separate and is distinct ethnically and/or culturally from the country administering it".

[162] See Shaw, *op. cit.*, Chapters 3 and 4.

[163] ICJ Reports, 1975, pp.12, 33 and 68. See also Judge Dillard, ibid., p.122; 59 *ILR*, pp.30, 50, 85, 138. See Assembly resolution 1541 (XV) and the 1970 Declaration on Principles of International Law.

for the resolution of disputes, and in the area of the permanent sovereignty of states over natural resources.[164]

INDIVIDUALS [165]

The question of the status in international law of individuals is closely bound up with the rise in the international protection of human rights. This section will be confined to some general comments about the former. The object theory in this regard maintains that individuals constitute only the subject-matter of intended legal regulation as such. Only states, and possibly international organisations, are subjects of the law.[166] This has been a theory of limited value. The essence of international law has always been its ultimate concern for the human being and this was clearly manifest in the Natural Law origins of classical international law.[167] The growth of positivist theories particularly in the nineteenth century obscured this and emphasised the centrality and even exclusivity of the state in this regard. Nevertheless, modern practice does demonstrate that individuals have become increasingly recognised as participants and subjects of international law. This has occurred primarily but not exclusively through human rights law.

The link between the state and the individual for international law purposes has historically been the concept of nationality. This was and remains crucial particularly in the spheres of jurisdiction and the international protection of the individual by the state. It is often noted that the claim of an individual against a foreign state,

---

[164] Note that on 22 February 1991 Portugal instituted proceedings against Australia at the International Court of Justice alleging, *inter alia,* that Australia's agreement with Indonesia dealing with the exploration and exploitation of the continental shelf in the "Timor Gap" has violated the right of the people of East Timor to self-determination. East Timor was a Portuguese colony that is now under the control of Indonesia. ICJ Press Communiqué No.91/6, 22 February 1991

[165] See e.g. Brownlie, *op. cit.,* Chapter XXIV; O'Connell, *op. cit.,* pp.106-12; Norgaard, *Position of the Individual in International Law,* 1962; Lauterpacht, *op. cit.* footnote 149 and *International Law; Collected Papers,* vol.II, 1975, p.487, and *The Individual's Duties to the Community and the Limitations on Human Rights and Freedoms under Article 29 of the Universal Declaration of Human Rights,* study prepared by Daes, 1983, E/CN.4/Sub.2/432/Rev.2. See also Chapter 6.

[166] See e.g. O'Connell, *op. cit.,* pp.106-7.

[167] See e.g. Grotius, *De Jure Praedae Commentarius,* 1604, cited in Daes, *op. cit.,* p.44 and Lauterpacht, *op. cit.* footnote 149, pp.9, 70 and 74.

for example, becomes subsumed under that of his national state.[168] Each state has the capacity to determine who are to be its nationals and this is to be recognised by other states in so far as it is consistent with international law, although in order for other states to accept this nationality there has to be a genuine connection between the state and the individual in question.[169]

States may, of course, agree to confer particular rights on individuals which will be enforceable under international law, independently of municipal law. Under article 304(b) of the Treaty of Versailles 1919, for example, nationals of the Allied and Associated Powers could bring cases against Germany before the Mixed Arbitral Tribunal in their own names for compensation, while the Treaty of 1907 between five Central American States establishing the Central American Court of Justice provided for individuals to bring cases directly before the Court.[170]

This proposition was reiterated in the *Danzig Railway Officials* case[171] by the Permanent Court of International Justice. In that case, there had been an agreement between Poland and Danzig relating to the conditions of employment of Danzig railway officials working on the Polish rail system. Poland agreed that since an international treaty was involved and since the particular rights conferred had not been incorporated into her municipal law, any failure to enforce such rights would be a matter between herself and Danzig alone and the individuals concerned would just have to make such representations as they could to Danzig. The Court dismissed this argument having regard to the particular circumstances of the treaty and the intentions at the time of agreement of the two parties to it. Whether a treaty does establish rights and duties as regards individuals will depend on the facts of the case and the intention of the parties.

Under the provisions concerned with minority protection in the 1919 Peace Treaties, it was possible for individuals to apply directly

---

[168] See the *Panevezys-Saldutiskis* case, PCIJ, Series A/B, no.76; 9 *ILR*, p.308. See also the *Mavrommatis Palestine Concessions* case (Jurisdiction), PCIJ, Series A, no.2 (1924); 2 *ILR*, p.27. See also *infra*, Chapter 13.

[169] See the *Nottebohm* case, ICJ Reports, 1955, pp.4, 22–23; 22 *ILR*, p.349 and *infra*, Chapter 13.

[170] See Whiteman, *op. cit.* vol.I, p.39.

[171] PCIJ, Series B, no.15 (1928); 4 *ILR*, p.287.

to an international court in particular instances. Similarly the Tribunal created under the Upper Silesia Convention of 1922 decided that it was competent to hear cases by the nationals of a state against that state.[172]

Since then a wide range of other treaties have provided for individuals to have rights directly and have enabled individuals to have direct access to international courts and tribunals. One may mention as examples the European Convention on Human Rights, 1950; the European Communities treaties, 1957; the Inter-American Convention on Human Rights, 1969; the Optional Protocol to the International Covenant on Civil and Political Rights, 1966; the International Convention for the Elimination of All Forms of Racial Discrimination, 1965 and the Convention on the Settlement of Investment Disputes, 1965.[173]

As far as obligations are concerned, international law has imposed direct responsibility upon individuals in certain specified matters.[174] In the case of piracy, offenders are guilty of a crime against the international society and can thus be punished by international tribunals or by any state at all. Jurisdiction to hear the charge is not confined to, for example, the state on whose territory the act took place, or the national state of the offender. The Nuremberg Tribunal following the Second World War pointed out that "international law imposes duties and liabilities upon individuals as well as upon states". This was because "crimes against international law are committed by men, not by abstract entities, and only by punishing individuals who commit such crimes can the provisions of international law be enforced".[175] Included in the relevant category for which individual responsibility was posited were crimes against peace, war crimes and crimes against humanity. The provisions of

---

[172] See e.g. *Steiner and Gross* v. *Polish State*, 4 *ILR*, p.291.

[173] *Infra*, Chapter 6 and Chapter 17.

[174] See e.g. Lauterpacht, *op. cit.* footnote 149, p.43; *International Criminal Law* (eds. Mueller and Wise), 1965, pp.621-22, and Brownlie, *op. cit.*, pp.561-64.

[175] See the Charter of the International Military Tribunal annexed to the London Agreement of 8 August 1945, providing for the prosecution and punishment of the major war criminals. See also Horowitz, *The Tokyo Trial*, International Conciliation no.465 (1950); Brownlie, *op. cit.*, p.562 and Lauterpacht, *op. cit.* footnote 15, p.6.

the Nuremberg Charter can now be regarded as part of international law, particularly since the General Assembly in 1946 affirmed the principles of this Charter and the decision of the Tribunal.[176] The Assembly also stated that genocide was a crime under international law bearing individual responsibility.[177] This was reaffirmed in the Genocide Convention of 1948, while the International Convention on the Suppression and Punishment of the Crime of Apartheid of 1973 declares apartheid to be an international crime with direct responsibility.

This vast array of practice with regard to the international rights and duties of the individual under customary and treaty law clearly demonstrates that individuals are subjects of international law. It remains only to determine the nature and extent of this personality, while recognising that the current structure of international relations militates against anything other than a limited personality for individuals.

INTERNATIONAL ORGANISATIONS

The nature, characteristics and forms of international organisations will be surveyed in Chapter 19, but such entities have played a crucial role in the sphere of international personality. Since the nineteenth century a growing number of such organisations have appeared and thus raised the question as to personality.[178] The answer in each instance will depend upon the particular circumstances of that case. Whether an organisation possesses personality before international law will hinge upon its constitutional status, its actual powers and practice. Significant factors in this context will include the capacity to enter into relations with states and other organisations and conclude treaties with them, and the status it has been given under municipal law. Such elements are known in international law as the indicia of personality.[179]

---

[176] Resolution 95(1). See also *Yearbook of the ILC,* 1950, vol.II, p.195, and the Convention on the Non-Applicability of Statutory Limitations to War Crimes Against Humanity, 1968.

[177] Resolution 96(1).

[178] See O'Connell, *op. cit.,* p.94. See further *infra,* Chapter 19.

[179] See the *Reparation for Injuries* case, ICJ Reports, 1949, p.174; 16 *ILR,* p.318.

THE ACQUISITION, NATURE AND CONSEQUENCES OF LEGAL PERSONALITY— SOME CONCLUSIONS

The above survey of existing and possible subjects of international law demonstrates both the range of interaction upon the international scene by entities of all types and the pressures upon international law to come to terms with the contemporary structure of international relations. The International Court clearly recognised the multiplicity of models of personality in stressing that "the subjects of law in any legal system are not necessarily identical in their nature or in the extent of their rights".[180] There are, however, two basic categories – objective and qualified personality. In the former case, the entity is subject to a wide range of international rights and duties and it will be entitled to be accepted as an international person by any other international person with which it is conducting relations. In other words, it will operate *erga omnes*. The creation of objective international personality will of necessity be harder to achieve and will require the action in essence of the international community as a whole or a substantial element of it. The Court noted in the *Reparation* case that:

> fifty states, representing the vast majority of the members of the international community, have the power, in conformity with international law, to bring into being an entity possessing objective international personality and not merely personality recognised by them alone, together with capacity to bring international claims.[181]

The attainment of qualified personality, on the other hand, binding only the consenting subject, may arise more easily and it is clear that in this respect at least theory ought to recognise existing practice. Any legal person may accept that another entity possesses personality in relation to itself and that determination will operate only *in personam.*

States are the original and major subjects of international law. Their personality derives from the very nature and structure of the international system. Statehood will arise as a result of the factual

---

[180] *Ibid.*, p.178; 16 *ILR*, p.321.
[181] *Ibid.*, p.185; 16 *ILR*, p.330.

satisfaction of the stipulated legal criteria. The constitutive theory of recognition is not really acceptable, although recognition, of course, contributes valuable evidence of adherence to the required criteria. All states, by virtue of the principle of sovereign equality, will enjoy the same degree of international legal personality. It has been argued that some international organisations, rather than being derivative subjects of international law, will as sovereign or self-governing legal communities possess an inherent personality directly from the system and will thus constitute general and even objective subjects of international law. Non-sovereign persons, including non-governmental organisations and individuals, would be derived subjects possessing only such international powers as conferred exceptionally upon them by the necessary subjects of international law.[182] This view may be questioned, but it is true that the importance of practice via the larger international organisations cannot be underestimated.

Similarly the role of the Holy See (particularly prior to 1929) as well as the UN experience demonstrates that the derivative denomination is unsatisfactory. The significance of this relates to their ability to extend their international rights and duties on the basis of both constituent instruments and subsequent practice and to their capacity to affect the creation of further international persons and to play a role in the norm-creating process.

Recognition, acquiescence and estoppel are important principles in the context of international personality, not only with regard to states and international organisations but throughout the range of subjects. They will affect not only the creation of new subjects but also the definition of their nature and rights and duties.

Personality may be acquired by a combination of treaty provisions and recognition or acquiescence by other international persons. For instance, the International Committee of the Red Cross, a private non-governmental organisation subject to Swiss law, was granted special functions under the 1949 Geneva Red Cross Conventions and has been accepted as being able to enter into international agreements under international law with international persons,

---

[182] See e.g. Seversted, "International Personality of Intergovernmental Organisations", 4 *Indian Journal of International Law*, 1964, p.19.

such as with the EEC under the World Food Programme.[183] Another possible method of acquiring international personality is by subjecting an agreement between a recognised international person and a private party directly to the rules of international law. This would have the effect of rendering the latter into an international person in the context of the arrangement in question so as to enable it to invoke in the field of international law the rights it derives from that arrangement.[184] While this currently may not be entirely acceptable to Third World states, this is probably because of a perception of the relevant rules of international law which may very well alter.[185] Personality may also be acquired by virtue of being directly subjected to international duties. This would apply to individuals in specific cases such as war crimes, piracy and genocide, and might in the future constitute the method by which transnational corporations may be accepted as international persons. One variation of the draft Code of Conduct under discussion would make the document a binding one and would impose duties directly upon such entities.[186]

Community needs with regard to the necessity to preserve international stability and life may well be of relevance in certain exceptional circumstances. In the case of non-state territorial entities that are not totally dominated by a state, there would appear to be a community need to ensure that at least the rules relating to the resort to force and the laws of war operate. Not to accept some form of qualified personality in this area might be to free such entities from having to comply with such rules and that clearly would affect community requirements. Just as municipal law has sometimes to face the facts of the existence of particular entities for certain humanitarian purposes,[187] so also international law may have to come

---

[183] See e.g. Whiteman, *op. cit.* vol.I, p.48 and *Yearbook of the ILC,* 1981, vol.II, p.125.

[184] See in particular the *Texaco* v. *Libya* case, 53 *ILR,* pp.389, 457-62.

[185] Note the intriguing suggestion raised in the study prepared for the Economic Commission for Asia and the Far East, that an agreement between autonomous public entities (not being subjects of international law) might create an international person; *UNJYB,* 1971, pp.215-18. The study was very cautious about this possibility.

[186] See 22 *ILM,* 1983, p.192.

[187] See e.g. *Hesperides Hotels* v. *Aegean Turkish Holidays Ltd,* [1978] QB 205; 73 *ILR,* p.9; *Luigi Monta of Genoa* v. *Cechofracht Ltd,* [1956] 2 QB 552; 23 ILR, p.71; *Re Al-Fin Corporation's Patent,* [1970] Ch. 160; 52 ILR, p.68 and *Reel* v. *Holder,* [1981] 1 WLR 1226; 74 *ILR,* p.105. See also Merrills, "Recognition and Construction", 10 *ICLQ,* p.476 and Shaw, "Legal Acts of an Unrecognised Entity", 94 *LQR,* 1978, p.500.

to terms with such bodies for such purposes.[188] The determining point here, it is suggested, must be the degree of effective control maintained by the entity in its territorial confines. However, even so, recognition may overcome this hurdle, as the recognition of Byelorussia and the Ukraine as non-sovereign state entities demonstrates.[189]

All these entities may be easily contained within the category of qualified personality, possessing a limited range of rights and duties valid as against those accepting their personality. There are no pre-set rules governing the extent of rights and duties of international persons. This will depend upon the type of entity concerned, its claims and expectations, functions and attitude adopted by the international community. The exception here would be states which enter upon life with an equal range of rights and obligations. Those entities with objective personality will, it is suggested, benefit from a more elastic perception of the extent of their rights and duties in the form of a wider interpretation of implied powers through practice. However, in the case of qualified subjects implied powers will be more difficult to demonstrate and accept and the range of their rights and duties will be much more limited. The presumption, thus, will operate the other way.

The precise catalogue of rights and duties is accordingly impossible to list in advance; it will vary from case to case. The capacity to function on the international scene in legal proceedings of some description will not be too uncommon, while the power to make treaties will be less widespread. As to this the International Law Commission noted that "agreements concluded between entities other than states or than international organisations seem too heterogeneous a group to constitute a general category, and the relevant body of international practice is as yet too exiguous for the characteristics of such a general category to be inferred from it".[190] The extent to which subjects may be internationally responsible is

---

[188] See the *Namibia* case, ICJ Reports, 1971, pp.16, 56, 134 and 149; 49 *ILR*, pp.3, 46, 124, 139. See also Security Council resolutions 326 (1973); 328 (1973); 403 (1977); 406 (1977); 411 (1977); and 424 (1978) in which the Council condemned Rhodesian attacks against neighbouring states and recognised that the entity was subject to the norms relating to the use of force.

[189] See e.g. UKMIL, 49 *BYIL*, 1978, p.340. Byelorussia and the Ukraine are separate members of the UN and are parties to a number of conventions; *ibid.*

[190] *Yearbook of the ILC,* 1981, vol.II, pp.125-26.

also unclear, although in general such an entity will possess responsibility to the extent of its rights and duties, but many problem areas remain. Similarly controversial is the norm-creating role of such diverse entities, but the practice of all international persons is certainly relevant material upon which to draw in an elucidation of the rules and principles of international law, particularly in the context of the entity in question.

International personality thus centres, not so much upon the capacity of the entity as such to possess international rights and duties, as upon the actual attribution of rights and/or duties on the international plane as determined by a variety of factors ranging from claims made to prescribed functions. Procedural capacity with regard to enforcement is important but not essential,[191] but in the case of non-individual entities the claimant will have to be in "such a position that it possesses, in regard to its members, rights which it is entitled to ask them to respect".[192] This, noted the International Court, expressed "the essential test where a group, whether composed of states, of tribes or of individuals, is claimed to be a legal entity distinct from its members".[193]

---

[191] See e.g. Norgaard, *op. cit.*, p.35. See also the *Peter Pázmány University* case, PCIJ, Series A/B, no.61 (1933); 7 *ILR*, p.490.

[192] ICJ Reports, 1949, pp.174, 178; 16 *ILR*, pp.318, 321.

[193] ICJ Reports, 1975, pp.12, 63; 59 *ILR*, pp.14, 80.

CHAPTER SIX

International Human Rights [1]

THE NATURE OF HUMAN RIGHTS

The preamble to the Universal Declaration of Human Rights adopted on 10 December 1948 emphasises that "recognition of the inherent dignity and of the equal and inalienable rights of all members of the human family is the foundation of freedom, justice and peace in the world". While there is widespread acceptance of the importance of human rights in the international structure, there is considerable confusion as to their precise nature and role in international law.[2] The question of what is meant by a "right" is itself controversial and the subject of intense jurisprudential debate.[3] Some "rights", for example, are intended as immediately enforceable binding commitments, others merely as specifying a possible future pattern of behaviour.[4] The problem of enforcement and sanctions with regard to human rights in international law is another issue which can affect the characterisation of the phenomenon. There are writers who regard the high incidence of non-compliance with human rights norms as evidence of state practice that argues against the existence of a structure of human rights principles in international law.[5] Although sight must not be lost of violations of human rights laws, such an approach is not only academically

[1] See e.g. Lauterpacht, *International Law and Human Rights*, 1950; Lillich and Newman, *International Human Rights*, 1979; McDougal, Lasswell and Chen, *Human Rights and World Public Order*, 1980; Sohn and Buergenthal, *International Protection of Human Rights*, 1973; Sieghart, *The International Law of Human Rights*, 1983; *The Human Rights Reader* (eds. Laquer and Rubin), 1977 and *Human Rights in International Law* (ed. Meron), 2 vols., 1984. See also Robertson and Merrills, *Human Rights in the World*, 3rd ed., 1989.

[2] See e.g. Moskowitz, *The Policies and Dynamics of Human Rights*, 1968; pp.98-99 and McDougal, Lasswell and Chen, *op. cit.*, pp.63-68.

[3] See e.g. Hohfeld, "Fundamental Legal Conceptions as Applied to Judicial Reasoning", 23 *Yale Law Journal*, 1913, p.16 and Dworkin, *Taking Rights Seriously*, 1977. See also Shestack, "The Jurisprudence of Human Rights" in *Human Rights in International Law, op. cit.* vol.1, p.69, and Cranston, *What Are Human Rights?*, 1973.

[4] Compare, for example, article 2 of the International Covenant on Civil and Political Rights with article 2 of the International Covenant on Economic, Social and Cultural Rights.

[5] See e.g. Watson, "Legal Theory, Efficacy and Validity in the Development of Human Rights Norms in International Law", *University of Illinois Law Forum*, 1979, p.609 and "Autointerpretation, Competence and the Continuing Validity of Article 2(7) of the UN Charter", 71 *AJIL*, 1977, p.60.

incorrect but also profoundly negative.[6] The concept of human rights is closely allied with ethics and morality. Those rights that reflect the values of a community will be those with the most chance of successful implementation. Of course, there is no necessary connection in particular instances, so that not all community values will be enshrined in law, nor will all legal rights reflect moral concerns, since many operate on a technical level as entitlements under specific conditions. However, this realisation does add to the uncertainty surrounding the definition of the nature and scope of rights. Positive rights may be taken to include those rights enshrined within a legal system, whether or not reflective of moral considerations, whereas a moral right does not necessarily exist as enforceable by law. One may easily discover positive rights. Deducing or inferring moral rights is another matter entirely and will depend upon the perception of the person seeking the existence of a particular right.[7] Rights may be seen as emanating from various sources, whether religious or the nature of man or the nature of society. The Natural Law view, as expressed in the traditional formulations of that approach or by virtue of the natural rights movement, is that certain rights exist as a result of a higher law than positive or man-made law. Such a higher law constitutes a universal and absolute set of principles governing all human beings in time and space. The natural rights approach of the seventeenth century, associated primarily with John Locke, founded the existence of such inalienable rights as the rights to life, liberty and property upon a social contract marking the end of the difficult conditions of the state of nature. This theory enabled recourse to be had to a superior type of law and thus was able to provide a powerful method of restraining arbitrary power.[8] Although this approach fell out of favour in the nineteenth century due to the problems of its non-empirical and diffuse methodology, it has proved of immense value this century in the establishment of human rights within the international community as universal principles. Positivism as a

---

[6] See e.g. Higgins, "Reality and Hope and International Human Rights: A Critique", 9 *Hofstra Law Review*, 1981, p.1485.

[7] See Cranston, "What are Human Rights?" in *The Human Rights Reader, op. cit.*, pp.17, 19.

[8] See e.g. Lauterpacht, *op. cit.*; Tuck, *Natural Rights Theories*, 1979; Finnis, *Natural Law and Natural Rights*, 1980 and McDougal, Lasswell and Chen, *op. cit.*, pp.68-71. See also *supra*, Chapter 1.

theory emphasised the authority of the state and as such left little place for rights in the legal system other than specific rights emanating from the constitutional structure of that system,[9] while the Marxist doctrine, although based upon the existence of certain immutable historical laws governing the development of society, nevertheless denied the existence of rights outside the framework of the legal order.[10] Modern rights theories cover a wide range of approaches, and this clearly emphasises the need to come to terms with the requirements of an evolving legal system that cannot be totally comprehended in terms of that system itself.[11]

Of particular interest is the work of the policy-orientated movement that seeks to identify, characterise and order a wide variety of relevant factors in the process of human rights creation and equipment. Eight interdependent values are noted (viz. demands relating to respect, power, enlightenment, well-being, health, skill, affection and rectitude) and various environmental influences stressed. Human dignity is seen as the key concept in relation to these values and to the ultimate goal of a world community in which a democratic distribution of values is sought.[12]

All these theories emphasise the complexity of the nature of the concept of human rights in the context of general legal and political processes, but also the importance and centrality of such notions. The broad issues are similarly raised within the framework of international law.

IDEOLOGICAL APPROACHES TO HUMAN RIGHTS IN INTERNATIONAL LAW

The view adopted by the western world with regard to international human rights law in general terms has tended to emphasise the basic civil and political rights of individuals, that is to say those rights that take the form of claims limiting the power of government over the

---

[9] See e.g. Lloyd, *Introduction to Jurisprudence*, 4th ed., 1979, Chapter 4. See also Hart, *The Concept of Law*, 1960, and McDougal, Lasswell and Chen, *op. cit.*, pp.73-75 and *supra*, Chapters 1 and 2.

[10] See e.g. Lloyd, *op. cit.*, Chapter 10 and McDougal, Lasswell and Chen, *op. cit.*, pp.76-79. See also *infra*, pp.190-91.

[11] See e.g. Rawls, *A Theory of Justice*, 1971; Cahn, *The Sense of Injustice*, 1949; Nozick, *Anarchy, State and Utopia*, 1974 and Dworkin, *op. cit.*

[12] See McDougal, Lasswell and Chen, *op. cit.*, especially pp.82-93.

governed. Such rights would include due process, freedom of expression, assembly and religion, and political participation in the process of government. The consent of the governed is seen as crucial in this process.[13] The approach of the Soviet Union has been to note the importance of basic rights and freedoms for international peace and security, but to emphasise the role of the state. Indeed, the source of human rights principles was seen as the state. Tunkin wrote that the content of the principle of respect for human rights in international law may be expressed in three propositions:

(1) all states have a duty to respect the fundamental rights and freedoms of all persons within their territories; (2) states have a duty not to permit discrimination by reason of sex, race, religion or language, and (3) states have a duty to promote universal respect for human rights and to co-operate with each other to achieve this objective.[14]

In other words, the focus is not upon the individual (as in western conceptions of human rights) but solely upon the state. Human rights are not directly regulated by international law and individuals are not subjects of international law. Indeed, human rights are implemented by the state and are matters basically and crucially within the domestic affairs of state. As Tunkin emphasised, "conventions on human rights do not grant rights directly to individuals".[15] Having stressed the central function of the state, the point is also made that the context of the international human rights obligations themselves is defined solely by the state in the light of the socio-economic advancement of that state. Accordingly, the nature and context of those rights will vary from state to state, depending upon the social system of the state in question. It is the particular socio-economic system of a state that will determine the concrete expression of an international human rights provision.[16] In other words, the Soviet Union was able and willing to enter into

[13] See e.g. Hauser, "A First World View", in *Human Rights and American Foreign Policy* (eds. Kommers and Loescher), 1979, p.85.
[14] *Theory of International Law*, 1974, p.81. See also Tedin, "The Development of the Soviet Attitude Towards Implementing Human Rights under the UN Charter", 5 *HRJ*, 1972, p.399; Dean, "Beyond Helsinki: The Soviet View of Human Rights in International Law", 21 *Va JIL*, 1980, p.55 and Reddaway, "Theory and Practice of Human Rights in the Soviet Union" in *Human Rights and American Foreign Policy, op. cit.*, p.115.
[15] *Op. cit.*, p.83.
[16] *Ibid.*, pp.82-83.

many international agreements on human rights, on the basis that only a state obligation was incurred, with no direct link to the individual, and that such an obligation was one that the country might interpret in the light of its own socio-economic system. The supremacy or centrality of the state is the key in this approach. As far as the different kinds of human rights are concerned, the Soviet approach has been to stress those dealing with economic and social matters and thus to minimise the importance of the traditional civil and political rights. However, there has recently been a new approach to the question of international human rights by Soviet writers. Vershchetin and Mullerson have written that human rights activity is one of the most important components of a comprehensive system of international security and that the role of the individual is "primary".[17] In particular, they have stated that:

> Soviet legal scholarship has always emphasised that international human rights treaties obligate signatories to ensure the applicable rights and freedoms. However, until now, Soviet scholars have unjustifiably advocated that these documents do not represent rights directly enforceable by the individual. This approach has been excessively legalistic. A citizen of a state based on the rule of law has the right to demand that state agencies observe voluntarily adopted international obligations which directly affect the individual's interests. Human rights treaties establish state obligations to citizens, not just to other state parties to the international agreements.[18]

The general approach of the Third World states has combined elements of both the previous perceptions.[19] Concern with the equality and sovereignty of states, together with a recognition of the importance of social and economic rights has characterised the Third World view. Such countries, in fact constituting a wide range of

[17] "International Law in an Interdependent World", 28 *Columbia Journal of Transnational Law*, 1990, pp.291, 300.

[18] *Ibid.* Note that on 10 February 1989, the USSR recognised the compulsory jurisdiction of the International Court of Justice with regard to six human rights treaties, including the Genocide Convention 1948; the Racial Discrimination Convention 1965; the Convention on Discrimination against Women 1979 and the Torture Convention 1984.

[19] See e.g. Emerson, "The Fate of Human Rights in the Third World", 27 *World Politics*, 1975, p.201; Mower, "Human Rights in Black Africa", 9 *HRJ*, 1976, p.33; Zvobgo, "A Third World View" in *Human Rights and American Foreign Policy, op. cit.*, p.90 and Nawaz, "The Concept of Human Rights in Islamic Law" in Symposium on International Law of Human Rights, 11 *Howard Law Journal*, 1965, p.257.

nations with differing interests and needs, and at different stages of development, have been much influenced by decolonisation and the struggle to obtain it and by the phenomenon of apartheid in South Africa. In addition, economic problems have played a large role in focusing their attention upon general developmental issues. Accordingly, the traditional civil and political rights have tended to lose their priority in the concerns of Third World states.[20]

THE DEVELOPMENT OF INTERNATIONAL HUMAN RIGHTS LAW [21]

In the nineteenth century, the positivist doctrines of state sovereignty and domestic jurisdiction reigned supreme. Very few issues were regarded as of international concern as such. Virtually all matters that today would be classified as human rights issues were at that stage universally regarded as within the internal sphere of national jurisdiction. The major exceptions to this were related to piracy *jure gentium* and slavery. In the latter case a number of treaties were entered into to bring about its abolition.[22] Concern also with the treatment of sick and wounded soldiers and with prisoners of war developed as from 1864 in terms of international instruments,[23] while states were required to observe certain minimum standards in the treatment of aliens.[24] In addition, certain agreements of a general welfare nature were beginning to be adopted by the turn of the century.[25] The nineteenth century also appeared to accept a right of humanitarian intervention, although its range and extent were unclear.[26]

An important change occurred with the establishment of the

[20] See generally Van Boven, "Some Remarks on Special Problems Relating to Human Rights in Developing Countries", *Revue des Droits de l'Homme*, 1970, p.383. See further *infra*, p.237 on the Banjul Charter on Human and Peoples' Rights.

[21] See e.g. *The International Protection of Human Rights* (ed. Luard), 1967; Sohn and Buergenthal, *op. cit.*, Lauterpacht, *op. cit.*, Moscowitz, *International Concern with Human Rights*, 1968 and Ganji, *The International Protection of Human Rights*, 1962.

[22] See e.g. Greenidge, *Slavery*, 1958 and Nanda and Bassiouni, "Slavery and the Slave Trade: Steps towards Eradication", 12 *Santa Clara Law Review*, 1972, p.424. See also ST/SOA/4.

[23] See generally Best, *Humanity in Warfare*, 1980 and *Studies and Essays on International Humanitarian Law and Red Cross Principles* (ed. Swinarski), 1984.

[24] See *infra*, Chapter 13.

[25] E.g. regarding the Prohibition of Night Work for Women in Industrial Employment and regarding the Prohibition of the Use of White Phosphorus in the Manufacture of Matches.

[26] See *infra*, Chapter 18.

League of Nations in 1919.[27] Article 22 of the Covenant of the League set up the mandates system for peoples in ex-enemy colonies "not yet able to stand by themselves in the strenuous conditions of the modern world". The mandatory power was obliged to guarantee freedom of conscience and religion and a Permanent Mandates Commission was created to examine the reports the mandatory authorities had undertaken to make. The arrangement was termed "a sacred trust of civilisation". Article 23 of the Covenant provided for just treatment of the native populations of the territories in question.[28] The 1919 peace agreements with Eastern European and Balkan states included provisions relating to the protection of minorities.[29] Persons belonging to racial, religious or linguistic minorities were to be given the same treatment and the same civil and political rights and security as other nationals in the state in question.[30] Such provisions constituted obligations of international concern and could not be altered without the assent of a majority of the League of Nations Council. The Council was to take action in the event of any infraction of minorities' obligations.[31] There also existed a petition procedure by minorities to the League, although they had no standing as such before the Council or the Permanent Court of International Justice.[32]

Part XIII of the Treaty of Versailles provided for the creation of the International Labour Organisation, among the purposes of

---

[27] See *infra*, Chapter 19.

[28] See *supra*, Chapter 5, p.156.

[29] The minorities regime of the League consisted of five special minorities treaties binding Poland, the Serbo-Croat-Slovene state, Romania, Greece and Czechoslovakia; special minorities clauses in the treaties of peace with Austria, Bulgaria, Hungary and Turkey; five general declarations made on admission to the League by Albania, Latvia, Lithuania, Estonia and Iraq; a special declaration by Finland regarding the Aaland Islands and treaties relating to Danzig, Upper Silesia and Memel. See generally, Thornberry, "Is There a Phoenix in the Ashes? – International Law and Minority Rights", 15 *Texas International Law Journal*, 1980, p.421; Macartney, *National States and National Minorities*, 1934 and Claude, *National Minorities: An International Problem*, 1955. See also Shaw, "The Definition of Minorities in International Law", 20 *Israel Yearbook on Human Rights*, 1991, p.13.

[30] See e.g. the *Minority Schools in Albania* case, PCIJ, Series A/B, 1935, no.64, p.17.

[31] See Thornberry, *op. cit.*, pp.433-54, and Jones, "National Minorities: A Case Study in International Protection", 14 *Law and Contemporary Problems*, 1949, pp.599, 610-24.

[32] In the early 1930s several hundred petitions were received but this dropped to virtually nil by 1939; see Thornberry, *op. cit.*, pp.434-36 and the Capotorti Report on the *Rights of Persons belonging to Ethnic, Religious and Linguistic Minorities*, 1979, E/CN.4/Sub.2/384/Rev.1, pp.20-22. See also Ermacora, "The Protection of Minorities before the United Nations", 182 *HR*, p.249 and Robertson and Merrills, *op. cit.*, Chapter 2.

which were the promotion of better standards of working conditions and support for the right of association.[33] The impact of the Second World War upon the development of human rights law was immense as the horrors of the war and the need for an adequate international system to maintain international peace and protect human rights became apparent to all.

THE UNITED NATIONS SYSTEM — GENERAL [34]

There are a number of human rights provisions in the Charter.[35] Article 1 includes in the purposes of the organisation the promotion and encouragement of respect for human rights and fundamental freedoms for all without distinction as to race, sex, language or religion. Article 13(1) notes that the General Assembly shall initiate studies and make recommendations regarding the realisation of human rights for all, while article 55 provides that the United Nations shall promote universal respect for and observance of human rights. In a significant provision, article 56 states that:

> all members pledge themselves to take joint and separate action in co-operation with the organisation for the achievement of the purposes set forth in article 55.[36]

The mandate system was replaced by the trusteeship system, one of the basic objectives of which was, by article 76, the encouragement of respect for human rights, while, with regard to non-self-governing territories, the administering powers under article 73 of the Charter recognised the principle that the interests of the inhabitants were paramount, and accepted as a sacred trust the obligation to promote the well-being of the inhabitants. It can thus be seen that the Charter provisions on human rights were very general and vague.

---

[33] See further *infra*, p.217.

[34] See generally Bowett, *The Law of International Institutions*, 4th ed., 1982; Lauterpacht, *op. cit.*, pp.145-220; *UN Action in the Field of Human Rights*, 1988; Lillich and Newman, *op. cit.*, pp.14-51 and *Human Rights: Thirty Years after the Universal Declaration* (ed. Ramcharan), 1979.

[35] Largely as a result of lobbying by non-governmental organisations at the San Francisco Conference: see Humphrey, "The United Nations Charter and the Universal Declaration of Human Rights" in *The International Protection of Human Rights* (ed. Luard), Chapter 3.

[36] Under article 62, the Economic and Social Council has the power to make recommendations for the purpose of promoting respect for and observance of human rights.

No enforcement procedures were laid down. Some have argued that the term "pledge" in article 56 had the effect of converting the enumerated purposes of article 55 into legal obligations,[37] but this has been disputed.[38] Certainly, as of 1946, this would have been a difficult proposition to sustain, particularly in view of the hortatory language used in the provisions and the fact that the respect for human rights stipulation does not identify precise legal rights.[39] However, in the *Namibia* case of 1971, the Court noted that under the UN Charter:

> the former Mandatory had pledged itself to observe and respect, in a territory having international status, human rights and fundamental freedoms for all without distinction as to race. To establish instead and to enforce, distinctions, exclusions, restrictions and limitations, exclusively based on grounds of race, colour, descent or national or ethnic origin which constitute a denial of fundamental human rights is a flagrant violation of the purposes and principles of the Charter.[40]

It may be that this provision can only be understood in the light of the special, international status of that territory, but in the light of extensive practice since the 1940s in the general area of non-discrimination and human rights, the broader interpretation is to be preferred.

The Charter does contain a domestic jurisdiction provision. Article 2(7) provides that:

> nothing contained in the present Charter shall authorise the United Nations to intervene in matters which are essentially within the domestic jurisdiction of any state

---

[37] See e.g. Lauterpacht, *op. cit.*, pp.47-49; Wright, "National Courts and Human Rights – the *Fujii* case", 45 *AJIL*, 1951, p.73 and Sloan, "Human Rights, the United Nations and International Law", 20 *Nordisk Tidsskrift for International Ret*, 1950, pp.30-31. See also Judge Tanaka, *South West Africa* cases, ICJ Reports, 1966, pp.6, 288-89; 37 *ILR*, pp.243, 451-52.

[38] See Hudson, "Integrity of International Instruments", 42 *AJIL*, 1948, pp.105-8 and *Yearbook of the ILC*, 1949, p.178. See also Kelsen, *The Law of the United Nations*, 1950, p.29.

[39] See Driscoll, "The Development of Human Rights in International Law" in *The Human Rights Reader, op. cit.*, pp.41, 43.

[40] ICJ Reports, 1971, pp.16, 57; 49 *ILR*, pp.3, 47. See also Brownlie, *Principles of Public International Law*, 4th ed., 1990, p.569; Schwelb, "The International Court of Justice and the Human Rights Clauses of the Charter", 66 *AJIL*, 1972, p.337 and Schachter, "The Charter and the Constitution", 4 *Vanderbilt Law Review*, 1951, p.443.

but as noted later[41] this has over the years been flexibly interpreted, so that human rights issues are no longer recognised as being solely within the domestic jurisdiction of states.

The Universal Declaration of Human Rights [42]

This Declaration was adopted by the UN General Assembly on 10 December 1948 without a dissenting vote (Byelorussian SSR, Czechoslovakia, Poland, Ukrainian SSR, USSR, Yugoslavia and Saudi Arabia abstained). It was intended not as a legally binding document as such but, as its preamble proclaims, "a common standard of achievement for all peoples and nations". Its thirty articles cover a wide range of rights, from liberty and security of the person (article 3), equality before the law (article 7), effective remedies (article 8), due process (articles 9 and 10), prohibitions on torture (article 5) and arbitrary interference with privacy (article 12) to rights protecting freedom of movement (article 13), asylum (article 14), expression (article 19), conscience and religion (article 18) and assembly (article 20). One should also note that included in the Declaration are social and economic rights such as the right to work and equal pay (article 23), right to social security (article 25) and the right to education (article 26). Although clearly not a legally enforceable instrument as such, the question arises as to whether the Declaration has subsequently become binding either by way of custom or general principles of law, or indeed by virtue of interpretation of the UN Charter itself by subsequent practice. The Declaration has had a marked influence upon the constitutions of many states and upon the formulation of subsequent human rights treaties and resolutions.[43] It is also to be noted that in 1968, the Proclamation of Tehran at the conclusion of the UN sponsored

[41] *Infra*, p.238.

[42] See e.g. Oppenheim, *International Law*, vol.1, 8th ed., 1955, p.744; Whiteman, *Digest of International Law*, vol.5, p.237; Humphrey, "The Universal Declaration on Human Rights" in *Human Rights: Thirty Years after the Universal Declaration, op. cit.*, p.21; Kunz, "The United Nations Declaration of Human Rights", 43 *AJIL*, 1949, p.316 and Schwelb, "The Influence of the Universal Declaration of Human Rights on International and National Law", *PASIL*, 1959, p.217.

[43] See e.g. Schwelb, *op. cit.* footnote 42; Humphrey, "The International Bill of Rights: Scope and Implementation", 17 *William and Mary Law Review*, 1975, p.527; Judge Tanaka, *South West Africa* cases, ICJ Reports, 1966, pp.6, 288 and 293; 37 *ILR*, pp.243, 451, 454 and the European Convention on Human Rights, 1950, *infra*, p.221.

International Conference on Human Rights stressed that the Declaration constituted "an obligation for members of the international community".[44] The Declaration has also been referred to in many cases,[45] and its importance within the context of United Nations human rights law should not be disregarded.

The intention had been that the Declaration would be followed immediately by a binding universal convention on human rights, but this process took considerably longer than anticipated. In the meantime, a selective human rights treaty approach was adopted. This led to the adoption of a number of important international conventions, some of which shall be briefly noted.

The Convention on the Prevention and Punishment of the Crime of Genocide [46]

This Convention signed in 1948 reaffirmed that genocide, whether committed in time of war or peace, was a crime under international law. Genocide was defined as any of the following acts committed "with intent to destroy, in whole or in part, a national, ethnic, racial or religious group as such":

(a) killing members of the group; (b) causing serious bodily or mental harm to members of the group; (c) deliberately inflicting on the group conditions of life calculated to bring about its physical destruction in whole or in part; (d) imposing measures intended to prevent births within

[44] 23 GAOR, A/Conf. 32/41. See also the non-governmental Montreal Statement, 9 *Review of the International Commission of Jurists*, 1968, p.94.

[45] See e.g. *In re Flesche*, 16 *ILR*, pp.266, 269; *The State (Duggan)* v. *Tapley*, 18 *ILR*, pp.336, 342; *Robinson* v. *Secretary-General of the UN*, 19 *ILR*, pp.494, 496; *Extradition of Greek National* case, 22 *ILR*, pp.520, 524 and *Beth El Mission* v. *Minister of Social Welfare*, 47 *ILR*, pp.205, 207. See also *Corfu Channel* case, ICJ Reports, 1949, pp.4, 22; 16 *ILR*, pp.155, 158 and *Filartiga* v. *Pena-Irala*, 630, F.2d 876 (1980).

[46] See e.g. Robinson, *The Genocide Convention*, 1960; Lemkin, *Axis Rule in Occupied Europe*, 1944; Kuper, *Genocide*, 1981 and *International Action Against Genocide*, Minority Rights Group Report no.53, 1984; *Genocide and Human Rights* (ed. Porter), 1982 and Horowitz, *Taking Lives: Genocide and State Power*, 1980. See also Ruhashyankiko, *Study on the Question of the Prevention and Punishment of the Crime of Genocide*, 1978, E/CN.4/Sub.2/416; Whittaker, *Revised and Updated Report on the Question of the Prevention and Punishment of the Crime of Genocide*, 1985, E/CN.4/Sub.2/1985/6; *Contemporary Practice of the United States Relating to International Law*, 79 *AJIL*, 1985, p.116 *et seq.* and Shaw, "Genocide and International Law" in *International Law at a Time of Perplexity* (ed. Dinstein), 1989, p.797. As of 1 March 1990, there were 102 ratifications to this Convention; ST/HR/5, 1990.

the group; (e) forcibly transferring children of the group to another group.

The Convention, which does not have an implementational system, provides that persons charged with genocide shall be tried by a competent tribunal of the state in the territory of which the act was committed or by an international penal tribunal. Several points should be noted. First, the question of intent is such that states may deny genocidal activity by noting that the relevant intent to destroy in whole or in part was in fact absent.[47] Secondly, the groups protected do not include political groups.[48] Thirdly, the concept of cultural genocide is not included[49] and fourthly there is virtually no mention of means to prevent the crime.

The International Convention on the Elimination of All Forms of Racial Discrimination [50]

This Convention was signed in 1965 and entered into force in 1969. It builds on the non-discrimination provisions in the UN Charter. Racial discrimination is defined as:

any distinction, exclusion, restriction or preference based on race, colour, descent or national or ethnic origin which has the purpose or effect of nullifying or impairing the recognition, enjoyment or exercise, on an equal footing, of human rights and fundamental freedoms in the political, economic, social, cultural or any other field of public life.

States parties undertake to prohibit racial discrimination and guarantee equality for all in the enjoyment of a series of rights and to assure to all within their jurisdiction effective protection and remedies regarding such human rights. A Committee on the

[47] See Kuper, *Genocide, op. cit.,* pp.32-35 and Lewis, "The Camp at Cecilio Baez", in *Genocide in Paraguay* (ed. Arens), 1976, p.58. See also Ruhashyankiko, *op. cit.,* p.25.

[48] See e.g. Kuper, *op. cit.* footnote 47, pp.25-30 and Ruhashyankiko, *op. cit.,* p.21. See also Robinson, *op. cit.,* p.59.

[49] See e.g. Kuper, *op. cit.* footnote 47, p.31; Robinson, *op. cit.,* p.64 and Ruhashyankiko, *op. cit.,* p.21 *et seq.*

[50] See e.g. Lerner, *The UN Convention on the Elimination of All Forms of Racial Discrimination,* 2nd ed., 1980. As of 1 March 1990, there were 129 ratifications; ST/HR/5, 1990.

Elimination of Racial Discrimination was established with eighteen expert members.[51]

The International Covenant on Economic, Social and Cultural Rights [52]

This was adopted in 1966 and entered into force in 1976. Article 2 provides that each state party undertakes to take steps to the maximum of its available resources "with a view to achieving progressively the full realisation of the rights recognised in the present Covenant". In other words, an evolving programme is envisaged depending upon the goodwill and resources of states rather than an immediate binding legal obligation with regard to the rights in question. The rights included range from self-determination (article 1), the right to work (articles 6 and 7), the right to social security (article 9), adequate standard of living (article 11) and education (article 13) to the right to take part in cultural life and enjoy the benefits of scientific progress and its applications (article 15).[53]

The International Covenant on Civil and Political Rights [54]

This important Covenant adopted in 1966 entered into force in 1976. By article 2, all states parties undertake to respect and to ensure to all individuals within its territory and subject to its jurisdiction the rights recognised in the Covenant. These rights are clearly intended as binding obligations. They include self-determination (article 1), the right to life (article 6), prohibitions on torture and

---

[51] See further *infra*, p.207 and note the Convention on the Suppression and Punishment of the Crime of Apartheid 1973. See also the Declaration on the Elimination of All Forms of Intolerance and of Discrimination Based on Religion or Belief, 1981, General Assembly resolution 36/55. See e.g. Neff, "An Evolving International Legal Norm of Religious Freedom: Problems and Prospects", 7 *California Western International Law Journal*, 1975, p.543; Krishnaswami, *Study of Discrimination in the Matter of Religious Rights and Practices*, 1960, E/CN.4/Sub.2/200/Rev.1; Lerner, "Towards a Draft Declaration against Religious Intolerance and Discrimination", 11 *Israel Yearbook on Human Rights*, 1981, p.82 and Odio Benito, *Elimination of All Forms of Intolerance and Discrimination based on Religion or Belief*, 1989. See also the Convention on the Elimination of All Forms of Discrimination against Women 1979, *infra*, p.213.

[52] As of 1 March 1990, it had 95 ratifications; ST/HR/5, 1990.

[53] As to the implementation system, see *infra*, p.203.

[54] *The International Bill of Rights* (ed. Henkin), 1981. As of 1 March 1990, there have been 90 ratifications; ST/HR/5, 1990.

slavery (articles 7 and 8), the right to liberty and security of the person (article 9), due process (article 14), freedom of thought, conscience and religion (article 18), freedom of association (article 22) and the right of minorities to enjoy their own culture (article 27). A Human Rights Committee was established under Part IV of the Covenant.[55]

The Convention against Torture and Other Cruel, Inhuman or Degrading Treatment or Punishment [56]

This Convention was signed on 10 December 1984 and entered into force in 1987. It built particularly upon the Declaration on the Protection of All Persons from being subjected to Torture and Other Cruel, Inhuman and Degrading Treatment or Punishment adopted by the General Assembly in 1975. Other relevant instruments preceding the Convention were the Standard Minimum Rules for the Treatment of Prisoners, 1955; the Code of Conduct for Law Enforcement Officers, 1979 (article 5) and The Principles of Medical Ethics, 1982 (Principles 1 and 2).[57]

Torture is defined in article 1 to mean:

> [a]ny act by which severe pain or suffering, whether physical or mental, is intentionally inflicted on a person for such purposes as obtaining from him or a third person information or a confession, punishing him for an act he or a third person has committed or is suspected of having committed, or intimidating or coercing him or a third person, or for any reason based on discrimination of any kind, when such pain or suffering is inflicted by or at the instigation of or with the consent or the acquiescence of a public official or other person acting in an official capacity. It does not include pain or suffering arising only from, inherent in or incidental to lawful sanctions.

The states parties to the Convention are under duties *inter alia* to take measures to prevent such activities in territories under their jurisdiction (article 2), not to return a person to a country where he may be subjected to torture (article 3), to make torture a criminal

---

[55] See *infra*, p.208. Note the Second Optional Protocol aiming at the abolition of the death penalty 1989, came into force July 1991.

[56] As of 1 March 1990, it had 51 ratifications; ST/HR/5, 1990.

[57] Note also the Principles on the Protection of Persons under Detention or Imprisonment adopted by the General Assembly in 1989.

offence and establish jurisdiction over it (articles 4 and 5),[58] to prosecute or extradite persons charged with torture (article 7) and to provide a remedy for persons tortured (article 14). A Committee against Torture was provided for in Part II of the Convention.[59]

It should also be noted that in 1985, the United Nations Commission on Human Rights appointed a Special Rapporteur on Torture to examine questions relevant to torture and to seek and receive credible and reliable information on such questions and to respond to that information without delay.[60] The work of the rapporteur includes the sending of urgent appeals and country visits. He is directed to co-operate closely with the Committee against Torture.[61]

The Convention on the Rights of the Child

This Convention was adopted by the General Assembly on 20 November 1989.[62] It provides that in all actions concerning children, the best interests of the child shall be a primary consideration. A variety of rights are stipulated including the inherent right to life (article 6); the right to a name and to acquire a nationality (article 7); the right to freedom of expression (article 13); the right to freedom of thought, conscience and religion (article 14); the right not to be subjected to arbitrary or unlawful interference with privacy, family, home or correspondence and the right to the enjoyment of the highest attainable standard of health (article 24).

The states parties agreed to take all appropriate measures to protect the child from all forms of physical and mental violence (article 19) and from economic exploitation (article 32) and the illicit use of drugs (article 33) and there are specific provisions relating to refugees and handicapped children. In addition, states parties agreed to respect the rules of international humanitarian law applicable to armed conflicts relevant to children. This provision was one response to the use of children in the Iran-Iraq war. A Committee was set up to oversee the application of the Convention.[63]

[58] See as far as the UK is concerned sections 134 and 135 of the Criminal Justice Act 1988.
[59] *Infra*, p.214.
[60] Resolution 1985/33.
[61] See e.g. Zoller, "46th Session of the United Nations Commission on Human Rights", 8(2) *NQHR*, 1990, pp.140, 166.
[62] The Convention came into force on 2 September 1990.
[63] *Infra*, p.215.

As can be seen, the United Nations system has successfully generated a wide-ranging series of international instruments dealing with the establishment of standards and norms in the human rights field.[64] The question of implementation will now be addressed.

THE UNITED NATIONS SYSTEM — IMPLEMENTATION [65]

The General Assembly has power under article 13 of the Charter to initiate studies and make recommendations regarding inter alia human rights. Human rights items on its agenda may originate in Economic and Social Council (ECOSOC) reports or decisions taken by the Assembly at earlier sessions to consider particular matters, or are proposed for inclusion by the UN organs, the Secretary-General or member-states. Most items on human rights go to the Assembly's Third Committee (Social, Humanitarian and Cultural Committee), but others may be referred to other committees such as the Sixth Committee (Legal) or the First Committee (Political and Security) or the Special Political Committee. The Assembly has also established subsidiary organs under Rule 161, several of which deal with human rights issues, such as the Special Committee on Decolonisation, the UN Council for Namibia, the Special Committee against Apartheid, the Special Committee to Investigate Israeli Practices in the Occupied Territories and the Committee on the Exercise of the Inalienable Rights of the Palestine People.[66] ECOSOC may under article 62 of the Charter make recommendations on human rights, draft conventions for the Assembly and call

---

[64] See also e.g. the Slavery Convention 1926 and Protocol, 1953; the Supplementary Convention on the Abolition of Slavery, the Slave Trade and Institutions and Practices Similar to Slavery 1956; the Convention for the Suppression of the Traffic in Persons and of the Exploitation of the Prostitution of Others 1949; the Convention on the Status of Refugees, 1951 and Protocol 1967; the Convention relating to the Status of Stateless Persons 1954 and the Convention on the Reduction of Statelessness 1961.

[65] See *United Nations Action in the Field of Human Rights*, 1988; Tardu, *Human Rights: The International Petition System*, 1979; *Human Rights: Thirty Years After the Universal Declaration, op. cit.*; *UN Law/Fundamental Rights*, (ed. Cassese), 1979; Robertson, "The Implementation System: International Measures", in *The International Bill of Rights, op. cit.*, p.332 and Golsong, "Implementation of International Protection of Human Rights", 110 *HR*, p.7. See also Lauterpacht, *op. cit.*, Chapter 11; Ermacora, "Procedure to Deal with Human Rights Violations" 7 *Revue des Droits de l'Homme*, 1974, p.670; Robertson and Merrills, *op. cit.*, and Trindade, "Co-existence and Co-ordination of Mechanisms of International Protection of Human Rights", 202 *HR*, 1987, p.9.

[66] See *UN Action, op. cit.*, Chapter 1. Note also the relevant roles of the other organs of the UN, the Security Council, Trusteeship Council, International Court and Secretariat, *ibid.*

international conferences on human rights matters. It consists of 54 members of the UN elected by the General Assembly and hears annually the reports of a wide range of bodies including the UN High Commissioner for Refugees, the UN Children's Fund, the UN Conference on Trade and Development, the UN Environment Programme and the World Food Council. Of its subsidiary bodies, the Commission on Human Rights and the Commission on the Status of Women have the most direct connection with human rights issues.[67]

Implementing the International Covenant on Economic, Social and Cultural Rights

Under the Covenant itself, states parties were obliged to send periodic reports to ECOSOC (articles 16-25). In 1978, a Sessional Working Group was set up, consisting of 15 members elected by ECOSOC from amongst states parties for three year renewable terms. The Group met annually and reported to the Council.[68] It was not a success, however, and in 1985 it was decided to establish a new committee of 18 members, this time composed of independent experts.[69] Accordingly in 1987 the new Committee on Economic, Social and Cultural Rights commenced operation.[70] But it is to be especially noted that unlike, for example, the Racial Discrimination Committee, the Human Rights Committee and the Torture Committee, the Economic Committee is not autonomous and it is responsible not to the states parties but to a main organ of the United Nations. As will be seen by comparison with the other bodies, the Economic Committee has at its disposal only relatively weak means of implementation.

The Committee hears states' reports, drawing upon a list of questions prepared by its pre-sessional working group, and it also

[67] *Ibid.*, pp.277-79. See also Assembly resolutions 1991B (XVIII) and 2847 (XXVI).

[68] See articles 16-22 of the Covenant; Sieghart, *op. cit.*, pp.427-29 and *UN Chronicle*, July 1982, pp.68-70; see also Ramcharan, "Implementing the International Covenants on Human Rights" in *Human Rights: Thirty Years After the Universal Declaration, op. cit.*, p.159 and Alston, "Out of the Abyss: The Challenge Confronting the New UN Committee on Economic, Social and Cultural Rights", 9 *HRQ*, 1987, p.332.

[69] See ECOSOC resolution 1985/17.

[70] See Alson and Simma, "First Session of the UN Committee on Economic, Social and Cultural Rights", 81 *AJIL*, 1987, p.747 and "Second Session of the UN Committee on Economic, Social and Cultural Rights", 82 *AJIL*, 1988, p.603.

prepares "General Comments", the second of which on international technical assistance measures was adopted at its fourth session in 1990. The Committee also holds general discussions on particular rights.[71] It cannot hear individual petitions, nor has it an inter-state complaints competence.

The Commission on Human Rights [72]

This was established in 1946 as a subsidiary organ of ECOSOC with extensive terms of reference, including making studies, preparing recommendations and drafting international instruments on human rights. It consists of 43 representatives of member-states of the UN selected by ECOSOC on the basis of equitable geographic distribution.[73] For its first twenty years, it took the view that it had no power to take any action with regard to complaints concerning human rights violations, despite receiving many via the Secretary-General.[74] However, in 1967, ECOSOC resolution 1235 (XLII) authorised the Commission and its Sub-Commission on Prevention of Discrimination and Protection of Minorities to examine information relevant to gross violations of human rights contained in communications and to study such situations as revealed a consistent pattern of violations with a view to making recommendations to ECOSOC.[75] The situations in question referred primarily to Southern Africa. In 1967, also, the Commission set up an *ad hoc* working group of experts on South Africa and has since established working groups on Chile; Situations revealing a Consistent Pattern of Gross Violations on Human Rights; Disappearances and the Right to Development. Special Rapporteurs have also been appointed to deal with summary executions, torture, mercenaries and religious intolerance.

---

[71] See Dommen, "Building from a Solid Basis: The Fourth Session of the Committee of Economic, Social and Cultural Rights", 8(2) *NQHR,* 1990, p.199.

[72] See e.g. Lauterpacht, *op. cit.,* Chapter 11; Buergenthal and Torney, *International Human Rights and International Education,* 1976, p.75 *et seq.* and Sieghart, *op. cit.,* p.423. See also *UN Action, op. cit.,* p.15 and Tolley, "The Concealed Crack in the Citadel", 6 *HRQ,* 1984, p.420. A Commission on the Status of Women was also created, see *ibid.,* pp.19-20.

[73] See ECOSOC resolutions 6(1), 1946; 9(II), 1946; 845 (XXXII), 1961; 1147(XLI), 1966 and 1979/36, 1979. Note that as from 1992, it is planned to increase the number to 53, the extra representatives coming from Third World states; see CCPR/C/SR.1009, p.4.

[74] See e.g. Report of the First Session of the Commission, E/259, para.22.

[75] See Tolley, *op. cit.,* p.421 *et seq.* and ECOSOC resolution 728F.

A series of informal working groups have also been created to prepare drafts of international instruments, such as the Declaration on Religious Intolerance, the Convention against Torture and proposed instruments on minority rights and the rights of the child.[76] The Commission has also established a Group of Three pursuant to article IX of the Apartheid Convention to consider states' reports under that Convention while a variety of country rapporteurs have been appointed, e.g. regarding Iran, Haiti, Romania and El Salvador.[77] In 1970 a new procedure for dealing with human rights complaints was introduced in ECOSOC resolution 1503 (XLVIII). By virtue of this resolution, a working group of not more than five members was set up by the Sub-Commission to meet to consider communications and government replies and to pass on to the Sub-Commission those communications together with replies of governments that appeared to reveal "a consistent pattern of gross and reliably attested violations of human rights". The Sub-Commission would at that stage consider such material and refer to the Commission those situations appearing to reveal the necessary consistent pattern of gross and reliably attested violations of human rights. The Commission, in its turn, under resolution 1503 is empowered to study such situations and make recommendations to ECOSOC and if it so decides to establish an *ad hoc* committee of investigation with the express consent of the government concerned.[78] The procedure, it is fair to say, which is confidential until the final stage, has not fulfilled the initial high expectations. The confidentiality requirement and the highly political nature of the Commission itself have combined to frustrate hopes that had been raised.[79]

Nevertheless, many human rights issues are discussed publicly at

---

[76] See e.g. *UN Action, op. cit.*, pp.15-18 and Report on the Fortieth Session of the Commission on Human Rights, E/CN.4/1984/77. See *supra*, p.201 on the 1989 Convention on the Rights of the Child.

[77] See also E/CN.4/1286.

[78] See also Sub-Committee resolution 1(XXIV), 1971.

[79] See e.g. Van Boven, "Human Rights Fora at the United Nations", in *International Human Rights Law and Practice* (ed. Tuttle), 1978, p.83; Möller, "Petitioning the United Nations", 1 *Universal Human Rights*, 1979, p.57; Rodley, "Monitoring Human Rights by the UN System and Non-governmental Organisations" in *Human Rights and American Foreign Policy, op. cit.*, p.157 and Tolley, *op. cit.*, p.429 *et seq.* Note that the Commission chairman now announces the names of the countries subject to complaints under resolution 1503, although no further details are disclosed: see e.g. E/CN.4/1984/77, p.151, naming Albania, Argentina, Benin, Haiti, Indonesia, Malaysia, Pakistan, Paraguay, the Philippines, Turkey and Uruguay.

sessions of the Commission and numerous resolutions are adopted,[80] although one cannot ignore the strong political currents that often prevent or mitigate criticism of particular states.[81] The events in Eastern Europe in 1989-90 led to an interesting change in the 1990 session of the Commission in that the earlier East-West axis of confrontation disappeared as the newly democratised states supported in the main western positions criticising human rights violations. It was replaced by a growing North-South friction and this reflects an unfortunate trend.

The Sub-Commission on Prevention of Discrimination and Protection of Minorities [82]

The Sub-Commission was established by the Commission in 1947 with wide terms of reference.[83] It is composed of 26 members elected by the Commission on the basis of nominations of experts made by the UN member-states. Members serve in their individual capacity for three year terms and the composition must reflect an agreed geographical pattern.[84] The Sub-Commission produces a variety of studies by rapporteurs[85] and has established a number of subsidiary bodies. The Working Group on Communications functions within the framework of the resolution 1503 procedure noted above, while the Working Groups on Slavery[86] and on Indigenous Populations[87] prepare material within the areas of their concern.[88]

---

[80] See generally, E/CN.4/1984/77 regarding the Commission's Fortieth Session.

[81] See e.g. the inability of the Commission in 1990 even to discuss draft resolutions relating to China and Iraq: Zoller, *op. cit.,* p.142.

[82] See e.g. Tolley, *op. cit.,* p.437 *et seq.*; Gardeniers, Hannum and Kruger, "The UN Sub-Committee on Prevention of Discrimination and Protection of Minorities: Recent Developments", 4 *HRQ,* 1982, p.353 and Garber and O'Conner, "The 1984 UN Sub-Commission on Prevention of Discrimination and Protection of Minorities", 79 *AJIL,* 1985, p.168. See also *UN Action, op. cit.,* pp.18-19. A Sub-Commission on Freedom of Information of the Press was discontinued in 1952, *ibid.,* p.18.

[83] See e.g. *UN Action, op. cit.,* p.18. See also resolutions E/259, 1947; E/1371, 1949, and 17 (XXXVII), 1981.

[84] See ECOSOC resolution 1334 (XLIV), 1968, and decision 1978/21, 1778.

[85] See e.g. the Capotorti Study, *supra* footnote 32 and the Ruhashyankiko Study, *supra* footnote 46. See also the Daes Study on the *Individual's Duties to the Community,* E/CN.4/Sub.2/432/Rev.2, 1983 and the Questiaux Study on *States of Emergency,* E/CN.4/Sub.2/1982/15, 1982.

[86] See resolution 11 (XXVII), 1974.

[87] See resolution 2 (XXXIV), 1981. See also E/CN.4/Sub.2/1982/33.

[88] The Sub-Commission has also established a practice of establishing sessional working groups in recent years: see *UN Action, op. cit.,* pp.18-19.

The Committee on the Elimination of Racial Discrimination [89]

Under Part II of the Convention on the Elimination of All Forms of Racial Discrimination, 1965, a Committee of eighteen experts was established consisting of persons serving in their personal capacity and elected by the states parties to the Convention. States parties undertook to submit reports every two years regarding measures adopted to give effect to the provisions of the Convention to the Committee, which itself would report annually through the UN Secretary-General to the General Assembly. The Committee may make suggestions and general recommendations based on the examination of the reports and information received from the states parties, which are reported to the General Assembly together with any comments from states parties.[90] Under article 11, one state party may bring a complaint against another state party and the Committee will seek to resolve the complaint. Should the matter not be so settled, either party may refer it back to the Committee and by article 12 an *ad hoc* Conciliation Commission may be established, which will report back to the Committee with any recommendation thought proper for the amicable solution of the dispute.[91] In addition to hearing states' reports and inter-state complaints, the Committee may hear also individual petitions under the article 14 procedure. This, however, is subject to the state complained of having made a declaration recognising the competence of the Committee to receive and consider such communications. If such a declaration has not been notified by a state, therefore, the Committee has no authority to hear a petition against the state. Indeed, article 14 as a whole would only come into effect when at least ten states had made such declarations.[92] The

[89] See Lerner, *op. cit.* and "Curbing Racial Discrimination — Fifteen Years Cerd", 13 *Israel Yearbook on Human Rights*, 1983, p.170; Burrowes, "Implementing the UN Racial Convention — Some Procedural Aspects", 7 *Australian Yearbook of International Law*, p.236 and Buergenthal, "Implementing the UN Racial Convention", 12 *Texas International Law Journal*, 1977, p.187.

[90] Articles 8 and 9 of the Convention.

[91] Article 13.

[92] The provision entered into force on 31 December 1982 upon the tenth declaration. As of 1 March 1990, fourteen states had made the necessary declarations (Algeria, Costa Rica, Denmark, Ecuador, France, Hungary, Iceland, Italy, Netherlands, Norway, Peru, Sweden, Senegal and Uruguay); ST/HR/5, 1990. The Committee has been formulating rules of procedure for article 14 petitions. See e.g. Report of the Committee, A/38/18, p.7 *et seq.* and p.138 *et seq.* See also *ibid.*, A/44/18, p.84 *et seq.*

Committee regularly meets twice a year and has interpreted articles of the Convention, discussed reports submitted to it, adopted decisions and recommendations, obtained further information from states parties and co-operated closely with the International Labour Organisation and UNESCO. Many states have enacted legislation as a consequence of the work of the Committee and its record of impartiality is very good.[93] The Committee also receives copies of petitions and reports sent to UN bodies dealing with trust and non-self-governing territories in the general area of Convention matters and may make comments upon them.[94] The general article 9 reporting system appears to work well, with large numbers of reports submitted and examined, but some states have proved tardy in fulfilling their obligations.[95] The Committee has published guidelines for states parties as to the structure of their reports.[96]

The Committee, in order to speed up consideration of states' reports, has instituted the practice of appointing country rapporteurs, whose function it is to prepare analyses of reports of states parties.[97] The Committee has also called for additional technical assistance to be provided by the UN to help in the reporting process, while it has expressed serious concern that financial difficulties are beginning to affect its functioning.[98]

The Human Rights Committee [99]

This Committee was established under Part IV of the International Covenant on Civil and Political Rights. It consists of eighteen independent and expert members, elected by the states parties to

---

[93] See e.g. Lerner, *op. cit.* footnote 89. Note that the Committee is not a subsidiary body of the UN, it (like for example the Human Rights Committee, *infra*), is an autonomous body established under a convention adopted by the UN. It also has close links with the UN bureaucracy and reports to the Assembly. It is often termed a "treaty organ of the UN".

[94] Article 15.

[95] See e.g. A/38/18, pp.14-24. Note, for example, that by late 1983 fifteen reminders had been sent to Swaziland requesting it to submit its fourth, fifth, sixth and seventh overdue periodic reports, *ibid.*, p.21. See also A/44/18, pp.10-16.

[96] See CERD/C/70/Rev.1, 6 December 1983.

[97] See e.g. A/44/18, 1990, p.7.

[98] *Ibid.*, p.91.

[99] See e.g. Robertson, *op. cit.*; Fischer, "Reporting under the Convention on Civil and Political Rights: the First Five Years of the Human Rights Committee", 76 *AJIL*, 1982, p.142; Ramcharan, "Implementing the International Covenants on Human Rights", *op. cit.*; Schwelb, "The International Measures of Implementation of the International Covenant on Civil and

the Covenant for four year terms, with consideration given to the need for equitable geographical distribution and representation of the different forms of civilisation and of the principal legal systems.[100] The Committee meets three times a year. The Covenant is primarily implemented by means of a reporting system, whereby states parties provide information on the measures adopted to give effect to the rights recognised in the Covenant. Initial reports are made within one year of the entry into force of the Covenant for the state in question and general guidelines have been issued.[101] The Committee has decided that subsequent reports would be required every five years,[102] and the first of the second periodic reports was due in 1983. The reports are discussed by the Committee with representatives of the state concerned (following upon the precedent established by the Committee on the Elimination of Racial Discrimination).[103] The Committee members informally receive information from sources other than the reporting state and the practice would appear to be that this is acceptable provided the source is not publicly identified. This enables the Committee to be more effective than would otherwise be the case.[104] Under article 40(4), the Committee is empowered to make such "general comments as it may deem appropriate". After some discussion, a consensus was adopted in 1980, which permitted such comments provided that they promoted co-operation between states in the implementation of the Covenant, summarised the experience of the Committee in examining states' reports and drew the attention of states parties to matters

---

Political Rights and of the Optional Protocol", 12 *Texas International Law Review*, 1977, p.141; Nowak, "The Effectiveness of the International Covenant on Civil and Political Rights — Stock-taking after the First Eleven Sessions of the UN Human Rights Committee", 2 *HRLJ*, 1981, p.168 and 5 *HRLJ*, 1984, p.199. See also Jhabvala, "The Practice of the Covenant's Human Rights Committee, 1976-82: Review of State Party Reports", 6 *HRQ*, 1984, p.81; Ghandhi, "The Human Rights Committee and the Right of Individual Communication", 57 *BYIL*, 1986, p.201 and McGoldrick, *The Human Rights Committee*, 1991.

[100] See articles 28-32 of the Covenant.

[101] See article 40 and CCPR/C/5. Supplementary reports may be requested, see Rule 70(2) of the provisional rules of procedure, CCPR/C/3/Rev.1.

[102] See CCPR/C/18; CCPR/C/19 and CCPR/C/19/Rev.1. See also CCPR/C/20 regarding guidelines. Several states have been lax about producing reports, e.g. Zaire and the Dominican Republic, while the initial report of Guinea was so short as to be held by the Committee as not providing sufficient information: see Nowak, 1984, *op. cit.*, p.200.

[103] See Buergenthal, *op. cit.*, pp.199-201, and Fischer, *op. cit.*, p.145.

[104] *Ibid.*, pp.146-47.

relating to the improvement of the reporting procedure and the implementation of the Covenant. The aim of the Committee was to engage in a constructive dialogue with each reporting state, and the comments would be non-country-specific.[105] A variety of comments have now been adopted by the Committee, which proceeds by way of consensus.[106] These comments are generally non-controversial. One interesting comment on article 6 (the right to life), however, emphasised the Committee's view that:

> the designing, testing, manufacture, possession and development of nuclear weapons are among the greatest threats to the right to life

and that the

> production, testing, possession and deployment and use of nuclear weapons should be prohibited and recognised as crimes against humanity.[107]

In April 1989, the Committee adopted a General Comment on the rights of the child, as the process of adopting the Convention on the Rights of the Child neared its climax. It noted the importance of economic, social and cultural measures, such as the need to reduce infant mortality and prevent exploitation. Freedom of expression was referred to, as was the requirement that children be protected against discrimination on grounds such as race, sex, religion, national or social origin, property or birth. Responsibility for guaranteeing the necessary protection lies, it was stressed, with the family, society and the state, although primarily incumbent upon the family. Special attention needed to be paid to the right of every child to acquire a nationality.[108] In November 1989, an important General Comment was adopted on non-discrimination. Discrimination was to be understood to imply for the purposes of the Covenant:

---

[105] CCPR/C/18.
[106] See e.g. Nowak, 1981, *op. cit.*, p.169; 3 *HRLJ*, 1982, p.209 and 1984, *op. cit.*, p.202. See also A/36/40, annex VII, Introduction; CCPR/C/21/Rev.1 and A/44/40, p.173.
[107] CCPR/C/21/Add.4, 14 November 1984.
[108] A/44/40, pp.173-75.

any distinction, exclusion, restriction or preference which is based on any ground such as race, colour, sex, language, religion, political or other opinion, national or social origin, property, birth or other status, and which has the purpose or effect of nullifying or impairing the recognition, enjoyment or exercise by all persons, on an equal footing, of all rights and freedoms.[109]

Identical treatment in every instance was not, however, demanded. The death sentence could not, under article 6(5) of the Covenant, be imposed on persons under the age of 18 or upon pregnant women. It was also noted that the principle of equality sometimes requires states parties to take affirmative action in order to diminish or eliminate conditions which cause or help to perpetuate discrimination prohibited by the Covenant. In addition, it was pointed out that not every differentiation constituted discrimination, if the criteria for such differentiation were reasonable and objective and if the aim was to achieve a purpose which was legitimate under the Covenant.[110]

Under article 41 of the Covenant, states parties may recognise the competence of the Committee to hear inter-state complaints. Both the complainant and object state must have made such declarations. The Committee will seek to resolve the issue and, if it is not successful, it may under article 42 appoint, with the consent of the parties, an *ad hoc* Conciliation Commission.[111]

The powers of the Human Rights Committee were extended by the Optional Protocol to the Civil and Political Rights Covenant with regard to ratifying states to include the competence to receive and consider individual communications, alleging violations of the Covenant by a state party to the Protocol.[112] The individual must have exhausted all available domestic remedies (unless unreasonably prolonged) and the same matter must not be in the process of

[109] CCPR/C/21/Rev.1/Add.1, p.3.

[110] *Ibid.*, p.4.

[111] As of 1 March 1990, twenty-six states had made such declarations; see ST/HR/5, 1990. The inter-state procedure has not been used to date.

[112] Signed in 1966 and in force as from 23 March 1976. As of 1 March 1990, forty-nine states had ratified the Optional Protocol; see ST/HR/5, 1990. See also de Zayas, Möller and Opsahl, "Application of the International Covenant on Civil and Political Rights under the Optional Protocol by the Human Rights Committee", 28 *German Yearbook of International Law*, 1985, p.9 and *Selected Decisions of the Human Rights Committee under the Optional Protocol*, vol.1, 1985 and vol.2, 1990.

examination under another international procedure.[113] The procedure under the Optional Protocol is divided into several stages. The gathering of basic information is done by the Secretary-General and laid before the Working Group on Communications of the Committee, which recommends whether, for example, further information is required from the applicant or the relevant state party and whether the communication should be declared inadmissible. The procedure before the Committee itself is divided into an admissibility and a merits stage. Interim decisions may be made by the Committee and ultimately a "final view" communicated to the parties.[114]

An increasing workload, however, began to cause difficulties as the number of parties to the Optional Protocol increased. By September 1989, 391 communications had been placed before the Committee, of which 98 were still pending at the pre-admissibility stage. Accordingly, the Committee felt the need to devise new methods of expediting its operations in this area. It was decided to appoint a Special Rapporteur for one year (which has been annually renewed) to process new communications as they were received (i.e. between sessions of the Committee) and this included requesting the state or individual concerned to provide additional written information or observations relevant to the question of the admissibility of the communication.[115] The Committee has also authorised its five member Working Group on Communications to adopt a decision declaring a communication admissible, providing there is unanimity.[116]

The Committee, however, is not a court with the power of binding decision on the merits of cases. Indeed, in instances of non-compliance with its final views, the Optional Protocol does not provide for an enforcement mechanism, nor indeed for sanctions.[117]

A variety of interesting decisions have so far been rendered. The first group of cases concerned complaints against Uruguay, in which the Committee found violations by that state of rights recognised

[113] Article 5, Optional Protocol.
[114] See Nowak, 1980, *op. cit.*, p.153 *et seq.* and 1981 Report of Human Rights Committee, A/36/40, pp.85-91.
[115] A/44/40, pp.139-40. See also rule 91 of the amended rules of procedure, *ibid.*, p.180.
[116] *Ibid.*, p.140.
[117] Note that in October 1990, the Committee appointed a Special Rapporteur to follow up cases, CCPR/C/SR.1002, p.8.

in the Covenant.[118] In the *Lovelace* case,[119] the Committee found Canada in breach of article 27 of the Covenant protecting the rights of minorities since its law provided that an Indian woman, whose marriage to a non-Indian had broken down, was not permitted to return to her home on an Indian reservation, and in the *Mauritian Women* case[120] a breach of Covenant rights was upheld where the foreign husbands of Mauritian women were liable to deportation whereas the foreign wives of Mauritian men would not have been. The Committee has also held that the Covenant's obligations cover the decisions of diplomatic authorities of a state party regarding citizens living abroad.[121] In the *Robinson* case,[122] the Committee considered whether a state was under an obligation itself to make provision for effective representation by counsel in a case concerning a capital offence, in circumstances where the counsel appointed by the author of the communication declines to appear. The Committee emphasised that it was axiomatic that legal assistance be available in capital cases and decided that the absence of counsel constituted unfair trial. The issue faced in the *Vuolanne* case[123] was whether the procedural safeguards in article 9(4) of the Covenant on Civil and Political Rights, whereby a person deprived of his liberty is to be allowed recourse to the courts, applied to military disciplinary detention. The Committee was very clear that it did.

It is already apparent that the Committee has proved a success and is performing a very important role in the field of human rights protection.

The Committee on the Elimination of All Forms of Discrimination Against Women

This Committee was established under article 22 of the 1979 Convention on the Elimination of all Forms of Discrimination

[118] These cases are reported in 1 *HRLJ*, 1980, p.209 *et seq*. See for other cases, 2 *HRLJ*, 1981, p.130 *et seq*.; *ibid.*, p.340 *et seq*.; 3 *HRLJ*, 1982, p.188; 4 *HRLJ*, 1983, p.185 *et seq*. and 5 *HRLJ*, 1984, p.191 *et seq*. See also Annual Reports of the Human Rights Committee, 1981-to date.
[119] 1981 Report of the Human Rights Committee, A/36/40, p.166.
[120] *Ibid.*, p.134.
[121] See e.g. the *Waksman* case, 1 *HRLJ*, 1980, p.220 and the *Lichtensztejn* case, 5 *HRLJ*, 1984, p.207.
[122] A/44/40, p.241 (1989).
[123] *Ibid.*, p.249.

Against Women,[124] which is implemented by means of states' reports. It is composed of 23 experts serving in individual capacities for four year terms. It held its first regular session in October 1982 and at its second session examined the reports of seven states parties regarding measures taken to comply with the terms of the Convention. It reports annually to the UN General Assembly through ECOSOC.[125]

The Committee in addition to hearing states' reports may make suggestions and general recommendations, which are included in the report. For example, General Recommendation 8 provided that states parties should take further measures to ensure to women, on equal terms with men and without discrimination, the opportunity to represent their government at the international level.[126] The Committee, however, meets only for two weeks a year, which is clearly inadequate. There is no right of individual petition or inter-state complaint under this Convention.

The Committee against Torture

This Committee was established under Part II of the Convention against Torture 1984 and commenced work in 1987. It consists of ten independent experts. In an interesting comment on the proliferation of international human rights committees and the dangers of inconsistencies developing, article 17(2) provides that in nominating experts, states parties should "bear in mind the usefulness of nominating persons who are also members of the Human Rights Committee".

The Committee receives states' reports (article 19), has an interstate complaint competence (article 21) and may hear individual communications (article 22). In both the latter cases, it is necessary that the state or states concerned should have made a declaration accepting the competence of the Committee. Article 20 of the Convention provides that if the Committee receives "reliable

---

[124] This came into force in 1981 and as of 1 March 1990 had 102 ratifications; see ST/HR/5, 1990.

[125] See articles 17-21 of the Convention and the first Report of the Committee, A/38/45 and *UN Chronicle,* November 1983, pp.65-86. See also Galey, "International Enforcement of Women's Rights", 6 *HRQ,* 1984, p.463 and Wadstein, "Implementation of the UN Convention on the Elimination of All Forms of Discrimination against Women", 6 *NQHR,* 1988, p.5.

[126] A/43/38 (1988).

evidence" that torture is being systematically practised in the territory of a state party, it may invite the state in question to co-operate in examining the evidence. The Committee may designate one or more of its members to make a confidential inquiry. In doing so, it shall seek the co-operation of the state concerned and with the latter's agreement, such an inquiry may include a visit to its territory. The Committee will transmit the findings of the inquiry to the state, together with appropriate comments or suggestions. The proceedings up to this point are to be confidential, but the Committee may after consulting the state decide to include a summary account of the results in its annual report.

This additional, if cautiously phrased, power may provide the Committee with a significant role. It remains to be seen whether this will happen.[127] The first three cases before the Committee were admissibility decisions concerning Argentinian legislation exempting junior military officers from liability for acts of torture committed during the 1976-83 period and its compatibility with the Torture Convention.[128] The Committee noted that there existed a general rule of international law obliging all states to take effective measures to prevent and punish acts of torture. However, the Convention took effect only from its date of entry (26 June 1987) and could not be applied retroactively to cover the enactment of legislation prior to that date. Therefore, the communications were inadmissible. However, the Committee did criticise the Argentinian legislation and stated that Argentina was morally bound to provide a remedy to the victims of torture.

The Committee on the Rights of the Child

Article 43 of the Convention on the Rights of the Child 1989 provides for the establishment of a Committee. This Committee, to be composed of ten independent experts, will have the competence to hear states' reports and will itself submit reports every two years to the General Assembly through ECOSOC (article 44). The Committee will also be able to recommend to the General

---

[127] See Zoller, "Second Session of the UN Commission against Torture", 7 *NQHR*, 1989, p.250.

[128] *O.R., M.M. and M.S.* v. *Argentina*, communications nos. 1-3/1988. Decisions of 23 November 1989. See 5 *Interights Bulletin*, 1990, p.12.

Assembly that the Secretary-General be requested to undertake on its behalf studies on specific issues relating to the rights of the child and will be able to make suggestions and general recommendations (article 45).

Conclusions

Most international human rights conventions obligate states parties to take certain measures with regard to the provisions contained therein, whether by domestic legislation or otherwise.[129] Several treaties require states parties to make periodic reports.[130] The number of treaties establishing committees specifically to oversee the implementation of particular conventions, however, is not large, while very few provide for the right of individual petition.[131]

It has sometimes been suggested that the committees that do exist should be amalgamated into a "super-committee". The aim of this would be two-fold: first, to save scarce resources, particularly within the hard-pressed UN system, and secondly, in order to minimise inconsistencies developing with regard to similar principles. The former is a worthy aim, but it should not dictate the future of international human rights supervision. The disadvantages of a "super-committee" include the danger of political influence, at present diffused over a range of organs and not particularly apparent in the case of the expert bodies, being sharply focused, and that is a risk that ought not to be taken. It is also true that the range of existing committees includes a wide range of specialisms and it is unlikely that a single committee would possess the skills necessary across the board in order to deal with the conventions in question.

The issue of resources is an important political one to be settled by states and not, one hopes, at the expense of human rights

[129] See e.g. article 2 of the Civil and Political Rights Covenant 1966; article 1 of the European Convention on Human Rights 1950; articles 1 and 2 of the American Convention on Human Rights 1969; article 5 of the Genocide Convention 1948; article 4 of the Convention on the Suppression and Punishment of the Crime of Apartheid 1973 and article 3 of the Slavery Convention 1926.

[130] See in addition to the conventions mentioned *supra*, article 7 of the Apartheid Convention 1973 and article 19 of the Convention against Torture 1984, Part II. Several conventions provide for the communication of information e.g. to the UN Secretary-General, see e.g. article 33 of the Convention Relating to the Status of Stateless Persons 1954 and articles 35 and 36 of the Convention Relating to the Status of Refugees 1951.

[131] See generally in addition to the above section, Tardu, *Human Rights: The International Petition System*, 1979.

implementation. The issue of discordant interpretations is one to be tackled seriously by building upon the developing links between the various committees and other relevant bodies.[132]

THE SPECIALISED AGENCIES

The International Labour Organisation [133]

The ILO was created in 1919 and expanded in 1946. The Declaration of Philadelphia of 1944 (which was incorporated in the ILO constitution in 1946) reaffirmed the basic principles of the organisation. These are: (a) that labour is not a commodity, (b) that freedom of expression and of association are essential to sustained progress and (c) that poverty anywhere constitutes a danger to prosperity everywhere. The ILO is composed of a unique tripartite structure involving governments, workers and employers and consists of three organs; a General Conference of representatives of member-states (the International Labour Conference), the Governing Body and the International Labour Office.[134] The ILO constitution enables the organisation to examine and elaborate international labour standards, whether Conventions or Recommendations. The former are the more formal method of dealing with important matters, while the latter consist basically of guidelines for legislation. Between 1919 and 1987, 166 Conventions and 174 Recommendations were adopted by the

---

[132] See e.g. the moves towards the harmonisation and consolidation of guidelines for states parties reports for the treaty bodies, following the recommendation adopted by the second meeting of persons chairing human rights treaty bodies, A/44/98, para. 79 and A/44/40, pp.117-78.

[133] See e.g. Jenks, "Human Rights, Social Justice and Peace", in the *International Protection of Human Rights* (eds. Schou and Eide), 1968, p.227, and *Social Justice in the Law of Nations*, 1970; Landy, *The Effectiveness of International Supervision: Thirty Years of ILO Experience*, 1966; Valticos, "The Role of the ILO: Present Action and Future Perspectives" in *Human Rights: Thirty Years After the Universal Declaration, op. cit.*, p.211, and "The International Labour Organisation", *The International Dimensions of Human Rights* (ed. Vasak), vol.1, 1982, p.363; Landy, "The Implementation Procedures of the International Labour Organisation", 20 *Santa Clara Law Review*, 1980, p.633; Wolf, "ILO Experience in Implementation of Human Rights", 10 *Journal of International Law and Economics*, 1975, p.599; Servais, "ILO Standards on Freedom of Association and Their Implementation", 123 *International Labour Review*, 1984, p.765; Valticos, *International Labour Law*, 1979 and Robertson and Merrills, *op. cit.*, p.236.

[134] See *UN Action, op. cit.*, pp.27-28. The tripartite structure means that the delegation of each member-state to the International Labour Conference includes two representatives of the government, one representative of workers and one representative of the employers.

ILO, all dealing basically with issues of social justice.[135] Under article 19 of the ILO constitution all members must submit Conventions and Recommendations to their competent national authorities within twelve to eighteen months of adoption. Under article 22, states which have ratified Conventions are obligated to make annual reports on measures taken to give effect to them to the International Labour Office,[136] while under article 19 members must also submit reports regarding both unratified Conventions and Recommendations. In 1926-7, a Committee of Experts on the Application of Conventions and Recommendations was established to consider reports submitted by member-states. The comments of the 20 member Committee, appointed by the Governing Body on the suggestion of the Director-General of the International Labour Office, on ratified Conventions take the form of "observations" included in the printed report of the Committee in the case of more important issues, or "requests" to the government concerned for information, which are not published in the report of the Committee. In the case of unratified Conventions and Recommendations a "general survey" of the application of the particular instrument in question is carried out.[137] A Committee on the Application of Conventions and Recommendations of the International Labour Conference is appointed at each of its annual sessions composed of tripartite representatives to discuss relevant issues based primarily upon the general report of the Committee of Experts. It may also draw up a "Special List" of cases to be drawn to the attention of the Conference.

Two types of procedure exist. Under articles 24 and 25, a representation may be made by employers' or workers' organisations to the Office to the effect that any of the members have failed to secure the effective observation of any Convention to which it is a party. These views are examined first by a committee of three of the Governing Body then by the Governing Body itself. States are invited to reply and both the original representation and the reply (if any) may be publicised by the Governing Body. There have not

---

[135] See Valticos, "The International Labour Organisation", *op. cit.*, p.365, and *UN Action, op. cit.*, p.326.

[136] However, in practice the annual rule is relaxed, see Valticos, *op. cit.*, p.368. Governments are obliged by article 23(2) to communicate copies of the reports to employers' and workers' organisations.

[137] *Ibid.*, pp.369-70 and Wolf, *op. cit.*, pp.608-10.

been many representations of this kind.[138] Under articles 26-29 and 31-33 any member may file a complaint against another member-state that the effective observance of a ratified Convention has not been secured. The Governing Body may call for a reply by the object state or establish a commission of inquiry. Such a commission is normally composed of three experts and the procedure adopted is of a judicial nature. Recourse may be had by the parties to the International Court of Justice. Ultimately the Governing Body may recommend to the Conference such action as it considers wise and expedient. The complaints procedure was first used by Ghana against Portugal regarding the Abolition of Forced Labour Convention 1957 in its African territories.[139]

A special procedure regarding freedom of association was established in 1951, with a Committee on Freedom of Association which examines a wide range of complaints. It consists of nine members (three from each of the tripartite elements in the ILO). The Committee submits detailed reports to the Governing Body with proposed conclusions and suggested recommendations to be made to the state concerned, and a considerable case-law has been build up.[140] A Fact-finding and Conciliation Commission has been created for more serious and politically delicate cases and operates with the consent of the state concerned. Accordingly, few questions have been dealt with.[141]

The United Nations Educational, Scientific and Cultural Organisation [142]

The constitution of UNESCO of 1945 is based on that of the ILO in the area of the implementation of the Conventions and

[138] But see e.g. Official Bulletin of the ILO, 1956, p.120 (Netherlands Antilles); *ibid.*, 1967, p.267 (Brazil) and *ibid.*, 1972, p.125 (Italy). See also *ibid.*, 1978, (Czechoslovakia).

[139] See Official Bulletin of the ILO, 1962; *ibid.*, 1963 (Liberia) and *ibid.*, 1971 (Greece).

[140] See e.g. Von Potobsky, "Protection of Trade Union Rights: Twenty Years Work of the Committee on Freedom of Association", 105 *International Labour Review*, 1972, p.69. Over 1,000 cases have been referred to the Committee, see Valticos, *op. cit.* footnote 135, p.383. See also Servais, *op. cit.* and *Freedom of Association: Digest of Decisions of the Freedom of Association Committee of the Governing Body of the ILO*, 3rd ed., 1985.

[141] See Valticos, "The International Labour Organisation", *op. cit.*, p.384 *et seq.* See also Official Bulletin of the ILO, 1966 (Japan); and Valticos, "Un Double Type d'Enquête de l'OIT au Chili", *AFDI*, 1975, p.483.

[142] See e.g. Alston, "UNESCO's Procedures for Dealing with Human Rights Violations", 20 *Santa Clara Law Review*, 1980, p.665; Saba, "UNESCO and Human Rights" in *The International Dimensions of Human Rights, op. cit.* vol.2, p.401; Robertson and Merrills, *op. cit.*, p.241 and *UN Action, op. cit.*, pp.331-34.

Recommendations adopted by the General Conference. For example, under article IV(4), member-states undertake to submit Conventions and Resolutions to the competent national authorities within a year of adoption and may be required to submit reports on action taken.[143] However, no complaints procedure was established until much later. In 1962 a Protocol instituting a Conciliation and Good Offices Commission was adopted to help resolve disputes arising between states parties to the 1960 Convention against Discrimination in Education. It entered into force in 1968 and the first meeting of the 11 member Commission was in 1971. It aims to make available its good offices in order to reach a friendly settlement between the states parties to the convention in question. In 1978 the Executive Board of UNESCO adopted decision 104 EX/3.3, by which it established a procedure to handle individual communications alleging violations of human rights. Ten conditions for admissibility are laid down, including the requirement that the human rights violated must fall within UNESCO's competence in the fields of education, science, culture and information, and the need for the communication to be compatible with international human rights interests. The investigating body is the Executive Board's Committee on Conventions and Recommendations, which meets twice a year.[144] It decides whether a communication is admissible and then makes a decision on the merits. The task of the Committee is to reach a "friendly solution designed to advance the promotion of the human rights falling within UNESCO's fields of competence".[145] Confidential reports are submitted to the Executive Board each session, which contain appropriate information plus recommendations.[146] It is also to be noted that under this procedure the Director-General generally has a role in seeking to strengthen the action of UNESCO in promoting human rights and initiating consultations in confidence to help reach solutions to

[143] See for example the 1960 Convention against Discrimination in Education, article 7, see also *UN Action, op. cit.,* p.167.

[144] Formerly the Committee on Conventions and Recommendations in Education, *ibid.,* pp.331-32.

[145] Decision 104.EX/3.3, para. 14(k).

[146] In the April 1980 session, for example, 45 communications were examined as to admissibility, of which 5 were declared inadmissible, 13 admissible, 20 suspended and 7 deleted from the agenda. Ten communications were examined on the merits, UNESCO doc.21 C/13, para. 65.

particular human rights problems.[147] A special procedure to deal with disappeared persons has been established by the Committee. Communications dealing with such persons are placed on a Special List, if insufficient information is forthcoming from the government in question, and examined by the Committee.[148] In addition to *cases* concerning violations of human rights which are individual and specific, UNESCO may also examine *questions* of massive, systematic or flagrant violations of human rights resulting either from a policy contrary to human rights applied by a state or from an accumulation of individual cases forming a consistent pattern.[149] In the instance of such *questions*, the issue is to be discussed by the Executive Board of the General Conference in public.[150]

REGIONAL ORGANISATIONS FOR THE PROTECTION OF HUMAN RIGHTS

A. *Europe*

1. *The European Convention on Human Rights* [151]

The Convention was signed on 4 November 1950 and entered into force in September 1953. Together with eight Protocols, it covers a wide variety of primarily civil and political rights.[152] The preamble notes that the European states are like-minded and have a common heritage of political tradition, ideals, freedoms and the rule of law. The rights covered in the Convention itself include the right to life (article 2), prohibition of torture and slavery (articles 3 and 4), right to liberty and security of person (article 5), right to a fair and public hearing within a reasonable time by an independent and

---

[147] *Ibid.*, paras 8 and 9.
[148] UNESCO doc.108 EX/CR/HR/PROC/2 Rev. (1979)
[149] Decision 104 ex/3.3, para. 10.
[150] *Ibid.*, para. 18.
[151] See e.g. Beddard, *Human Rights and Europe*, 2nd ed., 1980; Castberg, *The European Convention on Human Rights*, 1974; Drzemczewski, *The European Human Rights Convention in Domestic Law*, 1983; Jacobs, *The European Convention on Human Rights*, 1975; Nedjati, *Human Rights Under the European Convention*, 1978; Robertson, *Human Rights in Europe*, 2nd ed.,1977; Fawcett, *The Application of the European Convention on Human Rights*, 2nd ed., 1987 and Van Dijk and Van Hoof, *Theory and Practice of the European Convention on Human Rights*, 1984. See also Merrills, *The Development of International Law by the European Court of Human Rights*, 1988.
[152] Economic and Social rights are covered in the European Social Charter, 1961. See *infra*, p.228.

impartial tribunal established by law (article 6), prohibition of
retroactive criminal legislation (article 7), right to respect for private
and family life (article 8), freedom of thought, conscience and
religion (article 9), freedom of expression (article 10), freedom of
assembly and association (article 11), the right to marry and found
a family (article 12), the right to an effective remedy before a
national authority if one of the Convention rights or freedoms is
violated (article 13) and a non-discrimination provision regarding
the enjoyment of rights and freedoms under the Convention (article
14). In addition, Protocol I protects the rights of property, education
and free elections by secret ballots, Protocol IV prohibits
imprisonment for civil debt and protects *inter alia* the rights of free
movement and choice of residence and the right to enter one's own
country, Protocol VI provides for the abolition of the death penalty,
while Protocol VII provides *inter alia* that an alien lawfully resident
in a state shall not be expelled therefrom except in pursuance of
a decision reached in accordance with the law, that a person
convicted of a criminal offence shall have the right to have that
conviction or sentence reviewed by a higher tribunal and that no
one may be tried or punished again in criminal proceedings for an
offence for which he has already been finally acquitted or convicted.
Like other international treaties, the European Convention imposes
obligations upon states parties. In this instance the Convention
has been incorporated into the domestic legislation of a majority
of the 23 parties in one form or another,[153] although the Convention
does not provide as to how exactly the states parties are to implement
internally the relevant obligations.[154] However, it has been emphasised
that:

> unlike international treaties of the classic kind, the Convention comprises
> more than mere reciprocal engagements between contracting states.
> It creates, over and above a network of mutual and bilateral undertakings,
> objective obligations, which in the words of the preamble, benefit from
> a "collective enforcement".[155]

[153] See Drzemczewski, *op. cit.* The figure is 16 states, see H/Inf(90) 1, p.69. Note that Hungary
signed the Convention in late 1990 as the 24th state party.

[154] See e.g. the *Swedish Engine Drivers' Union* case, Series A, vol.20, 1976, p.18; 58 *ILR*, pp.19,
36. See also the *Belgian Linguistics* case, Series A, vol.6, 1968, p.35; 45 *ILR*, pp.136, 165.

[155] See article 1 and *Ireland* v. *UK*, Series A, vol.25, 1978, pp.90-91; 58 *ILR*, pp.188, 290-
91.

In addition, a more teleological and flexible approach to the interpretation of the Convention has been adopted.[156]

The Commission

The European Commission of Human Rights consists of 23 members (the number of members equal to the parties to the Convention),[157] who are elected by the Committee of Ministers from a list of names drawn up by the Bureau of the Consultative Assembly. They serve for six year terms in their individual capacity.[158] Article 24 provides for the right of inter-state complaint and to date eighteen applications have been lodged with the Commission by states, involving in fact six situations.[159] Only one of these has reached the Court.[160] Article 25 provides for the right of individual petition to the Commission, provided that the state complained against has declared that it recognises the competence of the Commission to receive such petitions.[161] It has proved to be a crucial provision. There is, however, no *actio popularis.* Individuals must claim to be the victim of a violation of one of the Convention rights. However, the Court has emphasised that:

> an individual may, under certain conditions, claim to be the victim of a violation occasioned by the mere existence of secret measures or of legislation permitting secret measures, without having to allege that such measures were in fact applied to him.[162]

It is also to be noted that a near relative of the victim, for example,

---

[156] See e.g. the *Tyrer* case, Series A, vol.26, 1978; 58 *ILR*, p.339, and see also the *Marckx* case, Series A, vol.31, 1979; 58 *ILR*, p.561.

[157] This will rise to 24 once Hungary ratifies the Convention, which it signed in late 1990.

[158] Articles 20-23.

[159] Cyprus case, *(Greece* v. *UK)*, 1956; *Austria* v. *Italy,* 1960; five applications against Greece, 1967-70; *Ireland* v. *UK,* 1971; *Cyprus* v. *Turkey,* 1974-7 and five applications against Turkey, 1982. See also *Stock-taking on the European Convention on Human Rights,* 1982, pp.13-27.

[160] *Ireland* v. *UK,* Series A, vol.25, 1978; 58 *ILR*, p.188.

[161] All the states parties have now made such a declaration.

[162] The *Klass* case, Series A, vol.28, 1979, pp.17-18; 58 *ILR*, pp.423, 442. See also e.g. the *Marckx* case, Series A, vol.31, 1979, pp.12-14; 58 *ILR*, pp.561, 576; the *Dudgeon* case, Series A, vol.45, 1982, p.18; 67 *ILR*, pp.395, 410 and the *Belgian Linguistics* case, Series A, vol.6, 1968; 45 *ILR*, p.136.

could raise an issue where the violation alleged was prejudicial to him or in which he had a valid personal interest.[163]

The Commission may only deal with a matter once all domestic remedies have been exhausted according to the generally accepted rules of international law and within a period of six months from the date on which the final decision was taken. In addition, no petition may be dealt with which is anonymous or is substantially the same as a matter already examined, and any petition which is incompatible with the Convention, manifestly ill-founded or an abuse of the right of petition is to be rendered inadmissible.[164]

Once a petition is accepted, the Commission examines the matter with the parties with a view to achieving a friendly settlement under article 28.[165] In urgent cases, the Commission may give precedence to a particular complaint and may indicate to the parties any interim measure deemed desirable.[166] In considering a friendly settlement, the Commission must also have regard to the general interest as well as the interests of the parties to the dispute.[167] Where a friendly settlement is reached a brief report is sent to the states concerned, the Committee of Ministers and to the Secretary of the Council of Europe.[168] If a solution is not found, a more detailed report is transmitted under article 31 to the Committee of Ministers. One cause for concern has been the very high rate of petitions rendered inadmissible as well as the increasing numbers of applications coming before the Commission.[169] To help deal with this situation, Protocol VIII of March 1985 provides *inter alia* that the Commission may set up Chambers of at least seven members each, which may

[163] See e.g. Application 100/55, *X* v. *FRG*, 1 *Yearbook of the ECHR*, 1955-7, p.162 and Application 1478/62, *Y* v. *Belgium*, *Yearbook of the ECHR*, 1963, p.590.

[164] Articles 26 and 27. See Van Dijk and Van Hoof, *op. cit.*, pp.60-90. See also e.g. the *Vagrancy* case, Series A, vol.12, 1971; 56 *ILR*, p.351.

[165] Under Rule 40 of the Rules of Procedure, 1973, a Rapporteur will be appointed to deal with the matter until it is brought to the Commission.

[166] See Rules 28, 36 and 41. The Court noted in *Cruz Varas* v. *Sweden* that although the power to order binding interim measures could not be derived either directly or by way of inference from the Convention, where a party chose not to comply with such an indication of interim measures under Rule 36, it knowingly assumed the risk of being found in breach of article 3; ECHR, Series A, No.201 (1991).

[167] See Van Dijk and Van Hoof, *op. cit.*, pp.101-10. See also the *Tyrer* case, Series A, vol.26, 1978, pp.12-14; 58 *ILR*, pp.339, 350.

[168] Article 30.

[169] By the end of 1989, 15,911 applications had been received; of these only 670 were declared admissible, see Council of Europe Press Communiqué, B(90), 31/1/90.

deal with petitions which raise no serious questions of interpretation of the Convention or which may be dealt with on the basis of existing case-law. In addition, committees of at least three members may agree to render petitions inadmissible when such a decision may be taken without further examination. This Protocol came into force on 1 January 1990. The Commission has gradually been transformed from a part-time into a semi-permanent body, sixteen session weeks being scheduled for 1990, for example, and the Committee of Ministers has been encouraged to adopt a series of measures, mainly of a financial nature, to enable members of the Commission to spend more of their time on Commission activities.

The Court

The Court consists of 23 judges (the number equal to the members of the Council of Europe),[170] elected by the Consultative Assembly, for a period of nine years. It is a judicial body, unlike the Commission, and it produces final and binding decisions.[171] The jurisdiction of the Court extends to all cases involving the interpretation and application of the Convention, but only as regards those states which have expressly recognised the jurisdiction of the Court.[172] All states parties have now done so. The Court may sit in Chambers of nine judges, but under Rule 50 of the Rules of the Court 1982 a Chamber may, or must under certain circumstances, relinquish jurisdiction in favour of the plenary Court. This had happened in 71 cases out of the 205 judgments delivered by the end of 1989.[173]

The Court may only deal with a case where a friendly settlement has not been reached and within three months of the Commission's report going to the Committee of Ministers.[174] Only the Commission or a relevant state party may bring a case before the Court.[175] Under the 1982 revised Rules of Court, the person or persons originally

[170] This will rise to 25 with Hungary's membership in late 1990 and Czechoslovakia's in early 1991.
[171] Articles 38, 39, 40, 52 and 53.
[172] Articles 45 and 46.
[173] See European Court of Human Rights, *Survey of Activities 1959-1989*, 1990. See also article 44.
[174] Articles 32 and 47.
[175] Articles 44 and 48. But note Protocol IX, signed in late 1990, which once in force would allow the applicant to take the case to the Court.

lodging the petition under article 25 may appear separately before the Court,[176] while third parties may address the Court with the leave of the President.[177] Both mark advances upon the pre-1983 situation. While the Court is not specifically given the power to order remedial measures under the Convention, article 50 does enable the Court to award "just satisfaction" to an injured party if the domestic law of the state in question does not provide an adequate remedy. This has enabled the Court to grant damages as well as costs to the complainant.

The Court has dealt with an ever-increasing number of cases, delivering one judgment in its first year of operation in 1960, six in 1976, seventeen in 1986 and twenty-five in 1989. By the end of 1989, 205 judgments had been delivered.[178] The average length of proceedings before the Court is around one year, but to this one must add, of course, the period during which the Commission has been considering the particular case, in order to obtain a proper perception of the time taken for any given case. This as a general rule has meant a total duration of proceedings of between five and six years.

The Court has developed a jurisprudence of considerable importance. In *Ireland* v. *UK*,[179] its only inter-state case to date, the Court found that the five interrogation techniques used by the UK Forces in Northern Ireland amounted to a practice of inhuman and degrading treatment, contrary to article 3. In *Golder* v. *UK*,[180] the Court inferred from article 6(1) a fundamental right of access to the courts and the Court has generally recognised a varying standard of the margin of appreciation allowed to domestic organs in dealing with internal law, so that in cases involving the protection of morals more scope would be left to domestic discretion than would be the case, for example, regarding the principle of contempt of court.[181] The Court has also developed a considerable jurisprudence in the

[176] See Rules 30 and 33. Cf. the *Lawless* case, Series A, vol.1, 1961, p.15; 31 *ILR*, pp.290.

[177] See Rules 37 and 40. See also the *Winterwerp* case, Series A, vol.33, 1979; 58 *ILR*, p.653; *Young, James and Webster*, Series A, vol.44, 1981;, 62 *ILR*, p.359, and the *Malone* case, Series A, vol.82, 1984; 74 *ILR*, p.346.

[178] *Survey of Activities*, *op. cit.*

[179] Series A, vol.25, 1978; 58 *ILR*, p.188.

[180] Series A, vol.18, 1975; 57 *ILR*, p.200.

[181] See e.g. *Handyside* v. *UK*, Series A, vol.24, 1981; 58 *ILR*, p.150; the *Dudgeon* case, Series A, vol.45, 1982; 67 *ILR*, p.395 and the *Sunday Times* case, Series A, vol.30, 1979; 58 *ILR*, p.491.

field of due process[182] that is having a significant impact upon domestic law, not least in the UK. A brief reference to some further examples will suffice. In the *Marckx* case[183] the Court emphasised that Belgian legislation discriminating against illegitimate children violated the Convention, while in the *Young, James and Webster* case[184] it was held that railway workers dismissed for refusing to join a trade union in the UK were entitled to compensation. In the *Brogan* case[185] the Court felt that periods of detention under anti-terrorist legislation in the UK before appearance before a judge or other judicial officer of at least four days violated the Convention. This decision, however, prompted a notice of derogation under article 15 of the Convention by the UK government.[186]

In the important *Soering* case[187] the Court unanimously held that the extradition of a German national from the UK to the United States, where the applicant feared he would be sentenced to death on a charge of capital murder and be subjected to the "death row" phenomenon, would constitute a breach of article 3 of the Convention (prohibiting torture and inhuman and degrading treatment and punishment). This seminal decision is likely to have significant consequences in the development of the Convention system.

The Committee of Ministers

Unlike the other two organs of the Convention system, this is a political body. It is the executive organ of the Council of Europe and consists of the Foreign Ministers, or their deputies, of all the member states. The Committee performs two tasks within the framework of the Convention, one controversial, the other not so. Under article 32, where a case is not taken to the Court, the Committee makes a final decision on a two-thirds majority basis, and this has also been the case where the state concerned has not accepted the jurisdiction of the Court under article 46. This has

---

[182] See e.g. Van Dijk and Van Hoof, *op. cit.*, pp.237-73 and *Digest of Strasbourg Case-law relating to the European Convention on Human Rights*, vol.II, (article 6), 1984.
[183] Series A, No. 31, 1979; 58 *ILR*, p.561.
[184] Series A, No. 44, 1981; 62 *ILR*, p.359.
[185] Series A, No. 145, 1988.
[186] For the text, see e.g. 7 *NQHR*, 1989, p.255.
[187] Series A, No. 161, 1989.

provoked some disquiet, since in some cases it has been suggested that decisions have been unduly influenced by non-legal factors.[188]

This is to be contrasted with the provision under article 54, where the Committee of Ministers supervises the execution of the decisions of the Court.

Future Developments of the European Convention System

The number of applications to the Commission is inevitably increasing, not only as the system becomes more widely known throughout the member states, but also because several newly democratised Eastern European states have applied to join the Council of Europe, which will in practice necessitate their acceptance of the Convention. It is, therefore, possible that within five years nearly thirty states parties to the Convention will exist, imposing even further strain upon the administrative and judicial system. A merger of the Commission and the Court has been suggested,[189] but problems with this are apparent. Whatever the approach taken, some solution will have to be found for the problems which are rapidly developing.

2. The European Social Charter [190]

The wide social and economic differences between the European states, coupled with the fact that economic and social rights often depend for their realisation upon economic resources, has meant that this area of concern has lagged far behind that of civil and political rights. Seven years of negotiations were necessary before the Charter was signed in 1961.[191]

The Charter consists of a statement of long-term objectives coupled with a list of more restricted rights. In an attempt to deal

---

[188] See Van Dijk and Van Hoof, *op. cit.*, pp.161-704 and Leuprecht, "The Protection of Human Rights by Political Bodies — the Example of the Committee of Ministers of the Council of Europe", in *Progress in the Spirit of Human Rights* (eds. Nowak, Steurer and Tretter), 1988, p.95.

[189] See e.g. 8 *HRLJ*, 1987, p.1 *et seq.*

[190] See e.g. Harris, *The European Social Charter*, 1984, and Wiebringhaus, "La Charte Sociale Européenne et la Convention Européenne des Droits de l'Homme", VIII *HRJ*, 1975, p.527. See also Robertson and Merrills, *op. cit.*, p.245.

[191] There are currently fourteen states parties to the Charter.

with economic disparities within Europe, the Charter provides for a system whereby only ten of the forty-five paragraphs (including five "key articles")[192] need to be accepted upon ratification.

The Charter is implemented by means of a Committee of Independent Experts, which receives every two years via the Secretary-General of the Council of Europe a report from contracting states on the way in which they are applying the Charter. Copies of these reports are sent to national organisations of employers and employees, whose comments the state in question must transmit to the Council of Europe. The reports of the governments and the comments of the Committee of Independent Experts are then examined by a Governmental Committee on the Social Charter. The conclusions of the experts are transmitted additionally to the Consultative Assembly of the Council of Europe, which sends its views to the Committee of Ministers, which in turn may make recommendations to each contracting party by a two-thirds majority.[193] The system works on the basis of two-yearly supervision cycles.

The process is complicated and the conclusions of the Committee of Independent Experts are often obscured by the Governmental Committee.[194] Although there has recently been an Additional Protocol to the Charter, perhaps the time is ripe to consider amalgamating this system with the operations of the Convention on Human Rights, by means of amending the latter to include social, economic and cultural rights on a comprehensive basis.

3. *The European Convention for the Prevention of Torture and Inhuman and Degrading Treatment or Punishment*

This innovative Convention was signed in 1987 and came into force on 1 February 1989.[195] The purpose of the Convention is to enable the supervision of persons deprived of their liberty and in particular to prevent the torture or other ill-treatment of such

---

[192] Out of the following seven rights: the rights to work, organise, bargain collectively, social security, social and medical assistance, and the rights of the family to special protection and of migrant workers and their families to protection and assistance; see article 20.

[193] See articles 27-29 of the Charter.

[194] See, for example, Betten, "European Social Charter", 6 *SIM Newsletter*, 1988, p.69.

[195] There are currently fifteen states parties to the Convention.

persons. The Convention established a Committee,[196] which is given a fact-finding and reporting function, rather than a judicial one. The Committee is empowered to carry out both visits of a periodic nature and *ad hoc* visits to places of detention in order to examine the treatment of persons deprived of their liberty with a view to strengthening, if necessary, the protection of such persons from torture and from inhuman or degrading treatment or punishment.[197]

The Committee plans in advance the periodic visits,[198] but the innovation lies in its competence to visit places of detention in an *ad hoc* fashion, when circumstances so warrant. When the Committee is not in session, the Bureau (i.e. the President and Vice-President of the Committee)[199] may in cases of urgency decide, on the Committee's behalf, on the carrying out of such an *ad hoc* visit.[200]

After each visit, the Committee will draw up a report for transmission to the party concerned. That report will remain confidential until the party concerned decides to make it public.[201] Subject to this requirement of obligation, the Committee is to make an annual general report on its activities to the Committee of Ministers, which will be transmitted to the Consultative Assembly and made public.

4. *The European Community*

The Treaty of Rome, 1957, which established the European Economic Community (now consisting of twelve member states) is not of itself a human rights treaty. However, in this brief survey of the mechanisms available in Europe for the protection of human rights, it is worth noting that the European Court of Justice has subsumed within Community law a variety of unwritten general

---

[196] See Resolution DH (89) 26 of the Committee of Ministers adopted on 19 September 1989 for the election of the members of the Committee.

[197] See articles 1 and 7. See also the Rules of Procedure of the Committee, 1989, CPT/Inf (89) 2, especially Rules 29-35.

[198] So that, for example, it is known that the Committee will visit Austria, Denmark, Malta, Spain and the UK during 1990, see 8 *NQHR*, 1990, p.189.

[199] Rule 10 of the Rules of Procedure.

[200] Rule 31 of the Rules of Procedure.

[201] See Rules 40-42.

principles, emanating from several sources, including the European Convention on Human Rights.[202]

5. *The CSCE (Conference on Security and Co-operation in Europe) Process* [203]

This process developed out of the Final Act of the Helsinki meeting, which was signed on 1 August 1975 after two years of discussions by the representatives of the thirty-five participating states.[204] The Final Act[205] dealt primarily with questions of international security and state relations, and was seen as the method by which the post-war European territorial settlement would be finally accepted. In the Western view, the Final Act constituted a political statement and accordingly it cannot be regarded as a binding treaty. None the less, the impact of the Final Act on developments in Europe has far exceeded the impact of most legally binding treaties.

The Final Act sets out in "Basket I" a list of ten fundamental principles dealing with relations between participating states, principle 7 of which refers to "respect for human rights and fundamental freedoms, including freedom of thought, conscience, religion and belief".

The Final Act also deals with human rights issues in "Basket III" dealing with Cooperation in Humanitarian and Other Fields. This covered family reunification, free flow of information and cultural and educational cooperation.

At the third "follow-up" meeting at Vienna in January 1989, great progress regarding human rights occurred,[206] primarily as a result of the changed attitudes in the USSR and in Eastern Europe, especially as regards the extent of the detailed provisions and the

---

[202] See e.g. *Internationale Handelsgesellschaft*, [1970] ECR 1125; *Nold* v. *EC Commission*, [1974] ECR 491; *Kirk*, [1984] ECR 2689 and *Johnston* v. *Chief Constable of the RUC*, [1986] 3 CMLR 240.

[203] See, for example, Buergenthal (ed.), *Human Rights, International Law and the Helsinki Accord*, 1977; Maresca, *To Helsinki: The Conference on Security and Cooperation in Europe, 1973-1975*, 1985, and Robertson, "The Helsinki Agreement and Human Rights" in Claude and Weston (eds.), *Human Rights in the World Community*, 1989, p.220.

[204] I.e. all the states of Western and Eastern Europe, except Albania, plus the United States and Canada.

[205] For the text, see, for example, 14 *ILM*, 1975, p.1292.

[206] See the text of the Concluding Document in 10 *HRLJ*, 1989, p.270.

recognition of concrete rights and duties. The part entitled "Questions Relating to Security in Europe" contains a Principles section, in which *inter alia* the parties confirmed their respect for human rights and their determination to guarantee their effective exercise. Paragraphs 13-27 contain in a detailed and concrete manner a list of human rights principles to be respected, ranging from due process rights to equality and non-discrimination and the rights of religious communities, and from the rights of minorities to the rights of refugees. The provision in which states agree to respect the right of their citizens to contribute actively, either individually or collectively, to the promotion and protection of human rights, constitutes an important innovation of great practical significance, as does the comment that states will respect the right of persons to observe and promote the implementation of CSCE provisions.

The part entitled "Cooperation in Humanitarian and Other Fields" includes an important section on Human Contacts in which the right to leave one's country and return thereto was reaffirmed. It was decided that all outstanding human contacts applications would be resolved within six months and that thereafter there would be a series of regular reviews. Family reunion issues are to be dealt with in as short a time as possible and in normal practice within one month. The parties committed themselves to publishing all laws and statutory regulations concerning movement by individuals within their territory and travel between states, an issue that had caused a great deal of controversy,[207] while the right of members of religions to establish and maintain personal contacts with each other in their own and other countries, *inter alia* through travel and participation in religious events, was proclaimed.[208]

In a further significant development, the Vienna Concluding Document contains a part entitled "Human Dimension of the CSCE" in which some implementation measures are provided for. The participating states decided to exchange information and to respond to requests for information and to representations made to them by other participating states on questions relating to the human dimension of the CSCE. Bilateral meetings would be held with other participating states that so request in order to examine such questions, while such questions could be brought to the

---

[207] Paragraph 18.
[208] Paragraph 32.

attention of other participating states through diplomatic channels or raised at further "follow-up" meetings or at meetings of the Conference on the Human Dimension.[209]

B. *The American Convention on Human Rights* [210]

The American Convention, which came into force in 1978, contains a range of rights to be protected by the states parties.[211] The rights are fundamentally those protected by the European Convention, with some interesting differences.[212] For example, under article 4 the right to life is deemed to start in general as from conception,[213] while the prohibition on torture and inhuman or degrading treatment is more extensively expressed and is in the context of the right to have one's physical, mental and moral integrity respected (article 5). In addition, articles 18 and 19 of the American Convention protect the right to a name and the specific rights of the child, article 23 provides for a general right to participation in the context of public affairs and article 26 provides for the progressive achievement of the economic, social and cultural rights contained in the Charter of the Organisation of American States (1948), as amended by the Protocol of Buenos Aires (1967).

The Inter-American Commission on Human Rights was created in 1959 and its first Statute approved by the OAS Council in 1960. In 1971, it was recognised as one of the principal organs of the OAS. Under its original Statute, it had wide powers to promote the awareness and study of human rights in America and to make recommendations to member-states. In 1965, the Statute was revised and the Commission's powers expanded to include *inter alia* the examination of communications. With the entry into force

[209] See also the Concluding Document of the Copenhagen Conference on the Human Dimension of the CSCE of June 1990, 8 *NQHR*, 1990, p.302 *et seq.* and the Charter of Paris, 1990, 30 *ILM*, 1991, p.190.

[210] See generally Buergenthal, Norris and Shelton, *Protecting Human Rights in the Americas*, 1982; Schreiber, *The Inter-American Commission on Human Rights*, 1970; *Human Rights in the Americas* (eds. Hennelly and Longman), 1982 and Buergenthal and Norris, *The Inter-American System*, 3 vols., 1983-4. See also Robertson and Merrills, *op. cit.*, Chapter 5.

[211] As of May 1990, there were 20 ratifications, see *Annual Report of the Inter-American Commission on Human Rights 1989-90*, 1990.

[212] See e.g. Frowein, "The European and the American Conventions on Human Rights — A Comparison", 1 *HRLJ*, 1980, p.44. See also the American Declaration of the Rights and Duties of Man, 1948.

[213] See e.g. 10 *DR*, 1977, p.100.

of the 1969 Convention, the Commission's position was further strengthened. The Commission has powers regarding all member-states of the OAS, not just those that have ratified the Convention, and its Statute emphasises that the human rights protected include those enumerated in both the Convention and the American Declaration of the Rights and Duties of Man.[214] Article 44 of the Convention provides that any person or group of persons or any non-governmental entity legally recognised in one or more of the OAS states may lodge petitions with the Commission alleging a violation of the Convention by a state party. Contrary to the European Convention, this right is automatic, whereas the right of inter-state complaint, again contrary to the European Convention, is under article 45 subject to a prior declaration recognising the competence of the Commission in this regard.[215] The admissibility requirements in articles 46 and 47 are very broadly similar to those in the European Convention, as is the procedure laid down in article 48 and the drawing up of a report in cases in which a friendly settlement has been achieved.[216] The Commission has, unlike its European counterpart, a wide-ranging competence to publicise human rights matters by way of reports, studies, lectures and so forth. It may also make recommendations to states on the adoption of progressive measures in favour of human rights and conduct on-site investigations with the consent of the state in question.[217] It provides states generally with advisory services in the human rights field and submits an annual report to the OAS General Assembly. Many special reports have been published dealing with human rights in particular states, e.g. Argentina, Bolivia, Chile, Colombia, Cuba, Dominican Republic, El Salvador, Guatemala, Haiti, Nicaragua, Paraguay, Surinam and Uruguay.[218] The Commission has also devoted attention to certain themes, such as disappearances, torture, refugees and economic

[214] See generally the OAS, *Handbook of Existing Rules Pertaining to Human Rights,* 1980. The competence of the Commission to hear petitions relates to the rights in the Convention for states parties and to rights in the American Declaration for states not parties to the Convention.

[215] There are currently 8 declarations, *Annual Report of the Inter-American Commission on Human Rights, 1989-90,* 1990, p.6.

[216] Articles 49-51. The Secretary-General of the OAS has played the role assigned in the European Convention to the Committee of Ministers.

[217] E.g. Guatemala, Paraguay and Haiti in 1990, *ibid.,* pp.16-22.

[218] *Ibid.,* Chapter IV.

and social rights.[219] In 1985, the OAS General Assembly adopted the Inter-American Convention to Prevent and Punish Torture, while in 1988 an Additional Protocol on Economic, Social and Cultural Rights was signed. Protection is envisaged by means of reports to be submitted to the OAS. Preparations are under way for a new Additional Protocol on the Abolition of the Death Penalty and a new Convention against Disappearances. Consideration is also being given to a juridical instrument dealing with the rights of indigenous peoples. The Commission itself consists of seven members elected in a personal capacity by the OAS General Assembly for four year terms.[220] Where in the case of petitions received, a friendly settlement has not been achieved, then under article 50 a report will be drawn up, together with such proposals and recommendations seen fit, and transmitted to the parties. A three month period is then available during which the Commission or the state concerned may go to the Inter-American Court of Human Rights.[221] The Court consists of seven judges serving in an individual capacity and elected by an absolute majority of the states parties to the Convention in the OAS General Assembly for six year terms.[222] The jurisdiction of the Court is subject to a prior declaration under article 62.[223] Under article 64, the Court also possesses an advisory jurisdiction with regard to the interpretation of the American Convention and other conventions concerning the protection of human rights in the American states.

The Court has to date given ten advisory opinions and dealt with three contentious cases.[224] In the former category several important issues have been covered. In *Definition of Other Treaties Subject to the Interpretation of the Inter-American Court*,[225] the Court took the view that the object of the Convention was to integrate the regional and universal systems of human rights protection and that, therefore, any human rights treaty to which American

---

[219] See e.g. *Annual Report 1983-4.* See also e.g. AG/Res.443, 1979 and AG/Res.666, 1983 and AG/Res.547, 1981, AG/Res.624, 1982 and AG/Res.644, 1983 (torture).

[220] See articles 34-38.

[221] Article 51. If this does not happen and the matter is not settled with the state concerned, the Commission by a majority vote may set forth its own opinion and conclusions on the matter, which may be published. See for example, *Annual Report 1983-4, op. cit.,* pp.23-75.

[222] Articles 52-54.

[223] There are currently 10 declarations, *Annual Report 1989-90, op. cit.,* p.6.

[224] See 5 *Interights Bulletin,* 1990, p.5.

[225] 22 *ILM,* 1983, p.51; 67 *ILR,* p.594.

states were parties could be the subject of an advisory opinion. In *The Effect of Reservations*,[226] the Court stressed that human rights treaties involve the establishment of legal orders within which obligations were created towards all individuals within their jurisdiction, while in an important discussion of freedom of expression in the *Licensing of Journalists* case,[227] the Court advised that the compulsory licensing of journalists was incompatible with the freedom of expression provision in the Convention (article 13) if it denied any person access to the full use of the media as a means of expressing opinions.

In the *Habeas Corpus* case[228] the Court declared that the writ of habeas corpus was a non-suspendable "judicial guarantee" for the protection of rights from which no derogation was permitted under the Convention (see article 27). Reference was made to the "inseparable bond between the principle of legality, democratic institutions and the rule of law". The Court has also addressed the issue of the relationship between itself and the American Declaration of the Rights and Duties of Man 1948 in the *Interpretation of the American Declaration* case.[229] In an opinion likely to be of significance in view of the fact that, for example, the US is not a party to the Convention but as a member of the OAS has signed the Declaration, the Court stressed that in interpreting the Declaration regard had to be had to the current state of the Inter-American system and that, by a process of authoritative interpretation, the member states of the OAS have agreed that the Declaration contains and defines the human rights norms referred to in the OAS Charter.[230] Since the Charter was a treaty, the Court could, therefore, interpret the Declaration under article 64.[231] This rather ingenious argument is likely to open the door to a variety of advisory opinions on a range of important issues.

The exercise of the Court's contentious jurisdiction has, however, been less successful. In the *Gallardo* case,[232] the Court remitted the claim to the Commission declaring it inadmissible,

---

[226] *Ibid.*, p.33; 67 *ILR*, p.559.

[227] 7 *HRLJ*, 1986, p.74; 75 *ILR*, p.31.

[228] 9 *HRLJ*, 1988, p.94.

[229] 28 *ILM*, 1989, p.378.

[230] *Ibid.*, p.388-89.

[231] The problem was that the Declaration clearly was not a treaty and article 64 provides for advisory opinions regarding the Convention itself and "other treaties".

[232] 20 *ILM*, 1981, p.1424; 67 *ILR*, p.578.

noting that a state could not dispense with the processing of the case by the Commission, while in the *Velasquez Rodriguez*[233] and *Godinez Cruz*[234] cases the Court in "disappearance" situations found that Honduras had violated the Convention.[235] It is to be hoped that the paucity of contentious cases will soon be remedied.[236]

C. *The Banjul Charter on Human and Peoples' Rights*

This was adopted by the Organisation of African Unity in 1981 and came into force in 1986.[237] The Charter contains a wide range of rights, including in addition to the traditional civil and political rights, economic, social and cultural rights and various peoples' rights. In this latter category are specifically mentioned the rights to self-determination, development and a generally satisfactory environment.[238] The reference to the latter two concepts is unusual in human rights instruments and it remains to be seen both how they will be interpreted and how they will be implemented.

One question that is immediately posed with respect to the notion of "peoples' rights" is to ascertain the definition of a people. If experience with the definition of self-determination in the context of the United Nations is any guide,[239] and bearing in mind the extreme sensitivity which African states have manifested with regard to the stability of the existing colonial borders,[240] then the principle is likely to be interpreted in the sense of independent states.

The African Charter is the first human rights convention that

---

[233] 9 *HRLJ*, 1988, p.212.

[234] H/Inf (90) 1, p.80.

[235] Note also the award of compensation to the victims in both of these cases, *ibid.*, pp.80-81.

[236] Note that the Court utilised the provisional measures power under article 63(2) for the first time in January 1988, against Honduras, following the killing of a person due to testify before it and concerns expressed about the safety of other witnesses, H/Inf. (88) 1, p.64. See also the provisional measures adopted by the Court against Peru, in similar circumstances, in August 1990, 11 *HRLJ*, 1990, p.257.

[237] See Gittleman, "The African Charter on Human and Peoples' Rights: A Legal Analysis", 22 *VaJIL*, 1981, p.667; Robertson and Merrills, *op. cit.*, p.200 and Umozurike, "The Protection of Human Rights under the Banjul (African) Charter on Human and Peoples' Rights", 1 *African Journal of International Law*, 1988, p.65.

[238] See article 19-2.

[239] *Supra*, Chapter 5, p.176.

[240] See Shaw, *Title to Territory in Africa*, 1986.

details the duties of the individual to the state, society and family.[241] Included are the duties to avoid compromising the security of the state and to preserve and strengthen social and national solidarity and independence. It remains to be seen whether this distinctive approach brings with it more problems than advantages.

The Charter set up the African Commission on Human and Peoples' Rights, consisting of eleven persons appointed by the Conference of the Heads of State and Government of the OAU, to implement the Charter. The Commission has important educational and promotional responsibilities,[242] including undertaking studies, organising conferences, disseminating information and making recommendations to governments. This is quite unlike the European Commission, but rather more similar to the Inter-American Commission. The Commission may hear as of right inter-state complaints,[243] although the clear preference for friendly settlement is expressed, and other non-state communications.[244] No provision was made for a Court. The Commission adopted Rules of Procedure in 1988.[245]

SOME BASIC PRINCIPLES

Domestic Jurisdiction [246]

The basic rule of international law providing that states have no right to encroach upon the preserve of other states' internal affairs is a consequence of the equality and sovereignty of states and is mirrored in article 2(7) of the UN Charter. It has, however, been subject to a process of reinterpretation in the human rights field[247] as this chapter has made apparent, so that states may no longer plead

[241] See articles 27-29.

[242] See article 45. See also Bello, "The Mandate of the African Commission on Human and Peoples' Rights", 1 *African Journal of International Law,* 1988, p.31.

[243] Articles 47-54.

[244] Articles 55-59.

[245] See 40 *The Review, International Commission of Jurists,* 1988, p.26.

[246] See e.g. Higgins, *The Development of International Law Through the Political Organs of the United Nations,* 1963; Rajan, *United Nations and Domestic Jurisprudence,* 1961 and Trindade, "The Domestic Jurisprudence of States in the Practice of the United Nations and Regional Organisations", 25 *ICLQ,* 1976, p.715.

[247] Note that the question of the extent and content of domestic jurisdiction is a matter for international law, see *Nationality Decrees in Tunis and Morocco* cases, PCIJ, Series B, no.4, 1923; 2 *ILR,* p.349. See also *infra,* Chapter 11, p.395.

this rule as a bar to international concern and consideration of internal human rights situations.[248]

The Exhaustion of Domestic Remedies Rule [249]

This rule flows from the above principles. It is a method of permitting states to solve their own internal problems in accordance with their own constitutional procedures before accepted international mechanisms can be invoked, and is well established in international law.[250] However, where such internal remedies are non-existent or unduly and unreasonably prolonged, the resort to international measures will not be obviated.[251] A provision regarding the need to exhaust domestic remedies before the various international mechanisms may be resorted to appears in all the international human rights instruments[252] and has been carefully analysed.[253]

Priorities of Rights

Certain rights may not be derogated from in the various human rights instruments even in times of war or other public emergency threatening the nation. In the case of the European Convention[254]

[248] See also the resolution of the Institut de Droit International, 1989, H/Inf (90) 1, p.131.

[249] See e.g. Trindade, *The Application of the Rule of Exhaustion of Local Remedies in International Law*, 1983; Law, *The Local Remedies Rule in International Law*, 1961 and Amerasinghe, "The Rule of Exhaustion of Local Remedies and the International Protection of Human Rights", 17 *Indian Yearbook of International Affairs*, 1974, p.3 and *Local Remedies in International Law*, 1990. See also *infra*, Chapter 13.

[250] See e.g. the *Ambatielos* case, 23 *ILR*, p.306; the *Finnish Ships* case, 3 *RIAA*, p.1479 and the *Interhandel* case, ICJ Reports, 1959, pp.26-27; 27 *ILR*, pp.475, 490.

[251] See e.g. the *Robert E. Brown* case, 6 *RIAA*, pp.120; 2 *ILR*, p.66. See also the *Salem* case, 2 *RIAA*, p.1161; 6 *ILR*, p.188 and the *Nielsen* case, 2 *Yearbook of the ECHR*, p.413; 28 *ILR*, p.210 and the *Second Cyprus* case, *ibid.*, p.186.

[252] See e.g. article 41(c), Civil and Political Rights Covenant and article 2, Optional Protocol; article 11(3), Racial Discrimination Convention; article 26, European Convention; article 50, American Convention and article 50, Banjul Charter. See also ECOSOC resolution 1503 and UNESCO decision 104 EX/3.3, 1978, para. 14(IX).

[253] See e.g. the *Nielsen* case, *op. cit.*; *Second Cyprus* case, *op. cit.*; *Donnelly* case, 16 *Yearbook of the ECHR*, p.212 and *Kjeldsen* v. *Denmark*, 15 *Yearbook of the ECHR*, p.428; 58 *ILR*, p.117. See also Van Dijk and Van Hoof, *op. cit.*, pp.72-84. See as regards the Human Rights Committee, e.g. the *Weinberger* case, Reports of the Human Rights Committee, A/36/40, p.114 and A/44/40, p.142.

[254] Article 15. See generally, Higgins, "Derogations Under Human Rights Treaties", 48 *BYIL*, 1976-7, p.281.

these are the rights to life (except in cases resulting from lawful acts of war), the prohibition on torture and slavery, and non-retroactivity of criminal offences.[255] In the case of the American Convention,[256] the following rights are non-derogable: the rights to judicial personality, life and humane treatment, freedom from slavery, freedom from *ex post facto* laws, freedom of conscience and religion, rights of the family, to a name, of the child, nationality and participation in government.[257] By article 4 of the Civil and Political Rights Covenant, the rights to life and recognition as a person before the law, the freedoms of thought, conscience and religion and the prohibition on torture, slavery, retroactivity of criminal legislation and imprisonment on grounds solely of inability to fulfil a contractual obligation are non-derogable.[258]

Such non-derogable rights clearly are regarded as possessing a special place in the hierarchy of rights.[259] In addition, it must be noted, many rights are subject to a limitation or clawback clause, whereby the absolute right provided for will not operate in certain situations.[260] Those rights therefore that are not so limited may be regarded as of particular value.[261]

It has sometimes been argued that a new "third generation" of rights, flowing on from the "first generation" of civil and political rights and the "second generation" of economic, social and cultural rights is in process of creation.[262] Such group or collective rights would include, for example, a right to development.[263] Whether this

---

[255] Articles 2, 3, 4(1) and 7.

[256] Article 27.

[257] Articles 3, 4, 5, 6, 9, 12, 17, 18, 19, 20 and 23.

[258] Articles 6, 7, 8(1) and (2), 11, 15, 16 and 18. Note that the Banjul Charter contains no specific derogations clause.

[259] The fact that a right may not be derogated from may constitute evidence that the right concerned is part of *jus cogens*.

[260] See e.g. articles 8-11 of the European Convention; articles 12-14, 15-16 and 21-22 of the American Convention and articles 12, 18, 19, 21 and 22 of the Civil and Political Rights Covenant. See also Higgins, *op. cit.* footnote 254.

[261] See e.g. the due process rights.

[262] See e.g. Alston, "A Third Generation of Solidarity Rights", 29 *NILR,* 1982, p.307 and "Conjuring Up New Human Rights: A Proposal for Quality Control", 78 *AJIL,* 1984, p.607; International Commission of Jurists, *Development, Human Rights and the Rule of Law,* 1981; and Rich, "The Right of Development as an Emerging Human Right", 23 *Va JIL,* 1983, p.287.

[263] See e.g. the report of the UN Secretary-General on "Global Consultation on the Right to Development as a Human Right", E/CN.4/1990/9/Rev.1, 26 September 1990.

process is occurring or not, sight must not be lost of the basic human rights of the individual under threat from the state.[264]

Customary International Law and Human Rights

It should also be noted that in addition to the treaty provisions relating to human rights, certain human rights may now be regarded as having entered into the category of customary law in the light of state practice. These would include the prohibition on torture, genocide and slavery and the principle of non-discrimination.[265]

---

[264] See *infra*, Chapter 11 with regard to international criminal law and the individual and *infra*, Chapter 18 with regard to international humanitarian law and the laws of war.

[265] See e.g. *Restatement (Third) of Foreign Relations Law of the United States*, 1987, vol.2, pp.161-83. Further suggestions are there made as to additional human rights as international customs.

CHAPTER SEVEN

Recognition[1]

International society is not an unchanging entity, but is subject to the ebb and flow of political life. New states are created and old units fall away. New governments come into being within states in a manner contrary to declared constitutions whether or not accompanied by force. Insurgencies occur and belligerent administrations are established in areas of territory hitherto controlled by the legitimate government. Each of these events creates new facts and the question that recognition is concerned with is how far legal effects should flow from such occurrences. Each state will have to decide whether or not to recognise the particular eventuality and the kind of legal entity it should be accepted as.

Recognition involves consequences both on the international plane and within municipal law. If an entity is recognised as a state in, for example, the United Kingdom, it will entail the consideration of rights and duties that would not otherwise be relevant. There are privileges permitted to a foreign state before the municipal courts that would not be allowed to other institutions or persons.

It is stating the obvious to point to the very strong political influences that bear upon this topic.[2] In more cases than not the decision whether or not to recognise will depend more upon political considerations than exclusively legal factors. Recognition is not merely applying the relevant legal consequences to a factual situation, for sometimes a state will not want such consequences to follow, either internationally or domestically.

To give one example, the United States refused for many years to recognise either the People's Republic of China or North Korea, not because it did not accept the obvious fact that these authorities exercised effective control over their respective territories, but rather because it did not wish the legal effects of recognition to come

---

[1] See generally, e.g. Lauterpacht, *Recognition in International Law*, 1947; Chen, *The International Law of Recognition*, 1951; Charpentier, *La Reconnaissance Internationale et l'Evolution du Droit des Gens*, 1956; Galloway, *Recognising Foreign Governments*, 1978 and Verhoeven, *La Reconnaissance Internationale dans la Pratique Contemporaine*, 1975. See also Dugard, *Recognition and the United Nations*, 1987.

[2] See e.g. Smith, *Great Britain and the Law of Nations*, vol.1, 1932, pp.77-80.

into operation.[3] It is purely a political judgment, although it has been clothed in legal terminology.

RECOGNITION OF STATES

There are basically two theories as to the nature of recognition. The constitutive theory maintains that it is the act of recognition by other states that creates a new state and endows it with legal personality and not the process by which it actually obtained independence. Thus, new states are established in the international community as fully-fledged subjects of international law by virtue of the will and consent of already existing states.[4] The disadvantage of this approach is that an unrecognised "state" may not be subject to the obligations imposed by international law and may accordingly be free from such restraints as, for instance, the prohibition on aggression. A further complication would arise if a "state" were recognised by some but not other states. Could one talk then of, for example, partial personality?

The second theory, the declaratory theory, adopts the opposite approach and is a little more in accord with practical realities.[5] It maintains that recognition is merely an acceptance by states of an already existing situation. A new state will acquire capacity in international law not by virtue of the consent of others but by virtue of a particular factual situation. It will be legally constituted by its own efforts and circumstances and will not have to await the procedure of recognition by other states. This doctrine owes a lot to traditional positivist thought on the supremacy of the state and the concomitant weakness or non-existence of any central guidance in the international community.

For the constitutive theorist, the heart of the matter is that fundamentally an unrecognised "state" can have no rights or obligations in international law. The opposite stance is adopted by

---

[3] See e.g. Kaplan and Katzenbach, *The Political Foundations of International Law*, 1961, p.109.

[4] See Oppenheim, *International Law*, vol.1, 8th ed., 1955, p.125. See also Crawford, *The Creation of States in International Law*, 1979, p.17 *et seq.*

[5] *Ibid.*, p.126. See Brierly, *The Law of Nations*, 6th ed., 1963, p.138; Brownlie, *Principles of Public International Law*, 4th ed., 1990, pp.89-91; O'Connell, *International Law*, vol.1, 2nd ed., 1970, p.128 *et seq.* and Crawford, *op. cit.*, p.20 *et seq.* See also the *Tinoco* arbitration, 1 *RIAA*, p.369; 2 *ILR*, p.34 and *Wulfsohn* v. *Russian Republic*, 138 NE 24; 2 *ILR*, p.39.

the declaratory approach, that emphasises the factual situation and minimises the power of states to confer legal personality.

Actual practice leads to a middle position between these two perceptions. The act of recognition by one state of another indicates that the former regards the latter as having conformed with the basic requirements of international law as to the creation of a state. Of course, recognition is highly political and is given in a number of cases for purely political reasons. This point of view was emphasised by the American representative on the Security Council during discussions on the Middle East in May 1948. He said that it would be:

> highly improper for one to admit that any country on earth can question the sovereignty of the United States of America in the exercise of the high political act of recognition of the *de facto* status of a state.

Indeed, he added that there was no authority that could determine the legality or validity of that act of the United States.[6] This American view that recognition is to be used as a kind of mark of approval was in evidence with regard to the attitude adopted towards Communist China for a generation.[7]

The United Kingdom, on the other hand, has often tended to extend recognition once it is satisfied that the authorities of the state in question have complied with the minimum requirements of international law, and have effective control which seems likely to continue over the country.[8] Recognition is constitutive in a political sense, for it marks the new entity out as a state within the international community and is evidence of acceptance of its new political status by the society of nations. This does not imply that the act of recognition is legally constitutive, because rights and duties do not arise as a result of the recognition.

Practice over the last century or so is not unambiguous but does point to the declaratory approach as the better of the two theories. States which for particular reasons have refused to recognise other states, such as the Arab world and Israel and the USA and certain

---

[6] See Whiteman, *Digest of International Law*, vol.2, p.10.

[7] See generally Young, "American Dealings with Peking", 45 *Foreign Affairs*, 1966, p.77 and Whiteman, *Digest, op. cit.* vol.2, p.551 *et seq.* See also A/CN.4/2, p.53, cited in Crawford, *op. cit.*, p.16.

[8] See Lauterpacht, *op. cit.*, p.6.

communist nations,[9] rarely contend that the other party is devoid of powers and obligations before international law and exists in a legal vacuum. The stance is rather that rights and duties are binding upon them, and that recognition had not been accorded for primarily political reasons. If the constitutive theory were accepted it would mean, for example, in the context of Arab non-recognition of Israel, that the latter was not bound by international law rules of non-aggression and non-intervention. This has not been adopted in any of the stances of non-recognition of "states".[10]

Of course, if an entity, while meeting the conditions of international law as to statehood, went totally unrecognised, this would undoubtedly hamper the exercise of its rights and duties, especially in view of the absence of diplomatic relations, but it would not seem in law to amount to a decisive argument against statehood itself.[11] For example, the Charter of the Organisation of American States adopted at Bogotá in 1948 notes in its survey of the fundamental rights and duties of states that:

the political existence of the state is independent of recognition by other states. Even before being recognised the state has the right to defend its integrity and independence.[12]

And the Institut de Droit International emphasised in its resolution on recognition of new states and governments in 1936 that the

existence of the new state with all the legal effects connected with that existence is not affected by the refusal of one or more states to recognise.[13]

In the period following the end of the First World War, the courts of the new states of eastern and central Europe regarded their states as coming into being upon the actual declaration of independence and not simply as a result of the Peace Treaties. The

[9] See 39 *Bulletin of the US Department of State,* 1958, p.385.
[10] See e.g. the *Pueblo* incident, 62 *AJIL,* 1968, p.756 and *Keesings Contemporary Archives,* p.23129; Whiteman, *Digest, op. cit.* vol.2, pp.604 *et seq.* and 651; "Contemporary Practice of the UK in International Law", 6 *ICLQ,* 1957, p.507, and *British Practice in International Law* (ed. E. Lauterpacht), 1963 II, p.90.
[11] See *supra,* Chapter 5.
[12] Article 9.
[13] 39 *Annuaire de L'Institut de Droit International,* 1936, p.300. See also *Restatement (Third) of Foreign Relations Law of the United States,* 1987, pp.77-78.

Tribunal in one case pointed out that the recognition of Poland in the Treaty of Versailles was only declaratory of the state which existed *"par lui-même"*.[14]

On the other hand, the constitutive theory is not totally devoid of all support in state practice. In some cases, the creation of a new state, or the establishment of a new government by unconstitutional means, or the occupation of a territory that is legally claimed will proceed uneventfully and be clearly accomplished for all to see and with little significant opposition. However, in many instances, the new entity or government will be insecure and it is in this context that recognition plays a vital role. Where the facts are unclear and open to different interpretations, recognition by a state will amount to a declaration by that state of how it understands the situation, and such an evaluation will be binding upon it. That is, it will not be able to deny later the factual position it has recognised (unless, of course, circumstances radically alter in the meantime). In this sense, recognition can be constitutive.

Another factor which leans towards the constitutive interpretation of recognition is the practice in many states whereby an unrecognised state or government cannot claim the rights available to a recognised state or government before the municipal courts. This means that the act of recognition itself entails a distinct legal effect and that after recognition a state or government would have enforceable rights within the domestic jurisdiction that it would not have had prior to the recognition.[15]

This theoretical controversy is of value in that it reveals the functions of recognition and emphasises the impact of states upon the development of international law. It points to the essential character of international law, poised as it is between the state and the international community. The declaratory theory veers towards the former and the constitutive doctrine towards the latter.

There have been a number of attempts to adapt the constitutive theory so that it accords more with reality. Lauterpacht maintained, for example, that once the conditions prescribed by international law for statehood have been complied with, there is actually a duty on the part of existing states to grant recognition. This is because, in the absence of a central authority in international law to assess

[14] *Deutsche Continental Gas-Gesellschaft* v. *Polish State*, 5 *ILR*, p.11.
[15] See *infra*, p.261.

and accord legal personality, it is the states that have to perform this function on behalf, as it were, of the international community and international law.[16]

This operation is both declaratory, in that it is based upon certain definite facts (i.e. the entity fulfils the requirements of statehood) and constitutive in that it is the acceptance by the recognising state of the particular community as an entity possessing all the rights and obligations that are inherent in statehood. Before the act of recognition, the community that is hoping to be admitted as a state will only have such rights and duties as have been expressly permitted to it, if any.

The Lauterpacht doctrine is an ingenious bid to reconcile the legal elements in a coherent theory. It accepts the realities of new creations of states and governments by practical (and occasionally illegal) means, and attempts to assimilate this to the supremacy of international law as Lauterpacht saw it. However, in so doing it ignores the political aspects and functions of recognition, that is, its use as a method of demonstrating or withholding support from a particular government or new community. The reality is that in many cases recognition is applied to demonstrate political approval or disapproval. Indeed, if there is a duty to grant recognition, would the entity involved have a right to demand this where a particular state or states is proving recalcitrant? If this were so, one would appear to be faced with the possibility of a non-state with as yet no rights or duties enforcing rights against non-recognising states.

Nevertheless, state practice reveals that Lauterpacht's theory has not been adopted.[17] The fact is that few states accept that they are obliged in every instance to accord recognition. In most cases they will grant recognition, but that does not mean that they have to. The position with regard to some communist nations and with respect to Israel should be sufficient illustration of this.

The approach of the United States was re-emphasised in 1976. The Department of State noted that:

[i]n the view of the United States, international law does not require a state to recognise another entity as a state; it is a matter for the

16   *Op. cit.*, pp.24, 55, 76-77.
17   See e.g. Waldock, "General Course on Public International Law", 106 *HR*, p.154. See also Mugerwa, "Subjects of International Law" in *Manual of Public International Law* (ed. Sørensen), 1968, pp.247, 266-90.

judgment of each state whether an entity merits recognition as a state. In reaching this judgment, the United States has traditionally looked to the establishment of certain facts. These facts include effective control over a clearly defined territory and population; an organised governmental administration of that territory and a capacity to act effectively to conduct foreign relations and to fulfil international obligations. The United States has also taken into account whether the entity in question has attracted the recognition of the international community of states.[18]

The view of the UK government was expressed as follows:

The normal criteria which the government apply for recognition as a state are that it should have, and seem likely to continue to have, a clearly defined territory with a population, a government who are able of themselves to exercise effective control of that territory, and independence in their external relations. Other factors, including some United Nations resolutions, may also be relevant.[19]

There are many different ways in which recognition can occur and it may apply in more than one kind of situation. It is not a single, constant idea but a category comprising a number of factors.

There are indeed different entities which may be recognised, ranging from new states, to new governments, belligerent rights possessed by a particular group and territorial changes.

Not only are there various objects of the process of recognition, but recognition may itself be *de facto* or *de jure* and it may arise in a variety of manners.

Recognition is an active process and should be distinguished from cognition, or the mere possession of knowledge, for example, that the entity involved complies with the basic international legal stipulations as to statehood. Recognition implies both cognition of the necessary facts and an intention that, so far as the acting state is concerned, it is willing that the legal consequences attendant upon recognition should operate. For example, the rules as to diplomatic and sovereign immunities should apply as far as the envoys of the entity to be recognised are concerned. It is not enough for the recognising state simply to be aware of the facts, it must desire the

[18] *DUSPIL*, 1976, pp.19-20.
[19] 102 HC Deb., col.977, Written Answer, 23 October 1986.

coming into effect of the legal and political results of recognition. This is inevitable by virtue of the discretionary nature of the act of recognition, and is illustrated in practice by the lapse in time that often takes place between the events establishing a new state or government and the actual recognition by other states. Timing in such cases is important since a premature recognition of a revolutionary take-over might constitute intervention in the affairs of a state and in any event would not be kindly regarded by the legitimate authorities. This, indeed, was the view adopted by the Nigerian Federal Government with respect to the recognition of "Biafra" by five states.[20]

RECOGNITION OF GOVERNMENTS

The recognition of a new government is quite different from the recognition of a new state. As far as statehood is concerned the factual situation will be examined in terms of the accepted criteria.[21] Different considerations apply where it is the government which changes. Recognition will only be relevant where the change in government is unconstitutional.

Political considerations have usually played a large role in the decision whether or not to grant recognition. However, certain criteria have emerged to cover recognition of illegal changes in government.

Such criteria amounted to an acceptance of the realities of the transfer of power and suggested that once a new government effectively controlled the country and that this seemed likely to continue, recognition should not be withheld. The United Kingdom on a number of occasions adopted this approach.[22] It was declared by the Under-Secretary of State for Foreign Affairs in 1970 that the test employed was whether or not the new government enjoyed:

with a reasonable prospect of permanence, the obedience of the mass

---

[20] See e.g. Stremlau, *The International Politics of the Nigerian Civil War, 1967-70*, 1977, pp.127-29, and Ijalaye, "Was 'Biafra' at any time a State in International Law?", 65 *AJIL*, 1971, p.51. See also Lauterpacht, *op. cit.*, pp.7-8 and Oppenheim, *op. cit.*, pp.128-29.

[21] See *supra*, Chapter 5, p.138.

[22] See the Morrison statement, 485 HC Deb., cols.2410-11, 21 March 1951.

of the population . . . effective control of much of the greater part of the territory of the state concerned.[23]

It is this attitude which prompted such policies as the recognition of the communist government of China and the Russian-installed government of Hungary in 1956 after the failure of the uprising. However, this general approach cannot be regarded as an absolute principle in view of the British refusal over many years to recognise as states North Vietnam, North Korea and the German Democratic Republic.[24] The effective control of a new government over the territory of the state is thus an important guideline to the problem of whether to extend recognition or not, providing such control appears well established and likely to continue. But it is no more than that and in most cases will yield to political considerations.

One example of the uses of the "effective control" concept took place in the *Tinoco* arbitration.[25] In 1919, the government of Tinoco in Costa Rica was overthrown and the new authorities repudiated certain obligations entered into by Tinoco with regard to British nationals. Chief Justice Taft, the sole arbitrator, referred to the problems of recognition or non-recognition as relating to the Tinoco administration. He decided that since the administration was in effective control of the country, it was the valid government irrespective of the fact that a number of states, including the United Kingdom, had not recognised it. This was so despite his opinion that:

the non-recognition by other nations of a government claiming to be a national personality, is usually appropriate evidence that it has not attained the independence and control entitling it by international law to be classed as such.[26]

Where recognition has been refused because of the illegitimacy or irregularity of origin of the government in question, rather than because of the lack of effectiveness of its control in the country, such

---

[23] 799 HC Deb., col.23, 6 April 1970. See also Foreign Office statements, 204 HL Deb., col.755, 4 July 1957 and 742 HC Deb., cols.6-7, Written Answer, 27 February 1967.

[24] See e.g. Greig, "The Carl-Zeiss Case and the Position of an Unrecognised Government in English Law", 83 *LQR*, 1967, pp.96, 128-30 and *Re Al-Fin Corporation's Patent*, [1970] Ch.160; 52 *ILR*, p.68.

[25] 1 *RIAA*, p.369 (1923); 2 *ILR*, p.34.

[26] *Ibid.*, p.380; 2 *ILR*, p.37.

non-recognition loses some of its evidential weight. In other words, where the degree of authority asserted by the new administration is uncertain, recognition by other states will be a vital factor. But where the new government is firmly established, non-recognition will not affect the legal character of the new government. The doctrine of effective control is an indication of the importance of the factual nature of any situation. But in those cases where recognition is refused upon the basis of the improper origins of the new government, it will have less of an impact than if recognition is refused because of the absence of effective control. Taft's view of the nature of recognition is an interesting amalgam of the declaratory and constitutive theories, in that recognition can become constitutive where the factual conditions (i.e. the presence or absence of effective control) are in dispute, but otherwise is purely declaratory or evidential.

A change in government, however accomplished, does not affect the identity of the state itself. The state does not cease to be an international legal person because its government is overthrown. That is not at issue. The recognition or non-recognition of a new administration is irrelevant to the legal character of the country. Accordingly one can see that two separate recognitions are involved and they must not be confused. Recognition of a state will affect its legal personality, whether by creating or acknowledging it, while recognition of a government affects the status of the administrative authority, not the state.

It is possible, however, for recognition of state and government to occur together in certain circumstances. This can take place upon the creation of a new state. Israel, to take one example, was recognised by the United States and the United Kingdom by the expedient of having its government recognised *de facto*.[27] Recognition of the government implies recognition of the state, but it does not work the other way.

It should be noted that recognition of a government has no relevance to the establishment of new persons in international law. Where it is significant is in the realm of diplomatic relations. If a government is unrecognised, there is no exchange of diplomatic envoys and thus problems can arise as to the enforcement of international rights and obligations.

[27] See e.g. Whiteman, *Digest, op. cit.* vol.2, p.168.

Although the effective control doctrine is probably accepted as the most reliable guide to recognition of governments, there have been other theories put forward, the most prominent amongst them being the Tobar doctrine or the so-called doctrine of legitimacy. This suggested that governments which came into power by extra-constitutional means should not be recognised.[28] This policy was applied particularly by the United States in relation to Central America and was designed to protect stability in that delicate area adjacent to the Panama Canal. Logically, of course, the concept amounts to the promotion of non-recognition in all revolutionary situations and it is, and was, difficult to reconcile with reality and political consideration. In American eyes it became transmuted into the Wilson policy of democratic legitimacy. Where the revolution was supported by the people, it would be recognised. Where it was not, there would be no grant of recognition. It was elaborated with respect to the Soviet Union until 1933, but gradually declined until it can now be properly accepted merely as a political qualification for recognition to be considered by the recognising state.[29]

A doctrine advocating the exact opposite, the automatic recognition of governments in all circumstances, was put forward by Estrada, the Mexican Secretary of Foreign Relations.[30] But this suffers from the same disadvantage as the legitimacy doctrine. It attempts to lay down a clear test for recognition in all instances excluding political considerations and exigencies of state and is thus unrealistic.

The problem, of course, was that recognition of a new government that has come to power in a non-constitutional fashion has been taken to imply approval. Allied with the other factors sometimes taken into account in such recognition situations,[31] an unnecessarily complicated process had resulted. Accordingly, in 1977 the United States declared that:

---

[28] See e.g. Mugerwa, *op. cit.*, p.271, and 2 *AJIL*, 1908, Supp., p.229.

[29] See e.g. Hackworth, *Digest of International Law*, vol.1, 1940, p.181 *et seq.* See also 17 *AJIL*, 1923, Supp., p.118; O'Connell, *op. cit.*, pp.137-39 and Whiteman, *Digest, op. cit.* vol.2, p.69.

[30] See e.g. 25 *AJIL*, 1931, Supp., p.203 and Whiteman, *Digest, op. cit.* vol.2, p.85. See also Chen, *op. cit.*, p.116 and O'Connell, *op. cit.*, pp.134-35.

[31] For example, the democratic requirement noted by President Wilson, President Rutherford Hayes' popular support condition and Secretary of State Seward's criterion of ability to honour international obligations, see statement by US Department of State, *DUSPIL*, 1977, pp.19, 20.

US practice has been to de-emphasise and avoid the use of recognition in cases of changes of governments and to concern ourselves with the question of whether we wish to have diplomatic relations with the new governments . . . The Administration's policy is that establishment of relations does not involve approval or disapproval but merely demonstrates a willingness on our part to conduct our affairs with other governments directly.[32]

In 1980, the UK government announced that it would no longer accord recognition to governments as distinct from states. This was primarily due to the perception that recognition meant approval, a perception that was often embarrassing, for example in the case of regimes violating human rights. There were, therefore, practical advantages in not according recognition to governments. The UK would continue to decide the nature of dealings with unconstitutional regimes:

in the light of [an] assessment of whether they are able of themselves to exercise effective control of the territory of the state concerned, and seem likely to continue to do so.[33]

The change, therefore, is that recognition of governments is abolished but that the criterion for dealing with such regimes is the same as the former test for the recognition of governments.[34] In that context, regard should also be had to the phrase "of themselves".[35]

---

[32] *Ibid.*, p.20. Note that Deputy Secretary of State Christopher stated in 1977 that unscheduled changes of government were not uncommon in this day and age and that "withholding diplomatic relations from these regimes after they have obtained effective control penalises us", *ibid.*, p.18. See also as regards Afghanistan and the continuation of diplomatic relations, 72 *AJIL*, 1978, p.879. Cf. the special circumstances of the recognition of the government of China, *DUSPIL*, 1978, pp.71-73 and *ibid.*, 1979, p.142 *et seq.* But see Petersen, "Recognition of Governments Should not be Abolished", 77 *AJIL*, 1983, p.31.

[33] See 408 HL Deb., cols.1121-22, 28 April 1980. See also Symmons, "United Kingdom Abolition of the Doctrine of Recognition of Governments: A Rose by Another Name?", *Public Law*, 1981, p.249.

[34] See *Gur Corporation* v. *Trust Bank of Africa*, [1987] 1 QB 599; 75 *ILR*, p.675.

[35] See as regards the different approaches adopted to the Cambodian and Ugandan experiences, Symmons, *op. cit.*, p.250 and UKMIL 1979, 50 *BYIL*, 1979, p.296. See also *supra*, Chapter 4, p.133. See as to recognition of belligerency and insurgency O'Connell, *op. cit.*, pp.148-53; Lauterpacht, *op. cit.*, p.270 and Oppenheim, *op. cit.*, pp.140-41. See also further, *infra*, Chapter 18.

DE FACTO AND DE JURE RECOGNITION

In addition to the fact that there are different entities to be recognised, recognition itself may take different forms. It may be either *de facto* or *de jure*. A more correct way of putting this might be to say that a government may be recognised as a *de facto* government or a *de jure* government.

Recognition *de facto* implies that there is some doubt as to the long-term viability of the government in question. Recognition *de jure* usually follows where the recognising state accepts that the effective control displayed by the government is permanent and firmly rooted and that there are no legal reasons detracting from this, such as constitutional subservience to a foreign power. *De facto* recognition involves a hesitant assessment of the situation, an attitude of wait and see, to be succeeded by *de jure* recognition when the doubts are sufficiently overcome to extend formal acceptance. To take one instance, the United Kingdom recognised the Soviet government *de facto* in 1921 and *de jure* in 1924.[36] A slightly different approach is adopted in cases of civil war where the distinction between *de jure* and *de facto* recognition is sometimes used to illustrate the variance between legal and factual sovereignty. For example, during the 1936-9 Spanish Civil War, the United Kingdom, while recognising the Republic government as the *de jure* government, extended *de facto* recognition to the forces under General Franco as they gradually took over the country. Similarly, the government of the Italian conquering forces in Ethiopia was recognised *de facto* by the UK in 1936, and *de jure* two years later.[37]

By this method a recognising state can act in accordance with political reality and its own interests while reserving judgment on the permanence of the change in government or its desirability or legality. It is able to safeguard the affairs of its citizens and institutions by this, because certain legal consequences will flow in municipal law from the recognition.[38]

There are few meaningful distinctions between a *de facto* and a *de jure* recognition. To point to one instance, only a government recognised *de jure* may enter a claim to property located in the

---

[36] See e.g. O'Connell, *op cit.*, p.161. See also the Morrison statement, *supra*, footnote 22.
[37] *Ibid.*
[38] See *infra*, p.261.

recognising state.[39] Additionally, it is generally accepted that *de facto* recognition does not of itself include the exchange of diplomatic relations.

IMPLIED RECOGNITION [40]

Recognition itself need not be express, that is in the form of an open, unambiguous and formal communication but may be implied in certain circumstances. This is due to the fact that recognition is founded upon the will and intent of the state that is extending the recognition. Accordingly, there are conditions in which it might be possible to declare that in acting in a certain manner, one state has by implication recognised another state or government. Because this facility of indirect or implied recognition is available, states may make an express declaration to the effect that a particular action involving another party is by no means to be interpreted as comprehending any recognition. This attitude has been maintained by the Arab countries with regard to Israel, and in certain other cases.[41] It automatically excludes any possibility of implied recognition but does suggest that without a definite and clear waiver, the result of some international actions may be recognition of a hitherto unrecognised entity.

The point can best be explained by mentioning the kind of conditions which may give rise to the possibility of a recognition where no express or formal statement has been made. A message of congratulations to a new state upon attaining sovereignty will imply recognition of that state, as will the formal establishment of diplomatic relations.[42] But the maintenance of informal and unofficial contacts (such as those between the United States and Communist China during the 1960s and early 1970s in Warsaw) will not. The issuing of a consular *exequatur*, the accepted authorisation

---

[39] See e.g. *Haile Selassie* v. *Cable and Wireless Ltd. (No.2)*, [1939] 1 Ch. 182; 9 *ILR*, p.94.

[40] See e.g. Lauterpacht, *op. cit.*, pp.369-408 and Chen, *op. cit.*, pp.201-16. See also Lachs, "Recognition and Modern Methods of International Co-operation", 35 *BYIL*, 1959, p.252.

[41] See e.g. UK and North Vietnam, Cmd. 9763, p.3, note 1 and e.g. Israel and Arab countries, International Convention on the Elimination of all Forms of Racial Discrimination, 1965, see *Human Rights International Instruments*, UN, ST/HR/4/rev.4, 1982. Note that Egypt withdrew its declarations regarding non-recognition of Israel with regard to this Convention on 18 January 1980, *ibid.*, p.86.

[42] See O'Connell, *op. cit.*, pp.154-55.

permitting the performance of consular functions, to a representative of an unrecognised state will usually amount to a recognition of that state, though not in all cases. A British Consul has operated in Taiwan, but the UK does not recognise the Taiwan government. It is possible that the conclusion of a bilateral treaty between the recognising and unrecognised state, as distinct from a temporary agreement, might imply recognition, but the matter is open to doubt since there are a number of such agreements between parties not recognising each other. One would have to study the circumstances of the particular case to clarify the issue.[43]

Recognition is not normally to be inferred from the fact that both states have taken part in negotiations and signed a multilateral treaty, for example the United Nations Charter. For practice has revealed that many of the member-states or their governments are not recognised by other member-states. Although Israel and many Arab countries are UN members, this has not affected Arab non-recognition of the Israeli state.[44] While to some extent this is a curious stance as regards universal membership and recognition, it emphasises how far the initiative remains with the individual state and how much political factors obtrude.

In the case of common participation in an international conference, similar considerations apply, although the element of doubt has often stimulated non-recognising states to declare expressly that their presence and joint signature on any agreement issuing forth from the meeting is in no way to be understood as implying recognition. Such has been the case particularly with the Arab states over the years with regard to Israel.

State practice has restricted the possible scope of operation of this concept of implied recognition to a few instances only and all the relevant surrounding circumstances will have to be carefully evaluated before one can deduce from conduct the intention to extend recognition. States like to retain their control of such an important political instrument as recognition and are usually not keen to allow this to be inferred from the way they behave. They prefer recognition to be, in general, a formal act accorded after due thought.

[43] See e.g. *Republic of China* v. *Merchants' Fire Assurance Corporation of New York*, 30 F.2d 278 (1929); 5 *ILR*, p.42.

[44] See e.g. Wright, "Some Thoughts about Recognition", 44 *AJIL*, 1950, p.548.

CONDITIONAL RECOGNITION

The political nature of recognition has been especially marked with reference to what has been termed conditional recognition. This refers to the practice of making the recognition subject to fulfilment of certain conditions, for example, the good treatment of religious minorities as occurred with regard to the independence of some Balkan countries in the late nineteenth century, or the granting of most-favoured-nation status to the recognised state. One well-known instance of this approach was the Litvinov agreement of 1933 whereby the United States recognised the Soviet government upon the latter undertaking to avoid acts prejudicial to the internal security of the USA, and to come to a settlement of various financial claims.

However, breach of the particular condition does not invalidate the recognition. It may give rise to a breach of international law and political repercussions but the law appears not to accept the notion of a conditional recognition as such. The status of any conditions will depend upon agreements specifically made by the particular parties.[45]

COLLECTIVE RECOGNITION [46]

The expediency of collective recognition has often been referred to. This would amount to recognition by means of an international decision, whether by an international organisation or not. It would, of course, signify the importance of the international community in its collective assertion of control over membership and because of this it has not been warmly welcomed, nor can one foresee its general application for some time to come. The idea has been discussed particularly since the foundation of the League of Nations and was re-emphasised with the establishment of the United Nations. However, it rapidly became clear that member-states reserved the right to extend recognition to their own executive authorities and

[45] See e.g. Lauterpacht, *op. cit.*, Chapter 19. See also the Treaty of Berlin 1878 concerning Bulgaria, Montenegro, Serbia and Romania and the provisions dealing with freedom of religion, articles V, XXVII, XXXV and XLIII.

[46] See e.g. Higgins, *The Development of International Law Through the Political Origins of the United Nations*, 1963; Dugard, *op. cit.*; Lauterpacht, *op. cit.*, p.400; Chen, *op. cit.*, p.211 and Oppenheim, *op. cit.*, pp.146-47.

did not wish to delegate it to any international institution. The most that could be said is that membership of the United Nations constitutes evidence of statehood. But that, of course, is not binding upon other member-states who are free to refuse to recognise any other member-state or government of the UN.

WITHDRAWAL OF RECOGNITION [47]

Recognition once given may in certain circumstances be withdrawn. This is more easily achieved with respect to *de facto* recognition, as that is by its nature a cautious and temporary assessment of a particular situation. Where a *de facto* government loses the effective control it once exercised, the reason for recognition disappears and it may be revoked. It is in general a preliminary acceptance of political realities and may be withdrawn in accordance with a change in political factors. *De jure* recognition, on the other hand, is intended to be more of a definitive step and is more difficult to withdraw.

Of course, where a government recognised *de jure* has been overthrown a new situation arises and the question of a new government will have to be faced, but in such instances withdrawal of recognition of the previous administration is assumed and does not have to be expressly stated, providing always that the former government is not still in existence and carrying on the fight in some way.

Withdrawal of recognition in other circumstances is not a very general occurrence but in exceptional conditions it remains a possibility. The United Kingdom recognised the Italian conquest of Ethiopia *de facto* in 1936 and *de jure* two years later. However, it withdrew recognition in 1940, with the intensification of fighting and the dispatch of military aid. Recognition of belligerency will naturally terminate with the defeat of either party, while the loss of one of the required criteria of statehood would affect recognition. It is to be noted that the 1979 recognition of the People's Republic of China as the sole legal government of China entailed the withdrawal of recognition or "derecognition" of the Republic of China (Taiwan). This was explained to mean that:

---

[47] *Ibid.*, pp.150-52. See also Lauterpacht, *op. cit.*, p.349.

so far as the formal foreign relations of the United States are concerned, a government does *not* exist in Taiwan any longer.[48]

Nevertheless, this was not to affect the application of the laws of the United States with respect to Taiwan in the context of US domestic law.[49] To some extent in this instance the usual consequences of non-recognition have not flowed, but this has taken place upon the background of a formal and deliberate act of policy. It does show how complex the topic of recognition has become.

The usual method of expressing disapproval with the actions of a particular government is to break diplomatic relations. This will adequately demonstrate aversion as, for example, the rupture in diplomatic relations between the UK and the US in 1927, and between some Arab countries and the United States in 1967, without entailing the legal consequences and problems that a withdrawal of recognition would initiate. But one must not confuse the ending of diplomatic relations with a withdrawal of recognition.

Since recognition is ultimately a political issue, no matter how circumscribed or conditioned by the law, it logically follows that, should a state perceive any particular situation as justifying a withdrawal of recognition, it will take such action as it regards as according with its political interests.

NON-RECOGNITION [50]

✓There has been developing since the 1930s a doctrine of non-recognition where under certain conditions a factual situation will not be recognised because of strong reservations as to the morality or legality of the actions that have been adopted in order to bring about the factual situation.

This approach was particularly stimulated by the Japanese invasion of Manchuria in 1931. The US Secretary of State declared in 1932 that the illegal invasion would not be recognised as it was contrary to the 1928 Pact of Paris (the Kellogg-Briand Pact) which had

[48] US reply brief in the Court of Appeals in *Goldwater* v. *Carter*, 444 US 996 (1979), quoted in *DUSPIL*, 1979, pp.143-44.

[49] Taiwan Relations Act, Pub. L. 96-8 Stat. 22 USC 3301-3316, s.4.

[50] See e.g. Lauterpacht, *op. cit.*, pp.416-20. See also Langer, *Seizure of Territory*, 1947 and Hackworth, *Digest, op. cit.* vol.1, p.334.

outlawed war as an instrument of national policy. The doctrine of not recognising any situation, treaty or agreement brought about by non-legal means was named the Stimson doctrine after the American Secretary of State who put it forward. It was reinforced not long afterwards by a resolution of the Assembly of the League of Nations stressing that League members should not recognise any situation, treaty or agreement brought about by means contrary to the League's Covenant or the Pact of Paris.[51]

However, state practice until the Second World War was not encouraging. The Italian conquest of the Empire of Ethiopia was recognised and the German takeover of Czechoslovakia accepted. The Soviet Union made a series of territorial acquisitions in 1940 ranging from areas of Finland to the Baltic States (of Lithuania, Estonia and Latvia) and Bessarabia. These were recognised *de facto* over the years by the Allies (though not by the United States).[52]

The doctrine was examined anew after 1945. The draft Declaration on the Rights and Duties of States, 1949, emphasised that territorial acquisitions by states were not to be recognised by other states where achieved by means of the threat or use of force or in any other manner inconsistent with international law and order. The Declaration on Principles of International Law, 1970, also included a provision to the effect that no territorial acquisition resulting from the threat or use of force shall be recognised as legal,[53] and resolution 242 (1967) on the solution to the Middle East conflict emphasised "the inadmissibility of the acquisition of territory by war".[54]

Rhodesia unilaterally proclaimed its independence in November 1965 and in the years of its existence did not receive official recognition from any state at all, although it did maintain diplomatic relations with South Africa and Portugal prior to the revolution of 1974. The day following the Rhodesian declaration of independence, the Security Council passed a resolution calling upon all states not to accord it recognition and to refrain from assisting it. The Council

[51] LNOJ, Sp. Suppl. no. 101, p.8. This principle was reiterated in a number of declarations subsequently, see e.g. 34 *AJIL*, 1940, Suppl. p.197. See also O'Connell, *op. cit.*, pp.143-46.
[52] *Ibid.*
[53] See also article 17 of the Bogotá Charter of the OAS, 1948, and article 52 of the Vienna Convention on the Law of Treaties, 1969.
[54] See also article 5(3) of the Consensus Definition of Aggression, 1974, adopted by the General Assembly.

imposed selective mandatory economic sanctions on Rhodesia and these were later made comprehensive.[55] MM

The role of non-recognition as an instrument of sanction as well as a means of pressure and a method of protecting the wronged inhabitants of a territory was discussed more fully in the Advisory Opinion of the International Court of Justice in the *Namibia* case, 1971, dealing with South Africa's presence in that territory. The Court held that since the continued South African occupancy was illegal, member-states of the United Nations were obliged to recognise that illegality and the invalidity of South Africa's acts concerning Namibia and were under a duty to refrain from any actions implying recognition of the legality of or lending support or assistance to the South African presence and administration.[56]

THE LEGAL EFFECTS OF RECOGNITION

In this section some of the legal results that flow from the recognition or non-recognition of an entity, both in the international sphere and within the municipal law of particular states, will be noted. Although recognition may legitimately be regarded as a political tool, it is one that nevertheless entails important consequences in the legal field.

Internationally

In the majority of cases, it can be accepted that recognition of a state or government is a legal acknowledgement of a factual state of affairs. Nevertheless, it should not be assumed that non-recognition of, for example, a state will deprive that entity of rights and duties

---

[55] See e.g. Security Council resolutions 217 (1965) and 232 (1966). See also Shaw, *Title to Territory in Africa*, 1986, p.160. Similar action has also been taken with regard to the Bantustans, see e.g. General Assembly resolution 31/6A and the Security Council statements of 21 September 1979 and 15 December 1981, Shaw, *op. cit.*, p.149. See also Security Council resolution 541 (1983) deploring the purported secession of part of Cyprus and terming the proposed Turkish Cypriot state "legally invalid", and Security Council resolution 662 (1990) declaring the Iraqi annexation of Kuwait "null and void" and calling on all states and institutions not to recognise the annexation.

[56] ICJ Reports, 1971, pp.16, 54, 56; 49 *ILR*, pp.2, 44, 46. Non member-states of the UN were similarly obliged, *ibid*. The non-recognition obligation did not extend, however, to certain acts of a humanitarian nature the effect of which could only be ignored to the detriment of the inhabitants of the territory, *ibid.*, p.56. See also *supra*, Chapter 5, p.157.

before international law, excepting, of course, those situations where it may be possible to say that recognition is constitutive of the legal entity.

In general, the political existence of a state is independent of recognition by other states, and thus an unrecognised state must be deemed subject to the rules of international law. It cannot consider itself free from restraints as to aggressive behaviour, nor can its territory be regarded as *terra nullius*. States which have signed international agreements are entitled to assume that states which they have not recognised but which have similarly signed the agreement are bound by that agreement. For example, the United Kingdom treated the German Democratic Republic as bound by its signature of the 1963 Nuclear Test Ban Treaty even when the state was not recognised by the UK.

Non-recognition, with its consequent absence of diplomatic relations, may affect the unrecognised state in asserting its rights or other states in asserting its duties under international law, but will not affect the existence of such rights and duties. The position is, however, different under municipal law.

Internally

Because recognition is fundamentally a political act, it is reserved to the executive branch of government. This means that the judiciary must accept the discretion of the executive and give effect to its decisions. The courts cannot recognise a state or government. They can only accept and enforce the legal consequences which flow from the executive's political decision.

To this extent, recognition is constitutive, because the act of recognition itself creates legal results within the domestic jurisdiction. In the United Kingdom and the United States particularly, the courts feel themselves obliged to accept the verdict of the executive branch of government as to whether a particular entity should be regarded as recognised or not. If the administration has recognised a state or government and so informs the judiciary by means of a certificate, the position of that state or government within the municipal structure is totally transformed.

It may sue in the domestic courts and be granted immunity from suit in certain instances. Its own legislative and executive acts will be given effect to in the courts of the recognising state and its own diplomatic representatives will be able to claim the various immunities accorded to the official envoys of a recognised state. In addition, it will be entitled to possession in the recognising state of property belonging to its predecessor.

The UK [57]

The English courts have adopted the attitude over many years that an entity unrecognised by the Foreign Office would be treated before the courts as if it did not exist and accordingly it would not be able to claim immunity before the courts. This meant in one case that ships of the unrecognised "Provisional Government of Northern Russia" would not be protected by the courts from claims affecting them.[58] Similarly an unrecognised state or government is unable to appear before the courts as a plaintiff in an action. This particular principle prevented the revolutionary government of Berne in 1804 from taking action to restrain the Bank of England from dealing with funds belonging to the previous administration of the city.[59]

The leading case in English law on the issue of effects of recognition of an entity within the domestic sphere is *Luther* v. *Sagor*.[60]

This concerned the operations and produce of a timber factory in Russia owned by the plaintiffs, which had been nationalised in 1919 by the Soviet government. In 1920 the defendant company purchased a quantity of wood from the USSR and this was claimed in England by the plaintiffs as their property since it had come from what had been their factory. It was argued by them that the 1919 Soviet decree should be ignored before the English courts since the United Kingdom had not recognised the Soviet government. The lower court agreed with this contention and the matter then came to the Court of Appeal.[61]

In the meantime the UK recognised *de facto* the Soviet government and the Foreign Office informed the Court of Appeal of this in

[57] See e.g. Greig, *op. cit.* and Merrills, "Recognition and Construction", 20 *ICLQ*, 1971, p.476.
[58] *The Annette*, [1919] P.105; 1 *ILR*, p.43.
[59] *The City of Berne* v. *The Bank of England*, (1804) 9 Ves. Jun. 347.
[60] [1921] 1 KB 456; 1 *ILR*, p.47.
[61] [1921] 3 KB 532; 1 *ILR*, p.49.

writing. The result was that the higher court was bound to take note of the Soviet decree and accordingly the plaintiffs lost their case, since a court must give effect to the legislation of a recognised state or government. The Court also held that the fact that the Soviet government was recognised *de facto* and not *de jure* did not affect the issue. Another interesting point is that since the Foreign Office certificate included a statement that the former Provisional Government of Russian recognised by the UK had been dispersed during December 1917, the Court inferred the commencement of the Soviet government from that date.

The essence of the matter was that the Soviet government was now accepted as the sovereign government of the USSR as from December 1917. And since recognition once given is retroactive and relates back to the date that the authority of the government was accepted as being established, and not the date on which recognition is granted, the Soviet decree of 1919 was deemed to be a legitimate act of a recognised government. This was so even though at that date the Soviet government was not recognised by the United Kingdom.

The purpose of the retroactivity provision[62] is to avoid possible influence in the internal affairs of the entity recognised, since otherwise legislation made prior to recognition might be rejected. However, this will depend always upon the terms of the executive certificate by which the state informs its courts of the recognition. Should the Foreign Office insist that the state or government in question is to be recognised as a sovereign state or government as of the date of the action the courts would be bound by this.

As in the case with legislation, contracts made by an unrecognised government will not be enforced in English courts. Without the required action by the political authorities an unrecognised entity does not exist as a legal person before the municipal courts.

The case of *Luther* v. *Sagor* suggested that in general the legal consequences of a *de facto* recognition would be the same as a *de jure* one. This was emphasised in *Haile Selassie* v. *Cable and Wireless Ltd (No.2)*,[63] but regarded as restricted to acts in relation to persons or property in the territory which the *de facto* government has been recognised as effectively controlling.

---

[62] See e.g. Oppenheim, *op. cit.*, p.150 and Whiteman, *Digest, op. cit.* vol.2, pp.728-45.
[63] [1939] 1 Ch. 182; 9 *ILR*, p.94.

In other words, a different situation would ensue with regard to persons or property situated outside the territory of the state or government. In the *Haile Selassie* case, the Emperor of Ethiopia was suing a British company for money owing to him under an agreement. The problem was that when the action was brought, the UK had recognised the Italian forces as the *de facto* authority in Ethiopia while Haile Selassie was still recognised as the *de jure* sovereign. The Court held that since the case concerned a debt recoverable in England and not the validity of acts with regard to persons or property in Ethiopia, the *de jure* authority, Emperor Haile Selassie, was entitled to the sum due from the company, and the *de facto* control of the Italians did not affect this.

However, before the defendant's appeal was heard, the United Kingdom extended *de jure* recognition to the Italian authorities in Ethiopia. The Court of Appeal accepted that this related back to, and was deemed to operate as from the date of the *de facto* recognition. Since this had occurred prior to the case starting, it meant that the Italian government was now to be recognised as the *de jure* government of Ethiopia, before and during the time of the hearing of the action. Accordingly, Haile Selassie was divested of any right whatsoever to sue for the recovery of the money owing.

This problem of the relationship between a *de facto* government and a *de jure* government as far as English courts were concerned, manifested itself again during the Spanish Civil War.

The case of the *Arantzazu Mendi* [64] concerned a private steam-ship registered in Bilbao in the Basque province of Spain. In June 1937, following the capture of that region by the forces of General Franco, the opposing Republican government issued a decree requisitioning all ships registered in Bilbao. Nine months later the Nationalist government of Franco also passed a decree taking control over all Bilbao vessels. In the meantime, the *Arantzazu Mendi* itself was in London when the Republican government issued a writ to obtain possession of the ship. The owners opposed this while accepting the Nationalists' requisition order.

It is an accepted rule of international law that a recognised state cannot be sued or otherwise brought before the courts of another state. Accordingly, the Nationalists argued that since their authority had been recognised *de facto* by the UK government over the areas

[64] [1939] AC 256; 9 *ILR*, p.60.

they actually controlled, their decree was valid and could not be challenged in the English courts. Therefore, the action by the Republican government must be dismissed.

The case came before the House of Lords, where it was decided that the Nationalist government, as the *de facto* authority of much of Spain including the region of Bilbao, was entitled to be regarded as a sovereign state and was able to benefit from the normal immunities which follow therefrom. Thus, the action by the Republican government failed. The House of Lords pointed out that it did not matter that the territory over which the *de facto* authority was exercising sovereign powers was from time to time increased or diminished.[65] This case marks the high-point in the attribution of characteristics to a *de facto* authority and can be criticised for its over-generous assessment of the status of such an entity.[66]

The problems faced by the English court when the rights and obligations of a *de jure* government and a *de facto* government, claiming the same territory, appear to be in conflict have been briefly noted. Basically the actions of a *de facto* authority with regard to people and property within this sphere of control will be recognised in an English court, but where property is situated and recoverable in England, the *de jure* sovereign will have precedence. A similarly complicated situation arises where the interests of two recognised *de jure* governments of the same state are involved, as one supersedes the other. Problems can arise concerning the issue of retroactivity, that is, how far the court will relate back actions of a *de jure* government, since recognition is normally retroactive to the moment of inception of the particular state or government.

The matter was discussed in the *Gdynia Ameryka Linie* v. *Boguslawski* case.[67] During the Second World War the Polish government in exile stationed in London was recognised by the UK as the *de jure* government of Poland. However, on 28 June 1945 the communist provisional government was established with effective control of the county and at midnight on 5 July the UK recognised that government as the *de jure* government of Poland. A couple of days prior to this recognition, the Polish government in exile made an offer to Polish

---

[65] See e.g. Lord Atkin, *ibid.*, pp.264-65.
[66] See e.g. Lauterpacht, *op. cit.*, pp.288-94.
[67] [1953] AC 11; 19 *ILR*, p.72.

seamen of compensation in the event of leaving the merchant navy service. The money was to be paid by the particular employers to seamen not wanting to work for the communist provisional government. In the *Boguslawski* case the employers refused to pay the compensation to seamen requesting it, and argued that the UK recognition *de jure* of the provisional government was retroactive to 28 June, this being the date that the government effectively took control of the country. If this was the case, then acts of the government in exile after 28 June ceased to be of effect and thus the offers of compensation could not be enforced in the English courts.

The House of Lords emphasised the general proposition that recognition operates retroactively. However, they modified the statement by declaring that the courts had to give effect not only to acts done by the new government after recognition, but also to acts done before the recognition "in so far as those acts related to matters under its control at the time when the acts were done".[68] It was stated that while the recognition of the new government had certain retroactive effects, the recognition of the old government remained effective down to the date when it was in fact withdrawn. Problems might have arisen had the old government, before withdrawal of recognition, attempted to take action with respect to issues under the control of the new government. However, that was not involved in the present case.

In other words, and in the circumstances of the case, the principle of retroactivity of recognition was regarded as restricted to matters within the effective control of the new government. Where something outside the effective control of the new government is involved, it would appear that the recognition does not operate retroactively and that prior to the actual date of recognition one would have to accept and put into effect the acts of the previous *de jure* government.

This could lead to many complicated situations especially where a court was faced with conflicting courses of action, something which is not hard to envisage when one *de jure* government has been superseded by another. It could permit abuses of government such as where a government, knowing itself to be about to lose recognition, awards its supporters financial or other awards in decrees that may

---

[68] Lord Reid, *ibid.*, pp.44-45; 19 *ILR*, pp.81, 83.

be enforced in English courts. What would happen if the new government issued contrary orders in an attempt to nullify the effect of the old government's decrees is something that was not examined in the *Boguslawski* case.

Another case which came before the courts in the same year was *Civil Air Transport Inc* v. *Central Air Transport Corporation*,[69] and it similarly failed to answer the question mentioned above. It involved the sale of aircraft belonging to the nationalist government of China, which had been flown to the British Crown Colony of Hong Kong. Such aircraft were sold to an American company after the communist government established effective control over the country but before it had been recognised by the UK. The Court accepted that the nationalist government had been entitled to the aircraft and pointed out that:

> retroactivity of recognition operates to validate acts of a *de facto* Government which has subsequently become the new *de jure* Government, and not to invalidate acts of the previous *de jure* Government.[70]

It is to be noted that the communist government did not attempt to nullify the sale to the American company. Had it done so, a new situation would have been created but it is as yet uncertain whether that would have materially altered the legal result.

The general doctrine adhered to by the UK with regard to recognition (and now diplomatic dealings) is that it will be accorded upon the evidence of effective control. It is used to acknowledge factual situations and not as a method of exhibiting approval or otherwise. However, this is not so in all cases and there are a number of governments in effective control of their countries and unrecognised by the UK. One major example was the German Democratic Republic. Since the prime consequence of non-recognition is that the English courts will not give effect to any laws of an unrecognised entity, problems are thus likely to arise in ordinary international political and commercial life.

The issue came before the Court in the *Carl Zeiss Stiftung* v. *Rayner and Keeler Ltd (No.2)* case.[71] It concerned the Carl Zeiss

---

[69] [1953] AC 70; 19 *ILR*, pp.85, 93, 110. See also Mann, "Recognition of Sovereignty", 16 *MLR*, 1953, p.226.

[70] [1953] AC 70, 90; 19 *ILR*, pp.110, 113.

[71] [1967] AC 853; 43 *ILR*, p.42. See also Greig, *op. cit.*

foundation which was run by a special board, reconstituted in 1952 as the Council of Gera. The problem was that it was situated in the German Democratic Republic (GDR) and the establishment of the Council of Gera as the governing body of the Carl Zeiss foundation was effected by a reorganisation of local government in the GDR. When Carl Zeiss brought a claim before the English courts, the issue was at once raised as to whether, in view of the UK non-recognition of the GDR, the governing body of the foundation could be accepted by the courts. The Court of Appeal decided that since the Foreign Office certified that the UK recognised "the State and Government of the Union of Soviet Socialist Republics as *de jure* entitled to exercise governing authority in respect of that zone"[72] (i.e. the GDR, being the former Soviet zone of occupation) it was not possible to give effect to any rules or regulations laid down by the GDR. The House of Lords, however, extricated the English courts system from a rather difficult position by means of an elaborate fiction.

It stated that as a Foreign Office certificate is binding on the courts as to the facts it contains, it logically followed that the courts must recognise the USSR as the *de jure* governing authority of East Germany, irrespective of the creation of the GDR. The courts were not entitled to enter into a political examination of the actual situation but were obliged to accept and give effect to the facts set out in the Foreign Office certificate. Thus, the Soviet Union was the *de jure* sovereign and the GDR government must be accepted as a subordinate and dependent body.

Accordingly, the Court could recognise the existence of the Carl Zeiss Stiftung by virtue of the UK recognition of the *de jure* status of the Soviet Union, the GDR as an administrative body being relevant only as a legal creature of the USSR.

The problem brought out in the *Carl Zeiss* case and sidestepped there, was raised again in a series of cases concerning Rhodesia, following the unilateral declaration of independence by the Smith regime in 1965. Basically, if a government or state which exercises effective control over its own territory is unrecognised by the UK a strict enforcement of the "no recognition, no existence" rule could lead to much hardship and inconvenience. Accordingly, in

---

[72] [1966] 1 Ch. 596; 43 *ILR*, p.25.

Adams v. *Adams* [73] a Rhodesian divorce decree was not recognised in an English court. However, in *Hesperides Hotels Ltd* v. *Aegean Turkish Holidays*,[74] concerning an action in trespass with respect to hotels owned by Greek Cypriots but run by Turkish Cypriots following the Turkish invasion of 1974, Lord Denning stated *obiter* that he believed that the courts could recognise the laws and acts of an unrecognised body in effective control of territory, at least with regard to laws regulating the day to day affairs of the people.[75] It is certainly an attractive approach, if carefully handled and if strictly limited to determinations of a humanitarian and non-sovereign nature.[76]

Since the UK decision to abandon recognition of governments in 1980, the question arises as to the attitude of the courts on this matter. In particular, it appears that they may be called upon to examine the nature of the UK government's dealings with a new regime in order to determine its status for municipal law purposes.[77]

In *Gur Corporation* v. *Trust Bank of Africa* [78] the Court was in fact called upon to decide the status of Ciskei. This territory, part of South Africa, was one of the Bantustans granted "independence" by South Africa. This was accomplished by virtue of the Status of Ciskei Act 1981. The preliminary issue that came before the Court in a commercial dispute was whether Ciskei had *locus standi* to sue or be sued in England. The Foreign and Commonwealth Office certified that Ciskei was not recognised as an independent sovereign state either *de facto* or *de jure* and that representations were made to South Africa in relation to matters occurring in Ciskei. The Court of Appeal held that it was able to take account of such declarations and legislation as were not in conflict with the certificates.

The effect of that, noted Lord Donaldson, was that the Status of Ciskei Act 1981 could be taken into account, except for those

[73] [1971] P.188; 52 *ILR*, p.15.

[74] [1978] QB 205; 73 *ILR*, p.9. See also Shaw, "Legal Acts of an Unrecognised Entity", 94 *LQR*, 1978, p.500.

[75] [1978] QB 205, 218; 73 *ILR*, pp.9, 15. See also Steyn J, *Gur Corporation* v. *Trust Bank of Africa Ltd.*, [1986] 3 WLR 583, 589, 592; 75 *ILR*, p.675.

[76] On a number of occasions the question of interpretation of a statutory provision containing the words 'state' or 'government' has arisen. In general, the courts have given an answer based upon construction of the relevant instrument rather than upon the Foreign Office certificate, see e.g. *Re Al-Fin Corporation's Patent*, [1970] Ch. 160; 52 *ILR*, p.68 and *Reel* v. *Holder*, [1981] 1 WLR 1226; 74 *ILR*, p.105. See Merrills, *op. cit.*

[77] See 409 HL Deb., cols.1097-98 and Symmons, *op. cit.*, pp.254-60.

[78] [1987] 1 QB 599; 75 *ILR*, p.675.

provisions declaring the territory independent and relinquishing South African sovereignty. This led to the conclusion that the Ciskei legislature was in fact exercising power by virtue of delegation from the South African authorities.[79] Accordingly, the government of Ciskei could sue or be sued in the English courts "as being a subordinate body set up by the Republic of South Africa to act on its behalf".[80] Clearly the Court felt that the situation was analogous to the *Carl Zeiss* case. Whether this was in fact so is an open question. It is certainly open to doubt whether the terms of the certificates in the cases were on all fours. In the *Gur* case, the executive was far more cautious and non-committal. Indeed, one of the certificates actually stated that the UK government did not have a formal position regarding the exercise of governing authority over the territory of Ciskei,[81] whereas in *Carl Zeiss* the certificate noted expressly that the USSR was recognised as *de jure* entitled to exercise governing authority in respect of the territory (the GDR).[82] The gap was bridged by construction and inference.

As far as the policy of executive certificates and the attitudes of the courts is concerned, the situation appears unsatisfactory. The executive no longer issues certificates in relation, for example, to governments that the courts are obliged to accept. On the other hand, *Gur* suggests that the courts are not willing to examine for themselves the realities of any given situation, but would seek to infer from the terms of any certificate what the answer ought to be.[83]

The USA

The situation in the United States with regard to the recognition or non-recognition of foreign entities is similar to that pertaining in the UK, with some important differences. While an unrecognised state or government cannot sue, it may in certain circumstances be permitted immunity before the American courts from being sued.

---

[79] *Ibid.*, p.623; 75 *ILR*, p.696.

[80] *Ibid.*, p.624. See also Nourse LJ, *ibid.*, pp.624-66; 75 *ILR*, pp.696-699.

[81] *Ibid.*, pp.618-19; 75 *ILR*, p.690.

[82] [1966] 1 Ch. 596; 43 *ILR*, p.25.

[83] See e.g. Mann, "The Judicial Recognition of an Unrecognised State", 36 *ICLQ*, 1987, p.349 and Beck, "A South African Homeland Appears in the English Court: Legitimation of the Illegitimate?", *ibid.*, p.350.

This would appear to depend on the facts of each case and a practical appreciation of the entity in question.[84]

As in the UK, a declaration by the executive will be treated as binding the courts, but in the USA, the courts appear to have a greater latitude. In the absence of the "suggestion" clarifying how far the process of non-recognition is to be applied, the courts are more willing than their UK counterparts to give effect to particular acts of an unrecognised body. Indeed, in the *Carl Zeiss* case Lords Reid and Wilberforce referred in approving terms to the trend evident in decisions of US courts to give recognition to the "actual facts or realities found to exist in the territory in question", in the interests of justice and common sense. Such recognition did not apply to every act, but in Lord Wilberforce's words, it did apply to "private rights, or acts of everyday occurrence, or perfunctory acts of administration".[85] How far this extends, however, has never been precisely defined.

It was the difficulties engendered by the American Civil War that first stimulated a reappraisal of the "no recognition, no existence" doctrine. It was not possible to ignore every act of the Confederate authorities and so the idea developed that such rules adopted by the Confederate states as were not hostile to the Union or the authority of the Central Government, or did not conflict with the terms of the US Constitution, would be treated as valid and enforceable in the courts system.[86] The doctrine was developed in a case before the New York Court of Appeals, when, discussing the status of the unrecognised Soviet government, Judge Cardozo noted that an unrecognised entity which had maintained control over its territory,

> may gain for its acts and decrees a validity quasi-governmental, if violence to fundamental principles of justice or to our public policy might otherwise be done.[87]

This thesis progressed rapidly in the period immediately preceding the American recognition of the USSR and led in *Salimoff* v. *Standard*

---

[84] See *supra*, p.258, regarding Taiwan after 1 January 1979. See also *Wulfsohn* v. *Russian Republic*, 234 NY 372 (1924); 2 *ILR*, p.39.

[85] [1967] AC 853, 954; 43 *ILR*, pp.23, 66.

[86] See e.g. *Texas* v. *White*, 74 US 700 (1868).

[87] *Sokoloff* v. *National City Bank of New York*, 239 NY 158 (1924); 2 *ILR*, p.44.

Oil Co of New York[88] to the enforcement of a Soviet oil nationalisation decree, with the comment that:

> to refuse to recognise that Soviet Russia is a government regulating the internal affairs of the country, is to give to fictions an air of reality which they do not deserve.

This decision, diametrically opposed to the *Luther* v. *Sagor* approach,[89] constituted a step towards the abolition of differences between the judicial treatment of the acts of recognised and unrecognised governments.

However, the limits of this broad doctrine were more carefully defined in *The Maret*[90] where the Court refused to give effect to the nationalisation of an Estonian ship by the government of the unrecognised Soviet Republic of Estonia. However, the ship in dispute was located in an American port at the date of the nationalisation order, and there appears to be a difference in treatment in some cases depending upon whether the property was situated inside or outside the country concerned.

One can mention, in contrast to *The Maret,* the case of *Upright* v. *Mercury Business Machines*,[91] in which the non-recognition of the German Democratic Republic was discussed in relation to the assignment of a bill to the plaintiff by a state-controlled company of the GDR. The judge of the New York Supreme Court declared, in upholding the plaintiff's claim, that a foreign government, although unrecognised by the executive:

> may nevertheless have *de facto* existence which is judicially cognisable. The acts of such a *de facto* government may affect private rights and obligations arising either as a result of activity in, or with persons or corporations within, the territory controlled by such *de facto* government.

However, the creation of judicial entities by unrecognised states will not be allowed to circumvent executive policy. In *Kunstsammlungen zu Weimar* v. *Elicofon*,[92] the KZW was an East

---

88 262 NY 220 (1933); 7 *ILR,* pp.22, 26.
89 [1921] 1 KB 456; 1 *ILR,* p.47; *supra,* p.263.
90 145 F.2d 431 (1944); 12 *ILR,* p.29.
91 213 NYS (2d) 417 (1961); 32 *ILR,* p.65.
92 358 F.Supp. 747 (1972); 61 *ILR,* p.143.

German governmental agency until 1969, when it was transformed into a separate juristic person in order to avoid the problems relating to unrecognised states in the above litigation. This concerned the recovery of pictures stolen from a museum during the American occupation of Germany.

As a branch of an unrecognised state, the KZW could not of course be permitted to sue in an American court, but the change of status in 1969 was designed to circumvent this. The Court, however, refused to accept this and emphasised that to allow the KZW to intervene in the case "would render our government's non-recognition of the German Democratic Republic a meaningless gesture".[93]

In *Ministry of Defense of the Islamic Republic of Iran* v. *Gould*,[94] the Court was faced with an action in which the unrecognised Iranian government sought to enforce an award. However, the US intervened and filed a statement of interest supporting Iran's argument and this proved of significant influence. This general approach was reinforced in *National Petrochemical* v. *The M/T Stolt Sheaf*,[95] where the Court stressed that the executive must have the power to deal with unrecognised governments and that therefore the absence of formal recognition did not necessarily result in a foreign government being barred from access to US courts.[96] However, where the executive has issued a non-recognition certificate and makes known its view that in the instant case the unrecognised party should not be permitted access to the courts, the courts appear very willing to comply.[97]

It is somewhat difficult to reconcile the various American cases or to determine the extent to which the acts of an unrecognised state or government may be enforced in the courts system of the United States. But two factors should be particularly noted. First of all, the declaration of the executive is binding. If that intimates that

---

[93] *Ibid.*, p.757; 61 *ILR*, p.154. See also *Federal Republic of Germany* v. *Elicofon*, 14 *ILM*, 1976, p.806, following the US recognition of the GDR in which KZW was permitted to intervene in the litigation in progress. See also *Transportes Aereos de Angola* v. *Ronair*, 544 F.Supp. 858.

[94] 1988 *Iranian Assets Litig. Rep.* 15, 313. See also 82 *AJIL*, 1988, p.591.

[95] 860 F.2d 551 (1988).

[96] *Ibid.*, p.554.

[97] See e.g. *Republic of Panama* v. *Republic National Bank of New York*, 681 F.Supp. 1066 (1988) and *Republic of Panama* v. *Citizens & Southern International Bank*, 682 F.Supp. 1144 (1988). See also Fountain, "Out From the Precarious Orbit of Politics: Reconsidering Recognition and the Standing of Foreign Governments to Sue in US Courts", 29 *Va JIL*, 1989, p.473.

no effect is to be given to acts of the unrecognised entity, the courts will be obliged to respect this. It may also be the case that the State Department "suggestions" will include some kind of hint or indication which, while not clearly expressed, may lead the courts to feel that the executive is leaning more one way than another in the matter of the government's status, and this may influence the courts. For example, in the *Salimoff*[98] case the terms of the certificate tended to encourage the court to regard the Soviet government as a recognised government, whereas in the case of *The Maret*[99] the tone of the executive's statement on the Soviet Republic of Estonia was decidedly hostile to any notion of recognition or enforcement of its decrees.

The second point is the location of the property in question. There is a tendency to avoid the enforcement of acts and decrees affecting property situated outside the unrecognised state or government and in any event the location of the property often introduces additional complications as regards municipal law provision.[100]

There is some uncertainty in the United States as to the operation of the retroactivity doctrine, particularly as it affects events occurring outside the country. There is a line of cases suggesting that only those acts of the unrecognised government performed in its own territory could be validated by the retroactive operation of recognition[101] while, on the other hand, there are cases illustrating the opposite proposition decided by the Supreme Court.[102]

[98] 262 NY 220 (1933); 7 *ILR*, p.22.

[99] 145 F.2d 431 (1944); 12 *ILR*, p.29.

[100] See e.g. *Civil Air Transport Inc* v. *Central Air Transport Corporation*, [1953] AC 70; 19 *ILR*, p.85.

[101] See e.g. *Lehigh Valley Railroad Co* v. *Russia*, 21 F.2d 396 (1927); 4 *ILR*, p.58.

[102] See e.g. *US* v. *Pink*, 315 US 203 (1942); 10 *ILR*, p.48, and *US* v. *Belmont*, 301 US 324 (1937); 8 *ILR*, p.34.

CHAPTER EIGHT

Territory[1]

THE CONCEPT OF TERRITORY IN INTERNATIONAL LAW

International law is based on the concept of the state. The state in its turn lies upon the foundation of sovereignty, which expresses internally the supremacy of the governmental institutions and externally the supremacy of the state as a legal person.

But sovereignty itself, with its retinue of legal rights and duties, is founded upon the fact of territory. Without territory a legal person cannot be a state.[2] It is undoubtedly the basic characteristic of a state and the one most widely accepted and understood. There are currently some one hundred and sixty distinct territorial units, each one subject to a different territorial sovereignty and jurisdiction.

Since such fundamental legal concepts as sovereignty and jurisdiction can only be comprehended in relation to territory, it follows that the legal nature of territory becomes a vital part in any study of international law. Indeed, the principle whereby a state is deemed to exercise exclusive power over its territory can be regarded as a fundamental axiom of classical international law.[3] The development of international law upon the basis of the exclusive authority of the state within an accepted territorial framework meant that territory became "perhaps the fundamental concept of international law".[4] Most nations indeed developed through a close relationship with the land they inhabited.[5]

One may note the central role of territory in the scheme of international law by remarking on the development of legal rules protecting its inviolability. The principle of respect for the territorial

---

[1] See e.g. Jennings, *The Acquisition of Territory in International Law*, 1963; Verzijl, *International Law in Historical Perspective*, vol.3, 1970, p.297 *et seq.*; Shaw, "Territory in International Law", 13 *Netherlands Yearbook of International Law*, 1982, p.61; Hill, *Claims to Territory in International Law and Relations*, 1945; Gottman, *The Significance of Territory*, 1973 and Schoenborn, "La Nature Juridique du Territoire", 30 *HR*, p.85.

[2] See Oppenheim, *International Law*, vol.1, 8th ed., 1955, p.451.

[3] See Delbez, "Du Territoire dans ses Rapports avec l'État", 39 *Revue Générale de Droit International Public*, 1932, p.46. See also Hill, *op. cit.*, p.3.

[4] O'Connell, International Law, 2nd ed., vol.1, 1970, p.403. See also Jennings, *op. cit.*, p.87 and Judge Huber, *The Island of Palmas* case, 2 *RIAA*, pp.829, 838 (1928).

[5] See generally, Gottman, *op. cit.*

integrity of states is well-founded as one of the linch-pins of the international system, as is the norm prohibiting interference within the internal affairs of other states.[6] A number of factors, however, have tended to reduce the territorial exclusivity of the state in international law. Technological and economic changes have had an impact as interdependence becomes more evident and the rise of such transnational concerns as human rights and self-determination have tended to impinge upon this exclusivity.[7] The growth of international organisations is another relevant factor, as is the development of the "common heritage" concept in the context of the law of the sea and air law.[8] Nevertheless, one should not exaggerate the effects upon international law doctrine today of such trends.[9] Territorial sovereignty remains as a key concept in international law.

Since the law reflects political conditions and evolves, in most cases, in harmony with reality, international law has had to develop a series of rules governing the transfer and control of territory. Such rules, by the very nature of international society, have often (although not always) had the effect of legitimising the results of the exercise of power. The lack of a strong, central authority in international law has emphasised, even more than municipal legal structures, the way that law must come to terms with power and force.

The rules laid down by municipal legislation and judicial decisions regarding the transfer and control of land within a particular state are usually highly detailed, for they deal with one of the basic resources and wealth-creating factors of the nation. Land law has often reflected the power balance within a society, with feudal arrangements being succeeded by free market contracts and latterly the introduction of comprehensive provisions elaborating the rights and duties of landlords and their tenants, and the development of more sophisticated conveyancing techniques. A number of legal

[6] See e.g. articles 2(4) and 2(7) of the UN Charter; the 1970 Declaration on Principles of International Law adopted by the UN General Assembly, resolution 2625 (XXV) and article 1 of the 1974 Consensus Definition of Aggression adopted by the General Assembly, resolution 3314 (XXIX).

[7] See e.g. Falk, "A New Paradigm for International Legal Studies: Prospects and Proposals", 84 *Yale Law Journal*, 1975, pp.969, 973, 1020. See also Lauterpacht, *International Law and Human Rights*, 1950 and Jenks, *The Common Law of Mankind*, 1958.

[8] See e.g. the Treaty on Outer Space, 1967 and the Convention on the Law of the Sea, 1982. See also Shaw, *op. cit.*, pp.65-66; *infra*, p.306.

[9] See e.g. the *Asylum* case, ICJ Reports, 1950, pp.266, 275; 17 *ILR*, pp.280, 283.

interests are capable of existing over land and the possibility exists of dividing ownership into different segments.[10]

The treatment of territory in international law has not reached this sophisticated stage for a number of reasons, in particular the horizontal system of territorial sovereignty that subsists internationally as distinct from the vertical order of land law that persists in most municipal systems.

One point that flows from this and is basic to an understanding of territory in international and domestic law, is the difference in the consequences that result from a change in the legal ownership of land in international law and in municipal law.

In international law a change in ownership of a particular territory involves also a change in sovereignty, in the legal authority governing the area. This means that the nationality of the inhabitants is altered, as is the legal system under which they live, work and conduct their relations, whereas in municipal law no such changes are involved in an alteration of legal ownership. Accordingly international law must deal also with all the various effects of a change in territorial sovereignty and not confine its attentions to the mere mechanism of acquisition or loss of territory.

TERRITORIAL SOVEREIGNTY

Judge Huber noted in the *Island of Palmas* case[12] that:

> sovereignty in relation to a portion of the surface of the globe is the legal condition necessary for the inclusion of such portion in the territory of any particular state.

Brierly defined territorial sovereignty in terms of the existence of rights over territory rather than the independence of the state itself or the relation of persons to persons. It was a way of contrasting "the fullest rights over territory known to the law" with certain minor territorial rights, such as leases and servitudes.[13] Territorial sovereignty has a positive and a negative aspect. The former relates

---

[10] See e.g. Megarry and Wade, *The Law of Real Property*, 5th ed., 1984.

[11] See *infra*, Chapter 16, dealing with the problems of state succession.

[12] 2 *RIAA*, pp.829, 838 (1928); 4 *ILR*, pp.103, 104. See also the Report of the Commission of Jurists in the *Aaland Islands* case, LNOJ, Suppl. no.3, p.6.

[13] *The Law of Nations*, 6th ed., 1963, p.162.

to the exclusivity of the competence of the state regarding its own territory,[14] while the latter refers to the obligation to protect the rights of other states.[15]

The international rules regarding territorial sovereignty are rooted in the Roman law provisions governing ownership and possession, and the classification of the different methods of acquiring territory is a direct descendant of the Roman rules dealing with property.[16] This has resulted in some confusion. Law, being so attached to contemporary life, cannot be easily transposed into a different cultural milieu.[17] And, as shall be noted, the Roman method of categorising the different methods of acquiring territory faces difficulties when applied in international law.

The essence of territorial sovereignty is contained in the notion of title. This term relates to both the factual and legal conditions under which territory is deemed to belong to one particular authority or another. In other words, it refers to the existence of those facts required under international law to entail the legal consequences of a change in the juridical status of a particular territory.[18]

One interesting characteristic that should be noted and which again points to the difference between the treatment of territory under international and municipal law is that title to territory in international law is more often than not relative rather than absolute.[19] Thus, a court, in deciding to which of contending states a parcel of land legally belongs, will consider all the relevant arguments and will award the land to the state which relatively speaking puts forward the better (or best) legal case. Title to land in municipal law is much more often the case of deciding in uncertain or contentious circumstances which party complies with the legal requirements as to ownership and possession, and in that sense title is absolute. It is not normally a question of examining

---

[14]   See Judge Huber, *Island of Palmas* case, 2 *RIAA*, pp.829, 838 (1928); 4 *ILR*, pp.103, 104.

[15]   *Ibid.*, p.839. See also Shaw, *op. cit.*, p.73 *et seq.* and Bastid, "Les Problèmes Territoriaux dans la Jurisprudence de la Cour Internationale", 107 *HR*, pp.360, 367.

[16]   See e.g. Schoenborn, *op. cit.*, p.96. See also O'Connell, *op. cit.*, pp.403-4. Note in particular the Roman law distinction between *imperium* and *dominium*, Shaw, *op. cit.*, p.74.

[17]   See as regards the theories concerning the relationship between states and territory, *ibid.*, pp.75-79.

[18]   See e.g. Jennings, *op. cit.*, p.4. See also *Salmond on Jurisprudence*, 12th ed., 1966, p.331 and Brownlie, *Principles of Public International Law*, 4th ed., 1990, pp.123-24.

[19]   See e.g. the *Eastern Greenland* case, PCIJ, Series A/B, no.53, 1933, p.46; 6 *ILR*, p.95.

the facts to see which claimant can under the law put forward a better claim to title.

Disputes as to territory in international law may be divided into different categories. The contention may be over the status of the country itself, that is, all the territory comprised in a particular state, as for example Arab claims against Israel and claims formerly pursued by Morocco against Mauritania.[20] Or the dispute may refer to a certain area on the borders of two or more states, as for example Somali claims against the north-east of Kenya and south-east of Ethiopia.[21] Similarly, claims to territory may be based on a number of different grounds, ranging from the traditional method of occupation or prescription to the newer concepts such as self-determination, with various political and legal factors, for example, geographical contiguity, historical demands and economic elements possibly being relevant. These issues will be noted during the course of this chapter.

Apart from territory actually under the sovereignty of a state, international law also recognises territory over which there is no sovereign. Such territory is known as *terra nullius*. In addition there is a category of territory called *res communis* which is (in contrast to *terra nullius*) generally not capable of being reduced to sovereign control. The prime instance of this is the high seas, which belong to no-one and may be used by all. Another example would be outer space. The concept of common heritage of mankind has also been raised and will be examined in this chapter.

NEW STATES AND TITLE TO TERRITORY [22]

The problem of how a state actually acquires its own territory in international law is a difficult one and one that may ultimately only be explained in legal-political terms. While with long-established states one may dismiss the question on the basis of recognition and acceptance, new states pose a different problem since under classical international law, until a new state is created, there is no legal person in existence competent to hold title. None of the traditional

---

[20] See *infra*, p.305.

[21] See *infra*, p.304.

[22] See Jennings, *op. cit.*, p.36 *et seq.*; Starke, "The Acquisition of Title to Territory by Newly Emerged States", 41 *BYIL*, 1965-6, p.411; Crawford, *The Creation of States in International Law*, 1979 and Shaw, *Title to Territory in Africa*, 1986, pp.168-73.

modes of acquisition of territorial title satisfactorily resolve the dilemma, which has manifested itself particularly in the post-Second World War period with the onset of decolonisation. The international community has traditionally approached the problem of new states in terms of recognition, rather than in terms of acquisition of title to territory. This means that states have examined the relevant situation and upon ascertainment of the factual conditions have accorded recognition to the new entity as a subject of international law. There has been relatively little discussion of the method by which the new entity itself acquires the legal rights to its lands. The stress has instead been on compliance with factual requirements as to statehood coupled with the acceptance of this by other states.[23]

One approach to this problem has been to note that it is recognition that constitutes the state, and that the territory of the state is, upon recognition, accepted as the territory of a valid subject of international law irrespective of how it may have been acquired.[24] While this theory is not universally or widely accepted,[25] it does nevertheless underline how the emphasis has been upon recognition of a situation and not upon the method of obtaining the rights in law to the particular territory.[26]

One major factor that is relevant is the crucial importance of the doctrine of domestic jurisdiction. This constitutes the legal prohibition on interference within the internal mechanisms of an entity and emphasises the supremacy of a state within its own frontiers. Many of the factual and legal processes leading up to the emergence of a new state are therefore barred from international legal scrutiny and this has proved a deterrent to the search for the precise method by which a new entity obtains title to the territory in question.[27]

In recent years, however, the scope of the domestic jurisdiction rule has been altered. Discussions in international conferences and institutions, such as the United Nations, have actively concerned themselves with conditions in non-independent countries and it has been accepted that territorial sovereignty in the ordinary sense of

---

[23] See e.g. Oppenheim, *op. cit.*, p.544
[24] *Ibid.*
[25] *Supra*, Chapter 7.
[26] See e.g. Jennings, *op. cit.*, p.37 and Starke, *op. cit.*, p.413.
[27] See Shaw, *op. cit.* footnote 22, pp.168-69.

the words does not really exist over mandate or trust territories.[28] This is beginning to encourage a re-examination of the procedures of acquiring title. However, the plea of domestic jurisdiction does at least illustrate the fact that not only international law but also municipal law is involved in the process of gaining independence.

There are basically two methods by which a new entity may gain its independence as a new state; by constitutional means, that is by agreement with the former controlling administration in an orderly devolution of power, or by non-constitutional means, usually by force, against the will of the previous sovereign.

The granting of independence according to the constitutional provisions of the former power may be achieved either by agreement between the former power and the accepted authorities of the emerging state, or by a purely internal piece of legislation by the previous sovereign. In many cases a combination of both procedures is adopted. For example, the independence of Burma was preceded by a Burmese-United Kingdom agreement and treaty (June and October, 1947) and by the Burma Independence Act of 1947 passed by the British legislature, providing for Burmese independence to take effect on 4 January 1948. In such cases what appears to be involved is a devolution or transfer of sovereignty from one power to another and the title to the territory will accordingly pass from the previous sovereign to the new administration in a conscious act of transference.

However, a different situation arises where the new entity gains its independence contrary to the wishes of the previous authority, whether by secession or revolution. It may be that the dispossessed sovereign may ultimately make an agreement with the new state recognising its new status, but in the meantime the new state might well be regarded by other states as a valid state under international law.[29]

The principle of self-determination is also very relevant here. Where a state gains its sovereignty in opposition to the former power, new facts are created and the entity may well comply with the international requirements as to statehood, such as population,

[28] See e.g. *International Status of South West Africa*, ICJ Reports, 1950, p.128; 17 *ILR*, p.47; the *South West Africa* cases, ICJ Reports, 1966, p.6; 37 *ILR*, p.243; the *Namibia* case, ICJ Reports, 1971, p.16; 49 *ILR*, p.2, and the *Western Sahara* case, ICJ Reports, 1975, p.12; 59 *ILR*, p.14. See further *supra*, Chapter 5, p.156.

[29] *Ibid*. See also Greig, *International Law*, 2nd ed., 1976, p.156.

territory and government. Other states will then have to make a decision as to whether or not to recognise the new state and accept the legal consequences of this new status. But at this point a serious problem emerges.

For a unit to be regarded as a state under international law it must conform with the legal conditions as to settled population, a definable area of land and the capacity to enter into legal relations. However, under traditional international law, until one has a state one cannot talk in terms of title to the territory, because there does not exist any legal person capable of holding the legal title. So to discover the process of acquisition of title to territory, one has first to point to an established state. A few ideas have been put forward to explain this. One theory is to concentrate upon the factual emergence of the new state and to accept that since a new state is in existence upon a certain parcel of land, international law should look no further but accept the reality of possession at the moment of independence as denoting ownership, that is, legal title.[30] While in most cases this would prove adequate as far as other states are concerned, it can lead to problems where ownership is claimed of an area not in possession and it does little to answer the questions as to the international legal explanation of territorial sovereignty. Another approach is to turn to the constitutive theory of recognition, and declare that by recognition not only is a new state in the international community created, but its title to the territory upon which it is based is conclusively determined.[31] The disadvantage of this attitude is that it presupposes the acceptance of the constitutive theory by states in such circumstances, something which is controversial.[32]

One possibility that could be put forward here involves the abandonment of the classical rule that only states can acquire territorial sovereignty, and the substitution of a provision permitting a people to acquire sovereignty over the territory pending the establishment of the particular state. By this method the complicated theoretical issues related to recognition are avoided. Some support for this view can be found in the provision in the 1970 Declaration on Principles of International Law that the territory of a colony or

---

[30] See e.g. Oppenheim, *op. cit.*, p.544 and Starke, *op. cit.*, p.413.
[31] *Ibid.* See also Jennings, *op. cit.*, p.37 and Starke, *op. cit.*, p.413.
[32] *Supra*, Chapter 7, p.243.

other non-self-governing entity possesses, under the United Nations Charter, a status separate and distinct from that of the administering power, which exists until the people have exercised the right of self-determination.[33] However, the proposition is a controversial one and must remain tentative.[34]

THE ACQUISITION OF ADDITIONAL TERRITORY

The classical technique of categorising the various modes of acquisition of territory is based on Roman law and is not altogether adequate.[35] Many of the leading cases do not specify a particular category or mode but tend to adopt an overall approach. Five modes of acquisition are usually detailed: occupation of *terra nullius*, prescription, cession, accretion and subjugation (or conquest); and these are further divided into original and derivative modes.[36]

Accretion [37]

This describes the geographical process by which new land is formed and becomes attached to existing land, as for example the creation of islands in a river mouth or the change in direction of a boundary river leaving dry land where it had formerly flowed. Where new land comes into being within the territory of a state, it forms part of the territory of the state and there is no problem. When, for example, an island emerged in the Pacific after an under-sea volcano erupted in January 1986, the UK government noted that:

> We understand the island emerged within the territorial sea of the Japanese island of Iwo Jima. We take it therefore to be Japanese territory.[38]

As regards a change in the course of a river forming a boundary, a different situation is created depending whether it is imperceptible and slight or a violent shift (*avulsion*). In the latter case, the general

---

[33] See the *Namibia* case, ICJ Reports, 1971, pp.16, 31; 49 *ILR*, pp.2, 21.
[34] See Shaw, *op. cit.* footnote 22, pp.171-73.
[35] See O'Connell, *op. cit.*, p.405.
[36] See Oppenheim, *op. cit.*, p.546 and Brownlie, *op. cit.*, pp.131-32.
[37] See e.g. Hyde, *International Law*, 2nd ed., 1947, vol.1, pp.355-56; O'Connell, *op. cit.*, pp.428-30, and Oppenheim, *op. cit.*, pp.563-66.
[38] 478 HL Deb., col.1005, Written Answer, 17 July 1986.

rule is that the boundary stays at the same point along the original
river bed. However, where a gradual move has taken place the
boundary may be shifted. If the river is navigable, the boundary will
be the middle of the navigable channel, whatever slight alterations
have occurred, while if the river is not navigable the boundary will
continue to be the middle of the river itself. This aspect of acquiring
territory is relatively unimportant in international law but these rules
have been applied in a number of cases involving disputes between
particular states of the United States of America.[39]

Cession [40]

This involves the peaceful transfer of territory from one sovereign
to another and has often taken place within the framework of a peace
treaty following a war. Indeed the orderly transference of sovereignty
by agreement from a colonial or administering power to
representatives of the indigenous population could be seen as a form
of cession.

Because cession has the effect of replacing one sovereign by
another over a particular piece of territory, the acquiring state
cannot possess more rights over the land that its predecessor had.
This is an important point, so that where a third state has certain
rights, for example, of passage over the territory, the new sovereign
must respect them. It is expressed in the land law phrase that the
burden of obligations runs with the land, not the owner. In other
words the rights of the territorial sovereign are derived from a
previous sovereign, who could not, therefore, dispose of more than
he had.

This contrasts with, for example, accretion which is treated as an
original title, there having been no previous legal sovereign over
the land.

The *Island of Palmas* case[41] emphasised this point. It concerned
a dispute between the United States and Holland. The claims of the
United States were based on an 1898 treaty with Spain, which
involved the cession of the island. It was emphasised by the arbitrator

---

[39] See e.g. *The Anna*, 5 C.Rob. 373 (1805); *Louisiana* v. *Mississippi*, 282 US 458 (1940)
and the *Chamizal* arbitration, 5 *AJIL*, 1911, p.782. See also E. Lauterpacht, "River Boundaries:
Legal Aspects of the Shatt-Al-Arab Frontier", 9 *ICLQ*, 1960, pp.208, 216.

[40] See e.g. Oppenheim, *op. cit.*, pp.546-54, and O'Connell, *op. cit.*, pp.436-40.

[41] 2 *RIAA*, p.829 (1928); 4 *ILR*, p.103.

and accepted by the parties that Spain could not thereby convey to the Americans greater rights than it itself possessed.

The basis of cession lies in the intention of the relevant parties to transfer the territory. Without this it cannot legally operate. Whether an actual delivery of the property is also required for a valid cession is less certain. It will depend on the circumstances of the case. For example, Austria ceded Venice to France in 1866, and that state within a few weeks ceded the territory to Italy. The cession to the Italian state through France was nonetheless valid.[42] In the *Iloilo* case,[43] it was held that the cession of the Philippines to the United States took place, on the facts of the case, upon the ratification of the Treaty of Paris of 1898, even though American troops had taken possession of the town of Iloilo two months prior to this.

Although instances of cession usually occur in an agreement following the conclusion of hostilities, it can be accomplished in other circumstances, such as the purchase of Alaska by the United States in 1867 from Russia or the sale by Denmark of territories in the West Indies in 1916 to the United States. It may also appear in exchanges of territories or pure gifts of territory.[44]

Conquest and the Use of Force

How far a title based on force can be regarded as a valid, legal right recognisable by other states and enforceable within the international system is a crucial question. Ethical considerations are relevant and the principle that an illegal act cannot give birth to a right in law is well established in municipal law and is an essential component of an orderly society.

However, international law has sometimes to modify its reactions to the consequences of successful violations of its rules to take into account the exigencies of reality. The international community has accepted the results of illegal aggression in many cases by virtue of recognition.

[42] See Oppenheim, *op. cit.*, pp.548-49. Note also that in 1859 Austria ceded Lombardy to France, which then ceded it to Sardinia without having taken possession, see O'Connell, *op. cit.*, p.438. Cf. *The Fama*, 5 C.Rob. 106, 115 (1804).

[43] 4 *RIAA*, p.158 (1925); 3 *ILR*, p.336.

[44] Oppenheim, *op. cit.*, pp.548-49. Cession of territory will automatically include all the appurtenances of the territory, for example the territorial sea, see the *Grisbadarna* case, Scott, *Hague Court Reports*, vol.1, 1916, p.121 and the *Beagle Channel* case, HMSO, 1977; 52 *ILR*, p.93.

Conquest, the act of defeating an opponent and occupying all or part of its territory, does not of itself constitute a basis of title to the land.[45] It does give the victor certain rights under international law as regards the territory, the rights of belligerent occupation,[46] but the territory remains the legal possession of the ousted sovereign.[47] Sovereignty as such does not merely pass by conquest to the occupying forces, although complex situations may arise where the legal status of the territory occupied is, in fact, in dispute prior to the conquest.[48] Conquest, of course, may result from a legal or illegal use of force. By the Kellogg-Briand Pact of 1928, war was outlawed as an instrument of national policy and by article 2(4) of the United Nations Charter all member-states must refrain from the threat or use of force against the territorial integrity or political independence of any state. However, force will be legitimate when exercised in self-defence.[49] Whatever the circumstances, it is not the successful use of violence that in international law constituted the valid method of acquiring territory. Under the classical rules, formal annexation of territory following upon an act of conquest would operate to pass title. It was a legal fiction employed to mask the conquest and transform it into a valid method of obtaining land under international law.[50] However, it is doubtful whether an annexation proclaimed while war is still in progress would have operated to pass a good title to territory. Only after a war is concluded could the juridical status of the disputed territory be finally determined. This follows from the rule that has developed to the effect that the control over the relevant territory by the state purporting to annex must be effective and that there must be no reasonable chance of the former sovereign regaining the land.

These points were emphasised by the Nuremburg War Crimes Tribunal after World War II, in discussing the various purported German annexations of 1939 and 1940. The Tribunal firmly declared

---

[45] See Oppenheim, *op. cit.*, pp.566-67.
[46] See e.g. Oppenheim, *op. cit.*, p.618: McDougal and Feliciano, *Law and Minimum World Public Order*, 1961, pp.733-36 and 739-44 and Stone, *Legal Controls of International Conflict*, 1959, pp.744-51.
[47] See generally *The Arab-Israeli Conflict* (ed. Moore), 3 vols., 1974.
[48] But cf. Blum, "The Missing Reversioner", *ibid.* vol.2, p.287.
[49] See article 51 of the UN Charter and *infra*, Chapter 18.
[50] See e.g. Oppenheim, *op. cit.*, pp.566-68. See also O'Connell, *op. cit.*, pp.431-36.

that annexations taking place before the conclusion of a war were ineffective and invalid in international law.[51] Intention to annex was a crucial aspect of the equation so that, for example, the conquest of Germany by the Allies in 1945 did not give rise to an implied annexation by virtue of the legislative control actually exercised (as it could have done) because the Allies had specifically ruled out such a course in a joint declaration.[52] It is, however, clear today that the acquisition of territory by force alone is illegal under international law. This may be stated in view of article 2(4) of the UN Charter and other practice. Security Council resolution 242, for example, emphasised the "inadmissibility of the acquisition of territory by war", while the 1970 Declaration of Principles of International Law adopted by the UN General Assembly provides that:

> the territory of a state shall not be the object of acquisition by another state resulting from the threat or use of force. No territorial acquisition resulting from the threat or use of force shall be recognised as legal.[53]

In Security Council resolution 662 (1990), adopted unanimously, the Council decided that the declared Iraqi annexation of Kuwait "under any form and whatever pretext has no legal validity and is considered null and void". All states and institutions were called upon not to recognise the annexation and to refrain from actions which might be interpreted as indirect recognition.[54]

Acquisition of territory following an armed conflict would require further action of an international nature in addition to domestic legislation to annex. Such further necessary action would be in the form either of a treaty of cession by the former sovereign or international recognition.[55]

---

[51] Ibid., p.436. See also e.g. Re Goering, 13 ILR, p.203 (1946).

[52] Cmd. 6648 (1945). See also Oppenheim, op. cit., p.568.

[53] See also article 5(3) of the Consensus Definition of Aggression adopted in 1974 by the UN General Assembly. Similarly, by article 52 of the Vienna Convention on the Law of Treaties, 1969, a treaty providing for the transfer of territory may be void for duress.

[54] See The Kuwait Crisis — Basic Documents (eds. Lauterpacht, Greenwood, Weller, Bethlehem), 1991, p.90.

[55] See, for example, Security Council resolution 497 (1981), condemning Israel's decision to extend its laws, jurisdiction and administration onto the occupied Golan Heights. The UN has also condemned Israel's policy of establishing settlements in the occupied territories, see e.g. Security Council resolution 465 (1980). See further infra, Chapter 18, with regard to self-determination and the use of force.

The Exercise of Effective Control

It is customary in the literature to treat the modes of occupation and prescription as separate categories. However, there are several crucial factors that link the concepts, so that the acquisition of territory by virtue of these methods, based as they are upon the exercise of effective control, is best examined within the same broad framework. The traditional definition of these two modes will be noted first.

Occupation is a method of acquiring territory which belongs to no one (*terra nullius*) and which may be acquired by a state in certain situations. The occupation must be by a state and not by private individuals, it must be effective and it must be intended as a claim of sovereignty over the area. The high seas cannot be occupied in this manner for they are *res communis*, but vacant land may be subjected to the sovereignty of a claimant state. It relates primarily to uninhabited territories and islands, but may also apply to certain inhabited lands.

The issue was raised in the *Western Sahara* case before the International Court of Justice.[56] The question was asked as to whether the territory in question had been *terra nullius* at the time of colonisation. It was emphasised by the Court that the concept of *terra nullius* was a legal term of art used in connection with the mode of acquisition of territory known as "occupation".[57] The latter mode was defined legally as an original means of peaceably acquiring sovereignty over territory otherwise than by cession or succession.[58] In an important statement, the Court unambiguously asserted that the state practice of the relevant period (i.e. the period of colonisation) indicated that territories inhabited by tribes or peoples having a social and political organisation were not regarded as *terrae nullius*.[59]

The point should also be made that in fact the majority of

---

[56] ICJ Reports, 1975, p.12; 59 *ILR*, p.14. See also Shaw, "The *Western Sahara* case", 49 *BYIL*, 1978, pp.119, 127-34.

[57] ICJ Reports, 1975, pp.12, 39; 59 *ILR*, pp.14, 56.

[58] *Ibid.*

[59] *Ibid.* This ran counter to some writers of the period, see e.g. Lindley, *The Acquisition and Government of Backward Territory in International Law*, 1926, pp.11-20; Westlake, *Chapters on the Principles of International Law*, 1894, pp.141-42; Jennings, *op. cit.*, p.20 and Oppenheim, *op. cit.*, p.555.

territories brought under European control were regarded as acquired by means of cessions especially in Asia and Africa.[60] However, there were instances of title by occupation, for example Australia, and many sparsely inhabited islands.

Occupation, both in the normal sense of the word and in its legal meaning, was often preceded by discovery, that is the realisation of the existence of a particular piece of land.[61] But mere realisation or sighting was never considered (except for periods in the fifteenth and sixteenth centuries and this is not undisputed) as sufficient to constitute title to territory. Something more was required and this took the form of a symbolic act of taking possession, whether it be by the raising of flags or by solemn proclamations or by more sophisticated ritual expressions. As time passed, the conditions changed and the arbitrator in the *Island of Palmas* case pointed to the modern effect of discovery as merely giving an inchoate title which had to be completed within a reasonable time by the effective occupation of the relevant region. Discovery only put other states on notice that the claimant state had a prior interest in the territory which to become legally meaningful had to be supplemented by effective occupation within a certain period.[62]

Prescription[63] is a mode of establishing title to territory which is not *terra nullius* and which has been obtained either unlawfully or in circumstances wherein the legality of the acquisition cannot be demonstrated. It is the legitimisation of a doubtful title by the passage of time and the presumed acquiescence of the former sovereign, and it reflects the need for stability felt within the international system by recognising that territory in the possession of a state for a long period of time and uncontested cannot be taken away from that state without serious consequences for the international order. It is the legitimisation of a fact. If it were not

---

[60] See Shaw, *op. cit.* footnote 22, Chapter 1 and Alexandrowicz, *The European-African Confrontation*, 1973.

[61] See e.g. Oppenheim, *op. cit.*, pp.558-59 and Van der Heydte, "Discovery, Symbolic Annexation and Virtual Effectiveness in International Law", 29 *AJIL*, 1935, p.448. See also Keller, Lissitzyn and Mann, *Creation of Rights of Sovereignty Through Symbolic Acts, 1400-1800*, 1938.

[62] 2 *RIAA*, pp.829, 846 (1928); 4 *ILR*, pp.103, 108.

[63] See generally e.g. Johnson, "Acquisitive Prescription in International Law", 27 *BYIL*, 1950, p.332.

for some such doctrine, the title of many states to their territory
would be jeopardised.[64]

Prescription differs from occupation, in that it relates to territory
which has previously been under the sovereignty of a state. In spite
of this, both concepts are similar in that they may require evidence
of sovereign acts by state over a period of time. And although
distinct in theory, in practice these concepts are often indistinct since
sovereignty over an area may lapse and give rise to doubts whether
an abandonment has taken place,[65] rendering the territory *terra
nullius*.

In fact, most cases do not fall into such clear theoretical categories
as occupation or prescription. Particular modes of acquisition that
can be unambiguously related to the classic definitions tend not to
be specified. Most cases involve contesting claims by states, where
both (or possibly all) the parties have performed some sovereign
acts.

As in the instance of occupation, so prescription too requires that
the possession forming the basis of the title must be by virtue of the
authority of the state or *à titre de souverain*, and not a manifestation
of purely individual effort unrelated to the state's sovereign claims.
And this possession must be public so that all interested states can
be made aware of it.

This latter requirement also flows logically from the necessity for
the possession to be peaceful and uninterrupted, and reflects the
vital point that prescription rests upon the implied consent of the
former sovereign to the new state of affairs. This means that protests
by the dispossessed sovereign may completely block any prescriptive
claim.[66]

In the *Chamizal* arbitration[67] between the United States and
Mexico, the Rio Grande River forming the border between the parties
changed course and the United States claimed the ground between

---

[64] As noted in the Grisbadarna case, "it is a settled principle of the law of nations that a
state of things which actually exists and has existed for a long time should be changed as
little as possible", Scott, *Hague Court Reports*, vol.1, 1916, pp.121, 130.

[65] For abandonment of territory, the fact of the loss plus the intention to abandon is
required. This is very rare; see e.g. the *Delagoa Bay* case, Parry, *British Digest of International
Law*, vol.5, 1965, p.535. See also the *Frontier Land* case, ICJ Reports, 1959, p.209.

[66] See Johnson, *op. cit.*, pp.343-48.

[67] 5 *AJIL*, 1911, p.782. See also the *Minquiers and Ecrehos* case, ICJ Reports, 1953, pp.47,
106-8; 20 *ILR*, pp.94, 142-144.

the old and the new river beds partly on the basis of peaceful and uninterrupted possession. This claim was dismissed in view of the constant protests by Mexico and in the light of a Convention signed by both parties that there existed a dispute as to the boundary which had to be resolved. The fact that Mexico did not go to war over the issue was not of itself sufficient to make the possession of the tract of land by the United States peaceful.

Thus acquiescence in the case of prescription, whether express or implied from all the relevant circumstances, is essential, whereas in the case of occupation it is merely an evidential point reinforcing the existence of an effective occupation, but not constituting the essence of the legal claim.

Precisely what form the protest is to take is open to question but resort to force is not acceptable in modern international law, especially since the 1928 Kellogg-Briand Pact and article 2(4) of the United Nations Charter.[68] The bringing of a matter before the United Nations or the International Court of Justice will be conclusive as to the existence of the dispute and thus of the reality of the protests, but diplomatic protests will probably be sufficient. This, however, is not accepted by all academic writers, and it may well be that in serious disputes further steps should be taken such as severing diplomatic relations or proposing arbitration or judicial settlement.

The requirement of a "reasonable period" of possession is similarly imprecise and it is not possible to point to any defined length of time.[70] It will depend, as so much else, upon all the circumstances of the case, including the nature of the territory and the absence or presence of any competing claims.

In the *Minquiers and Ecrehos* case[71] concerning disputed sovereignty over a group of islets and rocks in the English Channel, claimed by both France and the United Kingdom, the International Court of Justice exhaustively examined the history of the region since 1066.

---

[68] *Supra*, p.287 and *infra*, Chapter 18.

[69] See e.g. Johnson, *op. cit.*, pp.353-54 and MacGibbon, "Some Observations on the Part of Protest in International Law", 30 *BYIL*, 1953, p.293. Cf. Brownlie, *op. cit.*, p.157, who notes that "if acquiescence is the crux of the matter (and it is believed that it is) one cannot dictate what its content is to be".

[70] In the *British Guiana-Venezuela Boundary* case, the parties agreed to adopt a 50 year adverse holding rule, 89 *BFSP*, 1896, p.57.

[71] ICJ Reports, 1953, p.47; 20 *ILR*, p.94.

However, its decision was based primarily on relatively recent acts relating to the exercise of jurisdiction and local administration as well as the nature of legislative enactments referable to the territory in question. And upon these grounds, British sovereignty was upheld. The sovereign acts of the United Kingdom relating to the islets far outweighed any such activities by the French authorities and accordingly the claims of the latter were dismissed.

As in other cases, judgment was given not on the basis of clearly defined categories of occupation or prescription, but rather in the light of the balance of competing state activities.

De Visscher has attempted to render the theoretical classifications more consonant with the practical realities by the introduction of the concept of historical consolidation.[72] This idea is founded on proven long use, which reflects a complex of interests and relations resulting in the acquisition of territory (including parts of the sea). Such a grouping of interests and relations is considered by the courts in reaching a decision as of more importance than the mere passage of time and historical consolidation may apply to *terra nullius* as well as to territories previously occupied. Thus it can be distinguished from prescription. It differs from occupation in that the concept has relevance to the acquisition of parts of the sea, as well as of land. And it may be brought into existence not only by acquiescence and consent, but also by the absence of protest over a reasonable period by relevant states.[73]

However, de Visscher's discussion, based on the *Anglo-Norwegian Fisheries* case[74] does fail to note the important distinction between the acquisition of territory in accordance with the rules of international law, and the acquisition of territory as a permitted exception to the generally accepted legal principles. The passage in the *Anglo-Norwegian Fisheries* case relied upon[75] is really concerned with general acquiescence with regard to a maritime area, while the criticism has been made[76] that de Visscher has over-emphasised the aspect of "complex of interests and relations which *in themselves* have the effect of attaching a territory or an expanse of sea

[72] *Theory and Reality in Public International Law*, 1968, p.209.
[73] *Ibid.*
[74] ICJ Reports, 1951, pp.116, 138; 18 *ILR*, pp.86, 100.
[75] *Ibid.*
[76] See Jennings, *op. cit.*, pp.25-26. See also Johnson, "Consolidation as a Root of Title in International Law", *Cambridge Law Journal*, 1955, pp.215, 223.

to a given state".[77] Effectiveness, therefore, rather than consolidation would be the appropriate term. Both occupation and prescription rely primarily upon effective possession and control. The element of time is here also relevant as it affects the effectiveness of control.

1. *Intertemporal Law*

One question that arises is the problem of changing conditions related to particular principles of international law, in other words the relevant time period at which to ascertain the legal rights and obligations in question. This can cause considerable difficulties since a territorial title may be valid under, for example, sixteenth century legal doctrines but ineffective under nineteenth century developments. The general rule in such circumstances is that in a dispute the claim in question has to be examined according to the conditions and rules in existence at the time it was made and not at a later date.[78] This meant, for example, that in the *Island of Palmas* case, the Spanish claim to title by discovery, which the United States declared it had inherited, had to be tested in the light of international legal principles in the sixteenth century when the discovery was made.[79]

But it was also noted in this case that while the creation of particular rights was dependent upon the international law of the time, the continued existence of such rights depended upon their according with the evolving conditions of a developing legal system, although this stringent test would not be utilised in the case of territories with an "established order of things".[80] This proviso has in practice been carefully and flexibly interpreted within the context of all the relevant rules relating to the acquisition of territory including recognition and acquiescence.[81] However, the Court in

---

[77] *Op. cit.*, p.209. Emphasis added. See further *infra*, p.298.

[78] See e.g. the *Western Sahara* case, ICJ Reports, 1975, pp.12, 38-39; 59 *ILR*, pp.14, 55. See also Shaw, *op. cit.* footnote 56, pp.152-53; Jennings, *op. cit.*, pp.28-31; Elias, "The Doctrine of Intertemporal Law", 74 *AJIL*, 1980, p.285 and Brownlie, *op. cit.*, pp.129-30.

[79] 2 *RIAA*, pp.829, 845 (1928); 4 *ILR*, p.103.

[80] *Ibid.*, pp.839-45. See Jessup, "The Palmas Island Arbitration", 22 *AJIL*, 1928, p.735. See also the Resolution of the Institut de Droit International, *Annuaire*, 1975, p.536 *et seq.*

[81] Note that the 1970 Declaration on Principles of International Law provides that the concept of non-acquisition of territory by force was not to be affected *inter alia* by any international agreement made prior to the Charter and valid under international law.

the *Aegean Sea Continental Shelf* case[82] declared that the phrase "disputes relating to the territorial status of Greece" contained in a Greek reservation to the 1928 Kellogg-Briand Pact had to be interpreted "in accordance with the rules of international law as they exist today, and not as they existed in 1931". The evolution of international law concerning the continental shelf, therefore, had to be considered, so that the territorial status of Greece was taken to include its continental shelf, although that concept was completely unknown in the 1920s. How far this aspect of the principle of international law may be extended is highly controversial. The better view is to see it as one element in the bundle of factors relevant to the determination of effective control, but one that must be applied with care.

2. *Exercise of Authority*

The exercise of effective authority, therefore, is the crucial element. As Huber argued, "the actual continuous and peaceful display of state functions is in case of dispute the sound and natural criterion of territorial sovereignty".[83]

However, control, although needing to be effective, does not necessarily have to amount to possession and settlement of all of the territory claimed. Precisely what acts of sovereignty are necessary to found title will depend in each instance upon all the relevant circumstances of the case, including the nature of the territory involved, the amount of opposition (if any) that such acts on the part of the claimant state have aroused, and international reaction.

Indeed in international law many titles will be deemed to exist not as absolute but as relative concepts. The state succeeding in its claim for sovereignty over *terra nullius* over the claims of other states will in most cases have proved not an absolute title, but one relatively better than that maintained by competing states.

In the *Island of Palmas* arbitration[84] the dispute concerned sovereignty over a particular island in the Pacific. The United States declared that since by a Treaty of 1898 Spain had ceded to it all

---

[82] ICJ Reports, 1978, pp.3, 33-34; 60 *ILR*, pp.562, 592. See Elias, *op. cit.*, p.296 *et seq.* See also the Indian argument regarding the invalidity of Portugal's title to Goa, SCOR, S/PV-987, 11, 18 December 1961.

[83] 2 *RIAA*, pp.829, 840 (1928).

[84] *Ibid.*

Spanish rights possessed in that region and since that included the island discovered by Spain, the United States of America therefore had a good title. The Netherlands, on the other hand, claimed the territory on the basis of the exercise of various rights of sovereignty over it since the seventeenth century. The arbitrator, Max Huber, in a judgment which discussed the whole nature of territorial sovereignty, dismissed the American claims derived from the Spanish discovery as not effective to found title.[85] Huber declared that the Netherlands possessed sovereignty on the basis of "the actual continuous and peaceful display of state functions" evidenced by various administrative acts performed over the centuries.[86] It was also emphasised that manifestations of territorial sovereignty may assume different forms, according to conditions of time and place. Indeed,

> the intermittence and discontinuity compatible with the maintenance of the right necessarily differ according as inhabited or uninhabited regions are involved.

Additionally, geographical factors were relevant.[87]

The *Clipperton Island* arbitration[88] concerned a dispute between France and Mexico over an uninhabited island. The arbitrator emphasised that the actual, and not the nominal, taking of possession was a necessary condition of occupation, but noted that such taking of possession may be undertaken in different ways depending upon the nature of the territory concerned. In this case, a proclamation of sovereignty by a French Naval Officer later published in Honolulu was deemed sufficient to create a valid title. Relevant to this decision was the weakness of the Mexican claims to the guano-rich island, as well as the uninhabited and inhospitable nature of the territory.

These two cases, together with the *Eastern Greenland*[89] case, reveal that the effectivity of the occupation may indeed be relative and may in certain rare circumstances be little more than symbolic. In the

---

[85] *Ibid.*, p.846.

[86] *Ibid.*, pp.867-71.

[87] *Ibid.*, p.840. See also in this context, the American claim to the Howland, Baker and Jarvis Islands in the Pacific Ocean, where it was argued that the administration of the islands as part of the US Wildlife Refuge System constituted sufficient occupation, *DUSPIL*, 1975, pp.92-94.

[88] 26 *AJIL*, 1932, p.390; 6 *ILR*, p.105.

[89] PCIJ, Series A/B, no.53, 1933, p.46; 6 *ILR*, p.95.

Eastern Greenland case before the Permanent Court of International Justice, both Norway and Denmark claimed sovereignty over Eastern Greenland. Denmark had colonies in other parts of Greenland and had granted concessions in the uninhabited Eastern sector. In addition, it proclaimed that all treaties and legislation regarding Greenland covered the territory as a whole, as for example its establishment of the width of the territorial sea, and it sought to have its title to all of the territory recognised by other states. The Court felt that these acts were sufficient upon which to base a good title and were superior to various Norwegian actions such as the wintering of expeditions and the erection of a wireless station in Eastern Greenland, against which Denmark had protested. It is also to be noted that it was not until 1931 that Norway actually claimed the territory.

Such activity in establishing a claim to territory must be performed by the state or by individuals whose actions are subsequently ratified by their state, or by corporations or companies permitted by the state to engage in such operations. Otherwise, any acts undertaken are of no legal consequence.[90]

Another relevant factor, although one of uncertain strength, is the requirement of the intention by the state in performing various activities to assert claim in its sovereign capacity. In other words the facts are created pursuant to the will of the state to acquire sovereignty. This point was stressed in the *Eastern Greenland* case,[91] but appears not to have been considered as of first importance in the *Island of Palmas* case[92] or in the *Minquiers and Ecrehos* case,[93] where concern centred upon the nature and extent of the actual actions carried out by the contending states. Whatever the precise role of this subjective element, some connection between the actions undertaken and the assertion of sovereignty is necessary.

Account will also be taken of the nature of the exercise of the sovereignty in question, so that in the *Rann of Kutch* case, it was noted that:

---

[90] See McNair, the *Anglo-Norwegian Fisheries* case, ICJ Reports, 1951, pp.116, 184; 18 *ILR*, pp.86, 113 and *ibid.*, *International Law Opinions*, 1956, vol.1, p.21. See also O'Connell, *op. cit.*, pp.417-19.

[91] PCIJ, Series A/B, no.53, 1933, p.46; 6 *ILR*, p.95.

[92] 2 *RIAA*, p.829 (1928); 4 *ILR*, p.103.

[93] ICJ Reports, 1953, p.47; 20 *ILR*, p.94.

the rights and duties which by law and custom are inherent in and characteristic of sovereignty present considerable variations in different circumstances according to time and place, and in the context of various political systems.[94]

Similarly, the Court was willing to take into account the special characteristics of the Moroccan state at the relevant time in the *Western Sahara* case[95] in the context of the display of sovereign authority, but it was the exercise of sovereignty which constituted the crucial factor.

3. *Recognition, acquiescence and estoppel*

These three principles have a common foundation in that they all rest upon the notion of consent.[96] They reflect expressly or impliedly the presumed will of a state, which in turn may in some situations prove of great importance in the acquisition of title to territory. However, there are significant theoretical differences between the three principles, even if in practice the dividing lines are often blurred.

Recognition is a positive act by a state accepting a particular situation and even though it may be implied from all the relevant circumstances, it is nevertheless an affirmation of the existence of a specific factual state of affairs.[97] Acquiescence on the other hand, occurs in circumstances where a protest is called for and does not happen.[98] In other words, a situation arises which would seem to require a response denoting disagreement and since this does not transpire, the state making no objection is understood to have accepted the new situation. The idea of estoppel in general is that a party which has made or consented to a particular statement upon which another party relies in subsequent activity cannot thereupon change its position.

While, of course, the consent of a ceding state to the cession is essential, the attitude adopted by other states is purely peripheral

[94] Annex I, 7 *ILM*, 1968, pp.633, 674; 50 *ILR*, p.2.
[95] ICJ Reports, 1975, pp.12, 43-44; 59 *ILR*, pp.14, 60.
[96] Consent, of course, is the basis of cession, *supra*, p.285.
[97] See e.g. the *Eastern Greenland* case, PCIJ, Series A/B, no.53, 1933, pp.46, 51-52; 6 *ILR*, pp. 95, 100, and the *Western Sahara* case, ICJ Reports, 1975, pp.12, 49-57; 59 *ILR*, pp.14, 66. See also Schwarzenberger, "Title to Territory: Response to a Challenge", 51 *AJIL*, 1957, p.308.
[98] See Brownlie, *op. cit.*, p.160.

and will not effect the legality of the transaction. Similarly, in cases of the acquisition of title over *terra nullius*, the acquiescence of other states is not strictly relevant although of useful evidential effect. However, where two or more states have asserted competing claims the role of consent by third parties is much enhanced. In the *Eastern Greenland* case,[99] the International Court noted that Denmark was entitled to rely upon treaties made with other states (apart from Norway) in so far as these were evidence of recognition of Danish sovereignty over all of Greenland.

Recognition and acquiescence are also important in cases of acquisition of control contrary to the will of the former sovereign. Where the possession of the territory is accompanied by emphatic protests on the part of the former sovereign, no title by prescription can arise for such title is founded upon the acquiescence of the dispossessed state, and in such circumstances, consent by third states is of little consequence. However, over a period of time recognition may ultimately validate a defective title, although much will depend upon the circumstances including the attitude of the former sovereign. Where the territory involved is part of the high seas (i.e. *res communis*) acquiescence by the generality of states may affect the subjection of any part of it to another's sovereignty, particularly by raising an estoppel.[100]

Acquiescence and recognition[101] are also relevant where the prescriptive title is based on what is called immemorial possession, that is, the origin of the particular situation is shrouded in doubt and may have been lawful or unlawful but is deemed to be lawful in the light of general acquiescence by the international community.

Estoppel is a legal technique whereby states deemed to have consented to a state of affairs cannot afterwards alter their position. It is of evidential importance only and may help resolve disputes over territorial title, but it cannot found title by itself. Estoppel may arise either by means of a prior recognition or acquiescence, but the nature of the consenting state's interest is vital. Where, for example, two states put forward conflicting claims to territory, any acceptance by one of the other's position will serve as a bar to a renewal of contradictory assertions. This was illustrated in the

---

[99] PCIJ, Series A/B, no.53, 1933, pp.46, 51-52; 6 *ILR*, pp.95, 100.

[100] See the *Anglo-Norwegian Fisheries* case, ICJ Reports, 1951, p.116; 18 *ILR*, p.86.

[101] Note also the role of recognition in the context of new states and territory, *supra*, p.280.

Eastern Greenland case,[102] where the Court regarded the Norwegian acceptance of treaties with Denmark, which incorporated Danish claims to all of Greenland, as preventing Norway from contesting Danish sovereignty over the area.

The leading case on estoppel is the *Temple of Preah Vihear*[103] which concerned a border dispute between Cambodia and Thailand. The frontier was the subject of a treaty in 1904 between Thailand and France (as sovereign over French Indo-China which included Cambodia) which provided for a delimitation commission. The border was duly surveyed but was ambiguous as to the siting of the Preah Vihear temple area. Thailand called for a map from the French authorities and this placed the area within Cambodia. The Thai government accepted the map and asked for further copies.[104] A number of other incidents took place, including a visit by a Thai prince to the temple area for an official reception with the French flag clearly flying there, which convinced the International Court that Thailand had tacitly accepted French sovereignty over the disputed area.[105] In other words, Thailand was estopped by its conduct from claiming that it contested the frontier in the temple area.

However, it is to be noted that estoppel in that case was one element in a complexity of relevant principles which included prescription and treaty interpretation. The case also seemed to show that in situations of uncertainty and ambiguity, the doctrines of acquiescence and estoppel come into their own, but it would not appear correct to refer to estoppel as a rule of substantive law.[106]

Conclusions

It will be clear from the above that apart from the modes of acquisition that rely purely on the consent of the state and the consequences of sovereignty (cession or accretion), the method of acquiring additional territory is by the sovereign exercise of effective

---

[102] PCIJ, Series A/B, no.53, 1933, pp.46, 68; 6 *ILR*, pp.95, 102.
[103] ICJ Reports, 1962, p.6; 33 *ILR*, p.48. See Johnson, "The Case Concerning the Temple of Preah Vihear", 11 *ICLQ*, 1962, p.1183, and Bowett, "Estoppel before International Tribunals and its Relation to Acquiescence", 33 *BYIL*, 1975, p.176.
[104] ICJ Reports, 1962, pp.6, 23; 33 *ILR*, pp.48, 62.
[105] *Ibid.*, pp.30-32; 33 *ILR*, p.68.
[106] See e.g. Jennings, *op. cit.*, pp.47-51.

control. Both occupation and prescription are primarily based upon effective possession and although the time element is a factor in prescription, this in fact is really concerned with the effectiveness of control.

The principle of effective control applies in different ways to different situations, but its essence is that "the continuous and peaceful display of territorial sovereignty . . . is as good as title".[107] Such control has to be deliberate sovereign action, but what will amount to effectiveness is relative and will depend upon, for example, the geographical nature of the region, the existence or not of competing claims and other relevant factors, such as international reaction.[108] It will not be necessary for such control to be equally effective throughout the region.[109] The doctrine of effectiveness has displaced earlier doctrines relating to discovery and symbolic annexation as in themselves sufficient to generate title.[110] Effectiveness has also a temporal as well as a spatial dimension as the doctrine of intertemporal law has emphasised, while clearly the public or open nature of the control is essential. The acquiescence of a party directly involved is also a very important factor in providing evidence of the effectiveness of control. Where a dispossessed sovereign disputes the control exercised by a new sovereign, title can hardly pass. Effectiveness is related to the international system as a whole, so that mere possession by force is not the sole determinant of title. This factor also emphasises and justifies the role played by recognition.

Bilateral recognition is important as evidence of effective control and should be regarded as part of that principle. International recognition, however, involves not only a means of creating rules of international law in terms of practice and consent of states, but may validate situations of dubious origin. A series of recognitions could validate an unlawful acquisition of territory and could similarly prevent effective control from ever hardening

---

[107] Huber, *Island of Palmas* case, 2 *RIAA*, pp.829, 839 (1928); 4 *ILR*, p.103.

[108] *Ibid.*, p.840. See also the *Eastern Greenland* case, PCIJ, Series A/B, no.53, 1933, p.46; 6 *ILR*, p.95; the *Clipperton Island* case, 26 *AJIL*, 1932, p.390; 6 *ILR*, p.105 and the *Minquiers and Ecrehos* case, ICJ Reports, 1953, p.47; 20 *ILR*, p.94.

[109] See e.g. the *Island of Palmas* case, 2 *RIAA*, pp.829, 840 (1928).

[110] See in this context article 35 of the General Act of the Congress of Berlin, 1885, in which the parties recognised the obligation to "ensure the establishment of authority in the regions occupied by them on the coast of the African continent".

into title.[111] The significance of UN recognition is self-evident. Acquisition of title, therefore, rests upon the interplay of a number of rules, particularly effectiveness, sovereignty and recognition.

OTHER RELEVANT PRINCIPLES

There are a number of other concepts which may be of some relevance in territorial situations ranging from self-determination to historical and geographical claims. The major difference is that these concepts are not all necessarily legal principles but may be purely political or moral expressions. This means that although they may be extremely persuasive within the international political order, they would not necessarily be juridically effective.

The principle of the territorial integrity of states is well established and is protected by the rules prohibiting interference within the domestic jurisdiction of states as, for example, article 2(7) of the United Nations Charter and forbidding the threat or use of force against the territorial integrity and political independence of states, particularly article 2(4) of the United Nations Charter. This principle has been particularly emphasised by Third World states.[112]

It can be seen in the Latin American idea of *uti possidetis*, whereby the administrative divisions of the Spanish empire in South America were deemed to constitute the boundaries for the newly independent successor states, thus theoretically excluding any gaps in sovereignty which might precipitate hostilities and encourage foreign intervention.[113] It is more accurately reflected in the practice of African states, explicitly stated in a resolution of the Organisation of African Unity in 1964, which declared that colonial frontiers existing as at the date of independence constituted a tangible reality and that all member-states pledged themselves to respect such borders.[114]

Practice in Africa has reinforced this approach of emphasising the territorial integrity of the colonially defined territory, witness the widespread disapproval of the attempted creation of secessionist states whether in the former Belgian Congo, Nigeria or Sudan. Efforts

[111] See e.g as to Rhodesia, the Bantustans, Namibia and Kuwait, *supra*, pp.141-43, 157-59 and 261.

[112] See generally, Shaw, *op. cit.* footnote 22, Chapter 5.

[113] See the *Colombia-Venezuela* arbitral award, 1 *RIAA*, pp.223, 228 (1922); 1 *ILR*, p.84; the *Beagle Channel* case, HMSO, 1977; 52 *ILR*, p.93; Cukwurah, *The Settlement of Boundary Disputes in International Law*, 1967, p.114 and De La Pradelle, *La Frontière*, 1928, pp.86-87.

[114] AHG/Res.16(1). See Shaw, *op. cit.* footnote 22, pp.185-87.

to prevent the partition of the South African controlled territory of Namibia into separate Bantustans as a possible prelude to a dissolution of the unity of the territory are a further manifestation of this.[115]

The question of *uti possidetis* in the African context was discussed by the International Court in *Burkina Faso v. Republic of Mali*,[116] where the *compromis* (or special agreement) by which the parties submitted the case to the Court specified that the settlement of the dispute should be based upon respect for the principle of the "intangibility of frontiers inherited from colonisation".[117] The Court noted, however, that the principle had in fact developed into a general concept of contemporary customary international law and was unaffected by the emergence of the right of peoples to self-determination.[118] In the African contest particularly, the obvious purpose of the principle was "to prevent the independence and stability of new states being endangered by fratricidal struggles provoked by the challenging of frontiers following the withdrawal of the administering power".[119] Nevertheless, reference had been made to the principle in disputes between Asian states[120] and in European instruments.[121] The Court then proceeded to apply the principle by seeking to ascertain the delimitation of the former French colonies as at the end of the colonial period.

The principle of the territorial integrity of independent states is widely proclaimed and accepted in practice and can be regarded as a legal rule. However, it does not apply where the territorial dispute centres upon uncertain frontier demarcations, and it conflicts on the face of it with another principle of international law, that of the self-determination of peoples.[122]

This principle, noted in the United Nations Charter and emphasised in the 1960 Colonial Declaration, the 1966 International Covenant on Human Rights and the 1970 Declaration on Principles of International Law can be regarded as a rule of international law

---

[115] *Ibid.*, Chapter 5.
[116] ICJ Reports, 1986, p.554; 80 *ILR*, p.459.
[117] *Ibid.*, p.557; 80 *ILR*, p.462.
[118] *Ibid.*, p.565; 80 *ILR*, p.469.
[119] *Ibid.*
[120] E.g. the *Temple of Preah Vihear* case, ICJ Reports, 1962, p.6; 33 *ILR*, p.48 and the *Rann of Kutch* case, 7 *ILM*, 1968, p.633; 50 *ILR*, p.2.
[121] See Principle III of the Helsinki Final Act, 14 *ILM*, 1975, p.1292.
[122] See *Burkina Faso v. Mali*, ICJ Reports, 1986, pp.554, 565; 80 *ILR*, p.469.

in the light of, *inter alia*, the number and character of United Nations declarations and resolutions and actual state practice in the process of decolonisation. However, it has been interpreted as referring only to the inhabitants of non-independent territories. It has been rejected as a principle applying to independent states where identifiable groups demand the right to secede.[123]

Accordingly it fits in with the concept of territorial integrity[124] as it cannot apply once a colony or trust territory attains sovereignty and independence. Probably the most prominent exponent of the relevance of self-determination to post-independence situations is Somalia with its claims to those parts of Ethiopia and Kenya populated by Somali tribes, but that country has received very little support for its demands.[125]

Self-determination may be of some use in resolving cases of disputed frontier lines on the basis of the wishes of the inhabitants, but cannot be used to further larger territorial claims in defiance of internationally accepted boundaries of sovereign states.

Geographical claims have been raised throughout history.[126] France for long maintained that its natural frontier in the east was the west bank of the Rhine, and the European powers in establishing their presence upon African coastal areas often claimed extensive hinterland territories. Much utilised also was the doctrine of contiguity, whereby areas were claimed on the basis of the occupation of territories of which they formed a geographical continuation. However, such claims, although relevant in discussing the effectivity and limits of occupation, are not able in themselves to found title, and whether or not such claims will be taken into account at all will depend upon the nature of the territory and the strength of competing claims.[127]

Of some similarity are claims based upon historical grounds.[128] This was one of the grounds upon which Iraq sought to justify its

---

[123] See *supra*, Chapter 5, p.172.

[124] This analysis is supported by *Burkina Faso v. Mali*, ICJ Reports, 1986, pp.554; 80 *ILR*, p.459.

[125] Shaw, *op. cit.* footnote 22, Chapter 5. See also the Moroccan approach, *ibid.*

[126] See e.g. Shaw, *op. cit.* footnote 22, p.195; Jennings, *op. cit.*, p.74 and Hill, *op. cit.*, pp.77-80.

[127] See the *Eastern Greenland* case, PCIJ, Series A/B, no.53, 1933, p.46; 6 *ILR*, p.95 and the *Western Sahara* case, ICJ Reports, 1975, pp.12, 42-43; 59 *ILR*, pp.14, 59.

[128] See e.g. Shaw, *op. cit.* footnote 22, pp.193-94; Jennings, *op. cit.*, pp.76-78 and Hill, *op. cit.*, pp.81-91.

invasion and annexation of the neighbouring state of Kuwait in August 1990,[129] although the response of the United Nations demonstrated that such arguments were unacceptable to the world community as a whole.[130] Morocco too has made extensive claims to Mauritania, Western Sahara and parts of Algeria as territories historically belonging to the old Moroccan empire.[131] But such arguments are essentially political and are of but little legal relevance. The International Court of Justice in the *Western Sahara* case[132] of 1975 accepted the existence of historical legal ties between the tribes of that area and Morocco and Mauritania, but declared that they were not of such a nature as to override the right of the inhabitants of the colony to self-determination and independence.

THE FALKLAND ISLANDS [133]

The long dispute between the UK and Argentina over the Falkland Islands (or Las Malvinas) well illustrates the complex factors involved in resolving issues as to title to territory. The islands were apparently discovered by a British sea captain in 1592, but it is only in 1764 that competing acts of sovereignty commenced. In that year the French established a settlement on East Falklands and in 1765 the British established one on West Falklands. In 1767 the French sold their settlement to Spain. The British settlement was conquered by the Spaniards in 1770 but returned the following year. In 1774 the British settlement was abandoned for economic reasons, but a plaque asserting sovereignty was left behind. The Spaniards left in 1811. In 1816, the United Provinces of the River Plate (Argentina) declared their independence from Spain and four years later took

---

[129] See *Keesing's Record of World Events*, p.37635, 1990. Note that Iraq made a similar claim to Kuwait in the early 1960s, although not then taking military action, see Jennings, *op. cit.*, p.77, note 2.

[130] See e.g. Security Council resolution 662 (1990); *The Kuwait Crisis: Basic Documents, op. cit.*, p.90.

[131] Shaw, *op. cit.* footnote 22, pp.193-94. Note also the claims advanced by Indonesia to West Irian, *ibid.*, p.22.

[132] ICJ Reports, 1975, p.12; 59 *ILR*, p.14.

[133] See e.g. Goebel, *The Struggle for the Falklands*, 1927; Hoffmann and Hoffmann, *Sovereignty in Dispute*, 1984; The Falkland Islands Review, Cmnd. 8787 (1983); Chatham House, *The Falkland Islands Dispute — International Dimensions*, 1982; Reisman, "The Struggle for the Falklands", 93 *Yale Law Journal*, 1983, p.287 and Hassan, "The Sovereignty Dispute over the Falkland Islands", 23 *Va JIL* 1982, p.53. See also House of Commons Foreign Affairs Committee, Session 1983/4, 5th Report, 2681, and Cmnd. 9447 (1985).

formal possession of the islands. In 1829 the British protested and two years later, an American warship evicted Argentinian settlers from the islands, following action by the Argentinian Governor of the territory against American rebels: in 1833 the British captured the islands and have remained there ever since. The question has arisen therefore as to the basis of British title. It was originally argued that this lay in a combination of discovery and occupation, but this would be questionable in the circumstances.[134] It would perhaps have been preferable to rely on conquest and subsequent annexation for in the 1830s this was perfectly legal as a method of acquiring territory,[135] but for political reasons this was not claimed. By the 1930s the UK approach had shifted to prescription as the basis of title,[136] but of course this was problematic in the light of Argentinian protests made intermittently throughout the period since 1833.

The principle of self-determination as applicable to a recognised British non-self-governing territory has recently been much relied upon by the UK government,[137] but something of a problem is posed by the very small size of the territory's population (some 1,800) although this may not be decisive.

It would appear that conquest formed the original basis of title, irrespective of the British employment of other principles. This, coupled with the widespread recognition by the international community, including the United Nations, of the status of the territory as a British Colony would appear to resolve the legal issues, although the matter is not uncontroversial.

"THE COMMON HERITAGE OF MANKIND"

The proclamation of certain areas as the common heritage of mankind has raised the question as to whether a new form of territorial regime has been or is in process of being created.[138] In

---

[134] See McNair, *International Law Opinions*, vol.1, 1956, pp.299-300.
[135] See e.g. Lindley, *op. cit.*, pp.160-65 and *supra*, p.286.
[136] See e.g. Beck, *The Guardian*, 26 July 1982, p.7.
[137] See e.g. The Prime Minister, HC Deb., col.946, 13 May 1982.
[138] See e.g. Larschan and Brennan, "The Common Heritage of Mankind Principle in International Law", 21 *Columbia Journal of International Law*, 1983, p.305; Wolfrum, "The Principle of the Common Heritage of Mankind", *ZaöRV* 1983, p.312; Gorove, "The Concept of 'Common Heritage of Mankind'", 9 *San Diego Law Review*, 1972, p.390 and Joyner, "Legal Implications of the Common Heritage of Mankind", 35 *ICLQ*, 1986, p.190.

1970, the UN General Assembly adopted a Declaration of Principles Governing the Seabed and Ocean Floor in which it was noted that the area in question and its resources were the common heritage of mankind. This was reiterated in articles 136 and 137 of the 1982 Convention on the Law of the Sea, in which it was provided that no sovereign or other rights would be recognised with regard to the area (except in the case of minerals recovered in accordance with the Convention) and that exploitation could only take place in accordance with the rules and structures established by the Convention.[139] Article XI of the 1979 Moon Treaty emphasises that the moon and its natural resources are the common heritage of mankind, and thus incapable of national appropriation and subject to a particular regime of exploitation.[140] As is noted in the next section, attempts are currently being made to establish a common heritage regime over the Antarctic. There are certain common characteristics relating to the concept. Like *res communis*, the areas in question are incapable of national appropriation. Sovereignty is not an applicable principle and the areas in question would not be "owned", nor would any jurisdictional rights exist outside the framework of the appropriate common heritage regime institutional arrangements. However, while a *res communis* regime permits freedom of access, exploration and exploitation, a common heritage regime as envisaged in the examples noted above would strictly regulate exploration and exploitation, would establish management mechanisms and would employ the criterion of equity in distributing the benefits of such activity.

It is too early to predict the success or failure of this concept. The 1982 Law of the Sea Convention is not yet in force, while the Moon Treaty has the bare minimum of ratifications and its exploitation provisions are not yet operative. As a legal concept within the framework of the specific treaties concerned, it provides an interesting contrast to traditional *jus communis* rules, although the extent of the management structures required to operate the regime may pose considerable problems.

[139] See further *infra*, Chapter 10, p.387.
[140] See further *infra*, Chapter 9, p.332.

THE POLAR REGIONS [141]

The Arctic region is of some strategic importance, constituting as it does a vast expanse of inhospitable territory between North America and the Soviet Union. It consists to a large extent of ice packs beneath which submarines may operate.

Denmark possesses Greenland and its associated islands within the region,[142] while Norway has asserted sovereign rights over Spitzbergen and other islands. The Norwegian title is based on occupation and long exploitation of mineral resources and its sovereignty was recognised by nine nations in 1920, although the Soviet Union has protested.[143]

More controversial are the respective claims made by Canada[144] and Russia.[145] Use has been made of the concept of contiguity to assert claims over areas forming geographical units with those already occupied, in the form of the so-called sector principle. This is based on meridians of longitude as they converge at the North Pole and as they are placed on the coastlines of the particular nations, thus producing a series of triangular sectors with the coasts of the Arctic states as their baselines.

The other Arctic states of Norway, Finland, Denmark and the United States have abstained from such assertions. Accordingly it is exceedingly doubtful whether the sector principle can be regarded as other than a political proposition. Part of the problem is that such a large part of this region consists of moving packs of ice. Russia has made some claims to relatively immovable ice formations as being subject to its national sovereignty,[146] but the overall opinion remains that these are to be treated as part of the high seas open to all.[147]

[141] See e.g. O'Connell, *op. cit.*, pp.448-50 and Balch, "The Arctic and Antarctic Regions and the Law of Nations", 4 *AJIL*, 1910, p.165; Hayton, "Polar Problems and International Law", 52 *AJIL*, 1958, p.746 and Whiteman, *Digest of International Law*, vol.2, pp.1051-61. See also Lakhtine, "Rights over the Arctic", 24 *AJIL*, 1930, p.703; Mouton, "The International Regime of the Polar Regions," 101 *HR*, p.169; Auburn, *Antarctic Law and Politics*, 1982 and *International Law for Antarctica* (eds. Francioni and Scovazzi), 1987.

[142] See Hackworth, *Digest of International Law*, vol.1, 1940.

[143] *Ibid.*, p.465 *et seq.* See also O'Connell, *op. cit.*, p.499.

[144] Hackworth, *Digest, op. cit.*, p.463. But note Canadian Government statements denying that the sector principle applies to the ice, see e.g. 9 *ILM*, 1970, pp.607, 613. See also Head, "Canadian Claims to Territorial Sovereignty in the Arctic Regions", 9 *McGill Law Journal*, 1962-3, p.200.

[145] Hackworth, *Digest, op. cit.*, p.461.

[146] See e.g. Lakhtine, *op. cit.*, p.461.

[147] See e.g. Balch, *op. cit.*, pp.265-66.

Occupation of the land areas of the Arctic region may be effected by states by relatively little activity in view of the decision in the *Eastern Greenland* case[148] and the nature of the territory involved.

Claims have been made by seven nations (Argentina, Australia, Chile, France, New Zealand, Norway and the United Kingdom) to the Antarctic region, which is an ice-covered land mass in the form of an island.[149] Such claims have been based on a variety of grounds ranging from mere discovery to the sector principle employed by the South American states, and most of these are of rather dubious quality. Significantly, the United States of America has refused to recognise any claims at all to Antarctica and although the American Admiral Byrd discovered and claimed Marie Byrd Land for his country, the United States refrained from adopting the claim.[150] Several states have recognised the territorial aspirations of each other in the area, but one should note that the British, Chilean and Argentinian claims overlap.[151]

However, in 1959 the Antarctic Treaty was signed by all states concerned with territorial claims or scientific exploration in the region. Its major effect apart from the demilitarisation of Antarctica, is to suspend, although not to eliminate, territorial claims during the life of the treaty. Article IV(2) declares that:

> no acts or activities taking place while the present treaty is in force shall constitute a basis for asserting, supporting or denying a claim to territorial sovereignty in Antarctica or create any rights of sovereignty in Antarctica. No new claim or enlargement of an existing claim, to territorial sovereignty in Antarctica shall be asserted while the present treaty is in force.

Since the treaty does not provide for termination, an on-going regime has been created which because of its inclusion of all interested parties appears to have established an international regime binding on all. Subsequent meetings of the parties have

---

[148] PCIJ, Series A/B, no. 53, 1933, p.46; 6 *ILR,* p.95.

[149] See e.g. O'Connell, *op. cit.,* pp.450-53; Mouton, *op. cit.,* and Triggs, "Australian Sovereignty in Antarctica — Part I", 13 *Melbourne University Law Review,* 1981, p.123. See also UKMIL., 54 *BYIL,* 1983, p.488 *et seq.*

[150] See Hackworth, *Digest, op. cit.,* p.457. See also *DUSPIL,* 1975, pp.107-11 and Whiteman, *Digest of International Law,* vol.2, 1962, pp.250-54, 1254-56 and 1262.

[151] See e.g. Cmd. 5900.

resulted in a number of recommendations including proposals for the protection of flora and fauna in the region, and other environmental preservation measures.[152]

Of the 38 parties to the treaty in late 1989, 22 had consultative status. Full participation in the work of the consultative meetings of the parties is reserved to the original parties to the treaty and those contracting parties which demonstrate substantial scientific research activity in the area. Under article XII, any party entitled to participate in the consultative meetings may call for a review conference 30 years after the date the treaty came into force, that is in 1991.

The issue of a mineral resources regime has been under discussion since 1979 by the consultative parties and a series of special meetings on the subject held.[153] This resulted in the signing in June 1988 of the Convention on the Regulation of Antarctic Minerals Resource Activities.[154] The Convention provides for three stages of mineral activity, being defined as prospecting, exploration and development. Four institutions are to be established, once the treaty comes into force (following 16 ratifications or accessions, including the US, USSR and claimant states). The Commission is to consist of the 22 consultative parties, any other party to the Convention engaged in substantive and relevant research in the area and any other party sponsoring mineral resource activity. A Scientific, Technical and Environmental Advisory Committee consisting of all parties to the Convention is to be established, as are Regulatory Committees, which will regulate exploration and development activity in a specific area. Such committees will consist of ten members of the Commission, including the relevant claimant and additional claimants up to a maximum of four, the US, USSR and representation of developing countries. A system for Special Meetings of Parties, consisting of all parties to the Convention, is also provided for.

A framework for decision-making has thus been established and procedures provided for and several countries signed the

---

[152] See e.g. the 1980 Convention on the Conservation of Antarctic Marine Living Resources. See also Howard, "The Convention on the Conservation of Antarctic Marine Living Resources: A Five Year Review", 38 *ICLQ*, 1989, p.104.

[153] See e.g. *Keesings Contemporary Archives*, p.32834 and 21(9) *UN Chronicle*, 1984, p.45.

[154] See e.g. Joyner, "The Antarctic Minerals Negotiating Process", 81 *AJIL*, 1987, p.888.

Convention.[155] However, opposition to the Convention has been growing.

At a meeting of the consultative parties to the Antarctic Treaty in April 1991, a 50-year mining ban was agreed.[156] It would also appear that after that date mining could only be undertaken with the consent of all the parties. This would appear to mark the end of the limited mining approach which led to the signing of the Convention on the Regulation of Antarctic Mineral Resource Activities.

An initiative has been developing at the United Nations, headed by Malaysia, to consider establishing a common heritage of mankind regime over Antarctica. An extensive report on the area was issued by the Secretary-General of the UN in November 1984, detailing the operations of the regime created under the 1959 Treaty, and the subject is being further considered by the General Assembly. The parties to the treaty have emphasised the success of the system and the participation in it of the major powers. The possible disadvantages of a common heritage international regime have also been referred to, while the proponents of the common heritage regime have stressed the need for exploitation of the area in the interests of all mankind.[157]

The signing of the 1988 Convention on mineral resource activities stimulated opposition and in resolution 43/83, adopted by the General Assembly that year, "deep regret" was expressed that such a convention should have been signed despite earlier resolutions calling for a moratorium on negotiations to create a minerals regime in the Antarctic.

France and Australia proposed at the October 1989 meeting of the signatories of the Antarctic Treaty that all mining be banned in the area, which should be designated a global "wilderness reserve".[158] The issue has yet to be resolved. In the meantime, increasing environmental problems are arising. In 1989, the Argentine supply ship, the *Bahia Paraiso*, capsized in the area leaking a substantial amount of diesel fuel and causing damage to wildlife

---

[155] See e.g. the Antarctic Minerals Act 1989, which provided for a UK licensing system for exploration and exploitation activities in Antarctica.

[156] *The Guardian*, 30 April 1991, p.20.

[157] *Ibid*. See also Assembly resolutions 38/77 and 39/152, and A/39/583.

[158] See *Keesing's Record of World Events*, p.36989, 1989.

and krill, while criticisms have been made of certain states for the routine disposal of untreated sewage in the area.[159]

LEASES AND SERVITUDES [160]

This section is concerned with various legal rights exercisable by states over the territory of other states, which fall short of absolute sovereignty. Such rights are attached to the land and so may be enforced even though the ownership of the particular territory subject to the rights has passed to another sovereign. They are in legal terminology formulated as rights *in rem.*

Leases of land rose into prominence in the last century as a way of obtaining control of usually strategic points without the necessity of actually annexing the territory. Leases were used extensively in the Far East, as for example Britain's rights over the New Territories amalgamated with Hong Kong,[161] and sovereignty was regarded as having passed to the lessee for the duration of the lease, upon which event it would revert to the original sovereign who made the grant.

An exception to this usual construction of a lease in international law as limited to a defined period, occurred with regard to the Panama Canal, with the strip of land through which it was constructed being leased to the United States in 1903 "in perpetuity". However, by the 1977 Panama Canal Treaty, sovereignty over the Canal Zone was transferred to Panama. The United States will have certain operating and defensive rights until the treaty ends in 1999.[162]

A servitude exists where the territory of one state is under a particular restriction in the interests of the territory of another state. Such limitations are bound to the land as rights *in rem* and thus restrict the sovereignty of the state concerned, even if there is a change in

---

[159] *Ibid.*, p.37019, 1989.

[160] See e.g. Reid, *International Servitudes*, 1932 and Vali, *Servitudes in International Law*, 2nd ed., 1958. See also Parry, *Digest, op. cit.* vol.2B, 1967, p.373 *et seq.*, and article 12, Vienna Convention on Succession of States in Respect of Treaties, 1978.

[161] See 50 *BFSP*, 1860, p.10 and 90 *BFSP*, 1898, p.17. See now 23 *ILM*, 1984, p.1366 *et seq.* for the UK-China agreement on Hong Kong. See also Cmnd. 9543 (1985) and the 1985 Hong Kong Act, providing for the termination of British sovereignty and jurisdiction over the territory as from 1 July 1997.

[162] See e.g. 72 *AJIL*, 1978, p.225. This superseded treaties of 1901, 1903, 1936 and 1955 governing the Canal. See also Rubin, "The Panama Canal Treaties", *YBWA*, 1981, p.181.

control of the relevant territory, for instance upon merger with another state.

Examples of servitudes would include the right to use ports or rivers in, or a right of way across, the territory so bound, or alternatively an obligation not to fortify particular towns or areas in the territory.[163]

Servitudes may exist for the benefit of the international community or a large number of states. To give an example, in the *Aaland Islands* case in 1920, a Commission of Jurists appointed by the Council of the League of Nations declared that Finland since its independence in 1918 had succeeded to Russia's obligations under the 1856 treaty not to fortify the islands. And since Sweden was an interested state in that the islands are situated near Stockholm, it could enforce the obligation although not a party to the 1856 treaty. This was because the treaty provisions had established a special international regime with obligations enforceable by interested states and binding upon any state in possession of the islands.[164]

The situation of the creation of an international status by treaty, which is to be binding upon all and not merely upon the parties to the treaty, is a complex one and it is not always clear when it is to be presumed. However, rights attached to territory for the benefit of the world community were created with respect to the Suez and Panama Canals.

Article 1 of the Constantinople Convention of 1888[165] declared that "the Suez Maritime Canal shall always be free and open in time of war as in time of peace, to every vessel of commerce or of war without distinction of flag" and this international status was in no way affected by the Egyptian nationalisation of the Canal Company in 1956. Egypt stressed in 1957 that it was willing to respect and implement the terms of the Convention, although in fact it consistently denied use of the canal to Israeli ships and vessels bound for its shores or carrying its goods.[166] The canal was reopened in 1975 following the disengagement agreement with Israel, after a gap of eight years.[167] Under article V of the 1979 Peace Treaty between Israel and Egypt, it was provided that ships of Israel and

---

[163] See e.g. Brierly, *The Law of Nations*, 6th ed., 1963, p.191.
[164] LNOJ, Sp. Suppl. no.3, 1920, pp.3, 16-19.
[165] See e.g. O'Connell, *op. cit.*, pp.582-87.
[166] See Security Council Doc. S/3818, 51 *AJIL*, p.673.
[167] See *DUSPIL*, 1974, pp.352-54 and 760.

cargoes destined for or coming from Israel were to enjoy "the right of free passage through the Suez Canal . . . on the basis of the Constantinople Convention of 1888, applying to all nations".

In the *Wimbledon* case,[168] the Permanent Court of International Justice declared that the effect of article 380 of the Treaty of Versailles 1919 maintaining that the Kiel Canal was to be open to all the ships of all countries at peace with Germany was to convert the canal from an internal to an international waterway "intended to provide under treaty guarantee easier access to the Baltic for the benefit of all nations of the world".

Some of the problems relating to the existence of servitudes have arisen by virtue of the *North Atlantic Fisheries* arbitration.[169] This followed a treaty signed in 1818 between the United Kingdom and the United States, awarding the inhabitants of the latter country "forever . . . the liberty to take fish of every kind" from the southern coast of Newfoundland. The argument arose as to Britain's capacity under the treaty to issue fishing regulations binding American nationals. The arbitration tribunal decided that the relevant provision of the treaty did not create a servitude, partly because such a concept was unknown by American and British statesmen at the relevant period (i.e. 1818). However, the terms of the award do leave open the possibility of the existence of servitudes, especially since the tribunal did draw a distinction between economic rights (as in the case) and a grant of sovereign rights which could amount to a servitude in international law.

---

[168] PCIJ, Series A, no.1, 1923, p.24; 2 *ILR*, p.99. See generally Baxter, *The Law of International Waterways*, 1964.

[169] 11 *RIAA*, p.167 (1910).

CHAPTER NINE

Air Law and Space Law

AIR LAW [1]

Theories [2]

There were a variety of theories prior to the First World War with regard to the status of the airspace above states and territorial waters. One view was that the airspace was entirely free, another that there was, upon an analogy with the territorial sea, a band of "territorial air" appertaining to the state followed by a higher free zone, a third approach was that all the airspace above a state was entirely within its sovereignty, while a fourth view modified the third approach by positing a right of innocent passage through the air space for foreign civil aircraft.[3] There was a particular antagonism between the French theory of freedom of the air and the British theory of state sovereignty,[4] although all agreed that the airspace above the high seas and *terrae nullius* was free and open to all.

However, the outbreak of the First World War with its recognition of the security implications of use of the air changed this.

The approach that then prevailed, with little dissension, was based upon the extension of state sovereignty upwards into airspace. This was acceptable both from the defence point of view and in the light of evolving state practice regulating flights over national territory.[5] It was reflected in the 1919 Paris Convention for the Regulation of Aerial Navigation, which recognised the full sovereignty of states over the airspace above their land and territorial sea.[6]

---

[1] See generally Cheng, *The Law of International Air Transport,* 1962; Shawcross and Beaumont, *Air Law,* 4th ed., regularly up-dated; Lowenfield, *Aviation Law: Cases and Materials,* 1981; Matte, *Treatise on Air-Aeronautical Law,* 1981 and Cheng and Austin, "Air Law" in *The Present State of International Law* (ed. Bos), 1973, p.183.

[2] See e.g. Oppenheim, *International Law,* vol.1, 8th ed., 1955, p.517 and Matte, *op. cit.,* Chapters 4 and 5.

[3] See Oppenheim, *op. cit.,* pp.517-18 and Matte, *op. cit.,* Chapter 5.

[4] *Ibid.,* p.83.

[5] *Ibid.,* pp.91-96.

[6] Article 1. Each party also undertook to accord in peace time freedom of innocent passage to the private aircraft of other parties so long as they complied with the rules made by or under the authority of the Convention. Articles 5-10 also provided that the nationality of
(Footnote continued on p.316)

Sovereignty was understood to extend for an unlimited distance into the airspace (*usque ad coelum*),[7] although this has been modified by the new law of outer space.

One question that did arise immediately concerned the apparent similarity of treatment as regards sovereignty between the airspace and the territorial sea and centred upon the right of passage that exists through territorial waters. It questioned whether there existed a right of passage through the airspace above states. This issue had, of course, tremendous implications for the development of aerial transport and raised the possibility of some erosion of state exclusivity. However, it is now accepted that no such right may be exercised in customary international law.[8] Aircraft may only traverse the airspace of states with the agreement of those states, and where that has not been obtained an illegal intrusion will be involved which will justify interception, though not (save in very exceptional cases) actual attack. This is discussed later.

The Structure

The present regime concerning air navigation developed from the 1944 Chicago Conference and the conventions adopted there.

The Chicago Convention on International Civil Aviation, which does not apply to state aircraft (for example, military, customs and police aircraft),[9] emphasises the complete and exclusive sovereignty of states over their airspace[10] and article 6 reinforces this by providing that no scheduled international air service may be operated over or into the territory of a contracting state without that state's special authorisation. However, the states parties to the Convention qualified their sovereignty by agreeing in article 5 that aircraft of other contracting states:

> not engaged in scheduled international air service, shall have the right
> . . . to make flights into or in transit non-stop across [their territory and

(Footnote continued from p.315)

aircraft would be based upon registration and that registration would take place in the state of which their owners were nationals. An International Commission for Air Navigation was also established. See also the 1978 American Convention on Commercial Aviation.

[7] Based upon common law principles, see e.g. *Co. Litt.* 4 and Blackstone, *Commentaries*, vol.II, Chapter 2, p.18.

[8] See e.g. Oppenheim, *op. cit.*, p.523.

[9] Article 3.

[10] Article 1. This includes the airspace above territorial waters, article 2.

to make stops for non-traffic purposes without the necessity of obtaining prior permission and subject to the right of the state flown over to require landing.[11]

This provision has in practice been viewed as an exception to the general principle enumerated in article 6 of the Convention, particularly since states have required that permission be obtained prior to the acceptance of charter flights over or into their territory, even though such flights do not really come within the meaning of article 6 or within the definition of scheduled international air services put forward by the Council of the International Civil Aviation Organisation in 1952. It is one more example of state practice modifying the original interpretation of a treaty stipulation.[12]

The Chicago International Air Services Transit Agreement, 1944, dealing with scheduled international air services, specified that contracting states recognised the privileges of such services to fly across their territories without landing and to land for non-traffic purposes. This "two freedoms" agreement, as it has been termed, was accompanied by a "five freedoms" agreement, the 1944 Chicago International Air Transport Agreement, which added to the aforementioned provisions extensive privileges of taking on and putting down passengers, mail and cargo in the territories of contracting states. However, this agreement was not ratified by many countries and the USA withdrew from it in 1946[13] because it was felt that too much of commercial value had been granted away. Thus, that agreement is of little importance today.

This has meant in actual practice that the regulation of international scheduled services has been achieved by an extensive network of bilateral agreements such as the UK-USA Bermuda Agreement of 1946,[14] since the agreed "two freedoms" only relate to transit and not traffic rights. The hard bargaining that goes on in negotiations between states to arrange the operation of the remaining "three freedoms" attests to the commercial as well as

[11] Note also that under article 9, states may for reasons of military necessity or public safety prohibit or restrict the aircraft of other states on a non-discriminatory basis from flying over certain areas of its territory.

[12] The distinction between scheduled and non-scheduled international air services is not entirely clear, see here O'Connell, *International Law*, 2nd ed., 1970, vol.I, p.521. See also the non-binding ICAO Council definition of 1952, Doc. 7278-C/841, quoted in Greig, *International Law*, 2nd ed., 1976, p.349.

[13] See Oppenheim, *op. cit.*, p.527, note 5.

[14] Replaced by the Bermuda II agreement of 1977. See e.g. Matte, *op. cit.*, pp.229-50.

strategic significance connected with such privileges. But the technological advances of advanced design and "jumbo" jets as well as the proliferation of state airlines has put this somewhat unwieldy system under great strain.

The Chicago Conference also led to the creation of the International Civil Aviation Organisation (ICAO), a UN specialised agency based in Canada, which concentrates upon technical and administrative co-operation between states in the field of civil aviation, ranging from the adoption of agreed safety standards to the encouragement of the expansion of navigational facilities.[15] ICAO's aims and objectives are to develop the principles and techniques of international air navigation and to foster the planning and development of international air transport.[16] It has a range of powers from legal to technical and administrative and it consists of an Assembly, a Council and such other bodies as may be necessary.[17]

In the main, the Chicago Conference reaffirmed the principles agreed in the 1919 Convention with regard to, for example, the sovereignty of the state over its airspace and the need for permission to operate scheduled international air services. Air cabotage, i.e. the right to carry traffic between points within the territory of a state, can be reserved exclusively to the state as may traffic between the metropolitan and colonial areas. The Chicago Conference system was to some extent undermined by the growth of bilateral agreements as the means to regulate international air transport, but many common principles may be discerned in such agreements based as they are upon the Bermuda model.

The Bermuda principles, in general, provide that the air transport facilities available to the travelling public should bear a close relationship to the requirements of the public; that there shall be a fair and equal opportunity for the carriers of the two nations to operate on any route between their respective territories; that in the operation by the air carriers of either government of the trunk services described in the Annex of the Agreement, the interest of

---

[15] *Ibid.*, pp.187-201.

[16] Article 44 of the Chicago Convention 1944.

[17] Article 43. There are, for example, Committees dealing with Air Transport, Joint Support of Air Navigation Services and Legal Matters, and an Air Navigation Commission. Note the standard-setting work of ICAO, e.g. the 1948 Convention on the International Recognition of Rights in Aircraft and the 1955 Protocol to the 1929 Warsaw Convention. See generally Shawcross and Beaumont, *op. cit.*, DII (2)-(19).

the air carriers of the other government shall be taken into consideration, so as not to affect unduly the services which the latter provides on all or part of the same routes; and that it is the understanding of both governments that services provided by a designated air carrier under the Agreement and its Annex shall retain, as their primary objective, the provision of capacity adequate to the traffic demands between the country of which the carrier is a national and the country of ultimate destination of the traffic. The right to embark or to disembark on such services of international traffic destined for and coming from third countries at a point or points on the routes specified in the Annex to the Agreement, shall be applied in accordance with the general principles of orderly development to which both governments subscribe and shall be subject to the general principle that capacity should be related:

(a) to traffic requirements between the country of origin and the countries of destination;
(b) to the requirements of through airline operation; and
(c) to the traffic requirements of the area through which the airline passes after taking account of local and regional services; and that it is the intention of both governments that there should be regular and frequent consultation between their respective aeronautical authorities and that there should thereby be close collaboration in the observation of the principles and the implementation of the provisions outlined therein and in the Agreement and its Annex.[18]

The UK denounced the Bermuda Agreement in 1976 on grounds of inequity of share in the North Atlantic traffic and in 1977 a new agreement with the USA, Bermuda II, was signed.[19] The basic principles of Bermuda I were reaffirmed, but with new regulation techniques. British airlines were allowed new non-stop services and the freedom to combine their US points on each route as they choose. The problem of "excess capacity" was dealt with by a consultative process and a Tariff Working Group was established.

In additional to the International Civil Aviation Organisation there also exists the International Air Transport Association which consists

[18] See Matte, *op. cit.*, pp.591-95.
[19] See *DUSPIL*, 1977, pp.638-41. See generally as to dispute settlement in such cases, Cheng, "Dispute Settlement in Bilateral Air Transport Agreements" in *Settlement of Space Law Disputes* (ed. Böckstiegel), 1980, p.97. See also Shawcross and Beaumont, *op. cit.*, DIV.

of most of the airline companies acting together to establish uniform fares and tariffs subject to governmental approval. It is also an important forum for discussion of relevant topics such as hijacking and attacks upon civil aircraft.

The Warsaw Convention System [20]

An issue which has become of great importance in recent years relates to the liability of civil airline companies for death or injury suffered by passengers. The 1929 Warsaw Convention for the Unification of Certain Rules relating to International Carriage by Air established upper limits for such liability as well as dealing with other questions of responsibility and insurance. The Convention was modified by the Hague Amendment of 1955, but as this proved unacceptable to the United States a subsequent Agreement in Montreal was signed in 1966 raising the limits of liability as regards airlines flying in or to the USA.

Article 20 of the Convention lays down the general rule that the carrier is not liable if he proves that he and his agents have taken all necessary measures to avoid the damage or that it was impossible for him or them to take such measures The standard of proof is high.[21] Article 22 provides for limits to the carrier's liability, defined in terms of gold French francs (or Poincaré francs),[22] but liability is unlimited under article 25 if damage[23] results from the wilful misconduct of the carrier or of one of his agents.[24] Some help would undoubtedly be provided by the entry into force of the Montreal Additional Protocols 1975, which seek *inter alia* to substitute Special Drawing Rights for the gold franc, and the Guatemala Protocol 1971, which seeks to introduce absolute liability with

[20] See e.g. Matte, *op. cit.*, pp.377-496 and Miller, *Liability in International Air Transport,* 1977. See also the 1961 Guadalajara Convention, which deals with international carriage by air performed by a person other than the contracting carrier. See generally Shawcross and Beaumont, *op. cit.,* DVII.

[21] See e.g. *Grein* v. *Imperial Airways Ltd,* [1937] 1 KB 50; 8 *ILR,* p.453; *Ritts* v. *American Overseas Airlines,* US Av R, 1949, p.65 and *American Smelting and Refining Co* v. *Philippine Airlines Inc,* US and C Av R, 1954, p.221; 21 *ILR,* p.286.

[22] See e.g. *TWA Inc.* v. *Franklin Mint Corporation,* 23 *ILM,* 1984, p.814.

[23] Damage in this instance has been interpreted to include loss, see *Fothergill* v. *Monarch Airlines,* [1980] 2 All ER 696; 74 *ILR,* p.627.

[24] Dissatisfaction with the Warsaw system has led some municipal courts into the realms of judicial creativity, see e.g. *Chen* v. *Korean Air Lines Ltd,* 109 S Ct 1676 (1989) and *Coccia* v. *Turkish Airlines* [1985] Dir Mar 751 (Italian Constitutional Court).

increased limits in passenger and baggage cases. The ICAO Council and its Legal Committee did indeed discuss a plan to encourage the ratification of the Montreal Protocols in early 1990.[25]

But the situation respecting the airlines' liability outside the US is not at all satisfactory and the limits are low. This has meant that claimants are often tempted to sue not the airlines but, for example, the aircraft manufacturers in the hope of obtaining higher levels of compensation. However, here problems centre upon the choice of courts before which to bring the issue, since the sums available in personal injury cases vary considerably from country to country and the grounds for liability are not the same in all jurisdictions.

The whole position was graphically illustrated by the Turkish Airlines tragedy in 1974. The crash of the American-built plane near Paris and the loss of over three hundred lives emphasised the complexity of injustice of the situation respecting the amounts of compensation available for the death or injuries caused to passengers.

The sums that could have been obtained from Turkish Airlines were limited by the terms of the Warsaw Convention as amended, and accordingly the claimants turned to the American manufacturer of the defective aircraft. But the position was that if the case were brought in the UK, substantially less could have been obtained than if the matter came before the American courts, which have a much more progressive system of absolute liability and higher compensation limits with respect to personal injuries. In the end, a group of Britons succeeded in bringing their cases before Californian judges and were awarded satisfactory levels of compensation, in line with the American approach.[26]

The general significance of air transportation for the world community can be seen in the developing provisions relating to hijacking. The airspace has become a vital means of communication and the various attacks upon aircraft condemned as threatening this freedom of the air. The international community has adopted a series

[25] See Shawcross and Beaumont, *op. cit.*, DVII (57).

[26] See e.g. *DUSPIL*, 1975, pp.459-61 and *In re Paris Air Crash of March 2, 1974*, 399 F.Supp. 732 (1975). The Air Law Committee of the ILA has suggested 3 principles — (1) There should be a integrated system of civil aviation liability in international carriage by air and in respect of surface damage; (2) Claims should be channelled through the carrier and operator of the aircraft and (3) Compensation for personal injuries shall be based on the principle of absolute, unlimited and secured liability, see ILA, Report of the Sixteenth Conference, 1982, p.553.

of conventions outlawing hijacking and stipulating methods of enforcement, though with a limited degree of success. Nevertheless, it is likely that the law relating to hijacking will eventually turn that offence into a universal one on similar lines to piracy on the high seas.[27]

The Montreal Convention for the Suppression of Unlawful Acts against the Safety of Civil Aviation 1971 makes it an offence unlawfully and intentionally, *inter alia*, to perform an act of violence against a person on board an aircraft in flight where the act is likely to endanger the safety of the aircraft; to destroy an aircraft in service or to so damage it as to make flight unsafe or impossible; to destroy, damage or interfere with the operation of air navigation facilities or to communicate knowingly false information if this is likely to endanger an aircraft in flight.

The ambit of this convention was extended by the Montreal Protocol 1988 to include acts of violence against a person at an airport serving international civil aviation which cause or are likely to cause serious injury or death; destroying or seriously damaging the facilities of such an airport or aircraft not in service located thereon and disrupting the services of the airport.[28]

The terrorist attacks of the 1970s in particular gave rise to a series of cases, which have established, for example, that recovery for mental distress arising out of an airplane hijack was possible under the Warsaw Convention as amended by the Montreal Agreement of 1966[29] and that a carrier remains liable for injuries to passengers that occurred in a terrorist attack at Hellenikon Airport, Athens, at the departure gate of the terminal.[30] However, there was no liability in the case of an attack in the baggage retrieval area of an air terminal building while the passengers were waiting for their luggage as this was not "disembarking" within the meaning of article 17.[31]

The question of liability for damage caused by aircraft to persons on the surface has also been dealt with. The Rome Convention on Damage Caused by Foreign Aircraft to Third Parties on the Surface,

---

[27] See further, *infra*, Chapter 11, p.369.

[28] See the Aviation and Maritime Security Act 1990.

[29] *Krystal* v. *BOAC*, 403 F.Supp. 1322 (1975).

[30] *Day* v. *TWA Inc*, 528 F.2d 31 (1975), cert. denied 429 US 890.

[31] *Hernandez* v. *Air France*, 545 F.2d 279 (1976). See also *Mangrui* v. *Compagnie Nationale Air France*, 549 F.2d 1256 (1977), cert. denied, 45 Law Week 3801 (1977).

1952, and the Montreal Protocol of 1978, provide for compensation to be paid upon proof only of damage caused by an aircraft in flight or by any person or thing falling therefrom. It is the operator of the aircraft that bears the responsibility and under the 1952 Convention the registered owner of the aircraft is presumed to be the operator. The extent of liability is stipulated and one of the reasons for the low level of ratification has been the relatively limited level of compensation provided for. The system is based upon strict liability and on clear connection being established between the damage and the act causing the injury.

Unauthorised Aerial Intrusion and the Downing of Civilian Airliners [32]

A number of incidents have occurred since 1945 of the destruction of foreign aerial intruders. In 1955 a civil airliner of El Al Israel Airlines was shot down while intruding into Bulgarian airspace by Bulgarian warplanes. An action was commenced before the International Court of Justice which, however, dismissed the case on grounds of lack of jurisdiction. The Israeli Memorials emphasised that a state faced with an unauthorised aerial intrusion may deal with it in one or both of two ways: first, by informing the intruder that it is performing an unauthorised act (and this may include compelling it to land); secondly, by taking diplomatic action.[33]

In 1973, Israeli jets shot down a Libyan airliner straying several score miles into Israeli-occupied Sinai. It was alleged that the airliner had been warned to land but had refused to comply with the order. After an investigation the Council of ICAO condemned Israel's action and declared that "such actions constitute a serious danger against the safety of international civil aviation". Israel's attitude was criticised as a "flagrant violation of the principles enshrined in the Chicago Convention".[34]

On 1 September 1983, Soviet jets shot down a Korean Airlines airplane which had strayed several hundred miles into sensitive

---

[32] See e.g. Lissitzyn, "The Treatment of Aerial Intruders in Recent Practice and International Law", 47 *AJIL*, 1953, p.554; Greig, *op. cit.*, pp.356-60; Hassan, "The Shooting Down of Korean Airlines Flight 007 By the USSR and the Furtherance of Air Safety for Passengers", 33 *ICLQ* 1984, p.712 and de la Rochère, "L'Affaire de l'Accident du Boeing 747 de Korean Airlines", *AFDI*, 1983, p.749. See also Matte, *op. cit.*, pp.175-77.

[33] *Aerial Incident* case, ICJ Reports, 1959, pp.127, 130; 27 *ILR*, p.557.

[34] 12 *ILM*, 1973, p.1180. Israel apologised for the incident and paid compensation to the victims. See also *DUSPIL*, 1973, pp.312-13. As to the Chicago Convention, see *supra*, p.316.

Soviet airspace causing the deaths of 269 persons.[35] A week later, the USSR vetoed a draft Security Council resolution which reaffirmed the rules of international law prohibiting acts of violence against the safety of international civil aviation.[36] The Council of ICAO directed on 16 September that an investigation be held and that the Air Navigation Commission should review the Chicago Convention and related documents to prevent a recurrence of such a tragic incident and to seek to improve methods of communication between civil and military aircraft and air traffic control services.[37]

After the submission of the report,[38] the Council of ICAO adopted a resolution condemning the shooting down of the Korean airliner.[39] In addition, an amendment to the Chicago Convention was adopted.[40] This amendment was to article 3 of the Convention, which had laid down as one of its general principles that contracting states undertook to have due regard for the safety of navigation of civil aircraft. In addition to the general provision in article 3, Annex II to the Convention had provided for detailed procedures to be followed in cases of interception, procedures which were apparently not complied with in the case of the Korean Airlines tragedy.[41] Annex II also provided that "intercepting aircraft should refrain from the use of weapons in all cases of interception of civil aircraft". Despite this provision and ICAO Council action in 1973 regarding Israel's attack on a Libyan airliner over Sinai, the need was felt to strengthen the general principle in article 3 itself in order to add greater force to the concern felt. New article 3 *bis* provides that:

> (a) The contracting states recognise that every state must refrain from resorting to the use of weapons against the civil aircraft in flight, and that in case of interception, the lives of persons on board and the safety of aircraft must not be endangered. This provision shall not be interpreted as modifying in any way the rights and obligations of states set forth in the Charter of the United Nations.

[35] See the Report of the Secretary-General of ICAO, 23 *ILM,* 1984, p.864.

[36] 22 *ILM,* 1983, p.1148.

[37] See Leich, "Destruction of Korean Airliner: Action by International Organisations", 78 *AJIL,* 1984, pp.244-45.

[38] *Supra,* footnote 35.

[39] 23 *ILM,* 1984, p.937.

[40] *Ibid.,* p.705. This amendment, the Montreal Protocol 1984, needs to be ratified by two-thirds of the ICAO membership before it comes into force.

[41] See ICAO Report, 23 *ILM,* 1984, p.864 and de la Rochère, *op. cit.*

The right of states to require a civil aircraft to land at a designated airport, where the aircraft is flying above its territory without authority or where there are reasonable grounds to conclude that it is being used for any purpose inconsistent with the Convention, was reaffirmed in subsection (b). There are several points that may be made with regard to the amendment. First, it is to be noted that reference is made to "weapons" not force in the prohibition provision. Presumably this means that force may be used against civil aircraft in flight in pursuance of an interception, provided that weapons are not actually fired. Second, the wording appears to suggest that national as well as foreign civil aircraft fall within the scope of the provision, but the restriction to aircraft "in flight" leads one to assume that the need to distinguish this kind of situation from the recapture of hijacked aircraft on the ground was felt. Finally, the provision in subsection (b) stipulating when states may require aircraft to land appears to be more restrictive than article 4 of the 1963 Tokyo Convention on Offences and Certain Other Acts Committed on Board Aircraft, which permits interference in five defined situations, i.e. where:

(a) The offence has effect on the territory of such state;

(b) the offence has been committed by or against a national or permanent resident of such state;

(c) the offence is against the security of such state;

(d) the offence consists of a breach of any rules or regulations relating to the flight or manoeuvre of aircraft in force in such state;

(e) the exercise of jurisdiction is necessary to ensure the observance of any obligation of such state under a multilateral international agreement.

Article 82 of the Chicago Convention provides for the abrogation of all inconsistent obligations and understandings among ICAO members and it is a moot point whether this means that article 3 *bis* (when in force) would override the Tokyo provisions,[42] although it should be noted that the Tokyo Convention deals only with offences committed on board the aircraft.

Under article 25 of the Chicago Convention, an aircraft in distress is to be given necessary assistance, but this relies upon the fact of

[42] See e.g. Cheng, "The Destruction of KAL Flight KE007, and Article 3 *bis* of the Chicago Convention" in *Air Worthy* (eds. Van Gravesande and Van der Veen Vonk), 1985, p.49.

distress being evident or made known to the intercepting forces. In such a situation resort to the use of force would be illegal.

It is also clear that the doctrine of self-defence may be of relevance in certain situations, for example, if the intruding aircraft was clearly involved in an act of aggression or terrorism. The intercepting forces may have to take action, within the parameters of proportionality,[43] to forestall that threat and force may be necessary. However, a civilian airliner is unlikely to pose this level of threat justifying a shooting down. It appears that the USSR believed that the airliner was an American spy plane.[44] Even if that were true or if the belief were genuine, it would seem that the actions taken to require it to land were inadequate and the course actively embarked upon beyond the bounds of proportionality.

The general issue was again raised by the shooting down by the USS warship *Vincennes* in July 1988 of an Iranian civil airliner over the Persian Gulf, although it should be noted in this case that there was, of course, no unauthorised aerial intrusion into domestic airspace.[45] Both the US Defence Department and the ICAO reports into the incident in essence placed the blame for the incident upon the warship.[46] Mistakes made as to the identification of the aircraft and with regard to the warnings issued to it combined with the tense atmosphere in that region during the Iran-Iraq war to create the disaster. Suggestions have been made that the US should not be regarded as legally responsible, since proof of fault beyond reasonable doubt has yet to be established and the fact that the incident took place in a war zone is of the utmost relevance in assessing this.[47] However, it is undisputed that the airliner was shot down by a US warship and this is certainly contrary to article 3 *bis*, which could well now be regarded as a principle of customary law. While self-defence may well have been an initial consideration, its application is circumscribed by the principles of necessity and proportionality. The incident is currently before the International Court of Justice upon Iran's application on 17 May 1989.

[43] As to self-defence and proportionality, see *infra*, Chapter 18.

[44] See 22 *ILM*, 1983, pp.1126-28.

[45] See e.g. *Keesing's Record of World Events*, pp.36064, 36169, 36631 and 37423, and "Agora: The Downing of Iran Air Flight 655", 83 *AJIL*, 1989, p.318. See also 28 *ILM*, 1989, p.896.

[46] *Keesing's Record of World Events, op. cit.*, and 83 *AJIL*, 1989, p.332. See also Security Council resolution 616 (1988).

[47] See e.g. Maier, "*Ex Gratia* Payments and the Iranian Airline Tragedy", 83 *AJIL*, 1989, p.325.

Following the Iraqi invasion of Kuwait on 2 August 1990, the Security Council adopted a series of resolutions. Resolution 670 (1990) declared that permission to any aircraft to take off should be denied by all states from their territory where the aircraft was carrying any cargo to or from Iraq or Kuwait other than food in humanitarian circumstances or supplies strictly for medical purposes or solely for the UN Iran-Iraq Military Observer Group. All states were called upon to deny permission to overfly their territory to any aircraft destined to land in Iraq or Kuwait, unless it had been inspected to ensure it had no cargo on board which was in violation of Security Council resolution 661 (1990) establishing sanctions against Iraq, or unless the particular flight had been approved by the Sanctions Committee or had been certified by the UN as being solely for the purposes of the Military Observer Group. The Council would consider measures directed at states which evaded these provisions. However, this would not permit the shooting down of civilian airliners suspected of breaking the UN sanctions against Iraq.

The situation is different with regard to military aircraft intruding without authorisation into foreign airspace. The self-defence argument may be stronger and the burden of proof thus lower, but it is questionable whether the need for a prior warning has been dispensed with.[48]

THE LAW OF OUTER SPACE [49]

The fundamental principle of air law relates to the complete sovereignty of the subjacent state. This is qualified by the various multilateral and bilateral conventions which permit airlines to cross and land in the territories of the contracting states under recognised

[48] See e.g. Lissitzyn, Editorial Comment, 56 *AJIL*, 1962, pp.135, 138. See further *infra*, Chapter 18.

[49] See e.g. Christol, *The Modern International Law of Outer Space*, 1982; Fawcett, *Outer Space*, 1984; Goedhuis, "The Present State of Space Law" in *The Present State of International Law* (ed. Bos), 1973, p.201; Gorove, "International Space Law in Perspective", 181 *HR*, p.349; Marcoff, "Sources du Droit International de l'Espace", 168 *HR*, p.9; Matte, *Aerospace Law*, 1969; Cheng, "The 1967 Space Treaty", *Journal de Droit International*, 1968, p.532 and "The Moon Treaty", 33 *Current Legal Problems*, 1980, p.213. Note in particular the role of the UN Committee on the Peaceful Uses of Outer Space, established in 1958 and now consisting of representatives of 53 states. The Committee has a Legal Sub-Committee and a Scientific and Technical Sub-Committee, see Christol, *op. cit.*, pp.13-20. It operates by consensus. See also the Second UN Conference on the Exploration of Uses of Outer Space 1982, *UN Chronicle*, July 1982, p.49 *et seq.*

conditions and in the light of the accepted regulations. But there is also another qualification and one that substantially modifies the *usque ad coelum* concept, whereby sovereignty extended over the airspace to an unlimited height. This centres upon the creation and development of the law of outer space.

Ever since the USSR launched the first earth satellite in 1957, the pace of space exploration has developed at an ever-increasing rate. Satellites now control communications and observation networks, while landings have been made on the moon and information-seeking space probes dispatched to survey planets like Venus and Saturn. The amount of new knowledge obtained and collated by the various American, Soviet and European programmes has been vast and has demonstrated man's capacity to embark upon the discovery of his space environment.

The research material gathered upon such diverse matters as earth resources, ionospheric activities, solar radiation, cosmic rays and the general structure of space and planet formations has stimulated further efforts to understand the nature of space and the cosmos.[50]

This immense increase in available information has also led to the development of the law of outer space, formulating generally accepted principles to regulate the interests of the various states involved as well as taking into account the concern of the international community as a whole.

The Definition and Delimitation of Outer Space

It soon became apparent that the *usque ad coelum* rule, providing for state sovereignty over territorial airspace to an unrestricted extent, was not viable where space exploration was concerned. To obtain the individual consents of countries to the passage of satellites and other vehicles orbiting more than one hundred miles above their surface would prove cumbersome in the extreme and in practice states have acquiesced in such traversing. This means that the sovereignty of states over their airspace is limited in height at most to the point where the airspace meets space itself. Precisely where this boundary lies is difficult to say and will depend upon technological and other factors, but figures between fifty and one hundred miles have been put forward.

[50] See e.g. Fawcett, *op. cit.*, Chapter 7.

As conventional aircraft are developed to attain greater heights, so states will wish to see their sovereignty extend to those heights and, as well as genuine uncertainty, this fear of surrendering what may prove to be in the future valuable sovereign rights has prevented any agreement on the delimitation of this particular frontier.[51]

The Regime of Outer Space

Beyond the point separating air from space, states have agreed to apply the international law principles of *res communis*, so that no portion of outer space may be appropriated to the sovereignty of individual states.

This was made clear in a number of General Assembly resolutions following the advent of the satellite era in the late 1950s. For instance, UN General Assembly resolution 1962 (XVII) adopted in 1963 lays down a series of applicable legal principles which include the provisions that outer space and celestial bodies were free for exploration and use by all states on a basis of equality and in accordance with international law, and that outer space and celestial bodies were not subject to national appropriation by any means.[52] Such resolutions constituted in the circumstances expressions of state practice and *opinio juris* and thus part of customary law.[53]

The legal regime of outer space was clarified by the signature in 1967 of the Treaty on Principles Governing the Activities of States in the Exploration and Use of Outer Space, including the Moon and Other Celestial Bodies. This reiterates that outer space, including the moon and other celestial bodies, is not subject to national appropriation by any means and emphasises that the exploration and use of outer space must be carried out for the benefit of all countries. The Treaty does not provide a precise boundary between

[51] See generally Christol, *op. cit.*, Chapter 10. A variety of suggestions have been put forward regarding the method of delimitation, ranging from the properties of the atmosphere to the lowest possible orbit of satellites. They appear to fall within either a spatial or functional category, see *ibid.*, and UN Doc. A/AC.105/C.2/7/Add.1, 21 January 1977. Some states now argue for a 110 km. boundary, see e.g. USSR, 21(4) *UN Chronicle*, 1984, p.37; others feel it is premature to establish such a fixed delimitation, e.g. USA and UK, *ibid.* See also 216 HL Deb., 1958-9, col.975, and Goedhius, "The Problems of the Frontiers of Outer Space and Airspace", 174 *HR*, p.367.

[52] See also General Assembly resolutions 1721 (XVI) and 1884 (XVIII).

[53] See *supra*, Chapter 3, and Cheng, "United Nations Resolutions on Outer Space: 'Instant' International Customary Law?", 5 *Indian Journal of International Law*, 1965, p.23.

airspace and outer space but it provides the framework for the international law of outer space.[54]

Article IV provides that states parties to the Treaty agree:

not to place in orbit around the earth any objects carrying nuclear weapons or any other kinds of weapons of mass destruction, install such weapons on celestial bodies, or station such weapons in outer space in any other manner.

There are, however, disagreements as to the meaning of this provision.[55] The article bans only nuclear weapons and weapons of mass destruction from outer space, the celestial bodies and from orbit around the earth, but article I does emphasise that the exploration and use of outer space "shall be carried out for the benefit and in the interests of all countries" and it has been argued that this can be interpreted to mean that any military activity in space contravenes the treaty.[56]

Under article IV, only the moon and other celestial bodies must be used exclusively for peaceful purposes, although the use of military personnel for scientific and other peaceful purposes is not prohibited. There are minimalist and maximalist interpretations as to how these provisions are to be understood. The former, for example, would argue that only aggressive military activity is banned, while the latter would prohibit all military behaviour.[57]

Under article VIII, states retain jurisdiction and control over personnel and vehicles launched by them into space and under article VII they remain responsible for any damage caused to other parties to the Treaty by their space objects.

This aspect of space law was further developed by the Convention on International Liability for Damage Caused by Space Objects signed in 1972, article XII of which provides for the payment of compensation in accordance with international law and the principles of

[54] See e.g. Christol, *op. cit.,* Chapter 2.

[55] The issue has become particularly controversial in the light of the US Strategic Defence Initiative, ("Star Wars"), which aims to develop a range of anti-satellite and anti-missile weapons based in space. The UN Committee on the Peaceful Uses of Outer Space has recently considered the issue, although without the participation of the US, which objected to the matter being considered, see e.g. 21 (6) *UN Chronicle,* 1984, p.18.

[56] See e.g. Marcoff, *Traité de Droit International Public de l'Espace,* 1973, p.361 *et seq.* See also *Space Activities and Emerging International Law* (ed. Motte), 1984, p.290 *et seq.*

[57] See e.g. Christol, *op. cit.,* pp.25-26.

justice and equity for any damage caused by space objects. Article II provides for absolute liability to pay such compensation for damage caused by a space object on the surface of the earth or to aircraft in flight, whereas article III provides for fault liability for damage caused elsewhere or to persons or property on board a space object. This Convention was invoked by Canada in 1979 following the damage allegedly caused by Soviet Cosmos 954.[58] As a reinforcement to this evolving system of state responsibility, the Convention on the Registration of Objects Launched into Outer Space was was adopted by the General Assembly in 1975. This laid down a series of stipulations for the registration of information regarding space objects, such as, for example, their purpose, location and parameters, with the United Nations Secretary-General.

Such measures were preceded by the Agreement on the Rescue of Astronauts, the Return of Astronauts and the Return of Objects Launched into Outer Space signed in 1968, which set out the legal framework for the provision of emergency assistance to astronauts. This provides for immediate notification of the launching authority or, if that is not immediately possible, a public announcement regarding space personnel in distress as well as the immediate provision of assistance. It also covers search and rescue operations as well as a guarantee of prompt return. The Convention also provides for recovery of space objects.[59]

In 1979, the Agreement Governing the Activities of States on the Moon and other Celestial Bodies was adopted.[60] This provides for the demilitarisation of the moon and other celestial bodies, although military personnel may be used for peaceful purposes. This provision reiterates the principle established in the 1967 Outer Space Treaty. Under article IV, the exploration and the use of the moon shall be the province of all mankind and should be carried out for the

[58] The claim was for $6,401,174.70. See 18 *ILM*, 1979, p.899 *et seq*. See also Christol, *op. cit.*, p.59 *et seq* and "International Liability for Damage Caused by Space Objects", 74 *AJIL*, 1980, p.346. Note also that under article 3 of the 1967 Treaty, all states parties to the Treaty agree to carry on activities "in accordance with international law", which clearly includes rules relating to state responsibility.

[59] The Outer Space Act 1986 provides a framework for private sector space enterprises by creating a licensing system for outer space activities and by establishing a system for indemnification for damage suffered by third parties or elsewhere. The Act also establishes a statutory register of the launch of space objects.

[60] This came into force in July 1984, see Christol, "The Moon Treaty Enters into Force", 79 *AJIL*, 1985, p.163. There are currently 85 states parties to the 1967 Treaty, 78 to the 1968 Agreement, 69 to the 1972 Treaty and 34 to the 1975 Conventon, *ibid.*, pp.163-64.

benefit of all. Article XI emphasises that the moon and its natural resources are the common heritage of mankind and are not subject to national appropriation by any means. That important article emphasises that no private rights of ownership over the moon or any part of it or its natural resources in place may be created, although all states parties have the right to exploration and use of the moon. The states parties also agreed under article XI (5) and (7) to establish an international regime to govern the exploitation of the resources of the moon, when this becomes feasible.[61] The main purposes of the international regime to be established are to include:

(a) The orderly and safe development of the natural resources of the moon;
(b) The rational management of those resources;
(c) The expansion of opportunities in the use of those resources; and
(d) An equitable sharing by all states parties in the benefits derived from those resources, whereby the interests and need of the developing countries, as well as the efforts of those countries which have contributed either directly or indirectly to the exploration of the moon, shall be given special consideration.

Several points are worth noting. First, the proposed international regime is only to be established when exploitation becomes feasible. Second, it appears that until the regime is set up, there is a moratorium on exploitation, although not on "exploration and use", as recognised by articles XI(4) and VI(2). This would permit the collection of samples and their removal from the moon for scientific purposes. Thirdly, it is to be noted that private ownership rights of minerals or natural resources not in place are permissible under the Treaty.[62]

Telecommunications

Arguably the most useful application of space exploitation techniques has been the creation of telecommunications networks.

[61] See e.g. Cheng, "The Moon Treaty", *op. cit.*, pp.231-32, and Christol, *op. cit.* footnote 49, Chapters 7 and 8.
[62] See *infra*, Chapter 10, p.388, regarding the "common heritage" regime envisaged for the deep seabed under the 1982 Convention on the Law of the Sea.

This has revolutionised communications and has an enormous educational as well as entertainment potential.[63]

The legal framework for the use of space in the field of telecommunications is provided by the various INTELSAT (international telecommunications satellites) agreements which enable the member-states of the International Telecommunications Union to help develop and establish the system, although much of the work is in fact carried out by American corporations, particularly COMSAT. In 1971 the communist countries established their own network of telecommunications satellites, called INTER-SPUTNIK. The international regime for the exploitation of the orbit/spectrum resource[64] has built upon the 1967 Treaty, the 1973 Telecommunications Convention and Protocol and various International Telecommunication Union Radio Regulations. Regulation of the radio spectrum is undertaken at the World Administrative Radio Conferences and by the principal organs of the ITU.

However, there are a number of problems associated with these ventures ranging from the allocation of radio wave frequencies to the dangers inherent in direct broadcasting via satellites to willing and unwilling states alike. Questions such as the control of material broadcast by such satellites and the protection of minority cultures from "swamping" have yet to be answered, but are being discussed in various UN organs, for instance UNESCO and the Committee on the Peaceful Uses of Outer Space.[65]

Two principles are relevant in this context: freedom of information, which is a right enshrined in many international instruments,[66] and state sovereignty. A number of attempts have been made to reconcile the two.

In 1972, UNESCO adopted a Declaration of Guiding Principles on the Use of Satellite Broadcasting, in which it was provided that

[63] See e.g. the use by India of US satellites to beam educational television programmes to many thousands of isolated settlements that would otherwise not have been reached, *DUSPIL*, 1976, pp.427-28.

[64] See Christol, *op. cit.* footnote 49, Chapter 11.

[65] See Christol, *op. cit.* footnote 49, Chapter 12 and Matte, "Aerospace Law: Telecommunications Satellites", 166 *HR*, p.119. See also the study requested by the 1982 Conference, A/AC.107/341. See also the European Convention on Transfrontier Television 1988 and EEC Directive 89/552 on the Pursuit of Television Broadcasting Activities.

[66] See e.g. article 19, International Covenant on Civil and Political Rights, 1966; article 10, Universal Declaration on Human Rights, 1948 and article 10, European Convention on Human Rights, 1950.

all states had the right to decide on the content of educational programmes broadcast to their own peoples, while article IX declared that prior agreement was required for direct satellite broadcasting to the population of countries other than the country of origin of the transmission. Within the UN support for the consent principle was clear, but there were calls for a proper regulatory regime, in addition.[67]

In 1983, the General Assembly adopted resolution 37/92 entitled "Principles Governing the Use by States of Artificial Earth Satellites for International Direct Television Broadcasting". This provides that a state intending to establish or authorise the establishment of a direct television broadcasting satellite service must first notify the proposed receiving state or states and then consult with them. A service may only be established after this and on the basis of agreements and/or arrangements in conformity with the relevant instruments of the International Telecommunications Union. However, the value of these principles is significantly reduced in the light of the fact that nearly all the western states voted against the resolution.[68]

ITU regulations call for technical coordination between the sending and receiving states as to frequency and orbital positioning before any direct broadcasting by satellite can be carried out and thus do not affect regulation of the conduct of the broadcast activity as such, although the two elements are clearly connected.[69]

The question of remote sensing has also been under consideration for many years by several bodies, including the UN Committee on the Peaceful Uses of Outer Space. Remote sensing refers to the detection and analysis of the earth's resources by sensors carried in aircraft and spacecraft and covers, for example, meteorological sensing, ocean observation, military surveillance and land observation. It clearly has tremendous potential, but the question of the uses of the information received is highly controversial.[70]

---

[67] See e.g. *Space Activities and Emerging International Law, op. cit.*, p.438. See also A/8771 (1972).

[68] These included France, West Germany, the UK, US and Japan.

[69] See *Space Activities and Emerging International Law, op. cit.*, p.453 *et seq.* See also Chapman and Warren, "Direct Broadcasting Satellites: The ITU, UN and the Real World", 4 *Annals of Air and Space Law*, 1979, p.413.

[70] See e.g. Christol *op. cit.* footnote 49, Chapter 13 and 21(4) *UN Chronicle*, 1984, p.32. See also the Study on Remote Sensing, A/AC.105/339 and Add.1, 1985.

There are indeed a couple of issues to be noted. First is the question as to whether the prior consent of the observed state is required. Since the 1967 Outer Space Treaty provides for freedom of exploration and use, the answer would appear to be negative, although arguments based *inter alia* on permanent sovereignty over natural resources and exclusive sovereignty over airspace have challenged this.[71]

The second issue relates to control over the dissemination of information gathered by satellite. Some have called for the creation of an equitable regime for the sharing of information[72] and there is concern over the question of access to data about states by those, and other states. The USSR and France, for example, jointly proposed the concept of the inalienable right of states to dispose of their natural resources and of information concerning those resources,[73] while the US in particular points to the practical problems this would cause and the possible infringement of freedom of information. The UN Committee on the Peaceful Uses of Outer Space has been considering the problem for many years and general agreement has proved elusive.[74]

The increase in the use of satellites for all of the above purposes has put pressure upon the geostationary orbit. This is the orbit 22,300 miles directly above the equator, where satellites circle at the same speed as the earth rotates. It is the only orbit capable of providing continuous contact with ground stations via a single satellite. The orbit is thus a finite resource.[75] However, in 1976, Brazil, Colombia, the Congo, Ecuador, Indonesia, Kenya, Uganda and Zaire signed the Bogotá Declaration under which they stated that "the segments of geostationary synchronous orbit are part of the territory over which equatorial states exercise their sovereignty".[76]

Other states have vigorously protested against this and it

---

[71] See e.g. A/AC.105/171, Annex IV (1976) and A/AC.105/C.2/SR.220 (1984).

[72] See e.g. Gotlieb, "The Impact of Technology on the Development of Contemporary International Law", 170 *HR*, p.115.

[73] A/AC.105/C.2/L.99 (1974).

[74] See e.g. A/AC.105/320, Annex IV (1983).

[75] See e.g. article 33 of the 1973 International Telecommunications Convention and Christol, *op. cit.* footnote 49, p.451 *et seq.* See also the Study on the Feasibility of Closer Spacing of Satellites in the Geostationary Orbit, A/AC.105/340 (1985).

[76] *Ibid.*, pp.891-95. See also ITU Doc. WARC-155 (1977) 81-E.

therefore cannot be taken as other than an assertion and a bargaining counter.[77] Nevertheless, the increase in satellite launches and the limited nature of the geostationary orbit facility calls for urgent action to produce an acceptable series of principles governing its use.[78]

[77] See e.g. *DUSPIL*, 1979, pp.1187-88.
[78] See as to the question of nuclear power sources on aircraft, Christol, *op. cit.* footnote 49, Chapter 14 and 22(2) *UN Chronicle*, 1985, p.14.

CHAPTER TEN

The Law of the Sea[1]

The seas have historically performed two important functions: first, as a medium of communication, and secondly as a vast reservoir of resources, both living and non-living. Both of these functions have stimulated the development of legal rules.

The seas were at one time thought capable of subjection to national sovereignties. The Portuguese in particular in the seventeenth century proclaimed huge tracts of the high seas as part of their territorial domain, but these claims stimulated a response by Grotius who elaborated the doctrine of the open seas, whereby the oceans as *res communis* were to be accessible to all nations but incapable of appropriation.[2] This view prevailed, partly because it accorded with the interests of the North European states, which demanded freedom of the seas for the purposes of exploration and expanding commercial intercourse with the East.

The freedom of the high seas rapidly became a basic principle of international law, but not all the seas were so characterised. It was permissible for a coastal state to appropriate a maritime belt around its coastline as territorial waters, or territorial sea, and treat it as an indivisible part of its domain. Much of the history of the law of the sea has centred on the extent of the territorial sea or the precise location of the dividing line between it and the high seas and other recognised zones.

The original stipulation linked the width of the territorial sea to the ability of the coastal state to dominate it by military means from the confines of its own shore. But the present century has witnessed continual pressure by states to enlarge the maritime belt and thus subject more of the oceans to their exclusive jurisdiction.

---

[1] See e.g. O'Connell, *The International Law of the Sea*, 2 vols., 1982-4; Churchill and Lowe, *The Law of the Sea*, 2nd ed., 1988; Colombos, *The International Law of the Sea*, 6th ed., 1967; McDougal and Burke, *The Public Order of the Oceans*, 1962; Mangone, *Law for the World Ocean*, 1981; *The Maritime Dimension* (eds. Barston and Birnie), 1980; *New Directions in the Law of the Sea*, vols.1-6, (eds. Churchill, Nordquist and Lay), 1973-7; *ibid.*, 7-11 (eds. Nordquist and Simmons), 1980-1 and Oda, *The Law of the Sea in Our Time*, 2 vols., 1977. See also the series *Limits in the Seas*, published by the Geographer of the US State Department.

[2] *Mare Liberum*, 1609. See also O'Connell, *op. cit.* vol.1, p.9 *et seq.* The closed seas approach was put by e.g. Selden, *Mare Clausum*, 1635.

Beyond the territorial sea, other jurisdictional zones have been in process of development. Coastal states may now exercise particular jurisdictional functions in the contiguous zone, and the trend of international law today is moving rapidly in favour of even larger zones in which the coastal state may enjoy certain rights to the exclusion of other nations, such as fishery zones and more recently exclusive economic zones.

This gradual shift in the law of the sea towards the enlargement of the territorial sea (the accepted limit is now a width of twelve miles in contrast to three miles some thirty years ago), coupled with the continual assertion of jurisdictional rights over portions of what were regarded as high seas, reflects a basic change in emphasis in the attitude of states to the sea.

The predominance of the concept of the freedom of the high seas has been modified by the realisation of resources present in the seas and seabed beyond the territorial seas. Parallel with the developing tendency to assert ever greater claims over the high seas, however, has been the move towards proclaiming a "common heritage of mankind" regime over the seabed of the high seas. The law relating to the seas, therefore, has been in a state of flux for several decades as the conflicting principles have manifested themselves.

A series of conferences have been held, which led to the four 1958 Conventions on the Law of the Sea and then to the 1982 Convention on the Law of the Sea.[3] The 1958 Convention on the High Seas was stated in its Preamble to be "generally declaratory of established principles of international law", while the other three 1958 instruments can be generally accepted as containing both reiterations of existing rules and new rules.

The pressures leading to the Law of the Sea Conference, that lasted between 1974 and 1982 and involved a very wide range of states and international organisations, included a variety of economic, political and strategic factors. Many Third World states wished to develop the exclusive economic zone idea, by which coastal states would have extensive rights over a 200 mile zone beyond the territorial sea, and were keen to establish international control over the deep seabed, so as to prevent the technologically advanced states from being able

---

[3] The 1958 Convention on the Territorial Sea and the Contiguous Zone came into force in 1964; the 1958 Convention on the High Seas came into force in 1962; the 1958 Convention on Fishing and Conservation of Living Resources came into force in 1966 and the 1958 Convention on the Continental Shelf came into force in 1964.

to extract minerals from this vital and vast source freely and without political constraint. Western states were desirous of protecting their navigation routes by opposing any weakening of the freedom of passage through international straits particularly, and wished to protect their economic interests through free exploitation of the resources of the high seas and the deep seabed.

It was soon recognised that this Conference would be a highly political one. Unlike many other such conferences, such as the 1958 and 1960 conferences, for example, this one did not operate on the basis of a pre-existing report or other established document, and the question was dealt with in the United Nations framework via the First (Political and Security) Committee rather than the Sixth (Legal) Committee.[4]

Within the Conference itself, a variety of coalitions or groupings of states attending manifested themselves. The "Group of 77", consisting of well over 100 developing states, and the Western and Communist groups were particular examples. In addition, alliances of states with especial interests were very much in evidence. Examples here would include the landlocked and geographically disadvantaged states, archipelagic states and coastal states. The effect of this kaleidoscopic range of interests was very marked and led on to the "package deal" concept of the final draft. According to this approach, for example, the Third World accepted passage through straits and enhanced continental shelf rights beyond the 200 mile limit from the coasts in return for the internationalisation of deep sea mining.[5]

The 1982 Convention contains 320 articles and 9 Annexes. It was adopted by 130 votes to 4, with 17 abstentions. The Convention is not yet in force, having received, as of February 1991, 45 of the required 60 ratifications.

Many of the provisions in the 1982 Convention repeat principles enshrined in the earlier instruments and others have since become customary rules, but many new rules are proposed. Accordingly, a complicated series of relationships between the various states exists in this field, based on customary rules and treaty rules. Indeed when the 1982 Convention comes into force, a more problematic situation will probably exist. All states will *prima facie* be bound by the accepted

---

[4] See Churchill and Lowe, *op. cit.*, p.14.
[5] See, e.g. Caminos and Molitor, "Progressive Development of International Law and the Package Deal", 79 *AJIL*, 1985, p.871.

customary rules, while only the parties to the five treaties involved will be bound by the new rules contained therein, and since one must envisage some states not adhering to the 1982 Conventions, the 1958 rules will continue to be of importance.[6]

THE TERRITORIAL SEA

Internal Waters [7]

Internal waters are deemed to be such parts of the seas as are not either the high seas or relevant zones or the territorial sea, and are accordingly classed as appertaining to the land territory of the coastal state. Internal waters, whether harbours, lakes, or rivers, are such waters as are to be found on the landward side of the baselines from which the width of the territorial sea and other zones is measured,[8] and are assimilated with the territory of the state. They differ from the territorial sea primarily in that there does not exist any right of innocent passage from which the shipping of other states may benefit. There is an exception to this rule where the straight baselines enclose as internal waters what had been territorial waters.[9]

In general, a coastal state may exercise its jurisdiction over foreign ships within its internal waters to enforce its laws, although the judicial authorities of the flag-state (i.e. the state whose flag the particular ship flies) may also act where crimes have occurred on board ship. This concurrent jurisdiction may be seen in two cases.

In *R* v. *Anderson*,[10] in 1868, the Court of Criminal Appeal in the UK declared that an American national who had committed

---

[6] See the *North Sea Continental Shelf* cases, ICJ Reports, 1969, pp.3, 39; 41 *ILR*, pp.29, 68; the *Fisheries Jurisdiction (UK v. Iceland)* case, ICJ Reports, 1974, p.1; 55 *ILR*, p.238 and the *Anglo-French Continental Shelf* case, Cmnd. 7438, 1978; 54 *ILR*, p.6. See also *supra*, Chapter 3, p.66.

[7] See e.g. O'Connell, *op. cit.* vol.1, Chapter 9 and Churchill and Lowe, *op. cit.*, Chapter 3.

[8] Article 5(1) of the 1958 Convention on the Territorial Sea and article 8(1) of the 1982 Convention. Note the exception in the latter provision with regard to archipelagic states, *infra*, p.346.

[9] Article 5(2) of the 1958 Convention on the Territorial Sea and article 8(2) of the 1982 Convention. See *infra*, p.344.

[10] 1 Cox's Criminal Cases 198.

manslaughter on board a British vessel in French internal waters was subject to the jurisdiction of the British courts, even though he was also within the sovereignty of French justice (and American justice by reason of his nationality), and thus could be correctly convicted under English law. The US Supreme Court held in *Wildenhus'* case[11] that the American courts had jurisdiction to try a crew member of a Belgian vessel for the murder of another Belgian national, when the ship was docked in the port of Jersey City in New York.[12]

A merchant ship in a foreign port or in foreign internal waters is automatically subject to the local jurisdiction (unless there is an express agreement to the contrary), although where purely disciplinarian issues related to the ship's crew are involved, which do not concern the maintenance of peace within the territory of the coastal state, then such matters would by courtesy be left to the authorities of the flag-ship to regulate. Although some writers have pointed to theoretical differences between the Common Law and French approaches, in practice the same fundamental proposition applies.[13]

However, a completely different situation operates where the foreign vessel involved is a warship. In such cases, the authorisation of the captain or of the flag-state is necessary before the coastal state may exercise its jurisdiction over the ship and its crew. This is due to the status of the warship as a direct arm of the sovereign of the flag-state.[14]

Baselines

The width of the territorial sea is defined from the low-water mark around the coasts of the state. This is the traditional principle under customary international law and was reiterated in

[11] 120 US 1 (1887). See also *Armament Dieppe SA* v. *US*, 399 F.2d 794 (1968).

[12] See the Madrid incident, where US officials asserted the right to interview a potential defector from a Soviet ship in New Orleans, 80 *AJIL*, 1986, p.622.

[13] See e.g. Churchill and Lowe, *op. cit.*, pp.54-57. See also Lenoir, "Criminal Jurisdiction over Foreign Merchant Ships", 10 *Tulane Law Review*, 1935, p.13. See with regard to the right of access to ports and other internal waters, Lowe, "The Right of Entry into Maritime Ports in International Law", 14 *San Diego Law Review*, 1977, p.597, and O'Connell, *op. cit.* vol.2, Chapter 22. See also the Dangerous Vessels Act 1985.

[14] See *The Schooner Exchange* v. *McFaddon*, 7 Cranch 116 (1812). See also 930 HC Deb., col.450, Written Answers, 29 April 1977.

article 3 of the Geneva Convention on the Territorial Sea and the Contiguous Zone in 1958 and article 5 of the 1982 Convention, and the low-water line along the coast is defined "as marked on large-scale charts officially recognised by the coastal state".[15]

In the majority of cases, it will not be very difficult to locate the low-water line which is to act as the baseline for measuring the width of the territorial sea. Sometimes, however, the geography of the state's coasts will be such as to cause certain problems, for instance, where the coastline is deeply indented or there are numerous islands running parallel to the coasts, or where there exist bays cutting into the coastlines. Special rules have evolved to deal with this issue, which is of importance to coastal states, particularly where foreign vessels regularly fish close to the limits of the territorial sea. A more rational method of drawing baselines might have the effect of enclosing larger areas of the sea within the state's internal waters, and thus extend the boundaries of the territorial sea further than the traditional method might envisage.

This point was raised in the *Anglo-Norwegian Fisheries* case,[16] before the International Court of Justice. The case concerned a Norwegian decree delimiting its territorial sea along some 1000 miles of its coastline. However, instead of measuring the territorial sea from the low-water line, the Norwegians constructed a series of straight baselines linking the outermost parts of the land running along the skjaergaard (or fringe of islands and rocks) which parallels the Norwegian coastline. This had the effect of enclosing within its territorial limits parts of what would normally have been the high seas if the traditional method had been utilised. As a result certain disputes involving British fishing boats arose, and the United Kingdom challenged the legality of the Norwegian method of baselines under international law. The Court held that it was the outer line of the skjaergaard that was relevant in establishing the baselines, and not the low-water line of the mainland. This was dictated by geographic realities. The Court noted that the normal method of drawing baselines that are parallel to the coast (the *tracé parallèle*) was not applicable in this case because it would necessitate complex geometrical constructions in view of the extreme

---

[15] See e.g. Churchill and Lowe, *op. cit.*, Chapter 2 and O'Connell, *op. cit.* vol.1, Chapter 5.
[16] ICJ Reports, 1951, p.116; 18 *ILR*, p.86.

indentation of the coastline and the existence of the series of islands fringing the coasts.[17]

Since the usual methods did not apply, and taking into account the principle that the territorial sea must follow the general direction of the coasts, the concept of straight baselines drawn from the outer rocks could be considered.[18] The Court also made the point that the Norwegian system had been applied consistently over many years and had met no objections from other states, and that the UK had not protested until many years after it had first been introduced.[19] In other words, the method of straight baselines operated by Norway:

> had been consolidated by a constant and sufficiently long practice, in the face of which the attitude of governments bears witness to the fact that they did not consider it to be contrary to international law.[20]

Thus, although noting that Norwegian rights had been established through actual practice coupled with acquiescence, the Court regarded the straight baseline system itself as a valid principle of international law in view of the special geographic conditions of the area. The Court provided criteria for determining the acceptability of any such delimitations. The drawing of the baselines had not to depart from the general direction of the coast, in view of the close dependence of the territorial sea upon the land domain; the baselines had to be drawn so that the sea area lying within them had to be sufficiently closely linked to the land domain to be subject to the regime of internal waters and it was permissible to consider in the process "certain economic interests peculiar to a region, the reality and importance of which are evidenced by long usage".[21]

These principles emerging from the *Fisheries* case were accepted by states as part of international law within a comparatively short period.

Article 4 of the Geneva Convention on the Territorial Sea 1958 declared that the straight baseline system could be used in cases of indented coastlines or where there existed a skjaergaard, provided

---

[17] *Ibid.*, p.128; 18 *ILR*, p.91. Note also the Court's mention of the *courbe tangente* method of drawing arcs of circles from points along the low-water line, *ibid.*

[18] *Ibid.*, p.129; 18 *ILR*, p.92. Other states had already used such a system, see e.g. Waldock, "The Anglo-Norwegian Fisheries Case", 28 *BYIL*, 1951, pp.114, 148. See also Brownlie, *Principles of Public International Law*, 4th ed., 1990, p.183.

[19] ICJ Reports, 1951, p.138; 18 *ILR*, p.101. Cf. Judge McNair, *ibid.*, pp.171-80; 18 *ILR*, p.123.

[20] *Ibid.*, p.139; 18 *ILR*, p.102.

[21] *Ibid.*, p.133; 18 *ILR*, p.95.

that the general direction of the coast was followed and that there were sufficiently close links between the sea areas within the lines and the land domain to be subject to the regime of internal waters. In addition, particular regional economic interests of long-standing may be considered where necessary.[22]

A number of states now use the system including, it should be mentioned, the United Kingdom as regards areas on the west coast of Scotland.[23]

Where the result of the straight baseline method is to enclose as internal waters areas previously regarded as part of the territorial sea or high seas, a right of innocent passage shall be deemed to exist in such waters by virtue of article 5(2) of the 1958 Convention.[24]

Bays

Problems also arise as to the approach to be adopted with regard to bays,[25] in particular whether the waters of wide-mouthed bays ought to be treated as other areas of the sea adjacent to the coast, so that the baseline of the territorial sea would be measured from the low-water mark of the coast of the bay, or whether the device of the straight baseline could be used to "close off" the mouth of the bay of any width and the territorial limit measured from that line.

It was long accepted that a straight closing line could be used across the mouth of bays, but there was considerable disagreement as to the permitted width of the bay beyond which this would not operate.[26] The point was settled in article 7 of the 1958 Convention on the Territorial Sea. This declared that:

> if the distance between the low water-marks of the natural entrance points of a bay does not exceed twenty-four miles, a closing line may be drawn between these two low-water marks, and the waters enclosed thereby shall be considered as internal waters,

[22] See also article 7 of the 1982 Convention.
[23] Territorial Waters Order in Council, 1964, article 3, s.1, 1965, Part III, s.2, p.6452A. See also the Territorial Sea (Limits) Order 1989 regarding the Straits of Dover. See generally as regards state practice, Churchill and Lowe, *op. cit.*, pp.31-33 and Whiteman, *Digest of International Law*, vol.4, pp.21-35.
[24] See also article 8(2) of the 1982 Convention.
[25] See e.g. Churchill and Lowe, *op. cit.*, pp.33-38 and O'Connell, *op. cit.* vol.1, p.209.
[26] See e.g. the *North Atlantic Coast Fisheries* case, 11 *RIAA*, p.167 (1910) and the *Anglo-Norwegian Fisheries* case, ICJ Reports, 1951, p.116; 18 *ILR*, p.86, to the effect that no general rules of international law had been uniformly accepted.

otherwise a straight baseline of twenty-four miles may be drawn.[27] This provision, however, does not apply to historic bays. These are bays the waters of which are treated by the coastal state as internal in view of historic rights supported by general acquiescence rather than any specific principle of international law. A number of states have claimed historic bays, for example, Canada with respect to Hudson Bay (although the US has opposed this)[28] and certain American states as regards the Gulf of Fonseca.[29]

The United States Supreme Court has taken the view that where waters are outside the statutory limits for inland waters, the exercise of sovereignty required to establish title to a historic bay amounted to the exclusion of all foreign vessels and navigation from the area claimed. The continuous authority exercised in this fashion had to be coupled with the acquiescence of states. This was the approach in the *US* v. *State of Alaska* case[30] concerning the waters of Cook Inlet. The Supreme Court held that Alaska had not satisfied the terms and that the Inlet had not been regarded as a historic bay under Soviet, American or Alaskan sovereignty. Accordingly, it was the Federal State and not Alaska which was entitled to the subsurface of Cook Inlet.

In response to the Libyan claim to the Gulf of Sirte (Sidra) as an historic bay and consequent drawing of a closing line of nearly 300 miles in length in 1973, several states immediately protested, including the US and the states of the European Community.[31] The US in a note to Libya in 1974 referred to "the international law standards of past open, notorious and effective exercise of authority, and the acquiescence of foreign nations"[32] and has on several occasions sent naval and air forces into the Gulf in order to maintain its opposition to the Libyan claim and to assert that the waters of the Gulf constitute high seas.[33] Little evidence appears, in fact, to support the Libyan contention.

[27] See also article 10 of the 1982 Convention.
[28] See Whiteman, *Digest, op. cit.,* pp.250-57.
[29] See *El Salvador* v. *Nicaragua,* 11 *AJIL,* 1917, p.674.
[30] 422 US 184 (1975). See also Bouchez, *The Regime of Bays in International Law,* 1963 and the *Tunisia-Libya Continental Shelf* case, ICJ Reports, 1982, pp.18, 74; 67 *ILR,* pp.4, 67.
[31] See Churchill and Lowe, *op. cit.,* pp.37-38 and UKMIL, 57 *BYIL,* 1986, pp.579-80. See also Francioni, "The Gulf of Sidra Incident *(United States* v. *Libya)* and International Law", 5 *Italian Yearbook of International Law,* 1980-81, p.85.
[32] See 68 *AJIL,* 1974, p.510.
[33] See e.g. UKMIL, 57 *BYIL,* 1986, pp.581-82.

Islands [34]

As far as islands are concerned, the general provisions noted above regarding the measurement of the territorial sea apply. Islands are defined in the 1958 Convention on the Territorial Sea as consisting of "a naturally-formed area of land, surrounded by water, which is above water at high tide", and they can have a maritime belt.[35] Although islands may serve as the base for the measurement of the territorial sea, contiguous zone, exclusive economic zone and continental shelf, article 121(3) of the 1982 Convention notes that "rocks which cannot sustain human habitation or economic life of their own shall have no exclusive economic zone or continental shelf".[36]

Where only low-tide elevations are involved, that is areas of land visible at low-tide but submerged at high tide, they cannot have a territorial sea of their own. But they may be used as baselines if within the territorial sea of a coastal state and they may be utilised as a point on a straight baseline if installations permanently above sea level (for example, a lighthouse) have been constructed upon them.

Archipelagic States [37]

Problems have arisen as a result of efforts by states comprising a number of islands to draw straight baselines around the outer limits of their islands, thus "boxing in" the whole territory. Indonesia in particular has resorted to this method, against the protests of a number of states since it tends to reduce

---

[34] See e.g. Bowett, *The Legal Regime of Islands in International Law,* 1979, and Symmons, *The Maritime Zone of Islands in International Law,* 1979.

[35] Article 10(1). See also article 121(1) of the 1982 Convention.

[36] See the *Jan Mayen* report, 20 *ILM,* 1981, pp.797, 803; 62 *ILR,* pp.108, 114. Note as regards Rockall and the conflicting UK, Irish, Danish and Icelandic views, Symmons, *op. cit.,* pp.117-18, 126 and Brown, "Rockall and the Limits of National Jurisdiction of the United Kingdom", 2 *Marine Policy,* 1978, pp.181-211 and 275-303. See also 878, HC Deb., col.82, Written Answers and *The Times,* 8 May 1985, p.6 (Danish claims) and *The Guardian,* 1 May 1985, p.30 (Icelandic claims).

[37] See e.g. Churchill and Lowe, *op. cit.,* Chapter 6; O'Connell, *op. cit.* vol.1, Chapter 6; Bowett, *op. cit.,* Chapter 4; Amerasinghe, "The Problem of Archipelagos in the International Law of the Sea", 23 *ICLQ,* 1974, p.539 and O'Connell, "Mid-Ocean Archipelagos in International Law", 45 *BYIL,* 1971, p.1.

previously considered areas of the high seas extensively used as shipping lanes to the sovereignty of the archipelago state concerned.[38]

There has been a great deal of controversy as to which international law principles apply in the case of archipelagos and the subject was not expressly dealt with in the 1958 Geneva Convention.[39] Article 47 of the 1982 Convention, however, provides that an archipelagic state[40] may draw straight archipelagic baselines joining the outermost points of the outermost islands and drying reefs of the archipelago, which would then serve as the relevant baselines for other purposes. There are a number of conditions before this may be done, however, and article 47 provides as follows:

1. An archipelagic state may draw straight archipelagic baselines joining the outermost points of the outermost islands and drying reefs of the archipelago provided that within such baselines are included the main islands and an areas in which the ratio of the area of the water to the area of the land, including atolls, is between 1 to 1 and 9 to 1.

2. The length of such baselines shall not exceed 100 nautical miles, except that up to 3 per cent of the total number of baselines enclosing any archipelago may exceed that length, up to a maximum length of 125 nautical miles.

3. The drawing of such baselines shall not depart to any appreciable extent from the general configuration of the archipelago.

4. Such baselines shall not be drawn from low-tide elevations, unless lighthouses or similar installations which are permanently above sea level have been built on them or where a low-tide elevation is situated wholly or partly at a distance not exceeding the breadth of the territorial sea from the nearest island.

5. The system of such baselines shall not be applied by an archipelagic state in such a manner as to cut off from the high seas or the exclusive economic zone the territorial sea of another state.

6. If a part of the archipelagic waters of an archipelagic state lies between two parts of an immediately adjacent neighbouring state, existing rights and all other legitimate interests which the latter state has traditionally exercised in such waters and all rights stipulated by agreement between those states shall continue and be respected.

---

[38] *Ibid.*, pp.23-24, 45-47 and 51 and Whiteman, *Digest, op. cit.* vol.4, p.284.

[39] But see as regards "coastal archipelagos", article 4 of the 1958 Convention on the Territorial Sea.

[40] See article 46.

7. For the purpose of computing the ratio of water to land under paragraph 1, land areas may include waters lying within the fringing reefs of islands and atolls, including that part of a steep-sided oceanic plateau which is enclosed or nearly enclosed by a chain of limestone islands and drying reefs lying on the perimeter of the plateau.

8. The baselines drawn in accordance with this article shall be shown on charts of a scale or scales adequate for ascertaining their position. Alternatively, lists of geographic co-ordinates of points, specifying the geodetic datum, may be substituted.

9. The archipelagic states shall give due publicity to such charts or lists of geographical co-ordinates and shall deposit a copy of each such chart or list with the Secretary-General of the United Nations.

All the waters within such baselines are archipelagic waters[41] over which the state has sovereignty,[42] but existing agreements, traditional fishing rights and existing submarine cables must be reported.[43] In addition ships of all states shall enjoy the rights of innocent passage through archipelagic waters[44] and all the ships and aircraft are to enjoy a right of archipelagic sea lanes passage through such lanes and air routes designated by the archipelagic state for "continuous and expeditious passage".[45]

In response to a reported closure in 1988 of the Straits of Sunda and Lombok by Indonesia, the US stressed that the archipelagic provisions of the 1982 Convention reflected customary international law and that those straits were subject to the regime of archipelagic sea lanes passage. Accordingly, it was pointed out that any interference with such passage would violate international law.[46]

The Width of the Territorial Sea [47]

There has always been considerable disagreement as to how far the territorial sea may extend from the baselines. Originally, the

[41] But see article 50.
[42] Article 49.
[43] Article 51.
[44] Article 52.
[45] Article 53. For recent state practice, see Churchill and Lowe, *op. cit.*, pp.106-8.
[46] 83 *AJIL*, 1989, pp.559-61.
[47] See e.g. Churchill and Lowe, *op. cit.*, pp.65-68 and O'Connell, *op. cit.* footnote 1, vol.1, Chapter 4.

"cannon-shot" rule defined the width required in terms of the range of shore-based artillery, but at the turn of the nineteenth century, this was transmuted into the three-mile rule. This was especially supported by the United States and the United Kingdom, and any detraction had to be justified by virtue of historic rights and general acquiescence as, for example, the Scandinavian claim to four miles.[48]

However, the issue was much confused by the claims of many coastal states to exercise certain jurisdictional rights for particular purposes, for example, fisheries, customs and immigration controls. It was not until after the First World War that a clear distinction was made between claims to enlarge the width of the territorial sea and claims over particular zones.

Recently the three-mile rule has been discarded as a rule of general application to be superseded by contending assertions. The 1958 Geneva Convention on the Territorial Sea did not include an article on the subject because of disagreements among the states, while the 1960 Geneva Conference failed to accept a United States-Canadian proposal for a six-mile territorial sea coupled with an exclusive fisheries zone for a further six miles by only one vote.[49]

Article 3 of the 1982 Convention, however, notes that all states have the right to establish the breadth of the territorial sea up to a limit not exceeding twelve nautical miles from the baselines. This clearly accords with the evolving practice of states.[50] The UK adopted a twelve mile limit in the Territorial Sea Act 1987, for instance, as did the US by virtue of Proclamation No. 5928 in December 1988. There is little doubt that this now reflects customary international law.[51]

---

[48] See e.g. Kent, "Historical Origins of the Three-mile Limit", 48 *AJIL*, 1954, p.537 and *The Anna*, (1805) 165 ER 809. See also *US* v. *Kessler*, 1 Baldwin's C C Rep. 15 (1829).

[49] See O'Connell, *op. cit.* footnote 1, vol.1, pp.163-64.

[50] Churchill and Lowe give the following figures as at 1 June 1987: 3 miles — 13 states; 4 miles — 2 states; 6 miles — 4 states; 12 miles — 97 states; 15 to 200 miles claimed by 20 states; *op. cit.*, p.353. Brownlie gives the following figures: 3 miles — 9 states; 4 miles — 2 states; 6 miles — 4 states; 12 miles — 107 states; 15 — 200 miles claimed by 15 states, *op. cit.*, pp.189-90, note 53. See also the notice issued by the Hydrographic Department of the Navy in 1987, UKMIL, 59 *BYIL*, 1988, pp.519-22; this shows *inter alia* 107 states claiming a 12 mile territorial sea.

[51] Note that as of spring 1991, the 1982 Convention is not yet in force.

The Juridical Nature of the Territorial Sea [52]

There have been a number of theories as to the precise legal character of the territorial sea of the coastal state, ranging from treating the territorial sea as part of the *res communis,* but subject to certain rights exercisable by the coastal state, to regarding the territorial sea as part of the coastal state's territorial domain subject to a right of innocent passage by foreign vessels.[53] Nevertheless, it cannot be disputed that the coastal state enjoys sovereign rights over its maritime belt and extensive jurisdictional control, having regard to the relevant rules of international law. The fundamental restriction upon the sovereignty of the coastal state is the right of other nations to innocent passage through the territorial sea, and this distinguishes the territorial sea from the internal waters of the state, which are fully within the unrestricted jurisdiction of the coastal nation.

Articles 1 and 2 of the Convention on the Territorial Sea 1958[54] provide that the coastal state's sovereignty extends over its territorial sea and to the airspace and seabed and subsoil thereof, subject to the provisions of the Convention and of international law. The territorial sea forms an undeniable part of the land territory to which it is bound, so that a cession of land will automatically include any band of territorial waters.[55]

The coastal state may, if it so desires, exclude foreign nationals and vessels from fishing within its territorial sea and (subject to agreements to the contrary) from coastal trading (known as cabotage), and reserve these activities for its own citizens.

Similarly the coastal state has extensive powers of control relating to, amongst others, security and custom matters. It should be noted, however, that how far a state chooses to exercise the jurisdiction and sovereignty to which it may lay claim under the principles of international law will depend upon the terms of its own municipal legislation, and some states will not wish to take advantage of the full extent of the powers permitted them within the international legal system.

[52] See O'Connell, *op. cit.* footnote 1, vol.1, Chapter 3. See also Brownlie, *op. cit.,* p.194 and Churchill and Lowe, *op. cit.,* Chapter 4.

[53] O'Connell, pp.60-67.

[54] See also article 2 of the 1982 Convention.

[55] See the *Grisbadarna* case, 11 *RIAA,* p.147 (1909) and the *Beagle Channel* case, HMSO, 1977; 52 *ILR,* p.93. See also Judge McNair, *Anglo-Norwegian Fisheries* case, ICJ Reports, 1951, pp.116, 160; 18 *ILR,* pp.86, 113.

The Right of Innocent Passage

The right of foreign merchant ships (as distinct from warships) to pass unhindered through the territorial sea of a coastal state has long been an accepted principle in customary international law, the sovereignty of the coastal state notwithstanding. However, the precise extent of the doctrine is blurred and open to contrary interpretation, particularly with respect to the requirement that the passage must be "innocent".[56]

The doctrine was elaborated in article 14 of the Convention on the Territorial Sea 1958, which emphasised that the coastal state must not hamper innocent passage and must publicise any dangers to navigation in the territorial sea of which it is aware. Passage is defined as navigation through the territorial sea for the purpose of crossing that sea without entering internal waters or of proceeding to or from that sea without entering internal waters or of proceeding to or from internal waters. It may include temporary stoppages, but only if they are incidental to ordinary navigation or necessitated by distress or *force majeure*.[57]

The coastal state may not impose charges for such passage unless they are in payment for specific services, and ships engaged in passage are required to comply with the coastal state's regulations covering for example navigation in so far as they are consistent with international law.

Passage ceases to be innocent under article 14(4) of the 1958 Convention where it is "prejudicial to the peace, good order or security of the coastal state" and in the case of foreign fishing vessels when they do not observe such laws and regulations as the coastal state may make and publish to prevent these ships from fishing in the territorial sea. In addition, submarines must navigate on the surface and show their flag.

Where passage is not innocent, the coastal state may take steps to prevent it in its territorial sea and where ships are proceeding to internal waters, it may act to forestall any breach of the conditions to which admission of such ships to internal water is subject. Coastal states have the power temporarily to suspend innocent passage of

[56] See Churchill and Lowe, *op. cit.*, pp.68-77 and O'Connell, *op. cit.* footnote 1, Chapter 7.
[57] See articles 17 and 18 of the 1982 Convention.

foreign vessels where it is essential for security reasons, provided such suspension has been published and provided it does not cover international straits.

Article 19(2) of the 1982 Convention has developed the notion of innocent passage contained in article 14(4) of the 1958 Convention by the provision of examples of prejudicial passage such as the threat or use of force; weapons practice; spying; propaganda; breach of customs, fiscal, immigration or sanitary regulations; wilful and serious pollution; fishing; research or survey activities and interference with coastal communications or other facilities. In addition a wide-ranging clause also includes "any activity not having a direct bearing on passage". This would appear to have altered the burden of proof from the coastal state to the other party with regard to innocent passage as well as being somewhat difficult to define. By virtue of article 24 of the 1982 Convention, coastal states must not hamper the innocent passage of foreign ships, either by imposing requirements upon them which would have the practical effect of denying or impairing the right or by discrimination.

One major controversy of considerable importance revolves around the issue of whether the passage of warships in peace-time is or is not innocent.[58] The question was further complicated by the omission of an article on the problem in the 1958 Convention on the Territorial Sea, and the discussion of innocent passage in a series of articles headed "Rules applicable to all ships". This has led some writers to assert that this includes warships by inference, but other authorities maintain that such an important issue could not be resolved purely by omission and inference, especially in view of the reservations by many states to the Convention rejecting the principle of innocent passage for warships and in the light of comments in the various preparatory materials to the 1958 Geneva Convention.[59]

It is primarily the western states, with their preponderant naval power, that have historically maintained the existence of a right of innocent passage for warships, to the opposition of the communist and Third World nations. However, having regard to the rapid growth in their naval capacity in recent years and the ending of the

[58] See e.g. O'Connell, *op. cit.* footnote 1, pp.274-97.
[59] *Ibid.*, pp.290-92. See also Brownlie, *op. cit.*, pp.197-98.

Cold War, Soviet attitudes have undergone somewhat of a modification.[60]

In September 1989, the US and the USSR issued a joint "Uniform Interpretation of the Rules of International Law Governing Innocent Passage".[61] This reaffirms that the relevant rules of international law are stated in the 1982 Convention. It then provides that:

> [a]ll ships, including warships, regardless of cargo, armament or means of propulsion, enjoy the right of innocent passage through the territorial sea in accordance with international law, for which neither prior notification nor authorisation is required.

The statement notes that where a ship in passage through the territorial sea is not engaged in any of the activities laid down in article 19(2), it "is in innocent passage" since that provision is exhaustive. Ships in passage are under an obligation to comply with the laws and regulations of the coastal state adopted in conformity with articles 21, 22, 23 and 25 of the 1982 Convention, provided such laws and regulations do not have the effect of denying or impairing the exercise of the right of innocent passage.

This important statement lends considerable weight to the view that warships have indeed a right of innocent passage through the territorial sea and one that does not necessitate prior notification or authorisation.

Jurisdiction over Foreign Ships [62]

Where foreign ships are in passage through the territorial sea, the coastal state may only exercise its criminal jurisdiction as regards the arrest of any person or the investigation of any matter connected with a crime committed on board ship in defined situations. These

[60] See also Churchill and Lowe, *op. cit.*, pp.54-56. The issue was left open at the Third UN Conference on the Law of the Sea and does not therefore appear in the 1982 Convention. Note, however, that western and communist states both proposed including a reference to warships in early sessions of the Conference, see UNCLOS III, Official Records, vol.III, pp.183, 203, 192 and 196. See also article 29(2) of the 1975 Informal Single Negotiating Text. The right of warships to innocent passage was maintained by the US following an incident during which four US warships sailed through Soviet territorial waters off the Crimean coast, see *The Times*, 19 March, 1986, p.5.

[61] See 84 *AJIL*, 1990, p.239.

[62] See e.g. O'Connell, *op. cit.* footnote 1, Chapter 23 and 24. Note that these rules are applicable to foreign ships and government commercial ships.

are enumerated in article 19(1) of the 1958 Convention on the Territorial Sea as follows:

(a) If the consequences of the crime extend to the coastal state; or (b) If the crime is of a kind likely to disturb the peace of the country or the good order of the territorial sea; or (c) If the assistance of the local authorities has been requested by the captain of the ship or by the consul of the country whose flag the ship flies; or (d) If it is necessary for the suppression of illicit traffic in narcotic drugs.[63]

However, if the ship is passing through the territorial sea having left the internal waters of the coastal state, then the coastal state may act in any manner prescribed by its laws as regards arrests or investigations on board ship and is not restricted by the terms of article 19(1). But the authorities of the coastal state cannot act where the crime was committed before the ship entered the territorial sea, providing the ship is not entering or has not entered internal waters.[64]

The coastal state may not exercise its civil jurisdiction over a foreign ship passing through its territorial sea under article 20 of the 1958 Convention as regards any person on board ship, nor levy execution against or arrest the ship, unless obligations are involved which were assumed by the ship itself in the course of or for the purpose of its voyage through waters of the coastal state, or unless the ship is passing through the territorial sea on its way from internal waters. The above rules do not, however, prejudice the right of a state to levy execution against or to arrest, for the purpose of any civil proceedings, a foreign ship lying in the territorial sea or passing through the territorial sea after leaving internal waters.[65]

Warships and other government ships operated for non-commercial purposes are immune from the jurisdiction of the coastal state, although they may be required to leave the territorial sea immediately for breach of rules governing passage and the flag-state will bear international responsibility in cases of loss or damage suffered as a result.[66]

---

[63] Article 27(1) of the 1982 Convention has added to this provision "or psychotropic substances".

[64] These provisions are reaffirmed in article 27 of the 1982 Convention.

[65] See also article 28 of the 1982 Convention.

[66] Articles 29-32 of the 1982 Convention. See also articles 21-23 of the 1958 Convention.

INTERNATIONAL STRAITS [67]

Article 16(4) of the 1958 Convention on the Territorial Sea declares that:

> there shall be no suspension of the innocent passage of foreign ships through straits which are used for international navigation between one part of the high sea and another part of the high seas or the territorial sea of a foreign state.

This provision should be read in conjunction with the decision in the *Corfu Channel* case.[68] In this case, British warships passing through the straits were fired upon by Albanian guns. A number of months later, an augmented force of cruisers and destroyers sailed through the North Corfu Channel and two of them were badly damaged after striking mines. This impelled the British authorities to sweep the Channel three weeks later, and clear it of some twenty mines of German manufacture. The Court in a much-quoted passage emphasised that:

> states in time of peace have a right to send their warships through straits used for international navigation between two parts of the high seas without the previous authorisation of a coastal state, provided that the passage is innocent.[69]

It was also noted that the minesweeping operation was in no way "innocent" and was indeed a violation of Albania's sovereignty, although the earlier passages by British naval vessels were legal.[70]

The 1982 Convention established a new regime for straits used for international navigation. The principle is reaffirmed that the

---

[67] See e.g. Churchill and Lowe, *op. cit.*, Chapter 5; O'Connell, *op. cit.* footnote 1, vol.1, Chapter 8; Lapidoth, *Les Détroits en Droit International*, 1972; Koh, *Straits in International Navigation*, 1982; Moore, "The Regime of Straits and the Third United Nations Conference on the Law of the Sea", 74 *AJIL*, 1980, p.77 and Reisman, "The Regime of Straits and National Security", *ibid.*, p.48.

[68] ICJ Reports, 1949, p.4; 16 *ILR*, p.155.

[69] *Ibid.*, p.28; 16 *ILR*, p.161. The Court emphasised that the decisive criterion regarding the definition of "strait" was the geographical situation of the strait as connecting two parts of the high seas, coupled with the fact that it was actually used for international navigation, *ibid.*

[70] *Ibid.*, pp.30-31, 33; 16 *ILR*, pp.163, 166.

legal status of the waters of the straits in question is unaffected by the provisions dealing with passage.[71]

A new right of transit passage is posited with respect to straits used for international navigation between one part of the high seas or an exclusive economic zone and another part of the high seas or an exclusive economic zone.[72] It involves the exercise of the freedom of navigation and overflight solely for the purpose of continuous and expeditious transit of the strait and does not preclude passage through the strait to enter or leave a state bordering that strait.[73] States bordering the straits in question are not to hamper or suspend transit passage.[74]

These are two exceptions to the right, under article 36 where a route exists through the strait through the high seas or economic zone of similar navigational convenience and under article 38(1) in the case of a strait formed by an island of a state bordering the strait and its mainland, where there exists seaward of the island a route through the high seas or economic zone of similar navigational convenience.

Ships and aircraft in transit must observe the relevant international regulations and refrain from all activities other than those incidental to their normal modes of continuous and expeditious transit, unless rendered necessary by *force majeure* or by distress.[75]

Under article 45, the regime of innocent passage will apply with regard to straits used for international navigation excluded from the transit passage provisions by article 38(1) and to international straits between a part of the high seas or economic zone and the territorial sea of a foreign state. Such innocent passage is not to be suspended.

It is unclear whether the right of transit passage has passed into customary law. Practice is as yet ambiguous.[76] Some states have provided explicitly for rights of passage through international straits. When the UK extended its territorial sea in 1987 to twelve

---

[71] Articles 34 and 35.

[72] Article 37.

[73] Article 38.

[74] Article 44.

[75] Article 39. Under articles 41 and 42, the coastal state may designate sea lanes and traffic separation schemes.

[76] See Churchill and Lowe, *op. cit.*, p.94, but cf. Schachter, "International Law in Theory and Practice", 178 *HR*, 1982, pp.9, 281.

miles, one of the consequences was that the high seas corridor through the Straits of Dover disappeared. The following year an agreement was signed with France which related to the delimitation of the territorial sea in the Straits of Dover and a joint declaration was issued in which both governments recognised:

> rights of unimpeded transit passage for merchant vessels, state vessels and, in particular, warships following their normal mode of navigation, as well as the right of overflight for aircraft, in the Straits of Dover. It is understood that, in accordance with the principles governing this regime under the rules of international law, such passage will be exercised in a continuous and expeditious manner.[77]

A number of straits are subject to special regimes, which are unaffected by the above provisions.[78] One important example is the Montreux Convention of 1936 governing the Bosphorus and Dardanelles Straits. This provides for complete freedom of transit or navigation for merchant vessels during peacetime and for freedom of transit during daylight hours for some warships, giving prior notification to Turkey.[79]

THE CONTIGUOUS ZONE [80]

Historically some states have claimed to exercise certain rights over particular zones of the high seas. This has involved some diminution of the principle of the freedom of the high seas as the jurisdiction of the coastal state has been extended into areas of the high seas contiguous to the territorial sea, albeit for defined purposes only. Such restricted jurisdiction zones have been established or asserted for a number of reasons, for instance, to prevent infringement of customs, immigration or sanitary laws of the coastal state, or to conserve fishing stocks in a particular area, or to enable the coastal state to have exclusive or principal rights to the resources of the proclaimed zone.

---

[77] Cmnd. 557. See also 38 *ICLQ*, 1989, pp.416-17.
[78] Article 35(c).
[79] See e.g. Churchill and Lowe, *op. cit.*, pp.94-96. See also UKMIL, 57 *BYIL*, 1986, p.581.
[80] See Lowe, "The Development of the Concept of the Contiguous Zone", 52 *BYIL*, 1981, p.109; Churchill and Lowe, *op. cit.*, Chapter 7 and O'Connell, *op. cit.* footnote 1, vol.2, Chapter 27.

In each case they enable the coastal state to protect what it regards as its vital or important interests without having to extend the boundaries of its territorial sea further into the high seas. It is thus a compromise between the interests of the coastal state and the interests of other maritime nations seeking to maintain the status of the high seas, and it marks a balance of competing claims.

The extension of rights beyond the territorial sea has, however, been seen not only in the context of preventing the infringement of particular domestic laws, but also increasingly as a method of maintaining and developing the economic interests of the coastal state regarding maritime resources.

The idea of the contiguous zone (i.e. zone bordering upon the territorial sea) was virtually formulated as an authoritative and consistent doctrine in the 1930s by the French writer Gidel,[81] and it appeared in the Convention on the Territorial Sea. Article 24 declared that:

> In a zone of the high seas contiguous to its territorial sea, the coastal state may exercise the control necessary to:
>   (a) Prevent infringement of its customs, fiscal, immigration or sanitary regulations within its territory or territorial sea;
>   (b) Punish infringement of the above regulations committed within its territory or territorial sea.

Thus, such contiguous zones were clearly differentiated from claims to full sovereignty as parts of the territorial sea, by being referred to as part of the high seas over which the coastal state may exercise particular rights. Unlike the territorial sea, which is automatically attached to the land territory of the state, contiguous zones have to be specifically claimed.

While sanitary and immigration laws are relatively recent additions to the rights enforceable over zones of the high seas and may be regarded as stemming by analogy from customs regulations, in practice they are really only justifiable since the 1958 Convention. On the other hand customs zones have a long history and are recognised in customary international law as well. Many states, including the UK and the USA, have enacted legislation to enforce

---

[81] "La Mer Territoriale et la Zone Contigue", 48 *HR,* p.241.

customs regulations over many years, outside their territorial waters and within certain areas, in order to suppress smuggling which appeared to thrive when faced only with territorial limits of three or four miles.[82]

Contiguous zones, however, were limited to a maximum of twelve miles from the baselines from which the territorial sea is measured. So if the coastal state already claimed a territorial sea of twelve miles, the question of contiguous zones would not arise.

This limitation, plus the restriction of jurisdiction to customs, sanitary and immigration matters, is the reason for the decline in relevance of the contiguous zones in international affairs in recent years. Under article 33 of the 1982 Convention, however, a coastal state may claim a contiguous zone (for the same purpose as the 1958 provisions) up to twenty-four nautical miles from the baselines. In view of the accepted twelve miles territorial sea limit, such an extension was required in order to preserve the concept. One crucial difference is that while under the 1958 system the contiguous zone was part of the high seas, under the 1982 Convention it would form part of the exclusive economic zone complex.[83] This will clearly have an impact upon the nature of the zone.

THE EXCLUSIVE ECONOMIC ZONE [84]

This zone has developed out of earlier, more tentative claims, particularly relating to fishing zones,[85] and as a result of developments in the negotiating processes leading to the 1982 Convention.[86] It marks a compromise between those states seeking a 200 mile territorial sea and those wishing a more restricted system of coastal state power.

One of the major reasons for the call for a 200 mile exclusive economic zone has been the controversy over fishing zones. The 1958 Geneva Convention on the Territorial Sea did not reach

[82] E.g. the British Hovering Acts of the eighteenth and nineteenth century. See O'Connell, *op. cit.* footnote 1, vol.2, pp.1034-38 and the similar US legislation, *ibid.*, p.1038 *et seq.*

[83] See article 55, which states that the exclusive economic zone is "an area beyond and adjacent to the territorial seas".

[84] See e.g. Churchill and Lowe, *op. cit.*, Chapter 9; Attard, *The Exclusive Economic Zone in International Law*, 1986 and O'Connell, *op. cit.* footnote 1, vol.1, Chapter 15.

[85] *Ibid.*, Chapter 14.

[86] *Ibid.*, p.559 *et seq.*

agreement on the creation of fishing zones and article 24 of the Convention does not give exclusive fishing rights in the contiguous zone. However, increasing numbers of states have claimed fishing zones of widely varying widths. The European Fisheries Convention, 1964, which was implemented in the UK by the Fishing Limits Act, 1964, provided that the coastal state has the exclusive right to fish and exclusive jurisdiction in matters of fisheries in a six-mile belt from the baseline of the territorial sea; while within the belt between six and twelve miles from the baseline, other parties to the Convention have the right to fish, provided they had habitually fished in that belt between January 1953 and December 1962. This was an attempt to reconcile the interests of the coastal state with those of other states who could prove customary fishing operations in the relevant area. In view of the practice of many states in accepting at one time or another a twelve-mile exclusive fishing zone, either for themselves or for some other states, it seems clear that there has already emerged an international rule to that effect.

Indeed, the International Court in the *Fisheries Jurisdiction* cases[87] stated that the concept of the fishing zone, the area in which a state may claim exclusive jurisdiction independently of its territorial sea for this purpose, had crystallised as customary law in recent years and especially since the 1960 Geneva Conference, and that "the extension of that fishing zone up to a twelve mile limit from the baselines appears now to be generally accepted". That much is clear, but the question was whether international law recognised such a zone in excess of twelve miles.

In 1972, concerned at the proposals regarding the long-term effects of the depletion of fishing stocks around her coasts, Iceland proclaimed unilaterally a fifty mile exclusive fishing zone. This precipitated prolonged and acrimonious exchanges between that state, which depends upon fishing for some ninety per cent of its foreign earnings, and the UK and West Germany. The latter states referred the issue to the ICJ and specifically requested the Court to decide whether or not Iceland's claim was contrary to international law.

The Court did not answer that question and held that Iceland's fishing regulations extending the zone were not binding upon the UK and West Germany, since they had in no way acquiesced in them.

[87] ICJ Reports, 1974, pp.8, 175; 55 *ILR*, pp.238.

Indeed, they had vigorously protested and brought the matter before the Court. However, by implication the ICJ based its judgment on the fact that there did not exist any rule of international law permitting the establishment of a fifty mile fishing zone. Similarly, it appeared that there was no rule prohibiting claims beyond twelve miles and that the validity of such claims would depend upon all relevant facts of the case and the degree of recognition by other states.

The Court emphasised instead the notion of preferential rights, which it regarded as a principle of customary international law. Such rights arose where the coastal state was "in a situation of special dependence on coastal fisheries".[88] However, this concept was overtaken by developments at the UN Conference and the 1982 Convention. Article 55 of the 1982 Convention provides that the exclusive economic zone is an area beyond and adjacent to the territorial sea, subject to the specific legal regime established under the Convention.

Under article 56, the coastal state in the economic zone has *inter alia*:

(a) sovereign rights for the purpose of exploring and exploiting, conserving and managing the natural resources, whether living[89] or non-living of the waters superjacent to the seabed and of the seabed and its subsoil and with regard to other activities for the economic exploitation and exploration of the zone, such as the production of energy from the water, currents and winds;

(b) jurisdiction with regard to (i) the architecture and use of artificial islands, installations and structures;[90] (ii) marine scientific research;[91] (iii) the protection and preservation of the marine environment.[92]

Article 57 provides that the zone shall not extend beyond 200 nautical miles from the baselines from which the breadth of the territorial sea is measured.

Article 58 lays down the rights and duties of other states in the

---

[88] *Ibid.*, pp.23-29; 55 *ILR*, p.258.

[89] See also articles 61-69.

[90] See also article 60.

[91] See further Part XIII of the Convention and see Churchill and Lowe, *op. cit.*, Chapter 15.

[92] See further Part XII of the Convention and see Churchill and Lowe, *op. cit.*, Chapter 14.

exclusive economic zone. These are basically the high seas freedoms of navigation, overflight and laying of submarine cables and pipelines. It is also provided that in exercising their rights and performing their duties, states should have due regard to the rights, duties and laws of the coastal state. In cases of conflict over the attribution of rights and jurisdiction in the zone the resolution is to be on the basis of equity and in the light of all the relevant circumstances.[93]

It is also to be noted that landlocked and geographically disadvantaged states are to have the right to participate upon an equitable basis in the exploitation of an appropriate part of the surplus of the living resources of the economic zones of coastal states of the same sub-region or region, taking into account relevant economic and geographical factors.[94]

The delimitation of economic zones between states with opposite or adjacent coasts is to be effected by agreement on the basis of international law, as referred to in article 38 of the Statute of the ICJ, "in order to achieve an equitable solution".[95]

A wide variety of states have in the last decade claimed exclusive fishing or economic zones of 200 miles.[96] It would appear that such is the number and distribution of these states, that it is possible to talk of the establishment of a rule of customary law regarding the zones. This is especially important as the 1982 Convention is not yet in force.

The fact that the economic zone has become a norm of customary law is attested to, in addition to the weight of state practice, by the comment of the International Court of Justice in the *Libya* v. *Malta Continental Shelf* case[97] that "the institution of the exclusive economic

[93] Article 59.

[94] Articles 69 and 70. Note also articles 69(4) and 70(5) restricting such rights of development of landlocked states to developed coastal states of the same region.

[95] Article 74. See further on delimitation, *infra*, p.380.

[96] Churchill and Lowe point to around 70 such claims, *op. cit.*, p.353, but higher figures have been noted, see e.g. *AFDI*, 1978, pp.851, 858-65 and *The Maritime Dimension, op. cit.*, pp.45-46. See the figure of 92 states claiming 200 mile fisheries or economic zones cited in *Marine Fisheries Review*, May 1982, p.30. The Office of the Geographer of the US State Department reports that as at 1 March 1985, 62 states have claimed a 200 mile economic zone and 24 states a 200 mile fishing zone, *Keesings Contemporary Archives*, p.34016. See also the US Declaration of an Exclusive Economic Zone in March 1983. Note that the proclamation did not assert a right of jurisdiction over marine scientific research over the zone, 22 *ILM*, 1983, p.461 *et seq.*

[97] ICJ Reports, 1985, p.13; 81 *ILR*, p.239.

zone . . . is shown by the practice of states to have become a part of customary law".[98]

In addition to such zones, some other zones have been announced by states over areas of the seas. Canada has, for example, claimed a 100 mile deep zone along her Arctic coastline as a special, pollution-free zone.[99] Certain states have also asserted rights over what have been termed security or neutrality zones,[100] but these have never been particularly well received and are rare.

THE HIGH SEAS [101]

The closed seas concept proclaimed by Spain and Portugal in the fifteenth and sixteenth centuries, and supported by the Papal Bulls of 1493 and 1506 dividing the seas of the world between the two powers, was replaced by the notion of the open seas and the concomitant freedom of the high seas during the eighteenth century.

The essence of the freedom of the high seas is that no state may acquire sovereignty over parts of it.[102] This is the general rule, but it is subject to the operation of the doctrines of recognition, acquiescence and prescription, where, by long usage accepted by other nations, certain areas of the high seas bounding on the territorial waters of coastal states may be rendered subject to that state's sovereignty. This was emphasised in the *Anglo-Norwegian Fisheries* case.[103]

The high seas were defined in Article 1 of the Geneva Convention on the High Seas, 1958, as all parts of the sea that were not included in the territorial sea or in the internal waters of a state. This reflected customary international law, although as a result of developments the definition in article 86 of the 1982 Convention includes:

---

[98] *Ibid.*, p.33; 81 *ILR*, p.265.

[99] See O'Connell, *op. cit.* footnote 1, vol.2, pp.1022-25. See also the Canadian Arctic Waters Pollution Prevention Act 1970. The US has objected to this jurisdiction, see e.g. *Keesings Contemporary Archives*, pp.23961 and 24129. The Canadian claim was reiterated in September 1985, *ibid.*, p.33984.

[100] *Ibid.*, vol.1, p.578, note 95 regarding North Korea's proclamation of a 50 mile security zone in 1977. Note also the establishment of the "exclusion zone" around the Falkland Islands in 1982, see HC Deb., 28 April 1982, cols.296-97. See e.g. Barston and Birnie, "The Falkland Islands/Islas Malvinas Conflict. A Question of Zones", 7 *Marine Policy*, 1983, p.14.

[101] See e.g. *ibid.*, vol.2, Chapter 21, and Churchill and Lowe, *op. cit.*, Chapter 11.

[102] See article 2 of the 1958 High Seas Convention and article 89 of the 1982 Convention.

[103] ICJ Reports, 1951, p.116; 18 *ILR*, p.86. See *supra*, p.342.

all parts of the sea that are not included in the exclusive economic zone, in the territorial sea or in the internal waters of a state, or in the archipelagic waters of an archipelagic state.

Article 2 of the 1958 Geneva Convention on the High Seas provided a general explanation of the freedom of the seas. Apart from being open to all nations, the high seas could be used by all states for the purpose of navigation, fishing and the laying of submarine cables and pipelines. Additionally, there existed freedom to fly over the high seas. Such freedoms are not exhaustive, and others "recognised by the general principles of international law" could be exercised with regard to the high seas and with reasonable regard to the interests of other states.[104]

Australia and New Zealand alleged before the ICJ, in the *Nuclear Tests* case,[105] that French nuclear testing in the Pacific infringed the principle of the freedom of the seas, but this point was not decided by the Court. The 1963 Nuclear Test Ban Treaty prohibited the testing of nuclear weapons on the high seas as well as on land, but France was not a party to the treaty, and it appears not to constitute a customary rule binding all states, irrespective of the treaty. Nevertheless, article 88 of the 1982 Convention provides that the high seas shall be reserved for peaceful purposes.

Principles that are generally acknowledged to come within article 2 include the freedom to conduct naval exercises on the high seas and the freedom to carry out research studies.

The freedom of navigation[106] is a traditional and well-recognised facet of the doctrine of the high seas, as is the freedom of fishing.[107] This was reinforced by the declaration by the Court in the *Fisheries Jurisdiction* cases[108] that Iceland's unilateral extension of its fishing zones from twelve to fifty miles constituted a violation of article 2 of the High Seas Convention, which is, as the preamble states, "generally declaratory of established principles of international law". The freedom of the high seas applies not only to coastal states

[104] See also articles 87 and 89 of the 1982 Convention. Note particularly the freedoms to construct artificial islands and other installations and the freedom of scientific research.

[105] ICJ Reports, 1974, pp.253 and 457; 57 *ILR*, pp.350, 605.

[106] See the *Corfu Channel* case, ICJ Reports, 1949, pp.4, 22; 16 *ILR*, p.155, and *Nicaragua* v. *United States*, ICJ Reports, 1986, pp.14, 111-12; 76 *ILR*, pp.349, 445.

[107] See the *Anglo-Norwegian Fisheries* case, ICJ Reports, 1951, pp.116, 183; 18 *ILR*, pp.86, 131.

[108] ICJ Reports, 1974, p.3; 55 *ILR*, p.238.

but also to states that are landlocked.[109] Article 3 of the High Seas Convention provides that states having no sea coast should have free access to the sea, and accordingly states situated between the sea and landlocked countries should by common agreement accord to the latter free transit through their territory on a basis of reciprocity, and equal treatment to their ships as regards access to and use of ports. Problems have arisen on this issue not only because of reciprocity, and equal treatment to their ships as regards access to and use of ports. Problems have arisen on this issue not only because of the considerable number of landlocked states, especially in Africa, but also because many of the transit states (that is those states between the sea and the landlocked states) lack many of the essential communications and transportation facilities for the proper fulfilment of the access provisions.[110]

The question of freedom of navigation on the high seas in times of armed conflict was raised during the Iran-Iraq war, which during its latter stages involved attacks upon civilian shipping by both belligerents. Rather than rely on the classical and somewhat out-of-date rules of the laws of war at sea,[111] the UK in particular has analysed the issue in terms of the UN Charter. The following statement was made:[112]

The UK upholds the principle of freedom of navigation on the high seas and condemns all violations of the law of armed conflicts including attacks on merchant shipping. Under article 51 of the UN Charter, a state actively engaged in armed conflict (as in the case of Iran and Iraq) is entitled in exercise of its inherent right of self-defence to stop and search a foreign merchant ship on the high seas if there is reasonable ground for suspecting that the ship is taking arms to the other side for use in the conflict. This is an exceptional right: if the suspicion proves to be unfounded and if the ship has not committed acts calculated to give rise to suspicion, then the ship's owners have a good claim for compensation for loss caused by the delay. This right would not, however, extend to the imposition of a maritime blockade or other forms of economic warfare.

---

[109] See Churchill and Lowe, *op. cit.*, Chapter 18.
[110] See also article 125 of the 1982 Convention.
[111] See e.g. Colombos, *International Law of the Sea*, 6th ed. 1967, Part II.
[112] *Parliamentary Papers*, 1987-88, HC, Paper 179-II, p.120 and UKMIL, 59 *BYIL*, 1988, p.581.

Jurisdiction on the High Seas

The foundation of the maintenance of order on the high seas has rested upon the concept of the nationality of the ship, and the consequent jurisdiction of the flag state over the ship. It is, basically, the flag state that will enforce the rules and regulations not only of its own municipal law but of international law as well. A ship without a flag will be deprived of many of the benefits and rights available under the legal regime of the high seas.

Each state is required to elaborate the conditions necessary for the grant of its nationality to ships, for the registration of ships in its territory and for the right to fly its flag.[113] The nationality of the ship will depend upon the flag it flies, but article 5 of the High Seas Convention also stipulates that there must be a "genuine link" between the state and the ship, and "in particular the state must effectively exercise its jurisdiction and control in administrative, technical and social matters over ships flying its flag".[114] This provision was intended to check the use of flags of convenience operated by states such as Liberia and Panama which would grant their nationality to ships requesting such because of low taxation and the lack of application of most wage and social security agreements. This enabled the ships to operate at very low costs indeed.

However, what precisely the "genuine link" consists of and how one may regulate any abuse of the provisions of article 5 are unresolved questions. Some countries, for example the United States, maintain that the requirement of a "genuine link" really only amounts to a duty to exercise jurisdiction over the ship in an efficacious manner, and is not a pre-condition for the grant, or the acceptance by other states of the grant, of nationality.[115]

An opportunity did arise in 1960 to discuss the meaning of the provision in the *IMCO* case.[116] The International Court was called upon to define "largest ship-owning nations" for the purposes of the constitution of a committee of the Inter-Governmental Maritime Consultative Organisation. It was held that the term referred only to registered tonnage so as to enable Liberia and Panama to be

---

[113] Article 5 of the 1958 High Seas Convention and article 91 of the 1982 Convention.
[114] Note that the latter requirement was omitted in the 1982 Convention, see article 91.
[115] See Churchill and Lowe, *op. cit.*, pp.205-9.
[116] ICJ Reports, 1960, p.150; 30 *ILR*, p.426.

elected to the committee. Unfortunately, the opportunity was not taken of considering the problems of flags of convenience or the meaning of the "genuine link" in the light of the true ownership of the ships involved, and so the doubts and ambiguities remain.

The UN Conference on Conditions of Registration of Ships, held under the auspices of the UN Conference on Trade and Development, convened in July 1984 and an agreement was signed in 1986. It attempts to deal with the flags of convenience issue, bearing in mind that nearly one-third of the world's merchant fleet by early 1985 flew such flags. It specifies that flag states should provide in their laws and regulations for the ownership of ships flying their flags and that those should include appropriate provision for participation by nationals as owners of such ships, and that such provisions should be sufficient to permit the flag state to exercise effectively its jurisdiction and control over ships flying its flag.[117]

The issue of the genuine link arose in the context of the Iran-Iraq war and in particular Iranian attacks upon Kuwaiti shipping. This prompted Kuwait to ask the USSR and the USA to reflag Kuwaiti tankers. The USA agreed in early 1987 to reflag eleven such tankers under the US flag and to protect them as it did other US-flagged ships in the Gulf.[118] The UK also agreed to reflag some Kuwaiti tankers, arguing that only satisfaction of Department of Trade and Industry requirements was necessary.[119] Both states argued that the genuine link requirement was satisfied and in view of the ambiguity of state practice as to the definition of genuine link in such instances, it is hard to argue that the US and UK acted unlawfully.

Ships are required to sail under the flag of one state only and are subject to its exclusive jurisdiction (save in exceptional cases). Where a ship does sail under the flags of more than one state, according to convenience, it may be treated as a ship without nationality and will not be able to claim any of the nationalities concerned.[120] A ship that is stateless, and does not fly a flag, may be boarded and seized on the high seas. This point was accepted

---

[117] *Keesings Contemporary Archives*, p.33952.

[118] See 26 *ILM*, 1987, pp.1429-30, 1435-40 and 1450-52. See also 37 *ICLQ*, 1988, pp.424-45 and Nordquist and Wachenfeld, "Legal Aspects of Reflagging Kuwaiti Tankers and Laying of Mines in the Persian Gulf", 31 *German Yearbook of International Law*, 1988, p.138.

[119] See e.g. 119 HC Deb., col.645, 17 July 1987.

[120] Article 6 of the 1958 Convention and article 92 of the 1982 Convention.

by the Privy Council in the case of *Naim Molvan* v. *Attorney-General for Palestine*,[121] which concerned the seizure by the British navy of a stateless ship attempting to convey immigrants into Palestine.

The basic principle relating to jurisdiction on the high seas is that the flag state alone may exercise such rights over the ship.[122] This was elaborated in the *Lotus* case,[123] where it was held that "vessels on the high seas are subject to no authority except that of the state whose flag they fly". This exclusivity is without exception regarding warships and ships owned or operated by a state where they are used only on governmental non-commercial service. Such ships have, according to articles 8 and 9 of the High Seas Convention, "complete immunity from the jurisdiction of any state other than the flag state".[124]

Exceptions to the Exclusivity of Flag-State Jurisdiction

However, this basic principle is subject to exceptions regarding other vessels, and the concept of the freedom of the high seas is similarly limited by the existence of a series of exceptions.

1. Right of Visit

Since the law of the sea depends to such an extent upon the nationality of the ship, it is well recognised in customary international law that warships have a right of approach to ascertain the nationality of ships. However, this right of approach to identify vessels does not incorporate the right to board or visit ships. This may only be undertaken, in the absence of hostilities between the flag states of the warship and a merchant vessel and in the absence of special treaty provisions to the contrary, where the ship is engaged in piracy or the slave trade, or, though flying a foreign flag or no flag at all, is in reality of the same nationality as the warship or of no nationality. But the warship has to operate carefully in such circumstances, since

---

[121] [1948] AC 351; 13 *ILR*, p.51. See also e.g. *US* v. *Dominguez*, 604 F.2d 304 (1979); *US* v. *Cortes*, 588 F.2d 106, (1979); *US* v. *Monroy*, 614 F.2d 61 (1980) and *US* v. *Marino-Garcia*, 679 F.2d 1373 (1982). In the latter case, the Court referred to stateless vessels as "international pariahs", *ibid.*, p.1383.

[122] See article 6 of the 1958 Convention and article 92 of the 1982 Convention.

[123] PCIJ, Series A, no.10, 1927, p.25; 4 *ILR*, p.153.

[124] See articles 95 and 96 of the 1982 Convention.

it may be liable to pay compensation for any loss or damage sustained if its suspicions are unfounded and the ship boarded has not committed any act justifying them. Thus, international law has settled for a narrow exposition of the right of approach, in spite of earlier tendencies to expand this right, and the above provisions were incorporated into article 22 of the High Seas Convention.[125]

2. *Piracy*

The most formidable of the exceptions to the exclusive jurisdiction of the flag state and to the principle of the freedom of the high seas is the concept of piracy. Piracy is strictly defined in international law and was declared in article 15 of the High Seas Convention to consist of any of the following acts:

(1) Any illegal acts of violence, detention or any act of depredation, committed for private ends by the crew or the passengers of a private ship or private aircraft and directed: (a) on the high seas, against another ship or aircraft, or against persons or property on board such ship or aircraft; (b) against a ship, aircraft, persons or property in a place outside the jurisdiction of any state; (2) Any act of voluntary participation in the operation of a ship or of an aircraft with knowledge of facts making it a pirate ship or aircraft; (3) Any act of inciting or of intentionally facilitating an act described in sub-paragraph (1) or subparagraph (2) of this article.[126]

The essence of piracy under international law is that it must be committed for private ends. In other words, any hijacking or takeover for political reasons is automatically excluded from the definition of piracy. Similarly, any acts committed on the ship by the crew and aimed at the ship itself or property or persons on the ship do not fall within this category.

Any and every state may seize a pirate ship or aircraft whether on the high seas or on *terra nullius* and arrest the persons and seize

---

[125] See also article 110 of the 1982 Convention. This adds to the list a right of visit where the ship is engaged in unauthorised broadcasting and the flag state of the warship has under article 109 of the Convention jurisdiction to prosecute the offender.

[126] See also article 101 of the 1982 Convention. Note that article 105 deals with the seizure of pirate boats or aircraft. Article 106 provides for compensation in the case of seizure without adequate grounds. See also *Athens Maritime Enterprises Corporation* v. *Hellenic Mutual War Risk Association*, [1983] 1 All ER 590; 78 *ILR*, p.563.

the property on board. In addition, the courts of the state carrying out the seizure have jurisdiction to impose penalties, and may decide what action to take regarding the ship or aircraft and property, subject to the rights of third parties that have acted in good faith.[127] The fact that every state may arrest and try persons accused of piracy makes that crime quite exceptional in international law, where so much emphasis is placed upon the sovereignty and jurisdiction of each particular state within its own territory.

3. *The Slave Trade*

Although piracy may be suppressed by all states, most offences on the high seas can only be punished in accordance with regulations prescribed by the municipal legislation of states, even where international law requires such rules to be established. The slave trade, for instance, is to be repressed according to article 13 of the 1958 Convention by every state adopting effective methods to prevent and punish it. Though by article 22 of the Convention, warships may board foreign merchant ships where they are reasonably suspected of engaging in the slave trade, offenders must be handed over to the flag state for trial.[128]

4. *Unauthorised Broadcasting*

Under article 109 of the 1982 Convention, all states are to co-operate .in the suppression of unauthorised broadcasting from the high seas. This is defined to mean transmission of sound or TV from a ship or installation on the high seas intended for reception by the general public, contrary to international regulations but excluding the transmission of distress calls. Any person engaged in such broadcasting may be prosecuted by the flag state of the ship, the state of registry of the installation, the state of which the person is a national, any state where the transmission can be received or

---

[127] See article 19 of the 1958 Convention and article 105 of the 1982 Convention.

[128] See also articles 99 and 110 of the 1982 Convention. Several international treaties exist with the aim of suppressing the slave trade and some provide for reciprocal rights of visits and search on the high seas, see e.g. Churchill and Lowe, *op. cit.*, pp.171-72. Note also that under article 108 of the 1982 Convention all states are to co-operate in the suppression of the illicit drug trade.

any state where authorised radio communication is suffering interference.

Any of the above states having jurisdiction may arrest any person or ship engaging in unauthorised broadcasting on the high seas and seize the broadcasting apparatus.[129]

5. *Hot Pursuit* [130]

The right of hot pursuit of a foreign ship is a principle designed to ensure that a vessel which has infringed the rules of a coastal state cannot escape punishment by fleeing to the high seas. In reality it means that in certain defined circumstances a coastal state may extend its jurisdiction onto the high seas in order to pursue and seize a ship which is suspected of infringing its laws. The right, which has been developing in one form or another since the nineteenth century,[131] was comprehensively elaborated in article 23 of the High Seas Convention.

It notes that such pursuit may commence when the authorities of the coastal state have good reason to believe that the foreign ship has violated its laws. The pursuit must start while the ship, or one of its boats, is within the internal waters, territorial sea or contiguous zone of the coastal state and may only continue outside the territorial sea or contiguous zone if it is uninterrupted. However, if the pursuit commences while the foreign ship is in the contiguous zone, then it may only be undertaken if there has been a violation of the rights for the protection of which the zone was established. Under article 111 of the 1982 Convention, the right may similarly commence from the archipelagic waters. In addition, the right will apply *mutatis mutandis* to violations in the exclusive economic zone or on the continental shelf (including safety zones around continental shelf installations) of the relevant rules and regulations applicable to such areas.

Hot pursuit only begins when the pursuing ship has satisfied itself that the ship pursued or one of its boats is within the limits of the territorial sea or as the case may be in the contiguous zone, or economic zone or on the continental shelf.

---

[129] See also article 110 of the 1982 Convention. In addition, see the European Agreement for the Prevention of Broadcasting transmitted from Stations outside National Territories.

[130] See also Poulantzas, *The Right of Hot Pursuit in International Law*, 1969.

[131] See e.g. the *I'm Alone* case, 3 *RIAA*, p.1609 (1935); 7 *ILR*, p.203.

It is essential that prior to the chase a visual or auditory signal to stop has been given at a distance enabling it to be seen or heard by the foreign ship and pursuit may only be exercised by warships or military aircraft or by specially authorised government ships or places. The right of hot pursuit ceases as soon as the ship pursued has entered the territorial waters of its own or a third state.

6. Collisions

Where ships are involved in collisions on the high seas, article 11 of the High Seas Convention declares, overruling the decision in the *Lotus* case,[132] that penal or disciplinary proceedings may only be taken against the master or other persons in the service of the ship by the authorities of either the flag-state or the state of which the particular person is a national. It also provides that no arrest or detention of the ship, even for investigation purposes, can be ordered by other than the authorities of the flag-state.[133]

7. Treaty Rights

In many cases, states may by treaty permit each other's warships to exercise certain powers of visit and search as regards vessels flying the flags of the signatories to the treaty. For example, most of the agreements in the last century relating to the suppression of the slave trade provided that warships of the parties to the agreements could search and sometimes detain vessels suspected of being involved in the trade, where such vessels were flying the flags of the treaty states.[134] The Convention for the Protection of Submarine Cables of 1884 gave the warships of contracting states the right to stop and ascertain the nationality of merchant ships that were suspected of infringing the terms of the Convention, and other agreements dealing with matters as diverse as arms trading and liquor smuggling contained like powers.[135]

---

[132] PCIJ, Series A, no.10, 1927, p.25; 4 *ILR*, p.153.

[133] See also article 97 of the 1982 Convention.

[134] See e.g. Churchill and Lowe, *op. cit.*, pp.171-72 and 175.

[135] See the UK-US Agreement on Vessels Trafficking in Drugs 1981 and *US* v. *Biermann*, 83 *AJIL*, 1989, p.99.

Pollution [136]

Article 24 of the 1958 Convention on the High Seas called on states to draw up regulations to prevent the pollution of the seas by the discharge of oil or the dumping of radioactive waste, while article 1 of the Convention on the Fishing and Conservation of the Living Resources of the High Seas, of the same year, declared that all states had the duty to adopt, or co-operate with other states in adopting, such measures as may be necessary for the conservation of the living resources of the high seas. Although these provisions have not proved an unqualified success, they have been reinforced by an interlocking series of additional agreements covering the environmental protection of the seas.

The International Convention relating to Intervention on the High Seas in Cases of Oil Pollution Casualties, signed in 1969 and in force as of June 1975, provides that the parties to the Convention may take such measures on the high seas:

> as may be necessary to prevent, mitigate or eliminate grave and imminent danger to their coastline or related interests from pollution or threat of pollution of the sea by oil, following upon a maritime casualty or acts related to such a casualty, which may reasonably be expected to result in major harmful consequences.

This provision came as a result of the *Torrey Canyon* incident in 1967 [137] in which a Liberian tanker floundered off the Cornish coast, spilling massive quantities of oil and polluting large stretches of the UK and French coastlines. As a last resort to prevent further pollution, British aircraft bombed the tanker and set it ablaze. The Convention on Intervention on the High Seas provided for action to be taken to end threats to the coasts of states, while the Convention on Civil Liability for Oil Pollution Damage, also signed in 1969 and which came into effect in June 1975, stipulated that the owners of ships causing oil pollution damage were to be liable to pay compensation.

---

[136] See Churchill and Lowe, *op. cit.*, Chapter 15, and O'Connell, *op. cit.* footnote 1, vol.2, Chapter 25. See *infra*, Chapter 14.

[137] 6 *ILM*, 1967, p.480. See also the *Amoco Cadiz* incident in 1978, e.g. Churchill and Lowe, *op. cit.*, p.241.

The latter agreement was supplemented in 1971 by the Convention on the Establishment of an International Fund for Compensation for Oil Pollution Damage which sought to provide for compensation in circumstances not covered by the 1969 Convention and aid ship owners in their additional financial obligations.

These agreements are only a small part of the web of treaties covering the preservation of the sea environment. Other examples include the 1954 Convention for the Prevention of Pollution of the Seas by Oil, with its series of amendments designed to ban offensive discharges, the 1971 Oslo Convention for the Prevention of Marine Pollution by Dumping from Ships and Aircraft and the subsequent London Convention on the Dumping of Wastes at Sea the following year, the 1973 Convention for the Prevention of Pollution from Ships and the 1974 Paris Convention for the Prevention of Marine Pollution from Land-Based Sources.[138]

Under the 1982 Convention nearly 50 articles are devoted to the protection of the marine environment. Flag-states still retain the competence to legislate for their ships, but certain minimum standards are imposed upon them.[139] It is also provided that states are responsible for the fulfilment of their international obligations concerning the protection and preservation of the marine environment and are liable in accordance with international law. States must also ensure that recourse is available in accordance with their legal systems for prompt and adequate compensation or other relief regarding damage caused by pollution of the marine environment by persons under their jurisdiction.[140]

States are under a basic obligation to protect and preserve the marine environment.[141] Article 194 also provides that:

1. States shall take, individually or jointly as appropriate, all measures consistent with this Convention that are necessary to prevent, reduce and control pollution of the marine environment from any source, using for this purpose the best practicable means at their disposal and in accordance with their capabilities, and they shall endeavour to harmonise their policies in this connection,

---

[138] Also a variety of regional and bilateral agreements have been signed, *ibid.*, pp.263-64.
[139] See article 211. See also generally articles 192-238, covering *inter alia* global and regional co-operation, technical assistance, monitory and environmental assessment, and the development of the enforcement of international and domestic law preventing pollution.
[140] Article 235.
[141] Article 192.

2. States shall take all measures necessary to ensure that activities under their jurisdiction or control are so conducted as not to cause damage by pollution to other States and their environment, and that pollution arising from incidents or activities under their jurisdiction or control does not spread beyond the areas where they exercise sovereign rights in accordance with this Convention.

3. The measures taken pursuant to this Part shall deal with all sources of pollution of the marine environment. These measures shall include, *inter alia*, those designed to minimise to the fullest possible extent:

(a) the release of toxic, harmful, or noxious substances, especially those which are persistent, from land-based sources, from or through the atmosphere or by dumping;

(b) pollution from vessels, in particular measures for preventing accidents and dealing with emergencies, ensuring the safety of operations at sea, preventing intentional and unintentional discharges, and regulating the design, construction, equipment, operation and manning of vessels;

(c) pollution from installations and devices used in exploitation of the natural resources of the seabed and subsoil, in particular measures for preventing accidents and dealing with emergencies, ensuring the safety of operations at sea, and regulating the design, construction, equipment, operation and manning of such installations or devices;

(d) pollution from other installations and devices operating in the marine environment, in particular for preventing accidents and dealing with emergencies, ensuring the safety of operations at sea, and regulating the design, construction, equipment, operation and manning of such installations or devices.

4. In taking measures to prevent, reduce or control pollution of the marine environment, states shall refrain from unjustifiable interference with activities carried out by other states in the exercise of their rights and in pursuance of their duties in conformity with this Convention.

THE CONTINENTAL SHELF [142]

This is a geological expression referring to the ledges that project from the continental land mass into the seas and which are covered with only a relatively shallow layer of water (some 150-200 metres) and which eventually fall away into the ocean depths (some thousands

[142] See e.g. O'Connell, *op. cit.* footnote 1, vol.1, Chapter 13; Churchill and Lowe, *op. cit.*, Chapter 8; Mouton, *The Continental Shelf*, 1952; Slouka, *International Custom and the Continental Shelf*, 1968 and Lauterpacht, "Sovereignty over Submarine Areas", 27 *BYIL*, 1950, p.376.

of metres deep). These ledges or shelves take up some seven to eight per cent of the total area of ocean and their extent varies considerably from place to place. Off the western coast of the United States, for instance, it is less than five miles wide, while on the other hand the whole of the underwater area of the North Sea and Persian Gulf consists of shelf.

The vital fact about the continental shelves is that they are rich in oil and gas resources and quite often are host to extensive fishing grounds. This stimulated a round of appropriations by coastal states in the years following the Second World War, which gradually altered the legal status of the continental shelf from being part of the high seas and available for exploitation by all states until its current recognition as exclusive to the coastal state.

The first move in this direction, and the one that led to a series of similar and more extensive claims, was the Truman Proclamation of 1945.[143] This pointed to the technological capacity to exploit the riches of the shelf and the need to establish a recognised jurisdiction over such resources, and declared that the coastal state was entitled to such jurisdiction for a number of reasons. First, because utilisation or conservation of the resources of the subsoil and seabed of the continental shelf depended upon co-operation from the shore. Secondly, because the shelf itself could be regarded as an extension of the land mass of the coastal state, and its resources were often merely an extension into the sea of deposits lying within the territory. And finally, because the coastal state, for reasons of security, was profoundly interested in activities off its shores, which would be necessary to utilise the resources of the shelf.

Accordingly, the US government proclaimed that it regarded the "natural resources of the subsoil and seabed of the continental shelf beneath the high seas but contiguous to the coasts of the United States as appertaining to the United States, subject to its jurisdiction and control". However, this would in no way affect the status of the waters above the continental shelf as high seas.

This proclamation precipitated a whole series of claims by states to their continental shelves, some in similar terms to the US assertions, and others in substantially wider terms. Argentina and El Salvador, for example, claimed not only the shelf but also the

---

[143] Whiteman, *Digest, op. cit.* vol.4, p.756.

waters above and the airspace. Chile and Peru, having no continental shelf to speak of, claimed sovereignty over the seabed, subsoil and waters around their coasts to a limit of 200 miles, although this occasioned vigorous protests by many states.[144] The problems were discussed over many years leading to the 1958 Geneva Convention on the Continental Shelf.[145]

In the *North Sea Continental Shelf* cases,[146] the Court noted that:

> the rights of the coastal state in respect of the area of continental shelf that constitutes a natural prolongation of its land territory into and under the sea exist *ipso facto* and *ab initio*, by virtue of its sovereignty over the land, and as an extension of it in an exercise of sovereign rights for the purpose of exploring the seabed and exploiting its natural resources. In short there is here an inherent right.

The development of the concept of the exclusive economic zone has to some extent confused the issue, since under article 56 of the 1982 Convention the coastal state has sovereign rights over all the natural resources of its exclusive economic zone, including the seabed resources.[147] Accordingly, states possess two sources of rights with regard to the seabed, although claims with regard to the economic zone, in contrast to the continental shelf, need to be specifically maintained. It is also possible, as will be seen, that the geographical extent of the shelf may be different from that of the 200 mile economic zone.

Definition

The 1958 Convention defined the shelf, in article 1, in terms of its exploitability rather than relying upon the accepted geological definition, noting that the expression referred to the seabed and subsoil of the submarine areas adjacent to the coast but outside the territorial sea to a depth of 200 metres of "beyond that limit to where

---

[144] *Ibid.*, pp.794-99 and see also Oppenheim, *op. cit.*, p.632.

[145] Note that in the *Abu Dhabi* case, the arbitrator declared that the doctrine of the continental shelf in 1951 was not yet a rule of international law, 18 *ILR*, p.144. See also to the same effect (with regard to 1949), *Reference Re: The Seabed and Subsoil of the Continental Shelf Offshore Newfoundland*, 5 DLR (46), p.385 *per* Supreme Court of Canada (1984).

[146] ICJ Reports, 1969; pp.3, 22; 41 *ILR*, pp.29, 51.

[147] See *supra*, p.359.

the depth of the superjacent waters admits of the exploitation of the natural resources of the said areas".

This provision has caused problems, since developing technology is now in a position to extract resources to a much greater depth than 200 metres, and this means that the outer limits of the shelf, subject to the jurisdiction of the coastal state, would be unclear. This article was, however, regarded as reflecting customary law by the Court in the *North Sea Continental Shelf* case.[148] It is also important to note that the basis of title to continental shelf is now accepted as the geographical criterion, and not reliance upon, for example, occupation or effective control. The Court emphasised this and declared that:

> the submarine areas concerned may be deemed to be actually part of the territory over which the coastal state already has dominion in the sense that although covered with water, they are a prolongation or continuation of that territory, an extension of it under the sea.[149]

The 1982 Convention provides as to the outer limit of the continental shelf that:

> [t]he continental shelf of a coastal state comprises the seabed and subsoil of the submarine areas that extend beyond its territorial sea throughout the natural prolongation of its land territory to the outer edge of the continental margin, or to a distance of 200 nautical miles from the baselines from which the breadth of the territorial sea is measured where the outer edge of continental margin does not extend up to that distance.[150]

Thus, an arbitrary, legal and non-geographical definition is provided. Where the continental margin actually extends beyond 200 miles, geographical factors are to be taken into account in establishing the limit, which in any event shall not exceed either 350 miles from the baselines or 100 miles from the 2,500 metre isobath.[151]

---

[148] ICJ Reports, 1969, pp.3, 39; 41 *ILR*, pp.29, 68.

[149] *Ibid.*, p.31; 41 *ILR*, p.60.

[150] Article 76(1). See article 76(3) for a definition of the continental margin. See also Hutchinson, "The Seaward Limit to Continental Shelf Jurisdiction in Customary International Law", 56 *BYIL*, 1985, p.133.

[151] Article 76(4), (5), (6), (7), (8) and (9). See also Annex II to the Final Act.

The Rights of the Coastal State

The coastal state may exercise sovereign rights over the continental shelf for the purposes of exploring it and exploiting its natural resources under article 2 of the 1958 Convention and such rights are exclusive in that no other state may undertake such activities without the express consent of the coastal state. These sovereign rights (note the Convention does not talk in terms of "sovereignty" but of "sovereign rights") do not depend upon occupation or express proclamation.[152] Article 2(4) extends the Truman concept of resources, which referred only to mineral resources, to include organisms belonging to the sedentary species. However, this vague description did lead to disputes between France and Brazil over lobster, and between the USA and Japan over the Alaskan King Crab in the early 1960s.[153]

The Convention expressly states that the rights of the coastal state do not affect the status of the superjacent waters as high seas, or that of the airspace above the waters.[154] This is stressed in succeeding articles which note that, subject to its right to take reasonable measures for exploration and exploitation of the continental shelf, the coastal state may not impede the laying or maintenance of cables or pipelines on the shelf. In addition, such exploration and exploitation must not result in any unjustifiable interference with navigation, fishing or the conservation of the living resources of the sea.[155]

The coastal state may, under article 5 of the 1958 Convention, construct and maintain installations and other devices necessary for exploration on the continental shelf and is entitled to establish safety zones around such installations to a limit of 500 metres, which must be respected by ships of all nationalities. Within such zones, the state may take such measures as are necessary for their protection. But although under the jurisdiction of the coastal state, these installations are not to be considered as islands. This means that they have no territorial sea of their own and their presence in no

---

[152] See article 77 of the 1982 Convention.

[153] See e.g. O'Connell, *op. cit.* footnote 1, vol.1, pp.501-2. Note also article 77(4) of the 1982 Convention.

[154] Article 3. See also article 78 of the 1982 Convention, where the reference to "high seas" is omitted for reasons related to the new concept of the exclusive economic zone.

[155] Articles 4 and 5. See also articles 78 and 79 of the 1982 Convention.

way affects the delimitation of the territorial waters of the coastal state. Such provisions are, of course, extremely important when considering the status of oil rigs situated, for example, in the North Sea. To treat them as islands for legal purposes would cause difficulties.[156]

Where the continental shelf of a state extends beyond 200 miles, article 82 of the 1982 Convention provides that the coastal state must make payments or contributions in kind in respect of the exploitation of the non-living resources of the continental shelf beyond the 200 mile limit. The payments are to be made annually after the first five years of production at the site in question on a sliding scale up to the twelfth year, after which it is to remain at 7%. These payments and contributions are to be made to the International Seabed Authority, which shall distribute them amongst state parties on the basis of "equitable sharing criteria, taking into account the interests and needs of developing states, particularly the least developed and the landlocked among them".[157]

Delimitation of the Continental Shelf between Opposite and Adjacent States [158]

Article 6 of the Continental Shelf Convention 1958 declared that in the absence of agreement and unless another boundary line was justified by special circumstances, the boundary should be determined "by application of the principle of equidistance from the nearest points of the baselines from which the breadth of the territorial sea of each state is measured", that is to say by the introduction of the equidistance or median line which would operate in relation to the sinuosities of the particular coast lines.

This provision was considered in the *North Sea Continental Shelf* cases[159] between West Germany on the one side and Holland and Denmark on the other. The problem was that the application of the equidistance principle of article 6 would give West Germany only

---

[156] See also articles 60 and 80 of the 1982 Convention.

[157] Note also that by article 82(3) a developing state which is a net importer of the mineral resource in question is exempt from such payments and contributions.

[158] See Churchill and Lowe, *op. cit.*, Chapter 10; Brown, *Sea-Bed Energy and Mineral Resources and the Law of the Sea*, vols.I and III, 1984-86; Evans, *Relevant Circumstances and Maritime Delimitation*, 1989, and Weil, *The Law of Maritime Delimitation — Reflections*, 1989.

[159] ICJ Reports, 1969, p.3; 41 *ILR*, p.29.

a small share of the North Sea continental shelf, in view of its concave northern shoreline between Holland and Denmark. The question arose as to whether the article was binding upon West Germany at all, since it had not ratified the 1958 Continental Shelf Convention.

The Court held that the principles enumerated in article 6 did not constitute rules of international customary law and therefore West Germany was not bound by them.[160] The Court declared that the relevant rule was that:

> delimitation is to be effected by agreement in accordance with equitable principles, and taking account of all the relevant circumstances, in such a way as to leave as much as possible to each party all those parts of the continental shelf that constitute a natural prolongation of its land territory into and under the sea, without encroachment on the natural prolongation of the land territory of the other.[161]

In the *Anglo-French Continental Shelf* case,[162] both states were parties to the 1958 Convention, so that article 6 applied.[163] It was held that article 6 contained one overall rule, "a combined equidistance-special circumstances rule", which in effect:

> gives particular expression to a general norm that, failing agreement, the boundary between states abutting on the same continental shelf is to be determined on equitable principles.[164]

The choice of method of delimitation, whether by the equidistance or any other method, depended upon the relevant circumstances of the case. The fundamental norm under both customary law and the 1958 Convention was that the delimitation had to be in accordance with equitable principles.[165] The Court took into account "special circumstances" in relation to the situation of the

---

[160] See *supra*, Chapter 3, p.65.

[161] ICJ Reports, 1969, pp.3, 53; 41 *ILR*, p.83.

[162] Cmnd. 7438 (1978); 54 *ILR*, p.6. See also Bowett, "The Arbitration between the United Kingdom and France Concerning the Continental Shelf Boundary in the English Channel of South-Western Approaches", 49 *BYIL*, 1978, p.1.

[163] Although subject to a French reservation regarding the Bay of Granville to which the UK had objected, *ibid.*, p.50; 54 *ILR*, p.57.

[164] *Ibid.*, p.48; 54 *ILR*, p.55.

[165] *Ibid.*, pp.59-60; 54 *ILR*, p.66.

Channel Islands which justified a delimitation other than the median line proposed by the UK.[166] In addition, the situation of the Scilly Isles was considered and they were given only "half-effect" in the delimitation in the Atlantic area since

> what equity calls for is an appropriate abatement of the disproportionate effects of a considerable projection on the Atlantic continental shelf of a somewhat attenuated projection of the coast of the United Kingdom.[167]

In the *Tunisia-Libya Continental Shelf* case,[168] the Court, deciding on the basis of custom as neither state was a party to the 1958 Convention, emphasised that "the satisfaction of equitable principles is, in the delimitation process, of cardinal importance". The concept of natural prolongation was of some importance depending upon the circumstances, but not on the same plane as the satisfaction of equitable principles.[169] The Court also employed the "half-effect" principle for the Kerkennah Islands,[170] and emphasised that each continental shelf dispute had to be considered on its own merits having regard to its peculiar circumstance. No attempt should be made to "overconceptualise the application of the principles and rules relating to the continental shelf".[171]

The view of the Court that "the principles are subordinate to the goal" and that "[t]he principles to be indicated ... have to be selected according to their appropriateness for reaching an equitable result"[172] has led to criticism that the carefully drawn restriction on equity in the *North Sea Continental Shelf* cases[173] has been overturned and the element of predictability minimised. The dangers of an equitable solution based upon subjective assessments

---

[166] *Ibid.*, p.94; 54 *ILR*, p.101. This arose because of the presence of the British islands close to the French coast, which if given full effect would substantially reduce the French continental shelf. This was *prima facie* a circumstance creative of inequity, *ibid.*

[167] *Ibid.*, pp.116-17; 54 *ILR*, p.123.

[168] ICJ Reports, 1982, p.18; 67 *ILR*, p.4. See also Herman, "The Court Giveth and the Court Taketh Away", 33 *ICLQ*, 1984, p.825.

[169] *Ibid.*, p.47; 67 *ILR*, p.40. See also *Ibid.*, p.60; 67 *ILR*, p.53.

[170] *Ibid.*, p.89; 67 *ILR*, p.82. This was specified in far less constrained terms than in the *Anglo-French Continental Shelf* case, Cmnd. 7438, pp.116-17; 54 *ILR*, p.123. See e.g. Judge Gros' dissenting opinion, ICJ Reports, 1982, pp.18, 150; 67 *ILR*, p.143.

[171] *Ibid.*, p.92; 67 *ILR*, p.85.

[172] *Ibid.*, p.59; 67 *ILR*, p.52.

[173] ICJ Reports, 1969, pp.3, 49-50; 41 *ILR*, pp.29, 79.

of the facts, regardless of the law of delimitation, were pointed out by Judge Gros in his dissenting opinion.[174]

The Court in the *North Sea Continental Shelf* cases[175] in general discussed the relevance of the use of equitable principles in the context of the difficulty of applying the equidistance rule in specific geographical situations where inequity might result. In such a case, recourse may be had to equitable principles, provided a reasonable result was reached.

In the *Anglo-French Continental Shelf* case,[176] it was emphasised that:

> the appropriateness of the equidistance method or any other method for the purpose of effecting an equitable delimitation is a function or reflection of the geographical and other relevant circumstances of each particular case.

The methodological aspect here is particularly important, based as it is upon the requisite geographical framework.

A rigorous approach is rather less apparent in the *Tunisia-Libya* case, but the emphasis upon the solution, perhaps to the detriment of the method of reaching it, is reflected in recent cases. Indeed, article 83 of the 1982 Convention simply provides that delimitation "shall be effected by agreement on the basis of international law ... in order to achieve an equitable solution".

In the *Gulf of Maine* case,[177] which dealt with the delimitation of both the continental shelf and fisheries zones of Canada and the United States,[178] the Chamber of the ICJ produced two principles reflecting what general international law prescribes in every maritime delimitation. First, there could be no unilateral delimitations. Delimitations had to be sought and effected by agreement between the parties or if necessary with the aid of third parties. Secondly, it held that "delimitation is to be effected by the application of equitable criteria and by the use of practical methods capable of ensuring, with regard to the geographic configuration of the area

---

[174] ICJ Reports, 1982, pp.18, 153; 67 *ILR*, pp.4, 146.

[175] ICJ Reports, 1969, pp.3, 35-36; 41 *ILR*, pp.29, 64.

[176] Cmnd. 7438, p.59; 54 *ILR*, p.66.

[177] ICJ Reports, 1984, p.246; 71 *ILR*, p.74. See also Schneider, "The Gulf of Maine Case: The Nature of an Equitable Result", 79 *AJIL*, 1985, p.539.

[178] A "single maritime boundary" was requested by the parties, ICJ Reports, 1984, pp.246, 253; 71 *ILR*, p.80.

and other relevant circumstances, an equitable result".[179] The Court took as its starting point the criterion of the equal division of the areas of convergence and overlapping of the maritime projections of the coastlines of the states concerned, a criterion regarded as intrinsically equitable. This, however, had to be combined with the appropriate auxiliary criteria in the light of the relevant circumstances of the area itself. As regards the practical methods necessary to give effect to the above criteria, like the criteria themselves these had to be based upon geography and the suitability for the delimitation of both the seabed and the superjacent waters. Thus, it was concluded, geometrical methods would serve.[180] It will be noted that the basic rule for delimitation of the continental shelf is the same as that for the exclusive economic zone,[181] but the same boundary need not necessarily result.[182] The Chamber in the *Gulf of Maine* case indeed strongly emphasised "the unprecedented aspect of the case which lends it its special character", in that a single line delimiting both the shelf and fisheries zone was called for by the parties. Criteria found equitable with regard to a shelf delimitation need not necessarily possess the same properties with regard to a dual delimitation.[183] The above principles were reflected in the arbitral award in the *Guinea–Guinea-Bissau Maritime Delimitation* case in 1985.[184] The tribunal emphasised that the aim of any delimitation process was to achieve an equitable solution having regard to the relevant circumstances.[185] In the instant case, the concepts of natural prolongation and economic factors were in the circumstances of little assistance.[186]

In the *Libya-Malta Continental Shelf* case,[187] the International Court, in deciding the case according to customary law since Libya

[179] *Ibid.*, pp.299-300; 71 *ILR*, pp.126-27. This was regarded as the fundamental norm of customary international law governing maritime delimitation, *ibid.*, p.300.

[180] *Ibid.*, pp.328-29; 71 *ILR*, p.155. Note that the Chamber gave "half-effect" to Seal Island for reasons of equity, *ibid.*, p.337; 71 *ILR*, p.164.

[181] Article 74 of the 1982 Convention and *supra*, p.315.

[182] See e.g. the Australia-Papua New Guinea Maritime Boundaries Treaty of 1978, cited in Churchill and Lowe, *op. cit.*, p.160.

[183] ICJ Reports, 1984, pp.246, 326; 71 *ILR*, p.153.

[184] See 25 *ILM*, 1986, p.251; 77 *ILR*, p.636. The tribunal consisted of Judge Lachs, President and Judges Mbaye and Bedjaoui.

[185] *Ibid.*, p.289; 77 *ILR*, pp.675-76.

[186] *Ibid.*, pp.300-2; 77 *ILR*, p.686. It should be noted that the delimitation concerned a single line delimiting the territorial waters, continental shelves and economic zones of the respective countries.

[187] ICJ Reports, 1985, p.13; 81 *ILR*, p.239.

was not a party to the 1958 Convention on the Continental Shelf, emphasised the distance criterion. This arose because of the relevance of the economic zone concept, which was now held to be part of customary law, and the fact that an economic zone could not exist without rights over the seabed and subsoil similar to those enjoyed over a continental shelf. Thus the 200 mile limit of the zone had to be taken into account with regard to the delimitation of the continental shelf.[188] The fact that the law now permitted a state to claim a shelf of up to 200 miles from its coast, irrespective of geological characteristics, also meant that there was no reason to ascribe any role to geological or geographical factors within that distance.[189]

Since the basis of title to the shelf up to the 200 mile limit is recognised as the distance criterion, the Court felt that the drawing of a median line between opposite states was the most judicious manner of proceeding with a view to the eventual achievement of an equitable result. This provisional step had to be tested in the light of equitable principles in the context of the relevant circumstances.[190] The Court also followed the example of the *Tunisia-Libya* case[191] in examining the role of proportionality and in treating it as a test of the equitableness of any line.

However, the Court did consider the comparability of coastal lengths in the case as part of the process of reaching an equitable boundary, and used the disparity of coastal lengths of the parties as a reason for adjusting the median line so as to attribute a larger shelf area to Libya.[192] The general geographical context in which the islands of Malta exist as a relatively small feature in a semi-enclosed sea was also taken into account in this context.[193]

The Court in its analysis also referred to a variety of well-known examples of equitable principles, including abstention from refashioning nature, non-encroachment by one party on areas

---

[188] The Court emphasised that this did not mean that the concept of the continental shelf had been absorbed by that of the economic zone, but that greater importance had to be attributed to elements, such as distance from the coast, which are common to both, *ibid.*, p.33; 81 *ILR*, p.265.

[189] *Ibid.*

[190] *Ibid.*, p.47; 81 *ILR*, p.279.

[191] *Supra*, p.382.

[192] ICJ Reports, 1985, pp.48-50; 81 *ILR*, p.280.

[193] *Ibid.*, p.52; 81 *ILR*, p.284.

appertaining to the other, respect due to all relevant circumstances and the notions that equity did not necessarily mean equality and that there could be no question of distributive justice.[194] The Court, however, rejected Libya's argument that a state with a greater landmass would have a greater claim to the shelf and dismissed Malta's view that the relative economic position of the two states was of relevance.[195]

In conclusion, the Court reiterated in the operative provisions of its judgment, the following circumstances and factors that needed to be taken in account in the case:

(1) the general configuration of the coasts of the parties, their oppositeness, and their relationship to each other within the general context;

(2) the disparity in the lengths of the relevant coasts of the parties and the distance between them;

(3) the need to avoid in the delimitation any excessive disproportion between the extent of the continental shelf areas appertaining to the coastal state and the length of the relevant part of its coast, measured in the general direction of the coastlines.[196]

In discussing the variety of applicable principles, a distinction has traditionally been drawn between opposite and adjacent states for the purposes of delimitation. In the former case, the Court has noted that there is less difficulty in applying the equidistance method than in the latter, since the distorting effect of an individual geographical feature in the case of adjacent states is more likely to result in an inequitable delimitation. Accordingly, greater weight is to be placed upon equidistance in a delimitation of the shelf between opposite states in the context of equitable considerations,[197] than in the case of adjacent states where the range of applicable equitable principles may be more extensive and the relative importance of each particular

---

[194]   *Ibid.*, pp.39-40; 81 *ILR*, p.271.

[195]   *Ibid.*, pp.40-41; 81 *ILR*, p.272. The Court also noted that an equitable boundary between the parties had in the light of the general geographical situation to be south of a notional median line between Libya and Sicily, *ibid.*, p.51; 81 *ILR*, p.283.

[196]   *Ibid.*, pp.56-58; 81 *ILR*, p.288.

[197]   See *North Sea Continental Shelf* cases, ICJ Reports, 1969, pp.3, 36-37; 41 *ILR*, pp.29, 65; the *Anglo-French Continental Shelf* case, Cmnd. 7438, pp.58-59; 54 *ILR*, p.65; the *Tunisia-Libya Continental Shelf* case, ICJ Reports, 1982, pp.18, 88; 67 *ILR*, pp.4, 81, and the *Gulf of Maine* case, ICJ Reports, 1984, pp.246, 325; 71 *ILR*, pp.74, 152. See also article 6 of the Continental Shelf Convention, 1958.

principle less clear. Article 83 of the 1982 Convention, however, makes no distinction between delimitations on the basis of whether the states are in an opposite or adjacent relationship. The same need to achieve an equitable solution on the basis of international law is all that is apparent. Until the 1982 Convention comes into effect, one is obliged to have recourse to customary law, which posits the distinction. Once the 1982 Convention is in force, it will be interesting to note whether the distinction is totally eliminated or reappears within the framework of "international law".

The weight to be given to the criterion of proportionality between the length of the coastline and the area of continental shelf has also been the subject of some consideration and opinions have varied. It is a factor that must be cautiously applied.[198] It is as well to note that in the process of considering all the relevant factors in the attempt to reach an equitable solution, one is not seeking to do justice generally but to operate within the framework of legal rules, which themselves permit consideration of equitable matters.

Since the rule for delimitation of the economic zone in article 74 of the 1982 Convention is the same as for the continental shelf, one must assume that the same range of factors as noted above would similarly be relevant. However, it should be noted that treaty practice demonstrates that the equidistance principle tends to predominate.[199]

THE INTERNATIONAL SEABED [200]

Introduction

In recent years the degree of wealth contained beneath the high seas has become more and more apparent. It is estimated that some 175 billion dry tonnes of mineable manganese nodules are

---

[198] The Court in the *North Sea Continental Shelf* cases, in discussing this issue, called for a reasonable degree of proportionality, ICJ Reports, 1969, pp.3, 52; 41 *ILR*, pp.29, 82 while in the *Anglo-French Continental Shelf* case the Tribunal emphasised that it was disproportion rather than proportionality that was relevant in the context of the equities, Cmnd. 7438, pp.60-61; 54 *ILR*, pp.6, 67. But cf. the *Tunisia-Libya Continental Shelf* case, ICJ Reports, 1982, pp.18, 75; 67 *ILR*, pp.4, 75. See also the *Libya-Malta Continental Shelf* case, ICJ Reports, 1985, pp.48-50; 81 *ILR*, p.280.

[199] See Churchill and Lowe, *op. cit.*, pp.160-61.

[200] See e.g. O'Connell, *op. cit.* footnote 1, vol.1, Chapter 12; Churchill and Lowe, *op. cit.*, Chapter 12; Luard, *The Control of the Seabed*, 1974; Buzan, *Seabed Politics*, 1976; Kronmiller, *The Lawfulness of Deep Seabed Mining*, 2 vols., 1980, and Brown, *op. cit.*, vols.II and III.

in existence scattered over some 15 per cent of the seabed. This far exceeds the land-based reserves of the metals involved (primarily manganese, nickel, copper and cobalt).[201] While this source of mineral wealth is of great potential importance to the developed nations possessing or soon to possess the technical capacity to mine such nodules, it poses severe problems for developing states, particularly those who are dependent upon the export earnings of a few categories of minerals. Zaire, for example, accounts for over one third of total cobalt production, while Gabon and India each account for around 8 per cent of total manganese production.[202] At present there would appear to be six major deep sea mining consortia with the participation of numerous American, Japanese, Canadian, British, Belgian, West German, Dutch and French companies.[203] The technology to mine is at an advanced stage and some basic investment has been made, although it is unlikely that there will be considerable mining activity for several years to come.

In 1969, the UN General Assembly adopted resolution 2574 (XXIV) calling for a moratorium on deep seabed activities and a year later a Declaration of Principles Governing the Seabed and Ocean Floor and the Subsoil Thereof, beyond the Limits of National Jurisdiction[204] was adopted. This provided that the Area and its resources were the "common heritage of mankind" and could not be appropriated and that no rights at all could be acquired over it except in conformity with an international regime to be established to govern its exploration and exploitation.

The 1982 Law of the Sea Convention

Under the Convention, the Area[205] and its resources are deemed to be the common heritage of mankind and no sovereign or other rights may be recognised. Minerals recovered from the Area in accordance with the Convention are alienable, however.[206] Activities

---

[201] See e.g. *Seabed Mineral Resource Development*, UN Dept. of International Economic and Social Affairs, 1980, ST/ESA/107, pp.1-2.

[202] *Ibid.*, p.3.

[203] *Ibid.*, pp.10-12.

[204] Hereinafter "the Area".

[205] Defined in article 1 as the "seabed and ocean floor and subsoil thereof beyond national jurisdiction". This would start at the outer edge of the continental margin or at least at a distance of 200 nautical miles from the baselines.

[206] Articles 136 and 137.

in the Area are to be carried out for the benefit of mankind as a whole by or on behalf of the International Seabed Authority (the Authority) established under the Convention.[207] The Authority[208] is to provide for the equitable sharing of such benefits.[209] Activities in the Area are to be carried out under article 153 by the Enterprise (i.e. the organ of the Authority established as its operating arm) and by states parties or state enterprises, or persons possessing the nationality of state parties or effectively controlled by them, acting in association with the Authority. The latter "qualified applicants" will be required to submit formal written plans of work to be approved by the Council after review by the Legal and Technical Commission.[210]

This plan of work is to specify two sites of equal estimated commercial value. The Authority may then approve a plan of work relating to one of these sites and designate the other as a "reserved site" which may only be exploited by the Authority, via the Enterprise or in association with developing states.[211]

Resolution I of the Conference established a Preparatory Commission to make arrangements for the operation of the Authority and the International Tribunal for the Law of the Sea. It is currently preparing rules and regulations and carrying out research.[212]

Resolution II of the Conference makes special provision for eight "pioneer investors", four from France, Japan, India and the USSR and four from Belgium, Canada, the Federal Republic of Germany, Italy, Japan, the Netherlands, the UK and the USA, and possibly others from developing states, to be given pioneer status. Each investor must have invested at least $30 million in preparation for seabed mining at least ten per cent of which must be invested in a

---

[207] Articles 137 and 140. See also articles 156 and 157.

[208] The Authority is to consist of an Assembly (composed of all members of the Authority, i.e. all states parties to the Convention); a Council (36 members elected by the Assembly in accordance with certain criteria) acting as the executive organ and having an Economic Planning Commission and a Legal and Technical Commission and a Secretariat, see articles 158-169. The Enterprise which will be the organ of the Authority actually carrying out activities in the Area is also to be established, see article 170.

[209] Article 140. See also article 150.

[210] See also Annex III, articles 3 and 4. Highly controversial requirements for transfer of technology are also included, *ibid.*, article 5.

[211] *Ibid.*, articles 8 and 9. The production policies of the Authority are detailed in article 151 of the Convention.

[212] 21(4) *UN Chronicle*, 1984, p.44 *et seq.* See also 25 *ILM*, 1986, p.1329 and 26 *ILM*, 1987, p.1725.

specific site. Sponsoring states must provide certification that this has happened.[213] Such pioneer investors will be able to carry out exploration activities pending entry into force of the Convention and will have priority over the other applicants (apart from the Enterprise) in the allocation of exploitation contracts.[214] India, France, Japan and the USSR were registered as pioneer investors in 1987 on behalf of various consortia.[215]

The regime for the deep seabed, however, was opposed by the United States in particular and as a consequence it voted against the adoption of the 1982 Convention. The UK also declared that it would not sign the Convention until a satisfactory regime for deep seabed mining was established.[216] Concern was particularly expressed regarding the failure to provide assured access to seabed minerals, lack of a proportionate voice in decision-making for countries most affected and the problems that would be caused by not permitting the free play of market forces in the development of seabed resources.[217]

The Reciprocating States Regime

As a result of developments in the Conference on the Law of the Sea, many states began to enact domestic legislation with the aim of establishing an interim framework for exploration and exploitation of the seabed pending an acceptable international solution. The UK Deep Sea Mining (Temporary Provisions) Act, 1981, for example, provides for the granting of exploration licences (but not in respect of a period before 1 July 1981) and exploitation licences (but not in a period before 1 January 1988). The Act also provides for a Deep Sea Mining Levy to be paid by the holder of an exploitation licence into a Deep Sea Mining Fund. This fund may be paid over to an international organisation for the deep seabed if an agreement to create this has come into force for the UK. If this has not occurred within ten years, the fund will be wound up and paid into the

[213] See Churchill and Lowe, *op. cit.*, p.195.

[214] See 21(4) *UN Chronicle*, 1984, pp.45-47.

[215] See LOS/PCN/97-99 (1987). See also the Understanding of 5 September 1986 making various changes to the rules regarding pioneer operations, including extending the deadline by which the $30 million investment had to be made and establishing a Group of Technical Experts, LOS/PCN/L.41/Rev.1.

[216] See e.g. *The Times*, 16 February 1984, p.4.

[217] See e.g. the US delegate, *UN Chronicle*, June 1982, p.16.

Consolidated Fund. Section 3(1) provides that countries with similar legislation[218] may be designated as "reciprocating countries", which would allow for mutual recognition of licences.

A 1982 Agreement[219] calls for consultations to avoid overlapping claims under national legislation and for arbitration to resolve any dispute, while a 1984 Agreement[220] provides that no party shall issue an authorisation in respect of an application or seek registration of an area included in another application properly filed[221] and under consideration by another party; or within an area claimed in another application filed in conformity with national law and the instant Agreement before 3 April 1984 or earlier than the application or request for registration and which is still under consideration by another party; or within an authorisation granted by another party in conforming with the instant Agreement.

It is also provided that no party shall itself engage in deep seabed operations in an area for which it shall not issue an authorisation or seek registration, in accordance with the above provisions of the Agreement.

The Preparatory Commission, however, adopted a declaration in 1985 stating that any claim, agreement or action regarding the Area and its resources undertaken outside the Commission itself, which is incompatible with the 1982 Convention and its related resolutions, "shall not be recognised".[222] However, the Agreement on the Resolution of Practical Problems with respect to Deep Sea Mining Areas was signed in 1987 between Belgium, Italy, the Netherlands, Canada and the USSR, to which were attached Exchanges of Notes involving also the USA, UK and the Federal Republic of Germany.[223] It constituted an attempt to prevent

---

[218] A number of countries have adopted similar, unilateral legislation, e.g. the US in 1980, 19 *ILM*, 1980, p.1003; 20 *ILM*, 1981, p.1228 and 21 *ILM*, 1982, p.867; West Germany, 20 *ILM*, 1981, p.393 and 21 *ILM*, 1982, p.832; France, 21 *ILM*, 1982, p.808 and Japan, 22 *ILM*, 1983, p.102. Note that the USSR has also adopted similar unilateral legislation, but it is unlikely to join the reciprocating states system, see 21 *ILM*, 1982, p.551.

[219] The 1982 Agreement Concerning Interim Arrangements Relating to Polymetallic Nodules of the Deep Seabed (France, West Germany, UK, US), 21 *ILM*, 1982, p.950.

[220] Provisional Understanding Regarding Deep Seabed Mining (Belgium, France, West Germany, Italy, Japan, Netherlands, UK, USA), 23 *ILM*, 1984, p.1354. This was signed on 3 August 1984 and entered into force 2 September 1984.

[221] I.e. in conformity with the agreement for voluntary conflict resolution reached on 18 May 1983 and 15 December 1983.

[222] See *Law of the Sea Bulletin*, no.6, October 1985, p.85.

[223] 26 *ILM*, 1987, p.1502.

overlapping claims as between states within the Convention system and other states with regard to the Clarion-Clipperton Zone of the North-East Pacific, there being a particular problem, for example, between overlapping French and USSR claims.[224]

In any event, it is too early to determine how matters will evolve and the situation as a whole remains complex, confused and unsatisfactory.

SETTLEMENT OF DISPUTES [225]

The 1982 Convention contains detailed provisions regarding the resolution of law of the sea disputes. This involves conciliation procedures[226] or compulsory settlement under articles 286 and 287 relating to the International Tribunal for the Law of the Sea,[227] the ICJ, an arbitral tribunal[228] or a special arbitral tribunal to cover specific areas.[229]

There is a general obligation under article 279 for states to settle disputes by peaceful means, but they are able to choose methods other than those specified in the Convention.[230] States of the European Community, for example, have agreed to submit fisheries disputes amongst member states to the European Court of Justice under the EEC Treaty.

Outside the framework of the 1982 Convention, states may adopt a variety of means of resolving disputes, ranging from negotiations, inquiries,[231] conciliation,[232] arbitration,[233] and submission to the International Court of Justice.[234]

[224] See also 25 *ILM*, 1986, p.1326 and 26 *ILM*, 1987, p.1725.

[225] See e.g. Merrills, *International Dispute Settlement*, 2nd ed., 1991, Chapter 8; Churchill and Lowe, *op. cit.*, Chapter 19 and Adede, "Settlement of Disputes Arising Under the Law of the Sea Convention", 69 *AJIL*, 1975, p.798 and 72 *AJIL*, 1978, p.84.

[226] Article 284. See also Annex V.

[227] Annex VI. There is also provision for a Seabed Disputes Chamber of the Tribunal, *ibid.*, section 4.

[228] Annex VII.

[229] Annex VIII. The areas covered are fisheries, environmental protection, scientific research and navigation disputes.

[230] Article 280.

[231] E.g. the *Red Crusader* incident, 35 *ILR*, p.485.

[232] E.g. the *Jan Mayen Island Continental Shelf* dispute, 20 *ILM*, 1981, p.797; 62 *ILR*, p.108.

[233] E.g. the *Anglo-French Continental Shelf* case, Cmnd. 7438; 54 *ILR*, p.6.

[234] E.g. the *Anglo-Norwegian Fisheries* case, ICJ Reports, 1951, p.116; 18 *ILR*, p.84; the *North Sea Continental Shelf* cases, ICJ Reports, 1969, p.16; 41 *ILR*, p.29 and others referred to in this chapter.

CHAPTER ELEVEN

Jurisdiction [1]

Jurisdiction concerns the power of the state to affect people, property and circumstances and reflects the basic principles of state sovereignty, equality of states and non-interference in domestic affairs. Jurisdiction is a vital and indeed central feature of state sovereignty, for it is an exercise of authority which may alter or create or terminate legal relationships and obligations. It may be achieved by means of legislative action or by executive action or by judicial action. In each case, the recognised authorities of the state as determined by the legal system of that state perform certain functions permitted them which affect the life around them in various ways. In the UK, Parliament passes binding statutes, the courts make binding decisions and the administrative machinery of government has the power and jurisdiction (or legal authority) to enforce the rules of law. These differences, particularly between the capacity to make law (the prescriptive jurisdiction) and the capacity to ensure compliance with such law (the enforcement jurisdiction), are basic to an understanding of the legal competence of a state. This is to some extent because jurisdiction, although primarily territorial, may be based on other grounds, for example nationality, while enforcement is restricted by territorial factors.

To give an instance, if a man kills somebody in Britain and then manages to reach Holland, the British courts have jurisdiction to try him, but they cannot enforce it by sending officers to Holland to apprehend him. They must apply to the Dutch authorities for his arrest and despatch to Britain. If on the other hand, the murderer remains in Britain then he may be arrested and tried there, even if it becomes apparent that he is a German national. Thus, while the prescriptive jurisdiction may be exercised as regards events happening within the territorial limits irrespective of whether or not the actors are nationals or not, and may be founded on nationality as in the case of a British subject suspected of murder committed

---

[1] See e.g. Akehurst, "Jurisdiction in International Law", 46 *BYIL*, 1972-3, p.145; Mann, "The Doctrine of Jurisdiction in International Law", 111 *HR*, p.1 and "The Doctrine of International Law Revisited After Twenty Years", 186 *HR*, p.9; Bowett, "Jurisdiction: Changing Problems of Authority over Activities and Resources", 53 *BYIL*, 1982, p.1 and Jennings, "Extraterritorial Jurisdiction and the United States Antitrust Laws", 33 *BYIL*, 1957, p.146.

abroad who may be tried for the offence in the UK (if he is found in the UK, of course) enforcement jurisdiction is another matter entirely. It is restricted, fundamentally, to the presence of the suspect in the territorial limits.

However, there are circumstances in which it may be possible to apprehend a suspected murderer, but the jurisdictional basis is lacking. For example, if a Frenchman has committed a murder in Germany he cannot be tried for it in Britain, notwithstanding his presence in the country, although, of course, both France and Germany may apply for his extradition and return to their respective countries from Britain.

Thus, while jurisdiction is closely linked with territory it is not exclusively so tied. Many states have jurisdiction to try offences that have take place outside their territory, and in addition certain persons, property and situations are immune from the territorial jurisdiction in spite of being situated or taking place there. Diplomats, for example, have extensive immunity from the laws of the country in which they are working[2] and various sovereign acts by states may not be questioned or overturned in the courts of a foreign country.[3]

The whole question of jurisdiction is complex and unclear, not least because of the relevance also of constitutional issues and conflict of laws rules. International law tries to set down rules dealing with the limits of a state's exercise of governmental functions while conflict of laws (or private international law as it is sometimes referred to) will attempt to regulate in a case involving a foreign element whether the particular country has jurisdiction to determine the question, and secondly if it has, then the rules of which country will be applied in resolving the dispute.

The grounds for the exercise of jurisdiction are not identical in the cases of international law and conflict of laws rules. In the latter branch of legal study, specific subjects may well be regulated in terms of domicile or residence (for instance as regards the recognition of foreign marriages or divorces) but such grounds would not found jurisdiction where international law matters were concerned.[4] Although it is by no means impossible or in all cases difficult to keep apart the categories of international law and

---

[2] *Infra*, Chapter 12, p.462.
[3] *Ibid.*, p.430.
[4] See generally, Cheshire and North, *Private International Law*, 11th ed., 1987.

conflict of laws, nevertheless the often different definitions of jurisdiction involved are a confusing factor.

One should also be aware of the existence of disputes as to jurisdictional competence within the area of constitutional matters. These problems arise in federal court structures, as in the United States, where conflicts as to the extent of authority of particular courts may arise.

While the relative exercise of powers by the legislative, executive and judicial organs of government is a matter for the municipal legal and political system, the extraterritorial application of jurisdiction will depend upon the rules of international law and in this chapter we shall examine briefly the most important of these rules.

THE PRINCIPLE OF DOMESTIC JURISDICTION [5]

It follows from the nature of the sovereignty of states that while a state is supreme internally, that is within its own territorial frontiers, it must not intervene in the domestic affairs of another nation. This duty of non-intervention within the domestic jurisdiction of states provides for the shielding of certain state activities from the regulation of international law. State functions which are regarded as beyond the reach of international legal control and within the exclusive sphere of state management include the setting of conditions for the grant of nationality and the elaboration of the circumstances in which aliens may enter the country.

However, the influence of international law is beginning to make itself felt in areas hitherto regarded as subject to the state's exclusive jurisdiction. For example the treatment by a country of its own nationals is now viewed in the context of international human rights regulations, although in practice the effect of this has often been disappointing.[6]

Domestic jurisdiction is a relative concept, in that changing principles of international law have had the effect of limiting and reducing its extent[7] and in that matters of internal regulation may

[5] See e.g. Brownlie, *Principles of Public International Law*, 4th ed., 1990, p.291 and Rajan, *United Nations and Domestic Jurisdiction*, 2nd ed., 1961. See further *supra*, Chapter 4.

[6] *Supra*, Chapter 6.

[7] Whether a matter is or is not within the domestic jurisdiction of states is itself a question for international law, see *Nationality Decrees in Tunis and Morocco* case, PCIJ, Series B, no.4, 1923, pp.7, 23-24; 2 *ILR*, pp.349, 352.

well have international repercussions and thus fall within the ambit of international law. This latter point was mentioned in a couple of important cases before the International Court of Justice.

In the *Anglo-Norwegian Fisheries* case[8] it was stressed that:

> [a]lthough it is true that the act of delimitation [of territorial waters] is necessarily a unilateral act, because only the coastal state is competent to undertake it, the validity of the delimitation with regard to other states depends upon international law.[9]

The principle was also noted in the *Nottebohm* case,[10] where the Court remarked that while a state may formulate such rules as it wished regarding the acquisition of nationality, the exercise of diplomatic protection upon the basis of nationality was within the purview of international law.

There is also the basic rule that no state may plead its municipal laws as a justification for the breach of an obligation of international law.[11]

Accordingly, the dividing line between issues firmly within domestic jurisdiction on the one hand, and issues susceptible to international legal regulation on the other is by no means as inflexible as at first may appear.

Article 2(7) of the UN Charter declares that:

> [n]othing contained in the present Charter shall authorise the United Nations to intervene in matters which are essentially within the domestic jurisdiction of any state or shall require the members to submit such matters to settlement under the present Charter.

This paragraph, intended as a practical restatement and reinforcement of domestic jurisdiction, has constantly been reinterpreted in the decades since it was first enunciated. It has certainly not prevented the United Nations from discussing or adopting resolutions relating to the internal policies of member-states and the result of forty years of practice has been the further restriction and erosion of domestic jurisdiction.

---

[8] ICJ Reports, 1951, p.116; 18 *ILR*, p.86.
[9] *Ibid.*, p.132; 18 *ILR*, p.95.
[10] ICJ Reports, 1955, pp.4, 20-21; 22 *ILR*, pp.349, 357.
[11] *Supra*, Chapter 4, p.104.

In the late 1940s and 1950s, the European colonial powers fought a losing battle against the United Nations debate and adoption of resolutions concerning the issues of self-determination and independence for their colonies. The involvement of the United Nations in human rights matters is constantly deepening and South African domestic policies of apartheid have been continually criticised and condemned. The expanding scope of United Nations concern has succeeded in further limiting the extent of the doctrine of domestic jurisdiction.[12] Nevertheless, the concept does retain validity in recognising the basic fact that state sovereignty within its own territorial limits is the undeniable foundation of international law as it has evolved, and of the world political and legal system.[13]

LEGISLATIVE, EXECUTIVE AND JUDICIAL JURISDICTION

Legislative jurisdiction[14] refers to the supremacy of the constitutionally recognised organs of the state to make binding laws within its territory. Such acts of legislation may extend abroad in certain circumstances.[15] The state has legislative exclusivity in many areas. For example, a state lays down the procedural techniques to be adopted by its various organs, such as courts, but can in no way seek to alter the way in which foreign courts operate. This is so even though an English court might refuse to recognise a judgment of a foreign court on the grounds of manifest bias. An English law cannot then be passed purporting to alter the procedural conditions under which the foreign courts operate.

International law accepts that a state may levy taxes against persons not within the territory of that state, so long as there is some kind of real link between the state and the proposed taxpayer, whether it be nationality or domicile or whatever.[16] A state may nationalise foreign owned property situated within its borders,[17] but it cannot purport to take over foreign owned property situated abroad. It will be obvious that such a regulation could not be

[12] See e.g. Higgins, *The Development of International Law Through the Political Organs of the United Nations,* 1963.

[13] Note also the importance of the doctrine of the exhaustion of domestic remedies, see *supra,* Chapter 6, p.239.

[14] See e.g. Akehurst, *op. cit.,* p.179 *et seq.*

[15] See further *infra,* p.423.

[16] Akehurst, *op. cit.,* pp.179-80.

[17] See *infra,* Chapter 13, p.516.

enforced abroad, but the reference here is to the prescriptive jurisdiction, or capacity to pass valid laws.

The question of how far a court will enforce foreign legislation is a complicated one within, basically, the field of conflict of laws, but in practice it is rare for one state to enforce the penal or tax laws of another state.[18]

Although legislative supremacy within a state cannot be denied, it may be challenged. A state that adopts laws that are contrary to the provisions of international law, for example as regards the treatment of aliens or foreign property within the country, will render itself liable for a breach of international law on the international scene, and will no doubt find itself faced with protests and other action by the foreign state concerned. It is also possible that a state which abuses the rights it possesses to legislate for its nationals abroad may be guilty of a breach of international law. For example, if France were to order its citizens living abroad to drive only French cars, this would most certainly infringe the sovereignty and independence of the states in which such citizens were residing and would constitute an illegitimate exercise of French legislative jurisdiction.[19]

Executive jurisdiction relates to the capacity of the state to act within the borders of another state.[20] Since states are independent of each other and possess territorial sovereignty,[21] it follows that generally state officials may not carry out their functions on foreign soil (in the absence of express consent by the host state)[22] and may not enforce the laws of their state upon foreign territory. British policemen, for instance, cannot operate in France to arrest any

[18] See e.g. Cheshire and North, *op. cit.*, Chapter 8. English courts in general will not enforce the penal laws of foreign states. It will be for the court to decide what a foreign penal law is, *ibid.*, p.34. See also *Huntington* v. *Attrill*, [1893] AC 150, and Marshall CJ, *The Antelope*, 10 Wheat 123 (1825). As far as tax laws are concerned see *Government of India* v. *Taylor*, [1955] AC 491; 22 *ILR*, p.286. See in addition *Attorney-General of New Zealand* v. *Ortiz*, [1982] 31 All ER 432; 78 *ILR*, p.608, particularly Lord Denning, and *ibid.*, [1983] 3 All ER 93 (House of Lords); 78 *ILR*, p.631. See also *Williams & Humbert* v. *W & H Trade Marks*, [1985] 2 All ER 619 and [1986] 1 All ER 129 (House of Lords); 75 *ILR*, p.269 and *Re State of Norway's Application*, [1986] 3 WLR 452 and [1989] 1 All ER 745, 760-62 (House of Lords).

[19] See Mann, *op. cit.*, pp.36-62.

[20] See Akehurst, *op. cit.*, p.147.

[21] See e.g. *Lotus* case, PCIJ, Series A, no.10, 1927, p.18; 4 *ILR*, p.153 and the *Island of Palmas* case, 2 *RIAA*, pp.829, 838 (1928); 4 *ILR*, p.103.

[22] This cannot, of course, be taken too far. An official would still be entitled, for example, to sign a contract, see Akehurst, *op. cit.*, p.147.

person, and French tax inspectors are not able to collect taxes in Spain. It is also contrary to international law for state agents to apprehend persons or property abroad. The seizure of the Nazi criminal Eichmann by Israeli agents in Argentina in 1960 was a clear breach of Argentina's territorial sovereignty and an illegal exercise of Israeli jurisdiction.[23] Similarly, the unauthorised entry into a state of military forces of another state is clearly an offence under international law.

Judicial jurisdiction[24] concerns the power of the courts of a particular country to try cases in which a foreign factor is present. There are a number of grounds upon which the courts of a state may claim to exercise such jurisdiction. In criminal matters these range from the territorial principle to the universality principle and in civil matters from the mere presence of the defendant in the country to the nationality and domicile principles. It is judicial jurisdiction which forms the most discussed aspect of jurisdiction and criminal questions the most important manifestation of this.

CIVIL JURISDICTION [25]

Although jurisdiction in civil matters is enforced in the last resort by the application of the sanctions of criminal law, there are a number of differences between civil and criminal issues in this context.

In general it is fair to say that the exercise of civil jurisdiction has been claimed by states upon far wider grounds than has been the case in criminal matters, and the resultant reaction by other states much more muted.[26] This is partly due to the fact that public opinion is far more easily roused where a person is tried abroad for criminal offences than if a person is involved in a civil case.

In common law countries, such as the United States and Britain, the usual basis for jurisdiction in civil cases remains service of a writ upon the defendant within the country, even if the presence of the defendant is purely temporary and coincidental.[27] In continental

---

[23] See further, *infra*, p.413.

[24] See e.g. Akehurst, *op. cit.*, p.152 *et seq.*

[25] *Ibid.*, p.170 *et seq.*; Mann, *op. cit.*, pp.49-51 and Brownlie, *op. cit.*, p.299. See also Bowett, *op. cit.*, pp.1-4.

[26] See e.g. Akehurst, *op. cit.*, p.152 *et seq.*

[27] See e.g. *Maharanee of Baroda* v. *Wildenstein*, [1972] 2 All ER 689. See also the Civil Jurisdiction and Judgments Act, 1982.

European countries on the other hand, the usual ground for jurisdiction is the habitual residence of the defendant in the particular state.

Many countries, for instance Holland, Denmark and Sweden, will allow their courts to exercise jurisdiction where the defendant in any action possesses assets in the state, while in matrimonial cases the commonly accepted ground for the exercise of jurisdiction is the domicile or residence of the party bringing the action, as is clear from the 1970 Hague Convention on the Recognition of Divorces and Legal Separations.

In view of, for example, the rarity of diplomatic protests and the relative absence of state discussions, some writers have concluded that customary international law does not prescribe any particular regulations as regards the restriction of courts' jurisdiction in civil matters.[28]

CRIMINAL JURISDICTION [29]

The application by municipal courts of their own powers and the rules of their state to cases involving foreign persons, property or events is a crucial topic although complicated by the convergence of principles from international law and conflict of laws. A number of definite principles upon which to base jurisdiction have emerged, with varying degrees of support and of different historical legitimacy.

The Territorial Principle

This concept reflects one aspect of the sovereignty exercisable by a state in its territorial home, and is the indispensable foundation for the application of the series of legal rights that a state possesses.[30] That a country should be able to prosecute for offences committed upon its soil is a logical manifestation of a world order of independent

---

[28] See e.g. Akehurst, *op. cit.*, p.177. Cf. Mann, *op. cit.*, pp.49-51 and see also Brownlie, *op. cit.*, p.299, and Bowett, *op. cit.*, pp.3-4.

[29] See e.g. Akehurst, *op. cit.*, p.152 *et seq.*; Mann, *op. cit.*, p.82 *et seq.* and O'Connell, *International Law*, 2nd ed., 1970, vol.2, pp.823-31.

[30] See Lord Macmillan, *Compania Naviera Vascongado* v. *Cristina SS*, [1938] AC 485, 496-97; 9 *ILR*, pp.250, 259. Note also Bowett's view that the "dynamism and adaptability of the principle in recent years has been quite remarkable", *op. cit.*, p.5 and Marshall, CJ in *The Schooner Exchange* v. *McFaddon*, 7 Cranch 116, 136 (1812) to the effect that "[t]he jurisdiction of the nation within its own territory is necessarily exclusive and absolute".

states and is entirely reasonable since the authorities of a state are responsible for the conduct of law and the maintenance of good order within that state. It is also highly convenient since in practice the witnesses to the crime will be situated in the country and more often than not the alleged offender will be there too.

Thus, all crimes committed (or alleged to have been committed) within the territorial jurisdiction of a state may come before the municipal courts and the accused if convicted may be sentenced. This is so even where the offenders are foreign citizens.

The principle whereby criminal jurisdiction is based upon the territory of the state claiming to try the offence is the principal ground for the exercise of jurisdiction, although not the exclusive one. There are others, such as nationality, but the majority of prosecutions occurring where a crime has been involved take place because the crime was committed within the territory of the state.

However, the territorial concept is more extensive than at first appears since it encompasses not only crimes committed on the territory of a state but also crimes in which only part of the offence has occurred in the state, for example where a person fires a weapon across a frontier killing somebody.

Both the state where the gun was fired and the state where the injury actually took place have jurisdiction to try the offender, the former under the so-called objective territorial principle. Of course, which of the states will in the event exercise its jurisdiction will depend upon where the offender is situated, but the point remains that both the state where the offence was commenced and the state where the offence was concluded may validly try the offender.[31]

Such a situation would also apply in cases of offences against immigration regulations and in cases of conspiracy where activities have occurred in each of two, or more, countries.[32]

---

[31] See e.g. the *Lotus case*, PCIJ, Series A, no.10, 1927, pp.23, 30; 4 *ILR*, pp.153, 159 and Judge Moore, *ibid.*, p.73; the Harvard Research Draft Convention on Jurisdiction with Respect to Crime, 29 *AJIL*, 1935, Suppl., p.480 (article 3) and Akehurst, *op. cit.*, pp.152-53. See Lord Wilberforce, *DPP* v. *Doot*, [1973] AC 807, 817; 57 *ILR*, pp.117, 119; *R* v. *Berry*, [1984] 3 All ER 1008, and Restatement of the Foreign Relations Law of the US, 1965, para.17. See also *Strassheim* v. *Dailey*, 221 US 280 (1911); *US* v. *Columba-Colella*, 604 F.2d 356 and *US* v. *Perez-Herrera*, 610 F.2d 289.

[32] See e.g. *Board of Trade* v. *Owen*, [1957] AC 602, 634 and *DPP* v. *Stonehouse*, [1977] 2 All ER 909, 916; 73 *ILR*, p.252. Note also Akehurst, who would restrict the operation of the doctrine so that jurisdiction could only be claimed by the state where the primary effect is felt, *op. cit.*, p.154.

The nature of territorial sovereignty in relation to criminal acts was examined in the *Lotus* case.[33] The relevant facts may be summarised as follows. The French steamer, the *Lotus*, was involved in a collision on the high seas with the *Boz-Kourt*, a Turkish collier. The latter vessel sank and eight sailors and passengers died as a result. Because of this the Turkish authorities arrested the French officer of the watch (at the time of the incident) when the *Lotus* reached a Turkish port.

The French officer was charged with manslaughter and France protested strongly against this action, alleging that Turkey did not have the jurisdiction to try the offence. The case came before the Permanent Court of International Justice, which was called upon to decide whether there existed an international rule prohibiting the Turkish exercise of jurisdiction.

Because the basis of international law is the existence of sovereign states, the Court regarded it as axiomatic that restrictions upon the independence of states could not be presumed.[34] However, a state was not able to exercise its power outside its frontiers in the absence of a permissive rule of international law. But, continued the Court, this did not mean that "international law prohibits a state from exercising jurisdiction in its own territory, in respect of any case which relates to acts which have taken place abroad and in which it cannot rely on some permissive rule of international law". In this respect, states had a wide measure of discretion limited only in certain instances by prohibitive rules.[35]

Because of this, countries had adopted a number of different rules extending their jurisdiction beyond the territorial limits so that "the territoriality of criminal law, therefore, is not an absolute principle of international law and by no means coincides with territorial sovereignty".[36]

The Court rejected the French claim that the flag-state had exclusive jurisdiction over the ship on the high seas, saying that no rule to that effect had emerged in international law, and stated that the damage to the Turkish vessel was equivalent to affecting Turkish

---

[33] PCIJ, Series A, no.10, 1927; 4 *ILR*, p.153. See e.g. Mann, *op. cit.*, pp.33-36, 39, 92-93 and Verzijl, *The Jurisprudence of the World Court*, vol.1, 1965, pp.73-98.

[34] PCIJ, Series A, no.10, 1927, pp.18-19; 4 *ILR*, p.155.

[35] *Ibid.*, p.19; 4 *ILR*, p.156.

[36] *Ibid.*, p.20.

territory so as to enable that country to exercise jurisdiction on the objective territorial principle, unrestricted by any rule of international law prohibiting this.[37]

The general pronouncements by the Court leading to the dismissal of the French contentions have been criticised by writers for a number of years, particularly with respect to its philosophical approach in treating states as possessing very wide powers of jurisdiction which could only be restricted by proof of a rule of international law prohibiting the action concerned.[38] It is widely accepted today that the emphasis lies the other way around.[39]

It should also be noted that the *Lotus* principle as regards collisions at sea has been overturned by article 11(1) of the High Seas Convention 1958, which emphasised that only the flag-state or the state of which the alleged offender was a national has jurisdiction over sailors regarding incidents occurring on the high seas.

The territorial principle covers crimes committed not only upon the land territory of the state but also upon the territorial sea and in certain cases upon the contiguous and other zones and on the high seas where the state is the flag-state of the vessel.[40]

The Nationality Principle [41]

Since every state possesses sovereignty and jurisdictional powers and since every state must consist of a collection of individual human beings, it is essential that a link between the two be legally established. That link connecting the state and the people it includes in its territory is provided by the concept of nationality.

By virtue of nationality, a person becomes entitled to a series of rights ranging from obtaining a valid passport enabling him to

[37] *Ibid.*, p.24; 4 *ILR*, p.158.

[38] See e.g. Fitzmaurice, "The General Principles of International Law Considered from the Standpoint of the Rule of Law", 92 *HR*, pp.1, 56-57 and Lauterpacht, *International Law: Collected Papers*, vol.1, 1970, pp.488-89.

[39] See e.g. the *Anglo-Norwegian Fisheries* case, ICJ Reports, 1951, p.116; 18 *ILR*, p.86 and the *Nottebohm* case, ICJ Reports, 1955, p.4; 22 *ILR*, p.349.

[40] See *supra*, Chapter 10, pp.353, 358 and 366.

[41] Akehurst, *op. cit.*, pp.156-57; Harvard Research Draft Convention on Jurisdiction with Respect to Crime, 29 *AJIL*, 1935, Suppl., p.519 *et seq.*; Whiteman, *Digest, op. cit.*, vol.8, pp.1-22, 64-101, 105-113, 119-87; and Silving, "Nationality in Comparative Law", 5 *American Journal of Comparative Law*, 1956, p.410. See also further, *infra*, Chapter 13, p.503, and Brownlie, *op. cit.*, p.303 and Chapter XVIII.

travel abroad to being able to vote. In addition, nationals may be able to undertake various jobs (for example in the diplomatic service) that a non-national may be barred from. Nationals are also entitled to the protection of their state and to various benefits prescribed under international law. On the other hand, states may not mistreat the nationals of other states nor, ordinarily, conscript them into their armed forces, nor prosecute them for crimes committed outside the territory of the particular state.

The concept of nationality is important since it determines the benefits to which persons may be entitled and the obligations (such as conscription) which they must perform.

The problem is that there is no coherent, accepted definition of nationality in international law and only conflicting descriptions under the different municipal laws of states. Not only that, but the rights and duties attendant upon nationality vary from state to state.

Generally, international law leaves the conditions for the grant of nationality to the domestic jurisdiction of states.

This was the central point in the *Nationality Decrees in Tunis and Morocco* case.[42] This concerned a dispute between Britain and France over French nationality decrees which had the effect of giving French nationality to the children of certain British subjects. The Court, which had been requested to give an advisory opinion by the Council of the League of Nations, declared that:

> [t]he question of whether a certain matter is or is not solely within the jurisdiction of a state is an essentially relative question, it depends upon the development of international relations. Thus, in the present state of international law, questions of nationality are, in the opinion of this court, in principle within this reserved domain.[43]

However, although states may prescribe the conditions for the grant of nationality, international law is relevant, especially where other states are involved. As was emphasised in article I of the 1930 Hague Convention on the Conflict of Nationality Laws:

> it is for each state to determine under its own law who are its nationals. This law shall be recognised by other states in so far as it is consistent

---

[42] PCIJ, Series B, no.4, 1923; 2 *ILR*, p.349.
[43] *Ibid.*, p.24.

with international conventions, international custom and the principles of law generally recognised with regard to nationality.

The International Court of Justice noted in the *Nottebohm* case[44] that according to state practice, nationality was:

> a legal bond having as its basis a social fact of attachment, a genuine connection of existence, interests and sentiments, together with the existence of reciprocal rights and duties.

It was a legal manifestation of the link between the person and the state granting nationality and a recognition that the person was more closely connected with that state than with any other.

Since the concept of nationality provides the link between the individual and the benefits of international law, it is worth pointing to some of the basic ideas associated with the concept, particularly with regard to its acquisition.[45]

In general, the two most important principles upon which nationality is founded in states are first by descent from parents who are nationals (*jus sanguinis*) and second by virtue of being born within the territory of the state (*jus soli*).

It is commonly accepted that a child born of nationals of a particular state should be granted the nationality of that state by reason of descent. This idea is particularly utilised in continental European countries, for example, France, Germany and Switzerland, where the child will receive the nationality of his father, although many municipal systems do provide that an illegitimate child will take the nationality of his mother. On the other hand, in common law countries such as Britain and the US the doctrine of the *jus sanguinis* is more restricted, so that where a father has become a national by descent it does not always follow that that fact alone will be sufficient to make the child a national.

The common law countries have tended to adopt the *jus soli* rule, whereby any child born within the territorial limits of the state automatically becomes a national thereof.[46] The British Nationality

---

[44] ICJ Reports, 1955, pp.4, 23; 22 *ILR*, pp.349, 360. See also *infra*, p.505.

[45] See e.g. Brownlie, *op. cit.*, pp.386-89; Weiss, *Nationality and Statelessness in International Law*, 1956 and Van Panhuys, *The Role of Nationality in International Law*, 1959.

[46] See e.g. *United States* v. *Wong Kim Ark*, 169 US 649 (1898).

Act of 1948, for example, declared that "every person born within the United Kingdom and Colonies ... shall be a citizen of the United Kingdom and Colonies by birth".[47] There is an exception to this, however, which applies to virtually every country applying the *jus soli* rule, and that is with regard to persons entitled to immunity from the jurisdiction of the state. In other words, the children of diplomatic personnel born within the country do not automatically acquire its nationality.[48] Precisely how far this exception extends varies from state to state. Some countries provide that this rule applies also to the children of enemy alien fathers[49] born in areas under enemy occupation.[50]

Nationality may also be acquired by the wives of nationals, although here again the position varies from state to state. Some states provide for the automatic acquisition of the husband's nationality, others for the conditional acquisition of nationality and others merely state that the marriage has no effect as regards nationality. Problems were also caused in the past by the fact that many countries stipulated that a woman marrying a foreigner would thereby lose her nationality.

The Convention of 1957 on the Nationality of Married Women provides that contracting states accept that the marriage of one of its nationals with an alien shall not automatically affect the wife's nationality, although a wife may acquire her husband's nationality by special procedures should she so wish.

It should be noted also that article 9 of the Convention on the Elimination of All Forms of Discrimination against Women 1979 provides that states parties shall grant women equal rights with men to acquire, change or retain their nationality and that in particular neither marriage to an alien nor change of nationality by the husband during marriage shall automatically change the nationality of the wife, render her stateless or force upon her the nationality of the husband. It is also provided that women shall have

---

[47] But see now the British Nationality Act of 1981.

[48] See e.g. *In Re Thenault*, 47 F.Supp. 952 (1942) and article 12, Convention on Conflict of Nationality Law, 1930. See also article II, Optional Protocol on Acquisition of Nationality, (UN Conference on Diplomatic Law), 1961.

[49] But see *Inglis* v. *Sailor's Snug Harbour*, 3 Peters 99 (1830), US Supreme Court.

[50] Note the various problems associated with possible extensions of the *jus soli* rule, e.g. regarding births on ships, see Brownlie, *op. cit.*, pp.388-89. See also *Lam Mow* v. *Nagle*, 24 F.2d 316 (1928); 4 *ILR*, pp.295, 296.

equal rights with men with respect to the nationality of their children. As far as children themselves are concerned, article 24(3) of the International Covenant on Civil and Political Rights 1966 stipulated that every child has the right to acquire a nationality, while this is reaffirmed in article 7 of the Convention on the Rights of the Child 1989.

Nationality may be obtained by an alien by virtue of a naturalisation process usually involving a minimum period of residence, but the conditions under which this takes place vary considerably from country to country.[51]

Civil jurisdiction, especially as regards matters of personal status, in a number of countries depends upon the nationality of the parties involved. So that, for example, the appropriate matrimonial law in any dispute for a Frenchman anywhere would be French law. However, common law countries tend to base the choice of law in such circumstances upon the law of the state where the individual involved has his permanent home (domicile).

Many countries, particularly those with a legal system based upon the continental European model, claim jurisdiction over crimes committed by their nationals, notwithstanding that the offence may have occurred in the territory of another state. Common law countries tend, however, to restrict the crimes over which they will exercise jurisdiction over their nationals abroad to very serious ones. The English courts, for instance, generally limit such claims to treason, murder and bigamy committed by British nationals abroad.[52] But the common law countries have never protested against the extensive use of the nationality principle to found jurisdiction in criminal matters by other states.

[51] See e.g. Weiss, *op. cit.*, p.101.

[52] See e.g. Official Secrets Acts, 1911, (s.10); 1970 (s.8) and 1989 (s.15) and Offences Against the Person Act, 1861, ss.9 and 57. See also Merchant Shipping Act, 1894, s.686 (1) and *R* v. *Kelly*, [1982] AC 665; 77 *ILR*, p.284. Note that in *Skiriotes* v. *Florida*, 313 US 69, 73 (1941); 10 *ILR*, pp.258, 260, Hughes CJ declared that "the United States is not debarred by any rule of international law from governing the conduct of its own citizens upon the high seas or even in foreign countries when the rights of other nations or their nationals are not infringed". See also *DUSPIL*, 1976, pp.449-57, regarding legislation to subject US nationals and citizens to US district court jurisdiction for crimes committed outside the US, particularly regarding Antarctica.

The Passive Personality Principle [53]

Under this heading, a state will claim jurisdiction to try an individual for offences committed abroad which have affected or will affect nationals of the state.

The leading case on this particular principle is the *Cutting* case in 1886,[54] which concerned the publication in Texas of a defamatory statement by an American citizen of a Mexican. Cutting was arrested while in Mexico and convicted of the offence (a crime under Mexican law) with Mexico maintaining its right to jurisdiction upon the basis of the passive personality principle. The United States strongly protested against this, but there was an inconclusive end to the incident, the charges being withdrawn by the injured party.[55]

A strong attack on this principle was made by Judge Moore, in a dissenting opinion in the *Lotus* case,[56] since the Turkish criminal code provided for jurisdiction where harm resulted to a Turkish national. However, the Court did not resolve the issue and concentrated upon the objective territorial jurisdiction principle.[57]

The overall opinion has been that the passive personality principle is rather a dubious ground upon which to base claims to jurisdiction under international law and it has been strenuously opposed by the US[58] and Britain, although a number of states apply it.

However, article 9 of the International Convention against the Taking of Hostages 1979, in detailing the jurisdictional bases that could be established with regard to the offence, included the national state of a hostage "if that state considers it appropriate".[59] The possibility of using the passive personality concept was taken

---

[53] See e.g. Akehurst, *op. cit.*, pp.162-66; Mann, *op. cit.*, pp.40-41 and Bishop, "General Course of Public International Law, 1965", 115 *HR*, pp.151, 324. See also the *Eichmann* case, 36 *ILR*, pp.5, 49-57, 304.

[54] Moore, *Digest of International Law*, 1906, vol.2, p.228.

[55] See *US Foreign Relations*, 1886, p.viii; *ibid.*, 1887, p.757 and *ibid.*, 1888, vol.II, p.1114.

[56] PCIJ, Series A, no.10, 1927, p.92.

[57] *Ibid.*, pp.22-23. See also O'Connell, *op. cit.*, vol.2, pp.901-2.

[58] See, for example, US protests to Greece, concerning the service of summonses by Greek Consuls in the US on US nationals involved in accidents with Greek nationals occurring in the United States, *DUSPIL*, 1973, pp.197-98 and *DUSPIL*, 1975, pp.339-40.

[59] See generally, Lambert, *Terrorism and Hostages in International Law*, 1990. See also article 3(1)c of the Convention on the Prevention and Punishment of Crimes against Internationally Protected Persons 1973 and article 5(1)c of the Convention against Torture 1984.

up by the US in 1984 in the Comprehensive Crime Control Act[60] *inter alia* implementing the Convention and in the provision extending the special maritime and territorial jurisdiction of the US to include "[a]ny place outside the jurisdiction of any nation with respect to an offence by or against a national of the United States".[61] In 1986, following the *Achille Lauro* incident,[62] the US adopted the Omnibus Diplomatic Security and Anti-Terrorism Act,[63] inserting into the criminal code a new section which provided for US jurisdiction over homicide and physical violence outside the US where a national of the US is the victim. The section is less sweeping than it appears, since the written certification of the Attorney General is required, before a prosecution may commence by the US, to the effect that the offence was intended to coerce, intimidate or retaliate against a government or a civilian population.

In *US* v. *Yunis (No.2)*[64] the issue concerned the apprehension of a Lebanese citizen by US agents in international waters and his prosecution in the US for alleged involvement in the hijacking of a Jordanian airliner. The only connection between the hijacking and the US was the fact that several American nationals were on that flight. The Court accepted that both the universality principle[65] and the passive personality principle provided an appropriate basis for jurisdiction in the case. It was stated that although the latter principle was the most controversial of the jurisdictional principles in international law, "the international community recognises its legitimacy".[66] It was pointed out that although the US had historically opposed the passive personality principle, it had been accepted by the US and the international community in recent years in the sphere of terrorist and other internationally condemned crimes.[67]

---

[60] See new section 1203 of the Criminal Code, 18 USC para.1203, Pub.L. No.98-473, ch.19, para.2002(a), 98 Stat. 1976, 2186.

[61] Pub.L. No.98-473, para.1210, 98 Stat. at 2164.

[62] See *infra*, p.418.

[63] Pub.L. No.99-399, tit.XII, para.1202(a), 100 Stat. 853, 896.

[64] 681 F.Supp. 896 (1988); 82 *ILR*, p.344.

[65] *Infra*, p.411.

[66] *Ibid.*, p.901; 82 *ILR*, p.349.

[67] *Ibid.*, p.902; 82 *ILR*, p.350. Note that a comment to paragraph 402 of the *Restatement (Third) of Foreign Relations Law of the United States*, 1987, states that the passive personality principle "is increasingly accepted as applied to terrorist and other organised attacks on a state's nationals by reason of their nationality, or to assassinations of a state's diplomatic representatives or other officials", *ibid.*, Vol.I, p.240.

The Protective Principle [68]

This principle provides that states may exercise jurisdiction over aliens who have committed an act abroad which is deemed prejudicial to the security of the particular state concerned. It is a well established concept, although there are uncertainties as how far it extends in practice and particularly which acts are included within the net of the claimed jurisdiction.

The principle is justifiable on the basis of protection of a state's vital interests, since the alien might not be committing an offence under the law of the country where he is residing and extradition might be refused if it encompassed political offences.

However, it is clear that it is a principle that can easily be abused, although usually centred upon immigration and various economic offences, since far from protecting important state functions it could easily be manipulated to subvert foreign governments. Nevertheless, it exists partly in view of the insufficiency of most municipal laws as far as offences against the security and integrity of foreign states are concerned.[69]

This doctrine seems to have been applied in the British case of *Joyce* v. *Director of Public Prosecutions*,[70] involving the infamous pro-Nazi propagandist "Lord Haw-Haw". Joyce was born in America, but in 1933 fraudulently acquired a British passport by declaring that he had been born in Ireland. In 1939, he left Britain and started working for German radio. The following year, he claimed to have acquired German nationality. The case turned on whether the British court had jurisdiction to try him after the war, on a charge of treason. The House of Lords decided that jurisdiction did exist in this case. Joyce had held himself out to be a British subject and had availed himself of the protection (albeit fraudulently) of a British passport. Accordingly he could be deemed to owe allegiance to the Crown, and be liable for a breach of that duty. The fact that

[68] See e.g. Akehurst, *op. cit.*, pp.157-59; Harvard Research, *op. cit.*, pp.543-63 and Sahovic and Bishop, "The Authority of the State: its Range with Respect to Persons and Places" in *Manual of Public International Law* (ed. Sørensen), 1968, pp.311, 362-65. See also McDougal, Lasswell and Vlasic, *Law and Public Order in Space*, 1963, pp.699-701.

[69] See e.g. *Rocha* v. *US*, 288 F.2d 545 (1961); 32 *ILR*, p.112; *US* v. *Pizzarusso*, 62 *AJIL*, 1968, p.975, and *US* v. *Rodriguez*, 182 F.Supp. 479 (1960). See also the *Italian South Tyrol Terrorism* case, 71 *ILR*, p.242.

[70] [1946] AC 347; 15 *ILR*, p.91.

the treason occurred outside the territory of the UK was of no consequence since states were not obliged to ignore the crime of treason committed against it outside its territory. Joyce was convicted and suffered the penalty for his actions.

The Universality Principle [71]

Under this principle, each and every state had jurisdiction to try particular offences. This is accepted since the crimes involved are regarded as offensive to the international community as a whole. There are two categories that clearly belong to the sphere of universal jurisdiction. These are piracy and war crimes.

However, there is a growing number of other offences which by international treaty may be subject to the jurisdiction of contracting parties.

1. Piracy

Universal jurisdiction over piracy has been accepted under international law for many centuries and is one of the best established of the rules of the world community.[72] All states may both arrest and punish pirates, provided of course that they have been apprehended on the high seas or within the territory of the state concerned. The punishment of the offenders takes place whatever their nationality and wherever they happened to carry out their criminal activities.

Piracy under international law (or piracy *jure gentium*) must be distinguished from piracy under municipal law. Offences that may be characterised as piratical under municipal laws do not necessarily fall within the definition of piracy in international law, and thus are not susceptible to universal jurisdiction (depending of course upon the content and form of international conventions). Piracy *jure gentium* was defined in article 15 of the High Seas Convention 1958 as illegal acts of violence, detention or depredation committed for private ends by the crew or passengers of a private ship or private aircraft and directed against another ship or aircraft (or persons

---

[71] See e.g. Akehurst, *op. cit.*, pp.160-66; Bowett, *op. cit.*, pp.11-14; Harvard Research, *op. cit.*, pp.563-92 and Jennings, *op. cit.*, p.156.

[72] See e.g. *In re Piracy Jure Gentium*, [1934] AC 586; 7 *ILR*, p.213. See also Johnson, "Piracy in Modern International Law", 43 *Transactions of the Grotius Society*, 1957, p.63.

or property therein) on the high seas or *terra nullius*.[73] Attempts to commit such acts are sufficient to constitute piracy and it is not essential for the attempt to have been successful.[74]

2. War Crimes

In addition to piracy, war crimes are now accepted by most authorities as subject to universal jurisdiction, though of course the issues involved are extremely sensitive and highly political.[75] While there is little doubt about the legality and principles of the war crimes decisions emerging after the Second World War, a great deal of controversy arose over suggestions of war crimes guilt appertaining to American personnel connected with the Vietnam war,[76] and Pakistani soldiers involved in the Bangladesh war of 1971.

Article 6 of the Charter of the International Military Tribunal of 1945 referred to crimes against peace, violations of the law and customs of war and crimes against humanity as offences within the jurisdiction of the Tribunal for which there was to be individual responsibility. This article can now be regarded as part of international law. In a resolution unanimously approved by the General Assembly of the United Nations in 1946, the principles of international law recognised by the Charter of the Nuremberg Tribunal and the judgment of the Tribunal were expressly confirmed.[77] The General Assembly in 1968 adopted a Convention on the Non-Applicability of Statutory Limitations to War Crimes and Crimes Against Humanity, reinforcing the general conviction that war crimes form a distinct category under

---

[73] See further, *supra*, Chapter 10, p.369.

[74] *In re Piracy Jure Gentium*, [1934] AC 586; 7 *ILR*, p.213.

[75] See e.g. Akehurst, *op. cit.*, p.160; Sahovic and Bishop, *op. cit.*, pp.367-68; Cowles, "Universality of Jurisdiction over War Crimes", 33 *California Law Review*, 1945, p.177 and Brownlie, *op. cit.*, pp.304-5. Cf. Bowett, *op. cit.*, p.12. See also the *Eichmann* case, 36 *ILR*, p.5 and p.277 and the UN War Crimes Commission, 15 *Law Reports of Trials of War Criminals*, 1949, p.26.

[76] See e.g. *Calley* v. *Calloway*, 382 F.Supp. 650 (1974), rev'd 519 F.2d 184 (1975), cert. denied 425 US 911 (1976).

[77] Resolution 95(I). See also *Yearbook of the ILC*, 1950 II p.195; 253 HL Deb, col.831, 2 December 1963; the *British Manual of Military Law*, Part III, 1958, para.637 and Weiss, "Time Limits for the Prosecution of Crimes against International Law", 53 *BYIL*, 1982, pp.163, 188 *et seq.*

international law, susceptible to universal jurisdiction,[78] while the four Geneva "Red Cross" Conventions of 1949 also contain provisions for universal jurisdiction over grave breaches.[79]

The universality principle was to some extent applied in the *Eichmann* case[80] before the District Court of Jerusalem and the Supreme Court of Israel in 1961. Eichmann was prosecuted and convicted under an Israeli law of 1951 for war crimes, crimes against the Jewish people and crimes against humanity. The District Court declared that far from limiting states' jurisdiction with regard to such crimes, international law was actually in need of the legislative and judicial organs of every state to give effect to its criminal interdictions and bring the criminals to trial. The fact that the crimes were committed prior to the establishment of the state of Israel did not prevent the correct application of its powers pursuant to universal jurisdiction under international law. Israel's municipal law merely reflected the reiterated offences existing under international law.

The International Law Commission has been considering a Draft Code of Offences Against the Peace and Security of Mankind since 1982.[81] Such offences under the draft articles agreed to date are deemed to be universal so that every state is under a duty to prosecute an alleged offender arrested in its territory or extradite him to a state which will. Offences against the peace and security of mankind fall under three headings; crimes against peace, crimes against humanity and war crimes.[82] Crimes against peace consist of the commission by the authorities of a state of an act of aggression, including the organising or other support of international terrorism.[83] Crimes against humanity consist of genocide, apartheid, inhuman acts including extermination and deportation upon racial, religious or political grounds, and serious breaches of an

---

[78] See e.g. Weiss, *op. cit.*

[79] See e.g. Draper, *The Red Cross Conventions*, 1958, p.105. Cf. Bowett, *op. cit.*, p.12.

[80] 36 *ILR*, pp.5 and 277. See also the *Barbie* cases, 78 *ILR*, pp.78, 125, 136 and *Demjanjuk* v. *Petrovsky*, 776 F.2d 571 (1985); 79 *ILR*, p.534. See also *Keesing's Record of World Events*, p.36189 regarding the *Demjanjuk* case in Israel.

[81] See General Assembly resolution 36/106 of 10 December 1981. A Draft Code was formulated in 1954 by the ILC and submitted to the UN General Assembly, see *Yearbook of the ILC*, 1954, vol.II, p.150. The General Assembly postponed consideration of it until a definition of aggression had been formulated, resolution 897(IX). This was achieved in 1974, see resolution 3314(XXIX).

[82] Draft article 10. See *Yearbook of the ILC*, 1986, vol.II, Part 2, p.42.

[83] Draft article 11. See also draft article 16, adopted in 1990, 84 *AJIL*, 1990, p.933.

international obligation of essential importance for the preservation of the human environment.[84] War crimes are defined as serious violations of the conventions, rules and customs applicable to international or non-international armed conflicts and would include, for example, serious attacks on persons and property and the unlawful use of weapons.[85] Many of these items are controversial and it remains to be seen how the international community will deal with them.

3. Treaties Providing for Jurisdiction

In addition to the accepted universal jurisdiction to apprehend and try pirates and war criminals, there are a number of treaties which provide for the suppression by the international community of various activities, ranging from the destruction of submarine cables to drug trafficking and slavery.[86] These treaties provide for the exercise of state jurisdiction but not for universal jurisdiction. Some conventions establish what might be termed a quasi-universal jurisdiction or multiple exercise of jurisdiction.

For instance, the 1948 Genocide Convention declares that persons charged with genocide shall be tried by a competent tribunal of the state in the territory of which the offence was committed or "by such international penal tribunal as may have jurisdiction with respect to those contracting parties which shall have accepted its jurisdiction"[87] and treaties relating to currency counterfeiting[88] and drug trafficking[89] require the state claiming jurisdiction to have adopted municipal legislation accepting the prosecution of aliens for offences committed abroad.

Other examples of the recognition of a quasi-universal jurisdiction occur with regard to the offence of hijacking and crimes against diplomats and other internationally protected persons. These

---

[84] Draft article 12.
[85] Draft article 13.
[86] See e.g. Akehurst, *op. cit.*, pp.160-61.
[87] See further, *supra*, Chapter 6. See also the 1984 Convention against Torture, which similarly calls upon states either to prosecute an alleged offender or extradite him to a state which will prosecute him *(aut dedire aut punire)*.
[88] 112 LNTS, p.371.
[89] 198 LNTS, p.299 and 520 UNTS, p.151. See also the 1979 Convention against the Taking of Hostages and e.g. the UK Taking of Hostages Act, 1982.

offences are not like piracy *jure gentium,* in that all states automatically possess under international law the capacity to apprehend and try those suspected of them; rather, they stem from international treaties providing that jurisdiction with respect to them may be based upon any of several grounds.

The Convention on the Prevention and Punishment of Crimes against Internationally Protected Persons, including Diplomatic Agents was adopted in 1973 by the General Assembly of the United Nations and came into force in 1977.[90] This stipulates that contracting states should make acts such as assaults upon the person, premises and transport of such persons a crime under their domestic law (article 2). This, of course, will require little if any revision of existing penal statutes. Each state is to establish its jurisdiction over these crimes when committed in its territory or on board ships or aircraft registered in its territory, or when the alleged offender is a national or when the crimes have been committed against an internationally protected person functioning on behalf of that state (article 3). A person is regarded as internationally protected where he is a head of state or government, or foreign minister abroad, or state representative or official of an international organisation (article 1).

The International Convention against the Taking of Hostages 1979 came into force in 1983[91] and, like the Internationally Protected Persons Treaty, requires each state party to make the offence punishable under national law, and provides that states parties must either extradite or prosecute an alleged offender found on their territory and incorporate the offence of hostage-taking into existing and future extradition treaties. The grounds upon which a state party may exercise jurisdiction are laid down in article 5 and cover offences committed in its territory or on board a ship or aircraft registered in that state; by any of its nationals, or if that state considers it appropriate, by stateless persons having their habitual residence in its territory; in order to compel that state to do or abstain from doing any act; or with respect to a hostage who is a national of that state, if that state considers it appropriate.

[90] As of July 1989, there were 69 states parties to the Convention. See also the UK Internationally Protected Persons Act 1978.

[91] As of July 1990, it has 60 states parties. See also the UK Taking of Hostages Act 1982.

As far as hijacking of and other unlawful acts connected with aircraft is concerned, the relevant treaties are the Tokyo Convention on Offences and Certain Other Acts Committed on Board Aircraft, 1963; the Hague Convention for the Suppression of Unlawful Seizure of Aircraft, 1970 and the Montreal Convention for the Suppression of Unlawful Acts against the Safety of Civil Aviation, 1971. The latter two instruments arose as a result of the wave of aircraft hijacking and attacks upon civilian planes that took place in the later 1960s, and tried to deal with the problem of how to apprehend and punish the perpetrators of such deeds.

The Tokyo Convention[92] applies to both general offences and acts which, whether or not they are offences, may or do jeopardise the safety of the aircraft or of persons or property therein or which jeopardise good order and discipline on board. It provides for the jurisdiction of the contracting state over aircraft registered therein while the aircraft is in flight, or on the surface of the high seas or on any other area outside the territory of any state. Contracting states are called upon to take the necessary measures to establish jurisdiction by municipal law over such aircraft in such circumstances. In addition, the Convention permits interference with an aircraft in flight in order to establish criminal jurisdiction over an offence committed on board in certain specific circumstances by contracting states not being the state of registration. The circumstances specified are where the offence has effect on the territory of such state; has been committed by or against a national or permanent resident of such state; is against the security of such state; consists of a breach of any rules or regulations relating to the flight or manoeuvre of aircraft in force in such state or where the exercise of jurisdiction is necessary to ensure the observance of any obligation of such state under a multilateral international agreement.[93] No obligation to extradite is provided for.

The Hague Convention[94] provides that any person who, on board an aircraft in flight, is involved in the unlawful seizure of that aircraft (or attempts the same), commits an offence which contracting states undertake to make punishable by severe penalties. Each contracting state is to take such measures as may be necessary to

---

[92] As of July 1990, there were 131 contracting parties.

[93] Article 4. See Shuber, *Jurisdiction over Crimes on Board Aircraft*, 1973. See also the US Anti-Hijacking Act of 1974, and *supra*, Chapter 9, p.321.

[94] As of July 1990, there were 141 contracting parties.

establish its jurisdiction over the offence or related acts of violence when the offence is committed on board an aircraft registered in that state; when the aircraft in question lands in its territory with the alleged offender still on board or when the offence is committed on board an aircraft leased without a crew to a lessee who has his principal place of business, or if the lessee has no such place of business, his permanent residence, in that state. The Convention also provides that contracting states in the territory of which an alleged offender is found must either extradite or prosecute him.

The Montreal Convention[95] contains similar rules as to jurisdiction and extradition as the Hague Convention but is aimed at controlling and punishing attacks and sabotage against civil aircraft in flight and on the ground rather than dealing with hijacking directly.[96] A Protocol to the Montreal Convention was signed in 1988: it provides for the suppression of unlawful acts of violence at airports serving international civil aviation which cause or are likely to cause serious injury, and acts of violence which destroy or seriously damage the facilities of an airport serving international civil aviation or aircraft not in service located thereon or disrupt the service of the airport.[97]

The wide range of jurisdictional bases is to be noted, although it would appear that universality as such is not as yet included. Nevertheless, condemnation of this form of activity is widespread and it is likely that hijacking has become a crime of universal jurisdiction.[98]

Of course questions as to enforcement will arise where states fail either to respect their obligations under the above Conventions or if they are not parties to them then to respect customary law on the reasonable assumption that state practice now recognises hijacking as an unlawful act.[99]

[95] As of July 1990, there were 142 contracting parties.

[96] Note that neither the Tokyo nor the Hague Conventions apply to aircraft used in military, customs or police services, see articles 1(4) and 3(2) respectively.

[97] Note the Hindawi episode, where the European Community imposed sanctions upon Syria in a situation where it emerged during a court case in the UK that an attempt to smuggle a bomb on an Israeli airliner in 1986 in London had been supported by Syrian intelligence; see *Keesing's Contemporary Archives*, pp.34771-72 and pp.34883-84.

[98] See *US* v. *Yunis (No.2)*, 681 F.Supp. 896, 900-1 (1988); 82 *ILR*, pp.344, 348.

[99] See e.g. General Assembly resolution 2645 (XXV) and Security Council resolution 286 (1970).

A number of possibilities exist, in addition to recourse to the United Nations and the relevant international air organisations.[100] Like-minded states may seek to impose sanctions upon errant states. The 1978 Bonn Declaration, for example, agreed that "in cases where a country refuses the extradition or prosecution of those who have hijacked an aircraft and/or does not return such aircraft" action would be taken to cease all flights to and from that country and its airlines.[101] Bilateral arrangements may also be made, which provide for the return of, or prosecution of hijackers.[102] States may also, of course, adopt legislation which enables them to prosecute alleged hijackers found in their territory,[103] or more generally seeks to combat terrorism. The 1984 US Act to Combat International Terrorism, for example, provides for rewards for information concerning a wide range of terrorist acts primarily (although not exclusively) within the territorial jurisdiction of the US.

Other acts of general self-help have also been resorted to. In 1973, for example, Israeli warplanes intercepted a civil aircraft in Lebanese airspace in an unsuccessful attempt to apprehend a guerrilla leader held responsible for the killing of civilians aboard hijacked aircraft. Israel was condemned for this by the UN Security Council[104] and the International Civil Aviation Organisation.[105]

On the night of 10-11 October 1985, an Egyptian civil aircraft carrying the hijackers of the Italian cruise ship *Achille Lauro* was intercepted over the Mediterranean Sea by US Navy fighters and compelled to land in Sicily. The US justified its action generally by reference to the need to combat international terrorism, while the UK Foreign Secretary noted it was relevant to take into account the international agreements on hijacking and hostage taking.[106]

---

[100] See *supra*, Chapter 9, p.318.

[101] See UKMIL, 49 *BYIL*, 1978, p.423. The states making the Declaration were the UK, France, US, Canada, West Germany, Italy and Japan.

[102] See e.g. the US-Cuban Memorandum of Understanding on Hijacking of Aircraft and Vessels and Other Offences, 1973.

[103] See e.g. the US Anti-Hijacking Act of 1974 and the UK Civil Aviation Act, 1982, s.92 and the Aviation Security Act, 1982.

[104] Resolution 337 (1973).

[105] ICAO Doc. 9050-LC/169-1, at p.196 (1973).

[106] See *Keesing's Contemporary Archives*, p.34078 and *The Times*, 6 February 1986, p.4. In this context, one should also note the hijack of a TWA airliner in June 1985, the murder of a passenger and the prolonged detention in the Lebanon of the remaining passengers and the crew, see *Keesing's Contemporary Archives*, p.34130. See also Cassese, *Terrorism, Politics and Law*, 1989.

However, nothing in these conventions, it is suggested, would appear to justify an interception of a civilian aircraft over the high seas or over any area other than the territory of the intercepting state and for specified reasons. The apprehension of terrorists is to be encouraged, but the means must be legitimate. On 4 February 1986, the Israeli Airforce intercepted a Libyan civil aircraft en route from Libya to Syria in an attempt to capture terrorists, and argued that the aircraft in question was part of a terrorist operation.[107]

Nevertheless, there may be circumstances where an action taken by a state as a consequence of hostile hijacking or terrorist operations would be justifiable in the context of self-defence.[108]

4. *Illegal Apprehension of Suspects and the Exercise of Jurisdiction* [109]

It would appear that unlawful apprehension of a suspect by state agents acting in the territory of another state is not a bar to the exercise of jurisdiction. Such apprehension would, of course, constitute a breach of international law and the norm of non-intervention,[110] unless the circumstances were such that the right of self-defence could be pleaded.[111] It could be argued that the seizure, being a violation of international law, would only be compounded by permitting the abducting state to exercise jurisdiction,[112] but international practice demonstrates otherwise.[113] Domestic practice points the same way, but not invariably. The

---

[107] See *The Times*, 5 February 1986, p.1.

[108] See e.g. as to the 1976 Entebbe incident, *infra*, Chapter 18.

[109] See e.g. Morgenstern, "Jurisdiction in Seizures Effected in Violation of International Law", 29 *BYIL*, 1952, p.256; O'Higgins, "Unlawful Seizure and Irregular Extradition", 36 *BYIL*, 1960, p.279; Lowenfeld, "US Law Enforcement Abroad: The Constitution and International Law", 83 *AJIL*, 1989, p.880; "US Law Enforcement Abroad: The Constitution and International Law, Continued", 84 *AJIL*, 1990, p.444 and "Kidnapping by Government Order: A Follow-Up", 84 *AJIL*, 1990, p.712. See also Mann, "Reflections on the Prosecution of Persons Abducted in Breach of International Law" in *International Law at a Time of Perplexity* (ed. Dinstein), 1989, p.407.

[110] See e.g. article 2(4) of the United Nations Charter and *Nicaragua* v. *US*, ICJ Reports, 1986, p.110. See further *infra*, Chapter 18.

[111] Note, in particular, the view of the Legal Adviser of the US Department of State to the effect that "[w]hile international law therefore permits extraterritorial 'arrests' in situations which permit a valid claim of self-defence, decisions about any extraterritorial arrest entail grave potential implications for US personnel, for the United States, and for our relations with other states", 84 *AJIL*, 1990, pp.725, 727.

[112] See Mann, *op. cit.*, p.415.

[113] See the *Eichmann* case, 36 *ILR*, pp.5 and 277.

Court of Appeals in *US* v. *Toscanino*[114] held that the rule that jurisdiction was unaffected by an illegal apprehension[115] should not be applied where the presence of the defendant has been secured by force or fraud, but this approach has, it seems, been to a large extent eroded. In fact in *US ex rel. Lujan* v. *Gengler*[116] it was noted that the rule in *Toscanino* was limited to cases of "torture, brutality and similar outrageous conduct".[117] In *R* v. *Plymouth Justices, ex parte Driver*,[118] it was noted that once a person was in lawful custody within the jurisdiction, the court had no power to inquire into the circumstances in which he had been brought into the jurisdiction.

5. *The US Alien Tort Claims Act* [119]

Under this Act, the First Congress established original district court jurisdiction over all causes where an alien sues for a tort "committed in violation of the law of nations or a treaty of the United States". In *Filartiga* v. *Pena-Irala*,[120] the US Court of Appeals for the Second Circuit interpreted this provision to permit jurisdiction over a private tort action by a Paraguayan national against a Paraguayan police official for acts of torture perpetrated in that state, it being held that torture by a state official constituted a violation of international law. This amounted to an important move in the attempt to exercise jurisdiction in the realm of international human rights violations, although one clearly based upon a domestic statute permitting such court competence. The relevant issues in such actions would thus depend upon the definition of the "law of nations" in particular cases.

In *Tel-Oren* v. *Libyan Arab Republic*,[121] however, the Court dismissed

---

[114] 500 F.2d 267 (1974); 61 *ILR*, p.190.

[115] See in particular *Kerr* v. *Illinois*, 119 US 436 (1886) and *Frisbie* v. *Collins*, 342 US 519 (1952). These cases have given rise to the reference to the Kerr-Frisbie doctrine.

[116] 510 F.2d 62 (1975); 61 *ILR*, p.206. See also *US* v. *Lira*, 515 F.2d 68 (1975); Lowenfeld, *op. cit.*, 1990, p.712; *Afouneh* v. *Attorney-General*, 10 *ILR*, p.327 and *re Argoud*, 45 *ILR*, p.90.

[117] This approach was reaffirmed in *US* v. *Yunis* both by the district court, 681 F.Supp. 909, 918-21 (1988) and by the court of appeals, 30 *ILM*, 1991, pp.403, 408-9.

[118] [1986] 1 QB 95; 77 *ILR*, p.351.

[119] 28 USC, para.1350 (1982), originally enacted as part of the Judiciary Act of 1789. See also 28 USC, para.1331, and *supra*, Chapter 4, p.119.

[120] 630 F.2d 876 (2d Cir. 1980); 77 *ILR*, p.169. See also *ibid.*, 577 F.Supp. 860 (1984); 77 *ILR*, p.185, awarding punitive damages.

[121] 726 F.2d 774 (1984); 77 *ILR*, p.204. See also "Agora", 79 *AJIL*, 1985, p.92 *et seq.* for a discussion of the case.

an action under the same statute brought by survivors and representatives of persons murdered in an armed attack on an Israeli bus in 1978 for lack of subject-matter jurisdiction. The three judges differed in their reasoning. Judge Edwards held that the law of nations did not impose liability on non-state entities like the PLO. Judge Bork, in a departure from the *Filartiga* principles, declared that "an explicit grant of a cause of action [had to exist] before a private individual [will] be allowed to enforce principles of international law in a federal tribunal",[122] while Senior Judge Robb held that the case was rendered non-justiciable by the political question doctrine.

Further restrictions upon the *Filartiga* doctrine have also been manifested. It has, for example, been held that the Alien Tort Claims Act does not constitute an exception to the principle of sovereign immunity so that a foreign state could not be sued,[123] while it has also been held that US citizens could not sue for violations of the law of nations under the Act.[124]

In *Sanchez-Espinoza* v. *Reagan*,[125] suit was brought against a variety of present and former US executive officials for violation *inter alia* of domestic and international law with regard to the US support of the "contra" guerrillas fighting against the Nicaraguan government. The Alien Tort Claims Act was cited, but the Court of Appeals noted that the statute arguably only covered private, non-governmental acts that violated a treaty or customary international law and, relying on *Tel-Oren,* pointed out that customary international law did not cover private conduct "of this sort".[126] Thus the claim for damages could only be sustained to the extent that the defendants acted in an official capacity and even if the Alien Tort Claims Act applied to official state acts, the doctrine of domestic sovereign immunity precluded the claim.

The Act was relied upon again in the *Amerada Hess* case which concerned the bombing of a ship in international waters by

---

[122] *Ibid.,* p.801; 77 *ILR,* p.230.
[123] *Siderman* v. *Republic of Argentina,* no.CU82-1772-RMT (MCX) and *International Practitioner's Notebook,* July 1985, p.1.
[124] *Handel* v. *Artukovic,* 601 F.Supp. 1421 (1985); 79 *ILR,* p.397.
[125] 770 F.2d 202 (1985); 80 *ILR,* p.586.
[126] *Ibid.,* pp.206-7; 80 *ILR,* pp.590-91.

Argentina during the Falklands war and where it was claimed that the federal courts had jurisdiction under the Act. A divided Court of Appeals[127] held that the Act provided, and the Foreign Sovereign Immunities Act did not preclude,[128] federal subject matter jurisdiction over suits in tort by aliens against foreign sovereigns for violations of international law. However, the Supreme Court unanimously disagreed.[129] It was noted that the Act did not expressly authorise suits against foreign states and that at the time the Foreign Sovereign Immunities Act was enacted, the 1789 Act had never provided the jurisdictional basis for a suit against a foreign state.[130] Since the Congress had decided to deal comprehensively with sovereign immunity in the Foreign Sovereign Immunity Act, it appeared to follow that this Act alone provided the basis for federal jurisdiction over foreign states. This basis was thus exclusive. The Court did note, however, that the Alien Tort Claims Act was unaffected by the Foreign Sovereign Immunities Act insofar as non-state defendants were concerned.[131]

Extradition [132]

The practice of extradition enables one state to hand over to another suspected or convicted criminals who have fled abroad. It is based upon bilateral treaty law and does not exist as an obligation upon states in customary law. It is usual to derive from existing treaties on the subject certain general principles, for example that of double criminality, i.e. that the crime involved should be a crime in both states concerned[133] and that of specialty, i.e. a person surrendered may be tried and punished only for the offence for which extradition had been sought and granted. In general, offences of a political

---

[127] *Amerada Hess Shipping Corp.* v. *Argentine Republic,* 830 F.2d 421 (1987); 79 *ILR,* p.8.

[128] See *infra,* Chapter 12, p.439.

[129] *Argentine Republic* v. *Amerada Hess Shipping Corp.,* 109 S.Ct. 683 (1989); 81 *ILR,* p.658.

[130] *Ibid.,* p.689; 81 *ILR,* pp.664-65.

[131] *Ibid.,* p.690.

[132] See e.g. Shearer, *Extradition in International Law,* 1971 and Stanbrook and Stanbrook, *The Law and Practice of Extradition,* 1980.

[133] But see now the House of Lords decisions in *Government of Denmark* v. *Nielsen,* [1984] 2 All ER 81; 74 *ILR,* p.458 and *United States Government* v. *McCaffery,* [1984] 2 All ER 570.

character have been excluded, but this would not cover terrorist activities.[134]

EXTRATERRITORIAL JURISDICTION [135]

Claims have arisen in the context of economic issues whereby some states, particularly the United States, seek to apply their laws outside their territory in a manner which may precipitate conflicts with other states. Where the claims are founded upon the territorial and nationality theories of jurisdiction, problems do not often arise, but claims made upon the basis of the so-called "effects" doctrine have provoked considerable controversy. This goes beyond the objective territorial principle to a situation where the state assumes jurisdiction on the grounds that the behaviour of a party is producing "effects" within its territory. This is so even though all the conduct complained of takes place in another state. The effects doctrine has been energetically maintained particularly by the US in the area of antitrust regulation.[136] The classic statement of the American doctrine was in *US* v. *Aluminum Co. of America*,[137] in which the Court declared that:

---

[134] See e.g. the European Convention on the Suppression of Terrorism, 1976. See also the *McMullen* case, 74 *AJIL*, 1980, p.434; the *Eain* case, *ibid.*, p.435; *Re Piperno, ibid.*, p.683 and *US* v. *Mackin*, 668 F.2d 122 (1981); 79 *ILR*, p.459. A revised directive on international extradition was issued by the US Department of State in 1981; see 76 *AJIL*, 1982, pp.154-59. Note also the view of the British Home Secretary, *The Times*, 25 June 1985, p.1, that the political offences "loophole" as it applied to violent offences was not suitable to extradition arrangements between the democratic countries "sharing the same high regard for the fundamental principles of justice and operating similar independent judicial systems". The English law relating to extradition has now been consolidated in the Extradition Act 1989. See also *Government of Belgium* v. *Postlethwaite*, [1987] 2 All ER 985 and *R* v. *Chief Metropolitan Magistrate, ex parte Secretary of State for the Home Department*, [1988] 1 WLR 1204.

[135] See e.g. *Extraterritorial Jurisdiction* (ed. Lowe), 1983; Rosenthal and Knighton, *National Laws and International Commerce*, 1982; Meesen, "Antitrust Jurisdiction under Customary International Law", 78 *AJIL*, 1984, p.783; Lowe, "Blocking Extraterritorial Jurisdiction; The British Protection of Trading Interests Act, 1980", 75 *AJIL*, 1981, p.257 and Akehurst, *op. cit.*, p.190 *et seq.*

[136] See e.g. the US Sherman Antitrust Act, 1896, 15 USC, para.1 *et seq.* See also the controversy engendered by the US embargo imposed under the Export Administration Act on equipment intended for use on the Siberian gas pipeline, Bridge, "The Law and Politics of United States Foreign Policy Export Controls", 4 *Legal Studies*, 1984, p.2 and Lowe, "Public International Law and the Conflict of Laws", 33 *ICLQ*, 1984, p.575.

[137] 148 F.2d 416 (1945).

any state may impose liabilities, even upon persons not within its allegiance, for conduct outside its borders that has consequences within its borders which the state reprehends.[138]

The doctrine was to some extent modified by the requirement intention and the view that the effect should be substantial, but the wide-ranging nature of the concept aroused considerable opposition outside the US, as did American attempts to take evidence abroad under very broad pre-trial discovery provisions in US law[139] and the possibility of treble damage awards.[140] The US courts, perhaps in view of the growing opposition of foreign states, modified their approach in the *Timberlane Lumber Co.* v. *Bank of America*[141] and *Mannington Mills* v. *Congoleum Corporation*[142] cases. It was stated that in addition to the effects test, of the earlier cases, the courts had to take into account a balancing test, "a jurisdictional rule of reason", involving a consideration of other nations' interests and the full nature of the relationship between the actors concerned and the US.[143] A series of factors that needed to be considered in the process of balancing was put forward in the latter case.[144] The view taken by the Third Restatement of Foreign Relations Law,[145] it should be

---

[138] *Ibid.*, p.443. This approach was reaffirmed in a series of later cases, see e.g. *US* v. *Timken Roller Bearing Co.*, 83 F.Supp. 284, (1949) affirmed 341 US 593 (1951); *US* v. *The Watchmakers of Switzerland Information Center, Inc.* cases, s.77, p.414 (1963); 22 *ILR*, p.168 and *US* v. *General Electric Co*, 82 F.Supp. 753 (1949) and 115 F.Supp. 835 (1953). See also *Hazeltine Research Inc.* v. *Zenith Radio Corporation*, 239 F.Supp. 51 (1965), affirmed 395 US 100 (1969).

[139] See e.g. the statement of the UK Attorney-General that "the wide investigating procedures under the United States antitrust legislation against persons outside the United States who are not United States citizens constitute an "extraterritorial" infringement of the proper jurisdiction and sovereignty of the United Kingdom", *Rio Tinto Zinc* v. *Westinghouse Electric Corporation*, [1978] 2 WLR 81; 73 *ILR*, p.296. See also *Extraterritorial Jurisdiction, op. cit.*, pp.159-60 and 165-71. But see *Société Internationale* v. *Rogers*, 357 US 197 (1958); 26 *ILR*, p.123; *US* v. *First National City Bank*, 396 F.2d 897 (1968); 38 *ILR*, p.112; *In re Westinghouse Electric Corporation*, 563 F.2d 992 (1977) and *In re Uranium Antitrust Litigation*, 480 F.Supp. 1138 (1979).

[140] See e.g. Meessen, *op. cit.*, p.794.

[141] 549 F.2d 597 (1976); 66 *ILR*, p.270.

[142] 595 F.2d 1287 (1979); 66 *ILR*, p.487.

[143] See particularly Brewster, *Antitrust and American Business Abroad*, 1958.

[144] 595 F.2d 1287, 1297 (1979); 66 *ILR*, pp.487, 496. See also the *Timberlane* case, 549 F.2d 597, 614 (1976); 66 *ILR*, pp.270, 285. The need for judicial restraint in applying the effects doctrine in the light of comity was emphasised by the State Department, see 74 *AJIL*, 1980, pp.179-83. See also the US Foreign Trade Antitrust Improvements Act, 1982, where jurisdiction was said to be dependent on "direct, substantial and reasonably foreseeable effect".

[145] *Restatement (Third) of Foreign Relations Law of the United States*, 1987, para.402, p.239 and para.403, p.250.

noted, is that a state may exercise jurisdiction based on effects in the state, when the effect or intended effect is substantial and the exercise of jurisdiction is reasonable. It is noted that the principle of reasonableness calls for limiting the exercise of jurisdiction so as to minimise conflict with the jurisdiction of other states, particularly the state where the act takes place.

However, the assumption by the courts of a basically diplomatic function, that is, weighing and considering the interests of foreign states, has stimulated criticism.[146] Indeed, foreign states had started reacting to the effects doctrine by enacting blocking legislation, for example the UK Protection of Trading Interests Act 1980. Under this Act, the Secretary of State in dealing with extraterritorial actions by a foreign state may prohibit the production of documents or information to the latter's courts or authorities. In addition, a UK national or resident may sue in an English court for recovery of multiple damages paid under the judgment of a foreign court.[147]

The Protection of Trading Interests Act was used in connection with the action by the liquidator of Laker Airways to sue various major airlines, the Midland Bank and McDonnell Douglas in the US for conspiracy to violate the anti-trust laws of the United States. Two of the airlines, British Airways and British Caledonian, sought to prevent this suit in the US by bringing an action to restrain the liquidator in the UK. Thus, the effects doctrine was not actually in issue in the case, which centred upon the application of the US anti-trust law in connection with alleged conspiratorial activities in the US. The UK Government, holding the view that the Bermuda Two agreement regulating transatlantic airline activity[148] prohibited antitrust actions against UK airlines, issued instructions under the 1980 Act forbidding compliance with any requirement imposed pursuant to US anti-trust measures, including the provision of

---

[146] See e.g. Maier, "Interest Balancing and Extraterritorial Jurisdiction", 31 *American Journal of Comparative Law*, 1983, p.579 and "Resolving Extraterritorial Conflicts or There and Back Again", 25 *Va JIL*, 1984, p.7; Fugate, "Antitrust Aspect of the Revised Restatement of Foreign Relations Law", *ibid.*, p.49 and Bowett, *op. cit.*, pp.21-22. See also *Extraterritorial Jurisdiction, op. cit.*, pp.58-62.

[147] See Lowe, *op. cit.*, pp.257-82; 50 *BYIL*, 1979, pp.357-62 and 21 *ILM*, 1982, pp.840-50. In some cases, courts have applied aspects of domestic law to achieve the same aim, see. e.g. the *Fruehauf* case, 5 *ILM*, 1966, p.476. Several states have made diplomatic protests at extraterritorial jurisdictional claims, see e.g. *Report of the 51st Session of the International Law Association*, 1964, p.565 *et seq.*

[148] See *supra*, Chapter 9, p.319.

information.[149] The Court of Appeal felt that the order and directions required them in essence to prevent the *Laker* action in the US,[150] but the House of Lords disagreed.[151] It was held that the order and directions did not affect the appellant's right to pursue the claim in the US because the 1980 Act was concerned with "requirements" and "prohibitions" imposed by a foreign court,[152] so that the respondents would not be prohibited by the direction from paying damages on a "judgment" given against them in the US.[153] In fact the Court refused to restrain the US action.

The Court also refused to grant judicial review of the order and directions, since the appellant had failed to show that no reasonable minister would have issued such order and directions, this being the requisite test in ministerial decisions concerning international relations.[154] The case, however, did not really turn on the 1980 Act but it is the first time the issue has come before the judicial hierarchy.

The US Courts have, however, recently modified their approach. In *Laker Airways* v. *Sabena,*[155] the Court held *inter alia* that once US antitrust law was declared applicable, it could not be qualified or ignored by virtue of comity. The judicial interest balancing under the *Timberlane* precedent should not be engaged in since the courts on both sides of the Atlantic were obliged to follow the directions of the executive. Accordingly, the reconciliation of conflicting interests was to be undertaken only by diplomatic negotiations. Quite how such basic and crucial differences of opinion over the effects doctrine can be resolved is open to question. International fora have been suggested as the most appropriate way forward,[156] but it is an issue of considerable importance on which strongly held views are maintained.

---

[149] The Protection of Trading Interests (US Anti-trust Measures) Order 1983. Two directions were issued as well.

[150] *British Airways Board* v. *Laker Airways Ltd.,* [1983] 3 All ER 375; 74 *ILR,* p.36.

[151] [1984] 3 All ER 39; 74 *ILR,* p.65. But see also *Midland Bank plc* v. *Laker Airways Ltd.,* [1986] 2 WLR 707.

[152] S.1(3).

[153] [1984] 3 All ER 39, 55-56; 74 *ILR,* p.84.

[154] *Ibid.*, pp.54-55; 74 *ILR,* p.83. See also *Associated Provincial Picture Houses Ltd* v. *Wednesbury Corp.,* [1947] 2 All ER 680.

[155] 731 F.2d 909 (1984). However, cf. the continuation of the *Timberlane* litigation, 749 F.2d 1378 (1984), which reaffirms the approach of the first *Timberlane* case.

[156] See e.g. Bowett, *op. cit.,* pp.24-26 and Meessen, *op. cit.,* pp.808-10. See also *Extraterritorial Jurisdiction, op. cit.,* Part 3.

The dispute over extraterritoriality was affecting in particular the operation of the Western supervision of technological exports to the Communist bloc through COCOM, which links together fifteen states, since the US sought to exercise jurisdiction with respect to exports from third states to Communist states. In an attempt to resolve the issue, the US and the UK agreed in 1984 to consult should problems appear to arise with regard to the application of US export controls to individuals or businesses in the UK, or if the UK were contemplating resorting to the Protection of Trading Interests Act in relation to such controls.[157]

The European Community declared in a letter to the Congressional Committee considering changes in the US export control legislation in March 1984 that:

> US claims to jurisdiction over European subsidiaries of US companies and over goods and technology of US origin located outside the US are contrary to the principles of international law and can only lead to clashes of both a political and legal nature. These subsidiaries, goods and technology must be subject to the laws of the country where they are located.[158]

A substantial freeing of trade within the COCOM area was provided for in the US Omnibus Trade and Competitiveness Act of 1988.[159] In general, products that have already been exported can be re-exported to the COCOM area without advance permission, while those products that only required notification to COCOM may now be exported to the COCOM area without such permission. In addition, many forms of equipment were decontrolled. Trade sanctions were also provided for through the COCOM system for those who violated the provisions. However, the political revolution in Eastern Europe in 1989-90 would appear to have rendered most of the control system unnecessary.

It should also be noted that it is not only the US which has

---

[157] See 68 HC Deb., col.332, Written Answer, 23 November 1984 and 88 HC Deb., col.373, Written Answer, 6 December 1985. See also Current Legal Developments, 36 *ICLQ*, 1987, p.398.
[158] Cited in Current Legal Developments, *op. cit.*, p.399. See also UKMIL, 56 *BYIL*, 1985, pp.480-81.
[159] Pub.L. No.100-418, 102 Stat. 1107.

claimed extensive jurisdiction in economic matters.[160] The European Community itself has wrestled with the question of exercising jurisdiction over corporations not based in the Community in the field of competition law. In *ICI* v. *Commission*,[161] the European Court of Justice established jurisdiction with regard to a series of restrictive agreements to fix the price of dyestuffs on the ground that the defendant undertakings had corporate subsidiaries that were based within the Community, and declined to follow the Advocate General's suggestion[162] that jurisdiction should be founded upon direct and immediate, reasonably foreseeable and substantial effect.

The *Wood Pulp* case[163] concerned a number of non-EC companies and an association of US companies alleged to have entered into a price-fixing arrangement. The European Commission had levied fines on the jurisdictional basis that the effects of the price agreements and practices were direct, substantial and intended within the EC.[164] An action was then commenced before the European Court of Justice for annulment of the Commission's decision under article 173 of the EEC Treaty. Advocate General Darmon argued that international law permitted a state (and therefore the EC) to apply its competition laws to acts done by foreigners abroad if those acts had direct, substantial and foreseeable effects within the state concerned.[165]

The Court, however, took the view that the companies concerned had acted within the EC and were therefore subject to Community law. It was noted that where producers from third states sell directly to purchasers within the Community and engage in price competition in order to win orders from those customers, that constitutes competition within the Community, and, where such producers sell at prices that are actually co-ordinated, that restricts competition within the Community within the meaning of article 85 of the EEC Treaty. It was stressed that the decisive factor was the place where the price-fixing agreement was actually implemented, not where the

---

[160] But not the UK, see e.g. *Attorney General's Reference (No. 1 of 1982)*, [1983] 3 WLR 72, where the Court of Appeal refused to extend the scope of local jurisdiction over foreign conspiracies based on the effects principle.

[161] [1972] ECR 619; 48 *ILR*, p.106.

[162] *Ibid.*, pp.693-94.

[163] *A. Ahlstrom Oy* v. *Commission*, [1988] 4 CMLR 901.

[164] *Ibid.*, p.916.

[165] *Ibid.*, p.932.

agreement was formulated.[166] In other words, the Court founded its jurisdiction upon an interpretation of the territoriality principle, if somewhat stretched. It did not take the opportunity presented to it by the opinion of the Advocate General of accepting the effects principle of jurisdiction. Nevertheless, the case does appear to suggest that price-fixing arrangements intended to have an effect within the Community that are implemented there would be subject to the jurisdiction of the Community, irrespective of the nationality of the companies concerned and of the place where the agreement was reached.[167]

---

[166] *Ibid.*, pp.940-41. Note that the Court held that the association of US companies (KEA) was not subject to Community jurisdiction on the ground that it had not played a separate role in the implementation within the Community of the arrangements in dispute, *ibid.*, pp.942-43.

[167] See e.g. Lange and Sandage, "The *Wood Pulp* Decision and its Implications for the Scope of EC Competition Law", 26 *Common Market Law Review*, 1989, p.137 and Collins, *European Community Law in the United Kingdom*, 4th ed. 1990, p.7.

CHAPTER TWELVE

Immunities from Jurisdiction

In the previous chapter, the circumstances in which a state may seek to exercise its jurisdiction in relation to civil and criminal matters were considered. In this chapter the reverse side of this phenomenon will be examined, that is those cases in which jurisdiction cannot be exercised as it normally would because of special factors. In other words, the concern is with immunity from jurisdiction and those instances where there exist express exceptions to the usual application of a state's legal powers.

The concept of jurisdiction revolves around the principles of state sovereignty, equality and non-interference. Domestic jurisdiction as a notion attempts to define an area in which the actions of the organs of government and administration are supreme, free from international legal principles and interference. Indeed, most of the grounds for jurisdiction can be related to the requirement under international law to respect the territorial integrity and political independence of other states.

Immunity from jurisdiction, whether as regards the state itself or as regards its diplomatic representatives, is grounded in this requirement. Although constituting a derogation from the host state's jurisdiction, in that, for example, the UK cannot exercise jurisdiction over foreign ambassadors within its territory, it is to be construed nevertheless as an essential part of the recognition of the sovereignty of foreign states, as well as an aspect of the legal equality of all states.

SOVEREIGN IMMUNITY [1]

Sovereignty until comparatively recently was regarded as appertaining to a particular individual in a state and not as an abstract manifestation of the existence and power of the state. The sovereign was a definable person, to whom allegiance was due. As

---

[1] See generally e.g. Badr, *State Immunity*, 1984; Sucharitkul, *State Immunities and Trading Activities in International Law*, 1959 and "Immunities of Foreign States before National Authorities", 149 *HR*, p.87; Sinclair, "The Law of Sovereign Immunity: Recent Developments", 167 *HR*, p.113; UN Legislative Series, *Materials on Jurisdictional Immunities of States and Their Property*, 1982; 10 *Netherlands Yearbook of International Law*, 1979; Lauterpacht, "The Problem of Jurisdictional Immunities of Foreign States", 28 *BYIL*, 1951, p.220 and Higgins, "Certain

an integral part of this mystique, the sovereign could not be made subject to the judicial processes of his country. Accordingly, it was only fitting that he could not be sued in foreign courts. The idea of the personal sovereign would undoubtedly have been undermined had courts been able to exercise jurisdiction over foreign sovereigns. This personalisation was gradually replaced by the abstract concept of state sovereignty, but the basic mystique remained. In addition, the independence and equality of states made it philosophically as well as practically difficult to permit municipal courts of one country to manifest their power over foreign sovereign states, without their consent.

The classic case illustrating this relationship between territorial jurisdiction and sovereign immunity is *The Schooner Exchange* v. *McFaddon*,[2] decided by the US Supreme Court. Chief Justice Marshall declared that the jurisdiction of a state within its own territory was exclusive and absolute, but it did not encompass foreign sovereigns. He noted that the:

> perfect equality and absolute independence of sovereigns . . . have given rise to a class of cases in which every sovereign is understood to waive the exercise of a part of that complete exclusive territorial jurisdiction, which has been stated to be the attribute of every nation.[3]

It therefore followed that as concerned the case under litigation, "national ships of war entering the port of a friendly power open for their reception, are to be considered as exempted by the consent of that power from its jurisdiction". Such rules would not apply to private ships which are susceptible to foreign jurisdiction abroad.

Sovereign immunity is closely related to two other legal doctrines, non-justiciability and act of state. Reference has been made earlier to the interaction between the various principles,[4] but it is worth noting here that the concepts of non-justiciability and act of state

---

Unresolved Aspects of the Law of State Immunity", 29 *NILR*, 1982, p.265. See also ILA, *Report of the Sixtieth Conference*, 1982, p.325 *et seq.*; *ILR*, volumes 63-65; Crawford, "International Law of Foreign Sovereigns: Distinguishing Immune Transactions", 54 *BYIL*, 1983, p.75; Lewis, *State and Diplomatic Immunity*, 3rd ed., 1990 and Schreuer, *State Immunity: Some Recent Developments*, 1988.

  [2] 7 Cranch 116 (1812).
  [3] *Ibid.*, p.137.
  [4] *Supra*, p.128.

posit an area of international activity of states that is simply beyond the competence of the domestic tribunal in its assertion of jurisdiction, for example, that the courts would not adjudicate upon the transactions of foreign sovereign states.[5] On the other hand the principle of jurisdictional immunity asserts that in particular situations a court is prevented from exercising the jurisdiction that it possesses. Thus immunity from jurisdiction does not mean exemption from the legal system of the territorial state in question. The two concepts are distinct. In *International Association of Machinists & Aerospace Workers* v. *OPEC*,[6] it was declared that the two concepts are similar in that they reflect the need to respect the sovereignty of foreign states, but that they differ in that the former goes to the jurisdiction of the court and is a principle of international law, whereas the latter is a prudential doctrine of domestic law having internal constitutional roots.

In practice, however, the distinction is not always so evident and arguments presented before the court founded both upon non-justiciability and sovereign immunity are to be expected. It is also an interesting point to consider the extent to which the demise of the absolute immunity approach has affected the doctrine of non-justiciability.

As far as the act of state doctrine is concerned in particular in this context, some disquiet has been expressed by courts that the application of that principle may in certain circumstances have the effect of reintroducing the absolute theory of sovereign immunity. In *Letelier* v. *Republic of Chile*,[7] for example, Chile argued that even if its officials had ordered the assassination of Letelier in the US, such acts could not be the subject of discussion in the US courts as the orders had been given in Chile. This was not accepted by the Court since to do otherwise would mean emasculating the Foreign

---

[5] See e.g. *Buttes Gas and Oil Co.* v. *Hammer (No. 3)*, [1982] AC 888; 64 *ILR*, p.332; *Buck* v. *Attorney-General*, [1965] 1 Ch. 745; 42 *ILR*, p.11 and Goff J, *I° Congreso del Partido*, [1978] 1 QB 500, 527-28; 64 *ILR*, pp.154, 178-79. See also Sinclair, *op. cit.* footnote 1, p.198. See further *supra* p.128.

[6] 649 F.2d 1354, 1359; 66 *ILR*, pp.413, 418. Reaffirmed in *Asociacion de Reclamantes* v. *The United Mexican States*, 22 *ILM*, 1983, pp.625, 641-42. See also *Ramirez* v. *Weinberger*, 23 *ILM*, 1984, p.1274; *Goldwater* v. *Carter*, 444 US 996 (1979) and *Empresa Exportadora de Azucar* v. *Industria Azucarera Nacional SA*, [1983] 2 LL. R, 171; 64 *ILR*, p.368.

[7] 488 F.Supp. 665 (1980); 63 *ILR*, p.378. Note that the US Court of Appeals has held that the Foreign Sovereign Immunities Act 1976 does not supersede the act of state doctrine, see *Helen Liu* v. *Republic of China*, 29 *ILM*, 1990, p.192.

Sovereign Immunities Act by permitting a state to bring back the absolute immunity approach "under the guise of the act of state doctrine".[8] In somewhat different circumstances, Kerr LJ signalled his concern in *Maclaine Watson* v. *The International Tin Council*[9] that the doctrine of non-justiciability might be utilised to by-pass the absence of sovereign immunity with regard to a state's commercial activities.

Of course, once a court has determined that the relevant sovereign immunity legislation permits it to hear the case, it may still face the act of state argument. Such legislation implementing the restrictive immunity approach does not supplant the doctrine of act of state or non-justiciability,[10] although by accepting that the situation is such that immunity does not apply the scope for the non-justiciability plea is clearly much reduced.[11]

The Absolute Immunity Approach

The relatively uncomplicated role of the sovereign and of government in the eighteenth and nineteenth centuries logically gave rise to the concept of absolute immunity, whereby the sovereign was completely immune from foreign jurisdiction in all cases regardless of circumstances. However, the unparalleled growth in the activities of the state, especially with regard to commercial matters, has led to problems and in most countries to a modification of the above rule. The number of governmental agencies and public corporations, nationalised industries and other state organs created a reaction against the concept of absolute immunity, partly because it would enable state enterprises to have an advantage over private companies. Accordingly many states began to adhere to the doctrine of restrictive immunity, under which immunity was available as regards governmental activity, but not where the state was engaging in commercial activity. Governmental acts with regard to which immunity would be granted are termed acts *jure imperii*, while those relating to private or trade activity are termed acts *jure gestionis*.

---

[8] *Ibid.*, p.674.

[9] [1988] 3 WLR 1169, 1188; 80 *ILR*, pp.191, 209.

[10] See *International Association of Machinists & Aerospace Workers* v. *OPEC*, 649 F.2d 1354, 1359-60; 66 *ILR*, pp.413, 418. See also *Liu* v. *Republic of China*, 29 *ILM*, 1990, pp.192, 205.

[11] See the interesting discussion of the relationship between non-justiciability and immunity by Evans J in *Australia and New Zealand Bank* v. *Commonwealth of Australia*, 1989, Transcript, pp.59-60.

The leading practitioner of the absolute immunity approach has been the United Kingdom, and this position was established in a number of important cases.[12]

In the *Parlement Belge* case,[13] the Court of Appeal emphasised that the principle to be deduced from all the relevant preceding cases was that every state

> declines to exercise by means of its courts any of its territorial jurisdiction over the person of any sovereign or ambassador of any other state, or over the public property of any state which is destined to public use . . . though such sovereign, ambassador or property be within its jurisdiction.[14]

The wide principle expressed in this case gave rise to the question as to what kind of legal interest it was necessary for the foreign sovereign to have in property so as to render it immune from the jurisdiction of the British courts.

Commonly regarded as the most extreme expression of the absolute immunity doctrine is the case of the *Porto Alexandre*.[15] This concerned a Portuguese requisitioned vessel against which a writ was issued in an English court for non-payment of dues for services rendered by tugs near Liverpool. The vessel was exclusively engaged in private trading operations, but the Court felt itself constrained by the terms of the *Parlement Belge* principle to dismiss the case in view of the Portuguese government interest.

Differences of opinion as to the application of the immunity rules were revealed in the House of Lords in the *Cristina* case.[16] This followed a Spanish Republican Government decree requisitioning ships registered in Bilbao which was issued while the *Cristina* was on the high seas. On its arrival in Cardiff the Republican authorities took possession of the ship, whereupon its owners proceeded to issue a writ claiming possession. The case turned on

---

[12] But note a series of early cases which are not nearly so clear in their adoption of a broad absolute immunity doctrine, see e.g. *The Prins Frederik*, (1820) 2 Dod. 451; *Duke of Brunswick* v. *King of Hanover*, (1848) 2 *HLC* 1 and *De Haber* v. *Queen of Portugal*, (1851) 17 Cl B 171. See also Phillimore J in *The Charkieh*, (1873) LR 4A and E 59.

[13] (1880) 5 PD 197.

[14] Brett LJ, *ibid.*, pp.214-15. Note of course, that the principle relates to public property destined to public, not private use.

[15] [1920] P.30; 1 *ILR*, p.146. See e.g. Sinclair, *op. cit.*, p.126. See also *The Jupiter*, [1924] P.236, 3 *ILR*, p.136.

[16] [1938] AC 485; 9 *ILR*, p.250.

the argument to dismiss the case, by the Republican government, in view of its sovereign immunity. The majority of the House of Lords accepted this in view of the requisition decree taking over the ship.

However, two of the Lords criticised the *Porto Alexandre* decision and doubted whether immunity covered state trading vessels,[17] while Lord Atkin took more of a fundamentalist absolute approach.[18]

In *Krajina* v. *Tass Agency*[19] the Court of Appeal held that the Agency was a state organ of the USSR and was thus entitled to immunity from local jurisdiction. This was followed in *Baccus SRL* v. *Servicio Nacional del Trigo*,[20] where the Court felt that the defendants, although a separate legal person under Spanish law, were in effect a department of state of the Spanish government. How the entity was actually constituted was regarded as an internal matter, and it was held entitled to immunity from suit.

A different view from the majority was taken by Lord Justice Singleton who, in a dissenting opinion, condemned what he regarded as the extension of the doctrine of sovereign immunity to separate legal entities.[21]

There is some limitation to the absolute immunity rule to the extent that a mere claim by a foreign sovereign to have an interest in the contested property will have to be substantiated before the English court will grant immunity. Since this involves some submission by the foreign sovereign to the local jurisdiction, immunity is not unqualifiedly absolute. Once the court is clear that the claim by the sovereign is not merely illusory or founded on a manifestly defective title, it will dismiss the case. This was brought out in *Juan Ysmael* v. *Republic of Indonesia*[22] in which the asserted interest in a vessel by the Indonesian government was regarded as manifestly defective so that the case was not dismissed on the ground of sovereign immunity.[23]

American cases, however, have shown a rather different approach,

---

[17] See e.g. Lord Macmillan, *ibid.*, p.498; 9 *ILR*, p.260.

[18] *Ibid.*, p.490. See also *Berizzi Bros. Co* v. *SS Pesaro*, 271 US 562 (1926); 3 *ILR*, p.186 and *The Navemar*, 303 US 68 (1938); 9 *ILR*, p.176.

[19] [1949] 2 All ER 274; 16 *ILR*, p.129. See also Cohen LJ, *ibid.*, p.281.

[20] [1957] 1 QB 438; 23 *ILR*, p.160.

[21] *Ibid.*, p.461; 23 *ILR*, p.169.

[22] [1955] AC 72; 21 *ILR*, p.95. See also *USA and France* v. *Dollfus Mieg et Compagnie*, [1952] AC 582; 19 *ILR*, p.163.

[23] See Higgins, *op. cit.*, p.273, who raises the question as to whether this test would be rigorous in an era of restrictive immunity.

one that distinguishes between ownership on the one hand and possession and control on the other. In two cases particularly, immunity was refused where the vessels concerned, although owned by the states claiming immunity, were held subject to the jurisdiction since at the relevant time they were not in the possession or control of these states.[24]

Since the courts will not try a case in which a foreign state is the defendant, it is necessary to decide what a foreign state is in each instance. Where doubts are raised as to the status of a foreign entity and whether or not it is to be regarded as a state for the purposes of the municipal courts, the executive certificate issued by the UK government will be decisive.

The case of *Duff Development Company* v. *Kelantan*[25] is a good example of this point. Kelantan was a Malay state and firmly under British protection. Both its internal and external policies were subject to British direction and it could in no way be described as politically independent. However, the UK government had issued an executive certificate to the effect that Kelantan was an independent state and that the Crown neither exercised nor claimed any rights of sovereignty or jurisdiction over it. The House of Lords, to whom the case had come, declared that once the Crown recognised a foreign ruler as sovereign, this bound the courts and no other evidence was admissible or needed. Accordingly, Kelantan was entitled to sovereign immunity from the jurisdiction of the English courts.

The Restrictive Approach

A number of states in fact started adopting the restrictive approach to immunity, permitting the exercise of jurisdiction over non-sovereign acts, at a relatively early stage.[26] The Supreme Court of

---

[24] *The Navemar,* 303 US 68 (1938); 9 *ILR*, p.176 and *Republic of Mexico* v. *Hoffman,* 324 US 30 (1945); 12 *ILR*, p.143.

[25] [1924] AC 797; 2 *ILR*, p.124. By s.21 of the State Immunity Act, 1978, an executive certificate is deemed to be conclusive as to e.g. statehood in this context. See also *Trawnik* v. *Gordon Lennox,* [1985] 2 All ER 368 as to the issue of a certificate under s. 21 on the status of the Commander of UK forces in Berlin.

[26] See e.g. Belgium and Italy, Lauterpacht, *op. cit.*; Badr, *op. cit.,* Chapter 2; Sinclair, *op. cit.*; Brownlie, *Principles of Public International Law,* 4th ed., 1990, p.327 and the Tate letter, 26 *Department of State Bulletin,* 984 (1952). See also the Brussels Convention on the Immunity

Austria in 1950, in a comprehensive survey of practice, concluded that in the light of the increased activity of states in the commercial field the classic doctrine of absolute immunity had lost its meaning and was no longer a rule of international law.[27] In 1952, in the Tate letter, the United States Department of State declared that the increasing involvement of governments in commercial activities coupled with the changing views of foreign states to absolute immunity rendered a change necessary and that thereafter "the Department [will] follow the restrictive theory of sovereign immunity".[28] This approach was also adopted by the courts, most particularly in *Victory Transport Inc.* v. *Comisaria General de Abasteciementos y Transportes.*[29] In this case, the Court, in the absence of a State Department "suggestion" as to the immunity of the defendants, a branch of the Spanish Ministry of Commerce, affirmed jurisdiction since the chartering of a ship to transport wheat was not strictly a political or public act. The restrictive theory approach was endorsed by four Supreme Court Justices in *Alfred Dunhill of London Inc.* v. *Republic of Cuba.*[30]

As far as the UK was concerned, the adoption of the restrictive approach occurred rather later.[31]

In the *Philippine Admiral* case,[32] the vessel which was owned by the Philippine government had writs issued against it in Hong Kong by two shipping corporations. The Privy Council, hearing the case on appeal from the Supreme Court of Hong Kong, reviewed previous decisions on sovereign immunity and concluded that it

---

of State-owned Ships, 1926, which assimilated the position of such ships engaged in trade to that of private ships regarding submission to the jurisdiction and the 1958 Conventions on the Territorial Sea and on the High Seas. See now articles 31, 32, 95 and 96 of the 1982 Convention on the Law of the Sea.

[27] *Dralle* v. *Republic of Czechoslovakia,* 17 *ILR,* p.155. This case was cited with approval by the West German Supreme Constitutional Court in *The Empire of Iran,* 45 *ILR,* p.57 and by the US Court of Appeals in *Victory Transport Inc.* v. *Comisaria General de Abasteciementos y Transportes,* 35 *ILR,* p.110.

[28] 26 *Department of State Bulletin,* 984 (1952).

[29] 35 *ILR,* p.110. See also e.g. *National City Bank of New York* v. *Republic of China,* 22 *ILR,* p.210 and *Rich* v. *Naviera Vacuba,* 32 *ILR,* p.127.

[30] 15 *ILM,* 1976, pp.735, 744, 746-47; 66 *ILR,* pp.212, 221, 224.

[31] See for some early reconsiderations, Lord Denning in *Rahimtoola* v. *Nizam of Hyderabad,* [1958] AC 379, 422; 24 *ILR,* pp.175, 190.

[32] [1976] 2 WLR 214; 64 *ILR,* p.90. Sinclair describes this as an "historic landmark", *op. cit.,* p.154. See also Higgins, "Recent Developments in the Law of Sovereign Immunity in the United Kingdom", 71 *AJIL,* 1977, pp.423, 424.

would not follow the *Porto Alexandre* case.[33] Lord Cross gave four reasons for not following the earlier case. First, that the Court of Appeal wrongly felt that they were bound by the *Parlement Belge*[34] decision. Secondly, that the House of Lords in *The Cristina*[35] had been divided on the issue of immunity for state owned vessels engaged in commerce. Thirdly, that the trend of opinion was against the absolute immunity doctrine; and fourthly that it was "wrong" to apply the doctrine since states could in the western world be sued in their own courts on commercial contracts and there was no reason why foreign states should not be equally liable to be sued.[36] Thus, the Privy Council held that in cases where a state owned merchant ship involved in ordinary trade was the object of a writ, it would not be entitled to sovereign immunity and the litigation would proceed.

In the case of *Thai-Europe Tapioca Service Ltd* v. *Government of Pakistan*,[37] a German owned ship on charter to carry goods from Poland to Pakistan had been bombed in Karachi by Indian planes during the 1971 war. Since the agreement provided for disputes to be settled by arbitration in England, the matter came eventually before the English courts. The cargo had previously been consigned to a Pakistani corporation, and that corporation had been taken over by the Pakistani government. The shipowners sued the government for the 67 day delay in unloading that had resulted from the bombing. The government pleaded sovereign immunity and sought to have the action dismissed.

The Court of Appeal decided that since all the relevant events had taken place outside the jurisdiction and in view of the action being *in personam* against the foreign government rather than against the ship itself, the general principle of sovereign immunity would have to stand.

Lord Denning declared in this case that there were certain exceptions to the doctrine of sovereign immunity. It did not apply where the action concerned land situated in the UK or trust funds lodged in the UK or debts incurred in the jurisdiction for services

[33]   [1920] P.30; 1 *ILR*, p.146.
[34]   (1880) 5 PD 197.
[35]   [1938] AC 485; 9 *ILR*, p.250.
[36]   [1976] 2 WLR 214, 232; 64 *ILR*, pp.90, 108. Note that Lord Cross believed that the absolute theory still obtained with regard to actions *in personam, ibid.*, p.233.
[37]   [1975] 1 WLR 1485; 64 *ILR*, p.81.

rendered to property in the UK, nor was there any immunity when a commercial transaction was entered into with a trader in the UK "and a dispute arises which is properly within the territorial jurisdiction of our courts".[38]

This unfortunate split approach, absolute immunity for actions *in personam* and restrictive immunity for actions *in rem* did not, however, last long. In *Trendtex Trading Corporation Ltd.* v. *Central Bank of Nigeria*,[39] all three judges of the Court of Appeal accepted the validity of the restrictive approach as being consonant with justice, comity and international practice.[40] The problem of precedent was resolved for two of the judges by declaring that international law knew no doctrine of *stare decisis*.[41] The clear acceptance of the restrictive theory of immunity in *Trendtex* was reaffirmed in later cases,[42] particularly by the House of Lords in the *I° Congreso del Partido* case[43] and in *Alcom Ltd.* v. *Republic of Colombia*.[44]

The majority of states now have tended to accept the restrictive immunity doctrine[45] and this has been reflected in domestic legislation. The US Foreign Sovereign Immunities Act, 1976,[46] provides in section 1605 for the grounds upon which a state may be subject to the jurisdiction (as general exceptions to the jurisdiction immunity of a foreign state), while the UK State Immunity Act, 1978,[47] similarly provides for a general rule of

---

[38] *Ibid.*, pp.1490-91; 64 *ILR*, p.84.

[39] [1977] 2 WLR 356; 64 *ILR*, p.122.

[40] *Ibid.*, pp.366-67, (Denning MR), 380 (Stephenson LJ) and 385-86 (Shaw LJ).

[41] *Ibid.*, pp.365-66 and 380. But cf. Stephenson LJ, *ibid.*, p.381. See further *supra*, Chapter 4, p.112.

[42] See e.g. *Hispano Americana Mercantil SA* v. *Central Bank of Nigeria*, [1979] 2 LL. R 277; 64 *ILR*, p.221.

[43] [1981] 2 All ER 1064; 64 *ILR*, p.307, a case concerned with the pre-1978 Act common law. See also *Planmount Ltd* v. *Republic of Zaire*, [1981] 1 All ER 1110; 64 *ILR*, p.268.

[44] [1984] 2 All ER 6; 74 *ILR*, p.179.

[45] See e.g. the *Administration des Chemins de Fer du Gouvernement Iranien* case, 52 *ILR*, p.315 and the *Empire of Iran* case, 45 *ILR*, p.57; see also Sinclair, *op. cit.*; Badr, *op. cit.*; and UN *Materials, op. cit.*

[46] See e.g. Delaume, "Public Debt and Sovereign Immunity; The Foreign Sovereign Immunities Act of 1976", 71 *AJIL*, 1977, p.399; Sinclair, *op. cit.*, p.243 *et seq.* and Weber, "The Foreign Sovereign Immunities Act of 1976", 3 *Yale Studies in World Public Order*, 1976, p.1.

[47] See e.g. Bowett, "The State Immunity Act 1978", 37 *Cambridge Law Journal*, 1978, p.193; White, "The State Immunity Act 1978", 42 *MLR*, 1979, p.72; Sinclair, *op. cit.*, p.257 *et seq.* and Shaw, "The State Immunity Act 1978", *New Law Journal*, 23 November 1978, p.1136.

immunity from the jurisdiction of the courts with a range of exceptions thereto.[48]

The Soviet Union and some other countries generally adhere to the absolute immunity theory, and in practice have entered into many bilateral agreements permitting the exercise of jurisdiction in cases where a commercial contract has been signed on the territory of the other state party.[49]

Sovereign and Non-Sovereign Acts

With the acceptance of the restrictive theory, it becomes crucial to analyse the distinction between those acts that will benefit from immunity and those that will not. In the *Victory Transport* case,[50] the Court declared that it would (in the absence of a State Department suggestion)[51] refuse to grant immunity, unless the activity in question fell within one of the categories of strictly political or public acts; viz. internal administrative acts, legislative acts, acts concerning the armed forces or diplomatic activity and public loans. However, the basic approach of recent legislation[52] has been to proclaim a rule of immunity and then list the exceptions, so that the onus of proof falls on the other side of the line. This approach is mirrored in the articles of the Draft produced by the International Law Commission on "Jurisdictional Immunities of States and Their Property" in 1986. Draft article 6 notes that:

[48] See also the 1972 European Convention on State Immunity. The Additional Protocol to the European Convention, which establishes a European Tribunal in matters of State Immunity to determine disputes under the Convention, came into force on 22 May 1985. It will initially be composed of the same members as the European Court of Human Rights, see Council of Europe Press Release, C(85)39. See generally UN *Materials, op. cit.*, Part I "National Legislation", and Badr, *op. cit.*, Chapter 3. See also the Inter-American Draft Convention on Jurisdictional Immunity of States, 22 *ILM*, 1983, p.292. Note that the large number of cases precipitated by the 1979 Iran Hostages Crisis and the US freezing of assets were argued on the basis of the restrictive theory, before being terminated, see e.g. Edwards, "Extraterritorial Application of the US Iranian Assets Control Regulations", 75 *AJIL*, 1981, p.870. See also *Dames and Moore* v. *Regan*, 101 S. Ct. 1972 (1981); 72 *ILR*, p.270.

[49] See for a number of examples, UN *Materials, op. cit.*, pp.134-50. See also Boguslavsky, "Foreign State Immunity; Soviet Doctrine and practice", 10 *Netherlands Yearbook of International Law*, 1979, p.167.

[50] 336 F.2d 354(1964); 35 *ILR*, p.110. See also Lalive, "L'Immunité de Juridiction des Etats et des Organisations Internationales", 84 *HR*, p.205 and Lauterpacht, *op. cit.*, pp.237-39.

[51] Note that since the 1976 Foreign Sovereign Immunities Act, the determination of such status is a judicial, not executive act.

[52] See e.g. s.1 of the State Immunty Act 1978 and s.1604 of the US Foreign Sovereign Immunities Act 1976.

A state enjoys immunity in respect of itself and its property, from the jurisdiction of the courts of another state subject to the provisions of the present articles [and the relevant rules of general international law].[53]

The issue is, of course, crucial. Is the basic rule one of submission to the jurisdiction of another state subject to a list of exceptions in which immunity would be recognised, or is the basic rule one of immunity, subject to listed exceptions where jurisdiction could be exercised? There are many legal theories and extensive state practice on this point, depending on whether immunity is seen as a derogation from territorial sovereignty and thus to be justified in each particular case, or as a rule of international law as such, thus not requiring substantiation in each and every case.[54]

It would seem, however, that the approach positing a rule of immunity with exceptions providing for the exercise of the territorial state's jurisdiction in specific instances is the dominant one. In determining the characterisation of an activity as either sovereign *(jure imperii)* or non-sovereign *(jure gestionis),* the test is basically that of the nature of the transaction rather than its purpose.[55]

However, it should be noted that article 3(2) of the ILC Draft provides that:

In determining whether a contract for the sale or purchase of goods or the supply of services is commercial, reference should be made primarily to the nature of the contract, but the purpose of the contract should also be taken into account if, in the practice of that state, that purpose is relevant to determining the non-commercial character of the contract.[56]

[53] *Yearbook of the ILC,* 1986, vol.II, Part 2, p.9. Note that the reason for the square brackets is that the members of the ILC were divided as to the value of the inclusion of the phrase enclosed and thus left the issue to be resolved at a later date in the light of comments from governments, *ibid.,* p.16.

[54] See the Commentary to this draft article, *Yearbook of the ILC,* 1980, vol.II, Part 2, pp.142-57.

[55] See e.g. s.1603(d) of the US Foreign Sovereign Immunities Act of 1976. The Section-by-Section analysis of the Act emphasises that "the fact that goods or services to be procured through a contract are to be used for a public purpose is irrelevant; it is the initially commercial nature of an activity or transaction that is critical", reproduced in UN *Materials, op. cit.,* pp.103, 107. See also the *Empire of Iran* case, 45 *ILR,* pp.57, 80-81; *Trendtex Trading Corporation Ltd.* v. *Central Bank of Nigeria,* [1977] 2 WLR 356; 64 *ILR,* p.122; *Non-resident Petitioner* v. *Central Bank of Nigeria,* 16 *ILM,* 1977, p.501 (a West German case) and *Planmount Ltd.* v. *Republic of Zaire,* [1981] 1 All ER 1110; 64 *ILR,* p.268.

[56] *Yearbook of the ILC,* 1986, vol.II, Part 2, p.9.

The reason for the modified "nature" test was in order to provide an adequate safeguard and protection for developing countries, particularly as they attempt to promote national economic development. The ILC Commentary to this draft article notes that states should be given an opportunity to maintain that in their practice a particular contract or transaction should be treated as non-commercial since its purpose is clearly public and supported by reasons of state. Examples given include the procurement of arms for defence, materials for the construction of a base, medicaments to fight a spreading epidemic, and food supplies.[57]

This, if adopted, is likely to cause considerable confusion in certain situations and may be seen as something of a retreat from the restrictive immunity approach. It is a view that, as will be seen, appears to suggest a move against the current trend.

Lord Wilberforce in *P Congreso del Partido*[58] emphasised that in considering whether immunity should be recognised one had to consider the whole context in which the claim is made in order to identify the "relevant act" which formed the basis of that claim. In particular, was it an act *jure gestionis,* or in other words "an act of a private law character such as a private citizen might have entered into"?[59] This use of the private law/public law dichotomy,[59] familiar to civil law systems, was particularly noticeable, although different states draw the distinction at different points.[60] It should also be noted, however, that this distinction is less familiar to common law systems. In addition, the issues ascribed to the governmental sphere as distinct from the private area rest upon the particular political concept proclaimed by the state in question, so that a clear and comprehensive international consensus regarding the line of distinction is unlikely.[61] The characterisation of an act as *jure gestionis* or *jure imperii* will also depend upon the perception of the issue at hand by the courts.

The issue raised in the *Congreso* case was whether immunity could be granted where, while the initial transaction was clearly commercial,

[57] *Yearbook of the ILC,* 1983, vol.II, Part 2.

[58] [1981] 2 All ER 1064; 64 *ILR,* p.307.

[59] *Ibid.,* p.1070; 64 *ILR,* p.314.

[60] See e.g. Sinclair, *op. cit.,* pp.210-13 and the *Empire of Iran* case, 45 *ILR,* pp.57, 80. See also article 7 of the European Convention on State Immunity 1972.

[61] See e.g. Crawford, *op. cit.,* p.88; Lauterpacht, *op. cit.,* pp.220, 224-26 and Brownlie, *op. cit.,* pp.330-31.

the cause of the breach of the contract in question appeared to be an exercise of sovereign authority. In that case, two vessels operated by a Cuban state-owned shipping enterprise and delivering sugar to a Chilean company were ordered by the Cuban government to stay away from Chile after the Allende regime had been overthrown. The Cuban government pleaded sovereign immunity on the grounds that the breach of the contract was occasioned as a result of a foreign policy decision. The House of Lords did not accept this and argued that once a state had entered the trading field, it would require a high standard of proof of a sovereign act for immunity to be introduced. Lord Wilberforce emphasised that:

> in order to withdraw its action from the sphere of acts done *jure gestionis*, a state must be able to point to some act clearly done *jure imperii* [62]

and that the appropriate test was to be expressed as follows:

> it is not just that the purpose or motive of the act is to serve the purposes of the state, but that the act is of its own character a governmental act, as opposed to an act which any private citizen can perform.[63]

In the circumstances of the case, that test had not been satisfied. One of the two ships, the *Playa Larga*, had been owned at all relevant times by the Cuban Government, but the second ship, the *Marble Islands,* was owned by a trading enterprise not entitled to immunity. When this ship was on the high seas, it was taken over by the Cuban Government and ordered to proceed to North Vietnam, where its cargo was eventually donated to the people of that country. The Court was unanimous in rejecting the plea of immunity with regard to the *Playa Larga,* but was split over the second ship.

Two members of the House of Lords, Lord Wilberforce and Lord Edmund-Davies, felt that the key element with regard to the *Marble Islands,* as distinct from the *Playa Larga,* where the Government had acted as owner of the ship and not as governmental authority, was that the Republic of Cuba directed the disposal of the cargo in North Vietnam. This was not part of any commercial arrangement which was conducted by the demise charterer, who

---

[62] [1981] 2 All ER 1064, 1075; 64 *ILR*, p.320.
[63] *Ibid.*, quoting the judge at first instance, [1978] 1 All ER 1169, 1192; 64 *ILR*, p.179.

was thus responsible for the civil wrongs committed. The acts of the Government were outside this framework and accordingly purely governmental.[64]

However, the majority held that the Cuban Government had acted in the context of a private owner in discharging and disposing of the cargo in North Vietnam and had not regarded itself as acting in the exercise of sovereign powers. Everything had been done in purported reliance upon private law rights in that the demise charterers had sold the cargo to another Cuban state enterprise by ordinary private law sale and in purported reliance upon the bill of lading which permitted the sale in particular instances. It was the purchaser that donated the cargo to the Vietnamese people.[65]

In many respects, nevertheless, the minority view is the more acceptable one, in that in reality it was the Cuban Government's taking control of the ship and direction of it and its cargo that determined the issue and this was done as a deliberate matter of state policy. The fact that it was accomplished by the private law route rather than, for example, by direct governmental decree should not settle the issue conclusively. In fact, one thing that the case does show is how difficult it is in reality to distinguish public from private acts.[66]

In his discussion of the development of the restrictive theory of sovereign or state immunity in *Alcom* v. *Republic of Colombia*,[67] Lord Diplock noted that the critical distinction was between what a state did in the exercise of its sovereign authority and what it did in the course of commercial activities. The former enjoyed immunity, the latter did not.[68]

Commercial Acts

Of all state activities for which immunity is no longer to be obtained, that of commercial transactions is the primary example and the definition of such activity is crucial.

---

[64] [1981] 2 All ER 1064, 1077 and 1081; 64 *ILR*, pp.321, 327.

[65] *Ibid.*, pp.1079-80, 1082 and 1083; 64 *ILR*, pp.325, 328, 329.

[66] Note that if the State Immunity Act, 1978 had been in force when the cause of action arose in this case, it is likely that the claim of immunity would have completely failed, see s.10.

[67] [1984] 2 All ER 6; 74 *ILR*, p.180.

[68] *Ibid.*, p.9; 74 *ILR*, p.181.

Section 3(3) of the State Immunity Act 1978 defines the term "commercial transaction" to mean:

(a) any contract for the supply of goods or services;
(b) any loan or other transaction for the provision of finance and any guarantee or indemnity in respect of any such transaction or of any other financial obligation; and
(c) any other transaction or activity (whether of a commercial, industrial, financial, professional or other similar character) into which a state enters or in which it engages otherwise than in the exercise of sovereign authority.

Thus a wide range of transactions are covered[69] and as Lord Diplock pointed out,[70] the 1978 Act does not adopt the straightforward dichotomy between acts *jure imperii* and those *jure gestionis*. Any contract falling within section 3 would be subject to the exercise of jurisdiction and the distinction between sovereign and non-sovereign acts in this context would not be relevant, except in so far as transactions falling within section 3(3)c were concerned, in the light of the use of the term "sovereign authority". The Act contains no reference to the public/private question, but the *Congreso* case (dealing with the pre-Act law) would seem to permit examples from foreign jurisdictions to be drawn upon in order to determine the nature of "the exercise of sovereign authority".[71]

The key question as to the definition of sovereign authority, of course, still remains.

Section 3(1) of the State Immunity Act provides that a state is not immune as respects proceedings relating to:

(a) a commercial transaction entered into by the state; or
(b) an obligation of the state which by virtue of a contract (whether

---

[69] Thus, for example, the defence of sovereign immunity was not available in an action relating to a contract for the repair of an ambassador's residence, *Planmount Ltd* v. *Republc of Zaire*, [1981] 1 All ER 1110; 64 *ILR*, p.268.

[70] *Alcom* v. *Republic of Colombia*, [1984] 2 All ER 6, 10; 74 *ILR*, p.183.

[71] S.3(3). In *Sengupta* v. *Republic of India*, 65 *ILR*, pp.325, 360, it was emphasised that in deciding whether immunity applied one had to consider whether it was the kind of contract an individual might make, whether it involved the participation of both parties in the public functions of the state, the nature of the alleged breach and whether the investigation of the claim would involve an investigation into the public or sovereign acts of the foreign state.

a commercial transaction or not) falls to be performed wholly or partly in the United Kingdom.[72]

The scope of section 3(1)a was discussed by the court in *Australia and New Zealand Banking Group* v. *Commonwealth of Australia.*[73] This case arose out of the collapse of the International Tin Council in 1985. The ensuing litigation sought, by various routes, to ascertain whether the member-states of the ITC (which was itself an international organisation with separate personality[74]) could be held liable themselves for the debts of that organisation — a prospect vigorously opposed by the states concerned. The case in question concerned an attempt by the brokers and banks to hold the member-states of the ITC liable in tort for losses caused by misrepresentation and fraudulent trading.

It was argued by the defendants that as far as section 3(1) was concerned, the activity in question not only had to be commercial within the Act's definition but also undertaken "otherwise than in the exercise of sovereign authority". Evans J saw little difference in practice between the two terms in the context.[75] The defendants also argued that the term "activity" meant something more than a single act or sequence of acts. Evans J did not accept this, but did emphasise that the activity in question had to be examined in context. It was held that both the trading and loan contracts under discussion in the case were commercial and that if it could be demonstrated that the member states of the ITC had authorised them, such authorisation would amount to commercial activity within the meaning of section 3.[76]

The scope of section 3(1)b was discussed by the Court of Appeal in *Maclaine Watson* v. *Department of Trade and Industry,*[77] which concerned the direct action by the brokers and banks against the member-states of the ITC in respect of liability for the debts of the organisation on a contractual basis. It was held that the "contract" referred to need not have been entered into by the state as such. That particular phrase was absent from section 3(1)b. Accordingly,

---

[72] Note that by s.3(3), s.3(1) does not apply to a contract of employment between a state and an individual.

[73] 1989, Transcript, p.52 *et seq.*

[74] See *infra,* Chapter 19.

[75] *Ibid.,* p.54.

[76] *Ibid.,* pp.56-57.

[77] [1988] 3 WLR 1033; 80 *ILR,* p.49.

the member-states would not have been able to benefit from immunity in the kind of secondary liability of a guarantee nature that the plaintiffs were *inter alia* basing their case upon.[78] This view was adopted in the tort action against the member-states[79] in the more difficult context where the obligation in question was a tortious obligation on the part of the member-states, that is the authorisation or procuring of a misrepresentation inducing the creditors concerned to make a contract with another party (the ITC).[80]

Section 1603(d) of the US Foreign Sovereign Immunities Act, 1976 defines "commercial activity" as "a regular course of commercial conduct or a particular commercial transaction or act". It is also noted that the commercial character of an activity is to be determined by reference to the nature of the activity rather than its purpose. The courts have held that the purchases of food were commercial activities[81] as were purchases of cement,[82] the sending by a Government Ministry of artists to perform in the US under a US impresario[83] and activities by state airlines.[84]

The issuance of foreign governmental Treasury notes has also been held to constitute a commercial activity, but one which once validly statute-barred by passage of time cannot be revived or altered.[85]

In *Callejo* v. *Bancomer*,[86] a case in which a Mexican bank refused to redeem certificate of deposit, the District Court dismissed the action on the ground that the bank was an instrumentality of the Mexican government and thus benefited from sovereign immunity, although the Court of Appeals decided the issue on the basis that the act of state doctrine applied since an investigation of a sovereign act performed wholly within the foreign government's territory

[78] *Ibid.*, pp.1104-5 (Kerr LJ) and 1130 (Nourse LJ); 80 *ILR*, pp.119, 148.

[79] *Australia and New Zealand Banking Group* v. *Commonwealth of Australia*, 1989, Transcript pp.57-59.

[80] It should be noted that Evans J reached his decision on this point only with considerable hesitation and reluctance, *ibid.*, p.59.

[81] See e.g. *Gemini Shipping* v. *Foreign Trade Organisation for Chemicals and Foodstuffs*, 63 *ILR*, p.569 and *ADM Milling Co.* v. *Republic of Bolivia*, 63 *ILR*, p.56.

[82] *NAC* v. *Federal Republic of Nigeria*, 63 *ILR*, p.137.

[83] *United Euram Co.* v. *USSR*, 63 *ILR*, p.228.

[84] *Argentine Airlines* v. *Ross*, 63 *ILR*, p.195.

[85] *Schmidt* v. *Polish People's Republic*, 742 F.2d 67(1984). See also *Jackson* v. *People's Republic of China*, 596 F.Supp. 386 (1984); *Amoco Overseas Oil Co.* v. *Compagnie Nationale Algérienne*, 605 F.2d 648 (1979); 63 *ILR*, p.252 and *Corporacion Venezolana de Fomenta* v. *Vintero Sales*, 629 F.2d 786 (1980); 63 *ILR*, p.477.

[86] 764 F.2d 1101 (1985).

would otherwise be required. In other cases, US courts have dealt with the actions of Mexican banks consequent upon Mexican exchange control regulations on the basis of sovereign immunity.[87]

The purchase of military equipment by Haiti for use by its army[88] and a military training agreement whereby a foreign soldier was in the US were held not to be commercial activities.[89] It has also been decided that Somalia's participation in an Agency for International Development programme constituted a public or governmental act,[90] while the publication of a libel in a journal distributed in the US was not a commercial activity where the journal concerned constituted an official commentary of the Soviet Government.[91]

Many cases before the US courts have, however, centred upon the jurisdictional requirements of section 1605(a), which states that a foreign state is not immune in any case in which the action is based upon a commercial activity carried on in the US by a foreign state; or upon an act performed in the US in connection with a foreign state's commercial activity elsewhere; or upon an act outside the territory of the US in connection with a foreign state's commercial activity elsewhere, when that act causes a direct effect in the US.[92]

In *Zedan* v. *Kingdom of Saudi Arabia*,[93] for example, the US Court of Appeals in discussing the scope of section 1605(a)(2) emphasised that the commercial activity in question taking place in the US had to be substantial, so that a telephone call in the US which initiated a sequence of events which resulted in the plaintiff working in Saudi Arabia was not sufficient. Additionally, where an act is performed in the US in connection with a commercial activity of a foreign state elsewhere, this act must in itself be sufficient to form

---

[87] See e.g. *Braka* v. *Nacional Financiera*, No.83-4161 (SDNY July 9, 1984) and *Frankel* v. *Banco Nacional de Mexico*, No.82-6457 (SDNY May 31, 1983) cited in 80 *AJIL*, 1986, p.172, note 5.

[88] *Aerotrade Inc.* v. *Republic of Haiti*, 63 *ILR*, p.41.

[89] *Castro* v. *Saudi Arabia*, 63 *ILR*, p.419.

[90] *Transamerican Steamship Corp* v. *Somali Democratic Republic*, 590 F.Supp. 968 (1984) and 767 F.2d 998. This is based upon the legislative history of the 1976 Act, see the H.R. Rep. No. 1487, 94th Cong., 2d Sess. 16 (1976).

[91] *Yessenin-Volpin* v. *Novosti Press Agency*, 443 F.Supp. 849 (1978); 63 *ILR*, p.127.

[92] See e.g. *International Shoe Co* v. *Washington*, 326 US 310 (1945); *McGee* v. *International Life Insurance Co.*, 355 US 220 (1957); *Libyan-American Oil Co* v. *Libya*, 482 F.Supp. 1175 (1980); 62 *ILR*, p.220; *Perez et al* v. *The Bahamas*, 482 F.Supp. 1208 (1980); 63 *ILR*, p.350 and *Thos. P. Gonzalez Corp* v. *Consejo Nacional de Produccion de Costa Rica*, 614 F.2d 1247 (1980); 63 *ILR*, p.370, aff'd 652 F.2d 186 (1982).

[93] 849 F.2d 1511 (1988).

the basis of a cause of action,[94] while the direct effect in the US provision of an act abroad in connection with a foreign state's commercial activity elsewhere was subject to a high threshold. As the Court noted[95] in cases where this clause was held to have been satisfied, "something legally significant actually happened in the United States".[96]

It is interesting to note the approach adopted in the ILC Draft on Jurisdictional Immunities. Article 12 provides for immunity where a state enters into a "commercial contract" with a foreign natural or juridical person (but not another state, or a government to government arrangement) in a situation where by virtue of the rules of private international law a dispute comes before the courts of another state. Article 2(1)b provides that the term "commercial contract" means:

(i) any commercial contract or transaction for the sale or purchase of goods or the supply of services;

(ii) any contract for a loan or other transaction of a financial nature, including any obligation of guarantee in respect of any such loan or of indemnity in respect of any such transaction;

(iii) any other contract or transaction, whether of a commercial, industrial, trading or professional nature, but not including a contract of employment of persons.[97]

It should be noted that the expressions in draft articles 12 and 2(1)b exclude any reference to "trading or commercial activity". This was an attempt to narrow the scope of non-immunity situations[98] and can be seen as a further example of the rather more restrictive approach adopted by the ILC to the question of limiting immunity situations.

---

[94] *Ibid.*

[95] *Ibid.*, p.1515.

[96] Referring to the cases of *Transamerican Steamship Corp* v. *Somali Democratic Republic,* 767 F.2d 998, 1004, where demand for payment in the US by an agency of the Somali government and actual bank transfers were held to be sufficient, and *Texas Trading & Milling Corp.* v. *Federal Republic of Nigeria,* 647 F.2d 300, 312; 63 *ILR,* pp.552, 563, where refusal to pay letters of credit issued by a US bank and payable in the US to financially injured claimant was held to suffice.

[97] *Yearbook of the ILC,* 1986, vol.II, Part 2, p.8.

[98] See the ILC Commentary to draft article 12, *Yearbook of the ILC,* 1983, vol.II, Part 2, p.27.

Other Non-Immunity Areas

Sections 4-11 of the UK Act detail the remainder of the wide-ranging non-immunity areas and include contracts of employment made in the UK or where the work is to be performed wholly or in part in the UK (section 4); death or personal injury or damage to or loss of tangible property caused by an act or omission in the UK (section 5); proceedings relating to immovable property (section 6); patents, trademarks, designs, plant breeders' rights or copyrights (section 7); proceedings relating to a state's membership of a body corporate, an un-incorporated body or partnership, with members other than states which is incorporated or constituted under UK law or is controlled from or has its principal place of business in the UK (section 8); where a state has agreed in writing to submit to arbitration and with respect to proceedings in the UK courts relating to that arbitration (section 9); Admiralty proceedings with regard to state owned ships used or intended for use for commercial purposes (section 10) and proceedings relating to liability for various taxes, such as VAT (section 11). This, together with generally similar provisions in the legislation of other states,[99] demonstrates how restricted the concept of sovereign acts is now becoming in practice in the context of sovereign immunity, although definitional problems remain.

The Personality Issue

Whether the absolute or restrictive theory is applied, the crucial factor is to determine the entity entitled to immunity. If the entity, in very general terms, is not part of the apparatus of state, then no immunity can arise. Shaw LJ in *Trendtex Trading Corporation Ltd.* v. *Central Bank of Nigeria*[100] cautioned against too facile an attribution of immunity particularly in the light of the growth of governmental functions, since its acceptance resulted in a significant disadvantage to the other party.

A department of government would, however, be entitled to immunity, even if it had a separate legal personality under its own

---

[99] See e.g. section 1605(a)4 and 5 of the US Foreign Sovereign Immunities Act, 1976.
[100] [1977] 2 WLR 356, 383; 64 *ILR*, pp.122, 147.

law.[101] The issue was discussed in detail in the *Trendtex* case. It was emphasised that recourse should be had to all the circumstances of the case. The fact of incorporation as a separate legal identity was noted in *Baccus SrL* v. *Servicio Nacional del Trigo*[102] and both Donaldson J at first instance and Denning MR emphasised this.[103] The question arises in analysing whether a body is a corporation or not, and indeed whether it is or is not an arm of government, as to which law is relevant. Each country may have its own rules governing incorporation, and similarly with regard to government departments. Should English law therefore merely accept the conclusions of the foreign law? The majority of the Court in *Baccus* was of the view that foreign law was decisive in questions relating to incorporation and whether corporateness was consistent with the recognition of immunity, and to a certain extent this was accepted in *Trendtex*. Shaw LJ declared that "the constitution and powers of Nigerian corporation must be viewed in the light of the domestic law of Nigeria".[104] However, the status on the international scene of the entity in question must be decided, it was held, by the law of the country in which the issue as to its status has been raised. The Court had to determine whether the Nigerian Bank could constitute a government department as understood in English law.[105] It was also noted that where a material difference existed between English law and the foreign law, this would be taken into account, but the Court was satisfied that this was not the case in *Trendtex*.

This position of pre-eminence for English law must not be understood to imply the application of decisions of English courts relating to immunities granted internally. These could be at best only rough guides to be utilised depending on the circumstances of each case. If the view taken by the foreign law was not conclusive, neither was the attitude adopted by the foreign government. It was a factor to be considered, again, but no more than that. In this, the Court followed *Krajina* v. *Tass Agency*.[106] The point was also made that the evidence provided by Nigerian officials, including the High Commissioner, that the Bank was a government organ, was not

---

[101] *Baccus SrL* v. *Servicio Nacional del Trigo*, [1957] 1 QB 438; 23 *ILR*, p.160.
[102] *Ibid.*, p.467.
[103] [1977] 2 WLR 356, 370; 64 *ILR*, p.133.
[104] *Ibid.*, p.385; 64 *ILR*, p.149.
[105] *Ibid.*, pp.385 and 175.
[106] [1949] 2 All ER 274.

conclusive. This was because the officials might very well be
applying a test of governmental control which would not be decisive
for the courts of this country.[107]

Of more importance was the legislative intention of the
government in creating and regulating the entity and the degree
of its control. Stephenson LJ in fact based his decision upon this
point. An express provision in the creative legislation to the effect
that the Bank was an arm of government was not necessary, but the
Bank had to prove that the intention to make it an organ of the
Nigerian State was of necessity to be implied from the enabling
Central Bank of Nigeria Act, 1958 and subsequent decrees. This the
Bank had failed to do and Stephenson LJ accordingly allowed the
appeal.[108] It could be argued that the judge was placing too much
stress upon this aspect, particularly in the light of the overall
approach of the Court in applying the functional rather than the
personality test. In many ways, Stephenson LJ was also looking at
the attributes of the Bank but from a slightly different perspective.
He examined the powers and duties of the entity and denied it
immunity since the intention of the government to establish the
Bank as an arm of itself could not be clearly demonstrated. The other
judges were concerned with the functions of the Bank as implying
governmental status *per se*.

The Court clearly accepted the functional test as the crucial
guide to the determination of sovereign immunity. In this it was
following the modern approach which has precipitated the change
in emphasis from the personality of the entity for which immunity
is claimed to the nature of the subject matter. This functional test
looks to the powers, duties and control of the entity within the
framework of its constitution and activities.

In such difficult borderline decisions, the proposition put forward
by Shaw LJ is to be welcomed. He noted that:

> where the issue of status trembles on a fine edge, the absence of any
> positive indication that the body in question was intended to possess
> sovereign status and its attendant privileges must perforce militate
> against the view that it enjoys that status or is entitled to those privileges.[109]

---

[107] [1977] 2 WLR 356, 370 and 374; 64 *ILR*, p.137, 139.
[108] *Ibid.*, pp.374-76. See also Shaw LJ, *ibid.*, p.384; 64 *ILR*, p.149.
[109] *Ibid.*

In *Czarnikow Ltd.* v. *Rolimpex*,[110] the House of Lords accepted as correct the findings of the arbitrators that although Rolimpex had been established by the Polish Government and was controlled by it, it was not so closely connected with the Government as to be an organ or department of the state. It had separate legal personality and had considerable freedom in day-to-day commercial activities.

Under section 14 of the State Immunity Act of 1978, a state is deemed to include the sovereign or other head of state in his public capacity,[111] the government and any department of that government, but not any entity "which is distinct from the executive organs of the government of the state and capable of suing or being sued". This modifies the *Baccus* and *Trendtex* approaches to some extent. Such a separate entity would only be immune if the proceedings related to acts done "in the exercise of sovereign authority" and the circumstances are such that a state would have been so immune. The US Foreign Sovereign Immunities Act of 1976 provides in section 1603 that "foreign state" includes a political subdivision of such a state and its agencies or instrumentalities. This is defined to mean any entity which is a separate legal person and which is an organ of a foreign state or political subdivision thereof or a majority of whose shares or other ownership interest is owned by a foreign state or political subdivision thereof or a majority of whose shares or other ownership interest is owned by a foreign state or political subdivision thereof and which is neither a citizen of a state of the United States nor created under the laws of any third country. This issue of personality has occasioned problems and some complex decisions.[112]

In *First National City Bank* v. *Banco Para el Comercio Exterior de Cuba (Bancec)*,[113] for example, the Supreme Court suggested a presumption of separateness for state entities, under which their separate legal personalities were to be recognised unless applicable equitable principles mandated otherwise or the parent

[110] [1979] AC 351, 364 (Lord Wilberforce) and 367 (Viscount Dilhorne).

[111] See also e.g. *Re Honecker*, 80 *ILR,* p.365.

[112] See e.g. *Gittler* v. *German Information Centre*, 408 NYS 2d 600 (1978); 63 *ILR,* p.170; *Carey* v. *National Oil Co.*, 453 F.Supp. 1097 (1978); 63 *ILR,* p.164 and *Yessenin-Volpin* v. *Novosti Press Agency*, 443 F.Supp. 849 (1978); 63 *ILR,* p.127. See also Sinclair, *op. cit.*, pp.248-49 and 258-59. Note in addition, articles 6 and 7 of the European Convention on State Immunity, 1972.

[113] 462 US 611 (1983); 80 *ILR,* p.566.

entity so completely dominated the subsidiary as to render it an agent of the parent.[114]

In *Republic of the Philippines* v. *Marcos (No.1)*,[115] the US Court of Appeals for the Second Circuit held that the Marcoses, the deposed leader of the Philippines and his wife, were not entitled to claim sovereign immunity, but went on to note that even if they were to have standing it was uncertain that the immunity of a foreign state would go so far as to render a former head of state immune as regards his private acts. In a further decision on the same general issue of immunity and the Marcoses, the Court of Appeals for the Fourth Circuit held in *In Re Grand Jury Proceedings, Doe No. 770*[116] that head of state immunity was primarily an attribute of state sovereignty, not an individual right, and that accordingly full effect should be given to the revocation by the Philippines Government of the immunity of the Marcoses.

One particular issue that has caused controversy in the past relates to the status of component units of federal states.[117] There have been cases asserting immunity[118] and denying immunity[119] in such circumstances. In *Mellenger* v. *New Brunswick Development Corporation*,[120] Lord Denning emphasised that since under the Canadian constitution:

> (each) provincial government, within its own sphere, retained its independence and autonomy directly under the Crown . . . It follows that the Province of New Brunswick is a sovereign state in its own right and entitled if it so wishes to claim sovereign immunity.

However, article 28 of the European Convention on State Immunity 1972 provides that constituent states of a federal state do not enjoy immunity, although this general principle is subject

---

[114] See also *Foremost-McKesson Inc* v. *Islamic Republic of Iran*, 905 F.2d 438 (1990).

[115] 806 F.2d 344 (1986); 81 *ILR*, p.581.

[116] 817 F.2d 1108 (1987); 81 *ILR*, p.599.

[117] See e.g. Bernier, *International Legal Aspects of Federalism*, 1973, p.121 *et seq.* and Sucharitkul, *State Immunities and Trading Activities in International Law*, 1959, p.106.

[118] See e.g. *Feldman* c. *Etat de Bahia, Pasicrisie Belge*, 208, II, 55; *Etat de Céara* c. *Dorr et autres*, 4 *ILR*, p.39; *Etat de Céara* c. *D'Archer de Montgascon*, 6 *ILR*, p.162 and *Dumont* c. *Etat d'Amazonas*, 15 *ILR*, p.140. See also *Etat de Hesse* c. *Jean Negev*, 74 *Revue Générale de Droit International Public*, 1970, p.1108.

[119] See e.g. *Sullivan* v. *State of Sao Paulo*, 122 F.2d 355 (1941); 10 *ILR*, p.178.

[120] [1971] 2 All ER 593, 595; 52 *ILR*, pp.322, 324. See also *Swiss-Israel Trade Bank* v. *Salta*, 55 *ILR*, p.411.

to the proviso that federal state parties may declare by notification that their constituent states may invoke the benefits and carry out the obligations of the Convention.[121]

The State Immunity Act follows this pattern in that component units of a federation are not entitled to immunity. However, section 14(5) provides that the Act may be made applicable to the "constituent territories of a federal state by specific Order in Council".[122] Thus, *Mellenger* is reversed, but the international situation is rather less clear.[123]

The issue of the status of the European Community in this context was raised in the course of the ITC litigation as the EEC was a party to the sixth International Tin Agreement 1982 under which the ITC was constituted. The Court of Appeal in *Maclaine Watson v. Department of Trade and Industry*[124] held that the EEC's claim to sovereign immunity was untenable. It had been conceded that the EEC was not a state and thus could not rely on the State Immunity Act 1978, but it was argued that the Community was entitled to immunity analogous to sovereign immunity under the rules of common law. This approach was held by Kerr LJ to be "entirely misconceived".[125] Although the EEC had personality in international law and was able to exercise powers and functions analogous to those of sovereign states, this did not lead on to immunity as such. This was because sovereign immunity was "a derogation from the normal exercise of jurisdiction by the courts and should be accorded only in clear cases",[126] while the concept itself was based upon the equality of states. The EEC Treaty 1957 and the Merger Treaty 1965 themselves

---

[121] See e.g. Sinclair, "The European Convention on State Immunity", 22 *ICLQ*, 1973, pp.254, 279-80.

[122] An Order in Council has been made with respect to the constituent territories of Austria, S.1. 1979 no.457. The Act may also be extended to dependent territories, see e.g. the State Immunity (Overseas Territories) Order, 1979, S.1. 1979 no.458 and the State Immunity (Jersey) Order, 1985, S.1. 1985 no.1642.

[123] See section 1603(a) of the US Foreign Sovereign Immunities Act, 1976 in which the term "foreign state" is defined *inter alia* to include a political subdivision of a foreign state.

[124] [1988] 3 WLR 1033; 80 *ILR*, p.49. The issue of the personality of the EEC is addressed in Chapter 19, *infra*.

[125] *Ibid.*, p.1107; 80 *ILR*, p.122.

[126] *Victory Transport v. Comisaria General de Abastecimientos y Transportes*, 336 F.2d 354 (1964) cited with approval by Ackner LJ in *Empresa Exportadora de Azucar v. Industria Azucarera Nacional*, [1983] 2 LL. Rep. 171, 193 and Lord Edmund-Davies in *P Congreso del Partido*, [1983] 1 AC 244, 276.

made no claim for general immunity and nothing else existed upon which such a claim could be based.[127]

Waiver of Immunity

It is possible, of course, for a state to waive expressly or impliedly its immunity from the jurisdiction of the court. Express waiver of immunity from jurisdiction, however, does not of itself mean waiver of immunity from execution.[128] In the case of implied waiver, some care is required. Section 2 of the State Immunity Act provides for loss of immunity upon submission to the jurisdiction, either by a prior written agreement[129] or after the particular dispute has arisen. A state is deemed to have submitted to the jurisdiction where the state has instituted proceedings or has intervened or taken any step in the proceedings.[130] If a state submits to proceedings, it is deemed to have submitted to any counterclaim arising out of the same legal relationship or facts as the claim. A provision in an agreement that it is to be governed by the law of the UK is not to be taken as a submission. By section 9, a state which has agreed in writing to submit a dispute to arbitration is not immune from proceedings in the courts which relate to the arbitration.[131]

---

[127] [1988] 3 WLR 1033, 1108-12; 80 *ILR*, pp.49, 123. Nourse and Ralph Gibson LLJ agreed with Kerr LJ completely on this issue, *ibid.*, pp.1131 and 1158; 80 *ILR*, pp.150, 180.

[128] See e.g. article 22(2) of the ILC Draft Articles on Jurisdictional Immunities. Note, however, that the issue will turn upon the interpretation of the terms of the waiver, see *A Company* v. *Republic of X*, 1989, Transcript p.7. However, it is suggested that the principle that waiver of immunity from jurisdiction does not of itself constitute a waiver of immunity from the grant of relief by the courts is of the nature of a presumption, thus placing the burden of proof to the contrary upon the private party and having implications with regard to the standard of proof required.

[129] Overruling *Kahan* v. *Pakistan Federation*, [1951] 2 KB 1003; 18 *ILR*, p.210.

[130] But not where the intervention or step taken is only for the purpose of claiming immunity, or where the step taken by the state is in ignorance of facts entitling it to immunity if those facts could not reasonably have been ascertained and immunity is claimed as soon as reasonably practicable, s.2(5). See also article 1 of the European Convention on State Immunity and article 9 of the ILC Draft Articles on Jurisdictional Immunities.

[131] See also articles 2 and 14 of the European Convention on State Immunity 1972 and draft articles 8 and 9 of the ILC Draft Articles on Jurisdictional Immunities, see *Yearbook of the ILC*, 1981, vol.II, p.148 *et seq.* and *Yearbook of the ILC*, 1986, vol.II, Part 2, p.9. S.1605(a)(1) of the US Foreign Sovereign Immunities Act, 1976 provides that a foreign state is not immune where it has waived its immunity either expressly or by implication, notwithstanding any withdrawal of the waiver which the foreign state may purport to effect, except in accordance with the terms of the waiver. It should also be noted that a substantial number of bilateral treaties expressly waive immunity from jurisdiction. This is particularly the case where the states maintaining the absolute immunity approach are concerned, see e.g. UN *Materials, op. cit.*, Part III.

Pre-Judgment Attachment [132]

Section 1610(d) of the US Foreign Sovereign Immunities Act, 1976 prohibits the attachment of the property of a foreign state before judgment unless that state has explicitly waived its immunity from attachment prior to judgment and the purpose of the attachment is to secure satisfaction of a judgment that has been or may be entered against the foreign state. A variety of cases in the US have arisen over whether general waivers contained in treaty provisions may be interpreted as permitting pre-judgment attachment, in order to prevent the defendant from removing his assets from the jurisdiction. The courts generally require clear evidence of the intention to waive pre-judgment attachment, although that actual phrase need not necessarily be used.[133]

Under the UK State Immunity Act, 1978, no relief may be given against a state by way of injunction or order for specific performance, recovery of land or recovery of any property without the written consent of that state.[134] The question has therefore arisen as to whether a *Mareva* injunction,[135] ordering that assets remain within the jurisdiction pending the outcome of the case, may be obtained, particularly since this type of injunction is interlocutory and obtained *ex parte*. It is suggested that an application for a *Mareva* injunction may indeed be made *ex parte* since immunity may not apply in the circumstances of the case. In applying for such an injunction, a plaintiff is under a duty to make full and frank disclosure and the standard of proof is that of a "good and arguable case", explaining, for example, why it is contended that immunity would not be applicable. It is then for the defendant to seek to discharge the injunction by arguing that these criteria have not been met. The issue as to how the court should deal with

---

[132] See e.g Crawford, "Execution of Judgments and Foreign Sovereign Immunity", 75 *AJIL*, 1981, pp.820, 867 *et seq.*

[133] See e.g. *Behring International Inc.* v. *Imperial Iranian Air Force*, 475 F.Supp. 383 (1979); 63 *ILR*, p.261; *Reading & Bates Corp.* v. *National Iranian Oil Company*, 478 F.Supp. 724 (1979); 63 *ILR*, p.305; *New England Merchants National Bank* v. *Iran Power Generation and Transmission Company*, 19 *ILM*, 1980, p.1298; 63 *ILR*, p.408; *Security Pacific National Bank* v. *Government of Iran*, 513 F.Supp. 864 (1981); *Libra Bank Ltd* v. *Banco Nacional de Costa Rica*, 676 F.2d 47 (1982); 72 *ILR*, p.119 and *S & S Machinery Co.* v. *Masinexportimport*, 706 F.2d 411 (1981). See also *O'Connell Machinery* v. *M.V. Americana*, 734 F.2d 115 (1984).

[134] S.13(2).

[135] See *Mareva Compania Naviera* v. *International Bulkcarriers*, [1975] 2 LL. R 509. See also Gee, *Mareva Injunctions & Anton Piller Relief*, 2nd ed., 1990, especially at p.22.

such a situation was discussed in *A Company* v. *Republic of X*.[136] Saville J noted that the issue of immunity had to be finally settled at the outset[137] so that when a state sought to discharge a *Mareva* injunction on the grounds of immunity, the court could not allow the injunction to continue on the basis that the plaintiff has a good arguable case that immunity does not exist, for if immunity did exist "then the court simply has no power to continue the injunction".[138] Accordingly, a delay between the granting of the injunction *ex parte* and the final determination by the court of the issue was probably unavoidable.

Immunity from Execution [139]

Immunity from execution is to be distinguished from immunity from jurisdiction, particularly since it involves the question of the actual seizure of assets appertaining to a foreign state. As such it poses a considerable challenge to relations between states and accordingly states have proved unwilling to restrict immunity from enforcement judgment in contradistinction to the situation concerning jurisdictional immunity. Section 13(2)b of the State Immunity Act provides, for instance, that "the property of a state shall not be subject to any process for the enforcement of a judgment or arbitration award or, in an action *in rem*, for its arrest, detention or sale". Such immunity may be waived by written consent but not by merely submitting to the jurisdiction of the courts,[140] while there is no immunity from execution in respect of property which is for the time being in use or intended for use for commercial purposes.[141] It is particularly to be noted that this latter stipulation is not to apply to a state's central bank or other monetary institution.[142] Thus, a *Trendtex* type of situation could not arise again in the same form. It is also interesting that the corresponding provision in the US

---

[136] 21 December 1989, Transcript.

[137] *Ibid.*, p.12. See *infra* p.460.

[138] Transcript, p.12.

[139] See e.g. Sinclair, *op. cit.* footnote 1, Chapter IV; Crawford, *op. cit.*; Fox, "Enforcement Jurisdiction, Foreign State Property and Diplomatic Immunity", 34 *ICLQ*, 1985, p.115 and various articles in 10 *Netherlands Yearbook of International Law*, 1979.

[140] S.13(3). Singapore, Iran and South Africa, for example, have adopted similar legislation.

[141] S.13(4).

[142] S.14(4).

Foreign Sovereign Immunities Act of 1976 is more restrictive with regard to immunity from execution.[143]

In 1977, the West German Federal Constitutional Court in the *Philippine Embassy* case[144] declared that:

> forced execution of judgment by the state of the forum under a writ of execution against a foreign state which has been issued in respect of non-sovereign acts . . . of that state, or property of that state which is present or situated in the territory of the state of the forum is inadmissible without the consent of the foreign state if . . . such property serves sovereign purposes of the foreign state.

In particular it was noted that:

> claims against a general current bank account of the embassy of a foreign state which exists in the state of the forum and the purpose of which is to cover the embassy's costs and expenses are not subject to forced execution by the state of the forum.[145]

This was referred to approvingly by Lord Diplock in *Alcom Ltd. v. Republic of Colombia*,[146] a case which similarly involved the attachment of a bank account of a diplomatic mission. The House of Lords unanimously accepted that the general rule in international law was not overturned in the State Immunity Act. In *Alcom*, described as involving a question of law of "outstanding international importance",[147] it was held that such a bank account would not fall within the section 13(4) exception relating to commercial purposes, unless it could be shown by the person seeking to attach the balance that "the bank account was earmarked by the foreign state solely . . . for being drawn on to settle liabilities incurred in commercial transactions".[148] The onus of proof lies upon the applicant. It is also to be noted that under section 13(5) of the Act,

---

[143] Section 1610. Thus, for example, there would be no immunity with regard to property taken in violation of international law. See also articles 21 and 22 of the ILC Draft Articles on Jurisdictional Immunities, *Yearbook of the ILC*, 1986, vol.II, Part 2, pp.17-19.

[144] See UN *Materials, op. cit.*, p.297; 65 *ILR*, pp.146, 150.

[145] UN *Materials, op. cit.*, pp.300-1; 65 *ILR*, p.164.

[146] [1984] 2 All ER 6; 74 *ILR*, p.180, overturning the Court of Appeal Decision, [1984] 1 All ER 1; 74 *ILR*, p.170.

[147] *Ibid.*, p.14; 74 *ILR*, p.189.

[148] *Ibid.*, p.13; 74 *ILR*, p.187. But cf. *Birch Shipping Corporation* v. *Embassy of the United Republic of Tanzania*, 507 F.Supp. 311 (1980); 63 *ILR*, p.524.

a certificate by a head of mission to the effect that property was not in use for commercial purposes was sufficient evidence of that fact, unless the contrary was proven.[149] The question of determining property used for commercial purposes is a significant and complex one that will invariably depend upon an analysis of various factors, as seen in the light of the law of the forum state,[150] for example the present and future use of the funds and their origin.[151]

In *Benamar* v. *Embassy of the Democratic and Popular Republic of Algeria*,[152] the Italian Supreme Court reaffirmed the rule that customary international law forbids measures of execution against the property of foreign states located in the territory of the state seeking to exercise jurisdiction and used for sovereign purposes, and held that it lacked jurisdiction to enforce a judgment against a foreign state by ordering execution against bank accounts standing in the name of that state's embassy.

The Burden and Standard of Proof

Since section 1 of the State Immunity Act stipulates that a state is immune from the jurisdiction of the courts of the UK except as provided in the following sections, it is clear that the burden of proof lies upon the plaintiff to establish that an exception to immunity applies.[153]

As far as the standard of proof is concerned, the Court of Appeal in *Maclaine Watson* v. *Department of Trade and Industry*[154] held that whenever a claim of immunity is made, the court must deal with it as a preliminary issue and on the normal test of balance of probabilities.[155] It would be insufficient to apply the "good arguable case" test usual in Order 11[156] cases with regard to leave to serve.[157] To have decided otherwise would have meant that the state might

---

[149] Such certificate had been issued by the Colombian Ambassador. See *infra* p.462, with regard to diplomatic immunities.

[150] See the West German Federal Constitutional Court decision in the *National Iranian Oil Co.* case, 22 *ILM*, 1983, p.1279.

[151] See e.g. *Eurodif Corporation* v. *Islamic Republic of Iran*, 23 *ILM*, 1984, p.1062.

[152] 84 *AJIL*, 1990, p.573.

[153] See also Staughton J in *Rayner* v. *Department of Trade and Industry*, [1987] BCLC 667.

[154] [1988] 3 WLR 1033, 1103 and 1157; 80 *ILR*, pp.49, 118, 179.

[155] This would be done procedurally under Order 12, Rule 8 of the Rules of the Supreme Court, 1991.

[156] Rules of the Supreme Court, 1991.

[157] See e.g. *Vitkovice Horni* v. *Korner*, [1951] AC 869.

have lost its claim for immunity upon the more impressionistic "good arguable case" basis, which in practice is decided upon affidavit evidence only, and would have been precluded from pursuing its claim at a later stage since that could well be construed as submission to the jurisdiction under section 2(3) of the State Immunity Act.

The question of service of process upon a foreign state arose in *Westminster City Council* v. *Government of the Islamic Republic of Iran,*[158] where Peter Gibson J held that without prior service upon the Iranian Government, the court was unable to deal with the substantive issue before it which concerned the attempt by the Westminster City Council to recover from the Iranian Government charges incurred by it in rendering the Iranian embassy safe after it had been stormed in the famous 1980 siege. In the absence of diplomatic relations between the UK and Iran at that time and in the absence of Iranian consent, there appeared to be no way to satisfy the requirement in section 12 of the State Immunity Act that "any writ or other document required to be served for instituting proceedings against a state shall be served by being transmitted through the Foreign and Commonwealth Office to the Ministry of Foreign Affairs of the state". Clearly a procedural defect to be remedied.

Conclusion

Although sovereign immunity is in various domestic statutes proclaimed as a general principle, subject to wide-ranging exceptions, it is, of course, itself an exception to the general rule of territorial jurisdiction. The enumeration of non-immunity situations is so long, that the true situation of a rapidly diminishing exception to jurisdiction should be appreciated. In many instances, it has only been with practice that it has become apparent how much more extensive the submission to jurisdiction has become under domestic legislation. In *Letelier* v. *Republic of Chile,*[159] for example, section 1605(a)5 providing for foreign state liability for injury, death and loss of property occurring in the US was used to indict the secret service of Chile with regard to the murder of a former Chilean foreign minister in Washington. Similarly in *Verlinden* v. *Central Bank of*

---

[158] [1986] 3 All ER 284.
[159] 488 F.Supp. 665 (1980); 63 *ILR*, p.378.

Nigeria,[160] the Supreme Court permitted a Dutch company to sue the Central Bank of Nigeria in the US,[161] although the *Tel-Oren*[162] case may mark a modification of this approach. The principle of diplomatic immunity may often be relevant in a sovereign immunity case. This is considered in the next section.

DIPLOMATIC LAW [163]

Rules regulating the various aspects of diplomatic relations constitute one of the earliest expressions of international law. Whenever in history there has been a group of independent states co-existing, special customs have developed on how the ambassadors and other special representatives of other states were to be treated.[164]

Diplomacy as a method of communication between various parties, including negotiations between recognised agents, is an ancient institution and international legal provisions governing its manifestations are the result of centuries of state practice. The special privileges and immunities related to diplomatic personnel of various kinds grew up partly as a consequence of sovereign immunity and the independence and equality of states, and partly as an essential requirement of an international system. States must negotiate and consult with each other and with international organisations and in order to do so need diplomatic staffs. Since these persons represent their states in various ways, they thus benefit from the legal principle of state sovereignty. This is also an issue of practical convenience.

---

[160] 22 *ILM,* 1983, p.647; 79 *ILR,* p.548.

[161] Nevertheless, it would appear that the Foreign Sovereign Immunities Act of 1976 does require some minimum jurisdictional links, see generally *International Shoe Co* v. *Washington,* 326 US 310 (1945) and *Perez* v. *The Bahamas,* 482 F.Supp. 1208 (1980); 63 *ILR,* p.350, cf. State Immunity Act of 1978.

[162] 726 F.2d 774 (1984); 77 *ILR,* p.193. See further, *supra,* p.420.

[163] See e.g. Denza, *Diplomatic Law,* 1976; Hardy, *Modern Diplomatic Law,* 1968; *Satow's Guide to Diplomatic Practice* (ed. Gore-Booth), 5th ed. 1979; Wilson, *Diplomatic Privileges and Immunities,* 1967; Whiteman, *Digest of International Law,* vol. 7 and House of Commons Foreign Affairs Committee, *The Abuse of Diplomatic Immunities and Privileges,* 1984. See also Higgins, "The Abuse of Diplomatic Privileges and Immunities: Recent United Kingdom Experience", 79 *AJIL,* 1985, p.641 and the UK Government Response to the *Report,* Cmnd. 9497; Brown, "Diplomatic Immunity: State Practice under the Vienna Convention on Diplomatic Relations", 37 *ICLQ,* 1988, p.53, and McClanahan, *Diplomatic Immunity,* 1989.

[164] See e.g. Mattingley, *Renaissance Diplomacy,* 1955.

Diplomatic relations have traditionally been conducted through the medium of ambassadors and their staffs, but with the growth of trade and commercial intercourse the office of consul was established and expanded. The development of speedy communications stimulated the creation of special missions designed to be sent to particular areas for specific purposes, often with the head of state or government in charge. To some extent, however, the establishment of telephone, telegraph, telex and fax services has lessened the importance of the traditional diplomatic personnel by strengthening the centralising process. Nevertheless, diplomats and consuls do retain some useful functions in the collection of information and pursuit of friendly relations, as well as providing a permanent presence in foreign states, with all that that implies for commercial and economic activities.[165]

The field of diplomatic immunities is one of the most accepted and uncontroversial of international law topics, as it is in the interest of all states ultimately to preserve an even tenor of diplomatic relations, although not all states act in accordance with this. As the International Court noted in the *US Diplomatic and Consular Staff in Tehran* case:[166]

> the rules of diplomatic law, in short, constitute a self-contained regime, which on the one hand, lays down the receiving state's obligations regarding the facilities, privileges and immunities to be accorded to diplomatic missions and, on the other, foresees their possible abuse by members of the mission and specifies the means at the disposal of the receiving state to counter any such abuse.[167]

The Vienna Convention on Diplomatic Relations 1961

This treaty, which came into force in 1964,[168] emphasises the functional necessity of diplomatic privileges and immunities for the efficient conduct of international relations as well as pointing to

---

[165] See generally *Satow's Guide, op. cit.,* Chapter 1.
[166] ICJ Reports, 1980, p.3; 61 *ILR,* p.504. Hereinafter, the *Iran* case.
[167] *Ibid.,* p.40; 61 *ILR,* p.566.
[168] There were 152 parties to this treaty in January 1990. Many of its provisions are incorporated into English law by the Diplomatic Privileges Act, 1964. The importance of the Convention was stressed in the *Iran* case, ICJ Reports, 1980, pp.330-430; 61 *ILR,* p.556.

the character of the diplomatic mission as representing its state.[169] It both codified existing laws and established others.[170]

There is no right as such under international law to diplomatic relations, and they exist by virtue of mutual consent.[171] If one state does not wish to enter into diplomatic relations, it is not legally compelled so to do. Accordingly, the Convention specifies in article 4 that the sending state must ensure that the consent (or *agrément*) of the receiving state has been given for the proposed head of its mission, and reasons for any refusal of consent do not have to be given.

Similarly, by article 9 the receiving state may at any time declare any member of the diplomatic mission *persona non grata* without having to explain its decision, and thus obtain the removal of that person.

The main functions of a diplomatic mission are specified in article 3 and revolve around the representation and protection of the interests and nationals of the sending state, as well as the promotion of information and friendly relations.

Article 13 provides that the head of the mission is deemed to have taken up his functions in the receiving state upon presentation of credentials. Heads of mission are divided into three classes by article 14, viz. ambassadors or nuncios accredited to Heads of State and other heads of mission of equivalent rank; envoys, ministers and internuncios accredited to Heads of State and chargés d'affaires accredited to Ministers of Foreign Affairs.[172] It is customary for a named individual to be in charge of a diplomatic mission. When in 1979, Libya designated its embassies as "People's Bureaux" to be run by revolutionary committees, the UK insisted upon and obtained the nomination of a named person as the head of the mission.[173]

---

[169] See *Yearbook of the ILC*, 1958 vol.II, pp.94-95. The extraterritorial theory of diplomatic law, according to which missions constituted an extension of the territory of the sending state, was of some historic interest but not of practical use, *ibid.* See also *Radwan* v. *Radwan*, [1973] Fam. 24; 55 *ILR*, p.579 and *McKeel* v. *Islamic Republic of Iran*, 722 F.2d 582 (1983); 81 *ILR*, p.543.

[170] See e.g. the *Iran* case, ICJ Reports, 1980, pp.3, 24; 61 *ILR*, p.550.

[171] Article 2.

[172] The rules as to heads of missions are a modern restatement of the rules established in 1815 by the European powers, see Denza, *op. cit.*, p.58.

[173] Comment by Sir Antony Acland, Minutes of Evidence Taken Before the Foreign Affairs Committee, *Report, op. cit.*, p.20. See also *DUSPIL*, 1979, pp.571-73.

The Inviolability of the Mission

In order to facilitate the operations of normal diplomatic activities, article 22 of the Convention specifically declares that the premises of the mission are inviolable and that agents of the receiving state are not to enter them without the consent of the mission. This appears to be an absolute rule and in the Sun Yat Sen incident in 1896, the Court refused to issue a writ of habeas corpus with regard to a Chinese refugee held against his will in the Chinese legation in London.[174] Precisely what the legal position would be in the event of entry without express consent because, for example, of fire fighting requirements or of danger to persons within that area, is rather uncertain and justification might be pleaded by virtue of implied consent, but it is a highly controversial area.[175] The receiving state is under a special duty to protect the mission premises from intrusion or damage or "impairment of its dignity".

In 1979, the US Embassy in Tehran, Iran was taken over by several hundred demonstrators. Archives and documents were seized and 50 diplomatic and consular staff were held hostage. In 1980, the International Court declared that, under the 1961 Convention (and the 1963 Convention on Consular Relations):

> Iran was placed under the most categorical obligations, as a receiving state, to take appropriate steps to ensure the protection of the United States Embassy and Consulates, their staffs, their archives, their means of communication and the free movement of the members of their staffs.[176]

These were also obligations under general international law.[177] The Court in particular stressed the seriousness of Iran's behaviour

---

[174] McNair, *International Law Opinions*, vol.I, 1956, p.85. The issue was resolved by diplomatic means.

[175] The original draft of the article would have permitted such emergency entry, but this was rejected, see Denza, *op. cit.*, pp.82-84. In 1973 an armed search of the Iraqi embassy in Pakistan took place and considerable quantities of arms were found. As a result the Iraqi ambassador and an attaché were declared *personae non grata, ibid.*, p.84.

[176] The *Iran* case, ICJ Reports, 1980, pp.3, 30-31; 61 *ILR*, p.556. This the Iranians failed to do, *ibid.*, pp.31-32. See also *DUSPIL*, 1979, p.577 *et seq.*; Gryzbowski, "The Regime of Diplomacy and the Tehran Hostages", 30 *ICLQ*, 1981, p.42 and Gross, "The Case Concerning United States Diplomatic and Consular Staff in Tehran: Phase of Provisional Measures", 74 *AJIL*, 1980, p.395.

[177] See e.g. *Belgium* v. *Nicod and Another*, 82 *ILR*, p.124.

and the conflict between its conduct and its obligations under "the whole corpus of the international rules of which diplomatic and consular law is comprised, rules the fundamental character of which the Court must here again strongly affirm".[178]

On 17 April 1984, a peaceful demonstration took place outside the Libyan Embassy in London. Shots from the Embassy were fired that resulted in the death of a policewoman. After a siege, the Libyans inside left and the building was searched in the presence of a Saudi Arabian diplomat. Weapons and other relevant forensic evidence were found.[179] The issue raised here, in the light of article 45(a) which provides that after a break in diplomatic relations, "the receiving state must . . . respect and protect the premises of the mission", is whether that search was permissible. The UK view is that article 45(a) does not mean that the premises continue to be inviolable[180] and this would clearly appear to be correct. There is a distinction between inviolability under article 22 and respect and protection under article 45(a).

The suggestion has also been raised that the right of self-defence may also be applicable in this context. It was used to justify the search of personnel leaving the Libyan Embassy[181] and the possibility was noted that in certain limited circumstances it may be used to justify entry into an Embassy.[182]

A rather different issue arises where mission premises have been abandoned. The UK enacted the Diplomatic and Consular Premises Act in 1987, under which states wishing to use land as diplomatic or consular premises are required to obtain the consent of the Secretary of State. Once such consent has been obtained (although this is not necessary in the case of land which had this status prior to the coming into force of the Act), it could be subsequently withdrawn. The Secretary of State has the power to require that the

---

[178] The *Iran* case, ICJ Reports, 1980, p.42; 61 *ILR*, p.568. The Court particularly instanced articles 22, 25, 26 and 27 and analogous provisions in the 1963 Consular Relations Convention, *ibid.*

[179] See Foreign Affairs Committee, *Report, op. cit.,* p.xxvi.

[180] Memorandum by the Foreign and Commonwealth Office, Foreign Affairs Committee, *Report, op. cit.,* p.5.

[181] *Ibid.,* p.9. Such a search was declared essential for the protection of the police, *ibid.* Note the reference to self-defence is both to domestic and international law, *ibid.*

[182] See the comments of the Legal Adviser to the FCO, Minutes of Evidence, Foreign Affairs Committee, *Report, op. cit.,* p.28. Of course, entry can be made into the building with the consent of the receiving state, as for example when Iran requested the UK to eject militants who had taken over their London Embassy in 1980.

title to such land be vested in him where that land has been lying empty, or without diplomatic occupants, and could cause damage to pedestrians or neighbouring buildings because of neglect, providing that he is satisfied that to do so is permissible under international law (section 2). By section 3 of the Act, the Secretary of State is able to sell the premises, deduct certain expenses and transfer the residue to the person divested of his interest.

This situation occurred with respect to the Cambodian Embassy in London, whose personnel closed the building after the Pol Pot take-over of Cambodia in 1975, handing the keys over to the Foreign Office.[183] In 1979, the UK withdrew its recognition of the Cambodian government after the Vietnamese invasion and since that date has had no dealings with any authority as the government of that country. Squatters moved in shortly thereafter. These premises were made subject to section 2 of the Diplomatic and Consular Premises Act in 1988[184] and the Secretary of State vested the land in himself. This was challenged by the squatters and in *Rv. Secretary of State for Foreign and Commonwealth Affairs, ex parte Samuel*,[185] Henry J held that the Secretary of State had acted correctly and in accordance with the duty imposed under article 45 of the Vienna Convention. The Court of Appeal dismissed an appeal,[186] holding that the relevant section merely required that the Secretary of State be satisfied that international law permitted such action.[187]

In *Westminster City Council* v. *Government of the Islamic Republic of Iran*,[188] the issue concerned the payment of expenses arising out of repairs to the damaged and abandoned Iranian embassy in London in 1980. The council sought to register a land charge, but the question of the immunity of the premises under article 22 of the Vienna Convention was raised. Although the Court felt that

---

[183] See Warbrick, "Current Developments", 38 *ICLQ*, 1989, p.965.

[184] See s.2 of the Diplomatic and Consular Premises (Cambodia) Order, SI 30, 1988.

[185] *The Times*, 10 September 1988.

[186] *The Times*, 17 August 1989. Note that in *Secretary of State for Foreign and Commonwealth Affairs* v. *Tomlin, The Times*, 4 December 1990, the Court of Appeal held that in this situation, the extended limitation period of 30 years under s.15(1) of and Schedule 1 to the Limitation Act 1980 was applicable and the squatters could not rely on 12 years' adverse possession.

[187] Note that in the US, embassies temporarily abandoned due to broken relations may be sequestered and turned to other uses pending resumption of relations. This has been the case with regard to Iranian, Cambodian and Vietnamese properties that have been in the custody of the Office of Foreign Missions, see McClanahan, *op. cit.*, pp.53 and 110.

[188] [1986] 3 All ER 284.

procedurally it was unable to proceed,[189] reference was made to the substantive issue and it was noted that the premises had ceased to be diplomatic premises in the circumstances and thus the premises were not "used" for the purpose of the mission as required by article 22, since that phrase connoted the present tense.

The Diplomatic Bag

Article 27 provides that the receiving state shall permit and protect free communication on behalf of the mission for all official purposes. Such official communication is inviolable and may include the use of diplomatic couriers and messages in code and in cipher, although the consent of the receiving state is required for a wireless transmitter.[190]

Articles 27(3) and (4) deal with the diplomatic bag, and provide that it shall not be opened or detained and that the packages constituting the diplomatic bag "must bear visible external marks of their character and may contain only diplomatic documents or articles intended for official use". The need for a balance in this area is manifest. On the one hand, missions require a confidential means of communication, while on the other the need to guard against abuse is clear. Article 27, however, lays the emphasis upon the former.[191] This is provided that article 27(4) is complied with. In the Dikko incident on 5 July 1984, a former Nigerian minister was kidnapped in London and placed in a crate to be flown to Nigeria. The crate was opened at Stansted Airport, although accompanied by a person claiming diplomatic status. The crate[192] did not contain an official seal and was thus clearly not a diplomatic bag.[193]

---

[189] See *supra* p.461.

[190] There was a division of opinion at the Vienna Conference between the developed and developing states over this issue. The former felt that the right to install and use a wireless did not require consent, see Denza, *op. cit.*, pp.121-23.

[191] This marked a shift from earlier practice, *ibid.*

[192] An accompanying crate contained persons allegedly part of the kidnapping operation.

[193] See Foreign Affairs Committee, *Report, op. cit.*, pp.xxxiii-xxxiv. Note also the incident in 1964 when an Israeli was found bound and drugged in a crate marked "diplomatic mail" at Rome Airport. As a result, the Italians declared one Egyptian official at the Embassy *persona non grata* and expelled two others, *Keesings Contemporary Archives*, p.20580. In 1980, a crate bound for the Moroccan Embassy in London split open at Harwich to reveal £500,000 worth of drugs, *The Times*, 13 June 1980. In July 1984, a lorry belonging to the USSR was opened for inspection by West German authorities on the grounds that a lorry itself could not be a bag. The crates inside the lorry were accepted as diplomatic bags and not opened, Foreign Affairs Committee, *Report, op. cit.*, p.xiii, note 48.

In view of suspicions of abuse, the question has arisen as to whether electronic screening, not involving opening or detention, of the diplomatic bag is legitimate. The UK appears to take the view that electronic screening of this kind would be permissible, although it claims not to have carried out such activities, but other states do not accept this.[194] It is to be noted that after the Libyan Embassy siege in April 1984, the diplomatic bags leaving the building were not searched.[195] However, Libya had entered a reservation to the Vienna Convention, reserving its right to open a diplomatic bag in the presence of an official representative of the diplomatic mission concerned. In the absence of permission by the authorities of the sending state, the diplomatic bag was to be returned to its place of origin. Kuwait and Saudi Arabia made similar reservations which were not objected to.[196] This is to be contrasted with a Bahraini reservation to article 27(3) which would have permitted the opening of diplomatic bags in certain circumstances.[197] The Libyan reservation could have been relied upon by the UK in these conditions.

It is also interesting to note that after the Dikko incident, the UK Foreign Minister stated that the crates concerned were opened because of the suspicion of human contents. Whether the crates constituted diplomatic bags or not was a relevant consideration with regards to a right to search, but:

> the advice given and the advice which would have been given had the crate constituted a diplomatic bag took fully into account the overriding duty to preserve and protect human life.[198]

This appears to point to an implied exception to article 27(3) in the interests of humanity. It is to be welcomed, provided, of course, it is applied solely and strictly in these terms.

The issue of the diplomatic bag has been considered by the International Law Commission, in the context of article 27 and analogous provisions in the 1963 Consular Relations Convention,

---

[194] See the Legal Adviser, FCO, Foreign Affairs Committee, *Report, op. cit.*, p.23. See also 985, HC Deb., col.1219, 2 June 1980, and Cmnd. 9497.

[195] Foreign Affairs Committee, *Report, op. cit.*, p.xxx.

[196] Except by France, see Denza, *op. cit.*, p.128. The UK did not object and regarded the reservations in fact as reflective of customary law prior to the Convention, Memorandum of the FCO, Foreign Affairs Committee, *Report, op. cit.*, p.4.

[197] This was objected to, *ibid.*, and see Denza, *op. cit.*, p.128.

[198] See Foreign Affairs Committee, *Report, op. cit.*, p.50.

the 1969 Convention on Special Missions and the 1975 Convention on the Representation of States in their Relations with International Organisations. Article 28 of the Draft Articles on the Diplomatic Courier and the Diplomatic Bag, as finally adopted by the International Law Commission in 1989, provides that the diplomatic bag shall be inviolable wherever it may be. It is not to be opened or detained and "shall be exempt from examination directly or through electronic or other technical device". However, it is noted that if the competent authorities of the receiving or transit state have serious reason to believe that the bag contains something other than official correspondence and documents or articles intended exclusively for official use, they may request that the bag be opened in their presence by an authorised representative of the sending state. If this request is refused by the authorities of the sending state, the bag is to be returned to its place of origin.[199]

In effect the existing law is being reaffirmed and an opportunity to deal effectively with the problems raised by abuse of the diplomatic bag system has been missed. It remains to be seen to what extent the international conference that is to be organised to produce a convention on the basis of the draft wishes to settle this issue.[200]

As far as the diplomatic courier is concerned, that is, a person accompanying a diplomatic bag, the Draft Articles provide for a regime of privileges, immunities and inviolability that is akin to that governing diplomats. He is to enjoy personal inviolability and is not liable to any form of arrest or detention (draft article 10), his temporary accommodation is inviolable (draft article 17), and he will benefit from immunity from the criminal and civil jurisdiction of the receiving or transit state in respect of all acts performed in the exercise of his functions (draft article 18). In general, his privileges and immunities last from the moment he enters the territory of the receiving or transit state until he leaves such state (draft article 21).[201]

---

[199] See McCaffrey, "The Forty-First Session of the International Law Commission", 83 *AJIL*, 1989, p.937.

[200] See e.g. *Yearbook of the ILC*, 1980, vol.II, p.231 *et seq.*; *ibid.*, 1981, vol.II, p.151 *et seq.* and *ibid.*, 1985, vol.II, Part 2, p.30 *et seq.* See also A/38/10 (1983) and the Memorandum by Sir Ian Sinclair, member of the ILC, dealing with the 1984 session on this issue, Foreign Affairs Committee, *Report, op. cit.*, p.79 *et seq.*

[201] See e.g. McClanahan, *op. cit.*, p.64 and *Yearbook of the ILC*, 1985, vol.II, Part 2, p.36 *et seq.*

Diplomatic Immunities – Property

Under article 22 of the Vienna Convention, the premises of the mission are inviolable[202] and together with their furnishings and other property thereon and the means of transport are immune from search, requisition, attachment or execution. By article 23, a general exception from taxation in respect of the mission premises is posited. The court in the *Philippine Embassy* case explained that in the light of customary and treaty law, "property used by the sending state for the performance of its diplomatic functions in any event enjoys immunity even if it does not fall within the material or spatial scope" of article 22.[203] It should also be noted that the House of Lords in *Alcom Ltd. v. Republic of Colombia*[204] held that under the State Immunity Act 1978 a current account at a commercial bank in the name of a diplomatic mission would be immune unless the plaintiff could show that it had been earmarked by the foreign state solely for the settlement of liabilities incurred in commercial transactions. An account used to meet the day-to-day running expenses of a diplomatic mission would therefore be immune. This approach was also based upon the obligation contained in article 25 of the Vienna Convention on Diplomatic Relations, which provided that the receiving state "shall accord full facilities for the performance of the functions of the mission". The House of Lords noted that the negative formulation of this principle meant that neither the executive nor the legal branch of government in the receiving state must act in such manner as to obstruct the mission in carrying out its functions.[205]

Section 16 of the State Immunity Act provides, however, that the exemption from immunity in article 6 relating to proceedings involving immovable property in the UK did not extend to proceedings concerning "a state's title to or its possession of property used for the purposes of a diplomatic mission". It was held in *Intpro Properties (UK) Ltd. v. Sauvel*[206] by the Court of Appeal that the private residence of a diplomatic agent, even where

---

[202] By article 30(1) of the Convention, the private residence of a diplomatic agent shall enjoy the same inviolability and protection as the premises of the mission.

[203] See UN *Materials, op. cit.*, pp.297, 317; 65 *ILR*, pp.146, 187.

[204] [1984] 2 All ER 6; 74 *ILR*, p.180.

[205] *Ibid.*, p.9; 74 *ILR*, p.182.

[206] [1983] 2 All ER 495; 64 *ILR*, p.384.

used for Embassy social functions from time to time, did not constitute use for the purposes of a diplomatic mission and that in any event the proceedings did not concern the French government's title to or possession of the premises, but were merely for damages for breach of a covenant in a lease. Accordingly, there was no immunity under section 16.

It is to be noted that by article 24 of the Vienna Convention, the archives and documents of the mission are inviolable at any time and wherever they may be.[207]

The question of the scope of article 24 was discussed by the House of Lords in *Shearson Lehman* v. *Maclaine Watson (No. 2)*,[208] which concerned the intervention by the International Tin Council in a case on the grounds that certain documents it was proposed to adduce in evidence were inadmissible. This argument was made in the context of article 7 of the International Tin Council (Immunities and Privileges) Order 1972 which stipulates that the ITC should have the "like inviolability of official archives as . . . is accorded in respect of the official archives of a diplomatic mission". Lord Bridge interpreted the phrase "archives and documents of the mission" in article 24 as referring to the archives and documents "belonging to or held by the mission".[209] Such protection was not confined to executive or judicial action by the host state, but would cover, for example, the situation where documents were put into circulation by virtue of theft or other improper means.[210]

Diplomatic Immunities – Personal

The person of a diplomatic agent[211] is inviolable under article 29 of the Vienna Convention and he may not be detained or arrested. This principle is the most fundamental rule of diplomatic law.[212]

---

207 This goes beyond previous customary law, see e.g. *Rose* v. *R*, [1947] 3 DLR 618.

208 [1988] 1 WLR 16; 77 *ILR*, p.145.

209 *Ibid.*, p.24; 77 *ILR*, p.150.

210 *Ibid.*, p.27; 77 *ILR*, p.154. See also *Fayed* v. *Al-Tajir*, [1987] 2 All ER 396.

211 Defined in article 1(e) as the head of the mission or a member of the diplomatic staff of the mission.

212 See Denza, *op. cit.*, p.135. See also the 1973 Convention on the Prevention and Punishment of Crimes against Internationally Protected Persons, including Diplomatic Agents.

Article 30(1) provides for the inviolability of the private residence of a diplomatic agent, while article 30(2) provides that his papers, correspondence and property[213] are inviolable.

Section 4 of the Diplomatic Privileges Act 1964 stipulates that where a question arises as to whether a person is or is not entitled to any privilege or immunity under the Act, which incorporates many of the provisions of the Vienna Convention, a certificate issued by or under the authority of the Secretary of State stating any fact relating to that question shall be conclusive evidence of that fact.

As far as criminal jurisdiction is concerned, diplomatic agents enjoy complete immunity from the legal system of the receiving state.[214] This provision noted in article 31(1) merely reflects the accepted position under customary law. The only remedy the host state has in the face of offences alleged to have been committed by a diplomat is to declare him *persona non grata* under article 9.

Article 31(1) also specifies that diplomats are immune from the civil and administrative jurisdiction of the state in which they are serving, except in three cases. First, where the action relates to private immovable property situated within the host state (unless held for mission purposes),[215] secondly in litigation relating to succession matters in which the diplomat is involved as a private person (for example as an executor or heir) and finally, with respect to unofficial professional or commercial activity engaged in by the agent.[216] In a document issued by the Foreign Office in 1987, entitled *Memorandum on Diplomatic Privileges and Immunities in the United Kingdom*,[217] it was noted that a serious view was taken of any reliance on diplomatic immunity from civil jurisdiction to evade a legal obligation and that such conduct could call into question the continued acceptability in the UK of a particular diplomat.[218]

---

[213] Except that this is limited by article 31, see *infra*.

[214] See *Dickinson* v. *Del Solar*, [1930] 1 KB 376; 5 *ILR*, p.299. See also Denza, *op. cit.*, pp.149-82.

[215] See *Intpro Properties (UK) Ltd.* v. *Sauvel*, [1983] 2 All ER 495; 64 *ILR*, p.384. In *Hildebrend* v. *Champagne*, 82 *ILR*, p.121, it was held this provision did not cover the situation where a claim was made for payment for charges under a lease.

[216] See *Portugal* v. *Goncalves*, 82 *ILR*, p.115. Note that once a person ceases to be a diplomat, his immunity from jurisdiction is lost, see e.g. *Empson* v. *Smith*, [1965] 2 All ER 881; 41 *ILR*, p.407 and *Shaw* v. *Shaw*, [1979] 3 All ER 1; 78 *ILR*, p.483. See also Dinstein, "Diplomatic Immunity from Jurisdiction *Ratione Materiae*", 15 *ICLQ*, 1966, p.76.

[217] See UKMIL, 58 *BYIL*, 1987, p.549.

[218] Annex F, reproducing a memorandum dated February 1985, *ibid.*, p.558.

Article 37 provides that the members of a family of a diplomatic agent forming part of his household[219] shall enjoy the privileges and immunities specified in articles 29 to 36 if not nationals of the receiving state. Members of the administrative and technical staff (and their households) if not nationals or permanent residents of the receiving state may similarly benefit from articles 29-35, except that the article 31(1) immunities do not extend beyond acts performed in the course of their duties, while members of the service staff, who are not nationals or permanent residents of the receiving state benefit from immunity regarding acts performed in the course of official duties.[220]

Immunities and privileges start from the moment the person enters the territory of the receiving state on proceeding to take up his post or if already in the territory from the moment of official notification under article 39.[221] In *R* v. *Governor of Pentonville Prison, ex parte Teja*,[222] Lord Parker noted that it was fundamental to the claiming of diplomatic immunity that the diplomatic agent "should have been in some form accepted or received by this country".[223] This view was carefully interpreted by the Court of Appeal in *R* v. *Secretary of State for the Home Department, ex parte Bagga*[224] in the light of the facts of the former case so that as Parker LJ held if a person already in the country is employed as a secretary, for example, at an embassy, nothing more than notification is required before that person would be entitled to immunities. While it had been held in *R* v. *Lambeth Justices, ex parte Yusufu*[225] that article 39 in the words of Watkins LJ provided "at most some temporary immunity between entry and notification to a person who is without a diplomat", the court in *Bagga* disagreed strongly.[226] Immunity clearly did not depend upon notification and acceptance,[227] but under article 39 commenced upon

[219] See Brown, *op. cit.*, pp.63-66.

[220] Customary law prior to the Vienna Convention was most unclear on immunities of such junior diplomatic personnel and it was recognised that these provisions in article 37 constituted a development in such rules, see e.g. Denza, *op. cit.*, pp.226-33 and *Yearbook of the ILC*, 1958, vol.II, pp.101-2. See also *S.* v. *India*, 82 *ILR*, p.13.

[221] See also article 10.

[222] [1971] 2 QB 274; 52 *ILR*, p.368.

[223] *Ibid.*, p.282; 52 *ILR*, p.373.

[224] [1990] 3 WLR 1013, 1021.

[225] [1985] Crim. LR 510.

[226] [1990] 3 WLR 1013, 1022.

[227] *Ibid.*, p.1023, "save possibly in the case of a head of mission or other person of diplomatic rank", *ibid.*

entry. Article 40 provides for immunity where the person is in the territory in transit between his home state and a third state to which he has been posted.[228] Immunities and privileges normally cease when the person leaves the country or on expiry of a reasonable period in which to do so.[229] However, by article 39(2) there would be continuing immunity with regard to those acts that were performed in the exercise of his functions as a member of the mission. It follows from this formulation that immunity would not continue for a person leaving the host state for any act which was performed outside of the exercise of his functions as a member of a diplomatic mission even though he was immune from prosecution at the time. This was the view taken by the US Department of State with regard to an incident where the ambassador of Papua New Guinea was responsible for a serious automobile accident involving damage to five cars and injuries to two persons.[230] The ambassador was withdrawn from the US and assurances sought by Papua New Guinea that any criminal investigation of the incident or indictment of the former ambassador under US domestic law would be quashed were rejected. The US refused to accept the view that international law precluded the prosecution of the former diplomat for non-official acts committed during his period of accreditation.[231]

Although a state under section 4 of the State Immunity Act of 1978 is subject to the local jurisdiction with respect to contracts of employment made or wholly or partly to be performed in the UK, section 16(1)a provides that this is not to apply to proceedings concerning the employment of the members of a mission within the meaning of the Vienna Convention[232] and this was reaffirmed in *Sengupta* v. *Republic of India*,[233] a case concerning a clerk employed at the Indian High Commission in London.

---

[228] See Brown, *op. cit.*, p.59 and *Bergman* v. *de Sieyès*, 170 F.2d 360 (1948). See also *R* v. *Governor of Pentonville Prison, ex parte Teja*, [1971] 2 QB 274; 52 *ILR*, p.368. Note that such immunity only applies to members of his family if they were accompanying him or travelling separately to join him or return to their country, *Vafadar*, 82 *ILR*, p.97.

[229] Article 39, and see *Shaw* v. *Shaw*, [1979] 3 All ER 1; 78 *ILR*, p.483.

[230] See 81 *AJIL*, 1987, p.937.

[231] See also the *Tabatabai* case, 80 *ILR*, p.388.

[232] Or to members of a consular post within the meaning of the 1963 Consular Relations Conventions enacted by the Consular Relations Act of 1968.

[233] 64 *ILR*, p.352.

Waiver of Immunity

By article 32, the sending state[234] may waive the immunity from jurisdiction of diplomatic agents and others possessing immunity under the Convention. Such waiver must be express. Where a person with immunity initiates proceedings, he cannot claim immunity in respect of any counterclaim directly connected with the principal claim.[235] Waiver of immunity from jurisdiction in respect of civil or administrative proceedings is not to be taken to imply waiver from immunity in respect of the execution of the judgment, for which a separate waiver is necessary.

In general, waiver of immunity is unusual, especially in criminal cases.[236] In a memorandum entitled *Department of State Guidance for Law Enforcement Officers With Regard to Personal Rights and Immunities of Foreign Diplomatic and Consular Personnel* [237] the point is made that waiver of immunity does not "belong" to the individual concerned, but is for the benefit of the sending state. While waiver of immunity in the face of criminal charges is not common, "it is routinely sought and occasionally granted". However, Zambia speedily waived the immunity of an official at its London embassy suspected of drugs offences in 1985.[238]

In *Fayed* v. *Al-Tajir*,[239] the Court of Appeal referred to an apparent waiver of immunity by an ambassador made in pleadings by way of defence. Kerr LJ correctly noted that both under international and English law, immunity was the right of the sending state and that therefore "only the sovereign can waive the immunity of its diplomatic representatives. They cannot do so themselves."[240] It was also pointed out that the defendant's defence filed in the proceedings brought against him was not an appropriate vehicle for waiver of immunity by a state.[241] In *A Company* v. *Republic of X*,[242]

---

[234] See Denza, *op. cit.*, p.184.

[235] See e.g. *High Commissioner for India* v. *Ghosh*, [1960] 1 QB 134; 28 *ILR*, p.150.

[236] See McClanahan, *op. cit.*, p.137, citing in addition an incident where the husband of an official of the US embassy in London was suspected of gross indecency with a minor, where immunity was not waived, but the person concerned was returned to the US.

[237] Reproduced in 27 *ILM*, 1988, pp.1617, 1633.

[238] McClanahan, *op. cit.*, pp.156-57.

[239] [1987] 2 All ER 396.

[240] *Ibid.*, p.411.

[241] *Ibid.*, pp.408 (Mustill LJ) and 411-12 (Kerr LJ).

[242] 21 December 1989, Transcript p.10.

Saville J decided that no mere *inter partes* agreement could bind the state to a waiver of diplomatic immunities, but only an undertaking or consent given to the court itself at the time when the court is asked to exercise jurisdiction over or in respect of the subject-matter of the immunities.[243] In view of the concept that immunities adhere to the state and not the individual concerned (although they, of course, are beneficiaries) and thus waiver must be express and performed clearly by the state as such, this must be correct.

The Vienna Convention on Consular Relations 1963[244]

Consuls represent their state in many administrative ways, for instance, by issuing visas and passports and generally promoting the commercial interests of their state. They are based not only in the capitals of receiving states, but also in the more important provincial cities. However, their political functions are few and they are accordingly not permitted the same degree of immunity from jurisdiction as diplomatic agents. Consuls must possess a commission from the sending state and the authorisation *(exequatur)* of a receiving state.[245] They are entitled to the same exemption from taxes and customs duties as diplomats.

Article 31 emphasises that consular premises are inviolable and may not be entered by the authorities of the receiving state without consent. Like diplomatic premises, they must be protected against intrusion or impairment of dignity, and similar immunities exist with regard to archives and documents[246] and exemptions from taxes.[247]

Article 41 provides that consular officers may not be arrested or detained except in the case of a grave crime and following a decision by the competent judicial authority. If, however, criminal proceedings are instituted against a consul, he must appear before the competent authorities. The proceedings are to be conducted in a manner that respects his official position and minimises the inconvenience to

---

[243] Citing *Kahan* v. *Pakistan Federation*, [1951] 2 KB 1003; 18 *ILR,* p.210.

[244] See e.g. Lee, *Consular Law and Practice*, 2nd ed., 1991; *ibid.,* Vienna Convention on Consular Relations, 1963 and *Satow's Guide, op. cit.,* Book III. The International Court in the *Iran* case stated that this Convention codified the law on consular relations, ICJ Reports, 1980, pp.3, 24; 61 *ILR,* pp.504, 550. See also the Consular Relations Act 1968.

[245] Articles 10, 11 and 12.

[246] Article 33.

[247] Article 32.

the exercise of consular functions. Under article 43 their immunity from jurisdiction is restricted in both criminal and civil matters to acts done in the official exercise of consular functions.[248]

The Convention on Special Missions 1969 [249]

In many cases, states will send out special or *ad hoc* missions to particular countries to deal with some defined issue in addition to relying upon the permanent staffs of the diplomatic and consular missions. In such circumstances, these missions, whether purely technical or politically important, may rely on certain immunities which are basically derived from the Vienna Conventions by analogy with appropriate modifications. By article 8, the sending state must let the host state know of the size and composition of the mission, while according to article 17 the mission must be sited in a place agreed by the states concerned or in the Foreign Ministry of the receiving state.

By article 31 members of special missions have no immunity with respect to claims arising from an accident caused by a vehicle, used outside the official functions of the person involved and by article 27 only such freedom of movement and travel as is necessary for the performance of the functions of the special mission is permitted.

The question of special missions was discussed in the *Tabatabai* case before a series of German courts.[250] The Federal Supreme Court noted that the Convention had not yet come into force and that there were conflicting views as to the extent to which it reflected existing customary law. However, it was clear that there was a customary rule of international law which provided that an *ad hoc* envoy, charged with a special political mission by the sending state, may be granted immunity by individual agreement with the host state for that mission and its associated status and that therefore such envoys could be placed on a par with members of the permanent missions of states.[251] The concept of immunity protected not the

---

[248] See e.g. *Princess Zizianoff v. Kahn and Bigelow*, 4 *ILR*, p.384. See generally as to consular functions, *DUSPIL*, 1979, p.655 *et seq*. Note that waiver of consular immunities under article 45, in addition to being express, must also be in writing.

[249] See e.g. Hardy, *op. cit.*, p.89. The Convention came into force in June 1985.

[250] See 80 *ILR*, p.388. See also Böckslaff and Koch, "The Tabatabai Case: The Immunity of Special Envoys and the Limits of Judicial Review", 25 *German Yearbook of International Law*, 1982, p.539.

[251] 80 *ILR*, pp.388, 419.

diplomat as a person, but rather the mission to be carried out by that person on behalf of the sending state. The question thus turned on whether there had been a sufficiently specific special mission agreed upon by the states concerned, which the court found in the circumstances.[252]

The Vienna Convention on the Representation of States in their Relations with International Organisations of a Universal Character 1975 [253]

This treaty applies with respect to the representation of states in any international organisation of a universal character, irrespective of whether or not there are diplomatic relations between the sending and the host states.

There are many similarities between this Convention and the 1961 Vienna Convention. By article 30, for example, diplomatic staff enjoy complete immunity from criminal jurisdiction, and immunity from civil and administrative jurisdiction in all cases, save for the same exceptions noted in article 31 of the 1961 Convention. Administrative, technical and service staff are in the same position as under the latter treaty (article 36).

The mission premises are inviolable and exempt from taxation by the host state, while its archives, documents and correspondence are equally inviolable.

The Convention has received an unenthusiastic welcome, primarily because of the high level of immunities it provides for on the basis of a controversial analogy with diplomatic agents of missions.[254] The range of immunities contrasts with the general situation under existing conventions such as the Convention on the Privileges and Immunities of the United Nations 1946.[255]

The Immunities of International Organisations

As far as customary rules are concerned the position is far from

---

[252] *Ibid.*, p.420.

[253] See e.g. Fennessy, "The 1975 Vienna Convention on the Representation of States in their Relations with International Organisations of a Universal Character", 70 *AJIL*, 1976, p.62.

[254] It should be noted that among those states abstaining in the vote adopting the Convention were France, the US, Switzerland, Austria, Canada and the UK, all states that host the headquarters of important international organisations, see Fennessy, *op. cit.*, p.62.

[255] See in particular article IV. See also for a similar approach in the Convention on the Privileges and Immunities of the Specialised Agencies 1947, article V.

clear and the position is usually dealt with by means of a treaty, providing such immunities to the international institution sited on the territory of the host state as are regarded as functionally necessary for the fulfilment of its objectives.

Probably the most important example is the General Convention on the Privileges and Immunities of the United Nations of 1946, which sets out the immunities of the United Nations and its personnel and emphasises the inviolability of its premises, archives and documents.[256]

Internationally Protected Persons

The Convention on the Prevention and Punishment of Crimes against Internationally Protected Persons, including Diplomatic Agents, of 1973 came into force in 1977. It seeks to protect heads of state or government, foreign ministers abroad, state representatives and officials of international organisations from the offences of murder, kidnapping or other attack upon their person or liberty.[257]

---

[256] See further, *infra,* Chapter 19. See as to the privileges and immunities of foreign armed forces e.g. Brownlie, *Principles of Public International Law,* 4th ed. 1990, p.369 *et seq.* and the NATO Status of Forces Agreement, 1951, which provides for a system of concurrent jurisdiction. See also Lazareff, *Status of Military Forces under Current International Law,* 1971.

[257] See further *supra* p.415.

CHAPTER THIRTEEN

State Responsibility[1]

State responsibility is a fundamental principle of international law, arising out of the nature of the international legal system and the doctrines of state sovereignty and equality of states. It provides that whenever one state commits an internationally unlawful act against another state, international responsibility is established between the two. A breach of an international obligation gives rise to a requirement for reparation.

Accordingly, one is in the main dealing with a set of principles concerned with second-order issues, in other words the procedural and other consequences flowing from a breach of a substantive rule of international law.[2] In addition to the wide range of state practice in this area, the International Law Commission has been working extensively on this topic. In 1975 it took a decision for the draft articles on state responsibility to be divided into three parts: part I to deal with the origin of international responsibility, part II to deal with the content, forms and degrees of international responsibility and part III to deal with the settlement of disputes and the implementation of international responsibility.[3] Part I of the Draft Articles was provisionally adopted by the Commission in 1980 and work commenced on Part II.[4] Several articles have been provisionally adopted.[5] Thought has also been given to the structure of Part III, which has been affected by the change in Special Rapporteur in 1987.

---

[1] See generally, *International Law of State Responsibility for Injuries to Aliens* (ed. Lillich), 1983; Lillich, "Duties of States Regarding the Civil Rights of Aliens", 161 *HR*, p.329 and *The Human Rights of Aliens in Contemporary International Law*, 1984. See also Brownlie, *System of the Law of Nations: State Responsibility, Part I*, 1983; Cheng, *General Principles of Law as Applied by International Courts and Tribunals*, 1953 and Eagleton, *The Responsibility of States in International Law*, 1928. See also *United Nations Codification of State Responsibility* (eds. Spinedi and Simma), 1987.

[2] The issue of state responsibility for injuries caused by lawful activities will be noted in Chapter 14.

[3] *Yearbook of the ILC*, 1975, vol.II, pp.55-59. See also Allott, "State Responsibility and the Unmaking of International Law", 29 *Harvard International Law Journal*, 1988, p.1.

[4] *Yearbook of the ILC*, 1980, vol.II, Part 2, pp.30 *et seq.*

[5] See e.g. *Yearbook of the ILC*, 1985, vol.II, Part 2, pp.35 *et seq.*

THE NATURE OF STATE RESPONSIBILITY

The essential characteristics of responsibility hinge upon certain basic factors. First, the existence of an international legal obligation in force as between two particular states; secondly, that there has occurred an act or omission which violates that obligation and which is imputable to the state responsible, and finally that loss or damage has resulted from the unlawful act or omission.[6]

These requirements have been made clear in a number of leading cases. In the *Spanish Zone of Morocco* claims,[7] Judge Huber emphasised that:

> responsibility is the necessary corollary of a right. All rights of an international character involve international responsibility. Responsibility results in the duty to make reparation if the obligation in question is not met[8]

and in the *Chorzów Factory* case,[9] the Permanent Court of International Justice said that:

> it is a principle of international law, and even a greater conception of law, that any breach of an engagement involves an obligation to make reparation.

Article 1 of the International Law Commission's Draft Articles on State Responsibility reiterates the general rule that every internationally wrongful act of a state entails responsibility, while article 2 emphasises that every state is subject to the possibility of being held to have committed an internationally wrongful act entailing its international responsibility. These basic reaffirmations on the foundation of state responsibility are reinforced by two further articles. Article 3 provides that there is an internationally wrongful act of a state when

---

[6] See e.g. Mosler, *The International Society as a Legal Community,* 1980, p.157, and Aréchaga, "International Responsibility", in *Manual of Public International Law* (ed. Sørensen), 1968, pp.531, 534.

[7] 2 *RIAA,* p.615 (1923); 2 *ILR,* p.157.

[8] *Ibid.,* p.641.

[9] PCIJ, Series A, no.17, 1928, p.29; 4 *ILR,* p.258. See also the *Corfu Channel* case, ICJ Reports, pp.4, 23; 16 *ILR,* p.155.

(a) conduct consisting of an action or omission is attributable to the state under international law; and

(b) that conduct constitutes a breach of an international obligation of the state.[10]

It is, of course, international law that determines what constitutes an internationally unlawful act, irrespective of any provisions of municipal law.[11]

The general rules relating to responsibility are, as noted, second-level rules in that, while they seek to determine the consequences of a breach of those rules of international law stipulating standards of behaviour, they do not in themselves concern the content of the latter principle.[12]

The issue of the relationship between the rules of state responsibility and those relating to the law of treaties arose in the *Rainbow Warrior* Arbitration between France and New Zealand in 1990.[13] The arbitration followed the incident in 1985 in which French agents destroyed the vessel *Rainbow Warrior* in harbour in New Zealand. The UN Secretary-General was asked to mediate and his ruling in 1986[14] provided *inter alia* for French payment to New Zealand and for the transference of two French agents to a French base in the Pacific, where they were to stay for three years and not to leave without the mutual consent of both states.[15] However, both the agents were repatriated to France before the expiry of the three years for various reasons, without the consent of New Zealand. The 1986 Agreement contained an arbitration clause and this was invoked by New Zealand. The argument put forward by New Zealand centred upon the breach of a treaty obligation by France, whereas that state argued that only the law of state responsibility was relevant and that concepts of *force majeure* and distress exonerated it from liability.

The arbitral tribunal decided that the law relating to treaties was relevant, but that

---

[10] See *Yearbook of the ILC*, 1976, vol.II, p.75 *et seq.*

[11] Article 4. See generally *Yearbook of the ILC*, 1979, vol.II, p.90 *et seq.* and *ibid.*, 1980, vol.II, p.14 *et seq.*

[12] See *Yearbook of the ILC*, 1973, vol.II, pp.169-70.

[13] 82 *ILR*, p.499.

[14] See 81 *AJIL*, 1987, p.325 and 74 *ILR*, p.256.

[15] See also the Agreement between France and New Zealand of 9 July 1986, 74 *ILR*, p.274.

the legal consequences of a breach of a treaty, including the determination of the circumstances that may exclude wrongfulness (and render the breach only apparent) and the appropriate remedies for breach, are subjects that belong to the customary law of state responsibility.[16]

It was noted that international law did not distinguish between contractual and tortious responsibility, so that any violation by a state of any obligation of whatever origin gives rise to state responsibility and consequently to the duty of reparation.[17]

A distinction has been drawn between international crimes and international delicts within the context of internationally unlawful acts. Article 19 of the ILC Draft provides that all breaches of international obligations are internationally wrongful acts.

However, an internationally wrongful act which results from the breach by a state of

> an international obligation so essential for the protection of fundamental interests of the international community that its breach is recognised as a crime by that community as a whole

constitutes an international crime. All other internationally wrongful acts are international delicts, according to the Draft.[18] Article 19 gives some examples of situations that may give rise to international crimes. These include aggression, the establishment or maintenance by force of colonial domination, slavery, genocide, apartheid and massive pollution of the atmosphere or of the seas. The question as to whether states can be criminally responsible is highly controversial. Brownlie, for example, argues strongly that the concept is of no legal value and cannot be justified in principle. Although of use in the political and moral spheres, it is futile in the legal sphere. State responsibility was limited to the obligation to compensate. The problem of exacting penal sanctions from states, while in principle possible, could only be creative of instability.[19]

---

[16] *Ibid.*, p.551.

[17] *Ibid.* See further *infra* p.496.

[18] See Mohr, "The ILC's Distinction between 'International Crimes' and 'International Delicts' and Its Implications" in *UN Codification, op. cit.*, p.115 and Marek, "Criminalising State Responsibility", 14 *Revue Belge de Droit International*, 1978-79, p.460.

[19] *International Law and the Use of Force by States*, 1963, pp.150-54. But cf. Oppenheim, *International Law*, vol.I, 8th ed., 1955, pp.355-56. See also Gilbert, "The Criminal Responsibility of States", 39 *ICLQ*, 1990, p.345. As far as individual criminal responsibility is concerned, see *supra*, Chapter 11, p.411 and *infra*, Chapter 18.

However, others have argued that particularly since 1945, the attitude towards certain crimes by states has altered so as to bring it within the realm of international law.[20] The Rapporteur in his commentary to article 19 pointed to three specific changes since 1945 in this context; first, the development of the concept of *jus cogens* as a set of principles from which no derogation is permitted;[21] secondly, the rise of individual criminal responsibility directly under international law and thirdly, the UN Charter and its provision for enforcement action[22] against a state in the event of threats to or breaches of the peace or acts of aggression.[23] However, there are serious problems with regard to state criminal responsibility and the issue is unlikely to be easily resolved.[24]

A slightly different distinction in the area of responsibility was drawn in the *Barcelona Traction* case,[25] where the Court referred to the obligations of a state towards the international community as a whole as distinct from those vis-à-vis another state in the field of diplomatic protection. In the former case, obligations *erga omnes* are involved and aggression and human rights violations were instanced. Although the two distinctions to some extent overlap, the latter case was not concerned with the criminal liability of states as such but rather with the question of the requisite legal interest and standing of states in the particular situation.

The Question of Fault [26]

There are contending theories as to whether responsibility of the state for unlawful acts or omissions is strict or whether it is necessary to show some fault or intention on the part of the officials concerned.

---

[20] See e.g. Aréchaga, "International Law in the Past Third of the Century", 159 *HR*, p.1.

[21] See Article 53 of the Vienna Convention on the Law of Treaties 1969, *supra*, Chapter 3, p.98 and *infra*, Chapter 15, p.593.

[22] See *infra*, Chapters 18 and 19.

[23] *Yearbook of the ILC*, 1976, vol.II, pp.102-5.

[24] See also A/C.6/SR. 17, 14 October 1976. Note that the Special Rapporteur has proposed dealing with the consequences of international delicts and international crimes separately, see McCaffrey, "The Forty-first Session of the International Law Commission", 83 *AJIL*, 1989, pp.937, 943. See also *infra*, p.495.

[25] ICJ Reports, 1970, pp.3, 32; 46 *ILR*, p.178, 206.

[26] See e.g. Lauterpacht, *Private Law Sources and Analogies of International Law*, 1927, pp.135-43; Brownlie, *Principles of Public International Law*, 4th ed., 1990, pp.433-41 and *op. cit.* footnote 1, pp.38-46 and Aréchaga, *op. cit.* footnote 6, pp.534-40. See also Starke, "Imputability in International Delinquencies", 19 *BYIL*, 1938, p.104, and Cheng, *op. cit.*, pp.218-32.

The principle of objective responsibility (the so-called "risk" theory) maintains that the liability of the state is strict. Once an unlawful act has taken place, which has caused injury and which has been committed by an agent of the state, that state will be responsible in international law to the state suffering the damage irrespective of good or bad faith. To be contrasted with this approach is the subjective responsibility concept (the "fault" theory) and this emphasises that an element of intentional (*dolus*) or negligent (*culpa*) conduct on the part of the person concerned is necessary before his state can be rendered liable for any injury caused.

The relevant cases and academic opinions are divided on this question, although the majority tend towards the strict liability, objective theory of responsibility.

In the *Neer* claim[27] in 1926, an American superintendent of a Mexican mine was shot. The USA, on behalf of his widow and daughter, claimed damages because of the lackadaisical manner in which the Mexican authorities pursued their investigations. The General Claims Commission dealing with the matter disallowed the claim, in applying the objective test.

In the *Caire* claim,[28] the French-Mexican Claims Commission had to consider the case of a French citizen shot by Mexican soldiers for failing to supply them with 5,000 Mexican dollars. Verzijl, the presiding commissioner, held that Mexico was responsible for the injury caused in accordance with the objective responsibility doctrine, that is "the responsibility for the acts of the officials or organs of a state, which may devolve upon it even in the absence of any 'fault' of its own".[29]

A leading case adopting the subjective approach is the *Home Missionary Society* claim[30] in 1920 between Britain and the United States. In this case, the imposition of a "hut tax" in the protectorate of Sierra Leone triggered off a local uprising in which Society property was damaged and missionaries killed. The tribunal dismissed the claim of the Society (presented by the US) and noted that it was established in international law that no government was responsible for the acts of rebels where it itself was guilty of no breach of good faith or of no negligence in suppressing the revolt.

---

[27] 4 *RIAA*, p.60 (1926); 3 *ILR*, p.213.

[28] 5 *RIAA*, p.516 (1929); 5 *ILR*, p.146.

[29] *Ibid.*, pp.529-31. See also *The Jessie*, 6 *RIAA*, p.57 (1921); 1 *ILR*, p.175.

[30] 6 *RIAA*, p.42 (1920); 1 *ILR*, p.173.

It should, therefore, be noted that the view expressed in this case is concerned with a specific area of the law, viz. the question of state responsibility for the acts of rebels. Whether one can analogise from this generally is open to doubt.

In the *Corfu Channel* case,[31] the International Court appeared to tend towards the fault theory[32] by saying that:

> it cannot be concluded from the mere fact of the control exercised by a state over its territory and waters that that state necessarily knew, or ought to have known, of any unlawful act perpetrated therein, nor yet that it necessarily knew, or should have known, the authors. This fact, by itself and apart from other circumstances, neither involves *prima facie* responsibility nor shifts the burden of proof.[33]

However, it must be pointed out that the Court was concerned with Albania's knowledge of the laying of mines[34] and the question of *prima facie* responsibility for *any* unlawful act committed within the territory of the state concerned, irrespective of attribution, raises different issues. It cannot be taken as proof of the acceptance of the fault theory.

It is suggested that doctrine and practice support the objective theory and that this is right, particularly in view of the proliferation of state organs and agencies.[35]

Imputability [36]

Imposing upon the state absolute liability wherever an official is involved encourages that state to exercise greater control over its various departments and representatives. It also stimulates moves towards complying with objective standards of conduct in international relations.

---

[31] ICJ Reports, 1949, p.4; 16 *ILR*, p.155.

[32] See e.g. Oppenheim, *op. cit.*, p.343.

[33] ICJ Reports, 1949, pp.4, 18; 16 *ILR*, p.157. Cf. Judges Krylov and Ecer, *ibid.*, pp.71-72 and 127-28. See also Judge Azevedo, *ibid.*, p.85.

[34] See Brownlie, *op. cit.* footnote 26, pp.442-44.

[35] The question of intention is to be distinguished from the problem of causality, i.e. whether the act or omission in question actually caused the particular loss or damage, see e.g. the *Lighthouses* case, 23 *ILR*, p.352.

[36] See e.g. *Yearbook of the ILC*, 1973, vol.II, p.189. See also Brownlie, *op. cit.* footnote 26, p.435, and *op. cit.* footnote 1, pp.36-37 and Chapter VII.

State responsibility covers many fields. It includes unlawful acts or omissions directly committed by the state and directly affecting other states, for instance, the breach of a treaty, the violation of the territory of another state, or damage to state property. An example of the latter heading is provided by the incident in 1955 when Bulgarian fighter planes shot down an Israeli civil aircraft of its state airline, El Al.[37] Another example of state responsibility is illustrated by the *Nicaragua* case,[38] where the International Court of Justice found that acts imputable to the US included the laying of mines in Nicaraguan internal or territorial waters and certain attacks on Nicaraguan ports, oil installations and a naval base by its agents,[39] while in the *Corfu Channel* case[40] Albania was held responsible for the consequences of mine-laying in its territorial waters on the basis of knowledge possessed by that state as to the presence of such mines, even though there was no finding as to who had actually laid the mines. In the *Rainbow Warrior* incident,[41] the UN Secretary-General mediated a settlement in which New Zealand received *inter alia* a sum of $7 million for the violation of its sovereignty which occurred when that vessel was destroyed by French agents in New Zealand.[42] The state may also incur responsibility with regard to the activity of its officials in injuring a national of another state, and this activity need not be one authorised by the authorities of the state.

The doctrine depends on the link that exists between the state and the person or persons actually committing the unlawful act or omission. The state as an abstract legal entity cannot, of course, in reality "act" itself. It can only do so through authorised officials and representatives. The state is not responsible under international law for all acts performed by its nationals. If an Englishman were to attack and injure a Frenchman on holiday in London, the UK would not be held liable for the injury caused, unless the offender were, for example, a policeman or a soldier.

---

[37] See *supra*, Chapter 9, p.323.

[38] *Nicaragua* v. *United States*, ICJ Reports, 1986, p.14; 76 *ILR*, p.349.

[39] *Ibid.*, pp.48-51 and 146-49; 76 *ILR*, pp.382, 480.

[40] ICJ Reports, 1949, p.4; 16 *ILR*, p.155.

[41] See 81 *AJIL*, 1987, p.325 and 74 *ILR*, p.241 *et seq*. See also *supra* p.483.

[42] Note also the *USS Stark* incident, in which a US guided missile frigate on station in the Persian Gulf was attacked by Iraqi aircraft in May 1987. The Iraqi government agreed to pay compensation of $27 million, see 83 *AJIL*, 1989, pp.561-64.

Since the state is responsible only for acts of its servants that are imputable or attributable to it, it becomes necessary to examine the concept of imputability.

Imputability is the legal fiction which assimilates the actions or omissions of state officials to the state itself and which renders the state liable for damage resulting to the property or person of an alien.

Article 5 of the ILC Draft Articles on State Responsibility provides that the conduct of any state organ having that status under internal law shall be considered as an act of the state concerned under international law where the organ was acting in that capacity and the precise position of that organ in the constitutional structure and hierarchy of the state is irrelevant.[43] Similarly, organs of a "territorial governmental entity" within a state are assimilated to acts of the state, where acting in that capacity in the case in question.[44]

Article 7(2), in reaction to the proliferation of government organs and entities, notes that the conduct of an organ or of an entity not part of the formal structure of the state or a territorial governmental entity may still constitute acts of the state where internal law empowers them to exercise elements of governmental authority and they were so acting in the case in question. It is a little unclear how far this provision might extend, but the commentary to the article gives as an example the conduct of a railway company to which certain police powers have been granted.[45]

Article 9 provides that the conduct of an organ placed at the disposal of a state by another state or by an international organisation shall be considered as an act of the former state, if that organ was acting in the exercise of elements of the governmental authority of the former state. This would, for example, cover the

---

[43] Article 6. This reflects customary law, see e.g. the *Massey* case, 4 *RIAA*, p.155 (1927); 4 *ILR*, p.250. See also the *Salvador Commercial Company* case, 15 *RIAA*, p.477 (1902). Note that the state organ concerned may be from any branch of the state, including the judiciary, see e.g. the *Sunday Times* case, European Court of Human Rights, Series A, vol.30, 1979; 58 *ILR*, p.491, and the legislature, see e.g. the *Young, James and Webster* case, *ibid.*, vol.44, 1981; 62 *ILR*, p.359.

[44] Article 7(1). Thus, not only would communes, provinces and regions of a unitary state be concerned, see e.g. the *Heirs of the Duc de Guise* case, 13 *RIAA*, p.161 (1951); 18 *ILR*, p.423, but also the component states of a federal state, see e.g. the *Davy* case, 9 *RIAA*, p.468 (1903), the *Janes* case, 4 *RIAA*, p.86 (1925); 3 *ILR*, p.218 and the *Pellat* case, 5 *RIAA*, p.536 (1929); 5 *ILR*, p.145. See also *Yearbook of the ILC*, 1971, vol.II, Part I, p.257 *et seq.*

[45] *Yearbook of the ILC*, 1974, vol.II, pp.281-82.

UK Privy Council acting as the highest judicial body for certain Commonwealth countries.[46]

Ultra Vires Acts

An unlawful act may be imputed to the state even where it was beyond the legal capacity of the official involved, providing as Verzijl noted in the *Caire* case[47] that the officials "have acted at least to all appearances as competent officials or organs or they must have used powers or methods appropriate to their official capacity".

This was reaffirmed in the *Mossé* case,[48] where it was noted that:

> Even if it were admitted that . . . officials . . . had acted . . . outside the statutory limits of the competence of their service, it should not be deduced, without further ado, that the claim is not well founded. It would still be necessary to consider a question of law . . . namely whether in the international order the state should be acknowledged responsible for acts performed by officials within the apparent limits of their functions, in accordance with a line of conduct which was not entirely contrary to the instructions received.

In *Youman's* claim,[49] militia ordered to protect threatened American citizens in a Mexican town, instead joined the riot, during which the Americans were killed. These unlawful acts by the militia were imputed to the state of Mexico, which was found responsible by the General Claims Commission.

In the *Union Bridge Company* case,[50] a British official of the Cape Government Railway mistakenly appropriated neutral property during the Boer War. It was held that there was still liability despite the honest mistake and the lack of intention on the part of the authorities to appropriate the material in question. The key was that the action was within the general scope of duty of the official.

Article 10 of the ILC Draft provides that the conduct of an organ having the capacity to exercise elements of governmental authority and having so acted is still to be considered an act of the state

---

[46] *Ibid.*, p.288. See also articles 12 and 13, which in such circumstances deny the responsibility of the dispatching state or international organisation.

[47] 5 *RIAA*, pp.516, 530 (1929); 5 *ILR*, pp.146, 148.

[48] 13 *RIAA*, p.494 (1953); 20 *ILR*, p.217.

[49] 4 *RIAA*, p.110 (1926); 3 *ILR*, p.223.

[50] 6 *RIAA*, p.138 (1924); 2 *ILR*, p.170.

under international law even if, in the case in question, the organ exceeded its competence or contravened instructions.[51] This article appears to lay down an absolute rule of liability, one not limited by reference to the apparent exercise of authority and, in the context of the general acceptance of the objective theory of responsibility, is probably the correct approach.[52]

Although private individuals are not regarded as state officials so that the state is not liable for their acts, the state may be responsible for failing to exercise the control necessary to prevent such acts. This was emphasised in the *Zafiro* case[53] between Britain and America in 1925. The tribunal held the latter responsible for the damage caused by the civilian crew of a naval ship in the Philippines, since the naval officers had not adopted effective preventative measures.

Individuals

Article 8 of the ILC Draft provides that the conduct of a person or a group of persons shall also be considered as an act of the state if

(a) it is established that such person or group was in fact acting on behalf of that state; or

(b) such person or group was in fact exercising elements of the governmental authority in the absence of the official authorities and in circumstances which justified the exercise of those elements of authority.

The commentary to the article gives as examples of part (a) the crew of the *Zafiro* claim[54] and the Eichmann situation where Israelis kidnapped the war criminal in Argentina.[55]

In the *Iran* case, the International Court noted that the initial attack on the US Embassy by militants could not be imputable to Iran since they were clearly not agents or organs of the state.

---

[51] See also *Yearbook of the ILC*, 1975, vol.II, p.67.

[52] See *ibid.*, p.69 and the *Caire* case, 5 *RIAA*, p.516 (1929); 5 *ILR*, p.146. See also Meron, "International Responsibility of States for Unauthorised Acts of Their Officials", 33 *BYIL*, 1957, p.851.

[53] 6 *RIAA*, p.160 (1925); 3 *ILR*, p.221. See also *re Gill*, 5 *RIAA*, p.157 (1931); 6 *ILR*, p.203.

[54] 6 *RIAA*, p.160 (1925); 3 *ILR*, p.221.

[55] See *supra*, Chapter 11, p.413. See also the *Argoud* case, 45 *ILR*, p.90 where the accused had been kidnapped in Germany and brought to France for trial.

However, the subsequent approval of the Ayatollah Khomeini and other organs of Iran to the attack and the decision to maintain the occupation of the Embassy translated that action into a state act. The militants thus became agents of the Iranian state for whose acts the state bore international responsibility.[56]

Apart from such situations, "the conduct of a person or a group of persons not acting on behalf of the state shall not be considered as an act of the state under international law".[57]

Mob Violence, Insurrections and Civil Wars

Where the governmental authorities have acted in good faith and without negligence, the general principle is one of non-liability for the actions of rioters or rebels causing loss or damage.[58] The state, however, is under a duty to show due diligence. Quite what is meant by this is difficult to quantify and more easily defined in the negative.[59] It should also be noted that special provisions apply to diplomatic and consular personnel.[60]

Where an insurrectional movement is successful, it will be held responsible for its activities prior to its assumption of authority. Article 15 of the ILC Draft re-emphasises the rule and provides that the acts of such a movement which becomes the new government of a state shall be considered as acts of that state.[61]

The issue of the responsibility of the authorities of a state for activities that occurred prior to its coming to power was raised before the Iran-US Claims Tribunal. In *Short* v. *The Islamic Republic of Iran*,[62] the Tribunal noted that the international responsibility of a state can be engaged where the circumstances or events causing the departure of an alien are attributable to it, but that not all

---

[56] ICJ Reports, 1980, pp.3, 34-35; 61 *ILR*, pp.530, 560. See also *supra*, Chapter 12, p.465.

[57] Article 11.

[58] See e.g. the *Home Missionary Society* case, 6 *RIAA*, pp.42, 44 (1920); 1 *ILR*, p.173; the *Youmans* case, 4 *RIAA*, p.110 (1926); 3 *ILR*, p.223 and the *Herd* case, 4 *RIAA*, p.653 (1930). See also article 14 of the ILC Draft Articles on State Responsibility.

[59] E.g. Judge Huber, the *Spanish Zone of Morocco* claims, 2 *RIAA*, pp.617, 642 (1925); 2 *ILR*, p.157. See Brownlie, *op. cit.* footnote 26, pp.452-54 and the *Sambaggio* case, 10 *RIAA*, p.499 (1903). See also *Yearbook of the ILC*, 1957, vol.II, pp.121-23, and Schwarzenberger, *International Law*, 3rd ed., 1957, p.653 *et seq.*

[60] *Supra*, Chapter 12, p.472.

[61] See Borchard, *The Diplomatic Protection of Citizens Abroad*, 1927, p.241 and the *Bolivian Railway Company* case, 9 *RIAA*, p.445 (1903).

[62] 16 *Iran-US CTR*, p.76; 82 *ILR*, p.148.

departures of aliens from a country in a period of political turmoil would as such be attributable to that state.[63] In the instant case, it was emphasised that at the relevant time the revolutionary movement had not yet been able to establish control over any part of Iranian territory and the government had demonstrated its loss of control. Additionally, the acts of supporters of a revolution cannot be attributed to the government following the success of the revolution, just as acts of supporters of an existing government are not attributable to the government. Accordingly, and since the claimant was unable to identify any agent of the revolutionary movement the actions of whom forced him to leave Iran, the claim for compensation failed.[64]

In *Yeager* v. *The Islamic Republic of Iran*,[65] the Tribunal awarded compensation for expulsion, but in this case it was held that the expulsion was carried out by the Revolutionary Guards after the success of the revolution. Although the Revolutionary Guards were not at the time an official organ of the Iranian state, it was determined that they were exercising governmental authority with the knowledge and acquiescence of the revolutionary state, making Iran liable for their acts.[66] Falling somewhat between these two cases is *Rankin* v. *The Islamic Republic of Iran*,[67] where the Tribunal held that the claimant had not proved that he had left Iran after the revolution as a result of action by the Iranian Government and the Revolutionary Guards as distinct from leaving because of the general difficulties of life in that state during the revolutionary period. Thus Iranian responsibility was not engaged.

The Concept of the Injured State

Having noted the nature of imputability and thus the identity of the responsible party in the context of an internationally wrongful act, the identity of the state that has suffered in consequence needs to be looked at. Article 5(1) of Part II of the ILC Draft provides that the "injured state" is any state a right of which is infringed by the act of another state if such act constitutes an internationally wrongful

---

[63] *Ibid.*, p.83; 82 *ILR*, pp.159-60.
[64] *Ibid.*, p.85; 82 *ILR*, p.161.
[65] 17 *Iran-US CTR*, p.92; 82 *ILR*, p.178.
[66] *Ibid.*, p.104; 82 *ILR*, p.194.
[67] 17 *Iran-US CTR*, p.135; 82 *ILR*, p.204.

act of that state in accordance with Part I of the Draft. Only an injured state may invoked the responsibility of the "author" state and thus obtain compensation. Article 5(2) provides that:

> In particular 'injured state' means:
> (a) if the right infringed by the act of a state arises from a bilateral treaty, the other state party to the treaty;
> (b) if the right infringed by the act of a state arises from a judgment or other binding dispute-settlement decision of an international court or tribunal, the other state or states parties to the dispute and entitled to the benefit of that right;[68]
> (c) if the right infringed by the act of a state arises from a binding decision of an international organ other than an international court or tribunal, the state or states which, in accordance with the constituent instrument of the international organisation concerned, are entitled to the benefit of that right;[69]
> (d) if the right infringed by the act of a state arises from a treaty provision for a third state, that third state;[70]
> (e) if the right infringed by the act of a state arises from a multilateral treaty or from a rule of customary international law, any other state party to the multilateral treaty or bound by the relevant rule of customary international law, if it is established that:
> (i) the right has been created or is established in its favour,
> (ii) the infringement of the right by the act of a state necessarily affects the enjoyment of the rights or the performance of the obligations of the other states parties to the multilateral treaty or bound by the rule of customary law, or
> (iii) the right has been created or is established for the protection of human rights and fundamental freedoms;
> (f) if the right infringed by the act of a state arises from a multilateral treaty, any other state party to the multilateral treaty, if it is established that the right has been expressly stipulated in that treaty for the protection of the collective interests of the states parties thereto.[71]

---

[68] Note that, for example, article 59 of the Statute of the International Court of Justice provides that the decision of the Court "has no binding legal force except between the parties and in respect of that particular case".

[69] See e.g. with respect to the United Nations Security Council, *infra* Chapter 18.

[70] See also article 36 of the Vienna Convention on the Law of Treaties 1969, *infra* Chapter 15, p.581.

[71] See *Yearbook of the ILC,* 1985, vol.II, Part 2, pp.25-27. Draft article 5 was adopted at this session, but none of the succeeding draft articles, *ibid.* See also Simma, "Bilateralism and Community Interest in the Law of State Responsibility" in *International Law at a Time of Perplexity* (ed. Dinstein), 1989, pp.821, 829.

It should, of course, be noted that the provisions contained in draft article 5 form a sort of safety net, in that in many cases the legal consequences of a breach of a substantive rule of international law will be laid down by that rule itself. Of especial interest in article 5(2) is the reference to multilateral treaties and to customary international law, so that in certain circumstances all states parties to the treaty or bound by the relevant rule of international customary law may be regarded as injured states, thus enabling them to claim compensation or in particular situations to take counter-measures. In the case of human rights treaties, this would occur with no further requirement. The Commentary to the Draft specifically refers to the principle of self-determination in this context.[72]

Draft article 5(3) goes furthest of all in the direction of collective responsibility. It is also probably the most controversial. It provides that if the internationally wrongful act constitutes an international crime, then the term "injured state" means all other states. The Commentary, recognising some of the consequences that could be drawn from this, notes that the question arises as to whether all other states individually are entitled to respond to an international crime in the same manner as if their individual rights were infringed by the commission of the international crime. It is emphasised that article 5(3) does not and cannot prejudice the extent of the legal consequences otherwise to be attached to the commission of an international crime. These issues are to be addressed in some of the remaining articles of Part II.[73] However, the complexity and controversy of the issue is apparent. Some of these consequential issues will doubtless underline the difficulties inherent in the notion of state criminal responsibility.[74] Many, if not all, of the relevant situations likely to arise in the context of article 5(3) would fit into the provisions of article 5(2)e.[75]

---

[72] *Ibid.*, p.27.

[73] *Ibid.*

[74] *Supra* p.484.

[75] It should be emphasised that draft article 5(3) makes a reference in square brackets (indicating its provisional nature) to draft articles 14 and 15, which provide that an international crime entails an obligation for all states not to recognise the legality of that situation, not to assist the "criminal" state and to join together to carry out the above. Reference is also made to the United Nations and its regime for the maintenance of international peace and security. Note that these draft articles have not been approved by the International Law Commission.

Reparation[76]

The basic principle with regard to reparation, or the remedying of a breach of an international obligation for which the state concerned is responsible was laid down in the *Chorzów Factory* case,[77] where the Court emphasised that

> reparation must, as far as possible, wipe out all the consequences of the illegal act and re-establish the situation which would, in all probability, have existed if that act had not been committed.

Restitution in kind is the obvious method of performing the reparation, since it aims to re-establish the situation which ought to exist. While restitution has occurred in the past,[78] it is more rare today, if only because the nature of such disputes has changed. A large number of cases now involve expropriation disputes, where it is politically difficult for the state concerned to return to multinational companies expropriated property. Monetary compensation is clearly of importance in reparation. It is intended to replace the value of the asset confiscated and would probably include loss of expected profits, but not more remote prospective gains. Punitive damages are not usual in this context and go beyond the concept of reparation as such.[79] Monetary compensation may also be paid for non-material damage. In the *I'm Alone*[80] case, for example, a sum of $25,000 was suggested as recompense for the indignity suffered

[76] See e.g. Whiteman, *Damages in International Law*, 3 vols., 1937-43; Mann, "The Consequences of an International Wrong in International and National Law", 48 *BYIL*, 1978, p.1; Aréchaga, *op. cit.* footnote 6, p.564 *et seq.* and *op. cit.* footnote 20, pp.285-87. See also Cheng, *op. cit.*, p.233 *et seq.*, Brownlie, *op. cit.* footnote 1, Part VIII and Gray, *Judicial Remedies in International Law*, 1987.

[77] PCIJ, Series A, no.17, 1928, pp.47-48. See also the *Iran* case, ICJ Reports, 1980, pp.3, 45; 61 *ILR*, pp.530, 571, where the Court held that Iran was under a duty to make reparation to the US.

[78] See e.g. the post-1945 Peace Treaties with Hungary, Romania and Italy. See also the *Spanish Zone of Morocco* case, 2 *RIAA*, p.617 (1925); 2 *ILR*, p.157; the *Martini* case, 2 *RIAA*, p.977 (1930); 5 *ILR*, p.153; the *Palmagero Gold Fields* case, 5 *RIAA*, p.298 (1931) and the *Russian Indemnity* case, 11 *RIAA*, p.431 (1912). Brownlie notes that in certain cases, such as the illegal possession of territory or acquisition of objects of special cultural, historical or religious significance, restitution may be the only legal remedy, *op. cit.* footnote 1, p.210 and the *Temple* case, ICJ Reports, 1962, pp.6, 36-37; 33 *ILR*, pp.48, 73.

[79] See Aréchaga, *op. cit.* footnote 6, p.571. See also *Yearbook of the ILC*, 1956, vol.II, pp.211-12.

[80] 3 *RIAA*, p.1609 (1935); 7 *ILR*, p.203.

by Canada, in having a ship registered in Montreal unlawfully sunk. A further example of this is provided by the France-New Zealand Agreement of 9 July 1986, concerning the sinking of the vessel *Rainbow Warrior* by French agents in New Zealand, the second paragraph of which provided for France to pay the sum of $7 million as compensation to New Zealand for "all the damage which it has suffered".[81] It is clear from the context that it covered more than material damage.[82] In the subsequent arbitration in 1990, the Tribunal declared that

> an order for the payment of monetary compensation can be made in respect of the breach of international obligations involving . . . serious moral and legal damage, even though there is no material damage.[83]

However, the Tribunal declined to make an order for monetary compensation, primarily since New Zealand was seeking alternative remedies.[84]

A third form of reparation is termed satisfaction. This relates to non-monetary compensation and would include official apologies, the punishment of guilty minor officials or the formal acknowledgement of the unlawful character of an act.[85] In the *Rainbow Warrior* arbitration,[86] New Zealand sought *inter alia* an Order to the French Government to return its agents from France to their previous place of confinement in the Pacific as required by the original agreement of 9 July 1986. New Zealand termed this request *"restitutio in integrum"*. France argued that "cessation" of the denounced behaviour was the appropriate terminology and remedy, although in the circumstances barred by time.[87] The Tribunal pointed to the debate in the International Law Commission on the differences between the two concepts[88] and held that the French approach was correct.[89] The obligation to end an illegal situation

---

[81] 74 *ILR*, pp.241, 274.

[82] See the Arbitral Tribunal in the *Rainbow Warrior* case, 82 *ILR*, pp.499, 574.

[83] 82 *ILR*, pp.499, 575.

[84] *Ibid.*

[85] See Aréchaga, *op. cit.* footnote 6, p.572 and Schwarzenberger, *op. cit.*, p.653. See also the *I'm Alone* case, 3 *RIAA*, pp.1609, 1618 (1935); 7 *ILR*, p.206 and the *Corfu Channel* case, ICJ Reports, 1949, pp.4, 35; 16 *ILR*, pp.155, 167.

[86] 82 *ILR*, p.499.

[87] *Ibid.*, p.571.

[88] See e.g. *Yearbook of the ILC*, 1981, vol.II, Part 1, p.79 *et seq.*

[89] 82 *ILR*, p.572.

was not reparation but a return to the original obligation, that is cessation of the illegal conduct. However, it was held that since the primary obligation was no longer in force (in the sense that the obligation to keep the agents in the Pacific island concerned expired under the initial agreement on 22 July 1989), an order for cessation of the illegal conduct could serve no purpose.[90]

The Tribunal also pointed to the long established practice of states and international courts of using satisfaction as a remedy for the breach of an international obligation, particularly where moral or legal damage had been done directly to the state. In the circumstances of the case, it concluded that the public condemnation of France for its breaches of treaty obligations to New Zealand made by the Tribunal constituted "appropriate satisfaction".[91] The Tribunal also made an interesting "Recommendation" that the two states concerned establish a fund to promote close relations between their respective citizens and additionally recommended that the French Government "make an initial contribution equivalent to $2 million to that fund".[92] This suggestion, of course, does not constitute an order to France to pay damages, but it is a fascinating approach.

In some cases, a party to a dispute will simply seek a declaration that the activity complained of is illegal.[93] In territorial disputes, for example, such declarations may be of particular significance. The International Court, however, adopted a narrow view of the Australian submissions in the *Nuclear Tests* case,[94] an approach that was the subject of a vigorous dissenting opinion.[95]

---

[90] *Ibid.*, p.573. Note that the ILC draft article 6 of Part II provides that the injured state may require the other state to discontinue the internationally wrongful act. This draft article has not as yet been approved by the Commission, see e.g. *Yearbook of the ILC*, 1985, vol.II, Part 2, p.20.

[91] 82 *ILR*, p.577.

[92] *Ibid.*, p.578.

[93] See e.g. Rosenne, *The Law and Practice of the International Court*, vol.I, 1956 and *Certain German Interests in Polish Upper Silesia*, PCIJ, Series A, No.7, p.18 (1926). Note also that under article 50 of the European Convention on Human Rights 1950, the European Court of Human Rights may award "just satisfaction", which often takes the form of a declaration by the Court that a violation of the Convention has taken place, see e.g. the *Neumeister* case, European Court of Human Rights, Series A, No.17 (1974); 41 *ILR*, p.316. See also the *Pauwels* case, *ibid.*, No.135 (1989); the *Lamy* case, *ibid.*, No.151 (1989) and the *Huber* case, *ibid.*, No.188 (1990).

[94] ICJ Reports, 1974, p.253; 57 *ILR*, p.398.

[95] *Ibid.*, pp.312-19; 57 *ILR*, p.457.

The question of the appropriate reparation for expropriation was discussed in several recent cases. In the *BP* case,[96] the tribunal emphasised that there was

> no explicit support for the proposition that specific performance, and even less so *restitutio in integrum* are remedies of public international law available at the option of a party suffering a wrongful breach by a co-contracting party . . . the responsibility incurred by the defaulting party for breach of an obligation to perform a contractual undertaking is a duty to pay damages . . . the concept of *restitutio in integrum* has been employed merely as a vehicle for establishing the amount of damages.[97]

However, in the *Texaco* case,[98] which similarly involved Libyan nationalisation of oil concessions, the arbitrator held that restitution in kind under international law (and indeed under Libyan law) constituted

> the normal sanction for non-performance of contractual obligations and that it is inapplicable only to the extent that restoration of the *status quo ante* is impossible.[99]

This is an approach that in political terms, particularly in international contract cases, is unlikely to prove acceptable to states since it appears a violation of sovereignty. The problems, indeed, of enforcing such restitution awards against a recalcitrant state may be imagined.[100]

Circumstances Precluding Wrongfulness [101]

In certain situations, a breach of an international obligation attributable to a state may not give rise to responsibility. Generally

---

[96] 53 *ILR*, p.297. This concerned the expropriation by Libya of BP oil concessions.

[97] 53 *ILR*, pp.297, 347.

[98] 17 *ILM*, 1978, p.1; 53 *ILR*, p.389.

[99] *Ibid.*, p.36; 53 *ILR*, pp.507-8. In fact the parties settled the dispute by Libya supplying $152 million worth of crude oil, *ibid.*, p.2.

[100] These points were explained by the arbitrator in the *Liamco* case, 20 *ILM*, 1981, pp.1, 63-64; 62 *ILR*, pp.141, 198. See also the *Aminoil* case, 21 *ILM*, 1982, p.976; 66 *ILR*, p.519. See further e.g. Fatouros, "International Law and the International Contract", 74 *AJIL*, 1980, p.134. The issue of compensation for expropriated property is discussed further, *infra*, p.521.

[101] See e.g. Whiteman, *Digest, op. cit.* vol.8, p.837 *et seq.*: *Yearbook of the ILC*, 1979, vol.II, Part 1, p.21 *et seq.* and *ibid.*, 1980, vol.II, p.26 *et seq.*

the consent of the injured state, the legitimate application of a sanction, *force majeure,* self-defence and state of necessity are the circumstances which may preclude the inference of responsibility, or rather wrongfulness giving rise to responsibility. .

Where a state consents to an act by another state which would otherwise constitute an unlawful act, wrongfulness is precluded unless a rule of *jus cogens* is involved from which no derogation is permitted.[102] The most common example of this kind of situation is where troops from one state are sent to another at the request of the latter.[103] Similarly, under article 30 of Part I of the ILC Draft the international wrongfulness of an act is precluded where it is committed as a measure legitimate under international law, in consequence of an internationally wrongful act committed by the target state.

The institution of reprisals, certainly the pre-1945 use of force, provides an example of this situation, since an otherwise unlawful act is rendered legitimate by the prior application of unlawful force.[104] *Force majeure* has long been accepted as precluding wrongfulness,[105] although the standard of proof is high. In the *Serbian Loans* case,[106] for example, the Court declined to accept the claim that the First World War had made it impossible for Serbia to repay a loan. In 1946, following a number of unauthorised flights of US aircraft over Yugoslavia, both states agreed that only in cases of emergency could such entry be justified in the absence of consent.[107]

Article 31 of the ILC Draft provides for the preclusion of wrongfulness where the act was due to an irresistible force or to an unforeseen external event beyond the control of the state which made it materially impossible for the state concerned to conform with the international obligation in question. An example of the situation envisaged here is provided by the *Gill* case,[108] where a British

---

[102] See article 29 of Part I of the ILC Draft Articles. As to *jus cogens*, see *supra*, Chapter 3, p.98.

[103] See e.g. the dispatch of UK troops to Muscat and Oman in 1957, 574 HC Deb., col. 872, 29 July 1957, and to Jordan in 1958, SCOR, 13th Sess., 831st meeting, para. 28.

[104] See e.g. the *Naulilaa* case, 2 *RIAA*, p.1025 (1928); 4 *ILR*, p.466 and the *Cysne* case *ibid.,* p.1056; 5 *ILR*, p.150.

[105] See e.g. *Yearbook of the ILC,* 1961, vol.II, p.46.

[106] PCIJ, Series A, no.20, 1929, p.39. See also the *Brazilian Loans* case, PCIJ, Series A, no.20, 1929, p.120; 5 *ILR*, p.466.

[107] *Yearbook of the ILC,* 1979, vol.II, p.60.

[108] 5 *RIAA*, p.159 (1931); 6 *ILR*, p.203.

national residing in Mexico had his house destroyed as a result of sudden and unforeseen action by opponents of the Mexican government. The Commission held that failure to prevent the act was due not to negligence but to genuine inability to take action in the face of a sudden situation.

In its Commentary on this provision, the ILC emphasised that the event in question had to be an act which occurs and takes place without the state being able to do anything to rectify the event or avert its consequences. There had to be a constraint which the state was unable to avoid or to oppose by its own power.[109]

The issue of *force majeure* was raised by France in the *Rainbow Warrior* arbitration in 1990.[110] It was argued that one of the French agents repatriated to France without the consent of New Zealand had to be so moved as a result of medical factors which amounted to *force majeure*. The Tribunal, however, stressed that the test of applicability of this doctrine was one of "absolute and material impossibility" and a circumstance rendering performance of an obligation more difficult or burdensome did not constitute a case of *force majeure*.[111]

Article 32 of the Draft deals with situations of distress and provides that wrongfulness is precluded in the case of a state not acting in conformity with an international obligation binding upon it if the author of the conduct concerned had no other means "in a situation of extreme distress" of saving his life or that of persons entrusted to his care. This would cover, for example, emergency unauthorised entry into foreign airspace of the kind envisaged by the 1946 US-Yugoslav correspondence, or the seeking of refuge in a foreign port without authorisation by a ship's captain in storm conditions.[112]

The difference between distress and *force majeure* is that in the former case there is an element of choice. This, as the ILC points out, is illusory only, because this choice is one between observance of an obligation, which would lead to inevitable loss, since distress in this context is to be equated with extreme peril, and breach of

[109] *Yearbook of the ILC*, 1979, vol.II, p.133.
[110] 82 *ILR*, pp.499, 551.
[111] *Ibid.*, p.553.
[112] *Yearbook of the ILC*, 1979, vol.II, p.134.

that obligation.[113] The Tribunal in the *Rainbow Warrior* arbitration[114] noted that three conditions were required to be satisfied in order for this defence to be applicable to the French action in repatriating its two agents. First, the existence of very exceptional circumstances of extreme urgency involving medical and other considerations of an elementary nature, provided always that a prompt recognition of the existence of those exceptional circumstances is subsequently obtained from the other interested party or is clearly demonstrated. Secondly, the re-establishment of the original situation as soon as the reasons of emergency invoked to justify the breach of the obligation (i.e. the repatriation) had disappeared. Thirdly, the existence of a good faith effort to try to obtain the consent of New Zealand according to the terms of the 1986 Agreement.[115] It was concluded that France had failed to observe these conditions (except as far as the removal of one of the agents on medical grounds was concerned).

Article 33 of the Draft deals with the related issue of a state of necessity, where the act concerned was the "only means of safeguarding an essential interest of the state against a grave and imminent peril", provided that an essential interest of the second state is not seriously impaired by the act. An example of this kind of situation is provided by the *Torrey Canyon*,[116] where a Liberian oil tanker went aground off the UK coast but outside territorial waters, spilling large quantities of oil. After salvage attempts, the UK bombed the ship. The ILC took the view that this action was legitimate in the circumstances because of a state of necessity.[117] It was only after the incident that international agreements were concluded dealing with this kind of situation.[118]

The wrongfulness of an act of state would also be precluded if that act constitutes a lawful measure of self-defence taken in conformity with the UN Charter.[119]

[113] *Ibid.*, pp.133-35.

[114] 82 *ILR*, pp.499, 555.

[115] *Supra* p.483.

[116] Cmnd. 3246, 1967. See also *infra*, Chapter 14.

[117] *Yearbook of the ILC*, 1980, vol.II, p.39. See also the *Company General of the Orinoco* case, 10 *RIAA*, p.280.

[118] The defence of state necessity, however, has been characterised as "controversial": see the *Rainbow Warrior* arbitration, 82 *ILR*, pp.499, 554-55.

[119] See further *infra*, Chapter 18.

THE TREATMENT OF ALIENS[120]

The question of the protection of foreign nationals is one of those issues in international law most closely connected with the different approaches adopted to international relations by the western and Third World nations. Developing countries, as well as communist countries, have long been eager to reduce what they regard as the privileges accorded to capitalist states by international law. They lay great emphasis upon the sovereignty and independence of states and resent the economic influence of the west. The latter, on the other hand, have wished to protect their investments and nationals abroad and provide for the security of their property.

The diplomatic protection of nationals abroad arose after the decline of the grant of special letters of reprisal, by which individuals were authorised to engage in self-help activities.[121] Such diplomatic methods of assisting nationals abroad developed as the number of nationals overseas grew as a consequence of increasing trading activities and thus the relevant state practice multiplied. In addition, since the US-UK Jay Treaty of 1794 numerous mixed claims commissions were established to resolve problems of injury to aliens,[122] while a variety of national claims commissions were created to distribute lump sums received from foreign states in settlement of claims.[123] Such international and national claims procedures together with diplomatic protection therefore enabled nationals abroad to be aided in cases of loss or injury in state responsibility situations.

Nationality of Claims [124]

The doctrine of state responsibility rests upon twin pillars, the attribution to one state of the unlawful acts and omissions of its

[120] See references in footnote 1 and Guha Roy, "Is the Law of Responsibility of States for Injury to Aliens a Part of Universal International Law?", 55 *AJIL*, 1961, p.863. See also Fatouros, "International Law and the Third World", 50 *Virginia Law Review*, 1964, p.783.

[121] See generally Lillich, *HR, op. cit.*, p.344 *et seq.* See also the *Mavrommatis Palestine Concessions* case, PCIJ, Series A, no.2, 1924; 2 *ILR*, p.398.

[122] See e.g. Stuyt, *Survey of International Arbitrations*, 1972, p.IX.

[123] See e.g. *International Claims* (eds. Lillich and Weston), 1982 and Lillich and Weston, *International Claims: Their Settlements by Lump-Sum Agreements*, 2 vols., 1975. See also the US-People's Republic of China Claims Settlement Agreement of 1979, *DUSPIL*, 1979, pp.1213-15, and Whiteman, *Digest, op. cit.* vol.8, pp.933-69.

[124] See e.g. Brownlie, *op. cit.* footnote 26, pp.480-94.

officials and its organs (legislative, judicial and executive) and the capacity of the other state to adopt the claim of the injured party. The first part of this equation has been looked at above, the second will now be considered.

Nationality is the link between the individual and his state as regards particular benefits and obligations. It is also the vital link between the individual and the benefits of international law. Although international law is now moving to a stage whereby individuals may acquire rights free from the interposition of the state, the basic proposition remains that in a state-oriented world system, it is only through the medium of the state that the individual may obtain the full range of benefits available under international law, and nationality is the key.

A state is under a duty to protect its nationals and it may take up their claims against other states. However, once a state does this the claim then becomes that of the state. This is a result of the historical reluctance to permit individuals the right in international law to prosecute claims against foreign countries, for reasons relating to state sovereignty and non-interference in internal affairs.

This basic principle was elaborated in the *Mavrommatis Palestine Concessions* case.[125] The Permanent Court of International Justice pointed out that:

> by taking up the case of one of its subjects and by resorting to diplomatic action or international judicial proceedings on his behalf, a state is in reality asserting its own rights, its right to ensure, in the person of its subjects, respect for the rules of international law . . . .

Indeed, diplomatic protection was an elementary principle of international law. Once a state has taken up a case on behalf of one of its subjects before an international tribunal, in the eyes of the latter the state is sole claimant.

The corollary of this is that the right of a state to take over claims is limited to intervention on behalf of its own nationals. Diplomatic protection may not extend to the adoption of claims of foreign subjects. Such diplomatic protection is not a right, but merely a

---

[125] PCIJ, Series A, no.2, 1924, p.12. See the *Panevezys-Saldutiskis* case, PCIJ, Series A/B, no.76; 9 *ILR*, p.308. See also Vattel, who noted that "whoever ill-treats a citizen indirectly injures the state, which must protect that citizen", *The Law of Nations*, 1916 trans., p.136.

discretion exercised or not by the state as an extra-legal remedy.[126] On the other hand, its exercise cannot be regarded as intervention contrary to international law by the state concerned.

The scope of a state to extend its nationality to whomsoever it wishes is unlimited, except insofar as it affects other states. In the *Nottebohm* case,[127] the International Court of Justice decided that only where there existed a genuine link between the claimant state and its national could the right of diplomatic protection arise.

The Government of Liechtenstein instituted proceedings before the International Court of Justice, claiming restitution and compensation for Nottebohm against Guatemala for acts of the latter which were alleged to be contrary to international law. Guatemala replied that Nottebohm's right to Liechtenstein nationality and thus its diplomatic protection was questionable. The person in question was born in Germany in 1881 and, still a German national, applied for naturalisation in Liechtenstein in 1939. The point was, however, that since 1905 (and until 1943 when he was deported as a result of war measures) Nottebohm had been permanently resident in Guatemala and had carried on his business from there. The Court noted that Liechtenstein was entirely free, as was every state, to establish the rules necessary for the acquisition of its nationality, but the crux of the matter was whether Guatemala was obliged to recognise the grant of Liechtenstein nationality. The exercise of diplomatic protection by a state regarding one of its nationals brought the whole issue of nationality out of the sphere of domestic jurisdiction and onto the plane of international law.[128]

The Court emphasised that according to state practice, nationality was a legal manifestation of the link between the person and the state granting nationality and the recognition that the person was more closely connected with that state than with any other.[129]

---

[126] See *Administrative Decision no.V*, 7 *RIAA*, p.119; 2 *ILR*, pp.185, 191. See also *DUSPIL*, 1973, pp.332-34 and *US v. Dulles*, 222 F.2d 390.

[127] ICJ Reports, 1955, p.4; 22 *ILR*, p.349. The Court emphasised that to exercise protection, e.g. by applying to the Court, was to place oneself on the plane of international protection, *ibid.*, p.16. See the *Nationality Decrees in Tunis and Morocco* case, PCIJ, Series B, no.4, 1923, pp.7, 21; 2 *ILR*, p.349, where it was noted that while questions of nationality were in principle within the domestic jurisdiction of states, the right of a state to use its discretion was limited by obligations undertaken towards other states. See also the *Flegenheimer* case, 14 *RIAA*, p.327 (1958); 25 *ILR*, p.91, and article 1 of the 1930 Hague Convention on Nationality.

[128] *Ibid.*, pp.20-21; 22 *ILR*, p.357.

[129] *Ibid.*, p.23; 22 *ILR*, p.359.

Having brought out these concepts, the Court emphasised the tenuous nature of Nottebohm's links with Liechtenstein and the strength of his connection with Guatemala. Nottebohm had spent only a very short period of time in Liechtenstein and one of his brothers lived in Vaduz. Beyond that and the formal naturalisation process, there were no other links with that state. On the other hand, he had lived in Guatemala for some thirty years and had returned there upon obtaining his papers from Vaduz. Since the Liechtenstein nationality "was granted without regard to the concept . . . adopted in international relations" in the absence of any genuine connection, the Court held that Liechtenstein was not able to extend its diplomatic protection to Nottebohm as regards Guatemala.[130] The case has been subject to some criticism relating to the use of the doctrine of "genuine connection" by the Court. The doctrine had until then been utilised with regard to the problems of dual nationality, so as to enable a decision to be made on whether one national state may sue the other on behalf of the particular national. Its extension to the issue of diplomatic protection appeared to be a new move altogether.[131]

The nationality must exist at the date of the injury, and should continue until at least the date of the award settling the claim, although this latter point may depend upon a variety of other facts, for example any agreement between the contending states as regards the claim.[132]

Where an individual possesses dual nationality, either state of which he is a national may adopt a claim of his against a third state, and it may be that the state with which he has the more effective connection may be able to espouse his claim as against the other state. In the *Mergé* case,[133] it was emphasised that the principle

---

[130] *Ibid.*, pp.25-26; 22 *ILR*, p.362.

[131] See generally, Brownlie, *op. cit.* footnote 26, Chapter XVIII and Jennings, "General Course on Principles of International Law", 121 *HR*, pp.323, 459.

[132] See e.g. Borchard, *op. cit.*, p.660 *et seq.*; Whiteman, *Digest of International Law*, vol.8, 1967, pp.1243-47 and the *Nottebohm* case, ICJ Reports, 1955, p.4; 22 *ILR*, p.349. See also the view of the US State Department that it has consistently declined to espouse claims which have not been continuously owned by US nationals, see 76 *AJIL*, 1982, pp.836-39, and the Rules regarding International Claims issued by the UK Foreign and Commonwealth Office, 1971, to the same effect, cited in Harris, *Cases and Materials in International Law*, 3rd ed., 1983, p.448 and revised in 1983, see UKMIL, 54 *BYIL*, p.520 and in 1985, see 37 *ICLQ*, 1988, p.1006. See also Sinclair, "Nationality of Claims: British Practice", 27 *BYIL*, 1950, p.125.

[133] 14 *RIAA*, p.236 (1955); 22 *ILR*, p.443. See also the *Canevaro* case, 11 *RIAA*, p.397 (1912). Cf. the *Salem* case, 2 *RIAA*, p.1161 (1932); 6 *ILR*, p.188.

based on the sovereign equality of states, which excludes diplomatic protection in the case of dual nationality, must yield before the principle of effective nationality whenever such nationality is that of the claimant state. However, where such predominance is not proved, there would be no such yielding. In other words, the test for permitting protection by a state of a national against another state of which he is also a national is the test of effectiveness. This approach was reaffirmed by the Iran-US Claims Tribunal, where the Full Tribunal held that it had jurisdiction over claims against Iran by a dual national when the "dominant and effective nationality" at the relevant time was American.[134]

As far as a corporation is concerned, it appears that there must be some tangible link between it and the state seeking to espouse its claim. Different cases have pointed to various factors, ranging from incorporation of the company in the particular state to the maintenance of the administrative centre of the company in the state and the existence of substantial holdings by nationals in the company.[135]

The Court in the *Barcelona Traction* case[136] remarked that the traditional rule gave the right of diplomatic protection of a corporation to the state under the laws of which it is incorporated and in whose territory it has its registered office. Any application of the *Nottebohm* doctrine of the "genuine connection" was rejected as having no general acceptance. Nevertheless, it remains true that some meaningful link must bind the state to the company which seeks its protection. Just how far the traditionalist, rather restrictive approach adopted here by the International Court of Justice will be maintained has yet to be seen.

The position as regards the shareholders in a company was discussed in that case. It concerned a dispute between Belgium and Spain relating to a company established in 1911 in Canada, which was involved in the production of electricity in Spain and the majority of whose shares was owned by Belgian nationals. After the Second World War, the Spanish authorities took a number of

---

[134] *Islamic Republic of Iran* v. *USA, Case No. A/18*, 5 *Iran-US CTR*, p.251; 75 *ILR*, p.176. See also *Esphahanian* v. *Bank Tejarat*, 2 *Iran-US CTR*, p.157; 72 *ILR*, p.478, and *Malek* v. *Islamic Republic of Iran*, 19 *Iran-US CTR*, p.48.

[135] See e.g. Brownlie, *op. cit.* footnote 26, pp.485-88 and Schwarzenberger, *op. cit.*, pp.387-412.

[136] ICJ Reports, 1970, pp.3, 42; 46 *ILR*, pp.178, 216.

financial measures which resulted in harm to the company and in 1948 it was declared bankrupt. The case concerned a Belgian claim in respect of injury to the shareholders, who were Belgian nationals, because of the steps that Spain had adopted. Spain replied by denying that Belgium had any standing in the case since the injury had been suffered by the company and not the shareholders.

The Court rejected the Belgian claim on the grounds that it did not have a legal interest in the matter. Although shareholders may suffer if wrong is done to a company, it is only the rights of the latter that have been infringed and thus entitle it to institute action. If, on the other hand (as did not happen here), the direct rights of the shareholders were affected, for example as regards dividends, then they would have an independent right of action; but otherwise, only if the company legally ceased to exist.

The Court emphasised that the general rule of international law stated that where an unlawful act was committed against a company representing foreign capital, only the national state of the company could sue. In this case Canada had chosen not to intervene in the dispute. To accept the idea of the diplomatic protection of shareholders would, in the opinion of the International Court of Justice, result in the creation of an atmosphere of confusion and insecurity in economic relations especially since the shares of international companies are "widely scattered and frequently change hands".[137]

It is interesting to note that the United Kingdom, according to the set of Rules regarding the taking up of International Claims produced by the Foreign Office, most recently in 1985,[138] may intervene in *Barcelona Traction* situations where a national has an interest as a shareholder or otherwise, and the company is defunct, although this is regarded as an exceptional instance. The United Kingdom may also intervene where it is the national state of the company that actively wrongs the company in which a United Kingdom national has an interest as a shareholder or in some other respect; otherwise the UK would normally take up such a claim

---

[137] *Ibid.*, p.49; 46 *ILR*, p.223. See also the separate opinion of Judge Oda, the *Elettronica Sicula* case, *US* v. *Italy*, ICJ Reports, 1989, pp.15, 84.

[138] *Supra*, footnote 132. The increase in the number of bilateral investment treaties in the 1970s may be partly explained as the response to the post-*Barcelona Traction* need to protect shareholders. See e.g. Sornarajah, "State Responsibility and Bilateral Investment Treaties", 20 *Journal of World Trade Law*, 1986, pp.79, 87.

only in concert with the government of the state of incorporation of the company.

The Exhaustion of Local Remedies

It is a well established rule of customary international law that before international proceedings are instituted, the various remedies provided by the local state should have been exhausted.[139] This is both to enable the particular state to have an opportunity to redress the wrong that has occurred there within its own legal order and to reduce the number of international claims that might be brought. If claims could be brought on behalf of individuals or companies after the alleged violation and before the state responsible had a chance to rectify it, it could tax the international system as well as proving vexatious. Another factor, of course, is the respect that is to be accorded to the sovereignty and jurisdiction of foreign states by not pre-empting the operation of their legal systems.

The rule was well illustrated in the *Ambatielos* arbitration,[140] between Greece and Britain. The former brought proceedings arising out of a contract signed by Ambatielos, which were rejected by the tribunal since the remedies available under English law had not been fully utilised. In particular, he had failed to call a vital witness and he had not appealed to the House of Lords from the decision of the Court of Appeal.

The term local remedies applies only to available effective remedies. It will not be sufficient to dismiss a claim merely because the person claiming had not taken the matter to appeal, where the appeal would not have affected the basic outcome of the case. This was stressed in the *Finnish Ships* arbitration[141] where shipowners brought a claim before the Admiralty Transport Arbitration Board, but did not appeal against the unfavourable decision. It was held that since the appeal could only be on points of law, which could not overturn the vital finding of fact that there had been a British

---

[139] See further, *supra*, Chapter 6, p.239. See also article 22 of the ILC Draft, *Yearbook of the ILC*, 1980, vol.II, p.32. See also the *Panevezys Railway* case, PCIJ, Series A/B, No.76 (1939); 9 *ILR*, p.308; Whiteman, *op. cit.* vol.III, p.1558; Borchard, *The Diplomatic Protection of Citizens Abroad*, 1915, pp.817-18; Trindade, *The Application of the Rule of Exhaustion of Local Remedies in International Law*, 1983 and Amerasinghe, *Local Remedies in International Law*, 1990.

[140] 12 *RIAA*, p.83 (1956); 23 *ILR*, p.306.

[141] 2 *RIAA*, p.1479 (1934); 7 *ILR*, p.231.

requisition of ships involved, any appeal would have been ineffective. Accordingly the claims of the shipowners would not be dismissed for non-exhaustion of local remedies.

In the *Interhandel* case,[142] the United States seized the American assets of a company owned by the Swiss firm Interhandel, in 1942, which was suspected of being under the control of a German enterprise. In 1958, after nine years of litigation in the US courts regarding the unblocking of the Swiss assets in America, Switzerland took the matter to the International Court of Justice. However, before a decision was reached, the US Supreme Court readmitted Interhandel into the legal proceedings, thus disposing of Switzerland's argument that the company's suit had been finally rejected. The Court dismissed the Swiss government's claim since the local remedies available had not been exhausted. Criticism has been levelled against this judgment on the ground that litigation extending over practically ten years could hardly be described as constituting an "effective" remedy. However, the fact remains that the legal system operating in the United States had still something to offer the Swiss company even after that time.

The local remedies rule does not apply where one state has been guilty of a direct breach of international law causing immediate injury to another state, as for instance where its diplomatic agents are assaulted. But it does apply where the state is complaining of injury to its nationals. The local remedies rule may be waived by treaty stipulation, as for example in Article V of the US-Mexico General Claims Convention of 1923 and Article XI of the Convention on International Liability for Damage caused by Space Objects 1972.

The issue of local remedies was clarified in the *Elettronica Sicula S.p.A. (ELSI)* case,[143] which concerned an action brought by the US against Italy alleging injuries to the Italian interests of two US corporations. Italy claimed that local remedies had not been exhausted, while the US argued that the doctrine did not apply since

---

[142] ICJ Reports, 1959, p.6; 27 *ILR*, p.475. The Court declared that the "rule that local remedies must be exhausted before international proceedings may be instituted is a well-established principle of customary international law", *ibid.*, p.27; 27 *ILR*, p.490. See also Rules VII and VIII of the International Claims Rules of the FCO, *supra*, footnote 132; Pleadings, *Israel* v. *Bulgaria*, ICJ Reports, 1959, pp.531-32 and Meron, "The Incidence of the Rule of Exhaustion of Local Remedies", 25 *BYIL*, 1959, p.95. Note in addition, the *North American Dredging Co.* claim, 4 *RIAA*, p.26 (1926); 3 *ILR*, p.4.

[143] ICJ Reports, 1989, p.15.

the case was brought under the Treaty of Friendship, Commerce and Navigation 1948 between the two states which provided for the submission of disputes relating to the treaty to the International Court, with no mention of local remedies. The Court,[144] however, firmly held that while the parties to an agreement could if they so chose dispense with the local remedies requirement in express terms, it "finds itself unable to accept that an important principle of customary international law should be held to have been tacitly dispensed with".[145] In other words, the presumption that local remedies need to be exhausted can only be rebutted by express provision to the contrary.

The Court also dealt with a claim by the US that the doctrine did not apply to a request for a declaratory judgment finding that the treaty in question had been violated. This claim in effect was based on the view that the doctrine would not apply in cases of direct injury to a state. The Court felt unable to find in the case a dispute over alleged violation of the treaty resulting in direct injury to the US that was both distinct from and independent of the dispute with regard to the two US corporations.[146] The Court stressed that the matter "which colours and pervades the US claim as a whole" was the alleged damage to the two US corporations.[147] In the light of this stringent test, it therefore seems that in such mixed claims involving the interests both of nationals and of the state itself one must assume that the local remedies rule applies.

The Court also rejected the Italian claim that local remedies had not in fact been exhausted in the case because the two US corporations had not raised the treaty issue before the Italian courts. It was held that it was sufficient if the essence of the claim has been brought before the competent tribunals. Accordingly, identity of claims as distinct from identity of issues is not required. The Court was not convinced that there clearly remained some remedy which the corporations, independently of their Italian subsidiary (ELSI) ought to have pursued and exhausted.[148]

---

[144] The case was in fact decided by a Chamber of the Court, see further *infra* Chapter 17.

[145] ICJ Reports, 1989, pp.15, 42.

[146] *Ibid.*, pp.42-44.

[147] *Ibid.*, p.43.

[148] *Ibid.*, pp.46-48. See also Adler, "The Exhaustion of the Local Remedies Rule After the International Court of Justice's Decision in *ELSI*", 39 *ICLQ*, 1990, p.641.

The Relevant Standard of Treatment

The developed states of the west have argued historically that there exists an "international minimum standard" for the protection of foreign nationals that must be upheld irrespective of how the state treats its own nationals, whereas other states maintained that all the state need do is treat the alien as it does its own nationals (the "national treatment standard").

The reason for the evolution of the latter approach is to be found in the increasing resentment of western economic domination rather than in the necessary neglect of basic standards of justice. The Latin American states felt, in particular, that the international minimum standard concept had been used as a mean of interference in internal affairs.[149] Accordingly, the Calvo doctrine was formulated. This involved a reaffirmation of the principle of non-intervention coupled with the assertion that aliens were entitled only to such rights as were accorded nationals and thus had to seek redress for grievances exclusively in the domestic arena.[150] It was intended as a shield against external interference.

The international standard concept itself developed during the nineteenth century and received extensive support in case-law. In the *Neer* case,[151] for example, where the American Superintendent of a mine in Mexico had been killed, the Commission held "that the propriety of governmental acts should be put to the test of international standards", while in the *Certain German Interests in Polish Upper Silesia* case,[152] the Court recognised the existence of a common or generally accepted international law respecting the treatment of aliens, which is applicable to them despite municipal legislation. In the *Garcia* case,[153] the US-Mexican Claims Commission emphasised that there existed an international standard concerning the taking of human life and in the *Roberts* claim,[154] reference was made to the test as to whether aliens were treated in accordance with ordinary standards of civilisation.

---

[149] See e.g. Guha Roy, *op. cit.*; Castañeda, "The Underdeveloped Nations and the Development of International Law", 15 *International Organisation*, 1961, p.38 and Anand, *New States and International Law*, 1972.

[150] See e.g. Lillich, *HR, op. cit.*, p.349.

[151] 4 *RIAA*, p.60 (1926); 3 *ILR*, p.213.

[152] PCIJ, Series A, no.7, 1926; 3 *ILR*, p.429.

[153] 4 *RIAA*, p.119 (1926). See also the *Chattin* case, 4 *RIAA*, p.282 (1927); 4 *ILR*, p.248.

[154] 4 *RIAA*, p.77 (1926); 3 *ILR*, p.227.

If the principle is clear, the contents or definition of that principle are far from clear. In the *Neer* claim,[155] the Commission stated that the treatment of an alien, in order to constitute an international delinquency,

> should amount to an outrage, to bad faith, to wilful neglect of duty, or to an insufficiency of governmental action so far short of international standards that every reasonable and impartial man would readily recognise its insufficiency.

In other words, a fairly high threshold is specified before the minimum standard applies. Some indeed have argued that the concept never involved a definite standard with a fixed content, but rather a "process of decision",[156] a process which would involve an examination of the responsibility of the state for the injury to the alien in the light of all the circumstances of the particular case.[157] The issue of the content of such a standard has often been described in terms of the concept of denial of justice.[158] In effect, that concept refers to the improper administration of civil and criminal justice as regards an alien. It would include the failure to apprehend and prosecute those wrongfully causing injury to an alien, as in the *Janes* claim,[159] where an American citizen was killed in Mexico. The identity of the murderer was known, but no action had been taken for 8 years. The widow was awarded $12,000 in compensation for the non-apprehension and non-punishment of the murderer. It would also include unreasonably long detention and harsh and unlawful treatment in prison.[160]

A progressive attempt to resolve the divide between the national and international standard proponents was put forward by Garcia-Amador in a report on international responsibility to the International Law Commission in 1956. He argued that the two approaches were now synthesised in the concept of the international

---

[155] 4 *RIAA*, pp.60, 61-62 (1926); 3 *ILR*, p.213. See similarly, the *Chattin* case, 4 *RIAA*, p.282 (1927); 4 *ILR*, p.248.

[156] McDougal et al., *Studies in World Public Order*, 1960, p.869.

[157] See Lillich, *HR, op. cit.*, p.350.

[158] See e.g. Freeman, *The International Responsibility of States for Denial of Justice*, 1938.

[159] 4 *RIAA*, p.82 (1926); 3 *ILR*, p.218.

[160] See e.g. the *Roberts* claim, 4 *RIAA*, p.77 (1926); 3 *ILR*, p.227 and the *Quintanilla* claim, 4 *RIAA*, p.101 (1926); 3 *ILR*, p.224.

recognition of the essential rights of man.[161] He formulated two principles. First, that aliens had to enjoy the same rights and guarantees as enjoyed by nationals, which should not in any case be less than the fundamental human rights recognised and defined in international instruments. Secondly, international responsibility would only be engaged if internationally recognised fundamental human rights were affected.[162]

This approach did not prove attractive to the ILC at that time in the light of a number of problems. However, human rights law has developed considerably in recent years[163] and can now be regarded as establishing certain minimum standards of state behaviour with regard to civil and political rights. It is noticeable, for example, that the relevant instruments do not refer to nationals and aliens specifically, but to all individuals within the territory and subject to the jurisdiction of the state without discrimination.[164] One should also note the special efforts being made to deal with non-nationals, in particular the Elles Draft Declaration,[165] and the continuing concern with regard to migrant workers.

It is, of course, recognised that there must be some differences as regards the relative rights and obligations of nationals and aliens. Non-nationals do not have political rights and may be banned from employment in certain areas (e.g. the diplomatic corps), although they remain subject to the local law.

It is also unquestioned that a state may legitimately refuse to admit aliens, or may accept them subject to certain conditions being fulfilled. Whether a state may expel aliens with equal facility is more open to doubt.

A number of cases assert that states must give convincing reasons for expelling an alien. In for example the *Boffolo* case,[166] which concerned an Italian expelled from Venezuela, it was held that

---

[161] *Yearbook of the ILC,* 1956, vol.II, pp.173, 199-203.

[162] *Yearbook of the ILC,* 1957, vol.II, pp.104, 112-13.

[163] *Supra,* Chapter 6.

[164] See e.g. Article 2 of the International Covenant on Civil and Political Rights, 1966.

[165] E/CN.4/Sub.2/392 (1977). See also Lillich and Neff, "The Treatment of Aliens and International Human Rights Norms", 21 *German Yearbook of International Law,* 1978, p.97. The Elles Draft was ultimately taken to the UN, where a General Assembly Working Group is examining it.

[166] 10 *RIAA,* p.528 (1903). See also *Dr. Breger's* case, Whiteman, *Digest, op. cit.* vol.8, p.861; Plender, *International Migration Law,* 1972 and Goodwin-Gill, *International Law and the Movement of Persons Between States,* 1978.

states possess a general right of expulsion, but it could only be resorted to in extreme circumstances and accomplished in a manner least injurious to the person affected. In addition, the reasons for the expulsion must be stated before an international tribunal when the occasion demanded. Many municipal systems provide that the authorities of a country may deport aliens without reasons having to be stated. The position under customary international law is therefore somewhat confused. As far as treaty law is concerned article 13 of the International Covenant on Civil and Political Rights stipulates that an alien lawfully in the territory of a state party to the Convention

> may be expelled therefrom only in pursuance of a decision reached in accordance with law and shall, except where compelling reasons of national security otherwise require, be allowed to submit the reasons against his expulsion and to have his case reviewed by and be represented for the purpose before, the competent authority.

Article 3 of the European Convention on Establishment, 1956, provides that nationals of other contracting states lawfully residing in the territory may be expelled only if they endanger national security or offend against public order or morality, and Article 4 of the Fourth Protocol (1963) of the European Convention of Human Rights declares that "collective expulsion of aliens is prohibited".[167]

The burden of proving the wrongfulness of the expelling state's action falls upon the claimant alleging expulsion and the relevant rules would also apply where even though there is no direct law or regulation forcing the alien to leave, his continued presence in that state is made impossible because of conditions generated by wrongful acts of the state or attributable to it.[168]

Where states have expelled aliens, international law requires their national state to admit them. This is a general principle, although Lord Denning in the *Thakrar* case[169] did unfortunately

---

[167] Note also article 1 of Protocol 7 (1984) of the European Convention on Human Rights to the same general effect as article 13. See as regards refugees, the 1951 Convention Relating to the Status of Refugees and the 1967 Protocol and Goodwin-Gill, *The Refugee in International Law*, 1983.

[168] See *Rankin v. The Islamic Republic of Iran*, 17 Iran-US CTR, pp.135, 142; 82 *ILR*, pp.204, 214. See also Goodwin-Gill, *International Law and the Movement of Persons Between States*, 1978; Brownlie, *op. cit.*, pp.76-77 and Pellonpaa, *Expulsion in International Law*, 1984.

[169] [1974] QB 684; 59 *ILR*, p.450.

suggest that this might not apply in instances where mass expulsions of aliens have occurred and where the national state of these aliens is "an outgoing country with far-flung commitments abroad such as the United Kingdom".

However, the Lord Chancellor in dealing with the expulsion of British aliens from East Africa accepted that in international law a state was under a duty as between other states to accept expelled nationals.[170] The Denning dictum cannot be accepted as valid.

THE EXPROPRIATION OF FOREIGN PROPERTY[171]

The expansion of the western economies since the nineteenth century in particular stimulated an outflow of capital and consequent heavy investment in the developing areas of the world. This resulted in substantial areas of local economies falling within the ownership and control of western corporations. However, with the granting of independence to the various Third World countries and in view of the nationalisation measures taken by the Soviet Union after the success of the communist revolution, such properties and influence began to come under pressure.

In assessing the state of international law with regard to the expropriation of the property of aliens, one is immediately confronted with two opposing objectives, although they need not be irreconcilable in all cases. On the one hand, the capital-exporting countries require some measure of protection and security before they will invest abroad and on the other hand the capital-importing countries are wary of the power of foreign investments and the drain of currency that occurs, and are often stimulated to take over such enterprises.

Nationalisation for one reason or another is now a common feature not only in communist and Afro-Asian states, but also in western Europe. The need to acquire control of some key privately owned property is felt by many states to be an essential requirement

---

[170] 335 HL Deb., col. 497, 14 September 1972. See also *Van Duyn* v. *Home Office*, [1974] ECR 1337; 60 *ILR*, p.247.

[171] See e.g. White, *Nationalisation of Foreign Property*, 1961; Wortley, *Expropriation of Public International Law*, 1959; Brownlie, "Legal Status of Natural Resources", 162 *HR*, p.245; Higgins, "The Taking of Property by the State: Recent Developments in International Law", 176 *HR*, p.267, and *The Valuation of Nationalised Property in International Law* (ed. Lillich), 3 vols., 1972-75.

in the interests of economic and social reform. Indeed it is true to say that extensive sectors of the economies of most west European states are now under national control after having been taken under public ownership.

Since it can hardly be denied that nationalisation is a perfectly legitimate measure for a state to adopt, the problem arises where foreign property is involved. Not to expropriate such property in a general policy of nationalisation might be seen as equivalent to proposing a privileged status within the country for foreign property, as well as limiting the power of the state within its own jurisdiction.

There is no doubt that under international law, expropriation of alien property is legitimate. This is not disputed. However, certain conditions must be fulfilled.

The question, of course, arises as to the stage at which international law in fact becomes involved in such a situation. Apart from the relevance of the general rules relating to the treatment of aliens noted in the preceding section, the issue will usually arise out of a contract between a state and a foreign private enterprise. In such a situation, several possibilities exist. It could be argued that the contract itself by its very nature becomes "internationalised" and thus subject to international law rather than (or possibly in addition to) the law of the contracting state. The consequences of this would include the operation of the principle of international law that agreements are to be honoured (*pacta sunt servanda*) which would constrain the otherwise wide competence of a state party to alter unilaterally the terms of a relevant agreement. This proposition was adopted by the Arbitrator in the *Texaco v. Libya* case in 1977,[172] where it was noted that this may be achieved in various ways, for example, by stating that the law governing the contract referred to "general principles of law", which was taken to incorporate international law; by including an international arbitration clause for the settlement of disputes and by including a stabilisation clause in an international development agreement, preventing unilateral variation of the terms of the agreement.[173]

---

[172] 53 *ILR*, p.389.

[173] See e.g. Greenwood, "State Contracts in International Law — The Libyan Oil Arbitrations", 53 *BYIL*, 1982, pp.27, 41 *et seq*. See also Fatouros, "International Law and the Internationalised Contract", 74 *AJIL*, 1980, p.134.

However, this approach is controversial and case-law is by no means consistent.[174]

International law will clearly be engaged where the expropriation is unlawful, either because of, for example, the discriminatory manner in which it is carried out or the offering of inadequate or no compensation.[175]

The Property Question

Professor Higgins has pointed to "the almost total absence of any analysis of conceptual aspects of property".[176] Property would clearly include physical objects and certain abstract entities, for example, shares in companies, debts and intellectual property. The 1961 Harvard Draft Convention on the International Responsibility of States for Injuries to Aliens[177] discusses the concept of property in the light of "all movable and immovable property, whether tangible or intangible, including industrial, literary and artistic property as well as rights and interests in property". In the *Liamco* case the arbitration specifically mentioned concession rights as forming part of incorporeal property,[178] a crucial matter as many expropriation cases in fact involve a wide variety of contractual rights.[179]

---

[174] See e.g. Paulsson, "The ICSID *Klöckner* v. *Cameroon* Award: The Duties of Partners in North-South Economic Development Agreements", 1 *Journal of International Arbitration*, 1984, p.145; The *Aminoil* case, 21 *ILM*, 1982, p.976; 66 *ILR*, p.519 and Bowett, "State Contracts with Aliens: Contemporary Developments on Compensation for Termination or Breach", 59 *BYIL*, 1988, p.49.

[175] See in particular article 1 of Protocol I of the European Convention on Human Rights 1950 as regards the protection of the right to property and the prohibition of deprivation of possessions "except in the public interest and subject to the conditions provided for by law and by the general principles of international law". See e.g. the following cases, *Marckx*, European Court of Human Rights, Series A, No.31; 58 *ILR*, p.561 and *Sporrong and Lönnroth*, *ibid.*, No.52; 68 *ILR*, p.86. However, it has been held that the reference to international law did not apply to the taking by a state of the property of its own nationals; see *Lithgow*, European Court of Human Rights, Series A, No.102; 75 *ILR*, p.438; *James*, *ibid.*, No.98; 75 *ILR*, p.397 and *Mellacher*, *ibid.*, No.169. See also Brock, "The Protection of Property Rights Under the European Convention on Human Rights", *Legal Issues of European Integration*, 1986, p.52.

[176] *Op. cit.*, p.268.

[177] 55 *AJIL*, 1961, p.548 (article 10(7)).

[178] 20 *ILM*, 1981, pp.1, 53; 62 *ILR*, pp.141, 189. See also the *Shufeldt* case, 2 *RIAA*, pp.1083, 1097 (1930); 5 *ILR*, p.179.

[179] See also *infra* p.525 concerning the definition of "investments" in bilateral investment treaties.

The Nature of Expropriation

Expropriation involves taking property, but actions short of direct possession of the assets in question may also fall within the category. The 1961 Harvard Draft would include, for example, "any such unreasonable interference with the use, enjoyment or disposal of property as to justify an inference that the owner thereof will not be able to use, enjoy or dispose of the property within a reasonable period of time after the inception of such interference".[180] In 1965, for example, after a series of Indonesian decrees, the UK government stated that:

> in view of the complete inability of British enterprises and plantations to exercise and enjoy any of their rights of ownership in relation to their properties in Indonesia, Her Majesty's Government has concluded that the Indonesian Government has expropriated this property.[181]

In *Starrett Housing Corporation* v. *Government of the Islamic Republic of Iran* before the Iran-US Claims Tribunal,[182] it was emphasised by the Tribunal that:

> measures taken by a state can interfere with property rights to such an extent that these rights are rendered so useless that they must be deemed to have been expropriated, even though the state does not purport to have expropriated them and the legal title to the property formally remains with the original owner.

In that case, it was held that a taking had occurred by the end of January 1980 upon the appointment by the Iranian Housing Ministry of a temporary manager of the enterprise concerned, thus depriving the claimants of the right to manage and of effective control and use.[183] However, a series of events prior to that date, including armed incursions and detention of personnel, intimidation and

---

[180] *Op. cit.*, pp.553-54 (article 10(3)a).

[181] *BPIL*, 1964, p.200. See also 4 *ILM*, 1965, pp.440-47. Note also *Shanghai Power Co.* v. *US*, 4 Cl. Ct. 237 (1983), where it was held that the settlement of the plaintiff's claim by the US Government in an agreement with China for less than its worth did not constitute a taking for which compensation was required in the context of the Fifth Amendment.

[182] Interlocutory Award, 4 *Iran-US CTR*, p.122; 23 *ILM*, 1984, p.1090.

[183] 4 *Iran-US CTR*, p.154; 23 *ILM*, 1984, p.1116. See also *Harza Engineering Co.* v. *The Islamic Republic of Iran*, 1 *Iran-US CTR*, p.499 and *AIG* v. *The Islamic Republic of Iran*, 4 *Iran-US CTR*, p.96.

interference with supplies and needed facilities, did not amount
to a taking of the property, since investors in foreign countries
assume certain risks with regard to disturbances and even revolution.
The fact that the risks materialise, held the Tribunal, did not mean
that property rights affected by the events could be deemed to
have been taken.[184] There is clearly an important, but indistinct,
dividing line here. It has also been held that the seizure of a
controlling stock interest in a foreign corporation is a taking of
control of the assets and profits of the enterprise in question.[185] The
expropriation of a given property may also include a taking of
closely connected ancillary rights, such as patents and contracts,
which had not been directly nationalised.[186]

Public Purposes

The expropriation must be for "reasons of public utility, judicial
liquidation and similar measures" as noted in the *Certain German
Interests in Polish Upper Silesia* case.[187] But how far this extends is open
to dispute, although it will cover wartime measures.

The issue was raised in the *BP* case,[188] where the reason for the
expropriation of the BP property was the Libyan belief that the UK
had encouraged Iran to occupy certain Persian Gulf Islands. The
arbitrator explained that the taking violated international law "as
it was made for purely extraneous political reasons and was arbitrary
and discriminatory in character".[189] This is ambiguous as to the public
purpose issue, and in the *Liamco* case[190] it was held that "the public
utility principle is not a necessary requisite for the legality of a

---

[184] 4 *Iran-US CTR*, p.156; 23 *ILM*, 1984, p.117. Cf. the concurring opinion by Judge
Holtzmann on this issue, 4 *Iran-US CTR*, pp.159, 178; 23 *ILM*, p.1138.

[185] *Kalamazoo Spice Extraction Company* v. *The Provisional Military Government of Socialist
Ethiopia*, 24 *ILM*, 1985, p.1277. See also *Agip SpA* v. *The Government of the Popular Republic of
the Congo*, 67 *ILR*, p.319 and *Benvenuti and Bonfant* v. *The Government of the Popular Republic
of the Congo, ibid.*, p.345.

[186] PCIJ, Series A, no.7, 1926. See also the *Norwegian Shipowners' Claims* case, 1 *RIAA*, p.307
(1922) and the *Sporrong and Lönnroth* case before the European Court of Human Rights,
Series A, no.52 (1982); 68 *ILR*, p.86. Note in addition *Revere Copper* v. *Opic*, 56 *ILR*, p.258,
and see Christie, "What Constitutes a Taking of Property under International Law?", 38 *BYIL*,
1962, p.307, and *DUSPIL*, 1976, p.444.

[187] PCIJ, Series A, no.7, 1926, p.22.

[188] 53 *ILR*, p.297.

[189] *Ibid.*, p.329.

[190] 20 *ILM*, 1981, p.1; 62 *ILR*, p.141.

nationalisation".[191] It is to be noted, however, that the 1962 General Assembly Resolution on Permanent Sovereignty over Natural Resources mentions this requirement,[192] although the 1974 Charter of Economic Rights and Duties of States does not.[193] The question is thus still an open one.[194]

Compensation

The requirement often stipulated by western authorities is for prompt, adequate and effective compensation, the formula used by US Secretary of State Hull on the occasion of Mexican expropriations.[195] It is the standard maintained in particular by the US[196] and found in a number of bilateral investment treaties.[197] However, case-law is less clear. Early cases did not use the Hull formulation[198] and the 1962 Permanent Sovereignty Resolution referred to "appropriate compensation". This phrase, in fact, was cited with approval by the arbitrator in the *Texaco*

---

[191] *Ibid.*, pp.58-59; 62 *ILR*, p.194.

[192] Paragraph 4 of the 1962 Resolution provides that "[n]ationalization, expropriation or requisitioning shall be based on grounds or reasons of public utility, security or the national interest which are recognized as overriding purely individual or private interests, both domestic and foreign. In such cases the owner shall be paid appropriate compensation in accordance with the rules in force in the state taking such measures in the exercise of its sovereignty and in accordance with international law. In any case where the question of compensation gives rise to a controversy, the national jurisdiction of the state taking such measures shall be exhausted. However, upon agreement by sovereign states and other parties concerned, settlement of the dispute should be made through arbitration or international adjudication."

[193] Article 2(2)c of the 1974 Charter provides that every state has the right to "nationalise, expropriate or transfer ownership of foreign property in which case appropriate compensation should be paid by the state adopting such measures, taking into account its relevant laws and regulations and all circumstances that the state considers pertinent. In any case where the question of compensation gives rise to a controversy, it shall be settled under the domestic law of the nationalising state and by its tribunals, unless it is freely and mutually agreed by all states concerned that other peaceful means be sought on the basis of the sovereign equality of states and in accordance with the principle of free choice of means."

[194] See also *Agip SpA* v. *The Government of the Popular Republic of the Congo*, 67 *ILR*, pp.319, 336-39.

[195] Hackworth, *Digest of International Law*, vol.3, 1940-44, p.662.

[196] See e.g. *DUSPIL*,1976, p.444 and Robinson, "Expropriation in the Restatement (Revised)", 78 *AJIL*, 1984, p.176.

[197] *Ibid.*, p.178. See further *infra* p.524.

[198] See e.g. the *Chorzow Factory* case, PCIJ, Series A, no.17, 1928, p.46; 4 *ILR*, p.268 and the *Norwegian Shipowners' Claims* case, 1 *RIAA*, pp.307, 339-41 (1922). See also Schachter, "Compensation for Expropriation", 78 *AJIL*, 1984, p.121.

case[199] as a rule of customary law in view of the support it achieved. This was reinforced in the *Aminoil* case[200] where the tribunal said that the standard of "appropriate compensation" in the 1962 resolution "codifies positive principles".[201] It was stated that the determination of "appropriate compensation" was better accomplished by an inquiry into all the circumstances relevant to the particular concrete case than through abstract theoretical discussion.[202] This practical and acceptable formulation is likely to prove influential. It should, however, be noted that while the "appropriate compensation" formula of the 1962 resolution is linked to both national and international law, the 1974 Charter of Economic Rights and Duties of States links the formula to domestic law and considerations only. While the former instrument is accepted, as noted above, as a reflection of custom, the latter is not.[203] But in any event, it is unclear whether in practice there would be a substantial difference in result.[204]

In the sensitive and controversial process of assessing the extent of compensation, several distinct categories should be noted. There is generally little dispute about according compensation for the physical assets and other assets of the enterprise such as debts or monies due,[205] although there are differing methods as to how to value such assets in particular cases.[206] Interest on the value of such assets will also be normally paid. There is, however, disagreement with regard to the award of compensation for the loss of future profits.

---

[199] 17 *ILM*, 1978, pp.3, 29; 53 *ILR*, pp.389, 489. See also *Banco Nacional de Cuba* v. *Chase Manhattan Bank*, 658 F.2d 875 (1981); 66 *ILR*, p.421.

[200] 21 *ILM*, 1982, p.976; 66 *ILR*, p.519.

[201] *Ibid.*, p.1032; 66 *ILR*, p.601.

[202] *Ibid.*, p.1033.

[203] See e.g. the *Texaco* case, 17 *ILM*, 1978, pp.1, 29-31; 53 *ILR*, p.489. Note that the *Restatement (Third) of Foreign Relations Law of the United States*, 1987, vol.II, p.196, (para. 712) refers to the requirement of "just compensation" and not the Hull formula. This is defined as "an amount equivalent to the value of the property taken and to be paid at the time of taking or within a reasonable time thereafter with interest from the date of taking and in a form economically usable by the foreign national", *ibid.*, p.197. See also Schachter, *op. cit.*, p.121.

[204] See generally also Dolzer, "New Foundation of the Law of Expropriation of Alien Property", 75 *AJIL*, 1981, p.533 and Sornarajah, "Compensation for Expropriation", 13 *Journal of World Trade Law*, 1979, p.108.

[205] See e.g. the *Liamco* case, 62 *ILR*, pp.140, 201. See also Bowett, *op. cit.*, p.61 and Greenwood, *op. cit.*, pp.77-79.

[206] See e.g. the *Aminoil* case, 21 *ILM*, 1982, pp.976, 1038; 66 *ILR*, pp.519, 608-9.

In *Amco Asia Corporation* v. *The Republic of Indonesia*,[207] the Arbitral Tribunal held that:

> the full compensation of prejudice, by awarding to the injured party, the *damnum emergens* [loss suffered] and the *lucrum cessans* [expected profits] is a principle common to the main systems of municipal law, and therefore, a general principle of law which may be considered as a source of international law,

although the compensation that could be awarded would cover only direct and foreseeable prejudice and not more remote damage.[208] However, this approach needs to be carefully considered. In particular one may need to take into account whether the expropriation itself was lawful or unlawful. In *INA Corporation* v. *The Islamic Republic of Iran*,[209] the Tribunal suggested that in the case of a large-scale, lawful nationalisation "international law has undergone a gradual reappraisal, the effect of which may be to undermine the doctrinal value of any 'full' or 'adequate' (when used as identical to 'full') compensation standard". However, in a situation involving an investment of a small amount shortly before the nationalisation, international law did allow for compensation in an amount equal to the fair market value of the investment.[210] Fair market value meant the amount that a willing buyer would have paid a willing seller for the shares of a going concern, ignoring the expropriation situation completely.[211] However, Judge Lagergren noted that the "fair market value" standard would normally be discounted in cases of lawful large-scale nationalisations in taking account of "all circumstances".[212]

In *Amco International Finance Corporation* v. *The Islamic Republic of Iran*,[213] Chamber Three of the Iran-US Claims Tribunal held that the property in question had been lawfully expropriated and that

---

[207] 24 *ILM*, 1985, pp.1022, 1036-37. See also the *Chorzow Factory* case, PCIJ, Series A, no.17, 1928; 4 *ILR*, p.268; the *Sapphire* case, 35 *ILR*, p.136; the *Norwegian Shipowners' Claims* case, 1 *RIAA*, p.307 (1922); the *Lighthouses Arbitration*, 23 *ILR*, p.299, and *Benvenuti and Bonfant* v. *The Government of the Popular Republic of the Congo*, 67 *ILR*, pp.345, 375-79.

[208] 24 *ILM*, 1985, pp.1022, 1037.

[209] 8 *Iran-US CTR*, p.373; 75 *ILR*, p.595.

[210] *Ibid.*, p.378; 75 *ILR*, p.602.

[211] *Ibid.*, p.380; 75 *ILR*, p.603.

[212] *Ibid.*, p.390; 75 *ILR*, p.614.

[213] 15 *Iran-US CTR*, pp.189, 246-52; 82 *AJIL*, 1986, p.358.

"a clear distinction must be made between lawful and unlawful expropriations, since the rules applicable to the compensation to be paid by the expropriating state differ according to the legal characterisation of the taking".[214] In the case of an unlawful taking, full restitution in kind or its monetary equivalent was required in order to re-establish the situation which would in all probability have existed if the expropriation had not occurred,[215] while in the case of lawful taking, the standard was the payment of the full value of the undertaking at the moment of dispossession. The difference was interpreted by the Tribunal to mean that compensation for lost profits was only available in cases of wrongful expropriation. As far as the actual method of valuation was concerned, the Tribunal rejected the "discounted cash flow" method, which would involve the estimation of the likely future earnings of the company at the valuation date and discounting such earnings to take account of reasonably foreseeable risks, since it was likely to amount to restitution as well as being too speculative.[216]

Bilateral Investment Treaties and Lump-Sum Agreements

In practice many of the situations involving commercial relations between states and private parties fall within the framework of bilateral agreements.[217] These arrangements are intended to encourage investment in a way that protects the basic interests of both the capital-exporting and capital-importing states. Indeed, the British government has stated that it is its policy to conclude as many bilateral investment promotion and protection agreements as possible in order to stimulate investment flows. It has also been

---

[214] *Ibid.*, p.246; 82 *AJIL*, 1986, p.360.

[215] See also Judge Lagergren's separate opinion in *INA Corporation* v. *The Islamic Republic of Iran*, 8 *Iran-US CTR*, p.385; 75 *ILR*, p.609.

[216] But see e.g. *AIG* v. *The Islamic Republic of Iran*, 4 *Iran-US CTR*, pp.96, 109-10, where in a case of lawful expropriation lost profits were awarded. See also Brownlie, *op. cit.*, pp.537-39.

[217] See e.g. Denza and Brooks, "Investment Protection Treaties: United Kingdom Experience", 36 *ICLQ*, 1987, p.908; Akinsanya, "International Protection of Direct Foreign Investments in the Third World", *ibid.*, p.58; Mann, "British Treaties for the Promotion and Protection of Investments", 52 *BYIL*, 1981, p.241; Vagts, "Foreign Investment Risk Reconsidered: The View From the 1980s", 2 *ICSID Review – Foreign Investment Law Journal*, 1987, p.1; Gann "The US Bilateral Investment Treaties Program", 21 *Stanford Journal of International Law*, 1986, p.373 and Pogany, "The Regulation of Foreign Investment in Hungary", 4 *ICSID Review – Foreign Investment Law Journal*, 1989, p.39.

noted that they are designed to set standards applicable in international law.[218] The provisions of such agreements indeed constitute valuable state practice,[219] but great care has to be taken in inferring the existence of a rule of customary international law from a range of bilateral treaties.[220]

Bearing this important proviso in mind, it is interesting to note some of the features of such treaties. First, the concept of an investment is invariably broadly defined. In article 1(a) of the important UK-USSR bilateral investment treaty 1989,[221] for example, it is provided that:

> the term "investment" means every kind of asset and in particular, though not exclusively, includes:
>
> (i) movable and immovable property and any other related property rights such as mortgages;
>
> (ii) shares in, and stocks, bonds and debentures of, and any other form of participation in, a company or business enterprise;
>
> (iii) claims to money, and claims to performance under contract having a financial value;
>
> (iv) intellectual property rights, technical processes, know-how and any other benefit or advantage attached to a business;
>
> (v) rights conferred by law or under contract to undertake any commercial activity, including the search for, or the cultivation, extraction or exploitation of natural resources.[222]

Secondly, both parties undertake to encourage and create favourable conditions for investment, to accord such investments "fair and equitable treatment" and to refrain from impairing by unreasonable or discriminatory measures the management, maintenance, use, enjoyment or disposal of investments in its territory.[223] Thirdly, investments by the contracting parties are not to be treated less

---

[218] See the text of the Foreign Office statement in UKMIL, 58 *BYIL*, 1987, p.620.

[219] Some 300 such treaties now exist world-wide, see Denza and Brooks, *op. cit.*, p.913. The UK had signed 31 bilateral investment promotion and protection treaties by the end of 1987, see UKMIL, 58 *BYIL*, 1987, p.621.

[220] But cf. Dolzer, who argues that such agreements constitute state practice supporting the traditional view of compensation for expropriation, "New Foundations of the Law of Expropriation of Alien Property", 75 *AJIL*, 1981, pp.553, 565-66.

[221] Text reproduced in 29 *ILM*, 1989, p.366.

[222] See also, for example, the similar provisions in the UK-Philippines Investment Agreement 1981, and the UK-Hungary Investment Agreement 1987.

[223] See e.g. article 2 of the UK-USSR agreement.

favourably than those of other states.[224] As far as expropriation is concerned, article 5 of the UK-USSR agreement, by way of example, provides that investments of the contracting parties are not to be expropriated:

> except for a purpose which is in the public interest and is not discriminatory and against the payment, without delay, of prompt and effective compensation. Such compensation shall amount to the real value of the investment expropriated immediately before the expropriation or before the impending expropriation became public knowledge, whichever is the earlier, shall be made within two months of the date of expropriation, after which interest at a normal commercial rate shall accrue until the date of payment and shall be effectively realisable and be freely transferable. The investor affected shall have a right under the law of the contracting state making the expropriation, to prompt review, by a judicial or other independent authority of that party, of his or its case and of the valuation of his or its investment in accordance with the principles set out in this paragraph.

In other words, the traditional principles dealing with the conditions of a lawful expropriation and the provision for compensation are reaffirmed, together with an acceptance of the jurisdiction of the expropriating state over the issues of the legality of the expropriation and the valuation of the property expropriated.[225]

Many disputes over expropriation of foreign property have in fact been resolved directly by the states concerned on the basis of lump-sum settlements, usually after protracted negotiations and invariably at valuation below the current value of the assets concerned.[226] For example, the UK-USSR Agreement on the Settlement of Mutual Financial and Property Claims 1986[227] dealt with UK government claims of the order of £500 million in respect of Russian war debt and private claims of British nationals amounting to some £400

---

[224] See e.g. article 3 of the UK-USSR agreement.

[225] Note that provisions for compensation for expropriation may also be contained in Treaties of Friendship, Commerce and Navigation as part of a framework arrangement dealing with foreign trade and investment, see e.g. article IV(3) of the Convention of Establishment 1959 between the US and France, 11 UST 2398.

[226] See e.g. Lillich and Weston, *International Claims: Their Settlement by Lump-Sum Agreements*, 1975 and "Lump-Sum Agreements: Their Continuing Contribution to the Law of International Claims", 82 *AJIL*, 1988, p.69.

[227] Cm. 30. Note that this Agreement dealt with claims arising before 1939.

million.[228] In the event, a sum in the region of £45 million was made available to satisfy these claims.[229] The Agreement also provided that money held in diplomatic bank accounts in the UK belonging to the pre-revolutionary Russian embassy, amounting to some £2.65 million, was released to the Soviet authorities. As is usual in such agreements, each government was solely responsible for settling the claims of its nationals.[230] This was accomplished in the UK through the medium of the Foreign Compensation Commission, which acts to distribute settlement sums "as may seem just and equitable to them having regard to all the circumstances". A distinction was made as between bond and property claims and principles enunciated with regard to exchange rates at the relevant time.[231]

The question arises thus as to whether such agreements constitute state practice in the context of international customary rules concerning the level of compensation required upon an expropriation of foreign property. A Chamber of the Iran-US Claims Tribunal in *SEDCO* v. *National Iranian Oil Co.*[232] noted that deriving general principles of law from the conduct of states in lump-sum or negotiated settlements in other expropriation cases was difficult because of the "questionable evidentiary value . . . of much of the practice available". This was because such settlements were often motivated primarily by non-juridical considerations. The Chamber also held that bilateral investment treaties were also unreliable evidence of international customary standards of compensation. Views differ as to the value to be attributed to such practice,[233] but caution is required before accepting bilateral investment treaties and lump-sum agreements as evidence of customary law. This is particularly so with regard to the latter since they deal with specific situations rather than laying down a

---

[228] As against these claims, the USSR had made extensive claims in the region of £2 billion in respect of alleged losses caused by British intervention in the USSR between 1918 and 1921, see UKMIL, 57 *BYIL*, 1986, p.606.

[229] The British government waived its entitlement to a share in the settlement in respect of its own claims, *ibid.*, p.608.

[230] See also the UK-China Agreement on the Settlement of Property Claims 1987, see UKMIL, 58 *BYIL*, 1987, p.626.

[231] See with respect to the UK-USSR Agreement, the Foreign Compensation (USSR) (Registration and Determination of Claims) Order 1986, SI 1986/2222 and the Foreign Compensation (USSR) (Distribution) Order 1987.

[232] 10 *Iran-US CTR*, pp.180, 185; 80 *AJIL*, 1986, p.969.

[233] See e.g. Bowett, *op. cit.*, pp.65-66.

framework for future activity.[234] Nevertheless, it would be equally unwise to disregard them entirely. As with all examples of state practice and behaviour careful attention must be paid to all the relevant circumstances both of the practice maintained and the principle under consideration.

Non-Discrimination

It has been argued that non-discrimination is a requirement for a valid and lawful expropriation.[235] Although it is not mentioned in the 1962 resolution, the arbitrator in the *Liamco*[236] case strongly argued that a discriminatory nationalisation would be unlawful.[237] Nevertheless, in that case, it was held that Libya's action against certain oil companies was aimed at preserving its ownership of the oil and was non-discriminatory. Indeed, the arbitrator noted that the political motive itself was not the predominant motive for nationalisation and would not *per se* constitute sufficient proof of a purely discriminatory measure.[238] While the discrimination factor would certainly be a relevant factor to be considered, it would in practice often be extremely difficult to prove in concrete cases.

The Multilateral Investment Guarantee Agency [239]

One approach to the question of foreign investment and the balancing of the interests of the states concerned is provided by the Convention Establishing the Multilateral Investment Guarantee Agency 1985, which came into force in 1988.[240] Article 2 provides that the purpose of the Agency, which is an affiliate of the World Bank, is to encourage the flow of investment for productive purposes among member-countries and, in particular, to developing countries.

---

[234] Note the view of the International Court in the *Barcelona Traction* case that such settlements were *sui generis* and provided no guide as to general international practice, ICJ Reports, 1969, pp.4, 40.

[235] See e.g. White, *op. cit.*, p.119 *et seq.*

[236] 20 *ILM*, 1981, p.1; 62 *ILR*, p.141.

[237] *Ibid.*, pp.58-59; 62 *ILR*, p.194.

[238] *Ibid.*, p.60.

[239] See e.g. Chatterjee, "The Convention Establishing the Multilateral Investment Guarantee Agency", 36 *ICLQ*, 1987, p.76. The Convention came into force on 12 April 1988, see 28 *ILM*, 1989, p.1233.

[240] See e.g. the UK Multilateral Investment Guarantee Agency Act 1988.

This is to be achieved in essence by the provision of insurance cover "against non-commercial risks", such as restrictions on the transfer of currency, measures of expropriation, breaches of government contracts and losses resulting from war or civil disturbances.[241] It is also intended that the Agency would positively encourage investment by means of research and the dissemination of information on investment opportunities. It may very well be that this initiative could in the long term reduce the sensitive nature of the expropriation mechanism.[242]

[241] Article 11.
[242] Note that issues relating to the peaceful settlement of such disputes in general will be discussed in Chapter 17.

CHAPTER FOURTEEN

International Environmental Law[1]

An extensive range of environmental problems is now the subject of international concern. These include atmospheric pollution, marine pollution, global warming and ozone depletion, the dangers of nuclear and other extra-hazardous substances and threatened wildlife species.[2] Such problems have an international dimension in two obvious respects. First, pollution generated from within a particular state often has a serious impact upon other countries. The prime example would be acid rain, whereby chemicals emitted from factories rise in the atmosphere and react with water and sunlight to form acids. These are carried in the wind and fall eventually to earth in the rain, often thousands of miles away from the initial polluting event.

Secondly, it is now apparent that environmental problems cannot be resolved by states acting individually. Accordingly, co-operation between the polluting and the polluted state is necessitated. However, the issue becomes more complicated in those cases where it is quite impossible to determine from which country a particular form of environmental pollution has emanated. This would be the case, for example, with ozone depletion. In other words, the international nature of pollution, both with regard to its creation and the damage caused, is now accepted as requiring an international response.

---

[1] See generally Kiss, *Le Droit International de l'Environnement*, 1989 and "The International Protection of the Environment" in *The Structure and Process of International Law* (eds. Macdonald and Johnston), 1983, p.1069, and *Survey of Current Developments in International Environmental Law*, 1976; Caldwell, *International Environmental Policy*, 2nd ed., 1990; *International Environmental Diplomacy* (ed. Carroll), 1988; Barros and Johnston, *The International Law of Pollution*, 1974; *International Environmental Law* (eds. Teclaff and Utton), 1974; *Trends in Environmental Policy and Law* (ed. Bothe), 1980; Hague Academy of International Law Colloque 1973, *The Protection of the Environment and International Law* (ed. Kiss); *ibid.,* Colloque 1984, *The Future of the International Law of the Environment* (ed. Dupuy); Schneider, *World Public Order of the Environment*, 1979; Springer, *The International Law of Pollution: Protecting the Global Environment in a World of Sovereign States*, 1983; Brownlie, "International Customary Rules of Environmental Protection", *International Relations*, 1973, p.240; Brown Weiss, *In Fairness to Future Generations: International Law, Common Patrimony and Intergenerational Equity*, 1989; *Chernobyl: Law and Communication* (ed. Sands), 1988 and Boyle, "Nuclear Energy and International Law: An Environmental Perspective", 60 *BYIL*, 1989, p.257. See also *Selected Multilateral Treaties in the Field of the Environment*, 2 vols., 1991.

[2] See e.g. Carwardine, *The WWF Environment Handbook*, 1990. See also Lyster, *International Wildlife Law*, 1985.

The initial conceptual problem posed for international law lies in the state-oriented nature of the discipline. Traditionally, a state would only be responsible in the international legal sense for damage caused where it could be clearly demonstrated that this resulted from its own unlawful activity.[3] This has proved to be an inadequate framework for dealing with environmental issues for a variety of reasons, ranging from difficulties of proof to liability for lawful activities and the particular question of responsibility of non-state offenders. Accordingly, the international community has slowly been moving away from the classic state responsibility approach to damage caused towards a regime of international co-operation. The way in which this has occurred forms one of the major themes of this chapter.

It has also been argued that there now exists an international human right to a clean environment. Article 24 of the African Charter of Human and Peoples' Rights 1981 provides that "all people shall have the right to a general satisfactory environment favourable to their development". However, this provision is unclear in several respects, not least as to what constitutes a general satisfactory environment and how this relates to the need for development. It is also to be pointed out that none of the other human rights treaties contains such a provision.

The question of the relationship between the protection of the environment and the need for economic development is another factor underpinning the evolution of environmental law. States that are currently attempting to industrialise face the problem that to do so in an environmentally safe way is very expensive and the resources that can be devoted to this are extremely limited. The Stockholm Declaration of the United Nations Conference on the Human Environment 1972, a seminal instrument, emphasised in Principle 8 that "economic and social development is essential for ensuring a favourable living and working environment for man and for creating conditions on earth that are necessary for the improvement of the quality of life", while the sovereign right of states to exploit their own resources was also stressed.[4] The correct balance between development and

---

[3] See further *supra*, Chapter 13.
[4] Principle 21.

environmental protection is now one of the main challenges facing the international community.[5]

THE DEFINITION OF POLLUTION

The question of how one defines the term "pollution" has been addressed in several international instruments. In a recommendation adopted in 1974 by the Organisation for Economic Co-operation and Development,[6] pollution is broadly defined as "the introduction by man, directly or indirectly, of substances or energy into the environment resulting in deleterious effects of such a nature as to endanger human health, harm living resources and ecosystems, and impair or interfere with amenities and other legitimate uses of the environment".[7] This definition was substantially reproduced in the Geneva Convention on Long-Range Transboundary Air Pollution 1979[8] and in the Montreal Rules of International Law Applicable to Transfrontier Pollution adopted by the International Law Association in 1982.[9] Several points ought to be noted at this stage. First, actual damage must have been caused. Pollution likely to result as a consequence of certain activities is not included. Secondly, the harm caused must be of a certain level of intensity and thirdly, the question of interference with legitimate uses of the environment requires further investigation.

STATE RESPONSIBILITY AND THE ENVIRONMENT

The Basic Duty of States

Customary international law imposes several important fundamental obligations upon states in this area. The view that

---

[5] See e.g. D'Amato, "Do We Owe a Duty to Future Generations to Preserve the Global Environment?", 84 *AJIL*, 1990, p.190.

[6] OECD Doc.C(74)224, cited in *Chernobyl: Law and Communication, op. cit.*, p.150.

[7] *Ibid.*, Title A.

[8] The major difference being the substitution of "air" for "environment" in view of the focus of the Convention.

[9] Note that the term "air" was replaced by "environment". See also article 1 of the Paris Convention for the Prevention of Marine Pollution from Land-Based Sources 1974 and article 2 of the Barcelona Convention for the Protection of the Mediterranean Sea against Pollution 1976. The Institut de Droit International, in a draft resolution accompanying its final report

international law supports an approach predicated upon absolute territorial sovereignty, so that a state could do as it liked irrespective of the consequences upon other states, has long been discredited. The basic duty upon states is not to so act as to injure the rights of other states.[10] This duty has evolved partly out of the regime concerned with international waterways. In the *International Commission on the River Oder* case,[11] for example, the Permanent Court of International Justice noted that "this community of interest in a navigable river becomes the basis of a common legal right, the essential features of which are the perfect equality of all riparian states in the use of the whole course of the river and the exclusion of any preferential privileges of any riparian state in relation to others".[12] But the principle is of far wider application. It was noted in the *Island of Palmas* case[13] that the concept of territorial sovereignty incorporated an obligation to protect within the territory the rights of other states.

In the *Trail Smelter* arbitration,[14] the Tribunal was concerned with a dispute between Canada and the United States over sulphur dioxide pollution from a Canadian smelter, built in a valley shared by British Columbia and the state of Washington, which damaged trees and crops on the American side of the border. The Tribunal noted that "under principles of international law, as well as the law of the United States, no state has the right to use or permit the use of territory in such a manner as to cause injury by fumes in or to the territory of another or the properties

on Air Pollution Across National Frontiers, defines pollution as "any physical, chemical or biological alteration in the composition or quality of the atmosphere which results directly or indirectly from human action or omission and produces injurious or deleterious effects across national frontiers", 62 I *Annuaire de l'Institut de Droit International,* 1987, p.266.

[10] See the doctrine expressed by Judson Harmon, Attorney-General of the United States in 1895, 21 *Op. Att'y. Gen.* 274, 283 (1895), cited in *International Environmental Law, op. cit.,* pp.155-56.

[11] PCIJ, Series A, No.23 (1929); 5 *ILR,* p.83.

[12] *Ibid.,* p.27; 5 *ILR,* p.84.

[13] 2 *RIAA,* pp.829, 839.

[14] See 33 *AJIL,* 1939, p.182 and 35 *AJIL,* 1941, p.684; 9 *ILR,* p.315. See also Read, "The Trail Smelter Arbitration", 1 *Canadian Yearbook of International Law,* 1963, p.213; Kirgis, "Technological Challenge of the Shared Environment: US Practice", 66 *AJIL,* 1974, p.291 and Goldie, "A General View of International Environmental Law — A Survey of Capabilities, Trends and Limits" in *Hague Colloque 1973, op. cit.,* pp.26, 66-69.

of persons therein, when the case is of serious consequences and the injury established".[15]

The International Court reinforced this approach, by emphasising in the *Corfu Channel* case[16] that it was the obligation of every state "not to allow knowingly its territory to be used for acts contrary to the rights of other states".[17]

This judicial approach has now been widely reaffirmed in international instruments. Article 192 of the Law of the Sea Convention 1982 (which is not yet in force) provides that "states have the obligation to protect and preserve the marine environment", while article 194 notes that "states shall take all measures necessary to ensure that activities under their jurisdiction and control are so conducted as not to cause damage by pollution to other states and their environment".[18] The shift of focus from the state alone to a wider perspective including the high seas, deep sea-bed and outer space is a noticeable development.[19]

It is, however, Principle 21 of the Stockholm Declaration of 1972 that is of especial significance. It stipulates that in addition to the sovereign right to exploit their own resources pursuant to their own environmental policies, states have "the responsibility to ensure that activities within their jurisdiction or control do not cause damage to the environment of other states or of areas beyond the limits of national jurisdiction". Although a relatively modest formulation, it has been seen as an important turning-point in the development of international environmental law.[20] Several issues of importance are raised in the formulation contained in Principle 21 and to those we now turn.

---

[15] 35 *AJIL*, 1941, p.716; 9 *ILR*, p.317.

[16] ICJ Reports, 1949, pp.4, 22; 16 *ILR*, p.155, 158.

[17] See also the dissenting opinion of Judge de Castro in the *Nuclear Tests* case, ICJ Reports, 1974, pp.253, 388; 57 *ILR*, pp.350, 533 and the *Lac Lanoux* case, 24 *ILR*, p.101.

[18] See also Principle 3 of the UN Environment Programme Principles of Conduct in the Field of the Environment concerning Resources Shared by Two or More States 1978 and the Charter of Economic Rights and Duties of States adopted in General Assembly resolution 3281 (XXIX) and General Assembly resolution 34/186 (1979).

[19] See Boyle, "Nuclear Energy", *op. cit.*, p.271.

[20] See e.g. Kiss, *Survey, op. cit.*, p.25 and "The International Protection of the Environment", *op. cit.*, p.1075. See also the preamble to the Convention on Long-Range Transboundary Air Pollution 1979.

The Appropriate Standard

It is sometimes argued that the appropriate standard for the conduct of states in this field is that of strict liability. In other words, states are under an absolute obligation to prevent pollution and are thus liable for its effects irrespective of fault.[21] While the advantage of this is the increased responsibility placed upon the state, it is doubtful whether international law has in fact accepted such a general principle.[22] The leading cases are inconclusive. In the *Trail Smelter* case[23] Canada's responsibility was accepted from the start, the case focusing upon the compensation due and the terms of the future operation of the smelter,[24] while the strict theory was not apparently accepted in the *Corfu Channel* case.[25] In the *Nuclear Tests* case[26] the Court did not discuss the substance of the claims concerning nuclear testing in view of France's decision to end its programme.

It is also worth noting the *Gut Dam* arbitration between the US and Canada.[27] This concerned the construction of a dam by the Canadian authorities, with US approval, straddling the territory of the two states, in order to facilitate navigation in the St. Lawrence River, prior to the existence of the Seaway. The dam affected the flow of water in the river basin and caused an increase in the level of water in the river and in Lake Ontario. This, together with the incidence of severe storms, resulted in heavy flooding on the shores of the river and lake and the US government claimed damages. The tribunal awarded a lump sum payment to the US, without considering whether Canada had been in any way negligent or at fault with regard to the construction of the dam. However, one must be cautious in regarding this case as an example of a strict liability approach, since the US gave its approval to the construction

[21] See e.g. Goldie, "General View", *op. cit.*, pp.73-85 and Schneider, *op. cit.*, Chapter 6. See also Handl, "State Liability for Accidental Transnational Environmental Damage by Private Persons", 74 *AJIL*, 1980, p.525.

[22] See e.g. Boyle, "Nuclear Energy", *op. cit.*, pp.289-97 and Handl, *op. cit.*, pp.535-53.

[23] 33 *AJIL*, 1939, p.182 and 35 *AJIL*, 1941, p.681; 9 *ILR*, p.315.

[24] See Boyle, "Nuclear Energy", *op. cit.*, p.292 and Handl, "Balancing of Interests and International Liability for the Pollution of International Watercourses: Customary Principles of Law Revisited", 13 *Canadian Yearbook of International Law*, 1975, pp.156, 167-68.

[25] ICJ Reports, 1949, pp.4, 22-23.

[26] ICJ Reports, 1974, p.253; 57 *ILR*, p.350.

[27] 8 *ILM*, 1969, p.118.

of the dam on the condition that US citizens be indemnified for any damage or detriment incurred as a result of the construction or operation of the dam in question.[28]

Treaty practice is variable. The Convention on International Liability for Damage Caused by Space Objects 1972 provides for absolute liability for damage caused by space objects on the surface of the earth or to aircraft in flight (article II), but for fault liability for damage caused elsewhere or to persons or property on board a space object (article III). Most treaties, however, take the form of requiring the exercise of diligent control of sources of harm.[29]

The test of due diligence is in fact the standard that is accepted generally as the most appropriate one.[30] Article 194 of the Convention on the Law of the Sea 1982, for example, provides that states are to take "all measures . . . that are necessary to prevent, reduce and control pollution of the marine environment from any source, using for this purpose the best practicable means at their disposal and in accordance with their capabilities". Accordingly, states in general are not automatically liable for damage caused irrespective of all other factors. However, it is rather less clear what is actually meant by due diligence. In specific cases, such as the Convention on the Law of the Sea 1982, for example, particular measures are specified and references made to other relevant treaties. In other cases, the issue remains rather more ambiguous.[31] The test of due diligence undoubtedly imports an element of flexibility into the equation and must be tested in the light of the circumstances of the case in question. Other than that, it is only possible to provide generalities. States will be required to take all necessary steps to prevent substantial pollution and to demonstrate the kind of behaviour expected of "good government".[32] It is also important to note that elements of remoteness and foreseeability are part of

[28] See Schneider, *op. cit.*, p.165. Cf. Handl, "State Liability for Accidental Transnational Environmental Damage by Private Persons", 74 *AJIL*, 1980, pp.525, 538 *et seq.*

[29] See e.g. article 2, the Convention on Long-Range Transboundary Air Pollution 1979; article 2, the Vienna Convention for the Protection of the Ozone Layer 1985 and articles 139, 194 and 235, the Convention on the Law of the Sea 1982.

[30] See e.g. Handl, "State Liability", *op. cit.* at pp.539-40 and Boyle, "Nuclear Energy", *op. cit.*, p.272.

[31] See e.g. the Long-Range Transboundary Air Pollution Convention 1979.

[32] I.e. the standard of conduct expected from a government mindful of its international obligations, see Dupuy, "International Liability for Transfrontier Pollution", in *Trends in Environmental Policy and Law, op. cit.*, pp.363, 369.

the framework of the liability of states. The damage that occurs must have been caused by the pollution under consideration. The tribunal in the *Trail Smelter* case[33] emphasised the need to establish the injury "by clear and convincing evidence".

Damage Caused

The first issue is whether indeed any damage must actually have been caused before international responsibility becomes relevant. Can there be liability for risk of damage? It appears that at this stage international law in general does not recognise such a liability,[34] certainly outside of the category of ultra-hazardous activities.[35] This is for reasons both of state reluctance in general and with regard to practical difficulties in particular. It would be difficult, although not impossible, both to assess the risk involved and to determine the compensation that might be due.

However, it should be noted that article 1(4) of the Convention on the Law of the Sea 1982 defines pollution of the marine environment as "the introduction by man, directly or indirectly, of substances or energy into the marine environment . . . which results or is likely to result in . . . deleterious effects". In other words, actual damage is not necessary in this context. It is indeed possible that customary international law may develop in this direction, but it is too early to conclude that this has already occurred. Most general definitions of pollution rely upon damage or harm having been caused before liability is engaged.[36]

The next issue is to determine whether, before international law is infringed, a certain threshold of damage must have been caused. In the *Trail Smelter* case[37] the tribunal focused on the need to show that the matter was of "serious consequence", while article 1 of the Convention on Long-Range Transboundary Air Pollution 1979 provides that the pollution concerned must result "in deleterious effects of such a nature as to endanger human health, harm living resources and ecosystems and material property and

[33] 35 *AJIL*, 1941, p.716; 9 *ILR*, p.317.
[34] See e.g. Kiss, "International Protection", *op. cit.*, p.1076.
[35] See *infra* p.546.
[36] See also the commentary to the Montreal Rules adopted by the ILA in 1982, Report of the Sixtieth Conference, p.159.
[37] 35 *AJIL*, 1941, p.716; 9 *ILR*, p.317.

impair or interfere with amenities and other legitimate uses of the environment".[38] Article 3 of the ILA Montreal Rules 1982 stipulates that states are under an obligation to prevent, abate and control transfrontier pollution to such an extent that no substantial injury is caused in the territory of another state.[39] Such formulations do present definitional problems and the qualification as to the threshold of injury required is by no means present in all relevant instruments.[40] The issue of relativity and the importance of the circumstances of the particular case remain significant factors, but less support can be detected at this stage for linkage to a concept of reasonable and equitable use of its territory by a state occasioning liability for use beyond this.[41]

As far as the range of interests injured by pollution is concerned, the *Trail Smelter* case[42] focused upon loss of property. Later definitions of pollution in international instruments have broadened the range to include harm to living resources or ecosystems, interference with amenities and other legitimate uses of the environment or the sea. Article 1(4) of the Convention on the Law of the Sea 1982, for example, includes impairment of quality for use of sea water and reduction of amenities, while article 1(2) of the Vienna Convention on the Ozone Layer 1985 defines adverse effects upon the ozone layer as changes in the physical environment including climatic changes "which have significant deleterious effects on human health or on the composition, resilience and productivity of natural and managed ecosystems or on materials useful to mankind".[43] The type of harm that is relevant clearly now extends beyond

[38] Note also that General Assembly resolution 2995 (XXVII) refers to "significant harmful results".

[39] Note the formulation by Oppenheim, *International Law*, vol.I, 8th ed., 1955, p.291, that the interference complained of must be "unduly injurious to the inhabitants of the neighbouring state".

[40] See e.g. Principle 21 of the Stockholm Declaration and article 194 of the Convention on the Law of the Sea 1982.

[41] See the views of, e.g., Quentin-Baxter, *Yearbook of the ILC*, 1981, vol.II, Part 1, pp.112-19 and McCaffrey, *ibid.*, 1986, vol.II, Part 1, pp.133-34. See also Boyle, "Nuclear Energy", *op. cit.*, p.275 and "Chernobyl and the Development of International Environmental Law" in Butler (ed.), *Perestroika and International Law*, 1990, pp.203, 206.

[42] 35 *AJIL*, 1941, p.684; 9 *ILR*, p.315. See also Rubin, "Pollution by Analogy: The Trail Smelter Arbitration", 50 *Oregon Law Review*, 1971, p.259.

[43] See also the OECD Recommendation of Equal Right of Access in Relation to Transfrontier Pollution 1977 and article 1(15) of the Convention on the Regulation of Antarctic Mineral Resource Activities 1988.

damage to property, but problems do remain with regard to general environmental injury that cannot be defined in material form.[44]

Liability for Damage Caused by Private Persons

A particular problem relates to the situation where the environmental injury is caused not by the state itself but by a private party.[45] A state is, of course, responsible for unlawful acts of its officials causing injury to nationals of foreign states[46] and retains a general territorial competence under international law. In general, states must ensure that their international obligations are respected on their territory. Many treaties require states parties to legislate with regard to particular issues, in order to ensure the implementation of specific obligations. Where an international agreement requires, for example, that certain limits be placed upon emissions of a particular substance, the state would be responsible for any activity that exceeded the limit, even if it were carried out by a private party, since the state had undertaken a binding commitment.[47] Similarly where the state has undertaken to impose a prior authorisation procedure upon a particular activity, a failure so to act which resulted in pollution violating international law would occasion the responsibility of the state.

In some cases, an international agreement might specifically provide for the liability of the state for the acts of non-state entities. Article VI of the Outer Space Treaty 1967, for example, stipulates that states parties bear international responsibility for "national activities in outer space . . . whether such activities are carried out by governmental agencies or by non-governmental agencies".[48]

---

[44] Note that the Canadian claim for clean-up costs consequential upon the crash of a Soviet nuclear-powered satellite was settled, see 18 *ILM*, 1979, p.902.

[45] See e.g. Handl, "State Liability", *op. cit.* and Doeker and Gehring, "Private or International Liability for Transnational Environmental Damage — The Precedent of Conventional Liability Regimes", 2 *Journal of Environmental Law*, 1990, p.1.

[46] *Supra*, Chapter 13.

[47] See *infra*, p.557.

[48] See also article 1 of the Convention on International Liability for Damage Caused by Space Objects 1972 and article XIV of the Moon Treaty 1979. See further *infra* p.551 with regard to civil liability schemes.

The Duty to Co-operate

A developing theme of international environmental law, founded upon general principles, relates to the requirement for states to co-operate in dealing with transboundary pollution issues. Principle 24 of the Stockholm Declaration 1972 noted that "international matters concerning the protection and improvement of the environment should be handled in a co-operative spirit".

The *Corfu Channel* case[49] established the principle that states are not knowingly to allow their territory to be used for acts contrary to the rights of other states and from this can be deduced a duty to inform other states of known environmental hazards. A large number of international agreements reflect this proposition. Article 198 of the Convention on the Law of the Sea 1982, for example, provides that "when a state becomes aware of cases in which the marine environment is in imminent danger of being damaged or had been damaged by pollution, it shall immediately notify other states it deems likely to be affected by such damage, as well as the competent international authorities".[50] Article 13 of the Basle Convention on the Control of Transboundary Movement of Hazardous Wastes 1989 provides that states parties shall, whenever it comes to their knowledge, ensure that in the case of an accident occurring during the transboundary movement of hazardous wastes which are likely to present risks to human health and the environment in other states, those states are immediately informed.[51]

It is also to be noted that in 1974 the OECD (the Organisation for Economic Co-operation and Development) adopted a Recommendation that prior to the initiation of works or undertakings that might create a risk of significant transfrontier pollution, early information should be provided to states that are or may be affected.[52] In 1988, the OECD adopted a Council Decision in which it is

---

[49] ICJ Reports, 1949, pp.4, 22; 16 *ILR*, pp.155, 158.

[50] See also article 211(7).

[51] See also e.g. article 8 of the International Convention for the Prevention of Pollution from Ships 1973; Annex 6 of the Helsinki Convention on the Protection of the Marine Environment of the Baltic Sea 1974 and article 9 of the Barcelona Convention for the Protection of the Mediterranean Sea, Protocol of Co-operation in Case of Emergency 1976.

[52] Title E, para.6. See also the OECD Recommendation for the Implementation of a Regime of Equal Right of Access and Non-Discrimination in Relation to Transfrontier Pollution 1977, Title C, para.8.

provided that states must provide information for the prevention of and the response to accidents at hazardous installations and transmit to exposed countries the results of their studies on proposed installations. A duty to exchange emergency plans is stipulated, as well as a duty to transmit immediate warning to exposed countries where an accident is an imminent threat.[53]

One may also point to a requirement of prior consultation. Article 5 of the ILA Montreal Rules provides that states planning to carry out activities which might entail a significant risk of transfrontier pollution shall give early notice to states likely to be affected. This provision builds upon, for example, the *Lac Lanoux* arbitration between France and Spain,[54] which concerned the proposed diversion of a shared watercourse. The arbitral tribunal noted in particular the obligation to negotiate in such circumstances.[55] Some treaties establish a duty of prior notification, one early example being the Nordic Convention on the Protection of the Environment 1974. Article 5 of the Long-Range Transboundary Air Pollution Convention 1979 provides that consultations shall be held, upon request, at an early stage between the state within whose jurisdiction the activity is to be conducted and states which are actually affected by or exposed to a significant risk of long-range transboundary air pollution.[56] The increasing range of state practice[57] has led the International Law Association to conclude that "a rule of international customary law has emerged that in principle a state is obliged to render information on new or increasing pollution to a potential victim state".[58]

The evolution of a duty to inform states that might be affected by the creation of a source of new or increasing pollution has been

---

[53] C(88)84.

[54] 24 *ILR*, p.101.

[55] *Ibid.*, p.119. See also the *North Sea Continental Shelf* cases, ICJ Reports, 1969, pp.3, 46-47; 41 *ILR*, pp.29, 76.

[56] Note also that article 8(b) calls for the exchange of information *inter alia* on major changes in national policies and in general industrial development and on their potential impact, which would be likely to cause significant changes in long-range transboundary air pollution.

[57] See ILA, Report of the Sixtieth Conference, 1982, pp.172-73.

[58] *Ibid.*, p.173. See also Institut de Droit International, Resolution on Transboundary Air Pollution 1987, but cf. Sands, *op. cit.*, p.35. Note also e.g. the UNEP Recommendation concerning the Environment Related to Offshore Drilling and Mining within the Limits of National Jurisdiction 1981 and the Canada-Denmark Agreement for Co-operation Relating to the Marine Environment 1983.

accompanied by consideration of an obligation to make environmental impact assessments.[59] This requirement is included in several treaties.[60] Article 204 of the Convention on the Law of the Sea 1982 provides that states should "observe, measure, evaluate and analyse by recognised scientific methods, the risks or effects of pollution on the marine environment" and in particular "shall keep under surveillance the effects of any activities which they permit or in which they engage in order to determine whether these activities are likely to pollute the marine environment". Reports are to be published, while under article 206, when states have reasonable grounds for believing that planned activities under their jurisdiction or control may cause substantial pollution of or significant and harmful changes to the marine environment "they shall, as far as practicable, assess the potential effects of such activities on the marine environment and shall communicate reports of such assessments".[61]

INTERNATIONAL LIABILITY [62]

The International Law Commission has been considering since 1978 the topic of "International Liability for the Injurious Consequences of Acts Not Prohibited by International Law"[63] and the main focus of the work of the Commission has been on environmental harm.[64] International liability differs from state responsibility in that the latter is dependent upon a prior breach of international law,[65] while the former constitutes an attempt to

[59] See the UNEP Principles of Environmental Impact Assessment 1987.

[60] See e.g. the Kuwait Regional Convention for Co-operation on the Protection of the Marine Environment from Pollution 1978, article XI.

[61] A similar process is underway with regard to the siting of nuclear power installations, see e.g. the agreements between Spain and Portugal 1980; Netherlands and the Federal Republic of Germany 1977; Belgium and France 1966 and Switzerland and the Federal Republic of Germany 1982. See also Boyle, "Chernobyl", op. cit. at p.212. See infra p.547 with regard to the nuclear treaties.

[62] See e.g. Boyle, "State Responsibility and International Liability for Injurious Consequences of Acts not Prohibited by International Law: A Necessary Distinction?", 39 ICLQ, 1990, p.1; Akehurst, "International Liability for Injurious Consequences Arising out of Acts not Prohibited by International Law", 16 Netherlands Yearbook of International Law, 1985, p.3 and Magraw, "Transboundary Harm: The ILC Study", 80 AJIL, 1986, p.305.

[63] See Yearbook of the ILC, 1978, vol.II, Part 2, p.149.

[64] See e.g. Quentin-Baxter's preliminary report, Yearbook of the ILC, 1980, vol.II, Part 1, p.24.

[65] Supra, Chapter 13.

develop a branch of law in which a state may be liable internationally with regard to the harmful consequences of an activity which is in itself not contrary to international law.

It is a controversial approach. Its theoretical basis and separation from state responsibility have been questioned[66] and the capacity of this topic to subsume the law relating to environmental issues is open to criticism. In considering this aspect of international environmental law, it must also be remembered that states bear responsibility for activities that constitute violations of the law.

Article 1 of the 1989 Draft provides that the articles are to apply when the physical consequences of a particular activity "cause, or create the risk of causing, transboundary injury". Members of the Commission have been divided as to whether the focus of the topic should be upon risk or upon harm,[67] but indications are that the broader approach inherent in the latter concept is more likely to be accepted.[68] Under the Draft, states are to co-operate in good faith in trying to prevent such activities from causing transboundary injury and in minimising the effects of any such injury,[69] while reparation is to be made for "appreciable injury"[70] caused by such activities. Such reparation is to be decided by negotiation by the states concerned, bearing in mind in particular that reparation should seek to "restore the balance of interests affected by the injury".[71]

This conception of reparation differs, of course, from that considered in the context of state responsibility,[72] where the aim is to seek to restore the situation to what it was prior to the act in question. In the case of international liability, the purpose is to limit the compensation by the use of a "balance of interests" criterion and not necessarily to end the harmful activity.[73] This approach would

[66] See e.g. Boyle, "State Responsibility", *op. cit.*, p.3 and Brownlie, *System of the Law of Nations: State Responsibility, Part I*, 1983, p.50.

[67] See e.g. McCaffrey, "The Fortieth Session of the International Law Commission", 83 *AJIL*, 1989, pp.153, 170.

[68] McCaffrey, "The Forty-First Session of the International Law Commission", 83 *AJIL*, 1989, pp.937, 944.

[69] Draft article 7.

[70] Defined in article 2 as "the risk which may be identified through a simple examination of the activity and the substances involved, in relation to the place, environment or way in which they are used, and includes both the low probability of very considerable (disastrous) transboundary injury and the high probability of major appreciable injury".

[71] Draft article 9.

[72] *Supra* p.496. See also Gray, *Judicial Remedies in International Law*, 1987, p.233.

[73] See e.g. *Yearbook of the ILC*, 1986, vol.II, Part 1, p.147.

appear to draw heavily upon notions of equitable sharing developed in the context of the use of international watercourses,[74] but whether it could operate successfully in this rather different context is controversial. It is unclear how it might in practice work, nor how it relates to the issue of identifying the point at which the harmful activity becomes wrongful. Indeed many questions need to be resolved before this topic can proceed to a successful conclusion and the Commission is in effect only at a relatively early stage in bringing together all the necessary strands.

AIR POLLUTION

Perhaps the earliest perceived form of pollution relates to the pollution of the air. The burning of fossil fuels releases into the atmosphere sulphur dioxide and nitrogen oxides which change into acids and are carried by natural elements and fall as rain or snow or solid particles. Such acids have the effect of killing living creatures in lakes and streams and of damaging soils and forests.[75] In 1979, on the initiative of the Scandinavian countries and under the auspices of the UN Economic Commission for Europe, the Geneva Convention on Long-Range Transboundary Air Pollution was signed.[76] The definition of pollution is reasonably broad,[77] while article 1(b) defines long-range transboundary air pollution as air pollution whose physical origin is situated wholly or in part within the area under the national jurisdiction of one state and which has

[74] See e.g. Handl, "The Principle of 'Equitable Use' as Applied to Internationally Shared Natural Resources", 14 *Revue Belge de Droit International*, 1978-9, p.40; Kearney, "International Watercourses" in Dupuy (ed.), *A Handbook of International Organisations*, 1988, p.509 and Garretson, Olmstead and Hayton, *The Law of International Drainage Basins*, 1968. Draft article 6 of the ILC consideration of the topic of the Law of the Non-navigational Uses of International Watercourses (1987) provides that watercourse states shall participate in the use, development and protection of an international watercourse system in an equitable and reasonable manner, see *Yearbook of the ILC*, 1987, vol.II, Part 2, pp.31-38. See also *ibid.*, 1984, vol.II, Part 1, pp.110-12 and Principle IV of the Helsinki Rules on the Uses of the Waters of International Rivers 1966, which states that "each basin state is entitled, within its territory, to a reasonable and equitable share in the beneficial uses of the waters of an international drainage basin".

[75] See *Keesing's Record of World Events*, p.36782 *et seq.* (1989).

[76] See e.g. Rosencranz, "The ECE Convention of 1979 on Long-Range Transboundary Air Pollution", 75 *AJIL*, 1981, p.975; Tollan, "The Convention on Long-Range Transboundary Air Pollution", 19 *Journal of World Trade Law*, 1985, p.615 and Kiss, "La Convention sur la Pollution Atmosphérique Transfrontière à Longue Distance", *Revue Juridique de l'Environnement*, 1981, p.30.

[77] *Supra*, p.532.

adverse effects in the area under the jurisdiction of another state at such a distance that it is not generally possible to distinguish the contribution of individual emission sources or groups of sources.

The obligations undertaken under the Convention, however, are modest. States "shall endeavour to limit and, as far as possible, gradually reduce and prevent air pollution, including long-range transboundary air pollution".[78] The question of state liability for damage resulting from such pollution is not addressed. The Convention provides that states are to develop policies and strategies by means of exchanges of information and consultation[79] and to exchange information to combat generally the discharge of air pollutants.[80] Consultations are to be held upon request at an early stage between contracting parties actually affected by or exposed to a significant risk of long-range transboundary air pollution and contracting parties within which and subject to whose jurisdiction a significant contribution to such pollution originates or could originate, in connection with activities carried on or contemplated therein.[81]

The parties also undertook to develop the existing "Co-operative programme for the monitoring and evaluation of the long-range transmission of air pollutants in Europe" (EMEP) and in 1984 a Protocol was adopted dealing with the long-term financing of the project.

Two further Protocols to the Convention have been adopted. In 1985, the Helsinki Protocol was signed, dealing with the reduction of sulphur emissions or their transboundary fluxes by at least 30% and in 1988, the Sophia Protocol was adopted concerning the control of emissions of nitrogen oxides or their transboundary fluxes. Under this Protocol the contracting parties undertook to reduce their national annual emissions of nitrogen oxides or their transboundary fluxes so that by the end of 1994 these do not exceed those of 1987.

The European Community has also adopted instruments in this area. Under Council Directive 88/609, emissions of sulphur dioxide

---

[78] Article 2.
[79] Article 3. Note that under article 6, states undertake to develop the best policies and strategies using the "best available technology which is economically feasible".
[80] Article 4. See also article 8.
[81] Article 5. See also article 8(b).

and nitrogen oxide from existing large combustion plants are to be reduced by 15% by 1993 and by 30% by 1998, while other Council Directives deal with emissions from vehicle exhausts.[82]

In 1986 a Protocol to the Paris Convention for the Prevention of Marine Pollution from Land-Based Sources[83] extended that agreement to atmospheric emissions of pollutants.[84]

ULTRA-HAZARDOUS ACTIVITIES

It has been argued that ultra-hazardous activities form a distinct category in the field of international environmental law and one in which the principle of strict or absolute liability operates.[85] The definition of what constitutes such activity, of course, is somewhat uncertain, but the characterisation can be taken to revolve around the serious consequences that are likely to flow from any damage that results, rather than upon the likelihood of pollution occurring from the activity in question. The focus therefore is upon the significant or exceptional risk of severe transnational damage.[86] The effect of categorising a particular activity as ultra-hazardous would, it appears, be to accept the strict liability principle rather than the due diligence standard commonly regarded as the general rule in pollution situations.[87] In other words, the state under whose territory or jurisdiction the activity took place would be liable irrespective of fault.

This exception to the general principle can be justified as a method of moving the burden of proof and shifting the loss clearly from the victim to the state. It would also operate as a further incentive to states to take action in areas of exceptional potential harm.

---

[82] See e.g. Council Directives 88/76; 88/436 and 89/458.

[83] See *infra*, p.555.

[84] Note also that in 1987 the Second International Conference on the Protection of the North Sea urged states to ratify the Protocol, see 27 *ILM*, 1988, p.835, while in 1990 North Sea states agreed to achieve by 1999 a reduction of 50% or more in atmospheric and river-borne emissions of hazardous substances, provided that best available technology permitted this, see IMO Doc. MEPC 29/INF.26.

[85] See e.g. Jenks, "The Scope and Nature of Ultra-Hazardous Liability in International Law", 117 *HR*, 1966, p.99; Handl, "State Liability", *op. cit.*, p.553 *et seq.* and Dupuy, *La Responsabilité des Etats pour les Dommages d'Origine Technologique et Industrielle*, 1976, pp.206-9.

[86] Handl, "State Liability", *op. cit.*, p.554.

[87] *Supra*, p.535.

In determining what areas of activity could be characterised as ultra-hazardous, some caution needs to be exercised. There can be little doubt that nuclear activities fall within this category as a general rule, but beyond this there appears to be no agreement. The Convention on International Liability for Damage caused by Space Objects 1972 specifically provides that a launching state shall be absolutely liable to pay compensation for damage caused by its space objects on the surface of the earth,[88] but this is the only clear example of its kind.

Nuclear Activities [89]

The use of nuclear technology brings with it risks as well as benefits and the accident at the Chernobyl nuclear reactor in 1986[90] brought home to international opinion just how devastating the consequences of a nuclear mishap could be. Concern in this area had hitherto focused upon the issue of nuclear weapons. In 1963 the Treaty Banning Nuclear Weapons Testing in the Atmosphere, Outer Space and Under Water had been signed[91] and measures to prevent the spread of nuclear weapons were adopted in the Nuclear Non-Proliferation Treaty of 1968, although the possession of nuclear weapons themselves does not contravene international law.[92]

A variety of international organisations are now involved to some extent in the process of developing rules and principles concerning nuclear activities and environmental protection. The International Atomic Energy Agency, to take the prime example, was established in 1956 in order to encourage the development of nuclear power, but particularly since the Chernobyl accident its nuclear safety role

[88] See *supra*, p.536.
[89] See e.g. *Chernobyl: Law and Communication, op. cit.;* Boyle, "Nuclear Energy", *op. cit.* and "Chernobyl", *op. cit.*; Woodliffe, "Tackling Transboundary Environmental Hazards in Cases of Emergency: The Emerging Legal Framework" in *Current Issues in European and International Law* (eds. White and Smythe), 1990 and "Chernobyl: Four Years On", 39 *ICLQ*, 1990, p.461.
[90] See *Chernobyl: Law and Communication, op. cit.*, pp.1-2.
[91] Note, however, that France and China did not become parties to this treaty and continued atmospheric nuclear testing. Australia and New Zealand sought a declaration from the International Court that French atmospheric nuclear testing was contrary to international law, but the Court decided the case on the basis that a subsequent French decision to end such testing was binding and thus the issue was moot; see the *Nuclear Tests* cases, ICJ Reports, 1974, p.253.
[92] See e.g. Shaw, "Nuclear Weapons and International Law" in *Nuclear Weapons and International Law* (ed. Pogany), 1987, p.1.

has been emphasised. The Convention on Assistance in Cases of Nuclear Emergency 1986, for example, gave it a co-ordinating function and an obligation to provide appropriate resources where so requested.[93] The IAEA has established a series of standards and guidelines including, for example, in the context of the design, construction and operation of nuclear power plants, although such standards do not have the force of law.[94] Other international organisations also have a role to play in the sphere of nuclear activities.[95]

The Provision of Information

There appears to be a general principle requiring that information be provided in certain situations[96] and several bilateral agreements have expressed this in the context of nuclear accidents.[97] In general, such agreements provide that each state is to inform the other without delay of any emergency resulting from civil nuclear activities and any other incident that could have radiological consequences for the second state. Reciprocal information systems are set up and warning notification centres established. Such agreements, however, do not cover exchange of military information.[98]

Following the Chernobyl accident and the failure of the USSR to provide immediate information, the Vienna Convention on Early Notification of a Nuclear Accident 1986 was rapidly adopted, under the auspices of the IAEA. This provides that in the event of a nuclear accident, the relevant state shall "forthwith notify, directly or through the International Atomic Energy Agency . . . those states which are or may be physically affected . . . of the nuclear accident, its nature,

---

[93] See further *infra*, p.550.

[94] Note, however, that under the Geneva Convention on the High Seas 1958, states are to take account of IAEA standards in preventing pollution of the seas from the dumping of nuclear waste.

[95] E.g. EURATOM, the OECD and the ILO (International Labour Organisation). See Boyle, "Nuclear Energy", *op. cit.*, pp.266-68.

[96] See *supra*, p.541.

[97] The first was concluded between France and Belgium in 1966 concerning the Ardennes Nuclear Power Station. Other examples include Switzerland-Federal Republic of Germany 1978 and France-UK 1983. The latter agreement was supplemented by a formal arrangement between the UK Nuclear Installations Inspectorate and the French equivalent for the continuous exchange of information on safety issues.

[98] See Woodliffe, "Tackling Transboundary Environmental Hazards", *op. cit.* at pp.117-20.

the time of its occurrence and its exact location". Additionally, such states must be promptly provided with information relevant to minimising the radiological consequences.[99] States are to respond promptly to a request for further information or consultations sought by an affected state.[100]

It is also to be noted that although the Convention does not apply to military nuclear accidents, the five nuclear weapons states made Statements of Voluntary Application indicating that they would apply the Convention to all nuclear accidents, including those not specified in that agreement.[101]

Since this Convention was adopted, a variety of bilateral agreements have been signed which have been more wide-ranging than those signed beforehand and which in some cases have gone beyond the provisions specified in the Notification Convention. The agreements signed by the UK with Norway, the Netherlands and Denmark during 1988-9, for example, specify that there is an obligation to notify the other parties if there is an accident or activity in the territory of the notifying state from which a transboundary effect of radiological safety significance is likely and additionally where abnormal levels of radiation are registered that are not caused by release from facilities or activities in the notifying state's territory. Extensive provisions are also included dealing with exchanges of information.[102]

The Provision of Assistance

The earliest treaty providing for assistance in the event of radiation accidents was the Nordic Mutual Assistance Agreement 1963. This dealt with the general terms of assistance, the advisory and co-ordinating role of the IAEA, financing, liability and privileges and immunities. The United Nations established the UN Disaster Relief Office (UNDRO) in 1972[103] and this provides assistance in

[99] Article 2. See also article 5.
[100] Article 6.
[101] See text in 25 *ILM*, 1986, p.1394.
[102] See e.g. Woodliffe, "Chernobyl", *op. cit.*, p.464. See also the European Community Council Directive 87/600 of December 1987, which provides for the early exchange of information in the event of a radiological emergency.
[103] A Disaster Relief Co-ordinator was provided for in General Assembly resolution 2816 (XXVI). See *Chernobyl: Law and Communication, op. cit.*, p.45.

pre-disaster planning. In 1977 the IAEA concluded an agreement with UNDRO with the purpose of co-ordinating their assistance activities in the nuclear accident field and in 1984 published a series of guidelines[104] setting out the mechanics of co-operation between states, including references to the problems of costs, liability, privileges and immunities.

In 1986, following the Chernobyl accident and at the same time as the Notification Convention, the Vienna Convention on Assistance in the Case of a Nuclear Accident or Radiological Emergency was adopted. This provides that a state in need of assistance in the event of a nuclear accident or radiological emergency may call for such assistance from any other state party either directly or through the IAEA.[105] This applies whether or not such accident or emergency originated within its territory, jurisdiction or control. States requesting assistance (which may include medical assistance and help with regard to the temporary relocation of displaced persons[106]) must provide details of the type of assistance required and other necessary information.[107] The IAEA must respond to a request for assistance by making available appropriate resources allocated for this purpose and by transmitting promptly the request to other states and international organisations possessing the necessary resources. In addition, if requested by the state seeking assistance, the IAEA will co-ordinate the assistance at the international level. The IAEA is also required to collect and disseminate to the states parties information concerning the availability of experts, equipment and materials and with regard to methodologies, techniques and available research data relating to the response to such situations.[108] The general range of assistance that can be provided by the Agency is laid down in some detail.[109]

In general terms, the Assistance Convention seeks to balance considerations relating to the sovereignty of the requesting state,[110]

---

[104] Guidelines for Mutual Emergency Assistance Arrangements in Connection with a Nuclear Accident or Radiological Emergency, *Chernobyl: Law and Communication, op. cit.,* p.199.
[105] Article 2(1).
[106] Article 2(5).
[107] Article 2(2).
[108] Article 5.
[109] *Ibid.*
[110] Under article 3(a), and unless otherwise agreed, the requesting state has the overall direction, control, co-ordination and supervision of the assistance within its territory.

the legitimate rights of the assisting state or states[111] and the interests of the international community in rendering rapid assistance to affected states. Whether the balance achieved is a fair one is open to discussion.[112]

Civil Liability

In addition to the issue of the responsibility or liability of the state for the activity under consideration, the question of the proceedings that may be taken by the individual victims is also raised. One possible approach is to permit the victim to have access to the legal system of the foreign polluter and thus to all remedies available on a non-discriminatory basis. This would have the effect of transforming the transboundary pollution into a national matter.[113] This approach is evident in some treaties.[114] The problem is that while placing the foreign victim on a par with nationals within the domestic legal system of the offender, it depends for its value upon the legal system possessing internal legislation of appropriate substantive content. This is not always the case.

There are, however, several international agreements dealing specifically with the question of civil liability in the sphere of nuclear activities.

The OECD Paris Convention on Third Party Liability in the Field of Nuclear Energy 1960, together with the Brussels Supplementary Convention 1963, provides that the operator of a nuclear installation shall be liable for damage to or loss of life of any person and damage to or loss of any property (other than the nuclear installation and associated property or means of transport). The IAEA Vienna Convention on Civil Liability for Nuclear Damage 1963 has similar

[111] Under article 7, the assisting state is entitled, unless it offers its assistance without costs, to be reimbursed for all the costs incurred by it, which are to be provided promptly, and under article 10(2), unless otherwise agreed, a requesting state is liable to compensate the assisting state for all loss of or damage to equipment or materials and for the death of or injury to personnel of the assisting party or persons acting on its behalf. There is no provision dealing with liability for damage caused by the assisting state. See also article 8 dealing with privileges and immunities.

[112] See e.g. *Chernobyl: Law and Communication*, *op. cit.*, p.47 and Woodliffe, "Tackling Transboundary Environmental Hazards", *op. cit.*, p.127.

[113] See e.g. Boyle, "Nuclear Energy", *op. cit.*, pp.297-98.

[114] See e.g. the Nordic Convention on the Protection of the Environment 1974. See also OECD Recommendations C(74)224; C(76)55 and C(77)28.

provisions, but is aimed at global participation. However, the Paris Convention has only 14 parties, all European states, including the nuclear states of the UK and France, and the Vienna Convention has just 11 parties, with only Argentina and Yugoslavia possessing nuclear facilities.

Additionally, the Brussels Convention on the Liability of Operators of Nuclear Ships 1962 provides that the operator of a nuclear ship shall be absolutely liable for any nuclear damage upon proof that such damage has been caused by a nuclear incident involving the nuclear fuel of, or radioactive products or waste produced in such ship.[115]

These conventions operate upon similar principles. It is the actual operator of the nuclear installation that is to bear the loss[116] and this is done so upon the basis of absolute or strict liability. Accordingly, no proof of fault or negligence is required. The conventions require operators to possess appropriate liability insurance or other financial security under the conditions laid down by the competent public authorities, unless the operator is itself a state[117] and the relevant states are to ensure that claims up to the liability limits are met.[118] This recognition of the residual responsibility of the state is unique.[119] The amount of liability of the operator is, however, limited by the Paris Convention (as amended by the Brussels Supplementary Convention) to 120 million Units of Account (i.e. US dollars[120]).[121] In the case of the Vienna Convention regime, the installation state is permitted to limit the liability of the operator to a stated amount,[122] provided a minimum of liability is

---

[115] This Convention has 6 parties and is not yet in force. None of the states which licenses nuclear ships is a party. Note that the Convention Relating to Civil Liability in the Field of Maritime Carriage of Nuclear Material 1971 provides that a person held liable for damage caused by a nuclear incident shall be exonerated from such liability if the operator of a nuclear installation is liable for such damage under either the Paris or Vienna Conventions.

[116] A carrier or handler of nuclear material may be regarded as such an operator where the latter consents and the necessary legislative framework so provides, see e.g. article 4(d) of the Paris Convention.

[117] See e.g. article 10 of the Paris Convention; article VII of the Vienna Convention and article III of the Brussels Convention on Nuclear Ships.

[118] *Ibid.*

[119] Cf. the Convention on Civil Liability for Oil Pollution Damage 1969.

[120] Protocols signed in 1982 have changed this to Special Drawing Rights and increased the limit, but the Protocols are not yet in force.

[121] Article 7.

[122] Article V.

maintained.[123] Under the Brussels Convention on Nuclear Ships the liability of the operator as regards one nuclear ship is limited to 1500 million gold francs in respect of any one nuclear accident.[124]

The relevant conventions also determine which state has jurisdiction over claims against operators or their insurers. In general, jurisdiction lies with the state where the nuclear incident occurred, although where a nuclear incident takes place outside the territory of a contracting party or where the place of the nuclear incident cannot be determined with certainty, jurisdiction will lie with the courts of the contracting party in whose territory the nuclear installations of the operator liable is situated.[125] Judgments given by the competent courts are enforceable in the territory of any contracting party.

The main problem with the system of the nuclear conventions is the fact that only a very few states are parties to them. Accordingly, a Joint Protocol was adopted in 1988 linking the Paris and Vienna Convention regimes, so that parties under each of these conventions may benefit from both of them. This is, however, only a partial solution and it is to be hoped that major nuclear states such as the US, USSR and Japan, that are not parties to either convention, may reconsider their position.[126]

The issue of inter-state claims is more difficult as was demonstrated by the aftermath of the Chernobyl accident. Many states have paid compensation to persons affected within their jurisdiction by the fallout from that accident, but while positions have been reserved with regard to claims directly against the USSR, it seems that problems relating to the obligations actually owed by states and the doubt over the requisite standard of care have prevented such claims from having been actually made.[127]

Hazardous Wastes

The increasing problem of the disposal of toxic and hazardous wastes and the practice of dumping in the Third World, with its

[123] Article V fixes this at $5 million at 1963 values.

[124] Article III.

[125] Article 13 of the Paris Convention and article XI of the Vienna Convention.

[126] Note also that the Paris and Vienna Conventions do not provide for the costs of environmental clean-up.

[127] See e.g. *Chernobyl: Law and Communication, op. cit.*, pp.26-28.

attendant severe health risks, has prompted international action.[128] The Oslo Convention for the Prevention of Marine Pollution by Dumping from Ships and Aircraft 1972[129] provides for a ban on the dumping of certain substances[130] and for controls to be placed on the dumping of others.[131] The London Convention on the Prevention of Marine Pollution by Dumping of Wastes and Other Matter 1972[132] prohibits the dumping of wastes except as provided in the Convention itself, and this is strictly controlled.

In 1988, the Organisation of African Unity adopted a resolution proclaiming the dumping of nuclear and industrial wastes in Africa to be a crime against Africa and its people, while the OECD has adopted a number of Decisions and Recommendations concerning the transfrontier movements and exports of hazardous wastes.[133] In 1989 the OECD adopted a Recommendation[134] noting that the "polluter pays" principle should apply to accidents involving hazardous substances. The Basle Convention on the Control of Transboundary Movements of Hazardous Wastes and Their Disposal 1989 provides that parties shall prohibit the export of hazardous and other wastes to parties which have prohibited the import of such wastes and have so informed the other parties. In the absence of prohibition by the importing state, export to that state of such wastes is only permissible where consent in writing to the specific import is obtained.[135] The Convention also provides that any proposed transboundary movement of hazardous wastes must be notified to the competent authorities of the states concerned by the state of export. The latter shall not allow the generator or exporter of hazardous wastes to commence the transboundary movement without the written consent of the state of import and any state of transit.[136]

In 1990, the IAEA adopted a Code of Practice on the International Transboundary Movement of Radioactive Waste, emphasising that

---

[128] See *Keesing's Record of World Events,* pp.36788-9 (1989).
[129] This is limited essentially to the north-east Atlantic area.
[130] Listed in Annex I.
[131] Listed in Annex II.
[132] This is a global instrument.
[133] See e.g. 23 *ILM,* 1984, p.214; 25 *ILM,* 1986, p.1010 and 28 *ILM,* 1989, pp.277 and 259.
[134] C(89)88.
[135] Article 4.
[136] Article 6.

every state should ensure that such movements take place only with the prior notification and consent of the sending, receiving and transit states in accordance with their respective laws and regulations. Appropriate regulatory authorities are called for, as well as the necessary administrative and technical capacity to manage and dispose of such waste in a manner consistent with international safety standards.

MARINE POLLUTION[137]

Marine pollution can arise from a variety of sources, including the operation of shipping, dumping at sea,[138] activities on the sea-bed[139] and the effects of pollution originating on the land and entering the seas.[140] There are a large number of treaties, bilateral, regional and multilateral, dealing with such issues and some of the more significant of them in the field of pollution from ships will be briefly noted.

Pollution from Ships

The International Convention for the Prevention of Pollution of the Sea by Oil 1954[141] basically prohibits the discharge of oil within fifty miles of land. The International Convention for the Prevention of Pollution from Ships 1973[142] is concerned with all forms of non-accidental pollution from ships apart from dumping and supersedes the 1954 Convention as between parties to it. In five Annexes to the Convention, detailed standards are laid down covering oil, noxious liquid substances in bulk, harmful substances carried by sea in packaged form, sewage and garbage.

---

[137] See e.g. Churchill and Lowe, *The Law of the Sea*, 2nd ed., 1988, Chapter 15; *The Impact of Marine Pollution* (ed. Cusine and Grant), 1980; Timagenis, *International Control of Marine Pollution*, 1980 and Boyle, "Marine Pollution under the Law of the Sea Convention", 79 *AJIL*, 1985, p.347.

[138] See *supra* p.373, and Churchill and Lowe, *op. cit.*, pp.268-72.

[139] See Churchill and Lowe, *op. cit.*, pp.272-77.

[140] Articles 194 and 207 of the Convention on the Law of the Sea 1982 provide in general terms for states to reduce marine pollution from land-based sources. A number of regional conventions lay down specific rules dealing with the control of particular substances, see Churchill and Lowe, *op. cit.*, pp.277-81.

[141] As amended, see Churchill and Lowe, *op. cit.*, pp.248-49.

[142] Known as the MARPOL Convention.

Article 211(2) of the Convention on the Law of the Sea 1982 provides that states are to legislate for the prevention, reduction and control of pollution of the marine environment from vessels flying their flag or of their registry. Such rules are to have the same effect at least as that of generally accepted international rules and standards established through the competent international organisation[143] or general diplomatic conference. States are also to ensure that the ships of their nationality or of their registry comply with "applicable international rules and standards" and with domestic rules governing the prevention, reduction and control of pollution.[144] In addition, coastal states have jurisdiction to physically inspect, and, where the evidence so warrants, commence proceedings against ships in their territorial waters, where there are clear grounds for believing that the ship concerned has violated domestic or international pollution regulations.[145] It should also be noted that a state in whose port a vessel is may take legal proceedings against that vessel not only where it is alleged to have violated that state's pollution laws or applicable international rules in its territorial sea or economic zone,[146] but also in respect of any discharge outside its internal waters, territorial sea or exclusive economic zone in violation of applicable international rules and standards.[147]

Where an accident takes place, the Convention Relating to Intervention on the High Seas in Cases of Oil Pollution Casualties 1969[148] permits states parties to take such measures on the high seas as may be necessary to prevent, mitigate or eliminate grave and imminent danger to their coastline or related interests from pollution or threat of pollution of the sea by oil.[149]

As far as liability is concerned, the Convention on Civil Liability for Oil Pollution Damage 1969 provides that where oil from a ship causes damage on the territory or territorial sea of a contracting

[143] The International Maritime Organisation.

[144] Article 217.

[145] Article 220(2).

[146] Article 220(1).

[147] Article 218. A provision characterised as "truly innovatory" by Churchill and Lowe, *op. cit.*, p.259.

[148] The adoption of this Convention followed upon the *Torrey Canyon* incident in 1967 in which a ship aground, although on the high seas, was bombed in order to reduce the risk of oil pollution; see Churchill and Lowe, *op. cit.*, p.241.

[149] This was extended by a Protocol of 1973 to cover pollution from substances other than oil.

party, the shipowner is strictly liable for such damage and any preventive measures taken.[150] This liability is limited, however, unless the pollution is the result of the fault of the shipowner.[151]

An International Convention on Oil Pollution Preparedness, Response and Co-operation was signed in London in November 1990, with the purpose of ensuring prompt and effective action in the event of a pollution incident. It requires ships to carry detailed plans for dealing with pollution emergencies. Pollution incidents must be reported without delay and in the event of a serious incident, other states likely to be affected must be informed and details given to the International Maritime Organisation. National and regional systems for dealing with such incidents are encouraged and the contracting parties agree to co-operate and provide advisory services, technical support and equipment at the request of other parties.

GLOBAL WARMING AND OZONE DEPLETION[152]

The problem of global warming and the expected increase in the temperature of the earth in the decades to come has focused attention on the issues particularly of the consumption of fossil fuels and deforestation. In addition, the depletion of the stratospheric ozone layer, which has the effect of letting excessive ultraviolet radiation through to the surface of the earth, is a source of considerable concern.

In the first serious effort to tackle the problem of ozone depletion, the Vienna Convention for the Protection of the Ozone Layer was adopted in 1985, entering into force three years later. This Convention is a framework agreement, providing the institutional

---

[150] Except where the damage results from war or acts of God; is wholly caused by an act or omission done by a third party with intent to cause damage; or where the damage is wholly caused by the negligent or other wrongful act of any government or other authority responsible for the maintenance of navigational aids; articles II and III.

[151] The Convention on the Establishment of an International Fund for Compensation for Oil Pollution Damage 1971 enables compensation to be paid in certain cases not covered by the Civil Liability Convention.

[152] See e.g. Lawrence, "International Legal Regulation for Protection of the Ozone Layer: Some Problems of Implementation", 2 *Journal of Environmental Law*, 1990, p.17; Stoel, "Fluorocarbon: Mobilising Concern and Action" in *Environmental Protection, The International Dimension* (eds. Kay and Jacobson), 1983, p.45; Engelmann, "A Look at Some Issues Before an Ozone Convention", 8 *Environmental Policy and Law*, 1982, p.49 and Heimsoeth, "The Protection of the Ozone Layer", 10 *Environmental Policy and Law*, 1983, p.34.

structure for the elaboration of Protocols laying down specific standards concerning the production of chloroflourocarbons (CFCs), the agents which cause the destruction of the ozone layer. Under the Convention, contracting parties agree to take appropriate measures to protect human health and the environment against adverse effects resulting or likely to result from human activities which modify or are likely to modify the ozone layer.[153] The parties also agree to co-operate in the collection of relevant material and in the formulation of agreed measures, and to take appropriate legislative or administrative action to control, limit, reduce or prevent human activities under their jurisdiction or control "should it be found that these activities have or are likely to have adverse effects resulting from modification or likely modification of the ozone layer".[154] A secretariat and disputes settlement mechanism were also established.[155]

In 1987 the Montreal Protocol on Substances that Deplete the Ozone Layer was adopted and this called for a phased reduction of CFCs and a freeze on the use of halons.[156] The control measures of the Protocol are based on the regulation of the production of "controlled substances"[157] by the freezing of their consumption[158] at 1986 levels followed by a progressive reduction, so that by mid-1998 consumption is to be reduced by 20% in comparison with the 1986 figure. From mid-1998 onwards consumption is to be reduced to 50% of the 1986 level.[159] However, this was subsequently felt to have been insufficient and in 1989, the parties to the Convention and Protocol adopted the Helsinki Declaration on the Protection of the Ozone Layer in which the parties agreed to phase out the production and consumption of CFCs controlled by the Protocol as soon as possible, but not later than the year 2000, and to phase

---

[153] Article 2(1). "Adverse effects" is defined in article 1(2) to mean "changes in the physical environment or biota, including changes in climate, which have significant deleterious effects on human health or on the composition, resilience and productivity of natural and managed ecosystems or on materials useful to mankind".

[154] Article 2.

[155] Articles 7 and 11.

[156] See 26 *ILM*, 1987, p.1541 and 28 *ILM*, 1989, p.1301.

[157] I.e. ozone depleting substances listed in Annex A.

[158] This is defined to constitute production plus imports minus exports of controlled substances, see articles 1(5) and (6) and 3.

[159] There are two exceptions, however, first for the purposes of "industrial rationalisation between parties" and secondly with regard to certain developing countries, see article 5.

out halons and control and reduce other substances which contribute significantly to ozone depletion as soon as feasible.

The parties to the Montreal Protocol made a series of Adjustments and Amendments to the Protocol in June 1990, the main ones being that 1992 consumption and production levels are not to exceed 1986 levels, while 1995 levels are not to exceed 50% with 10% exception to satisfy basic domestic needs. 1997 levels are not to exceed 15%, with 10% exception permitted, and 2000 levels are not to exceed 0% with 15% exception permitted. Broadly similar consumption and production targets have also been laid down with regard to halons.

It should also be noted that European Community Council Regulation 594/91 of 4 March 1991 provides that after 30 June 1997 there shall be no production of CFCs unless the European Commission has determined that such production is essential.

Action with regard to the phenomenon of global warming has been a lot slower. General Assembly resolution 45/53, adopted on 6 December 1988, recognised that climate change is a common concern of mankind and determined that necessary and timely action should be taken to deal with this issue. It also called for the convening of a conference on world climate change, as did the UNEP Governing Council Decision on Global Climate Change of 25 May 1989. In addition, the Hague Declaration on the Environment 1989, signed by 24 states, called for the establishment of new institutional authority under the auspices of the UN to combat any further global warming and for the negotiation of the necessary legal instruments.

CHAPTER FIFTEEN

The Law of Treaties[1]

Unlike municipal law, the various methods by which rights and duties may be created in international law are relatively unsophisticated. Within a state, legal interests may be established by contracts between two or more persons, or by agreements under seal, or under the developed system for transferring property, or indeed by virtue of legislation or judicial decisions. International law is more limited as far as the mechanisms for the creation of new rules are concerned. Custom relies upon a measure of state practice supported by *opinio juris* and is usually, although not invariably, an evolving and timely process. Treaties, on the other hand, are a more direct and formal method of international law creation.

States transact a vast amount of work by using the device of the treaty, in circumstances which underline the paucity of international law procedures when compared with the many ways in which a person within a state's internal order may set up binding rights and obligations. For instance, wars will be terminated, disputes settled, territory acquired, special interests determined, alliances established and international organisations created all by means of treaties. No simpler method of reflecting the agreed objectives of states really exists and the international convention has to suffice both for straightforward bilateral agreements and complicated multilateral expressions of opinions. Thus, the concept of the treaty and how it operates becomes of paramount importance to the evolution of international law.

A treaty is basically an agreement between parties on the international scene. Although treaties may be concluded, or made, between states and international organisations, they are in essence concerned with relations between states.

An International Convention on the Law of Treaties was signed in 1969 and came into force in 1980, while a Convention on Treaties

---

[1] See generally McNair, *The Law of Treaties*, 1961; Brownlie, *Principles of Public International Law*, 4th ed., 1990, Chapter XXV; Detter, *Essays on the Law of Treaties*, 1967; Elias, *The Modern Law of Treaties*, 1974; O'Connell, *International Law*, 2nd ed., 1970, vol.1, p.195 *et seq.*; Sinclair, *The Vienna Convention on the Law of Treaties*, 2nd ed., 1984; Reuter, *Introduction to the Law of Treaties*, 1989; Bastid, *Les Traités Dans La Vie Internationale*, 1985 and Rosenne, *Developments in the Law of Treaties 1945-1986*, 1989.

between States and International Organisations was signed in 1986.[2] The emphasis, however, will be on the appropriate rules which have emerged as between states.

The 1969 Vienna Convention on the Law of Treaties partly reflects customary law[3] and constitutes the basic framework for any discussion of the nature and characteristics of treaties. Certain provisions of the Convention may be regarded as reflective of customary international law, such as the rules on interpretation,[4] material breach[5] and fundamental change of circumstances.[6] Others may not be so regarded, and constitute principles binding only upon state parties.

The fundamental principle of treaty law is undoubtedly the proposition that treaties are binding upon the parties to them and must be performed in good faith. This rule is known in legal terms as *pacta sunt servanda* and is arguably the oldest principle of international law. It was re-affirmed in article 26 of the 1969 Convention, and underlies every international agreement. It is not hard to see why this is so. In the absence of a certain minimum belief that states will perform their treaty obligations in good faith,[7] there is no reason for countries to enter into such obligations with each other.

The term "treaty" itself is the one most used in the context of international agreements but there are a variety of names which can be, and sometimes are, used to express the same concept, such as

[2] This was based upon the International Law Commission's Draft Articles on the Law of Treaties between States and International Organisations or between International Organisations, *Yearbook of the ILC*, 1982, vol.II, Pt.2, p.9 *et seq*. These articles were approved by the General Assembly and governmental views solicited and received. A plenipotentiary conference was held between 18 February and 21 March 1986 to produce a Convention based on those draft articles. See Assembly resolutions 37/112, 38/139 and 39/86. There are 6 parties to this Convention.

[3] See e.g. the *Namibia* case, ICJ Reports, 1971, pp.16, 47; 49 *ILR*, pp.2, 37 and the *Fisheries Jurisdiction* case, ICJ Reports, 1973, pp.3, 18; 55 *ILR*, pp.183, 198. See also Rosenne, *op. cit.*, p.121.

[4] See e.g. the *Beagle Channel* case, HMSO, 1977, p.7; 52 *ILR*, p.93; the *La Bretagne* case, 82 *ILR*, pp.590, 612; the *Golder* case, European Court of Human Rights, Series A, No.18, p.14; 57 *ILR*, pp.201, 213-14 and the *Lithgow* case, European Court of Human Rights, Series A, No.102, para.114; 75 *ILR*, pp.438, 482-83.

[5] See e.g. the *Namibia* case, ICJ Reports, 1971, pp.16, 47; 49 *ILR*, pp.2, 37.

[6] See e.g. the *Fisheries Jurisdiction* cases (jurisdictional phase), ICJ Reports, 1973, pp.3, 21; 55 *ILR*, pp.183, 201.

[7] Note also the references to good faith in articles 31, 46 and 69 of the 1969 Convention. See also the *Nuclear Tests* cases, ICJ Reports, 1974, pp.253, 268; 57 *ILR*, pp.398, 413 and the *Nicaragua* case, ICJ Reports, 1986, pp.392, 418; 76 *ILR*, pp.104, 129.

protocol, act, charter, covenant, pact and concordat. They each refer to the same basic activity and the use of one term rather than another often signifies little more than a desire for variety of expression.

A treaty is defined in article 2 (for the purposes of the Convention) as:

> an international agreement concluded between states in written form and governed by international law, whether embodied in a single instrument or in two or more related instruments and whatever its particular designation.[8]

In other words, in addition to excluding agreements involving international organisations, the Convention does not cover agreements between states which are to be governed by municipal law, such as a large number of commercial accords. This does not mean that such arrangements cannot be characterised as international agreements, or that they are invalid, merely that they are not within the purview of the 1969 Convention. Indeed, article 3 stresses that international agreements between states and other subjects of international law or between two or more subjects of international law, or oral agreements do not lose their validity by being excluded from the framework of the Convention. One important requirement is that the parties to the treaty intend to create legal relations as between themselves by means of their agreement. This is logical since many agreements between states are merely statements of commonly held principles or objectives and are not intended to establish binding obligations.

For instance, a declaration by a number of states in support of a particular political aim is in many cases bereft of legal (though not political) significance, as the states may regard it as a policy manoeuvre and not as setting up juridical relations between themselves. To see whether a particular agreement is intended to create legal relations, one has to examine carefully all the facts of the situation.[9]

---

[8] In the 1986 Convention on Treaties between States and International Organisations, the same definition is given, substituting states and international organisations for states alone, *supra*, footnote 2.

[9] Registration of the agreement with the United Nations under article 102 of the UN Charter is one useful indication.

It should be noted that the International Court regarded a mandate agreement as having the character of a treaty,[10] while in the *Anglo-Iranian Oil Co.* case[11] doubts were expressed about whether a concession agreement between a private company and a state constituted an international agreement in the sense of a treaty.[12] Optional declarations with regard to the compulsory jurisdiction of the International Court itself under article 36(2) of the Statute of the Court, have been regarded as treaty provisions,[13] while declarations made by way of unilateral acts concerning legal or factual situations may have the effect of creating legal obligations.[14] In the latter instance, of course, a treaty as such is not involved.

Where the parties to an agreement do not intend to create legal relations or binding obligations or rights thereby, the agreement will not be a treaty, although, of course, its political effect may still be considerable.[15] In fact a large role is played in the normal course of inter-state dealings by informal non-treaty instruments precisely because they are intended to be non-binding and are thus flexible, confidential and relatively speedy in comparison with treaties.[16] They may be amended with ease and without delay and may be terminated by reasonable notice (subject to provision to the contrary). It is this intention not to create a binding arrangement which marks the difference between treaties and informal international instruments.

The 1969 Convention also covers treaties which are the constituent instruments of international organisations, such as the United

---

[10] *South-West Africa* cases, ICJ Reports, 1962, pp.319, 330; 37 *ILR*, pp.3, 12.

[11] ICJ Reports, 1952, pp.93, 112; 19 *ILR*, pp.507, 517.

[12] But see *Texaco* v. *Libya*, 53 *ILR*, p.389 and *supra* p.517.

[13] The *Fisheries Jurisdiction* case, ICJ Reports, 1973, pp.3, 16; 55 *ILR*, pp.183, 196.

[14] The *Nuclear Tests* case, ICJ Reports, 1974, pp.253, 267; 57 *ILR*, pp.398, 412. See also the Ihlen Declaration, held to constitute a binding statement, in the *Eastern Greenland* case, PCIJ, Series A/B, no.53, 1933; 6 *ILR*, p.95 and *Burkina Faso* v. *Mali*, ICJ Reports, 1986, pp.554, 573-74; 80 *ILR*, pp.459, 477. See further *supra* p.98.

[15] See e.g. the Helsinki Final Act of 1975, which was understood to be non-binding and thus not a treaty by the parties involved, *DUSPIL*, 1975, pp.326-27. See Schachter, "The Twilight Existence of Non-binding International Agreements", 71 *AJIL*, 1977, p.296 and Rosenne, *op. cit.*, p.91.

[16] See e.g. Rosenne, *op. cit.*, p.107 *et seq.*; Aust, "The Theory and Practice of Informal International Instruments", 35 *ICLQ*, 1986, p.787; Baxter, "International Law in 'Her Infinite Variety'", 29 *ICLQ*, 1980, p.549 and Roessler, "Law, *De Facto* Agreements and Declarations of Principles in International Economic Relations", 21 *German Yearbook of International Law*, 1978, p.41.

Nations Charter, and internal treaties adopted within international organisations.[17]

THE MAKING OF TREATIES[18]

Formalities

Treaties may be made or concluded by the parties in virtually any manner they wish. There is no prescribed form or procedure, and how a treaty is formulated and by whom it is actually signed will depend upon the intention and agreement of the states concerned.

Treaties may be drafted as between states, or governments, or heads of states, or governmental departments, whichever appears the most expedient. For instance, many of the most important treaties are concluded as between heads of state, and many of the more mundane agreements are expressed to be as between government departments, such as minor trading arrangements.

Where precisely in the domestic constitutional establishment the power to make treaties is to be found depends upon each country's municipal regulations and varies from state to state. In the United Kingdom, the treaty making power is within the prerogative of the Crown,[19] whereas in the United States it resides with the President "with the advice and consent of the Senate" and the concurrence of two-thirds of the Senators.[20]

Nevertheless, there are certain rules that apply in the formation of international conventions. In international law, states have the capacity to make agreements, but since states are not identifiable human persons, particular principles have evolved to ensure that persons representing states have indeed the power so to do for the purpose of concluding the treaty in question. Such persons must produce what is termed "full powers" according to article 7 of the

---

[17] Article 5. See further Rosenne, *op. cit.*, Chapter 4.

[18] See e.g. Blix, *Treaty-Making Power*, 1960. See also Vierdag, "The Time of the Conclusion of a Multilateral Treaty: Article 30 of the Vienna Convention on the Law of Treaties and Related Provisions", 59 *BYIL*, 1988, p.75.

[19] See e.g. de Smith, *Constitutional and Administrative Law*, 3rd ed.; 1977, p.125.

[20] See Henkin, Pugh, Schachter and Smit, *International Law Cases and Materials*, 1980, p.580. See with regard to the Presidential power to terminate a treaty, *DUSPIL* 1979, p.724 *et seq.* and *Goldwater* v. *Carter*, 617 F.2d 697 and 100 S. Ct. 533 (1979). See also Henkin, "Restatement of the Foreign Relations Law of the United States (Revised)", 74 *AJIL*, 1980, p.954.

Convention, before being accepted as capable of representing their countries.[21] "Full powers" refers to documents certifying status from the competent authorities of the state in question. This provision provides security to the other parties to the treaty that they are making agreements with persons competent to do so.[22] However, certain persons do not need to produce such full powers, by virtue of their position and functions. This exception refers to heads of state and government, and foreign ministers for the purpose of performing all acts relating to the conclusion of the treaty; heads of diplomatic missions for the purpose of adopting the text of the treaty between their country and the country to which they are accredited; and representatives accredited to international conferences or organisations for the purpose of adopting the text of the treaty in that particular conference or organisation.

Sinclair notes that UK practice distinguishes between "general full powers" held by the Secretary of State for Foreign and Commonwealth Affairs, Ministers of State and Parliamentary Under-Secretaries in the Foreign and Commonwealth Office and UK Permanent Representatives to the UN, European Communities and General Agreement on Tariffs and Trade, which enable any treaty to be negotiated and signed, and "special full powers" granted to a particular person to negotiate and sign a specific treaty.[23]

Any act relating to the making of a treaty by a person not authorised as required will be without any legal effect, unless the state involved afterwards confirms the act.[24] One example of this kind of situation arose in 1951 with regard to a convention relating to the naming of cheeses. It was signed by a delegate of both Sweden and Norway, but it appeared that he had authority only from Norway. However, the agreement was subsequently ratified by both parties and entered into effect.[25]

Consent

Once a treaty has been drafted and agreed by authorised representatives, a number of stages are then necessary before it

---

[21] See Sinclair, *op. cit.*, p.29 *et seq.* and Jones, *Full Powers and Ratification*, 1946.
[22] See *Yearbook of the ILC*, 1966, vol.II, p.193.
[23] *Op. cit.*, p.32. See also *Satow's Guide to Diplomatic Practice*, 5th ed., 1979, p.62.
[24] Article 8.
[25] See *Yearbook of the ILC*, 1966, vol.II, p.195.

becomes a binding legal obligation upon the parties involved. The text of the agreement drawn up by the negotiators of the parties has to be adopted and article 9 provides that adoption in international conferences takes place by the vote of two-thirds of the states present and voting, unless by the same majority it is decided to apply a different rule. This procedure follows basically the practices recognised in the United Nations General Assembly[26] and carried out in the majority of contemporary conferences.

An increasing number of conventions are now adopted and opened for signature by means of UN General Assembly resolutions, such as the 1966 International Covenants on Human Rights and the 1984 Convention against Torture, using normal Assembly voting procedures.

Another significant point is the tendency in recent conferences to operate by way of consensus so that there would be no voting until all efforts to reach agreement by consensus have been exhausted.[27]

In cases other than international conferences, adoption will take place by the consent of all the states involved in drawing up the text of the agreement.[28]

The consent of the states parties to the treaty in question is obviously a vital factor, since states may (in the absence of a rule being also one of customary law) be bound only by their consent. Treaties are in this sense contracts between states and if they do not receive the consent of the various states, their provisions will not be binding upon them.

There are, however, a number of ways in which a state may express its consent to an international agreement. It may be signalled, according to article 11, by signature, exchange of instruments constituting a treaty, ratification, acceptance, approval or accession.

---

[26] See article 18 of the UN Charter.

[27] See e.g. the Third UN Conference on the Law of the Sea, see Sinclair, *op. cit.*, pp.37-39. See also the UN *Juridical Yearbook*, 1974, pp.163-64, where the Director of the General Legal Division, Office of Legal Affairs declared that the term "consensus" in UN organs, "was used to describe a practice under which every effort is made to achieve unanimous agreement; and if that could not be done, those dissenting from the general trend were prepared simply to make their position and reservations known and placed on the record".

[28] Article 9(1). This reflects the classic rule, Sinclair, *op. cit.*, p.33. See also articles 237 and 247 of the EEC Treaty.

In addition, it may be accomplished by any other means, if so agreed.

Consent by Signature [29]

A state may regard itself as having given its consent to the text of the treaty by signature in defined circumstances noted by article 12, that is, where the treaty provides that signature shall have that effect, or where it is otherwise established that the negotiating states were agreed that signature should have that effect, or where the intention of the state to give that effect to the signature appears from the full powers of its representative or was expressed during the negotiations.

Although consent by ratification is probably the most popular of the methods adopted in practice, consent by signature does retain some significance, especially in light of the fact that to insist upon ratification in each case before a treaty becomes binding is likely to burden the administrative machinery of government and result in long delays. Accordingly, provision is made for consent to be expressed by signature. This would be appropriate for the more routine and less politicised of treaties.

The act of signature is usually a very formal affair. Often in the more important treaties, the head of state will formally add his signature in an elaborate ceremony. In multilateral conventions, a special closing session will be held at which authorised representatives will sign the treaty.

However, where the convention is subject to acceptance, approval or ratification, signature will become a mere formality and will mean no more than that state representatives have agreed upon an acceptable text, which will be forwarded to their particular governments for the necessary decision as to acceptance or rejection. In such cases and pending ratification, acceptance or approval, a state must refrain from acts which would defeat the object and purpose of the treaty until such time as its intentions with regard to the treaty have been made clear.[30]

---

[29] See *Yearbook of the ILC*, 1966, vol.II, p.196.

[30] Article 18. See Sinclair, *op. cit.*, pp.42-44 and *Certain German Interests in Polish Upper Silesia*, PCIJ, Series A, no.7, 1926, p.30.

Consent by Exchange of Instruments

Article 13 provides that the consent of states to be bound by a treaty constituted by instruments exchanged between them may be expressed by that exchange when the instruments declare that their exchange shall have that effect or it is otherwise established that those states had agreed that the exchange of instruments should have that effect.

Consent by Ratification [31]

The device of ratification by the competent authorities of the state is historically well established and was originally devised to ensure that the representative did not exceed his powers or instructions with regard to the making of a particular agreement. Although ratification (or approval) was in years past a function of the sovereign, it has in modern times been made subject to constitutional control.

The advantages of waiting until a state ratifies a treaty before it becomes a binding document are basically twofold, internal and external. In the latter case, the delay between signature and ratification may often be advantageous in allowing extra time for consideration, once the negotiating process has been completed. But it is the internal aspects that are the most important, for they reflect the change in political atmosphere that has occurred in the last 150 years and has led to a much greater participation by a state's population in public affairs. By providing for ratification, the feelings of public opinion have an opportunity to be expressed with the possibility that a strong negative reaction may result in the state deciding not to ratify the treaty under consideration.

The rules relating to ratification vary from country to country. In the United Kingdom, although the power of ratification comes within the prerogative of the Crown, it has become accepted that treaties involving any change in municipal law, or adding to the financial burdens of the government or having an impact upon the private rights of British subjects will be first submitted to Parliament and subsequently ratified. There is, in fact, a procedure known as

[31] Defined in article 2(1)b as "the international act . . . whereby a state establishes on the international plane its consent to be bound by a treaty". It is thus to be distinguished as a concept from ratification in the internal constitutional sense, although clearly there is an important link, see *Yearbook of the ILC*, 1966, vol.II, pp.197-98. See also Brownlie, *op. cit.*, p.607.

the Ponsonby Rule which provides that all treaties subject to ratification are laid before Parliament at least 21 days before the actual ratification takes place.[32] Different considerations apply in the case of the United States.[33] However, the question of how a state effects ratification is a matter for internal law alone and outside international law.

Article 14 of the 1969 Vienna Convention notes that ratification will express a state's consent to be bound by a treaty where the treaty so provides; it is otherwise established that the negotiating states were agreed that ratification should be required; the representative of the state has signed the treaty subject to ratification or the intention of the state to sign the treaty subject to ratification appears from the full powers of its representative or was expressed during negotiations.

Within this framework, there is a controversy as to which treaties need to be ratified. Some writers maintain that ratification is only necessary if it is clearly contemplated by the parties to the treaty,[34] and this approach has been adopted by the United Kingdom.[35] On the other hand, it has been suggested that ratification should be required unless the treaty clearly reveals a contrary intention.[36] The United States, in general, will dispense with ratification only in the case of executive agreements.[37]

Ratification in the case of bilateral treaties is usually accomplished by exchanging the requisite instruments, but in the case of multilateral treaties the usual procedure is for one party to collect the ratifications of all states, keeping all parties informed of the situation. It is becoming more accepted that in such instances, the Secretary-General of the United Nations will act as the depositary for ratifications.

In some cases, signatures to treaties may be declared subject to "acceptance" or "approval". The terms, as noted in articles 11 and 14(2), are very similar to ratification and similar provisions apply.

---

[32] See *supra*, Chapter 4, p.116 *et seq.*

[33] *Ibid.*, p.120.

[34] See e.g. Fitzmaurice, "Do Treaties Need Ratification?", 15 *BYIL*, 1934, p.129, and O'Connell, *op. cit.*, p.222. See also Blix, "The Requirement of Ratification", 30 *BYIL*, 1953, p.380.

[35] See e.g. Sinclair, *op. cit.*, p.40 and O'Connell, *op. cit.*, p.222.

[36] See e.g. McNair, *op. cit.*, p.133.

[37] O'Connell, *op. cit.*, p.222. See also *DUSPIL* 1974, pp.216-17 and *ibid.*, 1979, p.678 *et seq.*

Such variation in terminology is not of any real significance and only refers to a somewhat simpler form of ratification.

Consent by accession [38]

This is the normal method by which a state becomes a party to a treaty it has not signed. Article 15 notes that consent by accession is possible where the treaty so provides, or the negotiating states were agreed or subsequently agree that consent by accession could occur in the case of the state in question.

Important multilateral treaties often declare that specific entities may accede to the treaty at a later date. For instance, the 1958 Geneva Conventions on the Sea provided for accession by any member-states of the United Nations or any of the Specialised Agencies of the United Nations.[39]

RESERVATIONS TO TREATIES[40]

A reservation is defined in article 2 of the Convention as:

> a unilateral statement, however phrased or named, made by a state, when signing, ratifying, accepting, approving or acceding to a treaty, whereby it purports to exclude or to modify the legal effect of certain provisions of the treaty in their application to that state.

This means generally that where a state is satisfied with most of a treaty, but is unhappy about one or two particular provisions, it may, in certain circumstances, wish to refuse to accept or be bound by such provisions, while consenting to the rest of the agreement. By this device of excluding certain provisions, states may agree to be bound by a treaty which otherwise they might reject entirely. This, obviously, may have very beneficial results in the cases of multilateral

---

[38] See *Yearbook of the ILC,* 1966, vol.II, p.199.

[39] See e.g. articles 26 and 28 of the Convention on the Territorial Sea and the Contiguous Zone.

[40] See e.g. Gamble, "Reservations to Multilateral Treaties: A Macroscopic View of State Practice", 74 *AJIL,* 1980, p.372; Fitzmaurice, "Reservations to Multilateral Treaties", 2 *ICLQ,* 1953, p.1; Bowett, "Reservations to Non-restricted Multilateral Treaties", 48 *BYIL,* 1976-7, p.67; Imbert, *Les Réserves Aux Traités Multilatéraux,* 1979; Sinclair, *op. cit.,* Chapter 3; O'Connell, *op. cit.,* p.229 *et seq.;* Ruda, "Reservations to Treaties", 146 *HR,* p.95 and Horn, *Reservations and Interpretative Declarations to Multilateral Treaties,* 1988.

conventions, by inducing as many states as possible to adhere to the proposed treaty. To some extent it is a means of encouraging harmony amongst states of widely differing social, economic and political systems, by concentrating upon agreed, basic issues and accepting disagreement on certain other matters.

The capacity of a state to make reservations to an international treaty illustrates the principle of sovereignty of states, whereby a state may refuse its consent to particular provisions so that they do not become binding upon it. On the other hand, of course, to permit a treaty to become honeycombed with reservations by a series of countries could well jeopardise the whole exercise. It could seriously dislocate the whole purpose of the agreement and lead to some complicated inter-relationships amongst states.

This problem does not really arise in the case of bilateral treaties, since a reservation by one party to a proposed term of the agreement would necessitate a renegotiation. An agreement between two parties cannot exist where one party refuses to accept some of the provisions of the treaty.[41] This is not the case with respect to multilateral treaties, and here it is possible for individual states to dissent from particular provisions, by announcing their intention either to exclude them altogether, or understand them in a certain way.

Reservations must be distinguished from other statements made with regard to a treaty that are not intended to have the legal effect of a reservation, such as understandings, political statements or interpretative declarations. In the latter instance, no binding consequence is intended with regard to the treaty in question. What is involved is a political manifestation for primarily internal effect.[42]

A distinction has been drawn between "mere" interpretative declarations and "qualified" interpretative declarations,[43] with the latter category capable in certain circumstances of constituting

[41] See *Yearbook of the ILC*, 1966, vol.II, p.203.

[42] See the *Temeltasch* case, 5 *European Human Rights Reports*, 1983, p.417 on the difference between reservations and interpretative declarations generally and in the context of the European Human Rights Convention. Cf. the *Ette* case, European Court of Human Rights, Series A, No.117. See also Imbert, "Reservations to the European Convention on Human Rights before the Strasbourg Commission", 33 *ICLQ*, 1984, p.558 and *UN Juridical Yearbook*, 1976, pp.220-21.

[43] See McRae, "The Legal Effect of Interpretative Declarations", 49 *BYIL*, 1978, p.155. See also the *Temeltasch* case, *op. cit.*, pp.432-33.

reservations. In the *Belilos* case[44] in 1988, the European Court of Human Rights considered the effect of one particular interpretative declaration made by Switzerland upon ratification.[45] The Court held that one had to look behind the title given to the declaration in question and to seek to determine its substantive content. It was necessary to ascertain the original intention of those drafting the declaration and thus recourse to the *travaux préparatoires* was required. In the light of these, the Court felt that Switzerland had indeed intended to "avoid the consequences which a broad view of the right of access to the courts . . . would have for the system of public administration and of justice in the cantons and consequently . . . put forward the declaration as qualifying [its] consent to be bound by the Convention".[46] Having so decided, the Court held that the declaration in question, taking effect as a reservation, did not in fact comply with article 64 of the Convention, which prohibited reservations of a general character[47] and required a brief statement of the law in force necessitating the reservation.[48] Accordingly, the declaration was invalid. It is hard to escape the conclusion that the Court has accepted a test favourable to states as to the situations under which a declaration may be regarded as a reservation, only to emphasise the requirements of article 64 concerning the validity of reservations to the European Convention. One should therefore be rather cautious before applying the easier test regarding interpretative declarations generally.

The problem is particularly acute, of course, since to constitute a reservation that word itself need not to be used. What is clearly required is the intention to modify the legal effect of a particular provision and this should not be too generously interpreted.

---

[44] European Court of Human Rights, Series A, No.132. See also Marks, "Reservations Unhinged: The *Belilos* Case Before the European Court of Human Rights", 39 *ICLQ,* 1990, p.300.

[45] Switzerland made in total two interpretative declarations and two reservations upon ratification of the European Convention on Human Rights. The declaration in question concerned article 6, paragraph 1 of the Convention dealing with the right to fair trial and provided that Switzerland considered that right was intended solely to ensure ultimate control by the judiciary over the acts or decisions of the public authorities. The issue concerned the right of appeal from the Lausanne Police Board to the Criminal Cassation Division of the Vaud Cantonal Court, which could not in fact hear fresh argument, receive witnesses or give a new ruling on the merits and whether the declaration prevented the applicant from relying on article 6 in the circumstances.

[46] *Op. cit.*, pp.18-19.

[47] *Ibid.*, pp.20-21.

[48] *Ibid.*, pp.21-22.

The general rule that became established historically was that reservations could only be made with the consent of all the other states involved in the process. This was to preserve as much as possible unity of approach to ensure the success of an international agreement and to minimise deviations from the text of the treaty. This reflected the contractual view of the nature of a treaty,[49] and the League of Nations supported this concept.[50] The effect of this was that a state wishing to make a reservation had to obtain the consent of all the other parties to the treaty. If this was not possible, that state could either become a party to the original treaty (minus the reservation, of course) or not become a party at all. However, this restrictive approach to reservations was not accepted by the International Court of Justice in the *Reservations to the Genocide Convention* case.[51] This was an advisory opinion by the Court, requested by the General Assembly after some states had made reservations to the 1948 Genocide Convention, which contained no clause permitting such reservations, and a number of objections were made.

The Court held that:

> a state which has made and maintained a reservation which has been objected to by one or more parties to the Convention but not by others, can be regarded as being a party to the Convention if the reservation is compatible with the object and purpose of the Convention.

Compatibility in the Court's opinion could be decided by states individually since it was noted that:

> if a party to the Convention objects to a reservation which it considers incompatible with the object and purpose of the Convention, it can . . . consider that the reserving state is not a party to the Convention.[52]

The Court did emphasise the principle of the integrity of a convention, but pointed to a variety of special circumstances with regard to the Genocide Convention in question, which called for

---

[49] See Sinclair, *op. cit.*, pp.54-55 and Ruda, *op. cit.*, p.112.

[50] Report of the Committee of Experts for the Progressive Codification of International Law, 8 LNOJ, pp.880-81 (1927).

[51] ICJ Reports, 1951, p.15; 18 *ILR*, p.364.

[52] *Ibid.*, pp.29-30.

a more flexible interpretation of the principle. These circumstances included the universal character of the UN under whose auspices the Convention had been concluded; the extensive participation envisaged under the Convention; the fact that the Convention had been the product of a series of majority votes; the fact that the principles underlying the Convention were general principles already binding upon states; that the Convention was clearly intended by the UN and the parties to be definitely universal in scope and that it had been adopted for a purely humanitarian purpose so that state parties did not have interests of their own but a common interest. All these factors militated for a flexible approach in this case.

The Court's approach, although having some potential disadvantages,[53] was in keeping with the move to increase the acceptability and scope of treaties and with the trend in international organisations away from the unanimity rule in decision-making and towards majority voting.[54] The 1969 Convention on the Law of Treaties accepted the Court's views.

By article 19, reservations may be made when signing, ratifying, accepting, approving or acceding to a treaty, but they cannot be made where the reservation is prohibited by the treaty, or where the treaty provides that only specified reservations may be made and these do not include the reservation in question, or where the reservation is not compatible with the object and purpose of the treaty.

In the instances where a reservation is possible, the traditional rule requiring acceptance by all parties will apply where, by article 20(2), "it appears from the limited number of the negotiating states and the object and purpose of a treaty that the application of the treaty in its entirety between all the parties is an essential condition of the consent of each one to be bound by the treaty".

Article 20(4) then outlines the general rules to be followed with regard to treaties not within article 20(2) and not constituent instruments of international organisations. These are that:

[53] See e.g. Fitzmaurice, *op. cit.*

[54] Although the International Law Commission was initially critical, it later changed its mind, see *Yearbook of the ILC*, 1951, vol.II, pp.130-31, cf. *ibid.*, 1962, vol.II, pp.62-65 and 178-79. Note also that the UN General Assembly in 1959 resolved that the Secretary-General as a depositary was to apply the Court's approach to all conventions concluded under UN auspices unless they contained provisions to the contrary.

(a) acceptance by another contracting state of a reservation constitutes the reserving state a party to the treaty in relation to that other state if or when the treaty is in force for those states;

(b) an objection by another contracting state to a reservation does not preclude the entry into force of the treaty as between the objecting and reserving states unless a contrary intention is definitely expressed by the objecting state;

(c) an act expressing a state's consent to be bound by the treaty and containing a reservation is effective as soon as at least one other contracting state has accepted the reservation.

The effect of reservations is outlined in article 21. This declares that a reservation established with regard to another party modifies, for the reserving state in its relations with the other party, the provisions of the treaty to which the reservation relates, to the extent of the reservation. The other party is similarly affected in its relations with the reserving state. An example of this was provided by the Libyan reservation to the 1961 Vienna Convention on Diplomatic Relations with regard to the diplomatic bag, permitting Libya to search the bag with the consent of the state whose bag it was, and insist that it be returned to its state of origin. Since the UK did not object to the reservation, it could have acted similarly with regard to Libya's diplomatic bags.[55] However, the reservation does not modify the provisions of the treaty for the other parties to the treaty as between themselves.

Article 21(3) provides that where a state objects to a reservation, but not to the entry into force of the treaty between itself and the reserving state, then, "the provisions to which the reservation relates do not apply as between the two states to the extent of the reservation". This provision was applied by the arbitration tribunal in the *Anglo-French Continental Shelf* case, where it was noted that:

the combined effect of the French reservations and their rejection by the United Kingdom is neither to render article 6 [of the Geneva Convention on the Continental Shelf, 1958] inapplicable *in toto*, as the French Republic contends, nor to render it applicable *in toto*, as the United Kingdom primarily contends. It is to render the article

---

[55] See Foreign Affairs Committee, *Report on the Abuse of Diplomatic Immunities and Privileges*, 1984, pp.23-24, and *supra*, Chapter 12, p.468.

inapplicable as between the two countries to the extent of the reservations.[56]

In general, reservations are deemed to have been accepted by states that have raised no objections to them at the end of a period of twelve months after notification of the reservation, or by the date on which consent to be bound by the treaty was expressed, whichever is the later.[57]

Reservations must be in writing and communicated to the contracting states and other states entitled to become parties to the treaty, as must acceptances of, and objections to, reservations.

Most multilateral conventions today will in fact specifically declare their position as regards reservations. Some, however, for example the Geneva Convention on the High Seas, 1958, make no mention at all of reservations, while others may specify that reservations are possible with regard to certain provisions only.[58] Still others may prohibit altogether any reservations.[59] Each of these solutions to the problem of reservations is equally valid.

ENTRY INTO FORCE OF TREATIES

Basically treaties will become operative when and how the negotiating states decide, but in the absence of any provision or agreement regarding this, a treaty will enter into force as soon as consent to be bound by the treaty has been established for all the negotiating states.[60]

In many cases, treaties will specify that they will come into effect upon a certain date or after a determined period following the last ratification. It is usual where multilateral conventions are involved to provide for entry into force upon ratification by a fixed number of states. To expect every state to ratify when there may have been

---

[56] Cmnd. 7438 (1979), p.45. See also Boyle, "The Law of Treaties and the Anglo-French Continental Shelf Arbitration", 29 *ICLQ*, 1980, p.498 and Sinclair, *op. cit.*, pp.70-76.

[57] Article 20(5). See the Inter-American Court of Human Rights, Advisory Opinion on *The Effect of Reservations on the Entry into Force of the American Convention on Human Rights*, 22 *ILM*, 1983, p.37; 67 *ILR*, p.559.

[58] E.g. the 1958 Geneva Convention on the Continental Shelf, article 12(1). See also *supra*, p.572, regarding article 64 of the European Convention on Human Rights, 1950.

[59] See e.g. article 37 of the Convention on Damage Caused by Foreign Aircraft to Third Parties on the Surface, 1952.

[60] Article 24. See Sinclair, *op. cit.*, pp.44-47.

over a hundred states participating in the negotiations and signature of a treaty could well consign such a treaty to oblivion since one country alone, by withholding ratification for any reason, could disrupt the whole process.

The Geneva Convention on the High Seas 1958, for example, provides for entry into force on the thirtieth day following the deposit of the twenty-second instrument of ratification with the United Nations Secretary-General, while the Convention on the Law of Treaties itself came into effect thirty days after the deposit of the thirty-fifth ratification.

It should be remembered at this point that even though the necessary number of ratifications has been received for the treaty to come into operation, only those states that have actually ratified the treaty will be bound. It will not bind those that have merely signed it, unless of course, signature is in the particular circumstances regarded as sufficient to express the consent of the state to be bound.

Article 80 of the 1969 Convention (following article 102 of the United Nations Charter) provides that after their entry into force, treaties should be transmitted to the United Nations Secretariat for registration and publication. These provisions are intended to end the practice of secret treaties, which was regarded as contributing to the outbreak of the First World War, as well as enabling the United Nations Treaty Series, which contains all registered treaties, to be as comprehensive as possible.[61]

THE APPLICATION OF TREATIES

Once treaties enter into force, a number of questions can arise as to the way in which they apply in particular situations. In the absence of contrary intention, the treaty will not operate retroactively so that its provisions will not bind a party as regards any facts, acts or situations prior to that state's acceptance of the treaty.[62]

---

[61] Article 102 of the UN Charter also provides that states may not invoke an unregistered treaty before any UN organ.

[62] Article 28. See *Yearbook of the ILC*, 1966, vol.II, pp.212-13 and the *Mavrommatis Palestine Concessions* case, PCIJ, Series A, no.2, 1924. Note article 4 of the Convention, which provides that, without prejudice to the application of customary law, the Convention will apply only to treaties concluded by states after the entry into force of the Convention with regard to such states.

Unless a different intention appears from the treaty or is otherwise established, article 29 provides that a treaty is binding upon each party in respect of its entire territory. This is the general rule, but it is possible for a state to stipulate that an international agreement will apply only to part of its territory. In the past, so-called "colonial application clauses" were included in some treaties by the European colonial powers, which declared whether or not the terms of the particular agreement would extend to the various colonies.[63]

With regard to the problem of successive treaties on the same subject-matter, article 30 provides that:

1. Subject to article 103 of the Charter of the United Nations,[64] the rights and obligations of states parties to successive treaties relating to the same subject-matter shall be determined in accordance with the following paragraphs.

2. When a treaty specifies that it is subject to, or that it is not to be considered as incompatible with, an earlier or later treaty, the provisions of that other treaty prevail.

3. When all the parties to the earlier treaty are parties also to the later treaty but the earlier treaty is not terminated or suspended in operation under article 59,[65] the earlier treaty applies only to the extent that its provisions are compatible with those of the later treaty.

4. When the parties to the later treaty do not include all the parties to the earlier one:

(a) as between states parties to both treaties the same rule applies as in paragraph 3;

(b) as between a state party to both treaties and a state party to only one of the treaties, the treaty to which both states are parties governs their mutual rights and obligations.

5. Paragraph 4 is without prejudice to article 41,[66] or to any question of the termination or suspension of the operation of a treaty under article

---

[63] See Sinclair, *op. cit.*, pp.87-92. See also e.g. article 63 of the European Convention on Human Rights, 1950. Practice would appear to suggest that in the absence of evidence to the contrary, a treaty would under customary law apply to all the territory of a party, including colonies, see e.g. McNair, *op. cit.*, pp.116-17.

[64] This stipulates that in the event of a conflict between the obligations of a member-state of the UN under the Charter and their obligations under any other international agreement, the former shall prevail.

[65] This deals with termination or suspension of a treaty by a later treaty, see further *infra*, p.596.

[66] This deals with agreements to modify multilateral treaties between certain of the parties only, see further *infra*, p.596.

60[67] or to any question of responsibility which may arise for a state from the conclusion or application of a treaty, the provisions of which are incompatible with its obligations towards another state under another treaty.

The problem raised by successive treaties is becoming a serious one with the growth in the number of states and the increasing numbers of treaties entered into, and the added complication of enhanced activity at the regional level.[68] The general rules laid down in article 30 provide a general guide and in many cases the problem will be resolved by the parties themselves expressly.

Third States

A point of considerable interest with regard to the creation of binding rules of law for the international community centres on the application and effects of treaties upon third states, i.e. states which are not parties to the treaty in question.[69]

The general rule is that international agreements bind only the parties to them. The reasons for this rule can be found in the fundamental principles of the sovereignty and independence of states, which posit that states must consent to rules before they can be bound by them. This, of course, is a general proposition and is not necessarily true in all cases. However, it does remain as a basic line of approach in international law. Article 34 of the Convention echoes the general rule in specifying that "a treaty does not create either obligations or rights for a third state without its consent".[70]

It is quite clear that a treaty cannot impose obligations upon third states and this was emphasised by the International Law Commission during its deliberations prior to the Vienna Conferences and Convention.[71] There is, however, one major exception to this and that is where the provisions of the treaty in question have entered into customary law.[72] In such a case, all states would be bound,

---

[67] This deals with material breach of a treaty, see further *infra*, p.596.

[68] See Sinclair, *op. cit.*, pp.93-98. See also McNair, *op. cit.*, p.219 *et seq.*

[69] See e.g. Sinclair, *op. cit.*, pp.98-106. The rule is sometimes referred to by the maxim *pacta tertiis nec nocent nec prosunt.*

[70] See also *infra*, Chapter 16 on succession of states in respect of treaties.

[71] *Yearbook of the ILC,* 1966, vol.II, p.227.

[72] Article 38. See *supra*, Chapter 3, p.81, and the *North Sea Continental Shelf* cases, ICJ Reports, 1969, p.3; 41 *ILR*, p.29. See also *Yearbook of the ILC,* 1966, vol.II, p.230.

regardless of whether they had been parties to the original treaty or not. One example of this would be the laws relating to warfare adopted by the Hague Conventions earlier this century and now regarded as part of customary international law.[73]

This point arises with regard to article 2(6) of the United Nations Charter which states that:

> the organisation shall ensure that states which are not members of the United Nations act in accordance with these principles so far as may be necessary for the maintenance of international peace and security.

It is sometimes maintained that this provision creates binding obligations rather than being merely a statement of attitude with regard to non-members of the United Nations.[74] This may be the correct approach since the principles enumerated in article 2 of the Charter can be regarded as part of customary international law, and in view of the fact that an agreement may legitimately provide for enforcement sanctions to be implemented against a state guilty of aggression. Article 75 of the Convention provides:

> the provisions of the Convention are without prejudice to any obligation in relation to a treaty which may arise for an aggressor state in consequence of measures taken in conformity with the Charter of the United Nations with reference to that state's aggression.

Article 35 notes that an obligation may arise for a third state from a term of a treaty if the parties to the treaty so intend and if the third state expressly accepts that obligation in writing.[75]

As far as rights allocated to third states by a treaty are concerned, the matter is a little different. The Permanent Court of International Justice declared in the *Free Zones* case[76] that:

> the question of the existence of a right acquired under an instrument drawn between other states is . . . one to be decided in each particular case: it must be ascertained whether the states which have stipulated in

---

[73] See *infra*, Chapter 18.

[74] See e.g. Kelsen, *The Law of the United Nations*, 1950, pp.106-10. See also McNair, *op. cit.*, pp.216-18.

[75] See as to the creation here of a collateral agreement forming the basis of the obligation, *Yearbook of the ILC*, 1966, vol.II, p.227.

[76] PCIJ, Series A/B, no.46, 1932, pp.147-48; 6 *ILR*, pp.362, 364.

favour of a third state meant to create for that state an actual right which the latter has accepted as such.

Article 36 of the Vienna Convention provides that:

a right arises for a third state from a provision of a treaty if the parties to the treaty intend the provision to accord that right either to the third state, or to a group of states to which it belongs, or to all states, and the third state assents thereto. Its assent shall be presumed so long as the contrary is not indicated, unless the treaty otherwise provides.

Instances of treaties providing benefits for third states would include those establishing the legal regimes over the Suez and Kiel canals.[77] In the *Wimbledon* case,[78] the Permanent Court noted that "an international waterway . . . for the benefit of all nations of the world" had been established. In other words, for an obligation to be imposed by a treaty upon a third state, the express agreement of that state in writing is required, whereas in the case of benefits granted to third states, their assent is presumed in the absence of contrary intention. This is because the general tenor of customary international law has leaned in favour of the validity of rights granted to third states, but against that of obligations imposed upon them, in the light of basic principles relating to state sovereignty, equality and non-interference.

THE AMENDMENT AND MODIFICATION OF TREATIES

Although the two processes of amending and modifying international agreements share a common aim in that they both involve the revision of treaties, they are separate activities and may be accomplished in different manners.

Amendments refer to the formal alteration of treaty provisions, affecting all the parties to the particular agreement, while modifications relate to variations of certain treaty terms as between particular parties only.

Where it is deemed desirable, a treaty may be amended by

---

[77] See further *supra*, Chapter 8, p.312.

[78] PCIJ, Series A, no.1, 1923, p.22; 2 *ILR*, p.99. See also *Yearbook of the ILC*, 1966, vol.II, pp.228-29 and Aréchaga, "International Law in the Past Third of a Century", 159 *HR*, pp.1, 54 and "Treaty Stipulations in favour of Third States", 50 *AJIL*, 1956, pp.338, 355-56.

agreement between the parties, but in such a case all the formalities as to the conclusion and coming into effect of treaties as described so far in this chapter will have to be observed except in so far as the treaty may otherwise provide.[79] It is understandable that as time passes and conditions change, the need may arise to alter some of the provisions stipulated in the international agreement in question. There is nothing unusual in this and it is a normal facet of international relations. The fact that such alterations must be effected with the same formalities that attended the original formation of the treaty is only logical since legal rights and obligations may be involved and any variation of them involves considerations of state sovereignty and consent which necessitate careful interpretation and attention. It is possible, however, for oral or tacit agreement to amend, providing it is unambiguous and clearly evidenced.

Many multilateral treaties lay down specific conditions as regards amendment. For example, the United Nations Charter in article 108 provides that amendments will come into force for all member-states upon adoption and ratification by two-thirds of the members of the organisation, including all the permanent members of the Security Council.

Problems can occur where, in the absence of specific amendment processes, some of the parties oppose the amendments proposed by others. Article 40 of the Vienna Convention specifies the procedure to be adopted in amending multilateral treaties, in the absence of contrary provisions in the treaty itself. Any proposed amendment has to be notified to all contracting states, each one of which is entitled to participate in the decision as to action to be taken and in the negotiation and conclusion of any agreements. Every state which has the right to be a party to the treaty possesses also the right to become a party to the amendment, but such amendments will not bind any state which is a party to the original agreement and which does not become a party to the amended agreement,[80] subject to any provisions to the contrary in the treaty itself.

The situation can become a little more complex where a state becomes a party to the treaty after the amendments have come into effect. That state will be a party to the amended agreement, except

---

[79] Article 39. See also Sinclair, *op. cit.*, pp.106-9; and *Yearbook of the ILC*, 1966, vol.II, p.232.
[80] See article 30(4)b.

as regards parties to the treaty that are not bound by the amendments. In this case the state will be considered as a party to the unamended treaty in relation to those states.

Two or more parties to a multilateral treaty may decide to change that agreement as between themselves in certain ways, quite irrespective of any amendment by all the parties. This technique, known as modification, is possible provided it has not been prohibited by the treaty in question and provided it does not affect the rights or obligations of the other parties. Modification, however, is not possible where the provision it is intended to alter is one "derogation from which is incompatible with the effective execution of the object and purpose of the treaty as a whole".[81] A treaty may also be modified by the terms of another later agreement[82] or by the establishment subsequently of a rule of *jus cogens*.[83]

TREATY INTERPRETATION[84]

One of the enduring problems facing courts and tribunals and lawyers, both in the municipal and international law spheres, relates to the question of interpretation.[85]

Accordingly, rules and techniques have been put forward to aid judicial bodies in resolving such problems.[86] As far as international law is concerned, there are three basic approaches to treaty interpretation.[87] The first centres on the actual text of the agreement and emphasises the analysis of the words used.[88] The second looks to the intention of the parties adopting the agreement as the

---

[81] Article 41.

[82] See article 30, and *supra*, p.578.

[83] See *supra*, Chapter 3, p.98 and *infra*, p.593.

[84] See e.g. Sinclair, *op. cit.*, Chapter 5; Fitzmaurice, "The Law and Procedure of the International Court of Justice, 1951-4", 33 *BYIL*, 1957, p.203 and 28 *BYIL*, 1951, p.1; Lauterpacht, "Restrictive Interpretation and the Principle of Effectiveness in the Interpretation of Treaties", 26 *BYIL*, 1949, p.48; McDougal, Lasswell and Miller, *The Interpretation of Agreements and World Public Order*, 1969; Gordon, "The World Court and the Interpretation of Constitutive Treaties", 59 *AJIL*, 1965, p.794; O'Connell, *op. cit.*, p.251 *et seq.* and Brownlie, *op. cit.*, p.626 *et seq.*

[85] Note that a unilateral interpretation of a treaty by the organs of one state would not be binding upon the other parties, see McNair, *op. cit.*, pp.345-50 and the *David J. Adams* claim, 6 *RIAA*, p.85 (1921); 1 *ILR*, p.331.

[86] But see Stone, "Fictional Elements in Treaty Interpretation", 1 *Sydney Law Review*, 1955, p.344.

[87] See Sinclair, *op. cit.*, pp.114-15 and Fitzmaurice, 1951, *op. cit.*

[88] See Fitzmaurice, 1957, *op. cit.*, pp.204-7.

solution to ambiguous provisions and can be termed the subjective approach in contradistinction to the objective approach of the previous school.[89] The third approach adopts a wider perspective than the other two and emphasises the objects and purpose of the treaty as the most important backcloth against which the meaning of any particular treaty provision should be measured.[90] This teleological school of thought has the effect of underlining the role of the judge or arbitrator, since he will be called upon to define the object and purpose of the treaty and it has been criticised for encouraging judicial lawmaking.

Nevertheless, any true interpretation of a treaty in international law will have to take into account all aspects of the agreement, from the words employed to the intention of the parties and the aims of the particular document. It is not possible to exclude completely any one of these components.

Articles 31 to 33 of the Vienna Convention comprise in some measure aspects of all three doctrines. Article 31(1) declares that a treaty shall be interpreted "in good faith in accordance with the ordinary meaning to be given to the terms of the treaty in their context and in the light of its object and purpose". The International Court noted in the *Competence of the General Assembly for the Admission of a State to the United Nations* case[91] that "the first duty of a tribunal which is called upon to interpret and apply the provisions of a treaty is to endeavour to give effect to them in their natural and ordinary meaning in the context in which they occur".[92] On the basis of this provision, for example, the European Court of Human Rights held in the *Lithgow* case[93] that the use of the phrase "subject to the conditions provided for ... by the general principles of international law" in article 1 of Protocol I of the European Convention in the context of compensation for interference with property rights, could not be interpreted as extending the general principles of international law in this field to establish standards of compensation for the nationalisation of property of nationals (as distinct from

---

[89] See e.g. Lauterpacht, "De l'Interprétation des Traités: Rapport et Projet de Résolutions", 43 *Annuaire de l'Institut de Droit International*, 1950, p.366.

[90] See e.g. Fitzmaurice, 1951, *op. cit.*, pp.7-8 and 13-14 and 1957, *op. cit.*, pp.207-9.

[91] ICJ Reports, 1950, pp.4, 8; 17 *ILR*, pp.326, 328.

[92] See also the *La Bretagne* arbitration (*Canada* v. *France*), 82 *ILR*, pp.590, 620.

[93] European Court of Human Rights, Series A, No.102, para.114; 75 *ILR*, pp.438, 482.

aliens).[94] The word "context" is held to include the preamble
and annexes of the treaty as well as any agreement or
instrument made by the parties in connection with the
conclusion of the treaty.[95] In addition, any subsequent agreement
or practice relating to the treaty together with any relevant
rules of international law must be considered together with the
context.[96]

The latter provision, whereby any relevant rules of international law applicable in the relations between the parties shall
be taken into account in interpreting a treaty, was applied in *Iran
v. United States*,[97] which was concerned with the question whether
a dual Iran-US national could bring a claim against Iran before
the Iran-US Claims Tribunal where the Claims Settlement
Agreement 1981 simply defined a US national as a "natural person
who is a citizen of . . . the United States".[98] The Full Tribunal
held that jurisdiction existed over claims against Iran by dual Iran-
US nationals when the dominant and effective nationality of the
claimant at the relevant period was that of the US. In reaching
this decision, the Tribunal cited article 31(3)c of the 1969 Vienna
Convention as the mechanism whereby the considerable body of
law and legal literature in the area could be analysed in the
context of interpreting the 1981 agreement and which led it to its
conclusion.

Where the interpretation according to the provisions of article
31 needs confirmation, or determination since the meaning is
ambiguous or obscure, or leads to a manifestly absurd or
unreasonable result, recourse may be had to supplementary
means of interpretation under article 32. These means include
the preparatory works (*travaux préparatoires*) of the treaty and the
circumstances of its conclusion and may be employed in the above

---

[94] See also the *James* case, European Court of Human Rights, Series A, No.98, para.61;
75 *ILR*, pp.397, 423 and the Advisory Opinions of the Inter-American Court of Human Rights
in the *Enforceability of the Right to Reply* case, 79 *ILR*, pp.335, 343, and the *Meaning of the Word
"Laws"* case, *ibid.*, pp.325, 329.

[95] Article 31(2). See also the *US Nationals in Morocco* case, ICJ Reports, 1952, pp.176, 196;
19 *ILR*, pp.255, 272; the *Beagle Channel* case, HMSO, 1977, p.12; 52 *ILR*, p.93 and the *Young
Loan* arbitration, 59 *ILR*, pp.495, 530.

[96] Article 31(3)a-c.

[97] Case No. A/18, 5 *Iran-US CTR*, p.251; 75 *ILR*, pp.175, 188.

[98] Article VII(1)a.

circumstances to aid the process of interpreting the treaty in question.[99]

Case-law provides some interesting guidelines to the above-stated rules. In the *Interpretation of Peace Treaties* case,[100] the Court was asked whether the UN Secretary-General could appoint the third member of a Treaty Commission upon the request of one side to the dispute where the other side (Bulgaria, Hungary and Romania) refused to appoint its own representative. It was emphasised that the natural and ordinary meaning of the terms of the Peace Treaties with the three states concerned envisaged the appointment of the third member after the other two had been nominated. The breach of a treaty obligation could not be remedied by creating a Commission which was not the kind of Commission envisaged by the Treaties. The principle of effectiveness could not be used by the Court to attribute to the provisions for the settlement of disputes in the Peace Treaties a meaning which would be contrary to their letter and spirit. The Court also stressed the nature of the disputes clause as being one that had to be strictly construed. Thus, the character of the provisions to be interpreted is significant in the context of utilising the relevant rules of interpretation.

The principle of effectiveness will be used, however, in order to give effect to provisions in accordance with the intentions of the parties.[101]

In two areas, it should be noted, the principle of effectiveness allied with the broader purposes approach has been used in an especially dynamic manner. In the case of treaties that also operate as the constitutional documents of an international organisation, a more flexible method of interpretation would seem to be justified, since one is dealing with an instrument that is being used in order to accomplish the stated aims of that organisation. In addition, of

---

[99] See *Yearbook of the ILC*, 1966, vol.II, p.223, doubting the rule in the *River Oder* case, PCIJ, Series A, no.23, 1929; 5 *ILR*, pp.381, 383, that the *travaux préparatoires* of certain provisions of the Treaty of Versailles could not be taken into account since three of the states before the Court had not participated in the preparatory conference. See also the *Young Loan* case, 59 *ILR*, pp.495, 544-45 and Sinclair, *op. cit.*, pp.141-47, and the *Lithgow* case, European Court of Human Rights, Series A, No.102, para.117; 75 *ILR*, pp.438, 484.

[100] ICJ Reports, 1950, pp.221, 226-30; 17 *ILR*, pp.318, 320-22. See also *Yearbook of the ILC*, 1966, vol.II, p.220.

[101] See e.g. the *Ambatielos* case, ICJ Reports, 1952, p.28; 19 *ILR*, p.416. See also the *Corfu Channel* case, ICJ Reports, 1949, pp.4, 24; 16 *ILR*, pp.155, 169 and *Yearbook of the ILC*, 1966, vol.II, p.219.

course, the concept and nature of subsequent practice possesses in such cases an added relevance.[102] This approach has been used as a way of inferring powers, not expressly provided for in the relevant instruments, which are deemed necessary in the context of the purposes of the organisation.[103] This programmatic interpretation doctrine in such cases is now well established and especially relevant to the United Nations, where forty years of practice related to the principles of the organisation by nearly one hundred and sixty states is manifest.

The more dynamic approach to interpretation is also evident in the context of the European Convention on Human Rights which created a system of implementation.[104] It has been held that a particular legal order was thereby established involving objective obligations to protect human rights rather than subjective, reciprocal rights.[105] Accordingly, a more flexible and programmatic or purpose-oriented method of interpretation was adopted, emphasising that the Convention constituted a living instrument that had to be interpreted "in the light of present-day conditions".[106]

Indeed, in this context, it was noted in the *Licensing of Journalists* case[107] that while it was useful to compare the Inter-American Convention on Human Rights with other relevant international

[102] Note that by article 5, the Vienna Convention is deemed to apply to any treaty which is the constituent instrument of an international organisation. See also Shaw, *Title to Territory in Africa*, 1986, pp.64-73 and Rosenne, "Is the Constitution of an International Organisation an International Treaty?", 12 *Communicazioni e Studi*, 1966, p.21.

[103] See e.g. the *Reparation* case, ICJ Reports 1949, p.174; 16 *ILR*, p.318; the *Certain Expenses of the UN* case, ICJ Reports, 1962, p.151; 34 *ILR*, p.281; the *Competence of the General Assembly for the Admission of a State* case, ICJ Reports, 1950, p.4; 17 *ILR*, p.326 and the *Namibia* case, ICJ Reports, 1971, p.16; 49 *ILR*, p.2. See further Shaw, *op. cit.* and Higgins, "The Development of International Law by the Political Organs of the United Nations", *PASIL*, 1965, p.119.

[104] See further, *supra*, Chapter 6, p.221.

[105] See e.g. *Austria* v. *Italy*, 4 *European Yearbook of Human Rights*, 1960, pp.116, 140. See also the Advisory Opinion of the Inter-American Court of Human Rights on the *Effect of Reservations on the Entry into Force of the American Convention on Human Rights*, 22 *ILM*, 1983, pp.37, 47; 67 *ILR*, pp.559, 568, which adopted a similar approach.

[106] See e.g. the *Tyrer* case, European Court of Human Rights, Series A, no.26, at p.15 (1978); 58 *ILR*, pp.339, 553; the *Marckx* case, *ibid.*, no.32, at p.14 (1979); 58 *ILR*, pp.561, 583 and the *Wemhoff* case, *ibid.*, no.7, (1968); 41 *ILR*, p.281. See also Waldock, "The Evolution of Human Rights Concepts and the Application of the European Convention on Human Rights" in *Mélanges Offerts à Paul Reuter*, 1981, p.535.

[107] Advisory Opinion of the Inter-American Court of Human Rights, 1985, 75 *ILR*, pp.30, 47-48.

instruments, this approach could not be utilised to read into the Convention restrictions existing in other treaties. In this situation, "the rule most favourable to the individual must prevail".

Article 31(4) provides that a special meaning shall be given to a term if it is established that the parties so intended. It would appear that the standard of proof is fairly high, since a derogation from the ordinary meaning of the term is involved. It is not enough that one party only uses the particular term in a particular way.[108]

Where a treaty is authenticated in more than one language, as often happens with multilateral agreements, article 33 provides that, in the absence of agreement, in the event of a difference of meaning that the normal processes of interpretation cannot resolve, the meaning which best reconciles the texts, having regard to the object and purpose of the treaty, shall be adopted.[109]

INVALIDITY, TERMINATION AND SUSPENSION OF THE OPERATION OF TREATIES

General Provisions

Article 42 states that the validity and continuance in force of a treaty may only be questioned on the basis of the provisions in the Vienna Convention.

Article 44 provides that a state may only withdraw from or suspend the operation of a treaty in respect of the treaty as a whole and not particular parts of it, unless the treaty otherwise stipulates or the parties otherwise agree. If the appropriate ground for invalidating, terminating, withdrawing from or suspending the operation of a treaty relates solely to particular clauses, it may only be invoked in relation to those clauses where:

(a) the said clauses are separable from the remainder of the treaty with regard to their application;

(b) it appears from the treaty or is otherwise established that acceptance of those clauses was not an essential basis of consent of the other party or parties to be bound by the treaty as a whole; and

---

[108] See the *Eastern Greenland* case, PCIJ, Series A/B, no.53, 1933, p.49; 6 *ILR*, p.95 and the *Anglo-French Continental Shelf* case, Cmnd. 7438, p.50; 54 *ILR*, p.6.

[109] See the *Mavrommatis Palestine Concessions* case, PCIJ, Series A, no.2, p.19, which called for the more restrictive interpretation in such cases and the *Young Loan* case, 59 *ILR*, p.495.

(c) continued performance of the remainder of the treaty would not be unjust.

Thus the Convention adopts a cautious approach to the general issue of separability of treaty provisions in this context.[110]

Article 45 in essence provides that a ground for invalidity, termination, withdrawal or suspension may no longer be invoked by the state where after becoming aware of the facts, it expressly agreed that the treaty is valid or remains in force or by reason of its conduct may be deemed to have acquiesced in the validity of the treaty or its continuance in force.[111]

Invalidity of Treaties

Municipal law

A state cannot plead a breach of its constitutional provisions as to the making of treaties as a valid excuse for condemning an agreement. There has been for some years disagreement amongst international lawyers as to whether the failure to abide by a domestic legal limitation by, for example, a head of state in entering into a treaty, will result in rendering the agreement invalid or not.[112] The Convention took the view that in general it would not, but that it could in certain circumstances.

Article 46 provides that:

> [a] state may not invoke the fact that its consent to be bound by a treaty has been expressed in violation of a provision of its internal law regarding competence to conclude treaties as invalidating its consent unless that violation was manifest and concerned a rule of its internal law of fundamental importance.

Violation will be regarded as manifest if it would be "objectively

---

[110] See Judge Lauterpacht, the *Norwegian Loans* case, ICJ Reports, 1957, pp.9, 55-59; 24 *ILR*, pp.782, 809 and Sinclair, *op. cit.*, pp.165-67.

[111] See e.g. the *Arbitral Award by the King of Spain* case, ICJ Reports, 1960, pp.192, 213-14; 30 *ILR*, pp.457, 473 and the *Temple* case, ICJ Reports, 1962, pp.6, 23-32; 33 *ILR*, pp.48, 62. See also the *Argentina-Chile* case, 38 *ILR*, p.10 and *supra*, Chapter 8.

[112] See Sinclair, *op. cit.*, pp.169-171, distinguishing between the constitutionalist and internationalist schools, and Holloway, *Modern Trends in Treaty Law*, 1967, pp.123-33. See also *Yearbook of the ILC*, 1966, vol.II, pp.240-41.

evident" to any state conducting itself in the matter in accordance with normal practice, and in good faith.

For example, where the representative of the state has had his authority to consent on behalf of the state made subject to a specific restriction which is ignored, the state will still be bound by that consent save where the other negotiating states were aware of the restriction placed upon his authority to consent prior to the expression of that consent.[113]

This particular provision applies as regards a person authorised to represent a state and such persons are defined in article 7 to include heads of state and government and foreign ministers in addition to persons possessing full powers.[114]

It should, of course, also be noted that a state may not invoke a provision of its internal law as a justification for its failure to carry out an international obligation. This is a general principle of international law[115] and finds its application in the law of treaties by virtue of article 27 of the 1969 Vienna Convention.

Error

Unlike the role of mistake in municipal laws of contract, the scope in international law of error as invalidating a state's consent is rather limited. In view of the character of states and the multiplicity of persons actually dealing with the negotiation and conclusion of treaties, errors are not very likely to happen, whether they be unilateral or mutual.

Article 48 declares that a state may only invoke an error in a treaty as invalidating its consent to be bound by the treaty, if the error relates to a fact or situation which was assumed by that state to exist at the time when the treaty was concluded and formed an essential basis of its consent to be bound by the treaty. But if the state knew or ought to have known of the error, or if it contributed

---

[113] Article 47. See e.g. the *Eastern Greenland* case, PCIJ, Series A/B, no.53, 1933; 6 *ILR*, p.95.

[114] *Supra*, p.564.

[115] See e.g. the *Alabama Claims* arbitration, Moore, *International Arbitrations*, vol.1, p.495 and the *Greco-Bulgarian Communities* case, PCIJ, Series B, No.17, p.32; 5 *ILR*, p.4. This has been recently reaffirmed in the *Applicability of the Obligation to Arbitrate under Section 21 of the United Nations Headquarters Agreement* case, ICJ Reports, 1988, pp.12, 34-35; 82 *ILR*, pp.225, 252.

to that error, then it cannot afterwards free itself from the obligation of observing the treaty by pointing to that error.

This restrictive approach is in harmony with the comments made in a number of cases, including the *Temple* case,[116] where the International Court of Justice rejected Thailand's argument that a particular map contained a basic error and therefore it was not bound to observe it, since "the plea of error cannot be allowed as an element vitiating consent if the party advancing it contributed by its own conduct to the error, or could have avoided it, or if the circumstances were such as to put that party on notice of a possible error".[117] The Court felt that in view of the character and qualifications of the persons who were involved on the Thai side in examining the map, Thailand could not put forward a claim of error.

Fraud and Corruption

Where a state consents to be bound by a treaty as a result of the fraudulent conduct of another negotiating state, that state may under article 49 invoke the fraud as invalidating its consent to be bound. Where a negotiating state directly or indirectly corrupts the representative of another state in order to obtain the consent of the latter to the treaty, that corruption may under article 50 be invoked as invalidating the consent to be bound.[118]

Coercion

Of more importance than error, fraud or corruption in the law of treaties is the issue of coercion as invalidating consent. Where consent has been obtained by coercing the representative of a state, whether by acts or threats directed against him, it shall, according to article 51 of the Convention, be without any legal effect.

The problem of consent obtained by the application of coercion against the state itself is a slightly different one. Prior to the League of Nations, it was clear that international law did not provide for the invalidation of treaties on the grounds of the use or threat of

---

[116] ICJ Reports, 1960, p.6; 33 *ILR*, p.48.

[117] *Ibid.*, p.26; 33 *ILR*, p.65.

[118] Such instances are very rare in practice, see *Yearbook of the ILC*, 1966, vol.II, pp.244-45 and Sinclair, *op. cit.*, pp.173-76.

force by one party against the other and this was a consequence of the lack of rules in customary law prohibiting recourse to war. With the signing of the Covenant of the League in 1919, and the Kellogg-Briand Pact in 1928 forbidding the resort to war to resolve international disputes, a new approach began to be taken with regard to the illegality of the use of force in international relations.

With the elucidation of the Nuremberg principles and the coming into effect of the Charter of the United Nations after the Second World War, it became clear that international law condemned coercive activities by states.

Article 2(4) of the United Nations Charter provides that:

> [a]ll members shall refrain in their international relations from the threat or use of force against the territorial integrity or political independence of any state, or in any other measure inconsistent with the purposes of the United Nations.

It followed that treaties based on coercion of a state should be regarded as invalid.[119]

Accordingly, article 52 of the Convention provides that "[a] treaty is void if its conclusion has been procured by the threat or use of force in violation of the principles of international law embodied in the Charter of the United Nations". This article was the subject of much debate in the Vienna Conference preceding the adoption of the Convention. Communist and certain Third World countries argued that coercion comprised not only the threat or use of force but also economic and political pressures.[120] The International Law Commission did not take a firm stand on the issue, but noted that the precise scope of the acts covered by the definition should be left to be determined in practice by interpretation of the relevant Charter provisions.[121]

The Vienna Conference came some way to accepting the approach of the communist and Third World states by issuing a Declaration on the Prohibition of Military, Political or Economic Coercion in the Conclusion of Treaties, which condemned the exercise of such

[119] See *Yearbook of the ILC*, 1966, vol.II, pp.246-47. See also the *Fisheries Jurisdiction* case, ICJ Reports, 1973, pp.3, 14; 55 *ILR*, pp.183, 194.
[120] See Sinclair, *op. cit.*, pp.177-79.
[121] *Yearbook of the ILC*, 1966, vol.II, pp.246-47.

coercion to procure the formation of a treaty. These points were not included in the Convention itself, which leaves one to conclude that the application of political or economic pressure to secure the consent of a state to a treaty may not be contrary to international law, but clearly a lot will depend upon the relevant circumstances.

In international relations, the variety of influences which may be brought to bear by a powerful state against a weaker one to induce it to adopt a particular line of policy is wide-ranging and may cover not only coercive threats but also subtle expressions of displeasure. The precise nuances of any particular situation will depend on a number of factors, and it will be misleading to suggest that all forms of pressure are as such violations of international law.

The problem was noted by Judge Padilla Nervo in the International Court in the *Fisheries Jurisdiction* case[122] when he stated that:

> there are moral and political pressures which cannot be proved by the so-called documentary evidence, but which are in fact indisputably real and which have, in history, given rise to treaties and conventions claimed to be freely concluded and subjected to the principle of *pacta sunt servanda*.[123]

It should also be noted that the phrase "in violation of the principles of international law embodied in the Charter" was used so that article 52 should by no means be construed as applying solely to members of the United Nations but should be treated as a universal rule.

Jus Cogens [124]

Article 53 of the Convention provides that:

---

[122] ICJ Reports, 1973, p.3; 55 *ILR*, p.183.

[123] *Ibid.*, p.47; 55 *ILR*, p.227.

[124] See e.g. Sztucki, *Jus Cogens and the Vienna Convention on the Law of Treaties*, 1974; Rozakis, *The Concept of Jus Cogens in the Law of Treaties*, 1976; Hannikainen, *Peremptory Norms (Jus Cogens) in International Law*, 1988; Robledo, "Le *Jus Cogens* International: Sa Genèse, Sa Nature, Ses Fonctions", 172 *HR*, p.9; Alexidze, "Legal Nature of *Jus Cogens* in Contemporary International Law'", *ibid.*, p.219 and Gaja, "*Jus Cogens* Beyond the Vienna Convention", *ibid.*, p.271. See also *Yearbook of the ILC*, 1966, vol.II, pp.247-48 and Sinclair, *op. cit.*, Chapter 7.

[a] treaty is void if, at the time of its conclusion, it conflicts with a peremptory norm of general international law. For the purposes of the present Convention, a peremptory norm of general international law is a norm accepted and recognised by the international community of states as a whole as a norm from which no derogation is permitted, and which can be modified only by a subsequent norm of general international law having the same character.

Article 64 declares that "(i)f a new peremptory norm of general international law emerges, any existing treaty which is in conflict with that norm becomes void and terminates".[125]

As noted in Chapter 3,[126] the concept of *jus cogens*, of fundamental and entrenched rules of international law, is well established in doctrine now, but controversial as to content and method of creation. The insertion of articles dealing with *jus cogens* in the 1969 Convention underlines the basic principles with regard to treaties.

Consequences of Invalidity

Article 69 provides that an invalid treaty is void and without legal force. If acts have nevertheless been performed in reliance on such a treaty, each party may require any other party to establish as far as possible in their mutual relations the position that would have existed if the acts had not been performed. Acts performed in good faith before the invalidity was invoked are not rendered unlawful by reason only of the invalidity of the treaty.

Where a treaty is void under article 53, article 71 provides that the parties are to eliminate as far as possible the consequences of any act performed in reliance on any provision which conflicts with *jus cogens* and bring their mutual relations into conformity with the peremptory norm. Where a treaty terminates under article 64, the parties are released from any obligation further to perform the treaty, but this does not affect any right, obligation or legal situation of the parties created through the execution of the treaty prior to its termination, provided that the rights, obligations or situations may be maintained thereafter in conformity with the new peremptory norm.

---

[125] See also article 71 and *infra*, pp.599-600.
[126] *Supra*, p.98.

The Termination of Treaties [127]

There are a number of methods available by which treaties may be terminated or suspended.

Termination by Treaty Provision or Consent

A treaty may be terminated or suspended in accordance with a specific provision in that treaty, or otherwise at any time by consent of all the parties after consultation.[128]

Where, however, a treaty contains no provision regarding termination and does not provide for denunciation or withdrawal specifically, a state may only denounce or withdraw from that treaty where the parties intended to admit such a possibility or where the right may be implied by the nature of the treaty.[129]

A treaty may, of course, come to an end if its purposes and objects have been fulfilled or if it is clear from its provisions that it is limited in time and the requisite period has elapsed. The Tribunal in the *Rainbow Warrior* case[130] held that the breach of the New Zealand-France Agreement 1986, concerning the two captured French agents that had sunk the vessel in question,[131] had commenced on 22 July 1986 and had run continuously for the three years period of confinement of the agents stipulated in the agreement. Accordingly, the period concerned had expired on 22 July 1989, so that France could not be said to be in breach of its international obligations after that date. However, this did not exempt France from responsibility for its previous breaches of its obligations, committed while these obligations were in force. Claims arising out of a previous infringement of a treaty which has since expired acquire an existence independent of that treaty.[132] The termination of a treaty does not affect any right, obligation or legal situation

[127] See e.g. David, *The Strategy of Treaty Termination*, 1975; Vamvoukis, *Termination of Treaties in International Law*, 1985, and Plender, "The Role of Consent in the Termination of Treaties", 57 *BYIL*, 1986, p.133.

[128] Articles 54 and 57.

[129] Article 56. Examples given by Brierly, *The Law of Nations*, 6th ed., 1963, p.331, include treaties of alliance and commerce.

[130] 82 *ILR*, pp.499, 567-68.

[131] See *supra* p.483.

[132] See the dissenting opinion of Judge McNair in the *Ambatielos* case, ICJ Reports, 1952, pp.28, 63; 19 *ILR*, pp.416, 433.

of the parties created through the execution of the treaty prior to its termination.[133]

Just as two or more parties to a multilateral treaty may modify as between themselves particular provisions of the agreement,[134] so they may under article 58 agree to suspend the operation of treaty provisions temporarily and as between themselves alone if such a possibility is provided for by the treaty. Such suspension may also be possible under that article, where not prohibited by the treaty in question, provided it does not affect the rights or obligations of the other parties under the particular agreement and provided it is not incompatible with the object and purpose of the treaty.

Where all the parties to a treaty later conclude another agreement relating to the same subject-matter, the earlier treaty will be regarded as terminated where it appears that the matter is to be governed by the later agreement or where the provisions of the later treaty are so incompatible with those of the earlier one that the two treaties are not capable of being applied at the same time.[135]

Material Breach[136]

There are two viewpoints here to be considered. First, if one state violates an important provision in an agreement, it is not unnatural for the other states concerned to regard that agreement as ended by it. It is in effect a reprisal, a rather unsubtle but effective means of ensuring the enforcement of a treaty. The fact that an agreement may be terminated where it is breached by one party may act as a discouragement to any party that might contemplate a breach of one provision but would be unwilling to forgo the benefits prescribed in others. On the other hand, there is the second point to consider, that to render treaties revocable because one party has acted contrary to what might very well be only a minor provision in the agreement taken as a whole, would be to place the states participating in a treaty in rather a vulnerable position. There is a need for flexibility as well as certainty in such situations.

Customary law supports the view that something more than a mere breach itself of a term in an agreement would be necessary to give

[133] Article 70(1)b of the 1969 Vienna Convention. See *infra* p.600.
[134] Article 41 and *supra*, p.583.
[135] Article 59.
[136] See e.g. Rosenne, *Breach of Treaty*, 1985.

the other party or parties the right to abrogate that agreement. In the *Tacna-Arica* arbitration,[137] between Chile and Peru, the arbitrator noted, in referring to an agreement about a plebiscite in former Peruvian territory occupied by Chile, that:

> [i]t is manifest that if abuses of administration could have the effect of terminating such an agreement, it would be necessary to establish such serious conditions as the consequence of administrative wrongs as would operate to frustrate the purpose of the agreement.[138]

Article 60(3) of the Vienna Convention declares that a material breach of a treaty consists in either a repudiation of the treaty not permitted by the Vienna Convention or the violation of a provision essential to the accomplishment of the object or purpose of the treaty.[139]

The second part of article 60(3) was applied in the *Rainbow Warrior* case,[140] where the obligation to confine the two French agents in question on a Pacific Island for a minimum period of three years was held to have constituted the object or purpose of the New Zealand-France Agreement 1986 so that France committed a material breach of this treaty by permitting the agents to leave the island before the expiry of the three year period.

Where such a breach occurs in a bilateral treaty, then under article 60(1) the innocent party may invoke that breach as a ground for terminating the treaty or suspending its operation in whole or in part. On the other hand, in the case of a multilateral treaty, a rather different situation obtains since a number of innocent parties are involved that might not wish the treaty to be denounced by one of them because of a breach by another state. To cover such situations, article 60(2) prescribes that a material breach of a multilateral treaty by one of the parties entitles:

> (a) the other parties by unanimous agreement to suspend the operation of the treaty in whole or in part or to terminate it either:
> (i) in the relations between themselves and the defaulting state, or
> (ii) as between all the parties;

---

[137] 2 *RIAA*, p.921 (1925).
[138] *Ibid.*, pp.943-44.
[139] See the *Namibia* case, ICJ Reports, 1971, pp.16, 46-47; 49 *ILR*, pp.2, 37.
[140] 82 *ILR*, pp.499, 564-66.

(b) a party specially affected by the breach to invoke it as a ground for suspending the operation of the treaty in whole or in part in the relations between itself and the defaulting state;

(c) any party other than the defaulting state to invoke the breach as a ground for suspending the operation of the treaty in whole or in part with respect to itself if the treaty is of such a character that a material breach of its provisions by one party radically changes the position of every party with respect to the further performance of its obligations under the treaty.[141]

It is interesting to note that the provisions of article 60 regarding the definition and consequences of a material breach do not apply, by article 60(5), to provisions relating to the "protection of the human person contained in treaties of a humanitarian character, in particular to provisions prohibiting any form of reprisals against persons protected by such treaties". This is because objective and absolute principles are involved and not just reciprocal rights and duties.[142]

Supervening Impossibility of Performance [143]

Article 61 of the Convention is intended to cover such situations as the submergence of an island, or the drying up of a river where the consequence of such events is to render the performance of the treaty impossible. Where the carrying out of the terms of the agreement becomes impossible because of the permanent destruction or disappearance of an object indispensable for the execution of the treaty, a party may validly terminate or withdraw from it. However, where the impossibility is only temporary, it may be invoked solely to suspend the operation of the treaty.

Impossibility cannot be used in this way where it arises from the breach by the party attempting to terminate or suspend the agreement of a treaty or other international obligation owed to any other party to the treaty.[144]

---

[141] See *Yearbook of the ILC*, 1966, vol.II, pp.253-55. See also the *Namibia* case, ICJ Reports, 1971, pp.16, 47; 49 *ILR*, p.37 and the *US-France Air Services Agreement* case, 54 *ILR*, pp.304, 331.

[142] See e.g. Fitzmaurice, "General Principles of International Law Considered from the Standpoint of the Rule of Law", 92 *HR*, pp.1, 125-26 and *supra*, Chapter 6.

[143] See e.g. McNair, *op. cit.*, pp.685-88 and Sinclair, *op. cit.*, pp.190-92.

[144] See *Yearbook of the ILC*, 1966, vol.II, p.256.

Fundamental Change of Circumstances [145]

There is a principle in customary international law that where there has been a fundamental change of circumstances since an agreement was concluded, a party to that agreement may withdraw from or terminate it. This is known as the doctrine of *rebus sic stantibus*. It is justified by the fact that some treaties may remain in force for long periods of time, during which fundamental changes might have occurred. Such changes might encourage one of the parties to adopt drastic measures in the face of a general refusal to accept an alteration in the terms of the treaty.

However, this doctrine has been criticised on the grounds that, having regard to the absence of any system for compulsory jurisdiction in the international order, it could operate as a disrupting influence upon the binding force of obligations undertaken by states. It might be used to justify withdrawal from treaties on rather tenuous grounds.[146]

The modern approach is to admit the existence of the doctrine, but severely restrict its scope.[147] The International Court in the *Fisheries Jurisdiction* case[148] declared that:

[i]nternational law admits that a fundamental change in the circumstances which determined the parties to accept a treaty, if it has resulted in a radical transformation of the extent of the obligations imposed by it, may, under certain conditions, afford the party affected a ground for invoking the termination or suspension of the treaty.[149]

Before the doctrine may be applied, the Court continued, it is necessary that such changes "must have increased the burden of the obligations to be executed to the extent of rendering the

---

[145] See e.g. Hill, *The Doctrine of Rebus Sic Stantibus in International Law*, 1934; Lissitzyn, "Treaties and Changed Circumstances (*Rebus Sic Stantibus*)", 61 *AJIL*, 1967, p.895 and Vamvoukis, *op. cit.*, Part 1. See also *Yearbook of the ILC*, 1966, vol.II, p.257 *et seq*. Note the decision in *TWA Inc.* v. *Franklin Mint Corporation*, 23 *ILM*, 1984, pp.814, 820, that a private person could not plead the *rebus* rule.

[146] This was apparently occurring in the immediate pre-1914 period, see Garner, "The Doctrine of *Rebus Sic Stantibus* and the Termination of Treaties", 21 *AJIL*, 1927, p.409 and Sinclair, *op. cit.*, p.193. See also Harastzi, "Treaties and the Fundamental Change of Circumstances", 146 *HR*, p.1.

[147] See e.g. the *Free Zones* case, PCIJ, Series A/B, No.46, pp.156-58; 3 *ILR*, pp.362, 365.

[148] ICJ Reports, 1973, p.3; 55 *ILR*, p.183.

[149] *Ibid.*, pp.20-21; 55 *ILR*, p.200.

performance something essentially different from that originally undertaken".[150]

Article 62 of the Vienna Convention, which the International Court of Justice regarded in many respects as a codification of existing customary law,[151] declares that:

1. A fundamental change of circumstances which has occurred with regard to those existing at the time of the conclusion of a treaty, and which was not foreseen by the parties, may not be invoked as a ground for terminating or withdrawing from the treaty unless:

(a) the existence of those circumstances constituted an essential basis of the consent of the parties to be bound by the treaty; and

(b) the effect of the change is radically to transform the extent of obligations still to be performed under the treaty.

2. A fundamental change of circumstances may not be invoked as a ground for terminating or withdrawing from a treaty:

(a) if the treaty establishes a boundary; or

(b) if the fundamental change is the result of a breach by the party invoking it either of an obligation under the treaty or of any other international obligation owed to any other party to the treaty.

The article also notes that instead of terminating or withdrawing from a treaty in the above circumstances, a party might suspend the operation of the treaty.

Consequences of the Termination or Suspension of a Treaty

Article 70 provides that:

1. Unless the treaty otherwise provides or the parties otherwise agree, the termination of a treaty under its provisions or in accordance with the present Convention:

(a) releases the parties from any obligation further to perform the treaty;

(b) does not affect any right, obligation or legal situation of the parties created through the execution of the treaty prior to its termination.

2. If a state denounces or withdraws from a multilateral treaty, paragraph 1 applies in the relations between that state and each of the

---

[150] *Ibid.*
[151] *Ibid.*

other parties to the treaty from the date when such denunciation or withdrawal takes effect.

Article 72 provides that:

1. Unless the treaty otherwise provides or the parties otherwise agree, the suspension of the operation of a treaty under its provisions or in accordance with the present Convention:

(a) releases the parties between which the operation of the treaty is suspended from the obligation to perform the treaty in their mutual relations during the period of the suspension;

(b) does not otherwise affect the legal relations between the parties established by the treaty.

2. During the period of the suspension the parties shall refrain from acts tending to obstruct the resumption of the operation of the treaty.[152]

DISPUTE SETTLEMENT

Article 66 provides that if a dispute has not been resolved within 12 months by the means specified in article 33 of the UN Charter[153] then further procedures will be followed. If the dispute concerns article 53 or 64 (*jus cogens*), any one of the parties may by a written application submit it to the International Court of Justice for a decision unless the parties by common consent agree to submit the dispute to arbitration. If the dispute concerns other issues in the Convention, any one of the parties may by request to the UN Secretary-General set in motion the conciliation procedure laid down in the Annex to the Convention.

TREATIES BETWEEN
STATES AND INTERNATIONAL ORGANISATIONS [154]

The International Law Commission completed Draft Articles on the Law of Treaties between States and International Organisations

---

[152] See also article 65 with regard to the relevant procedures to be followed.

[153] See *infra*, Chapter 17, p.634.

[154] See e.g. Gaja, "A 'New' Vienna Convention on Treaties Between States and International Organisations or Between International Organisations: A Critical Commentary", 58 *BYIL*, 1987, p.253 and Morgenstern, "The Convention on the Law of Treaties Between States and International Organisations or Between International Organisations"; *International Law at a Time of Perplexity* (ed. Dinstein), 1989, p.435.

or between International Organisations in 1982 and the Vienna Convention on the Law of Treaties between States and International Organisations was adopted in 1986.[155] Its provisions closely follow the provisions of the 1969 Vienna Convention *mutatis mutandis*. However, article 73 of the 1986 Convention notes that "as between states parties to the Vienna Convention on the Law of Treaties of 1969, the relations of those states under a treaty between two or more states and one or more international organisations shall be governed by that Convention". Whether this provision affirming the superiority of the 1969 Convention for states will in practice prejudice the interests of international organisations is an open question. In any event, there is no doubt that the strong wish of the Conference adopting the 1986 Convention was for uniformity, despite arguments that the position of international organisations in certain areas of treaty law was difficult to assimilate to that of states.[156]

Special concern in the International Law Commission focused on the effects that a treaty concluded by an international organisation has upon the member-states of the organisation. Article 36 *bis* of the ILC Draft[157] provided that:

> Obligations and rights arise for states members of an international organization from the provisions of a treaty to which that organization is a party when the parties to the treaty intend those provisions to be the means of establishing such obligations and according such rights and have defined their conditions and effects in the treaty or have otherwise agreed theron, and if:
>
> (a) the states members of the organization, by virtue of the constituent instrument of that organization or otherwise, have unanimously agreed to be bound by the said provisions of the treaty; and
>
> (b) the assent of the states members of the organization to be bound by the relevant provisions of the treaty has been duly brought to the knowledge of the negotiating states and negotiating organizations.

Such a situation would arise for example in the case of a customs union, which was an international organisation, normally concluding tariff agreements to which its members are not parties. Such

---

[155] *Supra,* footnote 2.

[156] See Morgenstern, *op. cit.,* pp.438-41.

[157] Described in the ILC Commentary as the article arousing the most controversy, *Yearbook of the ILC,* 1982, vol.II, Part 2, p.43.

agreements would be of little value if they were not to be immediately binding on member-states.[158]

However, despite the fact that the European Community was particularly interested in the adoption of this draft article, it was rejected at the Conference.[159] It was replaced by article 74(3) of the Convention, which provides:

> The provisions of the present Convention shall not prejudge any question that may arise in regard to the establishment of obligations and rights for states members of an international organisation under a treaty to which that organisation is a party.

Accordingly, the situation in question would fall to be resolved on the basis of the consent of the states concerned in the specific circumstances and on a case by case basis.

The other area of difference between the 1986 and 1969 Conventions concerns the provisions for dispute settlement. Since international organisations cannot be parties to contentious proceedings before the International Court, draft article 66 provided for the compulsory arbitration of disputes concerning issues relating to the principles of *jus cogens*, with the details of the proposed arbitral tribunal contained in the Annex. The provisions of the 1969 Convention relating to the compulsory conciliation of disputes relating to the other articles were incorporated in the draft with little change. The 1986 Convention itself, however, adopted a different approach. Under article 66(2), where an international organisation authorised under article 96 of the UN Charter to request advisory opinions is a party to a dispute concerning *jus cogens*, it may apply for an advisory opinion to the International Court, which "shall be accepted as decisive by all the parties to the dispute concerned". If the organisation is not so authorised under article 96, it may follow the same procedure acting through a member-state. If no advisory opinion is requested or the Court itself does not comply with the request, then compulsory arbitration is provided for.[160]

---

[158] *Ibid.*, pp.43-44.

[159] See e.g. Gaja, *op. cit.*, p.264.

[160] Note also *supra* Chapter 13, p.483 regarding the relationship between treaties and state responsibility. The issue of state succession to treaties is covered *infra* Chapter 16, p.606.

CHAPTER SIXTEEN

State Succession[1]

Political entities are not immutable. They are subject to change. New states appear and old states disappear. Federations, mergers and secessions take place. International law has to incorporate such events into its general framework with the minimum of disruption and instability. It is a situation which has come to the fore since the end of the Second World War and the establishment of some 100 new, independent countries.

Difficulties may result from the change in the political sovereignty over a particular territorial entity for the purposes of international law and the world community. For instance, how far is a new state bound by the treaties and contracts entered into by the previous sovereign of the territory? Does nationality automatically devolve upon the inhabitants to replace that of the predecessor? What happens to the public property of the previous sovereign, and to what extent is the new authority liable for the debts of the old?

State succession in international law cannot be confused with succession in municipal law and the transmission of property and so forth to the relevant heir. Other interests and concerns are involved and the principles of state sovereignty, equality of states and non-interference prevent a universal succession principle similar to domestic law from being adopted. Despite attempts to assimilate Roman law views regarding the continuity of the legal personality in the estate which falls by inheritance,[2] this approach could not be sustained in the light of state interests and practice. The opposing doctrine, which basically denied any transmission of rights, obligations and property interests between the predecessor and successor sovereigns, arose in the heyday of positivism in the nineteenth century. It manifested itself again with the rise of the

---

[1] See generally, O'Connell, *State Succession in Municipal Law and International Law*, 2 vols., 1967; Zemanek, "State Succession after Decolonisation", 116 *HR*, p.180; Udokang, *Succession of New States to International Treaties*, 1972; Verzijl, *International Law in Historical Perspective*, vol.7, 1974 and Brownlie, *Principles of Public International Law*, 4th ed., 1990, Chapter XXVIII. See also UN, *Materials on Succession of States*, 1967 and 1978; ILA, *The Effect of Independence on Treaties*, 1965 and Mériboute, *La Codification de la Succession d'Etats aux Traités*, 1984.

[2] See O'Connell, *op. cit.* vol.I, p.9 *et seq.*

decolonisation process in the form of the "clean slate" principle, under which new states acquired sovereignty free from incumbrances created by the predecessor sovereign.

The issue of state succession can arise in a number of defined circumstances, which mirror the ways in which political sovereignty may be acquired by, for example, decolonisation of all or part of an existing territorial unit, dismemberment of an existing state, secession, annexation and merger. In each of these cases a once recognised entity disappears in whole or in part to be succeeded by some other authority, thus precipitating problems of transmission of rights and obligations. However, it must be pointed out that the question of state succession does not infringe upon the normal rights and duties of states under international law. These exist by virtue of the fundamental principles of international law and as a consequence of sovereignty and not as a result of transference from the previous sovereign. The issue of state succession should also be distinguished from questions of succession of governments, particularly revolutionary succession, and consequential patterns of recognition and responsibility.[3]

In many cases, such problems will be dealt with by treaties, whether multilateral treaties dealing with primarily territorial dispositions as for example the Treaty of St. Germain, 1919, which resolved some succession questions relating to the dissolution of the Austro-Hungarian Empire,[4] or bilateral agreements as between, for instance, colonial power and new state, which, however, would not bind third states. The system of devolution agreements signed by the colonial power with the successor, newly decolonised state, was used by, for example, the UK, France and the Netherlands. Such agreements provided in general that all the rights and benefits, obligations and responsibilities devolving upon the colonial power in respect of the territory in question arising from valid international instruments, would therefore devolve upon the new state.[5] This system, however, was not seen as satisfactory by many

[3] *Supra*, Chapters 7 and 13.

[4] See O'Connell, *op. cit.* vol.II, pp.178-82. This treaty provided for the responsibility of the successor states of the Austro-Hungarian empire for the latter's public debts. See also the Italian Peace Treaty 1947.

[5] See e.g. the UK-Burma Agreement of 1947. See also Mugerwa, "Subjects of International Law" in *Manual of Public International Law* (ed. Sørensen), 1968, pp.247, 300-1, and *Yearbook of the ILC*, 1974, vol.II, p.186. See also O'Connell, *op. cit.* vol.II, pp.352-73, and Brownlie, *op. cit.*, p.656.

new states and several of them resorted to unilateral declarations, providing for a transitional period during which treaties entered into by the predecessor state would continue in force and be subject to review as to which should be accepted and which rejected.[6] In the case of bilateral treaties, those not surviving under customary law would be regarded as having terminated at the end of the period.

Where changes in political sovereignty do occur there are certain rules to guide the international community in its treatment of the situation. Where a new entity emerges, one has to decide whether it is a totally separate creature from its predecessor, or whether it is a continuation of it in a slightly different form. For example, it seems to be accepted that India is the same legal entity as British India and Pakistan a totally new state.[7] Yugoslavia was generally regarded as the successor state to Serbia,[8] and Israel as a completely different being from British mandated Palestine.[9]

SUCCESSION TO TREATIES

This has been probably the most difficult aspect of state succession as well as the most controversial and unsettled. State practice has been contradictory and has not recognised one particular approach, while doctrinal discussions were equally diverse. However, in 1978 the Vienna Convention on the Succession of States in Respect of Treaties was signed.

The definition of state succession adopted was based upon the factual criterion, that is "the replacement of one state by another in the responsibility for the international relations of territory",[10] and the Convention is only to apply under article 7 with regard to

---

[6] See e.g. the Tanganyika statement of December 1961, quoted in Mugerwa, *op. cit.,* p.302, subsequently followed by similar declarations by, for example, Uganda, Kenya and Burundi. See also *Yearbook of the ILC,* 1974, vol.II, p.192. In Zambia's case, it was stated that the question would be governed by customary international law, see O'Connell, *op. cit.* vol.II, p.115.

[7] See e.g. *Yearbook of the ILC,* 1962, vol.II, pp.101-3.

[8] See e.g. O'Connell, *op. cit.* vol.II, pp.378-79. See also *Artukovic* v. *Rison,* 784 F.2d 1354 (1986).

[9] O'Connell, *op. cit.* vol.II, pp.155-57.

[10] Article 2(1)b. See also article 2(1)a of the 1983 Vienna Convention on Succession of States in Respect of State Property, Archives and Debts.

a succession occurring after the entry in force of the Convention itself,[11] although, of course, such rules in it as reflect either customary law or treaty law in force for the particular state in question would be independently binding.[12]

As far as devolution agreements are concerned, article 8 provides that such agreements of themselves cannot affect third states and this reaffirms accepted principle, while article 9, dealing with unilateral declarations, emphasises that such a declaration by the successor state alone cannot of itself affect the rights and obligations of the state and third states. In other words, it would appear, the consent of the other parties to the treaties in question or an agreement with the predecessor state with regard to bilateral issues is required.

Certain treaties are, however, unaffected by a succession of states and thus bind the successor state automatically. These are territorial treaties. Article 11 declares that a boundary established by a treaty and obligations and rights established by a treaty and relating to the regime of a boundary are not affected by a succession. This provision reinforces international practice with regard to the sanctity of frontiers (in the absence of change by consent)[13] and may be linked with article 62(2) of the 1969 Convention on the Law of Treaties, which stipulates that a fundamental change of circumstances may not be invoked as a ground for terminating or withdrawing from a treaty that establishes a boundary. Not to have such a rule creating an objectively binding boundary regime, irrespective of the claims of the successor state and/or third states, would surely jeopardize the equilibrium of international relations. It is now well established practice that new states succeed to the borders of the predecessor state as such.[14] Article 12, in a slightly more controversial area, provides that a succession of states does not as such affect rights and obligations relating to the territory established by treaty with regard to other states. Examples of such arrangements

---

[11] As of the date of writing, the Convention has eight ratifications and is thus not yet in force. Fifteen ratifications are required for the Convention to enter into effect, under article 49.

[12] See articles 3 and 5.

[13] See *supra*, Chapter 8, p.302.

[14] See e.g. Shaw, *Title to Territory in Africa*, 1986, pp.240-44. See also *Burkina Faso* v. *Mali*, ICJ Reports, 1986, pp.554, 566; 80 *ILR*, pp.459, 470.

might include demilitarised zones, rights of transit, port facilities and other servitudes generally.[15]

Article 15, dealing with the "moving treaty-frontiers rule",[16] provides that where an existing state acquires territory, which is not itself a state, the treaties of the predecessor state cease to be applicable with regard to that territory, while the treaties of the successor state extend to the area, unless it appears from the treaty or is otherwise established that the application of the treaty to that territory would be incompatible with the object and purpose of the treaty or would radically change the conditions for its operation. When, for example, the US annexed Hawaii in 1898, its treaties were extended to the islands and Belgium was informed that US-Belgium commercial agreements were thenceforth to be applied to Hawaii also;[17] similarly it was held that after 1919 German treaties would not apply to Alsace-Lorraine, while French treaties would thereafter be extended to that territory.[18] Article 15 would therefore seem to reiterate existing custom.[19]

Newly Independent States

Such states, defined in the 1978 Convention as successor states, the territory of which immediately before the date of succession was a dependent territory for the international relations of which the predecessor state was responsible,[20] are deemed by virtue of article 16 to benefit from the "clean slate" rule. In other words, a newly decolonised state

---

[15] See Shaw, *op. cit.*, pp.244-48. See also the *Free Zones* case, PCIJ, Series A/B, no.46, 1932, p.145; 6 *ILR*, pp.362, 364 and the *Aaland Islands* case, LNOJ, Sp. Suppl. no.3, 1920, p.18. See *supra*, Chapter 8, p.312 and *Yearbook of the ILC*, 1974, vol.II, pp.157 and 196 *et seq*. Note, that by article 12(3), the provisions of article 12 do not apply to treaties providing for the establishment of foreign military bases on the territory concerned. See further Brownlie, *op. cit.*, p.669 and O'Connell, *op. cit.* vol.II, pp.12-23 and p.231 *et seq*.

[16] *Yearbook of the ILC*, 1974, vol.II, p.208.

[17] See e.g. O'Connell, *op. cit.* vol.II, pp.377-78.

[18] *Ibid.*, p.379.

[19] The exception to the "moving treaty-frontiers" rule reflects the concept that "political treaties" would not pass, *ibid.*, p.25. See further *infra*, p.624, with regard to the reunification of Germany 1990. See also article IX of Annex 1 of the Anglo-Chinese Agreement 1984 on Hong Kong, *infra*, p.623.

[20] Article 2(1)f.

is not bound to maintain in force, or to become a party to, any treaty by reason only of the fact that at the date of the succession of states the treaty was in force in respect of the territory to which the succession of states relates.

This is, of course, subject to the exceptions contained in articles 11 and 12 relating to territorial treaties. Having stated the general "clean slate" rule, Part III of the 1978 Convention proceeds to deal with newly independent states and existing multilateral and bilateral treaties. In essence, the situation is that such a state may become a party to multilateral treaties, which had previously been in force with respect to the territory in question, by notification of succession. This does not apply if it appears from the treaty or is otherwise established that the application of the treaty in respect of such a state would be incompatible with the object and purpose of the treaty or would radically change the conditions for its operation. In addition, where it appears from the nature of the treaty itself that the participation of any other state would require the consent of all the parties, such consent must be forthcoming for the new state to participate.[21]

The point thus is that a newly independent state is not required to succeed to an existing multilateral treaty in force for the territory with regard to which succession has occurred. It may, if it wishes, not do so under the Convention. What such a state has is a general right of option to be a party to multilateral treaties that do not fall within the exceptions noted above.[22] With regard to existing bilateral treaties, article 24[23] provides that succession will occur when the successor state and the third state (i.e. the other party to the treaty) expressly so agree, or by reason of their conduct are to be considered as having so agreed.[24]

---

[21] Article 17. See also article 27.

[22] See *Yearbook of the ILC*, 1974, vol.II, p.211 *et seq.* Note that no provision is made with respect to objections to such notifications, see e.g. *DUSPIL*, 1975, p.289.

[23] See also article 28.

[24] The above rules also apply to newly independent states (as defined in the Convention) formed from two or more territories, see article 30 (referring to articles 16-29). Where a treaty affects one or more but not all of the territories in question, there is a presumption that on succession it will apply to the newly independent state, *ibid.* See also *Re Bottali*, 78 *ILR*, p.105 and *M* v. *Federal Department of Justice and Police*, 75 *ILR*, p.107.

Uniting and Separating of States

Under article 31, where a new state, not being a newly independent decolonised state, is created by a merger of existing states, any treaty in force on the date of succession in respect of either or any of them continues in force in respect of the successor state unless all the parties to the treaty otherwise agree or unless it appears from the treaty or is otherwise established that the application of the treaty in respect of the successor state would be incompatible with the object and purpose of the treaty or would radically change the conditions for its operation. Such a treaty will only continue in force with respect to the particular territory to which it had previously applied, unless the successor state makes a notification that the treaty is to apply in respect of its entire territory,[25] or in the case of a bilateral treaty, both parties otherwise agree. The article 31 situation must be distinguished not only from the newly independent state category[26] but also from the situation envisaged in article 15 where territory not forming a state is transferred to an existing state. The precise form taken by the new state is not relevant in this context. The union of Egypt and Syria into the United Arab Republic between 1958 and 1961 and the union of Tanganyika and Zanzibar in 1964 provide examples of the operation of the principle that the treaties of the component territories continued in force within those territorial limits.[27]

Where a part (or parts) of the territory of a state separate to form one (or more) states, whether or not the predecessor state continues to exist, article 34 provides that any treaty in force at the date of succession in respect of the entire territory of the predecessor state continues in force for each of the successor states so formed. Any treaty which applied only to part of the territory of the predecessor state which has become a successor state will continue in force in respect of the latter only. These provisions will not apply if the states concerned otherwise agree or if it appears

---

[25] Where the treaty is such that the participation of any other party must be considered as requiring the consent of all the parties, the successor state and the other state parties must agree to the application of the treaty to all of the territory of the former, article 31(2)b. See also article 17(3).

[26] See article 29, and *supra*, footnote 24.

[27] See O'Connell, *op. cit.* vol.II, pp.71-78.

from the treaty or is otherwise established that the application of the treaty in respect of the successor state would be incompatible with the object and purpose of the treaty or would radically change the conditions for its operation.[28] The factual situations out of which a separation or dismemberment takes place are many and varied. They range from a break-up of a previously created entity into its previous constituent elements, as in the 1961 dissolution of the United Arab Republic into the pre-1958 states of Egypt and Syria or the dissolution of the Federation of Mali, to the complete fragmenting of a state into a variety of successors not being co-terminous with previous territorial units, such as the demise of Austria-Hungary in 1919.[29] The general principle in article 34 of succession to treaties of the predecessor state is by no means supported universally by state practice and it will be interesting to note how future dissolutions will be treated.

As far as the predecessor state is concerned in such a situation (assuming the predecessor state remains in existence), article 35 provides that existing treaties remain in force after the succession in respect of the remaining territory, unless the parties otherwise agree or it is established that the treaty related only to the territory which has separated from the predecessor state or it appears from the treaty or is otherwise established that the application of the treaty in respect of the predecessor state would be incompatible with the object and purpose of the treaty or would radically change the conditions for its operation.[30]

SUCCESSION WITH RESPECT TO MATTERS OTHER THAN TREATIES

Membership of International Organisations

Succession to membership of international organisations will proceed (depending upon the terms of the organisation's constitution) according to whether a new state is formed or an old state continues in a slightly different form. In the case of the partition of British India in 1947, India was considered by the UN

[28] See *Yearbook of the ILC,* 1974, vol.II, p.260 *et seq.*
[29] See O'Connell, *op. cit.* vol.II, Chapter 10.
[30] Part VI of the 1978 Convention deals with the settlement of disputes, see Lavalle, "Dispute Settlement under the Vienna Convention of Succession of States in Respect of Treaties", 73 *AJIL,* 1979, p.407.

General Assembly as a continuation of the previous entity, while Pakistan was regarded as a new state, which had then to apply for admission to the organisation.[31] Upon the merger of Egypt and Syria in 1958 to form the United Arab Republic, the latter was treated as a single member of the United Nations, while upon the dissolution of the merger in 1961, Syria simply resumed its separate membership of the organisation.[32]

The sixth (Legal) Committee of the General Assembly considered the situation of new states being formed through division of a member-state and the membership problem and produced the following principles:[33]

> 1. That, as a general rule, it is in conformity with legal principles to presume that a state which is a member of the Organization of the United Nations does not cease to be a member simply because its Constitution or frontier has been subjected to changes, and that the extinction of the state as a legal personality recognised in the international order must be shown before its rights and obligations can be considered thereby to have ceased to exist.
>
> 2. That when a new state is created, whatever may be the territory and the populations which it comprises and whether or not they formed part of a state member of the United Nations, it cannot under the system of the Charter claim the status of a member of the United Nations unless it has been formally admitted as such in conformity with the provisions of the Charter.
>
> 3. Beyond that, each case must be judged according to its merits.

State Property

Article 8 of the 1983 Vienna Convention on Succession of States in Respect of State Property, Archives and Debts (which is not yet in force)[34] defines state property of the predecessor state

---

[31] This issue, of a separation of part of an existing state to form a new state, was considered by the UN to be on a par with the separation from the UK of the Irish Free State and from the Netherlands of Belgium, where the remaining portions continued as existing states, see O'Connell, *op. cit.* vol.I, pp.184-87.

[32] *Ibid.*, pp.197-98. This situation, which differed from the India-Pakistan precedent of 1947, has been criticised, see e.g. Rousseau, "Secession de la Syrie et de la RUA", 66 *Revue Générale de Droit International Public*, 1962, p.413.

[33] A/CN.4/149, p.8, quoted in O'Connell, *op. cit.* vol.I, p.187.

[34] See e.g. Nathen, "The Vienna Convention on Succession of States In Respect of State Property, Archives and Debts" in *International Law at a Time of Perplexity* (ed. Dinstein), 1989, p.489. The Convention has no ratifications to date.

as "property, rights and interests, which at the date of the succession of states were, according to the internal law of the predecessor state owned by that state".[35] The general principle in customary law is that state property passes to the successor state.[36] Where the predecessor state is thereby extinguished, this rule is absolute, but where the successor state is established in part only of the predecessor state a rather more complicated situation arises. Where part of the territory of a state is transferred to another state, article 14 provides that in the absence of agreement both immovable state property of the predecessor state situated in the territory in question[37] and movable state property of the predecessor state connected with its activities in the territory[38] shall pass to the successor state.

Article 15 deals with newly independent states (as defined earlier) and basically provides that immovable and movable state property of the predecessor state within the territory shall pass to the successor state. Similarly, both immovable and movable property having belonged to the territory concerned, situated outside it and having become state property during the period of dependence, shall pass to the successor state. It is to be noted that article 15 does not, unlike other succession situations, refer to agreements between the predecessor and successor states. This was deliberate as the International Law Commission, which drafted the articles upon which the Convention is based, felt that this was required as a recognition of the special circumstances of decolonisation and the fact that many such agreements are unfavourable to the newly independent state.[39] Quite what effect this article would have in the event of an agreement is unclear, but it cannot be taken as either forbidding or rendering void such an agreement.

The article is also unusual in that it provides that immovable state property situated outside the territory and movable state property

---

[35] But note the *Peter Pazmany University* case, PCIJ, Series A/B, no.61, 1933, p.236, where the Court felt it need not rely upon the internal law of the predecessor state to decide whether the property in question was state or public property.

[36] *Ibid.*, p.237 and *Haile Selassie* v. *Cable and Wireless Ltd* (no.2), [1939] Ch. 182; 9 *ILR*, p.94. Note that under article 11, which basically reflects practice, no compensation is payable for the passing of state property unless otherwise agreed and article 12 provides that third states' property in the territory of the predecessor state remains unaffected by the succession.

[37] E.g. fixed military installations, prisons, airports, government offices, state hospitals and universities, see *Yearbook of the ILC*, 1981, vol.II, Pt.2, p.33.

[38] E.g. currency and state public funds, *ibid.*, pp.35-36.

[39] *Ibid.*, p.38.

other than that already covered in the article "to the creation of which the dependent territory has contributed" shall pass to the successor state in proportion to the contribution of the dependent territory. This was intended to introduce the application of equity to the situation and was designed to preserve *inter alia*, "the patrimony and the historical and cultural heritage of the people inhabiting the dependent territory concerned".[40] It is unclear how far this extends. It may cover contributions to international institutions made where the territory is a dependent territory, but beyond this one can only speculate.

When two or more states unite to form one successor state, the state property of the former will pass to the latter.[41] Where part of a state secedes to form another state then, in the absence of agreement, immovable property in the territory in question passes to the successor state, as does movable property of the predecessor state connected with the activity of that state in respect of the territory. Other movable property will pass to the successor state in an equitable proportion.[42] Similar rules apply where a state ceases to exist and is replaced by two or more successor states, except that immovable property situated outside the territory will pass to the successor states in equitable proportions.[43]

State Archives

Archives are state property with special characteristics. Many are difficult by their nature to divide up, but they may be relatively easily reproduced and duplicated. Archives are a crucial part of the heritage of a community and may consist of documents, numismatic collections, iconographic documents, photographs and films. The issue has been of great concern to UNESCO, which has called for the restitution of archives as part of the reconstitution and protection of the national cultural heritage and has appealed for the return of an irreplaceable cultural heritage to those that created it.[44] In

---

[40] *Ibid.*

[41] Article 16.

[42] Article 17.

[43] Article 18. See also O'Connell, *op. cit.* vol.I, Chapter 9.

[44] UNESCO, Records of the General Conference, 18th Session, Resolutions, 1974, p.68 *et seq.*, 20 C/102, 1978, paras. 18-19; and UNESCO Records of the General Conference, 20th Session, Resolutions, 1978, pp.92-93. See also *Yearbook of the ILC,* 1979, vol.II, Pt.1, pp.78-80.

this general context, one should also note articles 149 and 303 of the 1982 Convention on the Law of the Sea. The former provides that all objects of an archaeological and historical nature found in the International Sea-bed Area are to be preserved or disposed of for the benefit of mankind as a whole, "particular regard being paid to the preferential rights of the state or country of origin, or the state of historical and archaeological origin", while the latter stipulates that states have the duty to protect objects of an archaeological and historical nature found at sea and shall co-operate for this purpose.

In general, treaties between European states dealing with cessions of territory included archival clauses providing for the treatment of archives, while such clauses are very rare in cases of decolonisation.[45]

Article 20 of the 1983 Vienna Convention provides that state archives in the present context means:

> all documents of whatever date and kind, produced or received by the predecessor state in the exercise of its functions which, at the date of the succession of states, belonged to the predecessor state according to its internal law and were preserved by it directly or under its control as archives for whatever purpose.

Generally, such archives will pass as at the date of succession and without compensation, without as such affecting archives in the territory owned by a third state.[46]

Where part of the territory of a state is transferred by that state to another state, in the absence of agreement, the part of the state archives of the predecessor state which, for normal administration of the territory concerned, should be at the disposal of the state to which the territory is transferred, shall pass to the successor state, as shall any part of the state archives that relates exclusively or principally to the territory.[47] In the case of newly independent states, the same general provisions apply,[48] but with some alterations.

Note in addition the call for a New International Cultural Order, see e.g. Bedjaoui, *Towards a New International Economic Order*, 1979, pp.75 *et seq.* and 245 *et seq.*, and General Assembly Resolutions 3026A (XXVII); 3148 (XXVIII); 3187 (XXVIII); 3391 (XXX) and 31/40.

[45] *Yearbook of the ILC*, 1979, vol.II, Pt.1, p.93.

[46] Articles 21-24.

[47] Article 27.

[48] Article 28(1)b and c.

Archives having belonged to the territory in question and having become state archives of the predecessor state during the period of dependence are to pass to the successor state. The reference here to archives that became state archives is to pre-colonial material, whether kept by central government, local governments or tribes, religious ministers, private enterprises or individuals.[49] One may mention here the Treaty of Peace with Italy of 1947, which provided that Italy was to restore all archives and objects of historical value belonging to Ethiopia or its natives and removed from Ethiopia to Italy since October 1935.[50] In the case of Vietnam, the 1950 Franco-Vietnamese agreement provided for the return as of right of all historical archives,[51] while a dispute between France and Algeria has been in existence since the latter's independence over pre-colonial material removed to France.[52]

Article 28(2) provides that the passing or the appropriate reproduction of parts of the state archives of the predecessor state (other than those already discussed above) of interest to the territory concerned is to be determined by agreement, "in such a manner that each of these states [i.e. predecessor and successor] can benefit as widely and equitably as possible from those parts of the state archives of the predecessor state". The reference here is primarily to material relating to colonisation and the colonial period, and in an arrangement of 1975, the French specifically noted the practice of microfilming in the context of France's acquisition of Algeria.[53] Article 28(3) emphasises that the predecessor state is to provide the newly independent state with the best available evidence from its state archives relating to territorial title and boundary issues. This is important as many post-colonial territorial disputes will invariably revolve around the interpretation of colonial treaties delimiting frontiers and colonial administrative practice concerning the area in contention.[54]

Where two or more states unite to form one successor state, the state archives of the former will pass to the latter.[55] Where part

    [49] *Yearbook of the ILC*, 1981, vol.II, Pt.2, p.62.
    [50] 49 UNTS, p.142.
    [51] See *Yearbook of the ILC*, 1979, vol.II, Pt.1, p.113.
    [52] *Ibid.*, pp.113-14.
    [53] *Yearbook of the ILC*, 1981, vol.II, Pt.2, p.64.
    [54] See for example, the Mali-Upper Volta (Burkina Faso) border dispute, Shaw, *op. cit.*, pp.257-58 and the *Burkina Faso-Mali* case, ICJ Reports, 1986, p.554; 80 *ILR*, p.459.
    [55] Article 29.

of a state secedes to form another state, unless the states otherwise agree the part of the state archives of the predecessor state, which for normal administration of the territory concerned should be in that territory, will pass, as will those parts of the state archives that relate directly to the territory that is the subject of the succession.[56]

The same provisions apply in the case of a dissolution of a state, which is replaced by two or more successor states, in the absence of agreement, with the addition that other state archives are to pass to the successor states in an equitable manner, taking into account all relevant circumstances.[57]

Articles 28, 30 and 31 also contain a paragraph explaining that the relevant agreements over state archives "shall not infringe the right of the peoples of those states to development, to information about their history and to their cultural heritage". Despite the controversy over whether such a right does indeed exist in law as a right and precisely how such a provision might be interpreted in practice in concrete situations, the general concept of encouraging awareness and knowledge of a people's heritage is to be supported. The precise phraseology of the paragraphs, however, would not appear to promote this in the most acceptable manner.

State Debts [58]

These are defined in article 33 of the 1983 Vienna Convention as any financial obligation of a predecessor state arising in conformity with international law towards another state, an international organisation or any other subject of international law. Accordingly, debts to private persons are excluded from the Convention. Public debts generally have been divided into national debts owned by the state as a whole; local debts contracted by a local governmental body and localised debts, being those debts incurred by the central government for the purpose of

[56] Article 30.

[57] Article 31. Note in particular the dispute between Denmark and Iceland, after the disolution of their Union, over valuable parchments, see Verzijl, *op. cit.* vol.7, 1974, p.153 and *Yearbook of the ILC*, 1981, vol.II, Pt.1, pp.68-69, and the Treaty of St. Germain of 1919 with Austria which contained provisions relating to the succession to archives of various new or reconstituted states.

[58] See generally, O'Connell, *op. cit.* vol.I, Chapters 15-17; *Yearbook of the ILC*, 1977, vol.II, Pt.1, p.49 *et seq.* and Zemanek, *op. cit.*

local projects or areas.[59] The concept of state debts dealt with by the 1983 Convention is thus narrower than that of public debts generally. Where part of the territory of a state is transferred to another state, in the absence of agreement, the state debt of the predecessor state will pass to the successor state in an equitable proportion, taking into account, in particular, the property, rights and interests which pass to the successor state in relation to that state debt.[60] In general customary law, it would appear that, while a localised debt would pass to the successor state, there was no agreement on general state debts.[61] Accordingly, article 37 proposes an alteration to the previous approach and one based upon the concept of equity. It remains to be seen how in practice this would apply, especially since one would have thought that an agreement between the states concerned would be the way of achieving an equitable solution.

In common with the other parts of the 1983 Convention, a specific article is devoted to the situation of the newly independent state. Article 38 provides that no state debt of the predecessor state shall pass to the newly independent state, unless an agreement between them provides otherwise, "in view of the link between the state debt of the predecessor state connected with its activity in the territory to which the succession of states relates and the property, rights and interests which pass to the newly independent state". State practice generally in the decolonisation process dating back to the independence of the United States appears to show that there would be no succession to part of the general state debt of the predecessor state, but that this would differ where the debt related specifically to the territory in question.[62]

Where two or more states unite to form one successor state, then clearly the state debt of the former states will pass to the successor state.[63] Where part of a state secedes to form a new state, then, in

---

[59] See O'Connell, *op. cit.* vol.I, Chapters 15-17 and *Yearbook of the ILC*, 1981, vol.II, Pt.1, p.76. A variety of other distinctions have also been drawn, *ibid.* Note also that by article 36 a succession of states does not as such affect the right and obligations of creditors.

[60] Article 37. See also *Yearbook of the ILC*, 1981, vol.II, Pt.1, pp.84-91.

[61] See *ibid.*, p.90 and the *Ottoman Public Debt* case, 1 *RIAA*, p.529 (1925).

[62] See *Yearbook of the ILC*, 1981, vol.II, Pt.1, pp.91-105 and *ibid.*, 1977, vol.II, Pt.1, pp.86-107. Note the varied practice of succession to public debts in the colonisation process, *ibid.*, pp.87-88 and with regard to annexations, *ibid.*, pp.93-94. See also *West Rand Gold Mining Co.* v. *R*, [1905] 2 KB 391, and O'Connell, *op. cit.* vol.I, pp.373-83.

[63] Article 39.

the absence of agreement, the state debt of the predecessor state will pass to the successor state in an equitable proportion, taking into account, in particular, the property, rights and interests which pass to the successor state in relation to that state debt.[64] The same rule will apply also in the case of the dissolution of a state and its replacement by two or more states.[65] It is perhaps to be regretted that the Convention did not deal with public debt generally or with private debts chargeable to a state, since such areas could well have benefited from explanation and provision.

The Convention as a whole is an interesting attempt to deal with some succession problems. Certain parts of it are controversial and may not be acceptable to many states. In addition, the emphasis upon equity, while providing for flexibility and seeking justice, may give rise to some uncertainty as the guidance provided is minimal.

Private Rights

The question also arises as to how far a succession of states will affect, if at all, private rights. Principles of state sovereignty and respect for acquired or subsisting rights are relevant here and often questions of expropriation provide the context.

As far as those inhabitants who become nationals of the successor state are concerned, they are fully subject to its laws and regulations, and apart from the application of international human rights rules, they have little direct recourse to international law in these circumstances. Accordingly what does become open to discussion is the protection afforded to aliens by international provisions relating to the succession of rights and duties upon a change of sovereignty.

It is within this context that the doctrine of acquired rights[66] has been formulated. This relates to rights obtained by foreign nationals and has been held by some to include virtually all types of legal interests. Its import is that such rights continue after the succession and can be enforced against the new sovereign.

---

[64] Article 40.

[65] Article 41. See also *Yearbook of the ILC*, 1981, vol.II, Pt.1, pp.108-13. See with regard to public debts generally (over and above state debts), O'Connell, *op. cit.* vol.I, Chapters 15-17.

[66] See in particular, *ibid.*, Chapter 10 and Brownlie, *op. cit.*, pp.657-58 and 659-60.

Some writers declare this proposition to be a fundamental principle of international law,[67] while others describe it merely as a source of confusion.[68] And there is a certain amount of disagreement as to its extent. On the one hand, it has been held to mean that the passing of sovereignty has no effect upon such rights, and on the other that it implies no more than that aliens should be, as far as possible, insulated from the changes consequent upon succession.

The principle of acquired rights was discussed in a number of cases that came before the Permanent Court of International Justice between the two world wars, dealing with the creation of an independent Poland out of the former German, Russian and Austrian Empires. Problems arose specifically with regard to rights obtained under German rule, which were challenged by the new Polish authorities.

In the *German Settlers'* case,[69] the facts were that Poland had attempted to evict German settlers from its lands, arguing that since many of them had not taken transfer of title before the Armistice they could be legitimately ejected. According to the German system, such settlers could acquire title either by means of leases, or by means of an arrangement whereby they paid parts of the purchase price at regular intervals and upon payment of the final instalment the land would become theirs.

The Court held that German law would apply in the circumstances until the final transfer of the territory and that the titles to land acquired in this fashion would be protected under the terms of the 1919 Minorities Treaty. More importantly, the Court declared that even in the absence of such a treaty:

> private rights acquired under existing law do not cease on a change of sovereignty . . . even those who contest the existence in international law of a general principle of state succession do not go so far as to maintain that private rights, including those acquired from the state as the owner of the property, are invalid as against a successor in sovereignty.

---

[67] See e.g. O'Connell, *op. cit.*, vol.I, pp.239-40, and *International Law*, 2nd ed., 1970, vol.I, p.377. See also Oppenheim, *International Law*, vol.I, 8th ed., 1955, p.160, note 3.

[68] See e.g. Brownlie, *op. cit.*, p.658.

[69] PCIJ, Series B, no.6, 1923; 2 *ILR*, p.71. The proposition was reaffirmed in the *Certain German Interests in Polish Upper Silesia* case, PCIJ, Series A, no.7, 1926; 3 *ILR*, p.429 and the *Chorzów Factory* case, PCIJ, Series A, no.17, 1928; 4 *ILR*, p.268. See also the *Mavrommatis Palestine Concessions* case, PCIJ, Series A, no.5, 1924 and *US* v. *Percheman*, 7 Pet. 51 (1830).

The fact that there was a political purpose behind the colonisation scheme would not affect the private rights thus secured, which could be enforced against the new sovereign. It is very doubtful that this would be accepted today.

The principles emerging from such inter-war cases affirming the continuation of acquired rights, have modified the views expressed in the *West Rand Central Gold Mining Company* case[70] to the effect that upon annexation the new sovereign may choose which of the contractual rights and duties adopted by the previous sovereign it wishes to respect.

The inter-war cases mark the high-water mark of the concept of the continuation of private rights upon succession, but they should not be interpreted to mean that the new sovereign cannot alter such rights. The expropriation of alien property is possible under international law subject to certain conditions.[71] What the doctrine does indicate is that there is a presumption of the continuation of foreign acquired rights, though the matter is best regulated by treaty.

Only private rights that have become vested or acquired would be covered by the doctrine. Thus, where rights are to come into operation in the future, they will not be binding upon the new sovereign. Similarly, claims to unliquidated damages will not continue beyond the succession.

Claims to unliquidated damages occur where the matter in dispute has not come before the judicial authorities and the issue of compensation has yet to be determined by a competent court or tribunal. In the *Robert E. Brown* claim,[72] an American citizen's prospecting licence had been unjustifiably cancelled by the Boer republic of South Africa in the 1890s and Brown's claim had been dismissed in the Boer courts. In 1900 the United Kingdom annexed the republic and Brown sought (through the US government) to hold it responsible. This contention was rejected by the arbitration tribunal, which said that Brown's claim did not represent an acquired right since the denial of justice that had taken place by the Boer court's wrongful rejection of his case had prevented the claim from becoming liquidated. The tribunal also noted that liability for a

---

[70] [1905] 2 KB 391.

[71] *Supra*, Chapter 13, p.516.

[72] 6 *RIAA*, p.120 (1923); 2 *ILR*, p.66. See also the *Hawaiian Claims* case, 6 *RIAA*, p.157 (1925); 3 *ILR*, p.80.

wrongful act committed by a state did not pass to the new sovereign after succession.

The fact that the disappearance of the former sovereign automatically ends liability for any wrong it may have committed is recognised as a rule of international law, although where the new state adopts the illegal actions of the predecessor, it may inherit liability since it itself is in effect committing a wrong. This was brought out in the *Lighthouses* arbitration[73] in 1956 between France and Greece, which concerned the latter's liability to respect concessions granted by Turkey to a French company regarding territory subsequently acquired by Greece.

The problem of the survival of foreign nationals' rights upon succession is closely bound up with ideological differences and economic pressures. The western nations tend to support the doctrine of acquired rights rather more than communist or Third World states, and the issue is linked closely with state responsibility.

State Succession and Nationality [74]

The terms under which a state may award nationality are solely within its control but problems may arise in the context of a succession.

The issue of nationality will basically depend upon the municipal regulations of the predecessor and successor states. The laws of the former will determine the extent to which the inhabitants of an area to be ceded to another authority will retain their nationality after the change in sovereignty, while the laws of the successor state will prescribe the conditions under which the new nationality will be granted.

The general rule would appear to be that nationality will change with sovereignty, although it will be incumbent upon the new sovereign to declare the pertinent rules with regard to people born in the territory or resident there, or born abroad of parents who are nationals of the former regime. Similarly, the ceding state may well provide for its former citizens in the territory in question to retain their nationality, thus creating a situation

---

[73] 12 *RIAA*, p.155 (1956); 23 *ILR*, p.659.
[74] See *supra*, Chapters 11, p.403 and 13, p.505.

of dual nationality. This would not arise, of course, where the former state completely disappears.

Some states acquiring territory may provide for the inhabitants to obtain the new nationality automatically while others may give the inhabitants an option to depart and retain their original nationality. Actual practice is varied and much depends on the circumstances, but it should be noted that the 1961 Convention on the Reduction of Statelessness provides that states involved in the cession of territory should ensure that no person becomes stateless as a result of the particular change in sovereignty.[75]

HONG KONG

Of particular interest in the context of state succession and the decolonisation process is the situation with regard to Hong Kong. While Hong Kong island and the southern tip of the Kowloon peninsula (with Stonecutters island) were ceded to Britain in perpetuity,[76] the New Territories (comprising some 92% of the total land area of the territory) were leased to Britain for 99 years commencing 1 July 1898.[77] Accordingly, the British and Chinese governments opened negotiations and in 1984 reached an agreement. This Agreement took the form of a Joint Declaration and Three Annexes[78] and lays down the system under which Hong Kong will be governed as from 1 July 1997. It is specified that a Hong Kong Special Administrative Region (SAR) will be established, which will enjoy a high degree of autonomy, except in foreign and defence affairs. It will be vested with executive, legislative and independent judicial power, including that of final adjudication. The laws of Hong Kong will remain basically unaffected. The government of the SAR will be composed of local inhabitants and the current social and economic systems are to continue unchanged. The SAR will retain the status of a free port and a separate customs territory and is to remain an international financial centre with a freely convertible currency. Using the name of "Hong Kong, China", the

[75] See O'Connell, *op. cit.* vol.I, Chapters 20 and 21 and Weis, *Nationality and Statelessness in International Law,* 1956.
[76] See the Treaty of Nanking 1842, 30 BFSP, p.389 and the Convention of Peking 1860, 50 BFSP, p.10.
[77] 90 BFSP, p.17. All three treaties were denounced by China as "unequal treaties".
[78] See 23 *ILM*, 1984, p.1366.

SAR may on its own maintain and develop economic and cultural relations and conclude relevant agreements with states, regions and relevant international organisations. The existing systems of shipping management are to continue and shipping certificates relating to the shipping register will be issued under the name of "Hong Kong, China".

These policies are to be enshrined in a Basic Law of the SAR and will remain unchanged for fifty years. Annex I of the Agreement also provides that public servants in Hong Kong, including members of the police and judiciary, will remain in employment and upon retirement will receive their pension and other benefits due to them on terms no less favourable than before and irrespective of their nationality or place of residence. Airlines incorporated and having their principal place of business in Hong Kong may continue to operate and the current system of civil aviation management is to continue. The SAR will have extensive authority to conclude agreements in this field. Current rights and freedoms in Hong Kong are to be maintained, including freedoms of the person, of speech, of the press, of assembly, of belief, of movement, to strike and to form and join trade unions. In an important provision, article XIII of Annex I stipulates that the provisions of the International Covenants on Human Rights 1966 are to continue in force.

Accordingly, a high level of succession is provided for, but it is as well to recognise that the Hong Kong situation is unusual.

THE REUNIFICATION OF GERMANY 1990

In the dramatic period of political upheaval in Eastern Europe during 1989 and 1990, perhaps the most striking event was the reunification of Germany.

Following the conclusion of the Second World War, Germany was divided into the US, USSR, UK and French zones of occupation and a special Berlin area not forming part of any zone.[79] Supreme authority was exercised initially by the Commanders-in-Chief of

---

[79] See e.g. The Fourth Report of the Foreign Affairs Committee, Session 1989-90, June 1990. Note that part of the Soviet zone was placed under Soviet administration (i.e. the city of Konigsberg, now Kaliningrad, and the surrounding area) and the territory of Germany east of the Oder-Neisse line was placed under Polish administration.

the Armed Forces of the Four Allied Powers[80] and subsequently by the three Allied High Commissioners in Bonn, with parallel developments occurring in the Soviet zone. The Convention on Relations between the Three Powers and the Federal Republic of Germany, which came into force in 1955, terminated the occupation regime and abolished the Allied High Commission. The Three Allied Powers retained, however, their rights and obligations with regard to Berlin[81] and relating to "Germany as a whole, including the reunification of Germany and a peace settlement".[82] Recognition of the German Democratic Republic was on the same basis, i.e. as a sovereign state having full authority over internal and external affairs subject to the rights and responsibilities of the Four Powers in respect of Berlin and Germany as a whole.[83] Accordingly, it was accepted that in some sense Germany as a whole continued to exist as a state in international law.[84]

The question of the relation of the two German states to each other and with respect to the pre-1945 German state has occasioned considerable interest and generated no little complexity, not least because the Federal German Republic has always claimed to be the successor of the pre-1945 Germany.[85]

On 18 May 1990 a treaty between the two German states was signed establishing a Monetary, Economic and Social Union. In essence this integrated the GDR into the FRG economic system, with the Deutsche Mark becoming legal tender in the GDR and with the Bundesbank becoming the central bank for the GDR as well as for the FRG.[86] On 31 August 1990, a second treaty was signed between the two German states which provided for unification on 3 October 1990 by the accession of the GDR under article 23 of the

---

[80] Article 2 of the Agreement on Control Machinery in Germany of 14 November 1944, as amended by the Agreement of 1 May 1945.

[81] See in particular Hendry and Wood, *The Legal Status of Berlin*, 1987. See also Cmd. 8571, 1952 and the Quadripartite Agreement on Berlin, Cmnd. 5135, 1971.

[82] Article 2 of the Relations Convention. Parallel developments took place in the Soviet zone. Note the USSR-German Democratic Republic Treaty of 1955.

[83] See the Fourth Report, *op. cit.*, p.2.

[84] *Ibid.*, p.3.

[85] See e.g. Brownlie, *op. cit.*, pp.81, 84-85; Whiteman, *Digest of International Law*, vol.I, pp.332-38 and Mann, "Germany's Present Legal State Revisited", 16 *ICLQ*, 1967, p.760. See also the decision of the Federal Constitutional Court of the Federal Republic of Germany in *Re Treaty on the Basis of Relations Between the Federal Republic of Germany and the German Democratic Republic 1972*, 78 *ILR*, p.149.

[86] See 29 *ILM*, 1990, p.1108.

FRG Basic Law, while on 12 September 1990 the Treaty on
the Final Settlement With Respect to Germany was signed by the
two German states and the Four Allied Powers.[87] This latter
agreement settles definitively matters arising out of the Second
World War. It confirms the borders of the new Germany as those
of the FRG and the GDR (i.e. the post-war Oder-Neisse frontier
with Poland), provides for a reduction in the armed forces of
Germany and for the withdrawal of Soviet forces from the
territory of the GDR. The Four Allied Powers terminated their
rights and responsibilities regarding Berlin and Germany as a
whole so that the united Germany has full sovereignty over its
internal and external affairs.[88]

Treaties

As far as succession issues themselves are concerned, article 11
of the Unification Treaty of 31 August provides that all international
treaties and agreements to which the FRG is a contracting party are
to retain their validity and that the rights and obligations arising
therefrom will apply also to the territory of the GDR.[89] Article 12
provides that international treaties of the GDR are to be discussed
with the parties concerned with a view to regulating or confirming
their continued application, adjustment or expiry, taking into
account protection of confidence, the interests of the state
concerned, the treaty obligations of the FRG as well as the principles
of a free, democratic order governed by the rule of law, and
respecting the competence of the European Communities. The
united Germany would then determine its position after such
consultations. It is also stipulated that should the united Germany
intend to accede to international organisations or other multilateral
treaties of which the GDR, but not the FRG, is a member, agreement
is to be reached with the respective contracting parties and the

[87] See 29 *ILM*, 1990, p.1186.

[88] Note that by the Declaration of 1 October 1990, the Allied Powers suspended all
rights and responsibilities relating to Berlin and to Germany as a whole upon the unification
of Germany, pending the entry into force of the Treaty on the Final Settlement, see Annex
2 of the Observations by the Government to the Fourth Report, *op. cit.*, October 1990, Cm.
1246.

[89] However, Annex I to the Treaty provides that certain listed treaties are not to apply
to the territory of the former GDR. These treaties relate in essence to NATO activities.

European Communities, where the competence of the latter is affected.

The situation is thus different from the scenario referred to in article 31 of the 1978 treaty, under which in the case of a new state created by the merger of existing states there is a presumption of the continuance in force of treaties of the merging states in their respective territories. Here, no new state is created but an existing one has disappeared by means of merger with an existing and continuing state.[90]

Public Assets

Article 21 of the Unification Treaty provides that the assets of the GDR which served directly specified administrative tasks are to become Federal assets[91] and are to be used to discharge public tasks in the territory of the former GDR. Article 22 deals with public assets of legal entities in that territory, including the land and assets in the agricultural sectors which do not serve directly specified administrative tasks.[92] Such financial assets are to be administered in trust by the Federal Government and are to be appointed by federal law equally between the Federal Government on the one hand and the *Länder* of the former GDR on the other, with the local authorities receiving an appropriate share of the *Länder* allocation. The Federal Government is to use its share to discharge public tasks in the territory of the former GDR, while the distribution of the *Länder* share to the individual *Länder* is to take place upon the basis of population ratio. Publicly owned assets used for the housing supply become the property of the local authorities together with the assumption by the latter of a proportionate share of the debts, with the ultimate aim of privatisation.

---

[90] See *supra* p.610.

[91] Unless they were earmarked on 1 October 1989 predominantly for administrative tasks which under the Basic Law of the FRG are to be discharged by the *Länder,* local authorities or other public administrative bodies, in which case they will accrue to the appropriate institution of public administration. Administrative assets used predominantly for tasks of the former Ministry of State Security/Office for National Security are to accrue to the Trust Agency established under the Law on the Privatisation and Reorganisation of Publicly Owned Assets (Trust Law) of 17 June 1990 for the purpose of privatising former publicly owned companies.

[92] These are termed "financial assets" and deliberately exclude social insurance assets.

Debts

Article 23 provides that the total national budget debt of the GDR is to be assumed by a special Federal fund administered by the Federal Minister of Finance. The Federal Government is to be liable for the obligations of the special fund. The fund is to service the debt and may raise loans *inter alia* to redeem debts and to cover interest and borrowing costs. Until 31 December 1993, the Federal Government and the Trust Agency are to each reimburse one half of the interest payments made by the special fund. As from 1 January 1994, the Federal Government, the Trust Agency and the *Länder* of the former GDR are to assume the total debt accrued at that date by the special fund, which is to be dissolved.

The sureties, warranties and guarantees assumed by the GDR are to be taken over by the Federal Republic, while the interests of the GDR in the Berlin State Bank are to be transferred to the *Länder* of the former GDR. The liabilities arising from the GDR's responsibility for the Berlin State Bank are to be assumed by the Federal Government. If a claim is made on the Federal Government under this liability, the burden is to be included in the total debt of the GDR budget and assumed into the special fund.

In other words, the system of succession provides that the public assets and debts of the former GDR are to fall in essence to the authorities of the unified Germany with an apportionment between the Federal Government and the *Länder* of the former GDR.

Foreign Trade Relations

Article 29 provides that the existing foreign trade relations of the GDR, and in particular its contractual obligations towards the countries of the Council for Mutual Economic Assistance, are to be respected. The unified Germany is to ensure that such relations are settled in a suitable organisational form within the framework of its specialist competence.

Many queries still remain at the time of writing regarding the process of succession. It is unclear, for example, what the situation is with regard to succession to the state contracts of the GDR or with regard to air service agreements.

CHAPTER SEVENTEEN

The Settlement of Disputes by Peaceful Means[1]

It is fair to say that international law has always considered its fundamental purpose to be the maintenance of peace. Although ethical preoccupations stimulated its development and inform its growth, international law has historically been regarded by the international community primarily as a means to ensure the establishment and preservation of world peace and security. This chapter is concerned with the methods and procedures available within the international order for the peaceful resolution of disputes and conflicts.

Basically the techniques of conflict management fall into two categories: diplomatic procedures and adjudication. The former involves an attempt to resolve differences either by the contending parties themselves or with the aid of other entities by the use of the discussion and fact-finding methods. Adjudication procedures involve the determination by a disinterested third party of the legal and factual issues involved, either by arbitration or by the decision of judicial organs.

The political approach to conflict settlement is divided into two sections, so that the measures applicable by the United Nations may be separately looked at, since they do possess a distinctive character. The adjudication processes will be similarly divided so as to differentiate the techniques of arbitration and judicial settlement.

THE NATURE OF DISPUTES

Although it is not possible to point to a specific definition, the approach adopted by the Permanent Court in the *Mavrommatis Palestine Concessions (Jurisdiction)* case[2] should be noted. The Court

---

[1] See generally, Merrills, *International Dispute Settlement*, 2nd ed., 1991; David Davies Memorial Institute, *International Disputes: The Legal Aspects*, 1972; Raman, *Dispute Settlement Through the UN*, 1977; Young, *The Intermediaries*, 1967; Bowett, "Contemporary Developments in Legal Techniques in the Settlement of Disputes", 180 *HR*, p.171 and Murty, "Settlement of Disputes" in *Manual of Public International Law* (ed. Sørensen), 1968, p.673.

[2] PCIJ, Series A, no.2, 1924, p.11. See also the *South West Africa* cases, ICJ Reports, 1962, pp.319, 328; 37 *ILR*, pp.3, 10 and the *Nuclear Tests* case, ICJ Reports, 1974, p.253; 57 *ILR*, p.398.

declared that a dispute could be regarded as "a disagreement over a point of law or fact, a conflict of legal views or of interests between two persons". It is to be distinguished from a situation which might lead to international friction or give rise to a dispute. This is a subtle but important difference since, for the process of settlement to operate successfully, there has to be a specific issue or issues readily identifiable to be resolved.

In the *Interpretation of Peace Treaties* case[3] the Court noted that "whether there exists an international dispute is a matter for objective determination" and pointed out that in the instant case "the two sides hold clearly opposite views concerning the question of the performance or the non-performance of certain treaty obligations" so that "international disputes have arisen". A mere assertion is not sufficient; it must be shown that the claim of one party is positively opposed by the other.[4] This approach was reaffirmed in the *Applicability of the Obligation to Arbitrate under Section 21 of the United Nations Headquarters Agreement* case,[5] where the Court in an advisory opinion noted that the consistent challenge by the UN Secretary-General to the decisions contemplated and then taken by the US Congress and Administration with regard to the closing of the PLO offices in the US (which of necessity included the PLO Mission to the United Nations in New York) demonstrated the existence of a dispute between the US and the UN relating to the Headquarters Agreement.

The International Court has also noted that a legal dispute is one capable of being settled by the application of the principles and rules of international law and that it cannot concern itself with the political motivation of a state in seeking judicial settlement of a dispute.[6]

A dispute on the international scene may, of course, arise not only between states, but also between states and international organisations, or between such organisations themselves, or between states and private persons. As far as the second and third situations are involved, the basic principles applicable to disputes

---

[3] ICJ Reports, 1950, pp.65, 74; 17 *ILR*, pp.331, 336.

[4] *South West Africa* cases, ICJ Reports, 1962, pp.319, 328; 37 *ILR*, pp.3, 10.

[5] ICJ Reports, 1988, pp.12, 30; 82 *ILR*, pp.225, 248.

[6] See the *Case Concerning Border and Transborder Armed Actions (Nicaragua v. Honduras)*, ICJ Reports, 1988, pp.69, 91.

between states will be adopted subject to any special modifications as the case may be. Where the dispute is between a state and a private person, it is difficult to prescribe general rules since each situation will have to be examined in the light of its own specific circumstances. Accordingly, this chapter will be concerned with inter-state disputes.

However, states are not obliged to resolve their differences at all, and this applies in the case of serious legal conflicts as well as peripheral political disagreements. All the methods available to settle disputes are operative only upon the consent of the particular states. This, of course, can be contrasted with the situation within municipal systems. It is reflected in the different functions performed by the courts in the international and domestic legal orders respectively, and it is one aspect of the absence of a stable, central focus within the world community.

A distinction is sometimes made between legal and political disputes, or justiciable and non-justiciable disputes.[7] Although maintained in some international treaties, it is to some extent unsound, in view of the fact that any dispute will involve some political considerations and many overtly political disagreements may be resolved by judicial means.[8] Whether any dispute is to be termed legal or political may well hinge upon the particular circumstances of the case and the views adopted by the relevant parties. It is in reality extremely difficult to point to objective general criteria clearly differentiating the two.

This does not, however, imply that there are not significant differences between the legal and political procedures available for resolving problems. For one thing, the strictly legal approach is dependent upon the provisions of the law as they stand at that point, irrespective of any reforming tendencies the particular court may have, while the political techniques of settlement are not so restricted.

The role of political influences and considerations in inter-state disputes is obviously a vital one, and many settlements can only be properly understood within the wider international political context.

[7] See e.g. Lauterpacht, *The Function of Law in the International Community*, 1933, especially pp.19-20.
[8] See e.g. Henkin, Pugh, Schachter and Smit, *International Law Cases and Materials*, 1980, pp.829-31.

In addition, how a state proceeds in a dispute will be conditioned by political factors. If the dispute is perceived to be one affecting vital interests, for example, the state would be less willing to submit the matter to binding third party settlement than if it were a more technical issue, while the existence of regional mechanisms will often be of political significance.

Article 2(3) of the United Nations Charter provides that:

> [a]ll members shall settle their international disputes by peaceful means in such a manner that international peace and security and justice are not endangered.

The 1970 Declaration on Principles of International Law[9] develops this principle and notes that:

> states shall accordingly seek early and just settlement of their international disputes by negotiation, inquiry, mediation, conciliation, arbitration, judicial settlement, resort to regional agencies or arrangements or other peaceful means of their choice.

The same methods of dispute settlement are stipulated in article 33(1) of the UN Charter, although in the context of disputes the continuance of which are likely to endanger international peace and security. The 1970 Declaration, which is not so limited, asserts that in seeking an early and just settlement, the parties are to agree upon such peaceful means as they see appropriate to the circumstances and nature of the dispute.

There would appear, therefore, to be no inherent hierarchy with respect to the methods specified. In addition, it is to be noted that the parties to a dispute have the duty to continue to seek a settlement by other peaceful means agreed by them, in the event of the failure of one particular method. Should the means elaborated fail to resolve a dispute, the continuance of which is likely to endanger the maintenance of international peace and security, the parties under article 37(1) of the Charter, "*shall refer it to the Security Council*".[10]

---

[9] General Assembly resolution 2625 (XXV). See also the Manila Declaration on the Peaceful Settlement of International Disputes, General Assembly resolution 37/590.

[10] Emphasis added.

DIPLOMATIC METHODS OF DISPUTE SETTLEMENT

Negotiation [11]

Of all the procedures used to resolve differences, the simplest and most utilised form is understandably negotiation. It consists basically of discussions between the interested parties with a view to reconciling divergent opinions, or at least understanding the different positions maintained. It does not involve any third party, at least at that stage, and so differs from the other forms of dispute management.

In addition to being an extremely active method of settlement itself, negotiation is normally the precursor to other settlement procedures as the parties decide amongst themselves how best to resolve their differences.[12] It is eminently suited to the clarification, if not always resolution, of complicated disagreements. It is by mutual discussions that the essence of the differences will be revealed and the opposing contentions elucidated.

Negotiations are the most satisfactory means to resolve disputes since the parties are so directly engaged. Negotiations, of course, do not always succeed, since they do depend on a certain degree of mutual goodwill, flexibility and sensitivity. Hostile public opinion in one state may prevent the concession of certain points and mutual distrust may fatally complicate the process, while opposing political attitudes may be such as to preclude any acceptable negotiated agreement.

In certain circumstances there may exist a duty to enter into negotiations. This will usually arise on account of bilateral or multilateral agreements providing for the submission of disputes to various third party forms of settlement where negotiation has not succeeded.[13] Where disputes are by their continuance likely to

---

[11] See e.g. Merrills, *op. cit.*, Chapter 1 and Lachs, "The Law and Settlement of International Disputes" in *Dispute Settlement, op. cit.*, pp.287-89. See also Murty, *op. cit.*, pp.678-79; Watson, *Diplomacy*, 1982; Kirgis, *Prior Consultation in International Law*, 1983 and De Waart, *The Element of Negotiation in the Pacific Settlement of Disputes between States*, 1974. Note also that operative paragraph 10 of the Manila Declaration (*supra*, footnote 9) emphasises that direct negotiations are a "flexible and effective means of peaceful settlement".

[12] See e.g. Judge Nervo, *Fisheries Jurisdiction* case, ICJ Reports, 1973, pp.3, 45; 55 *ILR*, pp.183, 225.

[13] See e.g. the *Fisheries Jurisdiction* case, ICJ Reports, 1974, p.3; 55 *ILR*, p.238. See also article 41 of the Vienna Convention on Succession of States in Respect of Treaties, 1978.

endanger the maintenance of international peace and security, article 33 of the UN Charter provides that the parties to such disputes shall first of all seek a solution by negotiation, inquiry or mediation, and then resort, if the efforts have not borne fruit, to more complex forms of resolution.[14]

Good Offices and Mediation [15]

The employment of the procedures of good offices and mediation involves the use of a third party, whether an individual or individuals, a state or group of states or an international organisation, to encourage the contending parties to come to a settlement. Unlike the techniques of arbitration and adjudication, the process aims at persuading the parties to a dispute to reach satisfactory terms for its termination by themselves. Provisions for settling the dispute are not prescribed.

Technically, good offices are involved where a third party attempts to influence the opposing sides to enter into negotiations, whereas mediation implies the active participation in the negotiating process of the third party itself. In fact, the dividing line between the two approaches is often difficult to maintain as they tend to merge into one another, depending upon the circumstances. One example of the good offices method is the role played by the American President in 1906 in concluding the Russian-Japanese War.[16] Another might be the part played by France in encouraging US-North Vietnamese negotiations to begin in Paris in the early 1970s.[17]

A mediator, such as the US Secretary of State in the Middle East in 1973-74,[18] has an active and vital function to perform in seeking to cajole the disputing parties into accepting what are often his own

[14] See the *North Sea Continental Shelf* cases, ICJ Reports, 1969, pp.3, 47; 41 *ILR*, pp.29, 77 and the *Fisheries Jurisdiction* cases, ICJ Reports, 1974, pp.3, 32; 55 *ILR*, p.267.

[15] See e.g. Merrills, *op. cit.*, Chapter 2; Brierly, *The Law of Nations*, 6th ed., 1963, pp.373-76 and Murty, *op. cit.*, pp.680-81. See also *International Mediation in Theory and Practice* (eds. Touval and Zartman), 1985.

[16] Murty, *op. cit.*, p.681. See also Security Council resolution 367 (1975) requesting the UN Secretary-General to undertake a good offices mission to Cyprus.

[17] Note also the role played by Cardinal Samoré, a Papal mediator in the Beagle Channel dispute between Argentina and Chile, between 1978-85, see e.g. Merrills, *op. cit.*, p.29 and 24 *ILM*, 1985, p.1 *et seq*. See also *infra*, p.653.

[18] See e.g. *DUSPIL* 1974, pp.656-58 and *ibid.*, pp.759-62.

proposals. It is his responsibility to reconcile the different claims and improve the atmosphere pervading the discussions.

The Hague Conventions of 1899 and 1907 laid down many of the rules governing these two processes. It was stipulated that the signatories to the treaties had a right to offer good offices or mediation, even during hostilities, and that the exercise of the right was never to be regarded by either of the contending sides as an unfriendly act.[19] It was also explained that such procedures were not binding.

The Conventions laid a duty upon the parties to a serious dispute or conflict to resort to good offices or mediation as far as circumstances allow, before having recourse to arms.[20] This, of course, has to be seen in the light of the relevant Charter provisions regarding the use of force, but it does point to the part that should be played by these diplomatic procedures.

Inquiry [21]

Where differences of opinion on factual matters underlie a dispute between parties, the logical solution is often to institute a commission of inquiry to be conducted by reputable observers to ascertain precisely the facts in contention.[22] Provisions for such inquiries were first elaborated in the 1899 Hague Conference as a possible alternative to the use of arbitration.[23] However, the technique is limited in that it can only have relevance in the case of international disputes, involving neither the honour nor the vital interests of the parties where the conflict centres around a genuine disagreement as to particular facts which can be resolved by recourse to an impartial and conscientious investigation.[24]

---

[19] Article 3 of Hague Convention no.I, 1899 and Convention no.I, 1907.

[20] *Ibid.*, article 2.

[21] See e.g. Merrills, *op. cit.*, Chapter 3 and Bar-Yaacov, *The Handling of International Disputes by Means of Inquiry*, 1974.

[22] Inquiry as a specific procedure under consideration here is to be distinguished from the general process of fact-finding as part of other mechanisms for dispute settlement, such as through the UN or other institutions.

[23] See e.g. Bar-Yaacov, *op. cit.*, Chapter 2. The incident of the destruction of the US battleship *Maine* in 1898, which precipitated the American-Spanish War, was particularly noted as an impetus to the evolution of inquiry as an important "safety valve" mechanism, *ibid.*, pp.33-34. This was particularly in the light of the rival national inquiries that came to opposing conclusions in that episode.

[24] Article 9, 1899 Hague Convention for the Pacific Settlement of International Disputes.

Inquiry was most successfully used in the Dogger Bank incident of 1904 where Russian naval ships fired on British fishing boats in the belief that they were hostile Japanese torpedo craft.[25] The Hague provisions were put into effect[26] and the report of the international inquiry commission contributed to a peaceful settlement of the issue.[27] This encouraged an elaboration of the technique by the 1907 Hague Conference,[28] and a wave of support for the procedure.[29] The United States, for instance, between 1913 and 1940 concluded 48 bilateral treaties with provisions in each one of them for the creation of a permanent inquiry commission. These agreements were known as the 'Bryan Treaties'.[30]

However, the use of commissions of inquiry in accordance with the Hague Convention of 1907 proved in practice to be extremely rare. The *Red Crusader* inquiry of 1962[31] followed an interval of some forty years since the previous inquiry. This concerned an incident between a British trawler and a Danish fisheries protection vessel, which subsequently involved a British frigate. Although instituted as a fact-finding exercise, it did incorporate judicial aspects. A majority of the Commission were lawyers and the procedures followed a judicial pattern. In addition, aspects of the report reflected legal findings, such as the declaration that the firing on the trawler by the Danish vessel in an attempt to stop it escaping arrest for alleged illegal fishing, "exceeded legitimate use of armed force".[32] There have been no similar inquiries since 1962.

---

[25] Bar-Yaacov, *op. cit.*, Chapter 3. See also Merrills, *op. cit.*, pp.44-46.

[26] The Commission of Inquiry consisted of four naval officers of the UK, Russian, French and American fleets, plus a fifth member chosen by the other four (in the event an Austro-Hungarian). It was required to examine all the circumstances, particularly with regard to responsibility and blame.

[27] It was found that there was no justification for the Russian attack. In the event, both sides accepted the report and the sum of £65,000 was paid by Russia to the UK, Bar-Yaacov, *op. cit.*, p.70.

[28] *Ibid.*, Chapter 4. Note also the *Tavignano, Tiger* and *Tubantia* inquiries, Merrills, *op. cit.*, pp.46-50 and Bar-Yaacov, *op. cit.*, pp.141-79.

[29] *Ibid.*, Chapter 5.

[30] These were prefigured by the Taft or Knox Treaties of 1911 (which did not come into operation), *ibid.*, pp.113-17. The USSR has also signed a number of treaties which provide for joint inquiries with regard to frontier incidents, *ibid.*, pp.117-19.

[31] *Ibid.*, pp.179-95 and Merrills, *op. cit.*, pp.51-54. See also 35 *ILR*, p.485, Cmnd. 776 and E. Lauterpacht, "The Contemporary Practice of the UK in the Field of International Law", 1962, vol.1, pp.50-53.

[32] *Ibid.*, p.53, Merrills, *op. cit.*, p.54 and Bar-Yaacov, *op. cit.*, p.192.

The value of inquiry within specified institutional frameworks, nevertheless, has been evident. Its use has increased within the United Nations generally and in the specialised agencies. Inquiry is also part of other processes of dispute settlement in the context of general fact-finding. But inquiry as a separate mechanism in accordance with the Hague Convention of 1907 has fallen out of favour. In many disputes, of course, the determination of the relevant circumstances would simply not aid a settlement, whilst its nature as a third party involvement in a situation would discourage some states.

Conciliation [33]

The process of conciliation involves a third party investigation of the basis of the dispute and the submission of a report embodying suggestions for a settlement. As such it involves elements of both inquiry and mediation, and in fact the process of conciliation did emerge from treaties providing for permanent inquiry commissions.[34]

Conciliation reports are only proposals and do not constitute binding decisions. They are thus different from arbitration awards. The period between the World Wars was the heyday for conciliation commissions and many treaties made provision for them as a method for resolving disputes. But the process has not been widely employed and certainly has not justified the faith evinced in them by states between 1920 and 1938.[35]

Nevertheless, they do have a role to play. They are extremely flexible and by clarifying the facts and discussing proposals may stimulate negotiations between the parties. The rules dealing with conciliation were elaborated in the 1928 General Act on the Pacific Settlement of International Disputes. The function of the commissions was defined to include inquiries and mediation techniques. Such commissions were to be composed of five

[33] See e.g. Lauterpacht, *op. cit.*, pp.260-69; Merrills, *op. cit.*, Chapter 4 and Murty, *op. cit.*, pp.682-83. See also Fox, "Conciliation" in *International Disputes, op. cit.*, p.93; Cot, *International Conciliation*, 1968 and Bowett, *op. cit.*, Chapter II.

[34] See e.g. Murty, *op. cit.* Merrills notes that by 1940, nearly two hundred conciliation treaties had been concluded, *op. cit.*, p.61.

[35] But note e.g. the Chaco Commission, 1929, the Franco-Siamese Conciliation Commission, 1947 and the Franco-Swiss Commission, 1955, see Merrills, *op. cit.*, pp.62-65. See also Bar-Yaacov, *op. cit.*, Chapter 7.

persons, one appointed by each opposing side and the other three to be appointed by agreement from amongst the citizens of third states. The proceedings were to be concluded within six months and were not to be held in public. The conciliation procedure was intended to deal with mixed legal-factual situations and to operate quickly and informally.

There have of late been a number of proposals to reactivate the conciliation technique, but how far they will succeed in their aim remains to be seen.[36] A number of multilateral treaties do, however, provide for conciliation as a means of resolving disputes. The 1957 European Convention for the Peaceful Settlement of Disputes, the 1969 Vienna Convention on the Law of Treaties and the 1982 Convention on the Law of the Sea all contain provisions concerning conciliation. The conciliation procedure was used in the Iceland-Norway dispute over the continental shelf delimitation between Iceland and Jan Mayen island.[37] The agreement establishing the Conciliation Commission stressed that the question was the subject of continuing negotiations and that the Commission report would not be binding, both elements characteristic of the conciliation method. The Commission had also to take into account Iceland's strong economic interests in the area as well as other factors. The role of the concept of natural prolongation within continental shelf delimitation was examined as well as the legal status of islands and relevant state practice and court decisions. The solution proposed by the Commission was for a joint development zone, an idea that would have been unlikely to come from a judicial body reaching a decision solely on the basis of the legal rights of the parties. In other words, the flexibility of the conciliation process seen in the context of continued negotiations between the parties was demonstrated.

Although the various diplomatic procedures may be divided into negotiation, good offices, mediation, inquiry and conciliation, many situations will of course call for various combinations of these in efforts to settle international disputes.

---

[36] See e.g. the Regulations on the Procedure of Conciliation adopted by the Institut de Droit International, *Annuaire de l'Institut de Droit International*, 1961, p.374 *et seq.*

[37] 20 *ILM*, 1981, p.797; 62 *ILR*, p.108. The Commission Report was accepted by the parties, 21 *ILM*, 1982, p.1222.

THE UNITED NATIONS AND THE SETTLEMENT OF DISPUTES [38]

Many of the techniques elaborated in the preceding section are in fact used within the UN system of conflict management, but since the context is a special one and since the system itself is of vital importance, a separate section is required.

The provisions set out in the UN Charter are to a large degree based upon the terms of the Covenant of the League of Nations as amended in the light of experience. Accordingly, in order to be able better to understand the background of the UN system a brief summary of the procedures provided for within the League for solving disputes is necessary.[39]

Article 12 of the Covenant declared that any dispute likely to lead to a conflict between members was to be dealt with in one of three ways: by arbitration, by judicial settlement or by inquiry by the Council of the League. The third approach will be noted here, since arbitration and judicial settlement differ little from contemporary practice and will be reviewed in succeeding sections. Article 15 noted that the Council was to try to effect a settlement of the dispute in question, but if that failed, it was to publish a report containing the facts of the case and "the recommendations which are deemed just and proper in regard thereto". This report was not, however, binding upon the parties, but if it was a unanimous one the League members were not to go to war "with any party to the dispute which complies with the recommendations of the report". If the report was merely a majority one, League members reserved to themselves "the right to take such action as they shall consider necessary for the maintenance of right and justice".

In other words, in the latter case the Covenant did not absolutely prohibit the resort to war by members.

---

[38] See e.g. *Dispute Settlement through the United Nations*, *op. cit.*; Merrills, *op. cit.*, Chapter 9; Bar-Yaacov, *op. cit.*, Chapter 8; Murty, *op. cit.*, p.717 *et seq*; Goodrich and Simons, *The United Nations and the Maintenance of International Peace and Security*, 1955; *The Evolving United Nations – A Prospect for Peace?* (ed. Twitchett), 1971; Luard, *A History of the United Nations*, vol.1, 1982 and *The Strategy of World Order*, vol.3; *The United Nations* (ed. Falk and Mendlovitz), 1966. See also *La Charte des Nations Unies* (eds. Cot and Pellet), 1985, pp.567-643 and White, *The United Nations and the Maintenance of International Peace and Security*, 1990.

[39] See generally, e.g. Scott, *The Rise and Fall of the League of Nations*, 1973, and *The Strategy of World Order*, *op. cit.*, Chapter 1.

Where a member resorted to war in disregard of the Covenant, then the various sanctions prescribed in article 16 might apply, although whether the circumstances in which sanctions might be enforced had actually arisen was a point to be decided by the individual members and not by the League itself. Sanctions were in fact used against Italy in 1935-36, but in a half-hearted manner due to political considerations by the leading states at the time.[40]

The primary objective of the United Nations as stipulated under the Charter is the maintenance of international peace and security and disputes likely to endanger this are required under article 33 to be solved "by negotiation, inquiry, mediation, conciliation, arbitration, judicial settlement, resort to regional agencies or arrangements or other peaceful means". Indeed, the Charter declares as one of its purposes in article 1, "to bring about by peaceful means and in conformity with the principles of justice and international law, adjustment or settlement of international disputes or situations which might lead to a breach of the peace".

By article 24, the members of the UN conferred on the Security Council primary responsibility for the maintenance of international peace and security, and by article 25 agreed to carry out the decisions of the Security Council. Under the Charter, the role of the Security Council when dealing with the pacific settlement of disputes under Chapter VI is not the same as when the Council is contemplating action relating to threats to or breaches of the peace, or acts of aggression under Chapter VII. In the former instance there is no power to make binding decisions with regard to member-states. It may only make recommendations. This distinction is important. The functions of the Council under Chapter VII of the Charter will be noted later.[41]

In pursuance of its primary responsibility, the Security Council may, by article 34, "investigate any dispute, or any situation which might lead to international friction or give rise to dispute, in order to determine whether the continuance of the dispute or situation is likely to endanger the maintenance of international peace and security". In addition to this power of investigation, the

---

[40] See e.g. Scott, *op. cit.*, Chapter 15.
[41] *Infra*, Chapter 18, p.702-12.

Security Council can, where it deems necessary, call upon the parties to settle their dispute by the means elaborated in article 33.[42]

The Council may intervene if it wishes at any stage of a dispute or situation, the continuance of which is likely to endanger international peace and security and under article 36(1) recommend appropriate procedures or methods of adjustment. But in making such recommendations, which are not binding, it must take into consideration the general principle that legal disputes should be referred by the parties to the International Court of Justice. This process was involved when the Security Council recommended that the UK and Albania should take their case regarding the *Corfu Channel* incident to the International Court.[43] Nevertheless, this example proved to be exceptional.[44]

Where the parties to a dispute cannot resolve it by the various methods under article 33, they should refer it to the Security Council by article 37. The Council, where it is convinced that the continuance of the dispute is likely to endanger international peace and security, may recommend not only procedures and adjustment methods, but also such terms of settlement as it may consider appropriate.

Once the Council, however, has determined the existence of a threat to, or a breach of, the peace or act of aggression, it may make decisions which are binding upon member-states of the UN, but until that point it can issue recommendations only.

Any UN member-state may bring a dispute before the Council, while a non-member-state may do likewise under article 35 provided it is a party to the dispute in question and "accepts in advance, for the purposes of the dispute, the obligations of pacific settlement provided in the present Charter". The General Assembly may make recommendations to the Council regarding any questions or issues within the scope of the Charter or relating to the maintenance of international peace, so long as the Council itself is not already

[42] Note that under article 38, the Security Council may make recommendations to the parties with regard to the peaceful settlement of disputes generally if all the parties to the dispute so request.

[43] Security Council resolution 22 (1947). See SCOR, 2nd yr., 127th meeting, 9 April 1947, p.727. See also Luard, *op. cit.*, pp.209-12.

[44] See also Security Council resolution 395 (1976) calling for negotiations between Turkey and Greece over the Aegean Sea continental shelf dispute and inviting the parties to refer the question to the International Court.

exercising its functions with regard to the same question. The Assembly has the power, under article 11, to call the attention of the Council to situations likely to endanger international peace and security.

Similarly, the Secretary-General of the UN may, by article 99, bring to the Council's attention any matter which in his opinion may threaten the preservation of international peace and security.

In practice, the Security Council has applied all the diplomatic techniques available in various international disputes. This is in addition to open debates and the behind-the-scenes discussions and lobbying that take place. On numerous occasions it has called upon the parties to a dispute to negotiate a settlement and has requested that it be kept informed. The Council offered its good offices in the late 1940s with regard to the Dutch-Indonesian dispute[45] and has had recourse to mediation attempts in many other conflicts, for example with regard to the Kashmir[46] and Cyprus[47] questions.[48]

However, the cases where the Council has recommended procedures or methods of adjustment under article 36 have been comparatively rare. Only in the *Corfu Channel* and *Aegean Sea* disputes did the Council recommend the parties to turn to the International Court.[49]

Probably the most famous Security Council resolution recommending a set of principles to be taken into account in resolving a particular dispute is resolution 242 (1967) dealing with the Middle East. This resolution pointed to two basic principles to be applied in establishing a just and lasting peace in the Middle East: first, Israeli withdrawal "from territories occupied in the recent conflict",[50] and secondly the termination of all claims of belligerency and acknowledgment of the right of every state in the area to live in peace within secure and recognised

---

[45] See e.g. Luard, *op. cit.*, Chapter 9, and S/1156. See also S/514 and S/1234 and Murty, *op. cit.*, p.721

[46] *Ibid.* See also Luard, *op. cit.*, Chapter 14.

[47] See e.g. Murty, *op. cit.*, p.721. See also Ehrlich, *Cyprus 1958-1967*, 1974.

[48] Note also the appointment of Count Bernadotte and Dr. Jarring as UN mediators in the Middle East in 1948 and 1967 respectively. See Luard, *op. cit.*, Chapters 10 and 11, and *The Arab-Israeli Conflict* (ed. Moore), 3 vols., 1974.

[49] *Supra*, footnotes 43 and 44.

[50] I.e. the Six Day War of 1967.

frontiers. Various other points were referred to in resolution 242, including the need to guarantee freedom of navigation through international waterways in the area, achieve a just settlement of the refugee problem and reinforce the territorial inviolability of every state in the area through measures such as the use of demilitarised zones. As well as listing these factors, deemed important in any Middle East settlement by the Security Council, the Secretary-General of the UN was asked to designate a special representative to mediate in the dispute and keep the Council informed on the progress of his efforts. Thus, in this instance the Security Council proposed that a dispute be tackled by a combination of prescribed proposals reinforced by mediation.[51]

Although the primary responsibility with regard to international disputes lies with the Security Council, this should not be taken as meaning that the General Assembly, comprising all member-states of the UN organisation, is denied a role altogether. It may discuss any question or matter within the scope of the Charter, including the maintenance of international peace and security, and may make recommendations to the members of the UN or the Security Council, provided the Council is not itself dealing with the same matter.[52]

Under similar conditions, the Assembly may under article 14 "recommend measures for the peaceful adjustment of any situation regardless of origin, which it deems likely to impair the general welfare or friendly relations among nations".[53]

In practice, the resolutions and declarations of the General Assembly (which are not binding) have covered a very wide field, from colonial disputes to alleged violations of human rights and the need for justice in international economic affairs. The Assembly has also asserted its right to deal with a threat to or breach of the peace or act of aggression if the Security Council fails to act because of the exercise of the veto by a permanent member.[54]

---

[51] See as to resolution 242 (1967) and the Israeli-Arab conflict generally, the sources cited in footnote 48. Resolution 242 (1967) was reaffirmed in Security Council resolution 338 (1973).

[52] Articles 10, 11 and 12 of the UN Charter.

[53] Note e.g. the General Assembly resolution 181 (II) of 1947, recommending the partition of Palestine into Jewish and Arab states and an international area around Jerusalem.

[54] Resolution 377(V), the "Uniting for Peace" resolution. See further *infra*, Chapter 18, p.712.

The role of the General Assembly has increased over the years due to two factors. First, the existence of the veto in the Security Council has rendered that organ powerless in many important disputes since the permanent members (USA, UK, USSR, France and China) rarely agree with respect to any conflict, and secondly the vast increase in the membership of the UN, which has had the effect of radicalising the Assembly and its deliberations. For similar reasons, the functions performed by the UN Secretary-General have increased far beyond those originally envisaged.[55] In addition to constant exhortations and mediation attempts,[56] he has played the leading role in the despatch of UN troops to a number of conflict areas, in the hope of restoring order and enabling a lasting settlement to be achieved.[57]

The position of the United Nations has improved with the ending of the Cold War and the substantial changes in the approach of the USSR in particular.[58] More emphasis has been laid upon the importance of the UN in the context of an increased co-operation with the US. This is having a significant impact upon the work and achievements of the UN and provides the potential for a vastly increased role for the organisation. The new co-operative approach led to the agreements leading to the independence of Namibia,[59] while substantial progress has been made by the five permanent members of the Security Council in working out a solution to the Cambodian problem. This solution would involve the creation of a Supreme National Council consisting of representatives of various Cambodian factions, which would turn over most of its powers to the UN until the election of a new Cambodian government. The UN would probably administer defence, foreign affairs, finance, public security and information. This plan would of necessity require the involvement of substantial numbers of military and civilian UN personnel and if implemented would constitute the most extensive role the UN has played in resolving a crisis

[55] See e.g. Pechota, "The Quiet Approach" in *Dispute Settlement, op. cit.*, p.577; Murty, *op. cit.*, pp.724-25 and Merrills, *op. cit.*, pp.185-91. See also Gordentler, *The UN Secretary-General and the Maintenance of International Peace*, 1967.

[56] See e.g. Security Council resolution 505 (1982) requesting the Secretary-General *inter alia* to enter into contact with Argentina and the UK in order to negotiate a cease-fire in the Falklands conflict.

[57] See further *infra*, Chapter 18, p.715.

[58] See further *supra*, p.34.

[59] *Supra*, p.159.

situation.[60] The reaction of the UN to the Gulf crisis[61] is the most spectacular example of the impact of the changes wrought by the recent metamorphosis in international relations.

REGIONAL INSTITUTIONS AND DISPUTE SETTLEMENT [62]

Article 52 of the UN Charter provides that nothing in the Charter precludes the existence of regional arrangements or agencies for dealing with such matters relating to the maintenance of international peace and security as are appropriate for regional action, provided that such arrangements or agencies and their activities are consistent with the purposes and principles of the UN. It is also noted that members of the UN included in such arrangements or agencies are to make every effort to settle local disputes peacefully through such regional arrangements or by such regional agencies before referring them to the Security Council, and that the Security Council encourages the development of the peaceful settlement of local disputes through such regional arrangements. That having been said, article 52(4) stresses that the application of articles 34 and 35 of the UN Charter[63] remains unaffected. The supremacy of the Security Council is reinforced by article 53(1) which provides that while the Council may, where appropriate, utilise such regional arrangements or agencies for enforcement action under its authority, "no enforcement action shall be taken under regional arrangements or by regional agencies without the authorisation of the Security Council". It should also be noted that article 103 of the Charter emphasised that in the event of a conflict between the obligations of a UN member under the Charter and obligations under any other international agreement, the former are to prevail.

Various regional organisations have created machinery for the settlement of disputes.

[60] See e.g. *Keesing's Record of World Events*, p.37654 (1990). Note also the role played by the Personal Representative of the UN Secretary-General in the negotiating process leading to the signature of the Geneva Accords on the Settlement of the Situation Relating to Afghanistan 1988; see *The Geneva Accords* published by the United Nations, 1988, DPI/935-40420.

[61] *Infra*, p.706 and p.710.

[62] See e.g. Bowett, *The Law of International Institutions*, 4th ed., 1982; Merrills, *op. cit.*, Chapter 10 and Murty, *op. cit.*, pp.725-28. See also Oellers-Frahm and Wühler, *Dispute Settlement in Public International Law*, 1984, p.92 *et seq.*

[63] *Supra*, pp.640-42.

The Organisation of African Unity [64]

One of the principles of the OAU is "the peaceful settlement of disputes by negotiation, mediation, conciliation or arbitration" and accordingly a Commission of Mediation, Conciliation and Arbitration was established.[65] The jurisdiction of the Commission is not compulsory and indeed it has never been resorted to. African states have been unwilling to resort to judicial or arbitral methods of dispute settlement and have in general preferred informal third party involvement through the medium of the OAU. In the Algerian-Morocco boundary dispute,[66] for example, the OAU established an *ad hoc* commission consisting of the representatives of seven African states to seek to achieve a settlement of issues arising out of the 1963 clashes.[67] Similarly in the Somali-Ethiopian conflict,[68] a commission was set up by the OAU in an attempt to mediate.[69] This commission failed to resolve the dispute, although it did reaffirm the principle of the inviolability of frontiers of member states as attained at the time of independence.[70] In a third case, the Western Sahara dispute,[71] an OAU committee was established in July 1978, which has sought to reach a settlement in the conflict, so far unsuccessfully,[72] while the OAU has also established committees to try to mediate in the Chad civil war, again with little success.[73] Despite mixed success, it is fairly established practice that in a dispute involving African states, initial recourse will be made to OAU mechanisms, primarily *ad hoc* commissions or committees.

The Organisation of American States [74]

The Charter of the OAS, signed at Bogotá in 1948, provides that

[64] See generally Elias, *Africa and the Development of International Law*, 1972; Cervenka, *The Organisation of African Unity and its Charter*, 1968 and Shaw, "Dispute Settlement in Africa", 37 *YBWA*, 1983, p.149.

[65] Elias, *op. cit.*, Chapter 9.

[66] See Brownlie, *African Boundaries*, 1979, p.55 and Shaw, *Title to Territory in Africa*, 1986, pp.196-97.

[67] See *Keesings Contemporary Archives*, pp.19939-40 and Shaw, *op. cit.* footnote 64, p.153.

[68] See Brownlie, *op. cit.*, p.826. See also Shaw, *op. cit.* footnote 66, pp.197-201.

[69] *Africa Research Bulletin*, May 1973, p.2845 and *ibid.*, June 1973, pp.2883-4 and 2850.

[70] *Ibid.*, August 1980, pp.5763-64.

[71] See e.g. Shaw, *op. cit.* footnote 66, p.123 *et seq.*

[72] *Ibid.*, and Shaw, *op. cit.* footnote 64, pp.160-62.

[73] *Ibid.*, pp.158-60.

[74] See e.g. Merrills, *op. cit.*, pp.209-10 and Bowett, *op. cit.*, p.215 *et seq.*

disputes must be submitted to the Organisation for peaceful settlement before being referred to the UN Security Council. The 1948 American Treaty of Pacific Settlement (the Pact of Bogotá, to be distinguished from the Charter) sets out the procedures in detail, ranging from good offices, mediation and conciliation to arbitration and judicial settlement by the International Court of Justice. This treaty, however, has not been successful and in practice the OAS has utilised the Inter-American Peace Committee created in 1940 for peaceful resolution of disputes. This was replaced in 1970 by the Inter-American Committee on Peaceful Settlement, a subsidiary organ of the Council. Since the late 1950s the Council of the OAS, a plenary body at ambassadorial level, has played an increasingly important role.[75]

Other Regional Mechanisms

In the Middle East, the Arab League,[76] established in 1945, aims at increasing co-operation between the Arab states. Its facilities for peaceful settlement of disputes amongst its members are not, however, very well developed, and in practice consist primarily of informal conciliation attempts. One notable exception was the creation in 1961 of an Inter-Arab Force to keep the peace between Iraq and Kuwait.[77]

Within the NATO alliance,[78] there exist good offices facilities, and inquiry, mediation, conciliation and arbitration procedures may be instituted. In fact, the Organisation has proved of some use, for instance in the longstanding 'cod war' between Britain and Iceland, two NATO partners.[79]

The various specialised agencies[80] which encourage international co-operation in functional spheres have their own procedures for settling disputes between their members relating to the interpretation of their constitutional instruments. Such procedures vary from organisation to organisation. The UN Educational, Scientific and

---

[75] See e.g. Merrills, *op. cit.*, pp.214-16.

[76] See e.g. Bowett, *op. cit.*, p.229.

[77] Note also the pan-Arab "peacekeeping force" in the Lebanon between 1976-82, see *Keesings Contemporary Archives*, p.28117 *et seq.* See also Thakur, *International Peacekeeping in Lebanon*, 1987.

[78] See e.g. Bowett, *op. cit.*, p.180 and Merrills, *op. cit.*, p.208.

[79] *Ibid.*, p.213. See also the CSCE mechanisms following the Charter of Paris 1990.

[80] See e.g. Murty, *op. cit.*, pp.729-32. See further *infra*, Chapter 19.

Cultural Organisation (UNESCO) constitution refers to arbitration and judicial settlement,[81] while the International Labour Organisation has the power to set up Commissions of Inquiry to report on disputes.[82] It should also be noted that several international treaties expressly provide mechanisms and methods for the peaceful resolution of disputes arising therefrom.[83]

ARBITRATION [84]

The procedure of arbitration grew to some extent out of the processes of diplomatic settlement and represented an advance towards a developed international legal system. In its modern form, it emerged with the Jay Treaty of 1974 between Britain and America, which provided for the establishment of mixed commissions to solve legal disputes between the parties.[85]

The procedure was successfully used in the *Alabama Claims* arbitration[86] of 1872 between the two countries, which resulted in the UK having to pay compensation for the damage caused by a Confederate warship built in the UK. This success stimulated further arbitrations, for example the *Behring Sea*[87] and *British Guiana and Venezuela Boundary*[88] arbitrations at the close of the nineteenth century.[89]

The 1899 Hague Convention for the Pacific Settlement of Disputes

---

[81] See article 14 of the 1957 Constitution. But note that the 1962 Special Protocol to the Convention against Discrimination in Education provided for a Conciliation and Good Offices Commission. See also *supra*, Chapter 6, p.219.

[82] Murty, *op. cit.*, pp.729-30. See also Bowett, *op. cit.*, pp.152-54. See also *supra* Chapter 6, p.217.

[83] See e.g. *supra* p.392 with regard to the Convention on the Law of the Sea 1982, and *supra* p.601 and 611 with regard to the Conventions on the Law of Treaties 1969 and 1986.

[84] See e.g. Wetter, *The International Arbitral Process Public and Private*, 5 vols., 1979; Simpson and Fox, *International Arbitration*, 1959; Murty, *op. cit.*, p.684 *et seq.*; Merrills, *op. cit.*, Chapter 5; Ralston, *International Arbitration*, 1929; Carlston, *The Process of International Arbitration*, 1946 and Stuyt, *Survey of International Arbitrations*, 1972. See also Sohn, "International Arbitration Today", 108 *HR*, p.1 and Fox, "States and the Undertaking to Arbitrate", 37 *ICLQ*, 1988, p.1.

[85] See Simpson and Fox, *op. cit.*, pp.1-4. Note also the Treaty of Ghent, 1814, which incorporated the concept of a neutral element within the commission, *ibid.* See also Schwarzenberger, "Present-Day Relevance of the Jay Treaty Arbitrations", 53 *Notre Dame Lawyer*, 1978, p.715.

[86] Moore, *International Arbitrations*, vol.1, 1898, p.495.

[87] *Ibid.*, p.755.

[88] 92 *BFSP*, p.970.

[89] See also "Projet de Règlement pour la Procédure Arbitrale Internationale", *Annuaire de l'Institut de Droit International*, 1877, p.126.

included a number of provisions on international arbitration, the object of which was deemed to be under article XV, "the settlement of differences between states by judges of their own choice and on the basis of respect for law". International arbitration was held to be the most effective and equitable manner of dispute settlement, where diplomacy had failed. An agreement to arbitrate under article XVIII implied the legal obligation to accept the terms of the award. In addition, a Permanent Court of Arbitration was established.[90] It is not really a court since it is not composed of a fixed body of judges. It consists of a panel of persons, nominated by the contracting states (each one nominating a maximum of four), comprising individuals "of known competency in questions of international law, of the highest moral reputation and disposed to accept the duties of an arbitrator".[91] Where contracting states wish to go to arbitration, they are entitled to choose the members of the tribunal from the panel. Thus, it is in essence machinery facilitating the establishment of arbitral tribunals. The PCA also consists of an International Bureau, which acts as the registry of the Court and keeps its records, and a Permanent Administrative Council, exercising administrative control over the Bureau.[92]

Between 1900 and 1932 some twenty disputes went through the PCA procedure, but since then the numbers have fallen drastically so that only three cases have been heard since the early 1930s, although there have been suggestions in the last few years to revitalise the PCA arbitration system.[93]

Nevertheless, there has been continuing interest in the arbitration process itself. The International Law Commission formulated a set of Model Rules on Arbitral Procedure, which was adopted by the General Assembly in 1958.[94]

[90] See the UK-France Agreement of 1903, providing for referral of differences of a legal nature to the Permanent Court of Arbitration, so long as the "vital interests" of the parties were not involved, Cd. 1837.

[91] Article XLIV of the Convention as revised in 1907.

[92] See Murty, *op. cit.*, p.685. See also Hudson, *The Permanent Court of International Justice 1920-1942*, 1943, p.11.

[93] See generally Von Mangoldt, "Arbitration and Conciliation" in *The International Arbitral Process, op. cit.*, vol.V, p.243 *et seq.* and Johnson, "International Arbitration Back in Favour?", 34 *YBWA*, 1980, p.305.

[94] Resolution 1262(XI). These are, however, merely optional. See also Report of the ILC, 1958, A/3859. Note also the 1928 General Act, the 1929 General Treaty of Inter-American Arbitration and the 1949 Revised General Act. See also *Yearbook of the ILC*, 1953, vol.II, p.208.

Arbitration tribunals may be composed in different ways.[95] There may be a single arbitrator or a collegiate body. In the latter case, each party will appoint an equal number of arbitrators with the chairman or umpire being appointed by either the parties or the arbitrators already nominated. In many cases, a head of state will be suggested as a single arbitrator and he will then nominate an expert or experts in the field of international law or other relevant disciplines to act for him.[96]

Under the PCA system, and in the absence of agreement to the contrary, each party selects two arbitrators from the panel, only one of whom may be a national of the state. These arbitrators then choose an umpire, but if they fail to do so, this task will be left to a third party, nominated by agreement. If this also fails to produce a result, a complicated process then ensues culminating in the drawing of lots.

States are not obliged to submit a dispute to the procedure of arbitration, in the absence of their consent.[97] This consent may be expressed in arbitration treaties, in which the contracting states agree to submit certain kinds of disputes that may arise between them to arbitration, or in specific provisions of general treaties, which provide for disputes with regard to the treaty itself to be submitted to arbitration,[98] although the number of treaties dealing primarily with the peaceful settlement of disputes has declined since 1945.[99]

Consent to the reference of a dispute to arbitration with regard to matters that have already arisen is usually expressed by means of a *compromis*, or special agreement, and the terms in which it is couched are of extreme importance. This is because the jurisdiction of the tribunal is defined in relation to the provisions of the treaty or *compromis*, whichever happens to be the relevant document in the particular case. However, in general, the tribunal may determine

---

[95] See e.g. Merrills, *op. cit.*, pp.83-86. It is, of course, an issue for the parties to decide.

[96] E.g. the *Argentina-Chile* case, 38 *ILR*, p.10 and the *Beagle Channel* case, HMSO, 1977; 52 *ILR*, p.93. Note also the *Interpretation of Peace Treaties* case, ICJ Reports, 1950, p.221; 17 *ILR*, p.318.

[97] See e.g. the *Eastern Carelia* case, PCIJ, Series B, no.5, 1923, p.27; 2 *ILR*, p.394 and the *Ambatielos* case, ICJ Reports, 1953, p.19; 20 *ILR*, p.547.

[98] See *Arbitration and Security: The Systematic Survey of the Arbitration Conventions and Treaties of Mutual Security Deposited with the League of Nations*, 1927, and *Systematic Survey of Treaties for the Pacific Settlement of International Disputes 1928-1948*, 1949.

[99] See Sohn, "Report on the Changing Role of Arbitration in the Settlement of International Disputes", International Law Association, 1966, pp.325, 334.

its competence in interpreting the *compromis* and other documents concerned in the case.[100]

The law to be applied in arbitration proceedings is international law,[101] but the parties may agree upon certain principles to be taken into account by the tribunal and specify this in the *compromis*. In this case, the tribunal must apply the rules specified. For example, in the *British Guiana and Venezuela Boundary* dispute,[102] it was emphasised that occupation for fifty years should be accepted as constituting a prescriptive title to territory. And in the *Trail Smelter* case,[103] the law to be applied was declared to be US law and practice with regard to such questions as well as international law.[104]

Agreements sometimes specify that the decisions should be reached in accordance with "law and equity" and this means that the general principles of justice common to legal systems should be taken into account as well as the provisions of international law. Such general principles may also be considered where there are no specific rules covering the situation under discussion.[105] The rules of procedure of the tribunal are often specified in the *compromis* and decided by the parties by agreement as the process commences. Hague Convention I of 1899 as revised in 1907 contains agreed procedure principles, which would apply in the absence of express stipulation.

---

[100] In the absence of agreement to the contrary. See e.g. the *Nottebohm* case, ICJ Reports, 1953, pp.111, 119; 20 *ILR*, pp.567, 572. See also article 48 of the Hague Convention, 1899, and article 73 of the Hague Convention, 1907.

[101] See e.g. the *Norwegian Shipowners' Claims* case, 1 *RIAA*, 1921, p.309.

[102] 92 *BFSP*, p.970.

[103] 3 *RIAA*, 1938, p.1908; 9 *ILR*, p.315.

[104] Note that in international commercial arbitrations, the reference often incorporates municipal law, see e.g. the *BP* case, 53 *ILR*, p.297, where the basic reference was to "the principles of the Law of Libya common to the principles of international law". See also the wide reference to the Iran-United States Claims Tribunal to decide all cases "on the basis of respect for law, applying such choice of law rules and principles of commercial and international law as the Tribunal determines to be applicable, taking into account relevant usages of the trade, contract provisions and changed circumstances", Article V, Declaration of Algiers concerning the Settlement of Claims by the Government of the USA and the Government of the Islamic Republic of Iran, 1981, 1 *Iran-US CTR*, pp.9, 11; 20 *ILM*, 1981, p.232.

[105] See e.g. *Re Competence of the Conciliation Commission*, 22 *ILR*, p.867 and *supra* Chapter 3, p.81. See also article 28 of the 1928 General Act, article 10 of the ILC Model Articles and articles 26 and 28 of the European Convention for the Peaceful Settlement of Disputes. Note in addition the *Rann of Kutch* case, 50 *ILR*, p.520.

Once an arbitral award has been made, it is final and binding upon the parties,[106] but in certain circumstances the award itself may be regarded as a nullity.[107] There is disagreement amongst lawyers as to the grounds on which such a decision may be taken. It is, however, fairly generally accepted that where a tribunal exceeds its powers under the *compromis,* its award may be treated as a nullity, although this is not a common occurrence. Such excess of power (*excès de pouvoir*) may be involved where the tribunal decides a question not submitted to it, or applies rules it is not authorised to apply. The main example of the former is the *North-Eastern Boundary* case,[108] between Canada and the United States, where the arbitrator, after being asked to decide which of two lines constituted the frontier, in fact chose a third line.

It is sometimes argued that invalidity of the *compromis* is a ground of nullity,[109] while the corruption of a member of the tribunal or a serious departure from a fundamental rule of procedure are further possibilities as grounds of nullity.[110] Article 35 of the Model Rules on Arbitral Procedure drawn up by the International Law Commission, for example, provides for a successful plea of nullity in three cases: excess of power, corruption of a tribunal member or serious departure from a fundamental rule of procedure, including failure to state the reasons of the award.[111] "Essential error" has also been suggested as a ground of nullity, but the definition of this is far from unambiguous.[112] It would appear not to cover the evaluation of documents and

---

[106] Articles 81 and 84, Hague Convention I, 1907. The principle of *res judicata* also applies to arbitration awards, see e.g. the *Trail Smelter* case, 3 *RIAA,* 1938, p.1905; 9 *ILR,* p.324 and the *Orinoco Steamship Co.* case, 11 *RIAA,* 1910, p.227.

[107] See e.g. Reisman, *Nullity and Revision,* 1971; Nantwi, *The Enforcement of International Judicial Decisions and Arbitral Awards in Public International Law,* 1967 and Schachter, "The Enforcement of International Judicial and Arbitral Decisions", 54 *AJIL,* 1960, p.1.

[108] See Hyde, *International Law,* 2nd ed., 1945, vol.3, p.1636. See also the *Pelletier* case, *ibid.,* p.1640; the *Panama-Costa Rica Boundary* case, 11 *RIAA,* 1900, p.519 and *US Foreign Relations,* 1914, p.994; the *Chamizal* case, 11 *RIAA,* p.309, and the *Cerruti* arbitrations, 6 *AJIL,* 1912, p.965.

[109] See e.g. Murty, *op. cit.,* pp.693-64 and McNair, *The Law of Treaties,* 1961, pp.66-77.

[110] See Schachter, *op. cit.,* p.3. See also as regards corruption, Moore, *International Arbitrations,* vol.2, pp.1660-64 and the *Buraimi* arbitration, Wetter, *op. cit.* vol.3, p.357 and 545 HC Deb., vol.199, 1955.

[111] See the *British Guiana and Venezuela Boundary* case, 92 *BFSP,* p.160 and Wetter, *op. cit.* vol.3, p.81 *et seq.* See also the *Arbitral Award by the King of Spain* case, ICJ Reports, 1960, pp.188, 216; 30 *ILR,* pp.457, 476.

[112] See e.g. Murty, *op. cit.,* p.696 and Merrills, *op. cit.,* p.100.

evidence,[113] but may cover manifest errors[114] such as not taking into account a relevant treaty or a clear mistake as to the appropriate municipal law.[115] Of course, once a party recognises the award as valid and binding, it will not be able to challenge the validity of the award at a later stage.[116]

In certain circumstances, it may be open to a party to request a revision or re-opening of the award in order to provide for rectification of an error or consideration of a fact unknown at the time to the tribunal and the requesting party which is of such a nature as to have a decisive influence on the award.[117]

Arbitration as a method of settling disputes combines elements of both diplomatic and judicial procedures. It depends for its success on a certain amount of good-will between the parties in drawing up the *compromis* and constituting the tribunal, as well as actually enforcing the award subsequently made. A large part depends upon negotiating processes. On the other hand, arbitration is an adjudicative technique in that the award is final and binding and the arbitrators are required to base their decision on law.[118]

It will be seen in the following section just how close arbitration is to judicial settlement of disputes by the International Court of Justice, and it is no coincidence that the procedure of arbitration through the PCA began to decline with the establishment and consolidation of the Permanent Court of International Justice in the 1920s.

In recent years, there has been a rise in the number of inter-state arbitrations. The *Rann of Kutch* case,[119] the *Anglo-French Continental Shelf* case,[120] the *Beagle Channel* case[121] and the *Taba* case[122] were all the subject of arbitral awards, usually

---

[113] *Arbitral Award by the King of Spain*, ICJ Reports, 1960, pp.188, 215-16; 30 *ILR*, pp.457, 475. See also as regards the Argentinian claim of nullity of the *Beagle Channel* award, 17 *ILM*, 1978, p.738; 52 *ILR*, pp.267-285.

[114] See the *Trail Smelter* case, 3 *RIAA*, 1938, pp.1905, 1957; 9 *ILR*, p.331.

[115] See e.g. the *Schreck* case, Moore, *International Arbitrations*, vol.2, p.1357.

[116] *Arbitral Award by the King of Spain*, ICJ Reports, 1960, pp.188, 213; 30 *ILR*, p.473.

[117] See e.g. Wetter, *op. cit.* vol.2, p.539 *et seq.* See also article 29 of the ILC Model Rules.

[118] See the definition of arbitration in *Yearbook of the ILC*, 1953, vol.II, p.202.

[119] 50 *ILR*, p.2. See also Wetter, "The Rann of Kutch Arbitration", 65 *AJIL*, 1971, p.346.

[120] Cmnd. 7438, 1978; 54 *ILR*, p.6. See further *supra* Chapter 10, p.381.

[121] HMSO, 1977; 52 *ILR*, p.93. See Shaw, "The Beagle Channel Arbitration Award", 6 *International Relations*, 1978, p.415.

[122] 80 *ILR*, p.244.

successfully.[123] It may be that further such issues may be resolved in this fashion, although a lot depends on the evaluation of the parties as to the most satisfactory method of dispute settlement in the light of their own particular interests and requirements.

Arbitration is an extremely useful process where some technical expertise is required, or where greater flexibility than is available before the International Court is desired.[124] It may also be utilised as between states and international institutions, since only states may appear before the ICJ in contentious proceedings, or where one of the parties is not willing to go to the Court. The establishment of arbitral tribunals has often been undertaken in order to deal relatively quietly and cheaply with a series of problems within certain categories, for example, the mixed tribunals established after the First World War to settle territorial questions, or the Mexican Claims commissions which handled various claims against Mexico.

The Iran-United States Claims Tribunal was established in 1981 as an international arbitral body to adjudicate claims of US nationals against Iran and of Iranian nationals against the United States arising out of alleged violations of property rights as a result of the circumstances surrounding the hostage crisis.[125] The Tribunal also has jurisdiction to hear certain official claims between the US and Iran arising out of contractual arrangements for the purchase and sale of goods and services, and disputes relating to the interpretation and implementation of the Claims Settlement Agreement itself. Tribunal awards are final and binding and are enforceable under the Agreement in domestic courts. In order to ensure payment of awards to US nationals, a Security Account was established with one billion dollars capital from Iranian assets frozen in the US as a result of the hostages crisis. Once the sum falls below $500 million, Iran is under an obligation to replenish the

---

[123] Argentina initially rejected the award in the *Beagle Channel* case, but later mediation and negotiations resolved the issue, see 17 *ILM*, 1978, p.738 and 24 *ILM*, 1985, p.1.

[124] Note for example that in the *Argentina-Chile* case of 1966, the tribunal consisted of a lawyer and two geographical experts, 38 *ILR*, p.10.

[125] See 1 *Iran-US CTR*, pp.3-56; 20 *ILM*, 1981, p.223 *et seq.* See also e.g. Stewart and Sherman, "Development at the Iran-United States Claims Tribunal: 1981-1983", 24 *Va JIL*, 1983, p.1; Lloyd Jones, "The Iran-United States Claims Tribunal: Private Rights and State Responsibility", 24 *Va JIL*, 1984, p.259; *The Iran-US Claims Tribunal 1981-83* (ed. Lillich), 1984; Toope, *Mixed International Arbitration*, 1990, Chapter IX; Caron, "The Nature of the Iran-United States Claims Tribunal and the Evolving Structure of International Dispute Resolution", 84 *AJIL*, 1980, p.104 and the *Iran-United States Claims Tribunal Reports* (23 vols. to date), 1981-.

Account.[126] Under the terms of the Agreement, all claims had to be filed by 19 January 1982. The Tribunal is based at The Hague. This settlement procedure is highly complex and one of the most sophisticated attempts at resolving international claims attempted.[127]

A variety of important issues have been addressed by the Tribunal, including the treatment of dual nationality in claims[128] and in particular issues relating to expropriation.[129] A discussion of the precise nature of the Tribunal is beyond the confines of this work, but it should be noted that rather than being a typical inter-state arrangement, it constitutes a fusion of state and private party claims in the one procedure and in a way which ensures the security of the award. Although claims of under $250,000 are to be represented by the government of the national concerned, claims in excess of this are presented by the individual claimants themselves, while the agents of the two states are present during the hearing with the right of audience.[130] Nevertheless, the Tribunal has emphasised on several occasions that the claim remains that of the individual and is not that of the state, as would be normal in classical state responsibility situations.[131]

Whether this model will be used in other similar situations is an open question, particularly since the trend in the post-war era has tended towards the lump-sum settlement of such disputes.[132] But the value of the Tribunal in general terms in resolving the large number of claims in question and in addressing significant issues of international law cannot be denied.

Other Mechanisms

The International Centre for the Settlement of Investment Disputes was established under the auspices of the International Bank for Reconstruction and Development by the Convention on the Settlement of Investment Disputes Between States and the

[126] As of 28 March 1989, this had taken place on 26 occasions, see 83 *AJIL*, 1989, p.915.

[127] As of 30 June 1990, the total number of cases filed with the Tribunal Registry stood at 3,948. 486 awards had been made and a total of 3,662 cases had been finalised. See Annual Report of the Tribunal, 1990, pp.25-28.

[128] *Supra*, p.507.

[129] *Supra*, p.516.

[130] See Fox, *op. cit.*, p.21.

[131] See e.g. *State Party Responsibility for Awards Rendered Against Its Nationals, Case A/21*, 14 *Iran-US CTR*, pp.324, 330.

[132] See further *supra*, p.524.

Nationals of Other States 1965 and administers *ad hoc* arbitrations.[133] It provides an autonomous system free from municipal law, while states parties to the Convention undertake to recognise awards made by arbitration tribunals acting under the auspices of the Centre as final and binding in their territories and to enforce them as if they were final judgments of national courts.[134] The jurisdiction of the Centre extends to "any legal dispute arising directly out of an investment, between a contracting state . . . and a national of another contracting state, which the parties to the dispute consent in writing to submit to the Centre".[135] Bilateral investment treaties between states parties to the Convention frequently provide for recourse to arbitration under the auspices of the Centre in the event of an investment dispute.[136] The arbitration procedure afforded by the Centre has now been utilised in several interesting cases.[137]

Another procedure of growing importance is the Court of Arbitration of the International Chamber of Commerce.[138] A number of agreements provide for the settlement of disputes by arbitration under the Rules of the International Chamber of Commerce and several cases have been heard.[139]

JUDICIAL SETTLEMENT –
THE INTERNATIONAL COURT OF JUSTICE [140]

Judicial settlement comprises the activities of all international and regional courts deciding disputes between subjects of

[133] See e.g. Broches, "The Convention on the Settlement of Investment Disputes", 3 *Columbia Journal of Transnational Law*, 1966, p.263 and "The Convention on the Settlement of Investment Disputes Between States and Nationals of Other States", 136 *HR*, p.350; O'Keefe, "The International Centre for the Settlement of Investment Disputes", 34 *YBWA*, 1980, p.286 and Wetter, *op. cit.* vol.II, p.139.

[134] Wetter, *op. cit.* vol.II, p.139.

[135] Article 25(1) of the Convention.

[136] See e.g. Pogany, "The Regulation of Foreign Investment in Hungary", 4 *ICSID Review – Foreign Investment Law Journal*, 1989, pp.39, 51.

[137] See e.g. Lalive, "The First 'World Bank' Arbitration (*Holiday Inns* v. *Morocco*) – Some Legal Problems", 51 *BYIL*, 1980, p.123. See also *AGIP Spa* v. *Government of the Popular Republic of the Congo*, 67 *ILR*, p.318 and *Benvenuti and Bonfant* v. *Government of the Popular Republic of the Congo, ibid.*, p.345, dealing with questions of state responsibility and damages.

[138] See e.g. Wetter, *op. cit.* vol.II, p.145.

[139] See e.g. *Dalmia Cement* v. *National Bank of Pakistan*, 67 *ILR*, p.611 and the *Westland Helicopters* case, 80 *ILR*, p.595.

[140] See e.g. Rosenne, *The Law and Practice of the International Court*, 2 vols., 2nd ed., 1985 and *The World Court*, 4th ed., 1989; McWhinney, *The World Court and the Contemporary Law-*

international law, in accordance with the rules and principles of international law. There are a number of such bodies.[141] However, by far the most important of such bodies, both by prestige and jurisdiction, is the International Court of Justice.

The impetus to create a world court for the international community developed as a result of the atmosphere engendered by the Hague Conferences of 1897 and 1907. The establishment of the Permanent Court of Arbitration, although neither permanent nor, in fact, a court, marked an important step forward in the consolidation of an international legal system. However, no lasting concrete steps were taken until after the conclusion of the First World War.

The Covenant of the League of Nations called for the formulation of proposals for the creation of a world court and in 1920 the Permanent Court of International Justice (PCIJ) was created. It stimulated efforts to develop international arbitral mechanisms. Together with arbitration, the Permanent Court was intended to provide a reasonably comprehensive system serving the international community. It was intended as a way to prevent outbreaks of violence by enabling easily accessible methods of dispute settlement in the context of a legal and organisational framework to be made available.[142]

The PCIJ was superseded after the Second World War by the International Court of Justice (ICJ), described by the Charter as the United Nation's "principal judicial organ".[143] In essence, it is a continuation of the Permanent Court, with virtually the same statute and jurisdiction, and with a continuing line of cases, no distinction being made between those decided by the PCIJ and those by the ICJ.

Making Process, 1979; Elias, *The International Court of Justice and Some Contemporary Problems*, 1983; Merrills, *op. cit.*, Chapters 6 and 7; *The Future of the International Court of Justice* (ed. Gross), 2 vols., 1976; *The International Court of Justice at a Crossroads* (ed. Damrosch), 1987, and E. Lauterpacht, *Aspects of the Administration of International Justice*, 1991.

[141] E.g. the EEC Court of Justice, see *infra*, and Chapter 19; the European Court of Human Rights and the Inter-American Court of Human Rights, *supra*, Chapter 6, p.221 *et seq.*

[142] For an assessment of its work, see e.g. Rosenne, *Law and Practice, op. cit.* vol.I, p.10.

[143] Article 92 of the UN Charter.

ठ़ 1971 . 6 . R₿

The Organisation of the Court [144]

The ICJ is composed of 15 members:

elected regardless of their nationality, from among persons of high moral character, who possess the qualifications required in their respective countries for appointment to the highest judicial offices, or are jurisconsults of recognised competence in international law.[145]

The procedure for the appointment of judges is interesting in that it combines both legal and political elements, while seeking to exclude as far as possible the influence of national states over them. The system established by the Root-Phillimore plan in 1920 is in essence followed. This plan played a large part in the actual creation of the PCIJ and succeeded in allaying many suspicions regarding the composition of the proposed Court.[146]

The members of the Court are elected by the General Assembly and Security Council (voting separately) from a list of qualified persons drawn up by the national groups of the Permanent Court of Arbitration, or by specially appointed national groups in the case of UN members that are not represented in the PCA.[147] This provision was inserted to restrict political pressures in the selection of judges. The elections are staggered and take place once every three years, with respect to five judges each time. In this way some element of continuity amongst the Court is maintained.

In practice, there is close coordination between the Assembly and Security Council in electing judges and political factors do obtrude, especially in view of the requirement contained in Article 9 of the Statute that the

electors should bear in mind not only that the persons to be elected should individually possess the qualifications required, but also that in the body as a whole the representation of the main forms of civilisation and of the principal legal systems of the world should be assured.

This has engendered much bargaining at election time as well

---

[144] See e.g. Rosenne, *Law and Practice, op. cit.* vol.I, Chapter V.
[145] Article 2, Statute of the ICJ.
[146] See e.g. Murty, *op. cit.,* p.700.
[147] Articles 4 and 5 of the ICJ Statute. In practice, governments exercise a major influence upon the nominations process of the national groups, see Merrills, *op. cit.,* p.124.

as encouraging close scrutiny of the political stances of individual candidates. It has attracted much criticism[148] but in the circumstances it is difficult to see a way to avoid this completely. The opinions of the individual judges can be crucial, particularly in sensitive cases and the alteration in the stance adopted by the Court with regard to the *Namibia* case between 1966[149] and 1971[150] can be attributed in large measure to changes in the composition of the Court that took place in the intervening period.

Candidates must obtain an absolute majority of votes in both the Assembly and the Council,[151] and no two successful applicants may be of the same nationality.[152]

The members of the Court are elected for nine years and may be re-elected.[153] They enjoy diplomatic privileges and immunities when on official business,[154] and a judge cannot be dismissed unless it is the unanimous opinion of the other members of the Court that he has ceased to fulfil the required conditions.[155] These include the requirement that no member may exercise any political or administrative function or engage in any other professional occupation. No member may act as agent, advocate, or counsel in any case and no member may participate in the decision of any case in which he has previously taken part as agent, advocate or counsel for one of the parties, or as a member of a national or international court, or of a commission of inquiry, or in any other capacity.[156]

The Court elects a president and vice-president for a three year term which can be renewed,[157] and it is situated at The Hague.[158]

Since the aim of the election procedures relating to the composition of the Court is to produce a judicial body of independent

---

[148] See e.g. Rosenne, *Law and Practice, op. cit.* vol.I, p.184 *et seq.* and "The Composition of the Court", in *The Future of the International Court of Justice, op. cit.*, pp.377, 381-86.

[149] ICJ Reports, 1966, p.6; 37 *ILR*, p.243.

[150] ICJ Reports, 1971, p.16; 49 *ILR*, p.2.

[151] Article 10, Statute of the ICJ.

[152] Article 3, Statute of the ICJ.

[153] Article 13, Statute of the ICJ.

[154] Article 19, Statute of the ICJ.

[155] Article 18, Statute of the ICJ.

[156] Articles 16 and 17, Statute of the ICJ. Note the problem raised particularly in the *Namibia* case, ICJ Reports, 1971, pp.3, 6 and 9, of judges who had previously been involved in the dispute albeit in another capacity. The Court did not accept the need to remove the judges in question. See Rosenne, in *The Future of the International Court of Justice, op. cit.* vol.I, pp.388-90.

[157] Article 21, Statute of the ICJ.

[158] Article 22, Statute of the ICJ.

members rather than state representatives, the Statute provides in article 31 that judges of the nationality of each of the parties in a case before the Court shall retain their right to sit in that case. However, the effect of this is somewhat reduced by the provision in that article that the parties to a dispute before the ICJ are entitled to choose a person to sit as judge for the duration of that case, where they do not have a judge of their nationality there already.

This procedure of appointing *ad hoc* judges in cases to act, in reality, as representatives of their states, dilutes the character of the Court as an independent organ of legal experts.[159] The reason for the establishment and maintenance of the provision can be found solely within the realm of international politics and can only be understood as such.[160] It must be said, however, that in practice the procedure has not resulted in disruption of the functioning of the ICJ. The Court has also permitted the use of the *ad hoc* judges in advisory proceedings.[161]

Articles 26 and 29 of the Statute of the ICJ also permit the creation of Chambers of the Court, composed of three or more members as the Court may determine for dealing with particular categories of cases[162] or to deal with a particular case. This procedure was revised in the 1978 Rules of the Court and used for the first time in the *Gulf of Maine* case.[163] The question of the composition of the Chamber is decided by the Court after the parties have been consulted, and in such cases the identity of the judges to comprise the Chamber is clearly of critical value. In the

---

[159] It should also be distinguished from article 43 of the European Convention on Human Rights, which similarly provides for the appointment of an *ad hoc* judge to the Court. In this case, the Court deals with the provisions of municipal law of the member-states of the Council of Europe and measures their conformity with the Convention. It is thus necessary to retain some expertise as to the domestic system in the case in question. This is, of course, not true of the International Court, which concerns only international law.

[160] See e.g. Rosenne, *Law and Practice, op. cit.* vol.I, p.205 *et seq.* and Prott, *The Latent Power of Culture and the International Judge*, 1979.

[161] See the *Western Sahara* case, ICJ Reports, 1975, p.12; 59 *ILR*, p.30. Cf. the *Namibia* case, ICJ Reports, 1971, p.16; 49 *ILR*, p.2. See also Gross, "The International Court of Justice: Consideration of Requirements for Enhancing its Roles in the International Legal Order", in *The Future of the International Court of Justice, op. cit.* vol.1, p.61.

[162] Labour cases and cases relating to transit and communications are specifically mentioned.

[163] ICJ Reports, 1982, p.3 and *ibid.*, 1984, p.246; 71 *ILR*, p.58. The chamber consisted of Judge Ago (President) and Judges Gros, Mosler and Schwebel and Judge *ad hoc* Cohen.

Gulf of Maine case Canada and the US threatened to withdraw the case if their wishes as to composition were not carried out.[164] A Chamber was also formed to deal with the *Burkina Faso–Mali* frontier dispute.[165]

This trend may well amount to a significant element in the work of the Court. It provides the parties with flexibility in the choice of judges to hear the case and to that extent parallels arbitration.[166] Of the first two matters before Chambers of the Court, perhaps the more interesting from the perspective of the future development of the ICJ was the *Burkina Faso–Mali* case, since African states have hitherto been most reluctant in permitting third party binding settlement of their disputes. Chambers of the Court have also been utilised in the *Elettronica Sicula* case[167] and in the *Land, Island and Maritime Frontier Dispute* between El Salvador and Honduras.[168] In all cases, the request was for five judges with elections by secret ballot except in the case of *ad hoc* judges.

The Rules of the Court, which govern its procedure and operations, were adopted in 1946 and revised in 1972 and 1978.[169]

The Contentious Jurisdiction of the Court [170]

The jurisdiction of the International Court falls into two distinct parts: its capacity to decide disputes between states, and its capacity to give advisory opinions when requested so to do by particular qualified entities. The latter will be noted in the following section.

Article 34 of the Statute of the Court declares that only states may be parties in cases before the Court. This is of far-reaching importance

---

[164] See e.g. Merrills, *op. cit.*, p.126 and Brauer, "International Conflict Resolution: The ICJ Chambers and the Gulf of Maine Dispute", 23 *Va JIL*, 1982-3, p.463.

[165] See 22 *ILM*, 1983, p.1252 and Communiqué of the ICJ no.85/8, 1 May 1985. The chamber consisted of Judge Bedjaoui (President) and Judges Lachs and Ruda, with Judges *ad hoc* Luchaire and Abi-Saab, see ICJ Reports, 1986, p.554; 80 *ILR*, p.441.

[166] Although concern was expressed about the unity of the jurisprudence of the Court by frequent use of *ad hoc* Chambers, see Mosler, "The *Ad Hoc* Chambers of the International Court of Justice" in *International Law at a Time of Perplexity* (ed. Dinstein), 1989, p.449. See also Schwebel, "Chambers of the International Court of Justice formed for Particular Cases", *ibid.*, p.739.

[167] ICJ Reports, 1989, p.15 and see *supra* p.510.

[168] See ICJ Reports, 1987, p.10.

[169] See Rosenne, *Procedure in the International Court*, 1983.

[170] See e.g. Rosenne, *Law and Practice, op. cit.* vol.I, Part 3.

since it prohibits recourse to the Court by private persons and international organisations, save in so far as some of the latter may be able to obtain advisory opinions. The Court is open to all states that are parties to the Statute. Article 93 of the UN Charter provides that all UN members are *ipso facto* parties to the Statute of the ICJ, and that non-members of the UN may become a party to the Statute on conditions determined by the General Assembly upon the recommendation of the Security Council. In the case of Switzerland, for example, the Assembly and Security Council declared that it could become a party to the Statute of the ICJ provided it accepted the provisions of that Statute, accepted all the obligations of a UN member under Article 94 of the Charter (i.e. undertaking to comply with the decision of the Court), and agreed to pay a certain amount towards the expenses of the Court.[171]

As far as other states may be concerned, the Court may be open to them upon conditions laid down by the Security Council, which should not place the parties in a position of inequality before the Court.[172]

The Security Council has in fact resolved that access to the ICJ for a state not party to the Statute is possible provided that such state has previously deposited with the registrar of the Court a declaration (either general or particular) accepting the jurisdiction of the Court and undertaking to comply in good faith with the decision or decisions of the Court.[173]

West Germany filed a general declaration with the ICJ on this basis before it joined the UN,[174] while Albania[175] and Italy[176] filed particular declarations with respect to cases with which they were involved.

Although only states may be parties before the Court, the Court may request information relevant to cases before it from

---

[171] General Assembly resolution 91(I). See also Rosenne, *Law and Practice, op. cit.* vol.I, pp.271-74. Liechtenstein and San Marino are also in the same position, *ibid.*, and Assembly resolutions 363(IV) and 806(VIII) and also Nauru. Japan was also until it became a UN member-state in 1956.

[172] Article 35(2), Statute of the ICJ. See also Rosenne, *ibid.,* pp.278-82.

[173] Security Council resolution 9 (1946).

[174] The *North Sea Continental Shelf* case, ICJ Reports, Pleadings, vol.1, pp.6, 8.

[175] The *Corfu Channel* case, ICJ Reports, 1949, p.4; 16 *ILR,* p.155.

[176] The *Monetary Gold* case, ICJ Reports, 1954, p.19; 21 *ILR,* p.399.

public international organisations and may receive information presented by these organisations on their own initiative.[177]

Article 36(1)

The Court has jurisdiction under article 36(1) of its Statute in all cases referred to it by parties, and regarding all matters specially provided for in the UN Charter or in treaties or conventions in force. As in the case of arbitration, parties may refer a particular dispute to the ICJ by means of a special agreement or *compromis,* which will specify the terms of the dispute and the framework within which the Court is to operate. This method was used in the *Minquiers and Ecrehos* case,[178] and in a number of others.[179] However, the essence of the process is the consent of the parties to the dispute to submit to the jurisdiction of the ICJ. Their consent need not be in any particular form and in certain circumstances the Court will infer it from the conduct of the parties. In the *Corfu Channel (Preliminary Objections)* case,[180] the Court inferred consent from the unilateral application of the plaintiff state (the United Kingdom) coupled with subsequent letters from the other party involved (Albania) intimating acceptance of the Court's jurisdiction.

This idea, whereby the consent of a state to the Court's jurisdiction may be established by means of acts subsequent to the initiation of proceedings, is known as the doctrine of *forum prorogatum.*[181] It has been applied in other cases before the Court, but it is carefully interpreted to avoid giving the impression of a creeping extension by the Court of its own jurisdiction by means of fictions. Consent has to be clearly present, if inferred, and not merely a technical creation.[182] In the *Corfu Channel* case the UK sought to found the

[177] Article 34(2), Statute of the ICJ. See also Rosenne, *Law and Practice, op. cit.* vol.I, pp.284-90. Individuals, groups and corporations have no right of access to the Court, see here also Lauterpacht, *International Law and Human Rights,* 1950, p.48.

[178] ICJ Reports, 1953, p.47; 20 *ILR,* p.94.

[179] See e.g. the *Frontier Land* case, ICJ Reports, 1959, p.209, and the *Tunisia-Libya Continental Shelf* case, ICJ Reports, 1982, p.18; 67 *ILR,* p.4.

[180] ICJ Reports, 1948, p.15; 15 *ILR,* p.349.

[181] See e.g. Rosenne, *Law and Practice, op. cit.* vol.I, p.344 *et seq.*

[182] See e.g. the *Monetary Gold* case, ICJ Reports, 1954, pp.19, 31; 21 *ILR,* pp.399, 406. But cf. the *Treatment in Hungary of Aircraft of the USA* case, ICJ Reports, 1964, pp.99, 103; the *Aerial Incident (USA v. USSR)* case, ICJ Reports, 1956, pp.6, 9, 12, 15 and the two *Antarctic* cases, ICJ Reports, 1958, p.158 and *ibid.,* 1959, p.276. Note that article 38(2) of the 1978 Rules of the Court stipulates that the application shall specify as far as possible the legal grounds upon which the jurisdiction of the Court is said to be based.

Court's jurisdiction *inter alia* on the recommendation of the Security Council that the dispute be referred to the Court, which it was agreed was a "decision" binding upon member-states of the UN in accordance with article 25 of the Charter.[183] Accordingly, maintained the UK, Albania was obliged to accept the Court's jurisdiction irrespective of its consent. The ICJ did not deal with this point, since it actually inferred consent, but in a joint separate opinion, seven judges of the Court rejected the argument, which was regarded as an attempt to introduce a new meaning of compulsory jurisdiction.[184]

Apart from those instances where states specifically refer a dispute to it, the Court may also be granted jurisdiction over disputes arising from international treaties where such treaties contain a "compromissory clause" providing for this. In fact, quite a large number of international treaties, both bilateral and multilateral do include a clause awarding the ICJ jurisdiction with respect to questions that might arise from the interpretation and application of the agreements.[185] Examples of the more important of such conventions include the 1965 Convention on Investment Disputes, the 1965 International Convention on the Elimination of all forms of Racial Discrimination and the 1970 Hague Convention on Hijacking. For example, in the *US Diplomatic and Consular Staff in Tehran* case (the *Iran* case),[186] the Court founded jurisdiction on article 1 of the Optional Protocols[187] concerning the Compulsory Settlement of Disputes, which accompany both the Vienna Convention on Diplomatic Relations 1961 and the Vienna Convention on Consular Relations 1963. Common article 1 of the Protocol provides that disputes arising out of the interpretation or application of the Conventions lie within the compulsory jurisdiction of the International Court of Justice. The Court also

---

[183] Although not a member of the UN, Albania had agreed to assume the obligations of a member with regard to the dispute. This application was on the basis of that part of article 36(1) which specifies that the Court's jurisdiction also comprised "all matters specifically provided for in the Charter" of the UN.

[184] ICJ Reports, 1948, pp.15, 31-32; 15 *ILR*, pp.349, 354.

[185] See Rosenne, *Law of Practice, op. cit.* vol.I., Chapter X. Approximately 160 bilateral and trilateral treaties and 87 multilateral treaties refer to the Court in such a way, see e.g. 22(1) *UN Chronicle*, 1985, p.8. See also Charney, "Compromisory Clauses and the Jurisdiction of the International Court of Justice", 81 *AJIL*, 1989, p.85.

[186] ICJ Reports, 1980, pp.3, 24; 61 *ILR*, pp.530, 550.

[187] To which both Iran and the US were parties.

founded jurisdiction in the *Nicaragua*[188] case *inter alia* upon a treaty provision, article XXIV(2) of the 1956 US-Nicaragua Treaty of Friendship, Commerce and Navigation providing for submission of disputes over the interpretation or application of the treaty to the ICJ unless the parties agree to settlement by some other specific means.

In its judgment on jurisdiction and admissibility in the *Case Concerning Border and Transborder Armed Actions (Nicaragua v. Honduras)*,[189] the International Court emphasised that the existence of jurisdiction was a question of law and dependent upon the intention of the parties. The issue of jurisdiction in the case centred, in the view of the Court, upon article 31 of the Pact of Bogotá 1948, which declared that the parties "[i]n conformity with article 36(2) of the Statute of the International Court of Justice ... recognise, in relation to any other American state, the jurisdiction of the Court as compulsory *ipso facto* ... in all disputes of a juridical nature that arise among them". Objections to jurisdiction put forward by Honduras on the grounds that article 31 was not intended to have independent force, and was merely an encouragement to the parties to deposit unilateral declarations of acceptance of the Court's compulsory jurisdiction, and that article 31 would only operate after the exhaustion of conciliation procedures referred to in article 32, were rejected on the basis of interpretation.[190]

Article 31 nowhere envisaged that the undertaking contained therein might be amended subsequently by unilateral declaration and the reference to article 36(2) of the Statute was insufficient to have that effect,[191] while the reference in article 32 of the Pact to a right of recourse to the International Court upon the failure of conciliation provided a second basis for the jurisdiction of the Court and not a limitation upon the first.[192] In other words, the commitment contained in article 31 of the Pact was sufficient to enable the Court to exercise jurisdiction.

Where a treaty in force provides for reference of a matter to the PCIJ or to a tribunal established by the League of Nations, article

---

[188] ICJ Reports, 1984, pp.392, 426-29; 76 ILR, pp.104, 137. See Briggs, "*Nicaragua* v. *United States*: Jurisdiction and Admissibility", 79 *AJIL*, 1985, p.373.

[189] ICJ Reports, 1988, pp.69, 76.

[190] *Ibid.*, pp.78-90. The decision to affirm jurisdiction and admissibility was unanimous.

[191] *Ibid.*, pp.85-88.

[192] *Ibid.*, pp.88-90.

37 of the Statute declares that such matter shall be referred to the ICJ, provided the parties to the dispute are parties to the Statute. It is basically a bridging provision and provides some measure of continuity between the old Permanent Court and the new International Court.[193] Under article 36(6) of the Statute, the Court has the competence to decide its own jurisdiction in the event of a dispute.

Article 36(2)

Of great importance in extending the jurisdiction of the ICJ is article 36(2) of the Statute, the so-called "optional clause". This stipulates that:

> The states parties to the present Statute may at any time declare that they recognise as compulsory *ipso facto* and without special agreement, in relation to any other state accepting the same obligation, the jurisdiction of the Court in all legal disputes concerning:
>   (a) the interpretation of a treaty;
>   (b) any question of international law;
>   (c) the existence of any fact which, if established, would constitute a breach of an international obligation;
>   (d) the nature or extent of the reparation to be made for the breach of an international obligation.[194]

This provision was intended to operate as a method of increasing the Court's jurisdiction, by the gradual acceptance by more and more states of this clause. However, it has not worked out like that.

By the end of 1984, only 47 declarations were in force and deposited with the UN Secretary-General, comprising less than one-third of the parties to the ICJ Statute. Since 1951, nine declarations have expired or been terminated without renewal.

These declarations, pursuant to article 36(2), are in the majority of cases conditional and are dependent upon reciprocity for

---

[193] See e.g. the *Ambatielos* case (Preliminary Objections), ICJ Reports, 1952, p.28; 19 *ILR*, p.416 and the *Barcelona Traction* case (Preliminary Objections), ICJ Reports, 1964, p.6; 46 *ILR*, p.18. Cf. the *Aerial Incident* case, ICJ Reports, 1959, p.127; 27 *ILR*, p.557.

[194] See e.g. Rosenne, *Law and Practice, op. cit.* vol.I, Chapter XI. See also Merrills, "The Optional Clause Today", 50 *BYIL*, 1979, p.87; Gross, "Compulsory Jurisdiction under the Optional Protocol: History and Practice" in *The International Court of Justice at a Crossroads, op. cit.*, p.19 and Gordon, " 'Legal Disputes' Under Article 36(2) of the Statute", *ibid.*, p.183.

operation. This means that the Court will only have jurisdiction under article 36(2) where the declarations of the two parties in dispute meet. In other words, the doctrine of the lowest common denominator operates since the acceptance, by means of the optional clause, by one state of the jurisdiction of the Court is in relation to any other state accepting the same obligation. It is not that declarations in identical terms from the parties are necessary, but both declarations must grant jurisdiction to the Court regarding the dispute in question.

In practice, this can lead to the situation where one party may rely on a condition, or reservation, expressed in the declaration of the other party. This occurred in the *Norwegian Loans* case,[195] between France and Norway. The Court noted that:

> since two unilateral declarations are involved, such jurisdiction is conferred upon the Court only to the extent to which the declarations coincide in conferring it. A comparison between the two declarations shows that the French declaration accepts the Court's jurisdiction within narrower limits than the Norwegian declaration; consequently, the common will of the parties, which is the basis of the Court's jurisdiction, exists within these narrower limits indicated by the French reservation.[196]

Accordingly, Norway was entitled to invoked the French reservation to defeat the jurisdiction of the Court.

However, much will depend upon the precise terms of the declarations.

Declarations made under the optional clause in the Statute of the PCIJ and still in force are deemed to continue with respect to the ICJ,[197] but in the *Aerial Incident* case[198] between Israel and Bulgaria, the Court declared that this in fact only applied to states signing the ICJ Statute in 1945 and did not relate to states, like Bulgaria, which became a party to the Statute many years later as a result of admission to the United Nations.

[195] ICJ Reports, 1957, p.9; 24 *ILR*, p.782.

[196] *Ibid.*, p.23; 24 *ILR*, p.786. But note Judge Lauterpacht's individual opinion, *ibid.*, p.34; 24 *ILR*, p.793. See also the *Right of Passage* case, ICJ Reports, 1957, pp.125, 145; 24 *ILR*, pp.840, 845 and the *Interhandel* case, ICJ Reports, 1959, pp.6, 23; 27 *ILR*, pp.475, 487.

[197] Article 36(5), Statute of the ICJ.

[198] ICJ Reports, 1959, p.127; 27 *ILR*, p.557.

The issue also arose in the jurisdictional phase of the *Nicaragua* case.[199] That state had declared that it would accept the compulsory jurisdiction of the Permanent Court in 1929 but had not ratified this. The US argued that accordingly Nicaragua never became a party to the Statute of the Permanent Court and could not therefore rely on article 36(5). The Court in an interesting judgment noted that the Nicaraguan declaration, unconditional and unlimited as to time, had "a certain potential effect" and that the phrase in article 36(5) "still in force" could be so interpreted as to cover declarations which had only potential and not binding effect. Ratification of the Statute of the ICJ in 1945 by Nicaragua had the effect, argued the Court, of transforming this potential commitment into an effective one.[200] Since this was so, Nicaragua could rely on the US declaration of 1946 accepting the Court's compulsory jurisdiction as the necessary reciprocal element.[201]

The reservations that have been made in declarations by states under the optional clause, restricting the jurisdiction of the ICJ, vary a great deal from state to state, and are usually an attempt to prevent the Court becoming involved in a dispute which is felt to concern vital interests. One condition made by a number of states, particularly the United States of America, stipulates that matters within the domestic jurisdiction "as determined by" that particular state are automatically excluded from the purview of the Court. The validity of this type of reservation (known as the "Connally amendment" from the American initiator of the relevant legislation) has been questioned by many,[202] particularly since it appears to contradict the power of the Court under article 36(6) to determine

---

[199] ICJ Reports, 1984, pp.392, 403-12; 76 *ILR*, pp.104, 114.

[200] The Court also noted that since Court publications had placed Nicaragua on the list of states accepting the compulsory jurisdiction of the ICJ by virtue of article 36(5) and that no states had objected, one could conclude that the above interpretation had been confirmed, *ibid*. The Court also regarded the conduct of the parties as reflecting acquiescence in Nicaragua's obligations when article 36(5) was argued, *ibid.*, pp.411-15; 76 *ILR*, p.122.

[201] But see the separate opinions of Judges Mosler, *ibid.*, pp.461-63; Oda, *ibid.*, pp.473-89; Ago, *ibid.*, pp.517-27 and Jennings, *ibid.*, pp.533-45 and the dissenting opinion of Judge Schwebel, *ibid.*, pp.562-600; 76 *ILR*, pp.172, 184, 228, 244 and 273.

[202] See e.g. Henkin, "The Connally Reservation Revisited and, hopefully, Contained", 65 *AJIL*, 1971, pp.374, and Preuss, "The International Court of Justice, the Senate and Matters of Domestic Jurisdiction", 40 *AJIL*, 1946, p.720. See also Rosenne, *Law and Practice, op. cit.* vol.I, pp.395-99; Judge Lauterpacht, *Norwegian Loans* case, ICJ Reports, 1957, pp.9, 43-66; 24 *ILR*, pp.782, 800; the *Interhandel* case, ICJ Reports, 1959, pp.6, 77-78 and 93; 27 *ILR*, pp.475, 524, 534, and D'Amato, "Modifying US Acceptance of the Compulsory Jurisdiction of the World Court", 79 *AJIL*, 1985, p.385. See further, *infra*, footnote 236.

its own jurisdiction, and in reality it withdraws from the Court the jurisdiction conferred under the declaration itself. Indeed, it is a well established principle of international law that the definition of domestic jurisdiction is an issue of international and not domestic law.

Reservations often relate to requirements of time (*ratione temporis*)[203] since some are declared to expire automatically after a certain period or within a particular time after notice of termination has been given to the UN Secretary-General.[204] However, once the Court is dealing with a dispute, any subsequent expiry or termination of a party's declaration will not modify the jurisdiction of the case. Some states exclude the jurisdiction of the ICJ with respect to disputes arising before or after a certain date in their declarations, for example, where countries have made reservations about disputes arising out of war or hostilities, or certain disputes between member-states of the British Commonwealth.[205] One must note that the aim of the optional clause, which was to be the means for the establishment of a comprehensive and compulsory jurisdiction for the ICJ, has not been achieved.

A state may withdraw or modify its declaration.[206] The US declaration of 1946 provided for termination after a six-month period of notice. What the Court in the jurisdictional phase of the *Nicaragua* case[207] had to decide was whether a modifying notification[208] expressly deemed to apply immediately could have effect over the original declaration. It decided that the six-month notice provision remained valid and could be invoked by Nicaragua against the US, since it was an undertaking that constituted an integral part of the instrument that contained it.

---

[203] See Rosenne, *Law and Practice, op. cit.* vol.I, pp.399-400.

[204] *Ibid.*, pp.400-3. The UK for example, excluded disputes arising out of events occurring between 3 September 1939 and 2 September 1945 in its 1963 declaration, Cmnd. 2248. This was altered in the 1969 declaration, which is expressed to apply only to disputes arising after 24 October 1945, Cmnd. 3872.

[205] *Ibid.*

[206] See e.g. Rosenne, *Law and Practice, op. cit.* vol.I, pp.415-18.

[207] ICJ Reports, 1984, pp.392, 415-21; 76 *ILR*, p.126.

[208] Excluding disputes related to Central America for a two year period. See e.g. Chayes, "Nicaragua, The United States and the World Court", 85 *Columbia Law Review*, 1985, p.1445; Highet, "Litigation Implications of the US Withdrawal from the *Nicaragua* case", 79 *AJIL*, 1985, p.992 and US Department of State Statement on the US Withdrawal from the Proceedings Initiated by Nicaragua in the International Court of Justice, 22 *ILM*, 1985, p.246.

Sources of Law, Propriety and Legal Interest

In its deliberations, the Court will apply the rules of international law as laid down in article 38 (treaties, custom, general principles of law).[209] However, the Court may decide a case *ex aequo et bono,* i.e. on the basis of justice and equity untrammelled by technical legal rules.[210] This has not yet occurred, although it should not be confused with the ability of the ICJ to apply certain equitable considerations in a case within the framework of international law.

Quite often before dealing with the merits of a case, the Court will have to deal with preliminary objections as to whether in fact it has the jurisdiction to decide the case before it. Where it has established its right to exercise jurisdiction, the Court may well decline to exercise that right on grounds of propriety. In the *Northern Cameroons* case,[211] the Court declared that:

> it may pronounce judgment only in connection with concrete cases where there exists, at the time of adjudication, an actual controversy involving a conflict of legal interests between the parties. The Court's judgment must have some practical consequence in the sense that it can affect existing legal rights or obligations of the parties, thus removing uncertainty from their legal relations.[212]

In addition, and following the *South West Africa* cases (Second Phase) in 1966,[213] it may be necessary for the Court to establish that the claimant state has a legal interest in the subject matter of the dispute.[214]

The fact that political considerations may have motivated the application is not relevant, so long as a legal dispute is in evidence.[215] Similarly, the fact that a particular dispute has other important

---

[209] See further *supra* Chapter 3, p.59.

[210] *Ibid.*

[211] ICJ Reports, 1963, p.15; 35 *ILR*, p.353.

[212] *Ibid.*, pp.33-34; 35 *ILR*, p.369.

[213] ICJ Reports, 1966, p.6; 37 *ILR*, p.243.

[214] As to the requirement that the dispute be a legal dispute, see Rosenne, *Law and Practice, op. cit.* vol.I, pp.374-76. See also the *Nicaragua* case, ICJ Reports, 1984, pp.392, 429-41; 76 *ILR*, pp.104, 140 and *supra* p.629.

[215] See the *Case Concerning Border and Transborder Armed Actions (Nicaragua v. Honduras),* ICJ Reports, 1988, pp.16, 91.

aspects is not of itself sufficient to render the application in-admissible.[216]

Interim Measures [217]

Under article 41 of the Statute, the Court may grant provisional measures of protection in order to preserve the respective rights of the parties. In deciding upon a request for provisional measures, the Court need not finally satisfy itself that it has jurisdiction on the merits of the case, although it has held that it ought not to indicate such measures unless the provisions invoked by the applicant appear *prima facie* to afford a basis upon which the jurisdiction of the Court might be founded.[218] The purpose of exercising the power is to protect "rights which are the subject of dispute in judicial proceedings"[219] and thus the measures must be such that once the disputes over those rights has been resolved by the Court's judgment on the merits, they would no longer by required.[220] These are awarded to assist the Court to ensure the integrity of the proceedings. Such interim measures were granted by the Court in the *Fisheries Jurisdiction* case,[221] to protect British fishing rights in Icelandic-claimed waters, and in the *Nuclear Tests* case.[222] Interim measures would appear to be advisory only and are not to be regarded as judgments on the merits of the case. They may be indicated at the discretion of the Court if it feels circumstances

---

[216] *Ibid.,* p.92. See also the *Iran* case, ICJ Reports, 1980, pp.3, 19; 61 *ILR,* pp.530, 545.

[217] See e.g. Elias, *op. cit.,* Chapter 3; Merrills, "Interim Measures of Protection and the Substantive Jurisdiction of the International Court", 36 *Cambridge Law Journal,* 1977, p.86; Rosenne, *Law and Practice, op. cit.* vol.I, pp.224-28; Gross, "The Case Concerning United States Diplomatic and Consular Staff in Tehran: Phase of Provisional Measures", 74 *AJIL,* 1980, p.395, and Mendelson, "Interim Measures of Protection in Cases of Contested Jurisdiction", 46 *BYIL,* 1972-3, p.259. See also Rules 73-78 of the Court, 1978. See also Gray, *Judicial Remedies in International Law,* 1987, pp.69-74.

[218] See the request by Guinea-Bissau for the indication of provisional measures in the *Arbitral Award of 31 July 1989 (Guinea-Bissau v. Senegal)* case, ICJ Reports, 1990, pp.64, 68.

[219] The *Aegean Sea Continental Shelf* case, ICJ Reports, 1976, pp.3, 9; 60 *ILR,* pp.524, 530 and the *Iran* case, ICJ Reports, 1979, pp.7, 19; 61 *ILR,* pp.513, 525. See also the *Arbitral Award of 31 July 1989* case, ICJ Reports, 1990, pp.64, 69.

[220] *Arbitral Award of 31 July 1989* case, ICJ Reports, 1990, p.69.

[221] ICJ Reports, 1972, p.12; 55 *ILR,* p.160. See also the *Anglo-Iranian Oil Co.* case, ICJ Reports, 1951, p.89; 19 *ILR,* p.501.

[222] ICJ Reports, 1973, p.99; 57 *ILR,* p.360. They were also granted in the *Iran* case, ICJ Reports, 1979, pp.7, 19; 61 *ILR,* pp.513, 525 and in the *Nicaragua* case, ICJ Reports, 1980, p.169; 76 *ILR,* p.35.

so require. In the *Fisheries Jurisdiction* case, it emphasised that article 41 presupposes "that irreparable prejudice should not be caused to rights which are the subject of dispute in judicial proceedings".[223] Unfortunately the record of compliance with provisional measures is very poor.

Enforcement

Once given, the judgment of the Court under article 60 is final and without appeal. Although it has no binding force except between the parties and in respect of the particular case under article 59, such decisions are often very influential in the evolution of new rules of international law.

Under article 94 of the UN Charter, each member-state undertakes to comply with the decision of the Court in any case to which it is a party and if this does not occur, the other party may have recourse to the Security Council which may make recommendations or take binding decisions. In the event, the record of compliance with judgments is only marginally satisfactory. Examples of non-compliance would include Albania in the *Corfu Channel* case,[224] Iceland in the *Fisheries Jurisdiction* case[225] and Iran in the *Iran* case.[226] Nevertheless, on a political level such judgments have an impact and should not necessarily be exclusively evaluated on the legal plane.

Application for Interpretation of a Judgment

Under article 60 of the Statute, an application may be made to the Court for interpretation of a judgment, provided that the object of the request is solely to obtain clarification of the meaning and the scope of what the Court has decided with binding force and not to obtain an answer to questions not so decided. In addition, it is necessary that there should exist a dispute as to the meaning or scope of the judgment.[227]

---

[223] ICJ Reports, 1972, pp.12, 16, 30, 34; 55 *ILR*, pp.160, 164; 56 *ILR*, pp.76, 80. See also the *Iran* case, ICJ Reports, 1979, pp.7, 19; 61 *ILR*, p.525.

[224] ICJ Reports, 1949, p.4; 16 *ILR*, p.155.

[225] ICJ Reports, 1974, p.3; 55 *ILR*, p.238.

[226] ICJ Reports, 1980, p.3; 61 *ILR*, p.530.

[227] See *Request for Interpretation of the Judgment of 20 November 1950 in the Asylum* case, ICJ Reports, 1950, p.402; 17 *ILR*, p.339 and *Application for Revision and Interpretation of the Judgment of 24 February 1982 in the Case Concerning the Continental Shelf (Tunisia/Libya)*, ICJ Reports, 1985, pp.191, 214-20; 81 *ILR*, pp.420, 447.

Application for Revision of a Judgment

Under article 61 of the Statute, an application for revision of a judgment may only be made when based upon the discovery of some fact of such a nature as to be a decisive factor, which fact was, when the judgment was given, unknown to the Court and also to the party claiming revision, provided that such ignorance was not due to negligence. The application must be made within six months of the discovery of the new fact and within ten years of the date of the judgment. In the *Application for Revision and Interpretation of the Judgment of 24 February 1982 in the Case Concerning the Continental Shelf (Tunisia/Libya)*[228] the Court decided that the "new fact" in question, namely the text of a resolution of the Libyan Council of Ministers of 28 March 1968 setting out the western boundary of the Libyan oil concessions in the first sector of the delimitation, was a fact that could have been discovered through the application of normal diligence. If Tunisia was ignorant of the facts, it was due to its own negligence.[229] In addition, it could not be said that the new facts alleged were of such a nature as to be a decisive factor as required by article 61.[230]

Non-Appearance [231]

One unfortunate feature of the Court's work in recent years has been the reluctance of the defendant government to appear before the Court at all. This occurred in the *Fisheries Jurisdiction* case,[232] the *Nuclear Tests* case,[233] the *Aegean Sea Continental Shelf* case[234] and the *Iran* case.[235] Under article 53 of its Statute, the Court in such a situation may be called upon by the appearing party to decide in

[228] ICJ Reports, 1985, pp.191, 198-214; 81 *ILR*, p.431.

[229] *Ibid.*, pp.206-7; 81 *ILR*, p.439.

[230] *Ibid.*, pp.213-14; 81 *ILR*, p.446.

[231] See e.g. Thurlway, *Non-Appearance before the International Court of Justice*, 1985; Elias, *op. cit.*, Chapter 2; Fitzmaurice, "The Problem of the 'Non-appearing' Defendant Government", 51 *BYIL*, 1980, p.89 and Sinclair, "Some Procedural Aspects of Recent International Litigation", 30 *ICLQ*, 1981, p.338.

[232] ICJ Reports, 1974, p.3; 55 *ILR*, p.238.

[233] ICJ Reports, 1974, p.253; 57 *ILR*, p.350.

[234] ICJ Reports, 1978, p.3; 60 *ILR*, p.562.

[235] ICJ Reports, 1980, p.3; 61 *ILR*, p.530. See also the *Pakistani Prisoners of War* case, ICJ Reports, 1973, pp.328, 347; 57 *ILR*, p.606.

favour of its claim. Before doing so, the Court must satisfy itself not only that it has jurisdiction, but also that the claim is well founded in fact and law. This, of course, means that the Court is compelled to act on behalf of the absent defendant government in the sense of providing legal argumentation to support its case. This is controversial, although not to take into account the defendant's possible legal case in deciding would certainly discourage such state from accepting the judgment. It is a fine balance. The United States, after the Court decided it had jurisdiction to hear Nicaragua's claim, stated that it would withdraw from further proceedings in that case before the Court.[236] In view of the strong American attitude to Iran's non-appearance in the hostages dispute, it is perhaps surprising, although political changes may account for this. It is unfortunate and will not serve to alleviate the general problem.

Third Party Intervention [237]

Under article 62 of the Statute of the ICJ, any state which considers that it has an interest of a legal nature which may be affected by the decision in a case, may submit a request to be permitted to intervene, while under article 63 where the construction of a convention to which states other than those concerned in the case are parties is in question, the registrar of the Court shall notify all such states forthwith. Every state so notified has the right to intervene in the proceedings.[238] The Court, however, appears to have set a fairly high threshold of permitted intervention. In the *Nuclear Tests* case,[239] Fiji sought to intervene in the dispute between France on the one hand and New Zealand and Australia on the other, but the Court postponed consideration of this and, after its judgment that the issue was moot, it was clearly unnecessary to take any further

---

[236] See US statement in 24 *ILM*, 1985, p.246 *et seq*. See also e.g. Highet, *op. cit.* and Chayes *op. cit.* On 7 October 1985, the US announced that it was terminating its acceptance of the compulsory jurisdiction of the ICJ, although it would continue to accept the jurisdiction of the Court in "mutually submitted" legal disputes, *The International Herald Tribune,* 8 October, 1985, p.1. See also 24 *ILM*, 1985, p.1742 *et seq*.

[237] See e.g. Elias, *op. cit.,* Chapter 4, and Rosenne, *Law and Practice, op. cit.* vol.I, pp.430-34. See also Rules 81-86 of the Court, 1978, and Jessup, "Intervention in the International Court", 75 *AJIL,* 1981, p.903.

[238] See the *Wimbledon* case, PCIJ, Series A, no.1, 1923, pp.9-13, and the *Haya de la Torre* case, ICJ Reports, 1951, p.71; 18 *ILR,* p.349.

[239] ICJ Reports, 1974, p.253; 57 *ILR,* p.398.

steps regarding Fiji. Malta sought to intervene in the *Tunisia-Libya Continental Shelf* case[240] in the light of its shelf delimitation dispute with Libya in order to submit its views to the Court. The Court felt that the real purpose of Malta's intervention was unclear and did not relate to any legal interest of its own directly in issue as between Tunisia and Libya in the proceedings or as between itself and either one of those countries.[241] While Malta did have an interest similar to other states in the area in the case in question, the Court said[242] that in order to intervene under article 62 it had to have an interest of a legal nature which may be affected by the Court's decision in the instant case.

However, the Court has recently, for the very first time in the history of both the ICJ and its predecessor, granted permission to a third state to intervene under article 62 of the Statute. Nicaragua was permitted to intervene in the case concerning the *Land, Island and Maritime Frontier Dispute (El Salvador v. Honduras)* in certain respects, the Court having held unanimously that Nicaragua had demonstrated that it had an interest of a legal nature which may be affected by part[243] of the judgment of the Chamber on the merits of the case.[244] The Court noted that the burden of proof in such requests for intervention lies upon the applicant who must demonstrate convincingly what it asserts. Such applicant need only show that its interest may be affected, not that it will or must be so affected. It must identify the interest of a legal nature in question and show how that interest may be affected.[245]

The intervening state does not need to demonstrate a basis of jurisdiction, since the competence of the Court is founded here not upon the consent of the parties as such but is rather derived from the consent given by the parties in becoming parties to the Court's

---

[240] ICJ Reports, 1982, p.18; 67 *ILR*, p.4.

[241] ICJ Reports, 1981, pp.3, 12; 62 *ILR*, pp.612, 621.

[242] *Ibid.*, p.19; 62 *ILR*, p.628. The Court also refused Italy permission to intervene under article 62 in the *Libya-Malta* case, see ICJ Reports, 1984, p.3; 70 *ILR*, p.527. The Court also refused permission to El Salvador to intervene in the *Nicaragua* case under article 63, see ICJ Reports, 1984, p.215; 76 *ILR*, p.74, in as much as it related to the current phase of the proceedings. The Court here more controversially also refused to hold a hearing on the issue, *ibid.*, but see separate opinion of five of the judges, *ibid.*, p.219; 76 *ILR*, p.78.

[243] I.e. concerning the legal regime of the waters within the Gulf of Fonseca only and not the other issues in dispute, such as maritime delimitations and delimitation of the land frontier dispute between El Salvador and Honduras.

[244] ICJ Reports, 1990.

[245] *Ibid.*, paras. 61-63.

Statute to the Court's exercise of its powers conferred by the Statute. Thus the Court may permit an intervention by a third party even though it be opposed by one or both of the parties to the case. The purpose of such intervention is carefully circumscribed and closely defined in terms of the protection of a state's interest of a legal nature which may be affected by a decision in an existing case, and accordingly intervention cannot be used as a substitute for contentious proceedings, which are based upon consent. Thus the intervener does not as such become a party to the case.[246]

The Advisory Jurisdiction of the Court [247]

In addition to having the capacity to decide disputes between states, the ICJ may give advisory opinions. Article 65 of the Statute declares that "the Court may give an advisory opinion on any legal question at the request of whatever body may be authorised by or in accordance with the Charter of the United Nations to make such a request", while article 96 of the Charter notes that as well as the General Assembly and Security Council, other organs of the UN and specialised agencies established by the Assembly may request such opinions on legal questions arising within the scope of their activities.

The general rule established by the *Eastern Carelia* case[248] was that the Court would not exercise its advisory jurisdiction in respect of a central issue in a dispute between the parties where one of these parties refused to take part in the proceedings. However, the scope of this principle, which was intended to reflect the sovereignty and independence of states, has been reduced somewhat in a number of subsequent cases before the Court.

In the *Interpretation of Peace Treaties* case,[249] for example, which concerned the interpretation of the 1947 peace agreements with Bulgaria, Hungary and Romania, it was stressed that whereas the basis of the Court's jurisdiction in contentious proceedings rested upon the consent of the parties to the dispute, the same did not

---

[246] *Ibid.*, paras. 93-101.

[247] See e.g. Keith, *The Extent of the Advisory Jurisdiction of the International Court of Justice,* 1971; Pomerance, *The Advisory Jurisdiction of the International Court in the League and UN Eras,* 1973, and Rosenne, *Law and Practice, op. cit.* vol.II, Chapters XIX-XXI. See also Waldock, *Aspects of the Advisory Jurisdiction of the International Court of Justice,* 1976.

[248] PCIJ, Series B, no.5, 1923; 2 *ILR,* p.394.

[249] ICJ Reports, 1950, p.65; 17 *ILR,* p.331.

apply with respect to advisory opinions. Such opinions were not binding upon anyone and were given not to the particular states but to the organs which requested them.

The Court declared that "the reply of the Court, itself an 'organ of the United Nations', represents its participation in the activities of the organisation, and in principle should not be refused".[250] Similarly, the Court emphasised in the *Reservations to the Genocide Convention* case,[251] that the object of advisory opinions was "to guide the United Nations in respect of its own action". Thus, the Court would lean towards exercising its jurisdiction, despite the objections of a concerned party, where it would be providing guidance for an international body with respect to the application of an international treaty.[252]

In the *Western Sahara* case,[253] the ICJ gave an advisory opinion as regards the nature of the territory and the legal ties therewith of Morocco and Mauritania at the time of colonisation, notwithstanding the objections of Spain, the administering power. The Court distinguished the case from the *Eastern Carelia* dispute on a number of grounds. In the latter case, Russia, which had objected to the Court's jurisdiction, was neither a member of the League (at that time) nor a party to the Statute of the PCIJ, whereas in the *Western Sahara* case, Spain was a UN member and thus a party to the Statute of the ICJ. It had therefore given its consent in general to the exercise by the Court of its advisory jurisdiction. It was also to be noted that Spain's objection was to the restriction of the reference to the Court to the historical aspects of the Sahara question.[254] A vital point for the Court was that the dispute in the 1975 case had arisen within the framework of the General Assembly's decolonisation proceedings and the object of the request for the advisory opinion (by the Assembly) was to obtain from the Court an opinion which would aid the Assembly in the decolonisation of the territory.[255] Accordingly, the matter fell within the *Peace Treaties/Reservations* cases category of opinions to guide the UN.

[250] *Ibid.*, p.71; 17 *ILR*, p.335.
[251] ICJ Reports, 1951, p.15; 18 *ILR*, p.364.
[252] *Ibid.*, p.19; 18 *ILR*, p.366. See also the *Namibia* case, ICJ Reports, 1971, pp.16, 24; 49 *ILR*, pp.2, 14.
[253] ICJ Reports, 1975, p.12; 59 *ILR*, p.14.
[254] *Ibid.*, p.24; 59 *ILR*, p.41.
[255] *Ibid.*, p.25; 59 *ILR*, p.42.

The Court emphasised that the central core of the issue was not a dispute between Spain and Morocco, but rather the nature of Moroccan (and Mauritanian) rights at the time of colonisation. Thus, Spanish rights as administering power would be unaffected by the Court's judgment, which was aimed basically at assisting the Assembly to decolonise the territory.[256]

The Court noted that it was the fact that inadequate material was available for an opinion that impelled the PCIJ to refuse to consider the *Eastern Carelia* issue, notwithstanding that this arose because of a refusal of one of the parties to participate in the proceedings. In the *Western Sahara* case, an abundance of documentary material was available to the Court.[257]

It is therefore evident that the general rule expressed in the *Eastern Carelia* case has been to a very large extent eroded.

Apart from the cases already referred to, the ICJ has delivered a number of other advisory opinions which have greatly contributed to the development of international law. Examples include the *Reparation* case,[258] the *Admissions* case[259] and the *Certain Expenses* case.[260]

The Role of the Court [261]

The decisions and advisory opinions of the ICJ (and PCIJ before it) have played a vital part in the evolution of international law.

Having said that, the truth cannot be denied that the role of the ICJ within the international legal system is not as central as many would like. The declining number of cases and requests for advisory opinions coming before the Court and the acceptance by less than

[256] *Ibid.*, p.27; 59 *ILR*, p.44. Note that the Court dealt with the consent of an interested party in the context not of the competence of the Court, but of the propriety of giving an opinion, *ibid.*, p.25.

[257] *Ibid.*, pp.28-29; 59 *ILR*, p.45.

[258] ICJ Reports, 1949, p.174; 16 *ILR*, p.318.

[259] ICJ Reports, 1948, p.57; 15 *ILR*, p.333.

[260] ICJ Reports, 1962, p.151; 34 *ILR*, p.281. See also the *WHO-Egypt* case, ICJ Reports, 1980, p.73; 62 *ILR*, p.451; the *Administrative Tribunal* cases, ICJ Reports, 1973, p.166; 54 *ILR*, p.381; *ibid.*, 1982, p.325; 69 *ILR*, p.330; *ibid.*, 1987, p.18; 83 *ILR*, p.296 and the *Applicability of the Obligation to Arbitrate* case, ICJ Reports, 1988, p.12; 82 *ILR*, p.225.

[261] See e.g. Jenks, *The Prospects of International Adjudication*, 1964; Franck, *Judging the World Court*, 1986; Falk, *Reviving the World Court*, 1986 and *Forty Years International Court of Justice* (eds. Bloed and van Dijk), 1988.

a third of the parties to the Statute of the Court of the compulsory jurisdiction of the ICJ under article 36(2) is clear evidence of the often peripheral role of the Court within the world community. As far as the maintenance of international peace and security is concerned, the ICJ has indeed played a very minor part.

There are a number of reasons for this. Foremost amongst these is the character of the system itself, founded as it is upon over one hundred and fifty sovereign states jealously guarding their independence and fearful of any erosion of their status, real or imagined. This has meant that states will not consent to submit to the contentious jurisdiction of the Court on any significant issue unless they are sure the decision will go their way. The fact that in judicial proceedings one can rarely be sure is a further inhibiting factor. In view of the minimal enforcement measures available in practice to the Court, states often feel that a decision in their favour may in reality prove meaningless, since the other party may refuse to implement the judgment (as in fact happened to the Court's award of compensation to the UK in the *Corfu Channel* case).[262]

Many disputes are submitted to the various diplomatic processes for settlement or to arbitration because of the greater flexibility of these methods, particularly in technical matters. The time and expense involved in ICJ settlements are another factor militating against them, as is the growth in regional judicial arrangements.

Arguably most disheartening has been the deep suspicion with which the Court has been regarded by Third World nations, due not only to a strong adherence to the external manifestations of sovereignty but also to a perception that the ICJ is a traditionalist, developed world-dominated institution. This has been stimulated by the relative paucity of Afro-Asian representation on the Court over the years as well as by the effects of the decision in the 1966 *South West Africa* case,[263] which appeared to many, particularly in the Third World, to fail to grasp the essence of the dispute for arguable procedural reasons.

Nevertheless, there has been a rise in the number of developing states that have recently turned to the Court. One may note in this context Malta, Libya, Tunisia, Nicaragua, Mali, Burkina Faso,

[262] ICJ Reports, 1949, p.4; 16 *ILR*, p.155.
[263] ICJ Reports, 1966, p.6; 37 *ILR*, p.243.

El Salvador, Iran,[264] Honduras and Chad.[265] It thus appears that the earlier reluctance displayed by Third World states with regard to the International Court is being eroded. The development of the Chambers system within the Court and the prospect of financial assistance for poorer litigants via a UN Trust Fund are further examples of an important evolution and one may now envisage a steady increase in the workload of the Court. However, caution must be expressed against a belief that a legal decision by a permanent court will automatically resolve major political disputes.

[264] See the *Aerial Incident* case, *ICJ Press Communiqué*, 18 December 1989.
[265] In its border dispute with Libya, see *ICJ Press Communiqué*, 4 September 1990.

CHAPTER EIGHTEEN

International Law and the Use of Force[1]

The rules governing resort to force form a central element within international law, and together with other principles such as territorial sovereignty and the independence and equality of states provide the framework for international order. While domestic systems have, on the whole, managed to prescribe a virtual monopoly on the use of force for the governmental institutions, reinforcing the hierarchical structure of authority and control, international law is in a different situation. It must seek to minimise and regulate the resort to force by states, without itself being able to enforce its will. Reliance has to be placed on consent, consensus, reciprocity and good faith. The role and manifestation of force in the world community is, of course, dependent upon political and other non-legal factors as well as upon the current state of the law, but the law must seek to provide mechanisms to restrain and punish the resort to violence.

LAW AND FORCE FROM THE "JUST WAR" TO THE UNITED NATIONS[2]

The doctrine of the just war arose as a consequence of the Christianisation of the Roman Empire and the ensuing abandonment by Christians of their pacifism. Force could be used provided it complied with the divine will. The concept of the just war embodied elements of Greek and Roman philosophy and was employed as the ultimate sanction for the maintenance of an ordered society. St Augustine (354-430)[3] defined the just war

---

[1] See e.g. Bowett, *Self-Defence in International Law*, 1958; Brownlie, *International Law and the Use of Force by States*, 1963; Stone, *Aggression and World Order*, 1958 and *Legal Controls of International Conflict*, 2nd ed., 1959 and *Conflict Through Consensus*, 1977; McDougal and Feliciano, *Law and Minimum World Public Order*, 1961; Waldock, "The Regulation of the Use of Force by Individual States in International Law", 81 *HR*, p.415; Murphy, *The United Nations and the Control of International Violence*, 1982, and Falk, *Legal Order in a Violent World*, 1968. See also Dinstein, *War, Aggression and Self-Defence*, 1988 and *The Current Legal Regulations of the Use of Force* (ed. Cassese), 1986.

[2] See e.g. Bailey, *Prohibitions and Restraints in War*, 1972 and Walzer, *Just and Unjust Wars*, 1977. See also Brownlie, *op. cit.*, p.5 *et seq.* and Greenwood, "The Concept of War in Modern International Law", 36 *ICLQ*, 1987, p.283.

[3] See Eppstein, *The Catholic Tradition of the Law of Nations*, 1935, p.65 *et seq.*; Bailey, *op. cit.*, pp.6-9 and Brownlie, *op. cit.*, p.5.

in terms of avenging of injuries suffered where the guilty party has refused to make amends. War was to be embarked upon to punish wrongs and restore the peaceful *status quo* but no further. Aggression was unjust and the recourse to violence had to be strictly controlled.

St Thomas Aquinas[4] in the thirteenth century took the definition of the just war a stage further by declaring that it was the subjective guilt of the wrongdoer that had to be punished rather than the objectively wrong activity. He wrote that war could be justified provided it was waged by the sovereign authority, it was accompanied by a just cause (i.e. the punishment of wrongdoers) and it was supported by the right intentions on the part of the belligerents.

With the rise of the European nation-states, the doctrine began to change.[5] It became linked with the sovereignty of states and faced the paradox of wars between Christian states, each side being convinced of the justice of its cause. This situation tended to modify the approach to the just war. The requirement that serious attempts at a peaceful resolution of the dispute were necessary before turning to force began to appear. This reflected the new state of international affairs, since there now existed a series of independent states, uneasily co-existing in Europe in a primitive balance of power system. The use of force against other states, far from strengthening the order, posed serious challenges to it and threatened to undermine it. Thus the emphasis in legal doctrine moved from the application of force to suppress wrongdoers to a concern (if hardly apparent at times) to maintain the order by peaceful means. The great Spanish writer of the sixteenth century, Vitoria,[6] emphasised that "not every kind and degree of wrong can suffice for commencing war", while Suarez[7] noted that states were obliged to call the attention of the opposing side to the existence of a just cause and request reparation before action was taken.

The just war was also implied in immunity of innocent persons

---

[4] *Summa Theologica*, II, ii, 40. See Bailey, *op. cit.*, p.9. See also Von Elbe, "The Evolution of the Concept of the Just War in International Law", 33 *AJIL*, 1939, p.669, and Parry, "The Function of Law in the International Community" in *Manual of Public International Law* (ed. Sørensen), 1968, pp.1, 27.

[5] Brownlie, *op. cit.*, p.7 *et seq.*

[6] *De Indis et de Jure Belli Relectiones*, ss.14, 20-23, 29 and 60, cited in Bailey, *op. cit.*, p.11.

[7] See *ibid.*, pp.11-12. Suarez felt that the only just cause was a grave injustice that could not be avenged or repaired in any other way, *ibid.*

from direct attack and the proportionate use of force to overcome the opposition.[8]

Gradually it began to be accepted that a certain degree of right might exist on both sides, although the situation was confused by references to subjective and objective justice. Ultimately, the legality of the recourse to war was seen to depend upon the formal processes of law. This approach presaged the rise of positivism with its concentration upon the sovereign state, which could only be bound by what it had consented to.

Grotius,[9] in his systematising fashion, tried to exclude ideological considerations as the basis of a just war, in the light of the destructive seventeenth century religious conflicts, and attempted to redefine the just war in terms of self-defence, the protection of property and the punishment for wrongs suffered by the citizens of the particular state.

But with positivism and the definitive establishment of the European balance of power system after the Peace of Westphalia, 1648, the concept of the just war disappeared from international law as such.[10] States were sovereign and equal, and therefore no one state could presume to judge whether another's cause was just or not. States were bound to honour agreements and respect the independence and integrity of other countries, and had to try and resolve differences by peaceful methods.

But where war did occur, it entailed a series of legal consequences. The laws of neutrality and war began to operate as between the parties and third states and a variety of legal situations at once arose. The fact that the war may have been regarded as unjust by any ethical standards did not in any way affect the legality of force as an instrument of the sovereign state nor alter in any way the various rules of war and neutrality that sprang into operation once the war commenced.

Whether the cause was just or not became irrelevant in any legal way to the international community (though, of course, important in political terms) and the basic issue revolved around whether in fact a state of war existed.[11]

---

[8] *Ibid.*, pp.12-15.

[9] *Ibid.*, Chapter 2 and Brownlie, *op. cit.*, p.13. See *De Jure Belli ac Pacis*, 1625.

[10] See e.g. Brownlie, *op. cit.*, p.14 *et seq.* See also Gross, "The Peace of Westphalia, 1648-1948", 42 *AJIL*, 1948, p.20.

[11] Brownlie, *op. cit.*, pp.26-28.

The doctrine of the just war arose with the increasing power of Christianity and declined with the outbreak of the inter-Christian religious wars and the establishment of an order of secular sovereign states. Although war became a legal state of affairs which permitted force to be used and in which a series of regulatory conditions were recognised, there existed various other methods of employing force that fell short of war with all the legal consequences as regards neutrals and conduct that that entailed. Reprisals and pacific blockades[12] were examples of the use of force as "hostile measures short of war".

These activities were undertaken in order to assert or enforce rights or to punish wrongdoers. There were many instances in the nineteenth century in particular of force being used in this manner against the weaker states of Latin America and Asia.[13] There did exist limitations under international law of the right to resort to such measures but they are probably best understood in the context of the balance of power mechanism of international relations that to a large extent did help minimise the resort to force in the nineteenth century, or at least restrict its application.

The First World War marked the end of the balance of power system and raised anew the question of unjust war. It also resulted in efforts to rebuild international affairs upon the basis of a general international institution which would oversee the conduct of the world community to ensure that aggression could not happen again. The creation of the League of Nations reflected a completely different attitude to the problems of force in the international order.[14]

The Covenant of the League declared that members should submit disputes likely to lead to a rupture to arbitration or judicial settlement or inquiry by the Council of the League. In no circumstances were members to resort to war until three months after the arbitral award or judicial decision or report by the Council. This was intended to provide a cooling-off period for passions to subside and reflected the view that such a delay might well have

---

[12] *Ibid.*

[13] *Ibid.*, p.28 *et seq.*

[14] *Ibid.*, Chapter III. But note Hague Convention II of 1907, which provided that the parties would not have recourse to armed forces for the recovery of contract debts claimed from the government of one country by the government of another as being due to its nationals.

broken the seemingly irreversible chain of tragedy that linked the assassination of the Austrian Archduke in Sarajevo with the outbreak of general war in Europe.

League members agreed not to go to war with members complying with such an arbitral award or judicial decision or unanimous report by the Council.[15]

The League system did not, it should be noted, prohibit war or the use of force, but it did set up a procedure designed to restrict it to tolerable levels. It was a constant challenge of the inter-war years to close the gaps in the Covenant in an effort to achieve the total prohibition of war in international law and this resulted ultimately in the signing in 1928 of the General Treaty for the Renunciation of War (the Kellogg-Briand Pact).[16]

The parties to this treaty condemned recourse to war and agreed to renounce it as an instrument of national policy in their relations with one another.[17]

In view of the fact that this treaty has never been terminated and in the light of its widespread acceptance,[18] it is clear that prohibition of the resort to war is now a valid principle of international law. It is no longer possible to set up the legal relationship of war in international society. However, this does not mean that the use of force in all circumstances is illegal. Reservations to the treaty by some states made it apparent that the right to resort to force in self-defence was still a recognised principle in international law.[19] Whether in fact measures short of war such as reprisals were also prohibited or were left untouched by the treaty's ban on war was unclear and subject to conflicting interpretations.[20]

THE UN CHARTER

Article 2(4) of the Charter declares that:

---

[15] Brownlie, *op. cit.*, Chapter IV. See especially articles 10-16 of the Covenant.

[16] See e.g. Skubiszewski, "The Use of Force by States" in *Manual of Public International Law*, *op. cit.*, pp.739, 742-44 and Brownlie, *op. cit.*, pp.74-92.

[17] Article I.

[18] As of 1 January 1979, 64 states were parties to the Treaty. It came into force on 24 July 1929 and is still in effect. Many inter-war treaties reaffirmed the obligations imposed by the Pact, see Brownlie, *op. cit.*, pp.75-76.

[19] See e.g. Cmd. 3153, p.10.

[20] See *ibid.*, p.87. Cf. Bowett, *op. cit.*, p.136.

[a]ll members shall refrain in their international relations from the threat or use of force against the territorial integrity or political independence of any state, or in any other manner inconsistent with the purposes of the United Nations.

This provision is regarded now as a principle of customary international law and as such is binding upon all states in the world community.[21] The reference to "force" rather than war is beneficial and thus covers situations in which violence is employed which fall short of the technical requirements of the state of war.

Article 2(4) was elaborated as a principle of international law in the 1970 Declaration on Principles of International Law and analysed systematically. Firstly, wars of aggression constitute a crime against peace for which there is responsibility under international law.[22] Secondly, states must not threaten or use force to violate existing international frontiers (including demarcation or armistice lines) or to solve international disputes. Thirdly, states are under a duty to refrain from acts of reprisal involving the use of force. Fourthly, states must not use force to deprive peoples of their right to self-determination and independence. And fifthly, states must refrain from organising, instigating, assisting or participating in acts of civil strife or terrorist acts in another state and must not encourage the formation of armed bands for incursion into another state's territory. Many of these items are crucial, but ambiguous.

Although the Declaration is not of itself a binding legal document, it is important as an interpretation of the relevant Charter provisions.[23]

Important exceptions to article 2(4) exist in relation to collective measures taken by the United Nations and with regard to the right of self-defence.[24]

---

[21] See e.g. Skubiszewski, *op. cit.*, p.745, and Henkin, Pugh, Schachter and Smit, *International Law Cases and Materials*, 1980, p.910.

[22] Article 19(3) of the International Law Commission's Draft Articles on State Responsibility provides that a serious breach of an international obligation of essential importance for maintenance of international peace and security may constitute an international crime for which the state may be criminally liable. See *supra*, Chapter 13, p.484.

[23] See e.g. Arangio-Ruiz, *The UN Declaration on Friendly Relations and the System of Sources of International Law*, 1979 and Rosenstock, "The Declaration on Principles of International Law Concerning Friendly Relations", 65 *AJIL*, 1971, p.713.

[24] *Infra*, pp.702 and 691.

"Force"

One point that was considered in the past[25] and is now being reconsidered is whether the term "force" in article 2(4) includes not only armed force but, for example, economic force. Does the imposition of boycotts or embargoes against particular states or groups of states come within article 2(4), so rendering them illegal?[26]

Although that provision is not modified in any way, the preamble to the Charter does refer to the need to ensure that "armed force" should not be used except in the common interest, while article 51, dealing with the right to self-defence, specifically refers to armed force, although that is not of itself conclusive as to the permissibility of other forms of coercion.

The 1970 Declaration on Principles of International Law recalled the "duty of states to refrain . . . from military, political, economic or any other form of coercion aimed against the political independence or territorial integrity of any state" and the International Covenants on Human Rights adopted in 1966 emphasised the right of all peoples freely to pursue their economic, social and cultural development.

This approach was underlined in the Charter of Economic Rights and Duties of States, approved by the General Assembly in 1974, which particularly specified that "no state may use or encourage the use of economic, political or any other type of measures to coerce another state in order to obtain from it the subordination of the exercise of its sovereign rights".

The question of the legality of the open use of economic pressures to induce a change of policy by states was examined with renewed interest in the light of the Arab oil weapon used against states deemed favourable to Israel, in 1973-4.[27] It does seem that there is at least a case to be made out in support of the view that such actions are contrary to the United Nations Charter, as interpreted in numerous resolutions and declarations. But the issue is

[25] An attempt by Brazil to prohibit "economic measures" in article 2(4) itself was rejected, 6 *UNCIO,* Documents, p.335. See also Goodrich, Hambro and Simons, *Charter of the United Nations,* 3rd ed., 1969, p.49.

[26] See e.g. *Economic Coercion and the New International Economic Order* (ed. Lillich), 1976 and *The Arab Oil Weapon* (eds. Paust and Blaustein), 1977.

[27] *Ibid.*

controversial. It should, of course, also be noted that article 2(4) covers threats of force as well as use of force.

The provisions governing the resort to force internationally do not affect the right of a state to take measures to maintain order within its jurisdiction. Accordingly, such a state may forcibly quell riots, suppress insurrections and punish rebels without contravening article 2(4). In the event of injury to alien persons or property, the state may be required to make reparation to the state of the alien concerned,[28] but apart from this the prohibition on force in international law is not in general applicable within domestic jurisdictions.[29]

"Against the Territorial Integrity or Political Independence of any State"

Article 2(4) of the Charter prohibits the use of force "against the territorial integrity or political independence of any state, or in any other manner inconsistent with the purposes of the United Nations". There is a debate as to whether these words should be interpreted restrictively,[30] so as to permit force that would not contravene the clause, or as reinforcing the primary prohibition,[31] but the weight of opinion probably suggests the latter position. The 1965 Declaration on the Inadmissibility of Intervention in the Domestic Affairs of States[32] emphasised that:

[n]o state has the right to intervene, directly or indirectly, for any reason whatsoever, in the internal or external affairs of any other state. Consequently, armed intervention and all other forms of interference or attempted threats against the personality of the state or against its political, economic and cultural elements, are condemned.

This was reaffirmed in the 1970 Declaration on Principles in International Law,[33] with the proviso that not only were such manifestations condemned, but they were held to be in violation of international law.

---

[28] *Supra*, Chapter 13, p.503.
[29] But see *infra*, regarding self-determination, p.699 and civil wars, p.719.
[30] See e.g. Bowett, *op. cit.*, p.152.
[31] See Brownlie, *op. cit.*, p.268. See also Skubiszewski, *op. cit.*, pp.745-46.
[32] General Assembly resolution 2131 (XX).
[33] General Assembly resolution 2625 (XXV).

The International Court of Justice in the *Corfu Channel* case[34] declared specifically, in response to a British claim to be acting in accordance with a right of intervention in minesweeping the channel to secure evidence for judicial proceedings, that:

> the alleged right of intervention [was] the manifestation of a policy of force, such as has, in the past, given rise to most serious abuses and such as cannot . . . find a place in international law.

The Court noted that to allow such a right in the present case as a derogation from Albania's territorial sovereignty would be even less admissible:

> for, from the nature of things it would be reserved for the most powerful states, and might easily lead to perverting the administration of international justice itself.

The essence of international relations, concluded the Court, lay in the respect by independent states of each other's territorial sovereignty.[35]

CATEGORIES OF FORCE

Various measures of self-help ranging from economic retaliation to the use of violence pursuant to the right of self-defence have historically been used. Since the establishment of the Charter regime there are basically three categories of compulsion open to states under international law. These are retorsion, reprisal and self-defence.[36]

Retorsion [37]

Retorsion is the adoption by one state of an unfriendly and harmful act, which is nevertheless lawful, as a method of retaliation against the injurious legal activities of another state. Examples

[34] ICJ Reports, 1949, pp.4, 35; 16 *ILR*, pp.155, 167. See also Brownlie, *op. cit.*, pp.283-89 and Lauterpacht, *The Development of International Law by the International Court*, 1958, p.90.

[35] See the *Nicaragua* case, ICJ Reports, 1986, pp.14, 109-10 and see further, *infra*, p.719.

[36] As to the use of force by the UN, see *infra*, p.702.

[37] See e.g. Skubiszewski, *op. cit.*, p.753.

include the severance of diplomatic relations and the expulsion or restrictive control of aliens. Retorsion is a legitimate method of showing displeasure in a way that hurts the other state while remaining within the bounds of legality. The Hickenlooper Amendments to the American Foreign Assistance Act are often quoted as an instance of retorsion since they required the United States President to suspend foreign aid to any country nationalising American property without proper compensation.

This procedure was applied only once, as against Ceylon (now Sri Lanka) in 1963, and has now been effectively repealed by the American Foreign Assistance Act of 1973.[38]

Retorsion would also appear to cover the instance of a lawful act committed in retaliation to a prior unlawful activity.

Reprisals [39]

Reprisals are acts which are in themselves illegal and have been adopted by one state in retaliation for the commission of an earlier illegal act by another state. They are thus distinguishable from acts of retorsion, which are in themselves lawful acts.

The classic case dealing with the law of reprisals is the *Naulilaa* dispute[40] between Portugal and Germany in 1928. This concerned a German military raid on the colony of Angola, which destroyed property, in retaliation for the mistaken killing of three Germans lawfully in the Portuguese territory.

The tribunal, in discussing the Portuguese claim for compensation, emphasised that before reprisals could be undertaken, there had to be sufficient justification in the form of a previous act contrary to international law. If that was established, reprisals had to be preceded by an unsatisfied demand for reparation and accompanied by a sense of proportion between the offence and the reprisal. In fact, the German claim that it had acted lawfully was rejected on all three grounds.

---

[38] See e.g. Lillich, "Requiem for Hickenlooper", 69 *AJIL*, 1975, p.97, and Amerasinghe, "The Ceylon Oil Expropriations", 58 *AJIL*, 1964, p.445.

[39] See e.g. Skubiszewski, *op. cit.*, pp.753-55; Brownlie, *op. cit.*, pp.219-23 and 281-82 and Bowett, "Reprisals Including Recourse to Armed Force", 66 *AJIL*, 1972, p.1.

[40] 2 *RIAA*, p.1011 (1928); 4 *ILR*, p.526. See also Hackworth, *Digest of International Law*, vol.6, 1943, p.154.

Those general rules are still applicable but have now to be interpreted in the light of the prohibition on the use of force posited by article 2(4) of the United Nations Charter. Thus, reprisals short of force may still be undertaken legitimately, while reprisals involving armed force may be lawful if resorted to in conformity with the right of self-defence.[41]

Sometimes regarded as an aspect of reprisal is the institution of pacific blockade.[42] This developed during the nineteenth century and was extensively used as a forceful application of pressure against weaker states. In the absence of war or armed hostilities, the vessels of third states were probably exempt from such blockade, although this was disputed by some writers.

Pacific blockades may be instituted by the United Nations Security Council,[43] but cannot now be resorted to by states since the Charter of the United Nations. The legality of the so-called "quarantine" imposed by the United States upon Cuba in October 1962 to prevent certain weapons reaching the island appears questionable and should not be relied upon as an extension of the doctrine of pacific blockades.[44]

The Right of Self-defence [45]

The traditional definition of the right of self-defence in customary international law occurs in the *Caroline* case.[46] This dispute revolved around an incident in 1837 in which British subjects seized and

---

[41] But see Bowett, *op. cit.* footnote 39. See also SCOR, 19th Year, 111th meeting, 8 April 1964, in which the Security Council condemned reprisals as contrary to the UN Charter and deplored the UK bombing of Fort Harib, and Lillich, "Forcible Self-Help under International Law", 62 *US Naval War College International Law Studies*, 1980, p.129. As for episodes that appear to be on the borderline between self-defence and reprisals, see e.g. Falk, "The Beirut Raid and the International Law of Retaliation", 63 *AJIL*, 1969, p.415 and Blum, "The Beirut Raid and the International Double Standard", 64 *AJIL*, 1970, p.73.

[42] See e.g. Skubiszewski, *op. cit.*, pp.755-57 and Brownlie, *op. cit.*, pp.223-24.

[43] See *infra*, p.702.

[44] See e.g. Wright, "The Cuban Quarantine", 57 *AJIL*, 1963, p.546 and McDougal, "The Soviet-Cuban Quarantine and Self-Defence", *ibid.*, p.597. See also Chayes, *The Cuban Missile Crisis*, 1974. But note the rather different declaration by the UK of a Total Exclusion Zone during the Falklands conflict, *supra*, Chapter 10, p.363.

[45] See Bowett, *op. cit.*, and Brownlie, *op. cit.*, Chapter XIII. See also Brownlie, "The Use of Force in Self-Defence", 37 *BYIL*, 1961, p.183; Dinstein, *op. cit.*, p.165 and Schachter, "The Right of States to Use Armed Force", 82 *Michigan Law Review*, 1984, p.1620 and "Self-Defence and the Rule of Law", 83 *AJIL*, 1989, p.259.

[46] 29 *BFSP*, p.1137 and 30 *BFSP*, p.195. See also Jennings, "The Caroline and McLeod Cases", 32 *AJIL*, 1938, p.82.

destroyed a vessel in an American port. This had taken place because the *Caroline* had been supplying groups of American nationals, who had been conducting raids into Canadian territory. In the correspondence with the British authorities which followed the incident, the American Secretary of State laid down the essentials of self-defence. There had to exist "a necessity of self-defence, instant, overwhelming, leaving no choice of means, and no moment for deliberation".

Not only were such conditions necessary before self-defence became legitimate, but the action taken in pursuance of it must not be unreasonable or excessive, "since the act, justified by the necessity of self-defence must be limited by that necessity, and kept clearly within it". These principles were accepted by the British government at that time and are accepted as part of customary international law.[47]

There is extensive controversy as to the precise extent of the right of self-defence in the light of article 51. On the one hand, it is declared that article 51 in conjunction with article 2(4) now specifies the scope and limitations of the doctrine. In other words, self-defence can only be resorted to "if an armed attack occurs", and in no other circumstances.[48] On the other hand, there are writers who maintain that the opening phrase in article 51 specifying that "nothing in the present Charter shall impair the inherent right of . . . self-defence" means that there does exist in customary international law a right of self-defence over and above the specific provisions of article 51, which refer only to the situation where an armed attack has occurred.[49] This view is somewhat strengthened by an examination of the *travaux préparatoires* of the Charter, which seem to underline the validity of the use of force in legitimate self-

[47] See e.g. the Legal Adviser to the US Department of State, who noted that "the exercise of the inherent right of self-defence depends upon a prior delict, an illegal act that presents an immediate, overwhelming danger to an actual and essential right of the state. When these conditions are present, the means used must then be proportionate to the gravity of the threat or danger," *DUSPIL*, 1975, p.17.

[48] See e.g. Brownlie, *op. cit.*, pp.1123 and 264 *et seq.* and Aréchaga, "International Law in the Past Third of the Century", 159 *HR*, pp.1, 87-98. See also Skubiszewski, *op. cit.*, pp.765-68 and Kelsen, *The Law of the United Nations*, 1950, p.914.

[49] See e.g. Bowett, *op. cit.*, pp.185-86; Stone, *Aggression and World Order, op. cit.*, pp.43, 95-96. See also Waldock, "General Course on Public International Law", 166 *HR*, pp.6, 231-37; Brierly, *The Law of Nations*, 6th ed., 1963, pp.417-18 and O'Connell, *International Law*, 2nd ed., 1970, vol.1, p.3127.

defence.[50] A number of academics and some states have regarded article 51 as merely elaborating one kind of self-defence in the context of the primary responsibility of the Security Council for international peace and the enforcement techniques available under the Charter.[51]

The International Court of Justice in the *Nicaragua* case[52] has, however, clearly established that the right of self-defence exists as an inherent right under customary international law as well as under the UN Charter. It was stressed that:

> Article 51 of the Charter is only meaningful on the basis that there is a 'natural' or 'inherent' right of self-defence and it is hard to see how this can be other than of a customary nature, even if its present content has been confirmed and influenced by the Charter . . . It cannot, therefore be held that article 51 is a provision which 'subsumes and supervenes' customary international law.[53]

Accordingly, customary law continued to exist alongside treaty law (i.e. the UN Charter) in this field. There was not an exact overlap and the rules did not have the same content.

The Court also discussed the notion of an "armed attack" and noted that this included not only action by regular armed forces across an international border, but additionally the sending by or on behalf of a state of armed bands or groups which carry out acts of armed force of such gravity as to amount to an actual armed attack conducted by regular armed forces or its substantial involvement therein. However, the Court did not accept that this concept extended to assistance to rebels in the form of the provision of weapons or logistical support.[54]

The issue that is then raised is whether a right to anticipatory or pre-emptive self-defence exists. This would appear unlikely if one adopted the notion that self-defence is restricted to responses to actual armed attacks. The concept of anticipatory self-defence is of particular relevance in the light of modern weaponry, that can

---

[50] See e.g. 6 *UNCIO,* Documents, where it is noted that "the use of arms in legitimate self-defence remains admitted and unimpaired".

[51] *Supra,* footnote 49.

[52] ICJ Reports, 1986, pp.14, 94; 76 *ILR,* pp.349, 428.

[53] *Ibid.*

[54] *Ibid.,* pp.103-4; 76 *ILR,* p.437.

launch an attack with tremendous speed. An armoured column backed by supersonic aircraft can move swiftly from defence to attack. This could lead to a situation where a country faced with large concentrations of forces massing across its borders would be prevented, in law, from taking action until the attack had actually taken place. In view of the nature of modern weaponry this could, in certain circumstances, lead to extremely grave consequences for that state.[55]

States have employed pre-emptive strikes in self-defence. Israel, in 1967, launched such a strike upon its Arab neighbours, following the blocking of its southern port of Eilat and the conclusion of a military pact between Jordan and Egypt. This completed a chain of events precipitated by the mobilisation of Egyptian forces on Israel's border and the eviction of the United Nations peace-keeping forces from the area by the Egyptian President.[56] It could, of course, also be argued that the Egyptian blockade itself constituted the use of force, thus legitimising Israeli actions without the need for "anticipatory" conceptions of self-defence.

It is noteworthy that the United Nations in its debates in the summer of 1967 apportioned no blame for the outbreak of fighting and did not condemn the exercise of self-defence by Israel. The International Court in the *Nicaragua* case[57] expressed no view on the issue of the lawfulness of a response to an imminent threat of an armed attack since on the facts of the case that problem was not raised.

The trouble, of course, with the concept of anticipatory self-defence is that it involves fine calculations of the various moves by the other party. A pre-emptive strike embarked upon too early might constitute an aggression. There is a difficult line to be drawn. The problem is that the nature of the international system is such as to leave such determinations to be made by the states themselves, and in the absence of an acceptable, institutional alternative, it is difficult to foresee a modification of this.

[55] Contrast Bowett, *op. cit.*, pp.118-92, who emphasises that "no state can be expected to await an initial attack which, in the present state of armaments, may well destroy the state's capacity for further resistance and so jeopardise its very existence", with Brownlie, *op. cit.*, p.275, and Henkin, *How Nations Behave*, 2nd ed., 1979, pp.141-45. See also Higgins, *The Development of International Law Through the Political Organs of the United Nations*, 1963, pp.216-21.

[56] See generally, *The Arab-Israeli Conflict* (ed. Moore), 3 vols., 1974.

[57] ICJ Reports, 1986, pp.14, 103; 76 *ILR*, p.437.

States generally are not at ease with the concept of anticipatory self-defence, however,[58] and one possibility would be to concentrate upon the notion of "armed attack" so that this may be interpreted in a relatively flexible manner.[59] One suggestion has been to distinguish anticipatory self-defence, where an armed attack is foreseeable, from interceptive self-defence, where an armed attack is imminent and unavoidable so that the evidential problems and temptations of the former concept are avoided without dooming threatened states to making the choice between violating international law and suffering the actual assault.[60] According to this approach, self-defence is legitimate both under customary law and under article 51 of the Charter where an armed attack is imminent. It would then be a question of evidence as to whether that were an accurate assessment of the situation in the light of the information available at the relevant time. This would be rather easier to demonstrate than the looser concept of anticipatory self-defence and it has the merit of being consistent with the view that the right to self-defence in customary law exists as expounded in the *Caroline* case.[61]

In any event, much will depend upon the characterisation of the threat and indeed the nature of the response, for this has to be proportionate.[62]

The Protection of Nationals and Property Abroad [63]

In the last century, it was clearly regarded as lawful to use force to protect nationals and property situated abroad and many incidents

[58] See e.g. the Security Council debate on Israel's bombing of the Iraqi nuclear reactor in 1981, see 20 *ILM*, 1981, pp.965-67.

[59] See e.g. the dissenting opinion of Judge Schwebel, *Nicaragua* case, ICJ Reports, 1986, pp.14, 347-48; 76 *ILR*, pp.349, 681. But see Dinstein, *op. cit.*, pp.174-75.

[60] See Dinstein, *op. cit.*, p.180.

[61] *Supra* p.691.

[62] Note, for example, the US bombing raid on Libya on 15 April 1986 in retaliation for Libyan sponsored terrorist activities, see *infra* p.728.

[63] See e.g. Akehurst, "The Use of Force to Protect Nationals Abroad", 5 *International Relations*, 1977, p.3 and "Humanitarian Intervention" in *Intervention in World Politics* (ed. Bull), 1984, p.95; Green, "Rescue at Entebbe – Legal Aspects", 6 *Israel Yearbook on Human Rights*, 1976, p.312 and Shaw, "Some Legal Aspects of the Entebbe Incident", 1 *Jewish Law Annual*, 1978, p.232. See also D'Angelo, "Resort to Force to Protect Nationals", 21 *Va JIL*, 1981, p.485; Paust, "The Seizure and Recovery of the *Mayaguez*", 85 *Yale Law Journal*, 1976, p.774 and Ronzitti, *Rescuing Nationals Abroad Through Military Coercion and Intervention on Grounds of Humanity*, 1985.

occurred to demonstrate the acceptance of this position.[64] Since the adoption of the UN Charter, however, it has become rather more controversial since of necessity the "territorial integrity and political independence" of the target state is infringed,[65] while one interpretation of article 51 would deny that "an armed attack" could occur against individuals abroad within the meaning of that provision since it is the state itself that must be under attack, not specific persons outside the jurisdiction.[66]

The issue has been raised in recent years in several cases. In 1964, Belgium and the United States sent forces to the Congo to rescue hostages (including nationals of the states in question) from the hands of rebels, with the permission of the Congolese government,[67] while in 1975 the US used force to rescue an American cargo boat and its crew captured by Cambodia.[68] The most famous incident, however, was the rescue by Israel of hostages held by Palestinian and other terrorists at Entebbe, following the hijack of an Air France airliner.[69] The Security Council debate in that case was inconclusive. Some states supported Israel's view that it was acting lawfully in protecting its nationals abroad, where the local state concerned was aiding the hijackers;[70] others adopted the approach that Israel had committed aggression against Uganda or used excessive force.[71]

The United States has twice recently justified armed action in other states on the grounds partly of the protection of American citizens abroad. It was one of the three grounds announced for the invasion of Grenada in 1984[72] and one of the four grounds put forward for

[64] See e.g. Brownlie, *op. cit.,* p.289 *et seq.*

[65] There is, of course, a different situation where the state concerned has consented to the action.

[66] See e.g. Brownlie, *op. cit.,* p.289 *et seq.*

[67] See Whiteman, *Digest of International Law,* vol.5, p.475. See also Lillich, "Forcible Self-Help to Protect Human Rights", 53 *Iowa Law Review,* 1967, p.325.

[68] Paust, *op. cit.* See also *DUSPIL,* 1975, pp.777-83.

[69] See e.g. Akehurst, *op. cit.*; Green, *op. cit.,* and Shaw, *op. cit.*

[70] See e.g. S/PV.1939, pp.51-55; S/PV.1940, p.48 and S/PV.1941, p.31.

[71] See e.g. S/PV.1943, pp.47-50 and S/PV.1941, pp.4-10, 57-61 and 67-72. Note that Egypt attempted without success a similar operation in Cyprus in 1978, see *Keesings Contemporary Archives,* p.29305. In 1980, the US attempted to rescue its nationals held hostage in Iran but failed, see S/13908 and the *Iran* case, ICJ Reports, 1980, pp.3, 43; 61 *ILR,* pp.530, 569.

[72] See the statement of Deputy Secretary of State Dam, 78 *AJIL,* 1984, p.200. See also Gilmore, *The Grenada Intervention,* 1984 and *infra* p.722.

the intervention in Panama in December 1989.[73] However, in both cases the level of threat against the US citizens was such as to raise serious questions concerning the satisfaction of the requirement of proportionality.[74]

It is difficult to extract from the contradictory views expressed in these incidents the apposite legal principles. While some states affirm the existence of a rule permitting the use of force in self-defence to protect nationals abroad, others deny that such a principle operates in international law. There are states whose views are not fully formed or coherent on this issue. On balance and considering the opposing principles of saving the threatened lives of nationals and the preservation of the territorial integrity of states, it would seem preferable to accept the validity of the rule in carefully restricted, *Caroline*-style[75] situations.

Whether force may be used to protect property abroad is less controversial. It is probably universally accepted today that it is not lawful to have resort to force merely to save material possessions abroad.

Conclusions

Despite controversy and disagreement over the scope of the right of self-defence, there is an indisputable core and that is the competence of states to resort to force in order to repel an attack. A clear example of this was provided in the Falklands conflict. Whatever doubts may be entertained about the precise roots of British title to the islands, it is very clear that after the Argentinian invasion of the territory, the UK possessed in law the right to act to restore the *status quo ante* and remove the Argentinian troops.[76] Security Council resolution 502 (1982), in calling for an immediate withdrawal of Argentinian forces and determining that a breach of the peace existed, reinforced this. It should also be noted that it is

---

[73] See the statements by the US President and the Department of State, 84 *AJIL*, 1990, p.545.

[74] In the case of Grenada, it was alleged that some American students were under threat, see Gilmore, *op. cit.*, pp.55-64. In the Panama episode one American had been killed and several harassed, see Nanda, "The Validity of United States Intervention in Panama Under International Law", 84 *AJIL*, 1990, pp.494, 497.

[75] *Supra*, p.691.

[76] See *supra*, Chapter 8, p.305.

accepted that a state is entitled to rely upon the right of self-defence even while its possession of the territory in question is the subject of controversy.[77]

Collective Self-defence [78]

Historically the right of states to take up arms to defend themselves from external force is well established as a rule of customary international law. Article 51, however, also refers to "the inherent right of . . . collective self-defence" and the question therefore arises as to how far one state may resort to force in the defence of another. The idea of collective self-defence, however, is rather ambiguous.

It may be regarded merely as a pooling of a number of individual rights of self-defence within the framework of a particular treaty or institution, as some writers have suggested,[79] or it may form the basis of comprehensive regional security systems.

If the former were the case, it might lead to legal difficulties should Iceland resort to force in defence of Turkish interests, since actions against Turkey would in no way justify an armed reaction by Iceland pursuant to its individual right of self-defence.

In fact, state practice has adopted the second approach. Organisations such as NATO and the Warsaw Pact have been set up since the Second World War, specifically based upon the right of collective self-defence under article 51. By such agreements, an attack upon one party is treated as an attack upon all,[80] thus necessitating the conclusion that collective self-defence is something more than a collection of individual rights of self-defence, but another creature altogether.[81]

This approach finds support in the recent *Nicaragua* case.[82] The Court stressed that the right to collective self-defence was established

---

[77] See e.g. Brownlie, *op. cit.*, pp.382-83.

[78] See Dinstein, *op. cit.*, Chapter 9.

[79] See e.g. Bowett, *op. cit.*, p.245, cf. Goodrich, Hambro and Simons, *op. cit.*, p.348. See also Brownlie, *op. cit.*, pp.328-31.

[80] See e.g. article 5 of the NATO Treaty, 1949.

[81] Note article 52 of the UN Charter, which recognises the existence of regional arrangements and agencies, dealing with such matters relating to international peace and security as are appropriate for regional action, provided they are consistent with the purposes and principles of the UN, see further *infra*, p.718.

[82] ICJ Reports, 1986, p.14; 76 *ILR*, p.349.

in customary law but added that the exercise of that right depended both upon a prior declaration by the state concerned that it was the victim of an armed attack and a request by the victim state for assistance.[83] In addition, the Court emphasised that "for one state to use force against another, on the ground that that state has committed a wrongful act of force against a third state, is regarded as lawful, by way of exception, only when the wrongful act provoking the response was an armed attack".[84]

The invasion of Kuwait by Iraq on 2 August 1990 raised the issue of collective self-defence in the context of the response of the states allied in the coalition to end that conquest and occupation. The Kuwaiti government in exile appealed for assistance from other states.[85] Although the armed action taken as from 16 January 1991 was taken pursuant to UN Security Council resolutions,[86] it is indeed arguable that the right to collective self-defence is also relevant in this context.[87]

FORCE AND SELF-DETERMINATION [88]

Article 2(4) of the UN Charter calls upon states to refrain in their international relations from the threat or use of force against another state. It does not cover as such the self-determination situation where a people resorts to force against the colonial power. Until comparatively recently such situations were regarded as purely internal matters. The colonial authority could use such force as it deemed necessary to suppress a riot or rising without the issue impinging upon article 2(4). With the growing acceptance of self-determination as a legal right,[89] the question as to the legitimacy of the use of force was raised. It was argued indecisively in the Security Council upon the occasion of India's invasion of Goa[90] and

---

[83] *Ibid.*, pp.103-5; 76 *ILR*, p.437.

[84] *Ibid.*, p.110. See also *ibid.*, p.127; 76 *ILR*, pp.444 and 461.

[85] See *Keesing's Record of World Events*, p.37631 *et seq.* (1990).

[86] See *infra* p.710.

[87] See also the *Barcelona Traction* case, ICJ Reports, 1970, pp.3, 32; 46 *ILR*, pp.178, 206.

[88] See Wilson, *International Law and the Use of Force by National Liberation Movements*, 1988. As to the principle of self-determination, see *supra*, Chapter 5, p.172.

[89] See e.g. resolution 1514 (XV), the Colonial Declaration, 1960.

[90] SCOR, 16th Year, 897th meeting, pp.9-11. See also S/5032 and S/5033 and Wright, "The Goa Incident", 56 *AJIL*, 1962, p.617.

discussed at great length in the debates of the Special Committee leading to the adoption of the Declaration on Principles of International Law in 1970.[91] In the event, the Declaration emphasised that all states were under a duty to refrain from any forcible action which deprives people of their right to self-determination.[92] This can now be regarded as accepted by the international community. The Declaration also noted that "in their actions against, and resistance to, such forcible action" such peoples could receive support in accordance with the purpose and principles of the UN Charter. This modest and ambiguous formulation could not be taken as recognition of a right of self-defence inherent in peoples entitled to self-determination. The UN Charter neither confirms nor denies a right of rebellion. It is neutral. International law does not forbid rebellion, it leaves it within the purview of domestic law. The General Assembly, however, began adopting resolutions in the 1970s reaffirming the legitimacy of the struggle of peoples for liberation from colonial domination and alien subjugation, "by all available means including armed struggle".[93] This approach was intensively debated in the process leading to the adoption by the Assembly of the Consensus Definition of Aggression in 1974.[94] In particular the issue centred upon whether the use of force by peoples entitled to self-determination was legitimate as self-defence against the very existence of colonialism itself or whether as a response to force utilised to suppress the right of self-determination. The former view was taken by most Third World states and the latter by many western states. In the event, a rather cumbersome formulation was presented in article 7 of the Definition which referred *inter alia* and in ambiguous vein to the right of peoples entitled to but forcibly deprived of the right to self-determination, "to struggle to that end and to seek and receive support, in

[91] See e.g. A/5746, pp.20, 23 and 42-45 and A/7326, paras. 103, 105, 109, 175 and 177. See also A/7619, paras. 167 and 168.

[92] See also para. 4 of the 1960 Colonial Declaration and Schwebel, "Wars of Liberation as Fought in UN Organs" in *Law and Civil War in the Modern World* (ed. Moore), 1974, p.446.

[93] See e.g. resolutions 3070 (XXVIII), 3103 (XXVIII), 3246 (XXIX), 3328 (XXIX), 3481 (XXX), 31/91, 31/92, 32/42 and 32/154.

[94] See e.g. A/7185/Rev.1, para. 60 and A/7402, paras. 16 and 61. See also A/8019, para. 47 and A/8929, paras. 34, 73, 74, 142 and 143.

accordance with the principles of the Charter and in conformity" with the 1970 Declaration.[95]

The argument as to whether self-determination (or national liberation) wars could be regarded as international armed conflicts was also raised in the Diplomatic Conference on International Humanitarian Law,[96] which led to the adoption in 1977 of two Additional Protocols to the Geneva "Red Cross" Conventions of 1949. Ultimately, article 1(4) of Protocol I was approved. It provides that international armed conflict situations "include armed conflicts in which peoples are fighting against colonial domination and alien occupation and against racist regimes in the exercise of their right to self-determination" as enshrined in the Charter of the UN and the 1970 Declaration. The effect of this (within the clear self-determination context as defined in the Charter and the 1970 Declaration) is that the argument that valid self-determination conflicts are now to be accepted as within the international sphere of the activity of states has been greatly strengthened. The view that articles 2(4) and 51 of the Charter now apply to self-determination conflicts so that the peoples in question have a valid right to use force in self-defence is controversial and difficult to maintain. It is more likely that the principle of self-determination itself provides that where forcible action has been taken to suppress the right, force may be used in order to counter this and achieve self-determination. The use of force to suppress self-determination is now clearly unacceptable, as is help by third parties given to that end.

The question of third party assistance to peoples struggling to attain self-determination is highly controversial, and the subject of disagreement between western and some Third World states. A number of the UN General Assembly resolutions have called on states to provide all forms of moral and material assistance to such peoples,[97] but the legal situation is still far from clear

---

[95] Comments made following the adoption of the Definition clearly revealed the varying interpretations made by states of this provision, see e.g. A/C.6/SR.1472, paras. 5, 27 and 48 and A/C.6/SR.1480, paras. 8, 17, 25 and 73. See also Stone, *Conflict Through Consensus*, 1977, pp.66-86.

[96] See e.g. CDDH/SR.2 paras. 8-11 and 44-45.

[97] See e.g. resolutions 2105 (XX), 2160 (XX), 2465 (XXIII), 2649 (XXV), 2734 (XXV), 2787 (XXVI), 3070 (XXVIII), 3163 (XXVIII), 2328 (XXIX), 3421 (XXX), 31/29, 31/33, 32/10 and 32/154.

and the provision of armed help would appear to be unlawful.[98]

THE UNITED NATIONS SYSTEM [99]

The system established by the United Nations for the maintenance of international peace and security was intended to be comprehensive in its provisions and universal in its application. It has often been termed a collective security system, since a wronged state was to be protected by all, and a wrongdoer punished by all.

The Role of the Security Council

The original scheme by which this was achieved laid great stress upon the role of the Security Council, although this has been modified to some extent in practice. By article 24 of the United Nations Charter, the Council was granted primary responsibility for the maintenance of international peace and security, and its decisions are under article 25 binding upon all member states. It was thus intended to fulfil a dynamic, executive function.

While actions adopted by the Security Council in pursuance of Chapter VI of the Charter, dealing with the pacific settlement of disputes, are purely recommendatory,[100] matters concerning threats to, or breaches of, the peace or acts of aggression, under Chapter VII give rise to decision-making powers on the part of the Council. This is an important distinction and emphasises the priority accorded within the system to the preservation of peace and the degree of authority awarded to the Security Council to achieve this.

But before the Council can adopt measures relating to the enforcement of world peace, it must first "determine the existence of any threat to the peace, breach of the peace or act of aggression". This is the key to the collective security system. Once such a determination has been made, in accordance with article 39 of the

---

[98] See e.g. 17/8018, paras. 234 and 235, and *supra*, p.700 with regard to the phrase in the 1970 Declaration. See also Stone, *op. cit.* footnote 95, pp.66-86 and Ferencz, *Defining International Aggression*, vol.2, 1975, p.48, with regard to the ambiguous formulation in the 1974 Definition of Aggression.

[99] See e.g. Nicholas, *The United Nations as a Political Institution*, 5th ed., 1975; Luard, *A History of the United Nations*, vol.1, 1982; Goodrich, *The United Nations in a Changing World*, 1974 and Murphy, *op. cit.* See also White, *The United Nations and the Maintenance of International Peace and Security*, 1990.

[100] See *supra* Chapter 17, p.640.

Charter, the way is clear for the adoption of recommendations or decisions to deal with the situation. But this begs the question as to the definition of a threat to, or breach of the peace or act of aggression.

The answer that has emerged in practice is that it depends upon the circumstances of the case.[101] It also depends upon the relationship of the five permanent members of the Council (United Kingdom, United States of America, Soviet Union, China and France) to the issue under consideration, for a negative vote by any of the permanent members is sufficient to block all but procedural resolutions of the Council.[102] This is the veto, and it is one of the major causes of the failure of the Council in its appointed task of preserving international peace and security.

After several decades of discussion and deliberation, a definition of aggression was finally agreed upon by the United Nations General Assembly in 1974.[103] Article 1 provides that aggression is the use of armed force by a state against the sovereignty, territorial integrity or political independence of another state, or in any other manner inconsistent with the United Nations Charter. A number of examples of aggressive acts are given in article 3 and these include the use of weapons by a state against the territory of another state, the blockade of the ports or coasts of a state by the armed forces of another state,[104] and attack by the armed forces of a state on the land, sea or air forces of another state and the sending by, or on behalf of, a state of armed bands to carry out acts of armed force against another state.[105] A similar list of examples of aggression appears in article 12 of the Draft Code of Crimes Against the Peace and Security of Mankind, which is currently being formulated by the International Law Commission.[106]

This elucidation of some of the features of the concept of aggression might prove of some use to the Security Council, but the Council does retain the right to examine all the relevant circumstances, including the gravity of any particular incident,

---

[101] See White, *op. cit.*, Chapter 2.
[102] Article 27 of the UN Charter.
[103] General Assembly resolution 3314 (XXIX).
[104] As for example the blockade of the Israeli port of Eilat in May 1967, *supra*, p.694.
[105] See the *Nicaragua* case, ICJ Reports, 1986, pp.14, 103-4; 76 *ILR*, pp.349, 437.
[106] See McCaffrey, "The Fortieth Session of the International Law Commission", 83 *AJIL*, 1989, p.153.

before deciding on the determination to make pursuant to article 39.[107]

Findings as to actual breaches of the peace have occurred four times. In 1950, as a result of the invasion of South Korea by North Korea, the Security Council adopted resolutions determining that a breach of the peace had occurred and calling upon member-states to assist South Korea,[108] while in resolution 502 (1982) the Council determined that a breach of the peace in the Falkland Islands region had taken place following the Argentine invasion.[109] The third situation which prompted a finding by the Security Council of a breach of the peace was in resolution 598 (1987) dealing with the Iran-Iraq war, while the fourth occasion was in resolution 660 (1990) in which the Council determined that there existed "a breach of international peace and security as regards the Iraqi invasion of Kuwait".[110]

Once the Security Council has resolved that a particular dispute or situation involves a threat to the peace or act of aggression, the way is open to take further measures.

Such further measures may, however, be preceded by provisional action taken to prevent the aggravation of the situation. This action, provided for by article 40 of the Charter, is without prejudice to the rights or claims of the parties, and is intended as a provisional measure to stabilise a crisis situation. Usual examples of action taken by the Security Council under this provision include calls for cease-fires (as in the Middle East in 1967 and 1973),[111] and calls for the withdrawal of troops from foreign territory.[112]

However, the adoption of provisional measures by the Council often have an effect ranging far beyond the confines of a purely temporary action. They may induce a calmer atmosphere leading

---

[107] The first finding as to aggression by the Security Council was in 1976 with regard to South African action against Angola, Security Council resolution 387 (1976). See also Stone, *op. cit.* footnote 95 and Ferencz, *op. cit.* See as to the determination of a threat to international peace, resolution 221 (1966) regarding the proclamation of independence by minority white settlers in Rhodesia. See also Security Council resolution 667 (1990) condemning aggressive acts by Iraq against diplomatic premises and personnel in Kuwait.

[108] See Security Council resolutions of 25 June, 27 June and 7 July, 1950. See also Sohn, *Cases on United Nations Law*, 2nd ed., 1967, p.474 *et seq.*

[109] See further *supra*, p.697.

[110] See further *infra*, p.710.

[111] See resolutions 234 (1967) and 338 (1973).

[112] See e.g. resolution 509 (1982), with regard to Israel's invasion of Lebanon.

to negotiations to resolve the difficulties and they may set in train moves to settle the dispute upon the basis laid down in the Security Council resolution, which called for the provisional measures.

The action adopted by the Council, once it has decided that there exists with regard to a situation a threat to the peace, breach of the peace or act of aggression, may fall into either of two categories. It may amount to the application of measures not involving the use of armed force under article 41, such as the disruption of economic relations or the severance of diplomatic relations, or may call for the use of such force as may be necessary to maintain or restore international peace and security under article 42.

The Council has not utilised the powers it possesses under article 41 to any great extent. The first major instance of action not including the use of force occurred with respect to the Rhodesian situation following upon the Unilateral Declaration of Independence by the white minority government of that territory in 1965.[113] In two resolutions in 1965, the Council called upon member-states not to recognise or assist the illegal regime and in particular to break all economic and arms relations with it.[114] The next year, the Council went further and imposed selective mandatory economic sanctions upon Rhodesia,[115] which were extended in 1968 and rendered comprehensive,[116] although several states did act in defiance of these resolutions.[117] Sanctions were terminated in 1979 as a result of the agreement leading to the independence of Zimbabwe.[118]

However, the most comprehensive range of economic sanctions thus far imposed by the Security Council was adopted in the wake

[113] See e.g. Zacklin, *The United Nations and Rhodesia*, 1974; Fawcett, "Security Council Resolutions on Rhodesia", 41 *BYIL*, 1965-66, p.103; McDougal and Reisman, "Rhodesia and the United Nations: The Lawfulness of International Concern", 62 *AJIL*, 1968, p.1 and Murphy, *op. cit.*, p.139 *et seq*. See also Nkala, *The United Nations, International Law and the Rhodesia Independence Crisis*, 1985.

[114] Resolutions 216 (1965) and 217 (1965).

[115] Resolution 232 (1966). Note that under resolution 221 (1966) the Council *inter alia* called upon the UK "to prevent by the use of force if necessary" the arrival in Mozambique of vessels believed to be carrying oil for Rhodesia.

[116] Resolution 253 (1968). See also resolution 409 (1977).

[117] See Polakas, "Economic Sanctions: An Effective Alternative to Military Coercion?", 6 *Brooklyn Journal of International Law*, 1980, p.289. Note also the importation by the United States of Rhodesian chrome and other minerals under the Byrd Amendment between 1972 and 1977, see Murphy, *op. cit.*, pp.140-41 and *DUSPIL*, 1977, pp.830-34.

[118] Resolution 460 (1979). See also 19 *ILM*, 1980, p.287 *et seq*. Note in addition resolution 418 (1977), which imposed an arms embargo upon South Africa. See also White, *op. cit.*, pp.81-84.

of the invasion of Kuwait by Iraq on 2 August 1990.[119] Security Council resolution 661 (1990), noting that Iraq had failed to withdraw immediately and unconditionally from Kuwait[120] and acting specifically under Chapter VII of the Charter, imposed a wide range of economic sanctions upon Iraq, including the prohibition by states of all imports from and exports to Iraq and occupied Kuwait,[121] and the transfer of funds to Iraq and Kuwait for such purposes. Additionally, the Security Council decided that states should not make available to the Government of Iraq or to any commercial, industrial or public utility undertaking in Iraq or Kuwait any funds or any other financial or economic resources and should prevent their nationals and persons within their territories from remitting any other funds to persons or bodies within Iraq or Kuwait,[122] notwithstanding any existing contract or licence.

The Security Council also established a Committee consisting of all members of the Council to oversee the implementation of these measures. Under Security Council resolution 666 (1990), the Committee was instructed to keep the situation regarding foodstuffs in Iraq and Kuwait under constant review and to bear in mind that foodstuffs (as permitted under the terms of the previous resolutions) should be provided through the UN in co-operation with the International Committee of the Red Cross or other appropriate humanitarian agencies and distributed by them or under their supervision. The Committee was additionally given the task of examining requests for assistance under article 50 of the Charter[123] and making recommendations to the President of the Security Council for appropriate action.[124]

The binding economic sanctions imposed on Iraq because of its invasion and purported annexation of Kuwait were tightened in

---

[119] See *The Kuwait Crisis: Basic Documents* (eds. Lauterpacht, Greenwood, Weller, Bethlehem), 1991 and *The Kuwait Crisis: Sanctions and their Economic Consequences* (ed. Bethlehem), 1991.

[120] As required in Security Council resolution 660 (1990).

[121] Apart from supplies intended strictly for medical purposes and "in humanitarian circumstances" foodstuffs, paragraph 3(c).

[122] Except payments exclusively for strictly medical or humanitarian purposes and in humanitarian circumstances foodstuffs, *ibid.*, paragraph 4.

[123] Article 50 provides that if preventive or enforcement measures against any state are taken by the Security Council, any other state which finds itself confronted with special economic problems arising from the carrying out of those measures shall have the right to consult the Security Council with regard to a solution of those problems.

[124] Security Council resolution 669 (1990).

Security Council resolution 670 (1990), in which the Council decided that all states, irrespective of any international agreements or contracts, licences or permits in existence, were to deny permission to any aircraft to take off from their territory if the aircraft was carrying cargo to or from Iraq or Kuwait.[125] In addition, states were to deny permission to any aircraft destined to land in Iraq or Kuwait to overfly their territory.[126]

The economic sanctions were reinforced under Security Council resolution 665 (1990) which authorised those UN member-states deploying maritime forces in the area in co-operation with the legitimate government of Kuwait "to use such measures commensurate to the specific circumstances as may be necessary under the authority of the Security Council" in order to enforce the naval blockade on Iraq. The states concerned were requested to co-ordinate their actions "using as appropriate mechanisms of the Military Staffs Committee"[127] and after consultation with the UN Secretary-General to submit reports to the Security Council and the Committee established under resolution 661 (1990).

It is unclear whether given a substantial period of operation, this impressive range of sanctions would have sufficed to compel Iraq to withdraw from Kuwait, for on 16 January 1991 force was employed. Nevertheless, having once established a comprehensive set of economic and financial sanctions together with mechanisms of supervision, it is certainly conceivable that this response may be duplicated in other situations provided the same level of international political support is manifested. The machinery having once been put into operation may be re-used with less exertion on a subsequent occasion.

Where the Council feels that the measures short of armed forces as prescribed under Article 41 have been or would be inadequate, it may take "such action by air, sea or land forces as may be necessary to maintain or restore international peace and security". Article 42 also provides that such action may extend to demonstrations,

---

[125] Other than food in humanitarian circumstances subject to authorisation by the Council or the Committee or supplies intended strictly for medical purposes.

[126] Unless the aircraft lands for inspection or the flight has been approved by the Committee or the flight is certified by the UN as solely for the purposes of the UN Iran-Iraq Military Observer Group (UNIIMOG).

[127] See *infra* p.708.

blockades and other armed operations by members of the United Nations.

In order to be able to function effectively in this sphere, the United Nations organisation needed to be able to call upon an active and prepared reserve of troops and equipment, which could only be supplied by member-states. Consequently the Charter provides in Article 43 for member states to conclude agreements with the Security Council to make available armed forces, assistance and facilities. In this manner it was intended to create a United Nations corps to act as the arm of the Council to suppress threats to, or breaches of, the peace or acts of aggression.

Article 47 provides for the creation of a Military Staffs Committee, composed of the Chiefs of Staff of the five permanent members or their representatives, to advise and assist the Security Council on the military requirements relating to the maintenance of international peace and security, the employment and command of troops placed at its disposal, the regulation of armaments and possible disarmament. It was intended that the Military Staffs Committee should be responsible for the strategic direction of any armed force placed at the disposal of the Security Council. Until the Kuwait crisis of 1990-91, the Military Staffs Committee exercised no practical function. During the unfolding of that crisis, it played an important co-ordinating role as the permanent members of the Security Council sought to co-operate and align their positions, while under Security Council resolution 665 (1990) it was given a more general co-ordination function.

Because of great power disputes and other factors, none of the projected agreements has been signed and article 43 remains ineffective. This has weakened article 42 to the extent that the envisaged procedure for its implementation has had to be abandoned. Of course, there are other ways of carrying out the Council's decisions to employ force in any given situation, but actions under article 42 are likely to be few and far between.

The first example of this is the United Nations reaction to the North Korean invasion of the South in 1950,[128] and this only occurred because of a fortuitous combination of circumstances. In

---

[128] See e.g. Murphy, *op. cit.*, p.29 *et seq.*; Bowett, *United Nations Forces*, 1964, Chapter 3; Stone, *Legal Controls*, *op. cit.*, p.228 *et seq.* and White, *op. cit.*, pp.86-87. See also Luard, *op. cit.*, Chapter 13 and Sohn, *op. cit.*, p.474 *et seq.*

June 1950 North Korean forces crossed the 28th Parallel dividing North from South Korea and thus precipitated armed conflict. Almost immediately the Security Council debated the issue and after declaring that a breach of the peace had taken place, called upon member-states to assist the United Nations in achieving a North Korean withdrawal. Two days later, another resolution was adopted which recommended that United Nations members should furnish all necessary assistance to the South Korean authorities, while the third in the trio of Security Council resolutions on this issue authorised the United States to designate the commander of the unified forces established for the purpose of aiding the South Koreans and permitted the use of the United Nations flag by such forces.[129]

The only reason that these resolutions were in fact passed by the Council was the absence of the USSR in protest at the seating of the Nationalist Chinese delegation.[130] This prevented the exercise of the veto by the Soviet Union and permitted the creation of an authoritative United Nations umbrella for the American-commanded forces combating the North Korean armies. The USSR returned to the Council at the start of August 1950 and effectively blocked further action by the Council on this issue, but they could not reverse what had been achieved, despite claims that the resolutions were not constitutionally valid in view of the Soviet boycott.[131]

However, although termed United Nations forces, the contingents from the sixteen states which sent troops were under effective United States control, pursuant to a series of agreements concluded by that country with each of the contributing states, and were not in any real sense directed by the United Nations other than operating under a general Security Council authorisation.[132]

This improvised operation clearly revealed the deficiencies in the United Nations system of maintaining the peace. The lack of defined and clear procedures and the absence of the requisite organs meant that the formulation and establishment of the force could only be

---

[129] *Supra*, footnote 108.

[130] See e.g. Sohn, *op. cit.*, p.479 and Luard, *op. cit.*, p.242.

[131] *Ibid.*, p.481 *et seq.* See also *ibid.*, p.509 *et seq.* with regard to the situation following the Chinese involvement in the conflict.

[132] See e.g. Goodrich, *Korea in Collective Measures against Aggression*, 1953, p.157 *et seq.* and Bowett, *op. cit.* footnote 128, p.47. See also Stone, *op. cit.* footnote 128, pp.234-37, who argues that the UN force constituted an example of the right of collective self-defence.

attained under the aegis of the one superpower and the *de facto* abdication of the other. It was a combination of circumstances that was probably unique and it was recognised that the likelihood of its recurrence was minimal.

However, the changing relationship between the two superpowers and the new era of co-operation ushered in by the late 1980s suggested an increasing reliance upon the United Nations. This developing possibility was speedily concretised following the invasion of Kuwait by Iraq on 2 August 1990.[133] Resolution 660 (1990), adopted unanimously the same day by the Security Council, condemned the invasion and called for an immediate and unconditional withdrawal. Resolution 662 (1990) declared that the purported Iraqi annexation of Kuwait had no legal validity and was null and void. States and international organisations were called upon to refrain from any action or dealing that might be interpreted as an indirect recognition of the annexation. The Council, specifically acting under Chapter VII of the UN Charter, demanded in resolution 664 (1990) that Iraq permit the immediate departure of the nationals of third countries[134] and in resolution 667 (1990) condemned Iraqi aggressive acts against diplomatic premises and personnel in Kuwait, including the abduction of foreign nationals present in those premises, and demanded the protection of diplomatic premises and personnel.[135]

Eventually, the Security Council, feeling that the response of Iraq to all the foregoing resolutions and measures adopted had been unsatisfactory, adopted resolution 678 (1990) on 29 November 1990. This allowed Iraq a further period of grace within which to comply with earlier resolutions and withdraw from Kuwait. This "final opportunity" was to end on 15 January 1991. After this date, member-states co-operating with the government of Kuwait were authorised to use all necessary means to uphold and implement Security Council resolution 660 (1990) and to restore international peace and security in the area. All states were requested to provide appropriate support for the actions undertaken in pursuance of this resolution. The armed action commenced on 16 January 1991 by

---

133 See *The Kuwait Crisis: Basic Documents, op. cit.*
134 See also Security Council resolution 674 (1990).
135 See generally *Keesing's Record of World Events*, p.37631 *et seq.* and p.37694 *et seq.* (1990).

a coalition of states[136] under the leadership of the United States can thus be seen as a legitimate use of force authorised by the UN Security Council under its enforcement powers elaborated in Chapter VII of the UN Charter and binding upon all member-states of the UN by virtue of article 25. This is to be seen in the context of the purposes laid down by the Council in binding resolutions, that is the immediate and unconditional withdrawal of Iraq from Kuwait and the restoration of international peace and security in the area.

It is, in fact, an example of how the Security Council was intended to function from the start, with the proviso that it had been hoped initially that the Council would have had at its disposal UN-dedicated units rather than having to rely upon member-states to organise the logistical and operational aspects of the action. This operation constitutes therefore a watershed in UN history.

Security Council Resolution 687 (1991) laid down a series of conditions for the ending of the conflict in the Gulf. The resolution was adopted under Chapter VII of the Charter. The resolution demanded that Iraq and Kuwait respect the inviolability of the international boundary as laid down in the Agreed Minutes signed by Iraq and Kuwait on 4 October 1963. The Security Council in this resolution guaranteed the inviolability of this international boundary, a development of great significance in the history of the UN. The resolution also provided for the immediate deployment of a UN observer unit to monitor a demilitarised zone to be established extending ten kilometres into Iraq and five kilometres into Kuwait from the international boundary. Iraq was called upon to accept the destruction or removal of all chemical and biological weapons and all ballistic missiles with a range greater than 150 kilometres. A special commission was provided for to ensure that this happens. Iraq was to unconditionally agree not to acquire or develop nuclear weapons. The Security Council resolution reaffirmed that Iraq is liable under international law for any direct loss, damage, including environmental damage and the depletion of natural resources, or

---

[136] The following states supplied armed forces and/or warships or aircraft for the enforcement of the UN resolutions: USA, UK, France, Egypt, Syria, Saudi Arabia, Morocco, the Netherlands, Australia, Italy, Spain, Argentina, Belgium, Canada, Pakistan, Norway, Denmark, USSR, Bangladesh, Senegal, Niger, Czechoslovakia and the Gulf Co-operation Council (Kuwait, Qatar, Bahrain, Oman and the United Arab Emirates), see *The Sunday Times* "War in the Gulf" Briefing, 27 January 1991, p.9.

injury to foreign governments, nationals and corporations, as a result of Iraq's unlawful invasion and occupation of Kuwait. A fund to pay compensation for claims was created. In a further interesting but controversial provision, the resolution "decides that all Iraqi statements made since 2 August 1990, repudiating its foreign debt, are null and void, and demands that Iraq scrupulously adhere to all of its obligations concerning servicing and repayment of its foreign debt".

The scope and extent of this resolution, which is binding as adopted under Chapter VII, is a considerable development of the Security Council's efforts to resolve disputes. The demands that Iraq give up certain types of weapons and the requirement that repudiation of foreign debt is invalidated would appear to mark a new departure for the Council. In this category would also fall the guarantee given to the inviolability of an international border which is still the subject of dispute between the two parties concerned.

The General Assembly [137]

The focus of attention during the 1950s shifted from the Security Council to the General Assembly as the use of the veto by the permanent members led to a perception of the reduced effectiveness of the Council. Since it was never really envisaged that the General Assembly would play a large part in the preservation of international peace and security, its powers as defined in the Charter were vague and imprecise. Articles 10 to 14 provide that the Assembly may discuss any question within the scope of the Charter and may consider the general principles of co-operation in the maintenance of international peace and security. The Assembly may make recommendations with respect to questions relating to international peace to members of the United Nations or the Security Council or both, provided (except in the case of general principles of co-operation, including disarmament) the Council is not dealing with the particular matter. In addition, any question respecting international peace and security on which action is necessary has to be referred to the Security Council.

The Uniting for Peace resolution was adopted by the Assembly in 1950 because it was felt that such provisions had to be re-

---

[137] See e.g. White, *op. cit.*, Chapter 4.

interpreted more specifically if the Assembly was to strengthen its role in dealing with international peace in the event of a veto in the Security Council.

This resolution, organised by the western nations whose influence predominated in the Assembly at that time, was founded on the view that as the Security Council had the primary responsibility for the maintenance of peace under article 24, it could therefore be argued that the Assembly possessed a secondary responsibility in such matters, which could be activated in the event of obstruction in the Security Council.

The resolution[138] declared that where the Council failed to exercise its responsibility upon the occurrence of a threat to the peace, breach of the peace or act of aggression because of the exercise of the veto by any of its permanent members, the General Assembly was to consider the matter at once with a view to making appropriate recommendations to members for collective measures. Such measures could include the use of force when necessary in the case of a breach of the peace or act of aggression, and if not already in session, the Assembly would be able to meet within twenty-four hours in emergency special session.[139]

Certain aspects relating to this streamlining of the Assembly's procedures and elucidation of its substantive powers caused problems within a short time. Article 11 of the Charter emphasises that any question dealing with international peace and security on which action was necessary had to be referred to the Security Council and this appeared to cast some doubts upon the validity of the provision in the Uniting for Peace resolution under which the Assembly could call for collective measures involving the use of force. This point was particularly stressed by the Soviet Union and its allies. It became of vital significance with the creation by the Assembly in 1956 of the United Nations Emergency Force which was to supervise the cease-fire in the Middle East, and in 1960 of the United Nations Force in the Congo by the United Nations Secretary-General.

The constitutionality of such forces was questioned by a number

---

[138] General Assembly resolution 377(V). See e.g. Murphy, *op. cit.*, Chapter 4 and Andrassy, "Uniting for Peace", 50 *AJIL*, 1956, p.563. See also Petersen, "The Uses of the Uniting for Peace Resolution since 1950", 8 *International Organisation*, 1959, p.219 and Woolsey, "The Uniting for Peace Resolution of the United Nations", 45 *AJIL*, 1951, p.129.

[139] The General Assembly under article 20 of the UN Charter meets only in regular annual sessions and in such special sessions as occasion may require.

of states, who refused to pay their share of the expenses incurred, and the matter was referred to the International Court. In the *Certain Expenses*[140] case, the Court took the term "action"[141] to refer to "enforcement action", thus permitting action which did not amount to enforcement action to be called for by the General Assembly and the Secretary-General.[142]

This opinion, although leading to some interpretive problems, did permit the creation of United Nations peace-keeping forces[143] in situations where because of superpower rivalry it was not possible for the Security Council to reach a decision, provided such forces were not concerned with enforcement action. The adoption of this kind of action remains firmly within the prerogative of the Security Council.

In practice the hopes raised by the adoption of the Uniting for Peace resolution have not really been fulfilled.[144] The procedure prescribed within the resolution has been used with regard to the Suez and Hungarian crises of 1956, the Lebanese and Jordanian troubles of 1958, the Congo upheavals of 1960, the Middle East in 1967, the conflict leading to the creation of Bangladesh in 1971, Afghanistan in 1980, Namibia in 1981 and the Palestine question in 1980 and 1982. But it cannot be said that the Uniting for Peace system has in effect exercised any great influence regarding the maintenance of international peace and security. It has provided a method whereby disputes may be aired before the Assembly in a way that might not have otherwise been possible, but as a reserve mechanism for the preservation or restoration of international peace, it has not proved very successful. It arose as a result of the use of the veto in the Security Council in the context of superpower rivalry, but the expansion in the membership of the Assembly and

[140] ICJ Reports, 1962, p.151; 34 *ILR*, p.281.

[141] Article 11(2) of the Charter provides that the General Assembly may discuss any questions relating to the maintenance of international peace and security, but any such question "on which action is necessary" must be referred to the Security Council.

[142] Accordingly, the UN Emergency Force in the Middle East established in 1956 was not contrary to article 11(2) since it had not been intended to take enforcement action, ICJ Reports, 1962, pp.151, 165, 171-72. This precipitated a crisis over the arrears of the states refusing to pay their contributions, see Murphy, *op. cit.*, pp.82-84.

[143] See e.g. Bowett, *op. cit.* footnote 128 and Higgins, *United Nations Peacekeeping: Documents and Commentary*, 4 vols., 1969-81. See also James, *The Politics of Peacekeeping*, 1969 and Verier, *International Peacekeeping*, 1981.

[144] See White, *op. cit.*, pp.129-33.

the consequent shift in the balance of power against the west affected the use of the system.

The Secretary-General [145]

Just as the impotence of the Security Council stimulated a growing awareness of the potentialities of the General Assembly, it similarly underlined the role to be played by the United Nations Secretary-General. By article 99 of the Charter, he is entitled to bring to the attention of the Security Council any matter which he thinks may threaten the maintenance of international peace and security and this power is in addition to his function as the chief administrative officer of the United Nations organisation under article 79.[146]

In effect, the Secretary-General has considerable discretion and much has depended upon the views and outlook of the person filling the post at any given time. Dag Hammarskjöld was a particularly active holder of the office and expanded the role of Secretary-General in the circumstances created by the East-West deadlock.

In the Congo crisis of 1960, for example, which erupted soon after Belgium granted independence to the colony and resulted in mutinies, insurrections and much confused fighting, the Security Council adopted a resolution permitting the Secretary-General to provide military assistance to the Congo government.[147] This was interpreted by Dr. Hammarskjöld as a mandate to set up a peace-keeping force on an analogy with the earlier United Nations Emergency Force established in the Middle East. The exercise of the veto in the Council left the Secretary-General with little guidance

---

[145] See e.g. Rovine, *The First Fifty Years: The Secretary-General in World Politics, 1920-1970,* 1970; Murphy, *op. cit.,* Chapter 5 and *Public Papers of the Secretaries-General of the United Nations,* (eds. Cordier and Foote, and Cordier and Harrelson), 8 vols., 1969-77.

[146] Under article 98, the Secretary-General also performs such other functions as are entrusted to him by the General Assembly, Security Council, Economic and Social Council and the Trusteeship Council.

[147] S/4387, 14 July 1960. By resolution S/4405, 22 July 1960, the Council requested all states to refrain from action which might impede the restoration of law and order or undermine the territorial integrity and political independence of the Congo. By resolution S/4426, 9 August 1960, the Council confirmed the authority given to the Secretary-General by earlier resolutions and called on member-states to carry out the decisions of the Security Council. See e.g. Abi-Saab, *The United Nations Operation in the Congo 1960-1964,* 1978; Hoskyns, *The Congo Since Independence,* 1965 and Miller "Legal Aspects of UN Action in the Congo", 55 *AJIL,* 1961, p.1.

as to how to proceed in the situation. Accordingly, he performed many of the tasks that had in 1956 been undertaken by the General Assembly with respect to the Middle East.[148]

The development of the Congo crisis from mutiny to civil war faced the United Nations force (known as ONUC from the French initials) with many difficult decisions and these had in the main to be taken by the Secretary-General.

The role that could be played by the Secretary-General was emphasised in the succeeding crises in Cyprus (1964)[149] and the Middle East (1973)[150] and in the consequent establishment of United Nations peace-keeping forces for these areas under the general guidance of the Secretary-General.

Peace-Keeping Forces – Conclusions [151]

The creation of peace-keeping forces, whether in the Middle East in 1967 and again in 1973, in the Congo in 1960 or in Cyprus in 1964, was important in that such forces tended to stabilise particular situations for a certain time. Such United Nations forces are not intended to take enforcement action, but to act as an influence for calm by physically separating warring factions. They are dependent upon the consent of the state upon whose territory they are stationed and can in no way prevent a determined aggression.

The various United Nations peace-keeping operations have met with some limited success in temporarily preventing major disturbances, but they failed to prevent the 1967 Arab-Israeli war[152]

[148] See Abi-Saab, *op. cit.*, p.15 *et seq.*

[149] See Security Council resolution 186 (1964). See also Ehrlich, *op. cit.*, and Murphy, *op. cit.*, p.46 *et seq.* and Stranger, *The United Nations Force in Cyprus,* 1968. The force is known as the UN Force in Cyprus (UNICYP).

[150] The Security Council established the UN Emergency Force to monitor the Israel-Egyptian disengagement process in 1973, see resolution 340 (1973) and a Disengagement Observer Force with respect to the Israel-Syria disengagement process, see resolution 350 (1974). See generally Pogany, *The Security Council and the Arab-Israeli Conflict,* 1984. Note also the creation of the UN Interim Force in the Lebanon (UNIFIL) established by the Council in resolution 425 (1978) after Israel's incursion into the Lebanon in 1978.

[151] See White, *op. cit.*, Chapter 7; Franck, *Nation Against Nation,* 1985; Wiseman, *Peacekeeping: Appraisals and Proposals,* 1983; Higgins, *United Nations Peacekeeping,* 4 vols., 1969-81 and James, *Peacekeeping in International Politics,* 1990.

[152] In fact the hasty withdrawal of the UNEF in May 1967 by the Secretary-General following an Egyptian request did much to precipitate the conflict. UNEF was reconstituted in 1973, see footnote 150.

and the 1974 Turkish invasion of Cyprus.[153] One has to be careful not to overestimate their significance in difficult political situations. In addition to the consent of the host state, such forces also require the continuing support of the Security Council and if that is lost or not provided such forces cannot operate.[154]

Nevertheless, peace-keeping operations do have a role to play, particularly as a way of ensuring that conflict situations in the process of being resolved do not flare up as a result of misunderstandings or miscalculations. The most recent UN operations in this area demonstrate this. The UN Good Offices Mission in Afghanistan and Pakistan was established in the context of the Geneva Accords of 14 April 1988 dealing with the withdrawal of Soviet forces from Afghanistan, while the UN Iran-Iraq Military Observer Group was created the same year following the acceptance by the belligerent states of Security Council resolution 598 (1987) calling for a cease-fire. In 1989, in the context of the resolution of the Namibian problem, the UN Angola Verification Mission was established in order to verify the withdrawal of Cuban forces from Angola, while the UN Transition Assistance Group, although originally established in 1978 in Security Council resolution 435 (1978), in fact commenced operations with the Namibian independence process on 1 April 1989.[155] It is where the underlying political problems have not been settled that the long-term value of peace-keeping or observer operations is more questionable.

The functioning of the United Nations system for the preservation and restoration of world peace has not been a tremendous success

---

[153] See e.g. Security Council resolution 359 (1974) criticising the Turkish invasion. See also Murphy, *op. cit.*, pp.52-54. Note also the existence of the unarmed UN military observer missions, the UN Truce Supervision Organisation (UNTSO) in the Middle East and the Military Observer Group in India and Pakistan (UNMOGIP).

[154] The Israel-Egypt Peace Treaty of 1979 envisaged the deployment of a UN force such as UNEF to supervise the limited forces zones established by the parties but due to Soviet action the mandate of UNEF expired in July 1979, see e.g. Akehurst, "The Peace Treaty Between Egypt and Israel", 7 *International Relations*, 1981, pp.1035, 1046 and Shaw, "The Egyptian-Israeli Peace Treaty, 1979", 2 *Jewish Law Annual*, 1980, pp.180, 185. As a result, a special Multinational Force and Observers unit was established by the parties and the United States, independently of the UN, see 20 *ILM*, 1981, p.1190 *et seq*. See also Tabory, *The Multinational Force and Observers in the Sinai*, 1986. Note also the creation of the non-UN Multinational Force established in 1982 to supervise the evacuation of PLO forces from Beirut, Lebanon, 21 *ILM*, 1982, pp.1193-97. This force returned to Beirut for several months thereafter and was withdrawn after becoming involved in hostilities. See Thakur, *International Peacekeeping in the Lebanon*, 1987.

[155] See White, *op. cit.*, Chapter 8.

and is very far from being comprehensive. It constitutes merely one additional factor in international disputes management and one particularly subject to political pressures. The United Nations has played a minimal part in some of the major conflicts and disputes since its inception, whether it be the Cuban missiles crisis of 1962 or the Vietnam war, the Soviet intervention in Czechoslovakia and Afghanistan or the Nigerian and Angolan civil wars. And in those crises with which it has concerned itself, its effective influence has not been very high. The continuing Middle East conflict and Southern African problems attest to that.

The UN and Regional Agencies

Article 52 of the Charter provides for the existence of regional arrangements or agencies dealing with such matters relating to international peace and security as are appropriate for such arrangements or agencies. Article 53 permits the Security Council to utilise such arrangements or agencies for enforcement action under its authority. Without the authorisation of the Security Council, regional enforcement action is not possible.[156] In the Grenada episode, the United States argued that regional peace-keeping (as distinct from enforcement action) had occurred and that it constituted one of the legal grounds for its action there.[157] The issue is also raised in that case of the appropriate regional arrangement or agency. The Charter of the Organisation of American States emphasises the territorial inviolability of states and the prohibition of intervention,[158] but article 22 notes that such provisions would not be violated by measures adopted for the maintenance of peace and security "in accordance with existing treaties".[159] The US view was that the 1981 treaty establishing the Organisation of Eastern Caribbean states operated as the necessary "existing" or "special" treaty. However, the OECS Defence Committee can only act unanimously and in cases of external aggression and the Grenada episode whereby troops landed to overthrow the Marxist government

---

[156] See e.g. Akehurst, "Enforcement Action by Regional Agencies", 42 *BYIL*, 1967, p.175.
[157] See statement of Deputy Secretary of State Dam, 78 *AJIL*, 1984, p.200.
[158] Articles 20 and 18.
[159] See also article 28, whereby American states are to apply "special treaties on the subject" in the case of armed conflict or other act or situation endangering the peace of America.

on the island would not satisfy the requirements, while it is only with difficulty that other articles may be used.[160] It is therefore rather problematic to interpret the OECS treaty as including the necessary regional peace-keeping action in the Grenada situation.

INTERVENTION

The principle of non-intervention is part of customary international law and founded upon the concept of respect for the territorial sovereignty of states.[161] Intervention is prohibited where it bears upon matters in which each state is permitted to decide freely by virtue of the principle of state sovereignty. This includes, as the International Court of Justice noted in the *Nicaragua* case,[162] the choice of political, economic, social and cultural systems and the formulation of foreign policy. In addition, acts constituting a breach of the customary principle of non-intervention will also, if they directly or indirectly involve the use of force, constitute a breach of the principle of the non-use of force in international relations.[163]

Civil Wars [164]

International law treats civil wars as purely internal matters, with

---

[160] Article 3 includes among the functions and principles of the OECS "such other activities calculated to further the progress of the Organisation as the member-states may from time to time decide", while article 4 calls on parties to carry out the obligations arising out of the treaty; see Moore, *Law and the Grenada Mission*, 1984, pp.45-50 and Gilmore, *op. cit.* See also American Bar Association Section of International Law and Practice, Report on Grenada, 1984.

[161] See the *Corfu Channel* case, ICJ Reports, 1949, pp.4, 35; 16 *ILR*, pp.155, 167 and the *Nicaragua* case, ICJ Reports, 1986, pp.14, 106; 76 *ILR*, pp.349, 440. See also the Declaration on the Inadmissibility of Intervention in the Domestic Affairs of States 1965 and the Declaration on the Principles of International Law 1970, *supra* p.688.

[162] ICJ Reports, 1986, pp.14, 108; 76 *ILR*, p.442. See also article 14 of the Draft Code of Crimes Against the Peace and Security of Mankind currently being formulated by the International Law Commission, see McCaffrey, "The Forty-First Session of the International Law Commission", 83 *AJIL*, 1989, p.937.

[163] *Ibid.*, pp.109-10; 76 *ILR*, p.443.

[164] See e.g. *Law and Civil War in the Modern World*, (ed. Moore), 1974; *The International Regulation of Civil Wars* (ed. Luard), 1972; *The International Law of Civil Wars*, (ed. Falk), 1971; Fraser, "The Regulation of Foreign Intervention in Civil Armed Conflict", 142 *HR*, p.291 and Friedmann, "Intervention, Civil War and the Rule of International Law", *PASIL*, 1965, p.67. See also Higgins, "Intervention and International Law" in *Intervention in World Politics*, (ed. Bull), 1984, p.29 and Joyner and Grimaldi, "The United States and Nicaragua: Reflections on the Lawfulness of Contemporary Intervention", 25 *Va JIL*, 1985, p.621.

the possible exception of self-determination conflicts.[165] Article 2(4) of the UN Charter prohibits the threat or use of force in international relations, not in domestic situations. There is no rule against rebellion in international law. It is within the domestic jurisdiction of states and is left to be dealt with by internal law. Should the rebellion succeed, the resulting situation would be dealt with primarily in the context of recognition. As far as third parties are concerned, traditional international law developed the categories of rebellion, insurgency and belligerency.

Once a state has defined its attitude and characterised the situation, different international legal provisions would apply. If the rebels are regarded as criminals, the matter is purely within the hands of the authorities of the country concerned and no other state may legitimately interfere. If the rebels are treated as insurgents, then other states may or may not agree to grant them certain rights. It is at the discretion of the other states concerned, since an intermediate status is involved. The rebels are not mere criminals, but they are not recognised belligerents. Accordingly, the other states are at liberty to define their legal relationship with them. Insurgency is a purely provisional classification and would arise for example where a state needed to protect nationals or property in an area under the *de facto* control of the rebels.[166]

On the other hand, belligerency is a formal status involving rights and duties. In the eyes of classical international law, other states may accord recognition of belligerency to rebels when certain conditions have been fulfilled. These were defined as the existence of an armed conflict of a general nature within a state, the occupation by the rebels of a substantial portion of the national territory, the conduct of hostilities in accordance with the rules of war and by organised groups operating under a responsible authority and the existence of circumstances rendering it necessary for the states contemplating recognition to define their attitude to the situation.[167]

This would arise, for example, where the parties to the conflict are exercising belligerent rights on the high seas. Other maritime countries would feel compelled to decide upon the respective status

---

[165] See *supra*, p.699.

[166] See e.g. Lauterpacht, *Recognition in International Law*, 1947, p.275 *et seq.*

[167] See e.g. Mugerwa, "Subjects of International Law" in *Manual of Public International Law* (ed. Sørensen), 1968, pp.247, 286-88. See also Higgins, "International Law and Civil Conflict" in *International Regulation of Civil Wars, op. cit.*, pp.169, 170-71.

of the warring sides, since the recognition of belligerency entails certain international legal consequences.

Once the rebels have been accepted by other states as belligerents they become subjects of international law and responsible in international law for all their acts. In addition the rules governing the conduct of hostilities become applicable to both sides, so that, for example, the recognising states must then adopt a position of neutrality.

However, these concepts of insurgency and belligerency are lacking in clarity and are extremely subjective. The absence of clear criteria, particularly with regard to the concept of insurgency, has led to a great deal of confusion. The issue is of importance since the majority of conflicts in the years since the conclusion of the Second World War have been in essence civil wars.

The reasons for this are many and complex and ideological rivalry and decolonisation within colonially imposed boundaries are amongst them.[168] Intervention may be justified on a number of grounds, including response to earlier involvement by a third party. For instance, the USSR and Cuba justified their activities in the Angolan civil war of 1975-76 by reference to the prior South African intervention,[169] while the United States argued that its aid to South Vietnam grew in proportion to the involvement of North Vietnamese forces in the conflict.[170]

The international law rules dealing with civil wars depend upon the categorisation by third states of the relative status of the two sides to the conflict. In traditional terms, an insurgency means that the recognising state may, if it wishes, create legal rights and duties as between itself and the insurgents, while recognition of belligerency involves an acceptance of a position of neutrality (although there are some exceptions to this rule) by the recognising states.

But in practice, states very rarely make an express acknowledgement as to the status of the parties to the conflict, precisely in order to retain as wide a room for manoeuvre as possible. This means that the relevant legal rules cannot really operate as intended in classical law and that it becomes extremely difficult to decide whether a particular intervention is justified or not.

---

[168] See e.g. Shaw, *Title to Territory in Africa*, 1986.

[169] See e.g. Legum and Hodges, *After Angola*, 1976.

[170] See e.g. Moore, *Law and the Indo-China War*, 1972. See also *The Vietnam War and International Law* (ed. Falk), 4 vols., 1968-76.

Aid to the Authorities of a State

It would appear that in general outside aid to the government authorities to repress a revolt[171] is perfectly legitimate,[172] provided, of course, it was requested by the government. The problem of defining the governmental authority entitled to request assistance was raised in the Grenada episode. In that situation, the appeal for the US intervention was allegedly made by the Governor-General of the island,[173] but controversy exists as to whether this in fact did take place prior to the invasion and whether the Governor-General was the requisite authority to issue such an appeal.[174] The issue resurfaced in a rather different form regarding the Panama invasion of December 1989. One of the legal principles identified by the US Department of State as the basis for the US action was that of assistance to the "lawful and democratically elected government in Panama".[175] The problem with this was that this particular government had been prevented by General Noriega from actually taking office and the issue raised was therefore whether an elected head of state who is prevented from ever acting as such may be regarded as a governmental authority capable of requesting assistance including armed force from another state. This in fact runs counter to the test of acceptance in international law of governmental authority, which is firmly based upon effective control rather than upon the nature of the regime, whether democratic, socialist or otherwise.[176]

The general proposition, however, that aid to recognised governmental authorities is legitimate would be further reinforced where it could be shown that other states were encouraging or directing the subversive operations of the rebels. In such cases, it appears that the doctrine of collective self-defence would allow

---

[171] Except where the recipient state is forcibly suppressing the right to self-determination of a people entitled to such rights, *supra*, p.699.

[172] Until a recognition of belligerency, of course, although this has been unknown in modern times, see e.g. Lauterpacht, *op. cit.*, pp.230-33.

[173] See the statement by Deputy Secretary of State Dam, *op. cit.*

[174] See references cited in footnote 160. See also Higgins, *op. cit.* note 55, pp.162-64 regarding the Congo crisis of 1960, where that state's President and Prime Minister sought to dismiss each other.

[175] 84 *AJIL*, 1990, p.547.

[176] See *supra*, p.249.

other states to intervene openly and lawfully on the side of the government authorities.

Some writers have suggested that the traditional rule of permitting third party assistance to governments would not extend to aid where the outcome of the struggle has become uncertain.[177] While this may be politically desirable for the third state, it may put at serious risk entirely deserving governments. Practice, however, does suggest that many forms of aid, such as economic, technical and arms provision arrangements, to existing governments faced with civil strife, is acceptable.[178] There is an argument, on the other hand, for suggesting that substantial assistance to a government clearly in the throes of collapse might be questionable as intervention in a domestic situation that is on the point of resolution, but there are considerable definitional problems here.[179]

Aid to Rebels

The reverse side of the proposition is that aid to rebels is contrary to international law. The 1970 Declaration on Principles of International Law emphasised that:

[n]o state shall organise, assist, foment, finance, incite or tolerate subversive, terrorist or armed activities directed towards the violent overthrow of the regime of another state, or interfere in civil strife in another state.[180]

---

[177] See e.g. Wright, "US Intervention in the Lebanon", 53 *AJIL*, 1959, pp.112, 122. See also Hall, *International Law*, 8th ed., 1924, p.347 and Falk, *Legal Order in a Violent World*, 1968, pp.227-28 and 273.

[178] See with regard to the UK continuance of arms sales to Nigeria during its civil war, Higgins, *op. cit.* footnote 167, p.173. Note also the US policy of distinguishing between traditional supplier of arms and non-traditional supplier of arms in such circumstances. It would support aid provided by the former (as the UK in Nigeria), but not the latter, see *DUSPIL*, 1976, p.7.

[179] See Doswald-Beck, "The Legal Validity of Military Intervention by Invitation of the Government", 56 *BYIL*, 1985, p.189.

[180] See also in similar terms the Declaration on the Inadmissibility of Intervention in the Domestic Affairs of States, 1965, *supra*, p.688. Article 3(g) of the Consensus Definition of Aggression, 1974, characterises as an act of aggression "the sending by or on behalf of a state of armed bands, groups, irregulars or mercenaries, which carry out acts of armed force against another state". See also with regard to US aid to the Nicaraguan "contras", Chayes, *op. cit.*, and the *Nicaragua* case, ICJ Reports, 1986, p.14; 76 *ILR*, p.349.

The Declaration also provided that:

> [e]very state shall refrain from any action aimed at the partial or total disruption of the national unity and territorial integrity of any other state or country.

This would seem fairly conclusive, but in fact state practice is far from unanimous on this point.[181]

Where a prior, illegal intervention on the government side has occurred, it may be argued that aid to the rebels is acceptable. This was argued by a number of states with regard to the Afghanistan situation, where it was felt that the Soviet move into that state amounted to an invasion.[182]

Humanitarian Intervention

It has sometimes been argued that intervention in order to protect the lives of persons situated within a particular state and not necessarily nationals of the intervening state is permissible in strictly defined situations.[183] This has some support in pre-Charter law and it may very well have been the case that in the last century such intervention was accepted under international law.[184] However, it is difficult to reconcile today with article 2(4) of the Charter[185] unless one adopts a rather artificial definition of the "territorial integrity" criterion in order to permit temporary violations. Practice is also in general unfavourable to the concept, primarily because

---

[181] See e.g. Syrian intervention in the Jordanian civil war of 1970 and in the Lebanon in 1976.

[182] See e.g. *Keesings Contemporary Archives*, pp.30339, 30364 and 30385. See also General Assembly resolutions ES-62 and 36/34 condemning the USSR for its armed intervention in Afghanistan.

[183] See e.g. *Humanitarian Intervention and the United Nations* (ed. Lillich), 1973; Lillich, "Forcible Self-Help by States to Protect Human Rights", 53 *Iowa Law Review*, 1967, p.325 and "Intervention to Protect Human Rights", 15 *McGill Law Journal*, 1969, p.205; Fonteyne, "The Customary International Law Doctrine of Humanitarian Intervention", 4 *California Western International Law Journal*, 1974, p.203 and Chilstrom, "Humanitarian Intervention under Contemporary International Law", 1 *Yale Studies in World Public Order*, 1974, p.93. See also Tesón, *Humanitarian Intervention: An Enquiry into Law and Morality*, 1987.

[184] See e.g. Ganji, *International Protection of Human Rights*, 1962, Chapter 1 and references cited in previous footnote.

[185] See in particular, Brownlie, "Humanitarian Intervention" in *Law and Civil War in the Modern World, op. cit.*, p.217.

it might be used to justify interventions by more forceful states.[186] Nevertheless, it is not inconceivable that in some situations the international community might refrain from adopting a condemnatory stand where large numbers of lives have been saved in circumstances of gross oppression by a state of its citizens due to an outside intervention. This does not, of course, mean that it constitutes a legitimate principle of international law.

One variant of the principle of humanitarian intervention is the contention that intervention in order to restore democracy is permitted as such under international law. One of the grounds given for the US intervention in Panama in December 1989 was the restoration of democracy,[187] but apart from the problems of defining democracy, such a proposition is not acceptable in international law today in view of the clear provisions of the UN Charter. Nor is there anything to suggest that even if the principle of self-determination could be interpreted as applying beyond the strict colonial context[188] to cover "democracy", it could constitute a norm superior to that of non-intervention.[189]

TERRORISM AND INTERNATIONAL LAW [190]

The use of terror as a means to achieve political ends is not a new phenomenon, but it has recently acquired a new intensity. In many cases, terrorists deliberately choose targets in innocent third states as a means of pressurising the government of the state against which it is in conflict or its real or potential or assumed allies.[191]

As far as international law is concerned, there are a number of problems that can be identified. The first major concern is that of

---

[186] See e.g. Akehurst, "Humanitarian Intervention" in *Intervention in World Politics, op. cit.*, p.95. Note that the absence of the nationality link between the state intervening and the persons concerned makes an important difference, see *supra* p.695.

[187] See e.g. *Keesing's Record of World Events*, p.37112 (1989). See also Nanda, *op. cit.*, p.498.

[188] See *supra* p.176.

[189] See e.g. Schachter, "The Legality of Pro-Democratic Invasion", 78 *AJIL*, 1984, p.645.

[190] See e.g. *Legal Aspects of International Terrorism* (eds. Evans and Murphy), 1978; Friedlander, *Terrorism*, 1979 and Lillich and Paxman, "State Responsibility for Injuries to Aliens Caused by Terrorist Activity", 26 *American Law Review*, 1977, p.217. See also *International Terrorism and Political Crimes* (ed. Bassiouni), 1975; McWhinney, *Aerial Piracy and International Terrorism*, 2nd ed., 1987, and Cassese, *Terrorism, Politics and Law*, 1989. See also *supra* p.414.

[191] The hijack of TWA Flight 847 on 14 June 1985 by Lebanese Shi'ites is one example of this phenomenon, see e.g. *The Economist*, 22 June, 1985, p.34. See also *supra*, p.687.

definition.[192] Whether one terms a particular group of activists terrorists or freedom fighters depends upon one's political standpoint. Similarly difficult is the question of the width of definition one should accept with respect to acts undertaken. For example, should attacks against property as well as attacks upon persons be covered? The extent to which one should take into account the motives and intentions of the perpetrators is raised, as is the question as to whether one should distinguish purely criminal from politically inspired attacks.

There are, of course, also difficulties associated with the enforcement of such international law rules as may be agreed upon, since some states have supported terrorist activities.

However, some progress has been made to establish rules of international law applicable to particular manifestations of terrorism. The approach that has in practice been adopted by the international community in recent years can best be described as functional, or pragmatic, rather than comprehensive. This contrasts with the all-embracing view taken by the League of Nations in the 1937 Convention for the Prevention and Punishment of Terrorism, which in the event, and only partly because of the onset of the Second World War, never entered into force.[193]

The spread of aircraft hijacking in the 1950s and the 1960s stimulated a series of three international conventions in 1963, 1970 and 1971, to deal with this particular terrorist activity.[194] These can be regarded as partial successes, although efforts by the International Civil Aviation Organisation to reinforce these measures against hijackers and states harbouring them have so far failed.[195] It is

---

[192] See e.g. GAOR, 28th session, Suppl. no.28, 1973, pp.7-8.

[193] Terrorism was here defined as criminal acts directed against a state and intended to create a state of terror in the minds of particular persons, or a group of persons or the general public, see Murphy, *op. cit.*, p.179. See also Franck and Lockwood, "Preliminary Thoughts Towards an International Convention on Terrorism", 68 *AJIL*, 1974, p.69.

[194] See the Tokyo Convention of 1963, which requires parties to return hijacked aircraft and passengers; the Hague Convention of 1970 which declares that states should either extradite or prosecute hijackers and the Montreal Convention of 1971 which extends this requirement to those employed in aircraft sabotage activities, see further *supra*, Chapter 11, p.416. Note also the 1978 Bonn Declaration under which European Community states resolved that if a country failed to fulfil its obligations under the 1970 Convention, immediate action should be taken to cease flights to that country. See also the Convention for the Suppression of Unlawful Acts against the Safety of Maritime Navigation 1988.

[195] See e.g. Murphy, *op. cit.*, p.181.

enforcement rather than definition that constitutes the main bar to progress in this field.

In December 1972, the General Assembly set up an *ad hoc* committee on terrorism,[196] but this failed to arrive at any agreed recommendations and the matter passed to the Assembly itself, where the whole issue became further entangled with various political disputes, as Third World states concentrated their attention on state terror and in particular the use of force to deprive peoples of the right to self-determination.

However, in 1973 the General Assembly adopted a Convention on the Prevention and Punishment of Crimes against Internationally Protected Persons Including Diplomatic Agents. This was an attempt to stop the kidnapping and assaults upon diplomats that had spread throughout South America and parts of Europe and the Middle East. The treaty stipulates that alleged offenders should either be prosecuted or extradited and provides for an improved degree of international co-operation.[197]

In 1979, the General Assembly also adopted the International Convention against the Taking of Hostages.[198] Its aim is to ensure that persons taking hostages are either prosecuted or extradited where found within the jurisdiction of a state party. State parties are also obliged to co-operate in the prevention of such acts. However, one ambiguous provision is found in article 12 which declares that the Convention is not to apply where the Geneva Conventions of 1949 and its Additional Protocols of 1977[199] are relevant so that hostage-taking committed in the course of armed conflicts as defined in the 1949 and 1977 instruments (including self-determination wars) would fall outside the 1979 Hostage Convention.[200] The Assembly has also adopted a number of resolutions calling for ratification of the various conventions

---

[196] See General Assembly resolution 3034 (XXVII).

[197] This was modelled upon a similar Organisation of American States Convention in 1971, see 65 *AJIL*, 1971, p.898. See also the 1977 European Convention on the Suppression of Terrorism.

[198] See Lambert, *Terrorism and Hostages in International Law*, 1990.

[199] See e.g. article 34 of the Geneva Convention on the Protection of Civilians in Time of War, 1949, which provides that the taking of hostages is prohibited, and see also article 75 of the Protocol I, 1977. See also *infra*, p.730.

[200] States in such situations would be liable to prosecute or hand over hostage-takers under the 1949 and 1977 instruments.

and for improvement in co-operation between states in this area.[201] In resolution 40/61, for example, the Assembly condemned as criminal all acts, methods and practices of terrorism wherever and by whomever committed, while in resolution 579 (1985) the Security Council condemned unequivocally all acts of hostage-taking and abduction.

States may also adopt forceful measures in response to terrorist activities, and in certain situations actions against states sponsoring terrorism may be justifiable in the context of self-defence. However, the relevant international norms hardly envisage this kind of situation, but rather concentrate upon the dangers of large-scale state use of force. Since states generally are under an obligation not to sponsor terrorist activity or assist it in any way, the question of how to deal with a violator is posed. A major terrorist incident mounted or supported by one state against another will justify measures under the rubric of self-defence, provided that the necessary requirements as to, for example, proportionality are observed. A series of smaller-scale incidents may have the same effect, but it is unlikely that isolated, relatively minor terrorist activities would justify the use of force by the target state against the state supporting the activity in question.[202] It is on this area particularly that states need to concentrate in the formulation of relevant legal norms.

---

[201] See e.g. resolutions 34/145, 35/168 and 36/33. See also *supra*, p.696 with regard to the Iran hostages crisis. See also the statement made by the President of the Security Council on behalf of members condemning the hijacking of the *Achille Lauro* and generally "terrorism in all its forms, whenever and by whomever committed", 9 October 1985, S/17554, 24 *ILM*, 1985, p.1656. See also *supra*, pp.418 and 686.

[202] Note e.g. the US bombing raid on Libya on 15 April 1986 as a consequence of alleged Libyan involvement in an attack on US servicemen in West Berlin. This was justified by the US as an act of self-defence, see President Reagan's statement, *The Times*, 16 April 1986, p.6, and supported on this basis by the U.K., see *The Times*, 17 April 1986, p.4. However, the proportionality criterion is relevant in view of the injuries and damage caused in the air raid and is unlikely to have been met, in view of reports of one hundred casualties. One US serviceman was killed in the West Berlin action. The role of the UK in consenting to the use of British bases for the purposes of the raid is also raised and does cause problems of justification in the context of self-defence. See also UKMIL, 57 BYIL, 1986, pp.639-42 and 80 *AJIL*, 1986, pp.632-36.

THE LAWS RELATING TO ARMED CONFLICTS –
INTERNATIONAL HUMANITARIAN LAW [203]

In addition to prescribing laws governing resort to force, international law also seeks to regulate the conduct of hostilities. Relevant principles cover, for example, prisoners of war, civilians, sick and wounded personnel, prohibited methods of warfare and human rights in such situations.

Development

The law in this area developed from the middle of the last century. In 1864, as a result of the pioneering work of Henry Dunant, who had been appalled by the brutality of the battle of Solferino five years earlier, the Geneva Convention for the Amelioration of the Condition of the Wounded in Armies in the Field was adopted. This brief instrument was revised in 1906. In 1868 the Declaration of St Petersburg prohibited the use of small explosive or incendiary projectiles.

The laws of war were codified at the Hague Conferences of 1899 and 1907.[204] A series of conventions were adopted at these conferences concerning land and naval warfare, which still form the basis of the existing rules. It was emphasised that belligerents remained subject to the law of nations and forbade the use of force against undefended villages and towns. It defined those entitled to belligerent status and dealt with the measures to be taken as regards occupied territory. There were also provisions concerning the rights and duties of neutral states and persons in case of war, and an emphatic prohibition on the employment of "arms, projectiles or material calculated to cause unnecessary suffering". However, there were inadequate means to implement and enforce such rules

---

[203] See e.g. Best, *Humanity in Warfare*, 1980; *Studies and Essays on International Humanitarian Law and Red Cross Principles* (ed. Swinarski), 1984; *The New Humanitarian Law of Armed Conflict* (ed. Cassese), 1979; Draper, "The Geneva Convention of 1949", 114 *HR*, p.59 and "Implementation and Enforcement of the Geneva Conventions and of the two Additional Protocols", 164 *HR*, p.1; Karlshoven, *The Law of Warfare*, 1973; Bothe, Partsch and Solf, *New Rules for Victims of Armed Conflict*, 1982 and Pictet, *Humanitarian Law and the Protection of War Victims*, 1982. See also *Documents on the Laws of War* (ed. Roberts and Guelff), 2nd ed., 1989 and De Lupis, *The Law of War*, 1987.

[204] See e.g. Best, *op. cit.*, Chapter III.

with the result that much appeared to depend on reciprocal behaviour, public opinion and the exigencies of morale.[205]

Apart from the 1954 Hague Convention for the Protection of Cultural Property in Time of Armed Conflict, the rules of war remained as they had been formulated and codified in 1907.

A number of conventions in the inter-war period dealt with rules concerning the wounded and sick in armies in the field and prisoners of war.[206] Such agreements were replaced by the Four Geneva "Red Cross" Conventions of 1949 which dealt respectively with the amelioration of the condition of the wounded and sick in armed forces in the field, the amelioration of the condition of wounded, sick and ship-wrecked members of the armed forces at sea, the treatment of prisoners of war and the protection of civilian persons in time of war.

The Fourth Convention was an innovation and a significant attempt to protect civilians who, as a result of armed hostilities or occupation, were in the power of a state of which they were not nationals.

The essence of these Geneva Conventions is the principle that persons not actively engaged in warfare should be treated humanely. A number of practices ranging from the taking of hostages to torture, illegal executions and reprisals against persons protected by the Conventions are prohibited, while a series of provisions relate to more detailed points, such as the standard of care of prisoners of war and the prohibition of deportations and indiscriminate destruction of property in occupied territory.

In 1977, two Additional Protocols to the 1949 Conventions were adopted.[207] These built upon and developed the earlier Conventions. The "Law of the Hague", dealing primarily with interstate rules governing the use of force, and the "Law of Geneva" concerning

---

[205] Note, however, the Martens' Clause in the Preamble to the Hague Convention concerning the Laws and Customs of War on Land, which provided that "in cases not included in the Regulations . . . the inhabitants and the belligerents remain under the protection and the rule of the principles of the law of nations, as they result from the usages established among civilised peoples from the laws of humanity and the dictates of the public conscience".

[206] See e.g. the 1929 Conventions, one revising the 1864 and 1906 instruments on wounded and sick soldiers, the other on the treatment of prisoners of war.

[207] See e.g. *Studies and Essays, op. cit.*, Part B, and Draper, "Implementation and Enforcement", *op. cit.* See also Wortley, "Observations on the Revision of the 1949 Geneva 'Red Cross' Conventions", 54 *BYIL*, 1983, p.143.

the protection of persons from the effects of armed conflicts are to some extent merged, while certain other issues such as wars of liberation, mercenaries and apartheid, were also dealt with.

The Scope of Protection

The rules seek to extend protection to a wide range of persons. The basic distinction drawn has been between combatants and those who are not involved in actual hostilities. The Geneva Conventions of 1949 for the protection of war victims, as noted, cover the wounded and sick in land warfare; the wounded, sick and shipwrecked in warfare at sea; prisoners of war; and civilians. The first two of these Conventions are fairly self-explanatory and deal with the respect and protection due to medical personnel and establishments, the wounded and sick and the dead. The second instrument, on warfare at sea, also deals with hospital ships.[208] The provisions in these Conventions were supplemented by Protocol I, 1977, Parts I and II.

The Third Geneva Convention of 1949 is concerned with prisoners of war, and consists of a comprehensive code centred upon the requirement of humane treatment in all circumstances.[209] The definition of prisoners of war in article 4, however, is of particular importance since it has been regarded as the elaboration of combatant status. It covers members of the armed forces of a party to the conflict (as well as members of militias and other volunteer corps forming part of such armed force) and members of other militias and volunteer corps, including those of organised resistance movements, belonging to a party to the conflict providing the following conditions are fulfilled: (a) being commanded by a person responsible for his subordinates; (b) having a fixed distinctive sign recognisable at a distance; (c) carrying arms openly; (d) conducting operations in accordance with the laws and customs of war. This article reflected the experience of the Second World War, although the extent to which resistance personnel were covered was constrained by the need to comply with the four conditions.

---

[208] See with regard to the use of hospital ships in the Falklands conflict, Levie, "The Falklands Crisis and the Laws of the War" in *The Falklands War* (eds. Coll and Arend), 1985, pp.64, 67-68.

[209] It applies to all cases of declared war or any other armed conflict and to all cases of partial or total occupation of the territory of a party to the Convention (article 2).

Since 1949, the use of guerrillas spread to the Third World and the decolonisation experience. Accordingly, pressures grew to expand the definition of combatants entitled to prisoner of war status to such persons, who as practice demonstrated rarely complied with the four conditions. States facing guerrilla action, whether the colonial powers or others such as Israel, naturally objected. Articles 43 and 44 of Protocol I, 1977, provide that combatants are members of the armed forces of a party to an international armed conflict.[210] Such armed forces consist of all organised armed units under an effective command structure which enforces compliance with the rules of international law applicable in armed conflict. Article 44(3) further notes that combatants are obliged to distinguish themselves from the civilian population while they are engaged in an attack or in a military operation preparatory to an attack. When an armed combatant cannot so distinguish himself, the status of combatant may be retained provided that arms are carried openly during each military engagement and during such time as the combatant is visible to the adversary while engaged in a military deployment preceding the launching of an attack. This formulation is clearly controversial and was the subject of many declarations in the vote at the conference producing the draft.[211]

The framework of obligations covering prisoners of war is founded upon the following provisions. Article 13 provides that prisoners of war must at all times be humanely treated and must at all times be protected, particularly against acts of violence or intimidation and against "insults and public curiosity". This means that displaying prisoners of war on television confessing to "crimes" or criticising their own government must be regarded as a breach of the Convention.[212] While prisoners of war are bound to divulge their name, date of birth, rank and serial number, article 17 provides that

---

[210] *Infra*, p.737.

[211] See e.g. Verthy, *Guérrilla et droit Humanitaire*, 2nd ed., 1983 and Nahlik, "L'Extension du Statut de Combattant à la Lumière de Protocol I de Genève de 1977", 164 *HR*, p.171. Note that by article 45 any person taking part in hostilities and falling into the hands of an adverse party shall be presumed to be a prisoner of war and thus protected by the Third Geneva Convention of 1949. Where there are any doubts, such status shall be retained until conclusively determined by a competent tribunal. Where a person is a mercenary, there is no right to combatant or prisoner of war status under article 47. See also the International Convention against the Recruitment, Use, Financing and Training of Mercenaries 1989.

[212] See e.g. the treatment of allied prisoners of war by Iraq, *The Economist*, 26 January 1991, p.24.

"no physical or mental torture, nor any other form of coercion, may be inflicted . . . to secure from them information of any kind whatever. Prisoners of war who refuse to answer may not be threatened, insulted, or exposed to unpleasant or disadvantageous treatment of any kind." Once captured, prisoners of war are to be evacuated as soon as possible to camps situated in an area far enough from the combat zone for them to be out of danger,[213] while article 23 stipulates that "no prisoner of war may at any time be sent to, or detained in areas where he may be exposed to the fire of the combat zone, nor may his presence be used to render certain points or areas immune from military operations".[214]

The fourth of the Four Geneva Conventions of 1949 is concerned with the protection of civilians in time of war. This marked an extension to the pre-1949 rules, although limited under article 4 to those persons, "who, at a given moment and in any manner whatsoever, find themselves, in case of a conflict or occupation, in the hands of a party to the conflict or occupying power of which they are not nationals". Under article 50(1) of Protocol I, 1977, a civilian is defined as any person not a combatant,[215] and in cases of doubt a person is to be considered a civilian. The Fourth Convention provides a highly developed set of rules for the protection of such civilians, including the right to respect for person, honour, convictions and religious practices and the prohibition of torture and other cruel, inhuman or degrading treatment, hostage-taking and reprisals.[216] There are also various judicial guarantees as to due process.[217] The protection of civilians in occupied territories is covered in section III of the Fourth Geneva Convention, but what precisely occupied territory is may be open to dispute.[218] The situation with regard to the West Bank of Jordan,[219] for example, demonstrates the problems that may arise. By article 2, this

---

[213] Article 19.

[214] Thus the reported Iraqi practice during the 1991 Gulf War of sending allied prisoners of war to strategic sites in order to create a "human shield" to deter allied attacks was clearly a violation of the Convention, see e.g. *The Economist*, 26 January 1991, p.24.

[215] As defined in article 4 of the Third Geneva Convention, 1949 and article 43, Protocol I, 1977, *supra*, p.731.

[216] See articles 27-34.

[217] See articles 71-76. See also article 75 of Protocol I, 1977.

[218] Iraqi-occupied Kuwait is, of course, a prime example of the situation covered by this Convention.

[219] The area is sometimes known as Judaea and Samaria.

Convention is to apply to all cases of partial or total occupation "of the territory of a high contracting party". Israel has argued that since the West Bank has never been recognised internationally as Jordanian territory,[220] it cannot therefore be regarded as its territory to which the Convention would apply. In other words, to recognise that the Convention applies would be tantamount to a recognition of Jordanian sovereignty over the disputed land.[221] Amongst the provisions in Section III is a prohibition on "individual or mass forcible transfers" under article 49. Israel's policy of building settlements on the West Bank has been criticised on this basis.[222]

As far as the civilian population is concerned during hostilities,[223] the basic rule formulated in article 48 of Protocol I is that the parties to the conflict must at all times distinguish between such population and combatants and between civilian and military objectives and must direct their operations only against military objectives. Article 51 provides that the civilian population as such, as well as individual civilians, "shall not be the object of attack. Acts or threats of violence the primary purpose of which is to spread terror among the civilian population are prohibited." Additionally, indiscriminate attacks[224] are prohibited.[225] In addition, article 52 provides that civilian objects are not to be the object of attack or

[220] It was annexed by the Kingdom of Transjordan, as it then was, in 1949 at the conclusion of the Israeli War of Independence, but this annexation was recognised only by the UK and Pakistan. See e.g. Gerson, *Israel, the West Bank and International Law*, 1978.

[221] Note that Israel does observe the Convention *de facto*, see e.g. Shamgar, "The Observation of International Law in the Administered Territories", *Israel Yearbook on Human Rights*, 1977, p.262 and Meron, "West Bank and Gaza", *ibid.*, 1979, p.108. See also Fleiner-Gerster and Meyer, "New Developments in Humanitarian Law", 34 *ICLQ*, 1985, p.267 and Cohen, *Human Rights in the Israeli-Occupied Territories*, 1985.

[222] See e.g. UKMIL, 54 *BYIL*, 1983, pp.538-39.

[223] Apart from the inhabitants of occupied territories protected under the Fourth Geneva Convention 1949.

[224] These are defined in article 51(4) as: (a) those which are not directed at a specific military objective; (b) those which employ a method or means of combat which cannot be at a specific military objective; or (c) those which employ a method or means of combat the effects of which cannot be limited as required by Protocol I; and consequently in each such case are of a nature to strike military objectives and civilians or civilian objects without distinction.

[225] See 21(5) UN Chronicle, 1984, p.3 with regard to an appeal by the UN Secretary-General to Iran and Iraq to refrain from attacks on civilian targets. See also Security Council resolution 540 (1983). The above provisions apply to the use by Iraq in the 1991 Gulf War of missiles deliberately fired at civilian targets. The firing of missiles at Israeli cities in early 1991 constituted, of course, an act of aggression against a state not a party to that conflict, see e.g. *The Economist*, 26 January 1991, p.21.

of reprisals. Civilian objects are all objects which are not military objectives as defined in article 52(2).[226]

Cultural objects and places of worship are also protected,[227] as are objects deemed indispensable to the survival of the civilian population such as foodstuffs, agricultural areas for the production of foodstuffs, crops, livestock, drinking water installations and supplies, and irrigation works so long as they are not used as sustenance solely for the armed forces or in direct support of military action.[228] Attacks are also prohibited against works or installations containing dangerous forces, namely dams, dykes and nuclear generating stations.[229]

Methods of Warfare [230]

International law, in addition to seeking to protect victims of armed conflicts, also tries to constrain the conduct of military operations in a humanitarian fashion. In analysing the rules contained in the "Law of the Hague", it is important to bear in mind the delicate balance to be maintained between military necessity and humanitarian considerations. A principle of long standing, if not always honoured in practice, is the requirement to protect civilians against the effects of hostilities. The preamble of the St Petersburg Declaration of 1868, banning explosives or inflammatory projectiles below 400 grammes in weight, emphasises that the "only legitimate object which states should endeavour to accomplish during war is to weaken the military forces of the enemy", while article 48 of Protocol I provides that a distinction must at all times be drawn between civilians and combatants. The right of the parties to an armed conflict to choose methods of warfare is not unlimited. Article 22 of the Regulations annexed to the Hague Convention IV of 1907 points out that the "right of belligerents to adopt means of

---

[226] This provides that military objectives are limited to those objects which in their nature, location, purpose or use make an effective contribution to military action and whose total or partial destruction, capture or neutralisation in the circumstances ruling at the time offers a definite military advantage.

[227] See article 53 and the Hague Convention for the Protection of Cultural Property in the Event of Armed Conflict 1954.

[228] Article 54.

[229] Article 56.

[230] See e.g. Shaw, "The United Nations Convention on Prohibitions or Restrictions on the Use of Certain Conventional Weapons, 1981", 9 *Review of International Studies*, 1983, p.109.

injuring the enemy is not unlimited",[231] while article 23(e)[232] stipulates that it is especially prohibited to "employ arms, projectiles or material calculated to cause unnecessary suffering".[233] Quite how one may define such weapons is rather controversial and can only be determined in the light of actual state practice.[234] The balance between military necessity and humanitarian considerations is relevant here. A disproportionate amount of suffering in relation to a military advantage would violate this principle. Whether nuclear weapons would be covered by this is an open and highly controversial question, although the weight of state practice would seem to argue against it.[235]

In addition to the "unnecessary suffering" criterion, a number of specific bans have been imposed. Examples would include small projectiles under the St Petersburg formula of 1868, dum-dum bullets under the Hague Declaration of 1899 and asphyxiating and deleterious gases under the Hague Declaration of 1899 and the 1925 Geneva Protocol.[236] Under the 1981 Conventional Weapons Treaty, Protocol I, it is prohibited to use weapons that cannot be detected by X-rays while Protocol II prohibits the use of mines and booby-traps against civilians and Protocol III the use of incendiary devices against civilians or against military objectives located within a concentration of civilians where the attack is by air-delivered incendiary weapons.

Article 55 of Protocol I provides that care is to be taken in warfare to protect the natural environment against widespread, long-term and severe damage. This protection includes a prohibition of the use of methods or means of warfare which are intended or may be expected to cause such damage to the natural environment and

---

[231] This is repeated in virtually identical terms in article 35, Protocol I.

[232] It is generally recognised that the Regulations now form part of customary law, see e.g. 41 *AJIL,* 1947, pp.248-49 and Roberts and Guelff, *op. cit.,* p.54.

[233] See article 35(2) of Protocol I and the Preamble to the 1981 Convention on Conventional Weapons, see Shaw, *op. cit.* footnote 230, p.113.

[234] See e.g. the United States Department of the Army, *Field Manual, The Law of Land Warfare,* FM 27-10, 1956, p.18 and regarding the UK, *The Law of War on Land,* Part III of the Manual of Military Law, 1958, p.41.

[235] See Shaw, "Nuclear Weapons and International Law" in *Nuclear Weapons and International Law* (ed. Pogany), 1987, p.1.

[236] See also e.g. the 1972 Convention on the Prohibition of the Development, Production and Stockpiling of Bacteriological Weapons. See 21(3) *UN Chronicle,* 1984, p.3 with regard to the use of chemical weapons in the Iran-Iraq war.

thereby to prejudice the health or survival of the population.[237] The Convention on the Prohibition of Military or Any Other Hostile Use of Environmental Modification Techniques 1977 prohibits such activities having widespread, long-lasting or severe effects as the means of destruction, damage or injury to any other state party.

Non-International Armed Conflict

Although the 1949 Geneva Conventions were primarily aimed at international armed conflicts, common article 3 did provide in cases of non-international armed conflicts occurring in the territory of one of the parties a series of minimum guarantees for protecting those not taking an active part in hostilities, including the sick and wounded. Precisely where this article applied was difficult to define in all cases. Non-international armed conflicts could, it may be argued, range from full-scale civil wars to relatively minor disturbances. This poses problems for the state in question which may not appreciate the political implications of the application of the Geneva Conventions, and the lack of the reciprocity element due to the absence of another state adds to the problems of enforcement. Common article 3 was developed by Protocol II, 1977,[238] which applies by virtue of article 1 to all non-international armed conflicts which take place in the territory of a state party between its armed forces and dissident armed forces. The latter have to be under responsible command and exercise such control over a part of its territory as to enable them to carry out sustained and concerted military operations and actually implement Protocol II. It does not apply to situations of internal disturbances and tensions, such as riots, isolated and sporadic acts of violence and other acts of a similar nature, not being armed conflicts. The Protocol lists a series of fundamental guarantees and other provisions calling for the protection of non-combatants. It is in reality a fairly modest

---

[237] See, for example, the deliberate spillage of vast quantities of oil into the Persian Gulf by Iraq during the 1991 Gulf War; see *The Economist*, 2 February 1991, p.20.

[238] Note, of course, that by article 1(4) of Protocol I, 1977, international armed conflicts are now deemed to include wars against colonial domination, alien occupation and racist regimes. See Forsyth, "Legal Management of International War", 72 *AJIL*, 1978, p.272. Note also the UK view that "a high level of intensity of military operations" is required regarding Protocol I so that the Northern Ireland situation, for example, would not be covered, see 941 HC Deb., col. 237.

instrument which emphasises in practice the importance of the distinction between international and non-international armed conflicts. It remains to be seen whether parties will be willing to operate it.

It is also to be noted that there exists an area of civil conflict which is not covered by humanitarian law since it falls below the necessary threshold of common articles 3 and Protocol II. To bridge this gap, the International Committee of the Red Cross has been considering the elaboration of a new declaration on internal strife.[239] This process is also a further illustration of the way that this branch of international law is moving closer to human rights law.

Enforcement of Humanitarian Law

Parties to the 1949 Geneva Conventions and to Protocol I, 1977, undertake to respect and to ensure respect for the instrument in question,[240] and to disseminate knowledge of the principles contained therein.[241] A variety of enforcement methods also exist, although the use of reprisals has been prohibited.[242] One of the means of implementation is the concept of the Protecting Power, appointed to look after the interests of nationals of one party to a conflict under the control of the other, whether as prisoners of war or occupied civilians.[243] Sweden and Switzerland performed this role during the Second World War. Such a Power must ensure that compliance with the relevant provisions has been effected and that the system acts as a form of guarantee for the protected person as well as a channel of communication for him with the state of which he is a national.

The drawback of this system is its dependence upon the consent of the parties involved. Not only must the Protecting Power be prepared to act in that capacity, but both the state of which the protected person is a national and the state holding such persons

---

[239] See Hay, "The ICRC and International Humanitarian Issues", *International Review of the Red Cross*, Jan-Feb 1984, p.3. See also Meron, "Towards a Humanitarian Declaration on Internal Strife", 78 *AJIL*, 1984, p.859 and *Human Rights in Internal Strife: Their International Protection*, 1987.

[240] Article 1 in all instruments.

[241] See e.g. articles 127 and 144 of the Third and Fourth Geneva Conventions, article 83 of Protocol I and article 19 of Protocol II.

[242] See e.g. articles 20 and 51(6) of Protocol I.

[243] See e.g. Draper, "Implementation and Enforcement", *op. cit.*, p.13 *et seq.*

must give their consent for the system to operate.[244] Since the role is so central to the enforcement and working of humanitarian law, it is a disadvantage for it to be subject to state sovereignty and consent. It only requires the holding state to refuse its co-operation for this structure of implementation to be greatly weakened leaving only reliance upon voluntary operations. This has occurred on a number of occasions, for example the Chinese refusal to consent to the appointment of a Protecting Power with regard to its conflict with India in 1962, and the Indian refusal, of 1971 and subsequently, with regard to Pakistani prisoners of war in its charge.[245]

Protocol I also provides for an International Fact-Finding Commission for competence to inquire into grave breaches[246] of the Geneva Conventions and that Protocol or other serious violations, and to facilitate through its good offices the "restoration of an attitude of respect" for these instruments.[247] The parties to a conflict may themselves, of course, establish an *ad hoc* inquiry into alleged violations of humanitarian law.[248]

It is, of course, also the case that breaches of international law in this field may constitute war crimes for which universal jurisdiction is provided.[249] It is to be noted in particular that article 6 of the Charter of the Nuremberg Tribunal 1945 includes as examples of war crimes for which there is to be individual responsibility the murder, ill-treatment or deportation to slave labour of the civilian population of an occupied territory; the ill-treatment of prisoners of war; the killing of hostages and the wanton destruction of cities, towns and villages.

A great deal of valuable work in the sphere of humanitarian law has been accomplished by the International Red Cross.[250] This indispensable organisation consists of the International Committee

---

[244] See articles 8, 8, 8 and 9 of the Four Geneva Conventions 1949, respectively.

[245] Note that the system did operate in the Falklands conflict, with Switzerland acting as the Protecting Power of the UK and Brazil as the Protecting Power of Argentina, see e.g. Levie, *op. cit.*, pp.68-69.

[246] See articles 50, 51, 130 and 147 of the four 1949 Conventions respectively and article 85 of Protocol I, 1977.

[247] Article 90, Protocol I, 1977.

[248] Articles 52, 53, 132 and 149 of the four 1949 Conventions respectively.

[249] See e.g. Draper, *Implementation and Enforcement, op. cit.*, p.35 *et seq.* See also *supra*, Chapter 11, p.412.

[250] See e.g. Willemin and Heacock, *The International Committee of the Red Cross*, 1985 and Forsythe, "The Red Cross as Transnational Movement", 30 *International Organisation*, 1967, p.607.

of the Red Cross (ICRC), over one hundred national Red Cross (or Red Crescent) societies with a League co-ordinating their activities, and conferences of all these elements every four years.

The ICRC is the most active body and has a wide-ranging series of functions to perform, including working for the application of the Geneva Conventions and acting in natural and man-made disasters. It has operated in a large number of states, visiting prisoners of war[251] and otherwise functioning to ensure the implementation of humanitarian law. The largest operation it has undertaken since 1948 related to the Nigerian Civil war, and in that conflict nearly twenty of its personnel were killed on duty. Due to circumstances, the ICRC must act with great tact and discretion and in many cases states refuse their co-operation. It performed a valuable function in the exchange of prisoners after the 1967 and 1973 Middle East Wars, although for several years Israel did not accept the ICRC role regarding the Arab territories it occupied.[252]

Conclusion

The Red Cross recently formulated the following principles as a guide to the relevant legal rules:

1. Persons *hors de combat* and those who do not take a direct part in hostilities are entitled to respect for their lives and physical and moral integrity. They shall in all circumstances be protected and treated humanely without any adverse distinction.

2. It is forbidden to kill or injure an enemy who surrenders or who is *hors de combat*.

3. The wounded and sick shall be collected and cared for by the party to the conflict which has them in its power. Protection also covers medical personnel, establishments, transports and *matériel.* The emblem of the red cross (red crescent, red lion and sun) is the sign of such protection and must be respected.

4. Captured combatants and civilians under the authority of an adverse party are entitled to respect for their lives, dignity, personal rights and convictions. They shall be protected against all acts of violence and

---

[251] See e.g. articles 126 and 142 of the Third and Fourth Geneva Conventions respectively.

[252] See generally *Annual Report of the ICRC,* 1982. See also "Action by the ICRC in the Event of Breaches of International Humanitarian Law", *International Review of the Red Cross,* March-April 1981, p.1.

reprisals. They shall have the right to correspond with their families and to receive relief.

5. Everyone shall be entitled to benefit from fundamental judicial guarantees. No one shall be held responsible for an act he has not committed. No one shall be subjected to physical or mental torture, corporal punishment or cruel or degrading treatment.

6. Parties to a conflict and members of their armed forces do not have an unlimited choice of methods and means of warfare. It is prohibited to employ weapons or methods of warfare of a nature to cause unnecessary losses or excessive suffering.

7. Parties to a conflict shall at all times distinguish between the civilian population and combatants in order to spare civilian population and property. Neither the civilian populations as such nor civilian persons shall be the object for attack. Attacks shall be directed solely against military objectives.[253]

---

[253] See *International Review of the Red Cross*, Sept.-Oct. 1978, p.247.

CHAPTER NINETEEN

International Institutions[1]

HISTORICAL DEVELOPMENT

The evolution of the modern nation-state and the consequent development of an international order founded upon a growing number of independent and sovereign territorial units inevitably gave rise to questions of international co-operation. Diplomatic representation became more widespread as the system expanded and political and economic relationships multiplied. It soon became apparent, however, that diplomatic contacts in themselves were unable to cope completely with the complexities of the international system and the concept of the international conference evolved as a form of extended diplomacy. Such gatherings dealt with problems that concerned more than two or three states and in many cases resulted in an international treaty or formal peace. The first major instance of this occurred with the Peace of Westphalia in 1648, which ended the thirty year old religious conflict of central Europe and formally established the modern secular nation-state arrangement of European politics.[2]

The French wars of Louis XIV were similarly brought to an end by an international agreement of interested powers, and a century later the Napoleonic wars terminated with the Congress of Vienna in 1815. This latter conference can be taken as a significant turning-point, for it marked the first systematic attempt to regulate international affairs by means of regular international conferences.[3]

---

[1] See generally e.g. Bowett, *The Law of International Institutions*, 4th ed., 1982; Reuter, *International Institutions*, 1958; *Encyclopedia of Public International Law*, vols. 5 and 6, 1983; Claude, *Swords Into Ploughshares*, 3rd ed., 1964; Schermers, *International Institutional Law*, 2 vols., 2nd ed., 1981; Schwarzenberger, *International Law*, vol.3, 1976 and E. Lauterpacht, "The Development of the Law of International Organisations by the Decisions of International Tribunals", 152 *HR*, p.377. See also Kirgis, *International Organisations in their Legal Settings*, 1977; El Erian, "The Legal Organisation of International Society", in *Manual of Public International Law* (ed. Sørensen), 1968, p.55; Whiteman, *Digest of International Law*, vol.13, 1968; *A Handbook of International Organisations* (ed. Dupuy), 1988; Seidl-Hohenveldern, *Corporations In and Under International Law*, 1987 and Morgenstern, *Legal Problems of International Organisations*, 1986.

[2] See e.g. Gross, "The Peace of Westphalia, 1648-1948", 42 *AJIL*, 1948, p.20.

[3] See e.g. El Erian, *op. cit.*, p.58.

The Congress system lasted, in various guises, for practically a century and institutionalised not only the balance of power approach to politics, but also a semi-formal international order.[4]

Until the outbreak of the First World War, world affairs were to a large extent influenced by the periodic conferences that were held in Europe. The Paris conference of 1856 and the Berlin gathering of 1871 dealt with the problems of the Balkans, while the 1884-5 Berlin conferences imposed some order upon the scramble for Africa that had begun to develop.

These, and other such conferences, constituted an important prelude to the establishment of international institutions, but became themselves ever more inadequate to fulfil the job they had been intended to do. A conference could only be called into being upon the initiative of one or more of the states involved, usually following some international crisis, and this *ad hoc* procedure imposed severe delays upon the resolution of the issue. It meant that only states specifically invited could attend and these states made decisions upon the basis of unanimous agreement, a factor which severely restricted the utility of the system.[5]

The nineteenth century also witnessed a considerable growth in international non-governmental associations, such as the International Committee of the Red Cross (founded in 1863) and the International Law Association (founded in 1873). These private international unions, as they have been called,[6] demonstrated a wide-ranging community of interest on specific topics, and an awareness that co-operation had to be international to be effective. Such unions created the machinery for regular meetings and many established permanent secretariats. The work done by these organisations was, and remains, of considerable value in influencing governmental activities and stimulating world action.

This can be seen particularly with reference to the International Committee of the Red Cross and the efforts made by it to bring into being the Geneva Conventions and Additional Protocols[7] dealing with, for example, the treatment of prisoners and the regulation of military occupations. In fact, a number of these private

---

[4] See e.g. Reuter, *op. cit.*, pp.55-56. See also Bowett, *op. cit.*, pp.1-2.
[5] *Ibid.*, p.3.
[6] *Ibid.*, pp.4-65.
[7] *Supra*, Chapter 18, p.729.

international unions rather belie their name by including within their membership state representatives as well as national bodies and private individuals.[8]

To some extent impelled by the example of the private international unions, there developed during the course of the last century a series of public international unions. These were functional associations linking together governmental departments or administrations for specific purposes, and were set up by multilateral treaties. They fulfilled an increasingly felt need for more sophisticated methods of international co-operation and regulation in an interdependent world. The first instances of such intergovernmental associations were provided by the international commissions established for the more efficient functioning of such vital arteries of communication as the Rhine and Danube rivers, and later for other rivers of central and western Europe.[9]

The powers given to the particular commissions varied from case to case, but most of them performed important administrative and legislative functions. In 1865 the International Telegraphic Union was set up with a permanent bureau or secretariat and nine years later the Universal Postal Union was created. This combined a permanent bureau with periodic conferences, with decisions being taken by majority vote. This marked a step forward, since one of the weaknesses of the political order of *ad hoc* conferences had been the necessity for unanimity.

The latter half of the nineteenth century was especially marked by the proliferation of such public international unions, covering transportation, communications, health and economic co-operation. These unions restricted themselves to dealing with specific areas and were not comprehensive, but they introduced new ideas which paved the way for the universal organisations of the twentieth century. Such concepts as permanent secretariats, periodic conferences, majority voting, weighted voting and proportionate financial contributions, were important in easing administrative co-operation, and they laid the basis for contemporary international institutions.

The innovation of the present century has, of course, been the creation of the global, comprehensive organisations of the League

[8] For example, the International Council of Scientific Unions and the International Statistical Institute, Bowett, *op. cit.*, p.5.

[9] *Ibid.*, pp.6-9.

of Nations and the United Nations. These were, in many ways, the logical culmination of the pioneering work of the private and public international unions, the large numbers of which required some form of central co-ordination. This function both the League and the UN attempted to provide.

APPROACHES TO INTERNATIONAL INSTITUTIONS

There are a number of different ways in which one can approach the phenomenon of international organisation within the world order.

The rationalist approach[10] emphasises the notion of a world order of states that is moving towards the more sophisticated types of order found within states. It is progressive in that it believes in the transformation of a society of states into a true world community based upon the application of universally valid moral and legal principles. In other words, the development of the United Nations into a real world authority is seen not only as beneficial but also as, in the long run, inevitable. This is to be accomplished by the gradual increase in the influence and responsibility of the organisation in all fields of international peace and security. Thus international organisations have a profound substantive as well as procedural purpose, and are intended to function above and beyond mere administrative convenience. To put it another way, the rationalists emphasise the role of such institutions as active performers upon the world stage rather than as mechanisms to greater efficiency.

Another general line of approach is the revolutionary one, which regards international institutions in terms of specific policy aims.[11] Here, the primary aim is not the evolution of a world community of states based upon global associations as perceived by the rationalists, but rather the utilisation of such institutions as a means of attaining the final objective, whether it be the victory of the proletariat or the re-arrangement of existing states into, for example, continental units.

---

[10] See e.g. Goodwin, "World Institutions and World Order", in *The New International Actors* (eds. Cosgrove and Twitchett), 1970, pp.55-57. See also *The Concept of International Organisation* (ed. Abi-Saab), 1981 and Feld and Jordan, *International Organisations,* 1983.

[11] Goodwin, *op. cit.,* pp.57-61.

The third approach which may be noted is exemplified by the doctrine of realism.[12] This centres its attention on the struggle for power and supremacy and eschews any concern for idealistic views. The world stage is seen as a constant and almost chaotic inter-weaving of contentious state powers, and international institutions are examined within the context of the search for dominance. Both the League and the UN were created to reinforce the *status quo* established after the World Wars, it is stressed, although the latter institution is now seen as reflecting the new balance of power achieved with the growth of influence of the states of the Third World.

Since what can be described as a world order is merely a reflection of the operation of the principle of the balance of power, realists see the role of world organisations as reinforcing that balance and enabling it to be safely and gradually altered in the light of changing patterns of power; although, to be accurate, their overall attitude to such organisations is usually characterised by cynicism, as the inherent weaknesses in these organisations have become apparent.

A more hopeful way of looking at the international institutions is to concentrate upon those areas where the interdependence of states has impelled them to create viable organs for co-operation. By this means, by identifying such subjects for international agreement, it is hoped to be able to encourage growing circles of co-operation which may eventually impinge upon the basic political areas of world peace. This functional approach[13] appears as a cross between the nationalist and realist trends and is one much examined in recent years.

This approach also emphasises the pattern of institutional behaviour and the operations of the relevant bureaucracies, including the way in which the tasks set for the organisation are identified and completed. Decision-making analysis is another useful tool in this area.

It is also possible to examine international organisations in a variety of other ways, ranging from historical and comparative exposition to analysis of the legal rules underlying the establishment and operations of the particular institution.

---

[12] *Ibid.*, pp.61-64.

[13] See e.g. Mitrany, *A Working Peace System*, 1966 and "The Functional Approach to World Organisation" in *The New International Actors, op. cit.*, p.65.

Because of the great diversity of international and regional organisations, ranging from the United Nations to the North Atlantic Treaty Organisation and the International Labour Organisation, great difficulty has been experienced in classifying the relevant material. In this chapter, the simplest method of division into institutions of a universal character, regional institutions and the legal aspects of international institutions will be adopted. Within the relevant categories, the particular functions of different organisations, as well as their varying constitutional framework, will be noted. A brief survey only is proposed.

INSTITUTIONS OF A UNIVERSAL CHARACTER

The League of Nations [14]

The League of Nations, created in 1919, sought to promote international co-operation, peace and security upon the basis of disarmament, the peaceful resolution of disputes, a guarantee of the sovereignty and independence of member-states and sanctions.[15] In essence, it was left to each member to conclude whether a breach of the Covenant of the League had taken place or not, and in the last resort whether or not to apply sanctions. This system worked with regard to certain relatively minor crises in the Balkans and South America, but failed where European powers or Japan were directly involved. The German, Italian and Japanese aggressions in the 1930s, and the Russian invasion of Finland in the Winter War, evoked little meaningful response from the League.

The League consisted of three principal organs. The Council, a semi-executive body, consisted of the Principal Allied and Associated Powers plus a number of non-permanent members, and reached its decisions unanimously. Such decisions were not binding upon member-states. The Assembly consisted of representatives of all members and met annually, while the Secretariat functioned as an international civil service.

---

[14] See e.g. Bowett, *op. cit.*, Chapter 2; Scott, *The Rise and Fall of the League of Nations*, 1973; El Erian, *op. cit.*, p.60 *et seq.* and Walters, *A History of the League of Nations*, 2 vols., 1952.

[15] See articles 8 and 10-17 of the Covenant of the League of Nations. See also *supra*, Chapter 17, p.639.

Although an international organisation, it never became universal. It stayed to all intents and purposes a European-centred institution. It was formally dissolved in April 1946.

The United Nations [16]

The United Nations arose as an attempt to remedy the defects of the League system. It grew out of a series of war-time declarations and conferences, culminating in the San Francisco conferences of 1945, which finally adopted the UN Charter.[17]

The purposes of the UN are set out in article 1 of the Charter as follows:

1. To maintain international peace and security, and to that end, to take effective collective measures for the prevention and removal of threats to the peace, and for the suppression of acts of aggression or other breaches of the peace, and to bring about by peaceful means, and in conformity with the principles of justice and international law, adjustment or settlement of international disputes or situations which might lead to a breach of the peace;

2. To develop friendly relations among nations based on respect for the principle of equal rights and self-determination of peoples, and to take other appropriate measures to strengthen universal peace;

3. To achieve international co-operation in solving international problems of an economic, social, cultural or humanitarian character, and in promoting and encouraging respect for human rights and for fundamental freedoms for all without distinction as to race, sex, language, or religion; and

4. To be a centre for harmonizing the actions of nations in the attainment of these common ends.

[16] See e.g. Bowett, *op. cit.*, Chapter 3; Nicholas, *The United Nations as a Political Institution*, 5th ed., 1975; *The Strategy of World Order* (eds. Falk and Mendlovitz), 1966; Higgins, *The Development of International Law Through the Political Organs of the United Nations*, 1963; Goodrich, *The United Nations in a Changing World*, 1974; Hill, *The United Nations System*, 1978; Luard, *The United Nations*, 1979 and Sohn, *Cases on United Nations Law*, 2nd ed., 1967. See also the *Bertrand Report*, 1985, A/40/988. This critical report details a variety of structural problems at the UN, including the proliferation of competing organs and the lack of sufficient supervision of programmes and publications.

[17] See *UNCIO*, 15 vols., 1945. See also Goodrich, Hambro and Simons, *Charter of the United Nations*, 3rd ed., 1969.

While the purposes are clearly wide-ranging, they do provide a useful guide to the comprehensiveness of its concerns. The question of priorities as between the various issues noted is constantly subject to controversy and change, but this only reflects the continuing pressures and altering political balances within the organisation. In particular, the emphasis upon decolonisation, self-determination and apartheid mirrored the growth in UN membership and the dismantling of the colonial empires, while increasing concern with economic and developmental issues is now very apparent and clearly reflects the adverse economic conditions in various parts of the world.

The Charter of the United Nations is not only the multilateral treaty which created the organisation and outlined the rights and obligations of those states signing it, it is also the constitution of the UN, laying down its functions and prescribing its limitations. Foremost amongst these is the recognition of the sovereignty and independence of the member-states. Under article 2(7) of the Charter, the UN may not intervene in matters essentially within the domestic jurisdiction of any state (unless enforcement measures under Chapter VII are to be applied).

This provision has inspired many debates in the UN, and it came to be accepted that colonial issues were not to be regarded as falling within the article 2(7) restriction.[18]

In addition to the domestic jurisdiction provision, article 2 also lays down a variety of other principles in accordance with which both the UN and the member-states are obliged to act. These include the assertion that the UN is based upon the sovereign equality of states and the principles of fulfilment in good faith of the obligations contained in the Charter, the peaceful settlement of disputes and the prohibition on the use of force. It is also provided that member-states must assist the organisation in its activities taken in accordance with the Charter and must refrain from assisting states against which the UN is taking preventive or enforcement action.

The UN has six principal organs, these being the Security Council, General Assembly, Economic and Social Council, Trusteeship Council, Secretariat and International Court of Justice.

---

[18] See *supra*, Chapter 11, p.396.

The Security Council[19]

   The Council was intended to operate as an efficient executive organ of limited membership, functioning continuously. It was given primary responsibility for the maintenance of international peace and security.[20] The Security Council consists of fifteen members, five of them being permanent members (USA, UK, USSR, China and France). These permanent members, chosen on the basis of power politics in 1945, have the veto. Under article 27 of the Charter, on all but procedural matters, decisions of the Council must be made by an affirmative vote of nine members, including the concurring votes of the permanent members.

   This means that a negative vote by any of the permanent members is sufficient to veto any resolution of the Council, save with regard to procedural questions, where nine affirmative votes are all that is required. The veto was written into the Charter in view of the exigencies of power. The USSR, in particular, would not have been willing to accept the UN as it was envisaged without the establishment of the veto to protect it from the western bias of the Council and General Assembly at that time.[21] In practice, the veto has been exercised by the Soviet Union on a considerable number of occasions, and by the USA less frequently, and by the other members fairly rarely.

   The question of how one distinguishes between procedural and non-procedural matters has been a highly controversial one. In the statement of the Sponsoring Powers at San Francisco, it was declared that the issue of whether or not a matter was procedural was itself subject to the veto.[22] This "double-veto" constitutes a formidable barrier, but it is possible under the Rules of Procedure for the President of the Security Council to rule that a matter is procedural and if the ruling is supported by nine members the issue is resolved.[23]

---

[19] See e.g. Bailey, *Voting in the Security Council*, 1969, and *The Procedure of the Security Council*, 1975; Bowett, *op. cit.*, pp.26-42 and Higgins, "The Place of International Law in the Settlement of Disputes by the Security Council", 64 *AJIL*, 1970, p.1. See also *supra*, Chapter 17, p.640 and Chapter 18, p.702.

[20] Articles 23, 24, 25 and 28 of the UN Charter.

[21] See e.g. Nicholas, *op. cit.*, pp.10-13.

[22] *Repertory of Practice of UN Organs*, vol.II, 1955, p.104. See also Bowett, *op. cit.*, p.30.

[23] *Ibid.*, p.31.

Subsequent practice has interpreted the phrase "concurring votes of the permanent members" in article 27 in such a way as to permit abstentions. Accordingly, permanent members may abstain with regard to a resolution of the Security Council without being deemed to have exercised their veto against it.[24]

It does not, of course, follow that the five supreme powers of 1945 will continue to hold that rank. However, the complicated mechanisms for amendment of the Charter, coupled with the existence of the veto, make any change unlikely.[25]

Of the ten non-permanent seats, it is accepted that five should be allocated to Afro-Asian states, one to eastern Europe, two to Latin America, and two to western European and other powers.[26]

The Security Council acts on behalf of the members of the organisation as a whole in performing its functions, and its decisions (but not its recommendations)[27] are binding upon all member-states.[28] Its powers are concentrated in two particular categories, the peaceful settlement of disputes and the adoption of enforcement measures.[29] By these means, the Council conducts its primary task, the maintenance of international peace and security.

The Council has not fulfilled the expectations held of it in the years following the inception of the organisation. This has basically been because of the superpower rivalry which has prevented the Council from taking action on any matter regarded as of importance by any of the five members, and the veto has been the means by which this has been achieved.

However, this does tend to mean that initiatives taken by the Council are fairly highly regarded since they inevitably reflect a consensus of opinion amongst its members, and more particularly amongst its permanent members. The famous Council resolution 242 (1967)[30] laid down the basis for negotiations for a Middle East

[24] See e.g. Stavropoulos, "The Practice of Voluntary Abstentions by Permanent Members of the Security Council under article 27(3) of the Charter", 61 *AJIL*, 1967, p.737. See also the *Namibia* case, ICJ Reports, 1971, pp.16, 22; 49 *ILR*, pp.2, 12, recognising this practice as lawful.

[25] See articles 108 and 109 of the Charter, which require *inter alia* the consent of all the permanent members to any amendment to or alteration of the Charter.

[26] General Assembly resolution 1991(XVIII).

[27] Compare, for example, article 36 of the Charter (peaceful settlement) with articles 41, 42 and 44 (enforcement actions).

[28] Article 25 of the Charter.

[29] See *supra*, Chapter 17, p.640 and Chapter 18, p.702.

[30] As reiterated in resolution 338(1973).

peace settlement and is now regarded as the most authoritative expression of the principles to be taken into account.[31]

Hopes for the transformation of the Security Council into the body it was intended to be rose with the development of the *glasnost* and *perestroika* policies in the Soviet Union in the late 1980s. Increasing co-operation with the US ensued and this reached its highest point as the Kuwait crisis evolved and the Council adopted a series of twelve crucial and binding resolutions, culminating in resolution 678 (1990), which authorised the use of all necessary means in order to bring about an Iraqi withdrawal from Kuwait and the restoration of international peace and security in that region.[32] It remains to be seen whether such a transformation on a long-term basis will ensue.

The failure of the Council in its primary responsibility to preserve world peace stimulated a number of other developments. It encouraged the General Assembly to assume a residual responsibility for maintaining international peace and security, it encouraged the Secretary-General to take upon himself a more active role and it hastened the development of peace-keeping operations.

Another factor that can be pointed to outside the ambit of the UN itself has been the establishment of the military alliances, such as NATO and the Warsaw Pact, which arose as a consequence of the onset of the Cold War and constituted, in effect, regional enforcement systems by-passing the Security Council.

The General Assembly [33]

The General Assembly is the parliamentary body of the UN organisation and consists of representatives of all the member-states, of which there are now one hundred and sixty. Membership, as provided by article 4 of the Charter, is open to:

---

[31] See generally, Pogany, *The Security Council and the Arab-Israeli Conflict*, 1984, Chapter 5 and Shapira, "The Security Council Resolution of November 22, 1967 – Its Legal Nature and Implications", 4 *Israel Law Review*, 1969, p.229.

[32] *Supra* p.710. See also *The Kuwait Crisis: Basic Documents* (eds. Lauterpacht, Greenwood, Weller, Bethlehem), 1991.

[33] See e.g. Bowett, *op. cit.*, p.42 *et seq.*; Nicholas, *op. cit.*, Chapter 5; Finley, *The Structure of the United Nations General Assembly*, 3 vols., 1977 and Bailey, *The General Assembly*, 1960.

all other peace-loving states which accept the obligations contained in the present Charter and, in the judgment of the organisation, are able and willing to carry out these obligations,

and is effected by a decision of the General Assembly upon the recommendation of the Security Council.

However, in practice, the process of admitting states to membership became enmeshed in the rivalries of the Cold War and objections were raised as regards states of different ideological persuasions. Despite an advisory opinion by the International Court of Justice that only the conditions enumerated in article 4 were to be taken into account in considering a request for membership,[34] the practice continued until 1955, when a package deal was concluded and a group of sixteen new members was admitted.[35]

Voting in the Assembly is governed by article 18, which stipulates that each member has one vote only and that decisions on "important questions", including the admission of new members and recommendations relating to international peace and security, are to be made by a two-thirds majority of members present and voting. Other decisions may be taken by a simple majority.

This system of one state-one vote, although logical in view of the sovereign equality of states, has given rise to considerable criticism, especially when it is realised that in many cases the combined populations of two-thirds of member-states may be far less than that of the remaining one-third. Many members of the UN have populations of under two million, whereas the USA and the USSR have populations in the region of 250 million, not to mention India and China with their populations of over 600 millions each. This has led to complaints at the apparent inequity of having hostile Assembly resolutions adopted by what amounts to a minority of the world's population, even though something over ninety states may be involved.[36] The position has been underlined by the emergence

---

[34] The *Conditions of Admission of a State to Membership of the United Nations* case, ICJ Reports, 1948, p.57. See also the *Competence of the General Assembly for the Admission of a State to the United Nations* case, ICJ Reports, 1950, p.4, where the Court held that the General Assembly alone could not effect membership in the absence of a recommendation by the Security Council.

[35] See e.g. *op. cit.*, p.91 and Bowett, *op. cit.*, p.43. See also Luard, *History, op. cit.*, Chapter 19.

[36] *Ibid.*, p.44. See also Clarke and Sohn, *World Peace Through World Law*, 1958, pp.19-30; *The Strategy of World Order*, vol.3, *op. cit.*, p.272 *et seq.* and Sohn, *op. cit.*, p.248 *et seq.*

of bloc voting, whereby, for example, the Afro-Asian states agree to adopt a common stance on particular issues. This means that on a number of occasions resolutions have been passed against the wishes of those states that alone have the actual resources to carry out the terms of such resolutions.

Accordingly, a degree of unreality and what might be called false power has begun to pervade the General Assembly on occasions, as resounding majorities have been accumulated by states that are, in essence, weak in both population and means. On the other hand, this is probably the most effective way in which the developing nations of the Third World can assert their views. In any event, no acceptable alternative has been proposed and the interests of the five permanent members of the Security Council, at least, are safeguarded by the existence of the veto in the Council.

Except for certain internal matters, such as the budget,[37] the Assembly cannot bind its members. It is not a legislature in that sense, and its resolutions are purely recommendatory. Such resolutions, of course, may be binding if they reflect rules of customary international law and they are significant as instances of state practice that may lead to the formation of a new customary rule, but Assembly resolutions in themselves cannot establish binding legal obligations for member-states.[38]

The Assembly is essentially a debating chamber, a forum for the exchange of ideas and the discussion of a wide-ranging category of problems. It meets in annual sessions, but special sessions may be called by the Secretary-General at the request of the Security Council or a majority of UN members.[39] Such special sessions have been held, for example, to discuss the issues of Namibia (South West Africa) and the Middle East in 1967, and to debate the world economic order in 1974 and 1975. Emergency sessions may also be called by virtue of the Uniting for Peace machinery.[40]

The role of the Assembly has increased since its inception, due not only to the failure of the Security Council to function

[37] Article 17 of the Charter.
[38] See further *supra*, Chapter 3, p.93.
[39] Article 20 of the Charter.
[40] *Supra*, Chapter 18, p.712.

effectively in the light of East-West hostility, but also to the enormous growth in membership since the advent of decolonisation. These states are jealous of their independence and eager to play a significant part in world affairs, and the General Assembly is the ideal stage.

In the sphere of peace-keeping, the influence and activity of the Assembly have proved vital in the creation and consolidation of a new method of maintaining international peace.[41]

To aid it in its work, the Assembly has established a variety of organs covering a wide range of topics and activities. It has seven main committees that concern themselves with a broad tableau of political, economic, security, social, cultural, administrative and legal issues,[42] and there are a number of subsidiary organs dealing with relevant topics. The more well-known of these include the International Law Commission, the UN Commission on International Trade Law, the UN Institute for Training and Research, the Council for Namibia and the UN Relief and Works Agency.[43]

The Economic and Social Council [44]

Much of the work of the United Nations in the economic and social spheres of activity is performed by the Economic and Social Council, which is a principal organ of the UN. It has the capacity to discuss a wide range of matters, but its powers are restricted and its recommendations are not binding upon UN member-states. It consists of 54 members elected by the Assembly with staggered elections and each member has one vote.[45] The Council may, by article 62, initiate or make studies upon a range of issues and make recommendations to the General Assembly, the members of the UN and to the relevant specialised agencies. It may prepare draft conventions for submission to the Assembly and call international conferences. Arguably, however, its primary function rests in co-ordinating the activities of the various specialised agencies.

[41] *Supra*, Chapter 18, p.716.
[42] See e.g. Bowett, *op. cit.*, pp.54-55.
[43] *Ibid.*, pp.56-58.
[44] *Ibid.*, pp.58-72 and Sharp, *The UN Economic Council*, 1969. See also *supra*, Chapter 6, p.202.
[45] Article 61 of the Charter. Note that under article 69, any member of the UN may be invited to participate in its deliberations without a vote.

The Trusteeship Council [46]

The UN principal organ of the least significance today is the Trusteeship Council. This was intended to supervise the trust territories, which were to consist of mandated territories, areas detached from enemy states as a result of the Second World War and other territories voluntarily placed under the trusteeship system by the administering authority (of which there have been none).[47]

The only former mandated territory which was not placed under the new system or granted independence was South West Africa.[48]

The sole remaining trust territory is the Pacific Islands Territory, administered as a strategic area by the United States.[49]

The Secretariat [50]

The Secretariat of the UN consists of the Secretary-General and his staff, and constitutes virtually an international civil service. The staff are appointed by article 101 upon the basis of efficiency, competence and integrity, "due regard" being paid "to the importance of recruiting the staff on as wide a geographical basis as possible". All member-states have undertaken, under article 100, to respect the exclusively international character of the responsibilities of the Secretary-General and his staff, who are neither to seek nor receive instructions from any other authority but the UN organisation itself. This provision has not always been respected.

---

[46] See e.g. Bowett, *op. cit.*, pp.72-87 and Toussaint, *The Trusteeship System of the United Nations,* 1956.

[47] Article 77 of the Charter.

[48] *Supra,* Chapter 5, p.157.

[49] By article 83 of the Charter, the functions of the UN relating to strategic areas are exercised by the Security Council (where, of course, the United States has a veto) rather than, as normal for trust territories, under article 85 by the General Assembly with the assistance of the Trusteeship Council. The latter may also assist the Security Council with regard to strategic areas. See e.g. Dorrance, *Oceania and the United States,* 1980. See further *supra,* p.157.

[50] See e.g. Bailey, "The United Nations Secretariat" in *The Evolution of International Organisations* (ed. Luard), 1966, p.92 and *The Secretariat of the UN,* 1962. See also Meron, *The UN Secretariat,* 1977; Schwebel, *The Secretary-General of the United Nations,* 1952; Bowett, *op. cit.,* pp.87-104 and generally *Public Papers of the Secretaries-General of the United Nations* (eds. Cordier and Foote, and Cordier and Harrelson), 8 vols., 1969-77. See also *supra,* Chapter 18, p.715.

Under article 97, the Secretary-General is appointed by the General Assembly upon the unanimous recommendation of the Security Council and constitutes the chief administrative officer of the UN. He must accordingly be a personage acceptable to all the permanent members and this, in the light of effectiveness, is vital. Much depends upon the actual personality and outlook of the particular office holder, and the role played by the Secretary-General in international affairs has tended to vary according to the character of the person concerned. An especially energetic part was performed by Dr. Hammerskjöld in the late 1950s and very early 1960s until his untimely death in the Congo,[51] but since that time a rather lower profile has been maintained by the occupants of that position. The current holder of the office is Perez de Cuellar of Peru.

Apart from various administrative functions,[52] the essence of the Secretary-General's authority is contained in article 99 of the Charter, which empowers him to bring to the attention of the Security Council any matter which he feels may strengthen the maintenance of international peace and security, although this power has not often been used.[53]

In practice, the role of Secretary-General has extended beyond the various provisions of the Charter. In many disputes, the functions assigned to him by the other organs of the United Nations have enabled him to increase the influence of the organisation.[54]

One remarkable example of this occurred in the Congo crisis of 1960 and the subsequent Council resolution authorising the Secretary-General in very wide-ranging terms to take action.[55] Another instance of the capacity of the Secretary-General to take action was the decision of 1967 to withdraw the UN peace-keeping

[51] See e.g. Bailey, "The United Nations Secretariat", *op. cit.*

[52] These include servicing a variety of organs, committees and conferences; co-ordinating the activities of the secretariat, the specialised agencies and other inter-governmental organisations; the preparation of studies and reports and responsibility for the preparation of the annual budget of the UN. Note that the Secretary-General also acts as depositary for a wide range of multinational treaties, and under article 98, submits an annual report on the work of the organisation.

[53] Article 99 was invoked, for example, in 1950 in the Korean war crisis, in 1960 in the Congo crisis and in 1979 with regard to the Iranian hostage issue, see Bowett, *op. cit.*, p.92 and *Yearbook of the UN*, 1979, pp.307-12. See also S/13646.

[54] Article 98.

[55] See *supra*, Chapter 18, p.715.

force in the Middle East, thus removing an important psychological barrier to war, and provoking a certain amount of criticism.[56]

The sixth principal organ of the UN is the International Court of Justice, established in 1946 as the successor to the Permanent Court of International Justice.[57]

The Specialised Agencies [58]

This is the term used to define those organisations established by inter-governmental agreement and having wide international responsibilities in economic, social, cultural and other fields that have been brought into relationship with the United Nations.[59] This task is performed by the Economic and Social Council which also co-ordinates their activities with the approval of the General Assembly, and the agreements made usually specify the sending of regular reports by the agencies to the Economic and Social Council and provide for exchange of information in general.[60]

Specialised agencies are founded upon an international treaty between states that establishes the basic parameters of the organisation and deals *inter alia* with membership, purposes and structure.[61] Upon signing an agreement with the UN under articles 57 and 63 of the Charter, such an organisation will become a specialised agency. Most constituent instruments distinguish between original and subsequent members, while several agencies provide for associate membership[62] for non-self-governing territories, as for instance Namibia prior to its independence in 1990. Withdrawal is possible, as for example the United States withdrawal from the ILO between 1977-80 and from UNESCO in 1984. The usual structure of a specialised agency is based upon the

---

[56] See e.g. Bowett, *op. cit.,* p.93 and *supra,* Chapter 18, p.716.

[57] *Supra,* Chapter 17, p.656.

[58] See e.g. Bowett, *op. cit.,* Chapter 4; Alexandrowicz, *The Law-Making Functions of the Specialised Agencies of the United Nations,* 1973 and Luard, *International Agencies: The Emerging Framework of Interdependence,* 1977.

[59] Article 57 of the Charter.

[60] See articles 62-66.

[61] See e.g. Bowett, *op. cit.,* p.118 *et seq.*; Harrod, "Problems of the United Nations Specialised Agencies at the Quarter Century", 28 *YBWA,* 1974, p.187 and Klein, *Encyclopedia of Public International Law,* vol.5, 1983, pp.349-69. See also El Erian, *op. cit.,* pp.55, 96-106.

[62] See e.g. UNESCO and WHO.

plenary body, in which all members are represented. This organ elects a smaller executive council in which membership may be determined not only by geographical distribution but also functional conditions.

For instance, of the 24 members of the Council of the International Maritime Organisation, 6 must be governments of states with the largest interest in providing international shipping services, 6 must be governments of other states with the largest interest in international seaborne trade, while the remaining 12 have to be governments of states (not already elected) with special interests in maritime transport or navigation whose election will ensure an equitable geographical representation.[63] Similarly, the composition of the Council of the International Civil Aviation Organisation is weighted in favour of those states most active in the fields of air transport and the provision of facilities for international air navigation,[64] while the unique structure of the ILO has already been noted.[65]

Most of the specialised agencies have devised means whereby the decisions of the particular organisation can be rendered virtually binding upon members. This is especially so with regard to the International Labour Organisation, UNESCO and the World Health Organisation. Although such institutions are not able to legislate in the usual sense, they are able to apply pressures quite effectively to discourage non-compliance with recommendations or conventions. In the case of the ILO, treaties are submitted to member governments for ratification and within twelve or eighteen months must be laid before the state's legislative organs. The governments, in putting the convention before their parliaments, are required to outline their proposed line of action.

Although no obligations are imposed, considerable pressures often build up in favour of ratifying the ILO convention and this is reinforced by the comprehensive system of reporting back to the organisation that exists.

---

[63] See e.g. *The International Maritime Organisation* (ed. Mankabady), 1984.

[64] See e.g. Shenkmann, *International Civil Aviation Organisation*, 1955; Fitzgerald, "The International Civil Aviation Organisation" in *The Effectiveness of International Decisions* (ed. Schwebel), 1971, p.156 and Binaghi, "The Role of ICAO", in *The Freedom of the Air* (ed. McWhinney), 1968, p.17.

[65] *Supra*, Chapter 6, p.217.

Similarly, sanctions and enforcement procedures in the specialised agencies show much subtlety and sophistication and operate, on the whole, beyond the normal confines of strict legal obligations.[66]

The International Labour Organisation [67]

The International Labour Organisation was set up in 1919 with the aim of protecting and extending the rights of workers throughout the world. It has adopted well over a hundred conventions in pursuance of this, the vast majority of which are in force, which cover such topics as the general conditions of employment, rights to protect the interests of women and children, social security, industrial relations, safety regulations and provisions protecting the right to organise.

The World Health Organisation

The World Health Organisation was established in 1946 with the aim of unifying the standards of health care and it performs a variety of useful functions dedicated to this purpose. These range from the exchange of information to proposals for international treaties and the promotion of research and study in relevant areas.

The United Nations Educational, Scientific and Cultural Organisation [68]

The UN Educational, Scientific and Cultural Organisation (UNESCO) exists to further the increase and diffusion of knowledge by various activities including technical assistance and co-operative ventures with national governments. It also operates as a central bank of information. In the mid-1970s, however, the entrance of political considerations (mainly related to the Middle East) somewhat weakened the authority of UNESCO, which was never intended as a political arena, and brought intellectual and financial pressures to bear.[69]

---

[66] See e.g. Bowett, *op. cit.*, p.140 *et seq.* See also Alexandrowicz, *op. cit.* and Detter, *Law Making by International Organisations*, 1965.

[67] See *supra*, Chapter 6, p.217.

[68] See *supra*, Chapter 6, p.219.

[69] Note that at the end of 1984, the United States withdrew from UNESCO, see 34 *ILM*, 1985, p.489 *et seq.* The UK withdrew as from December 1985.

The Food and Agriculture Organisation [70]

The Food and Agriculture Organisation was created in 1943 and it works to collect and distribute information related to agricultural and nutritional matters. A World Food Programme was established in 1963 and in 1974 a World Food Conference was held in Rome. This called for the establishment of a World Food Council as an organ within the UN system to co-ordinate policies concerning food production, nutrition and other connected topics. It also suggested the creation of an international fund for agricultural development and urged support for the FAO's international fertilizer supply scheme. The increase attention devoted to agricultural issues is due to a growing awareness of the danger of world hunger and starvation, as well as a realisation of the extent to which rural development has been neglected in attempts to industrialise and urbanise in the Third World.

Economic and Financial Organisations

There are a number of international organisations concerned with economic and financial affairs. The International Bank for Reconstruction and Development (the World Bank) emerged from the Bretton Woods Conference of 1944 to encourage financial investment, and it works in close liaison with the International Monetary Fund, which aims to assist monetary co-operation and increase world trade. These agencies are assisted by the International Development Association and the International Finance Corporation, which are affiliated to the World Bank and encourage financial investment and the obtaining of loans on easy terms. These financial organisations differ from the rest of the specialised agencies in that authority lies with the Board of Governors, and voting is determined on a weighted basis according to the level of subscriptions made.[71]

[70] See e.g. Phillips, *FAO, Its Origins, Formation and Evolution 1945-1981*, 1981.
[71] See e.g. Bowett, *op. cit.*, pp.109-12. See also Scammell, "The International Monetary Fund" in the *Evolution of International Organisation, op. cit.*, Chapter 9; Shofield, "The World Bank", *ibid.*, Chapter 10 and Townley, "The Economic Organs of the United Nations", *ibid.*, Chapter 11; and Alexandrowicz, *op. cit.*, Chapter IX.

REGIONAL INSTITUTIONS

The proliferation of regional institutions, linking together geographically and ideologically related states, since the close of the Second World War, has been impressive. A number of factors can help explain this. The onset of the Cold War and the failure of the Security Council's enforcement procedures stimulated the growth of regional defence alliances and bloc politics. NATO, and its various sister organisations covering the Middle and Far East, confronted the Warsaw Pact. The decolonisation process resulted in the independence of scores of states, most of which were eager to play a non-aligned role between East and West. And to this end, regional organisations developed to reflect common interests (and sometimes common hostilities) in a super-power world. These included the Arab League, the Organisation of American States and the Organisation of African Unity, in particular.

But it was in Europe that regionalism became most constructive and political. The establishment of the European Economic Community, in particular, was intended to lay the basis for a resurgent western Europe with meaningful economic and political integration.

Europe

The North Atlantic Treaty Alliance [72]

This was created in 1949 to counter possible threats from the East. It associated the United States and Canada with a group of European powers for the protection, in essence, of western Europe (although Greece and Turkey are also involved). By the Treaty,[73] the parties agreed to consult where the territorial integrity, political independence or security of any of them has been threatened,[74] and accepted that an armed attack against one or more of them in Europe or North America should be considered an attack against all.[75]

---

[72] See e.g. Bowett, *op. cit.*, p.180 *et seq.*; Myers, *NATO, The Next Thirty Years*, 1980 and Kaplan and Clawson, *NATO After Thirty Years*, 1981.

[73] 43 *AJIL*, 1949, Suppl. p.159.

[74] Article IV.

[75] Article V.

The alliance consists of a Council which is the supreme organ and on which all members are represented, and a series of civil and military committees covering all aspects of security work. However, in 1966 France withdrew from the military side of the alliance while remaining a member of the organisation itself.[76] There also exists a NATO parliamentary conference which acts as an official consultative body.

European defence matters are also discussed within the framework of the seven nation Western European Union,[77] which possesses a Council and an Assembly. It was originally created in 1954 to exercise some kind of control over the extent of German rearmament. However, its effective functions today are few and its activities overlap with those of other European organisations.

The Council of Europe [78]

This was created in 1949 and embodied a wide-ranging series of co-operative moves in many fields. The powers of the 24-member[79] Council are very limited, however, and the organisation can best be characterised as a discussion forum. The Committee of Ministers consists of governmental representatives, while the Assembly is composed, unusually, of members representing the Parliaments of the member states. It is purely a deliberative body.

The most important part of the Council's work is the preparation and conclusion of conventions and protocols. There are a large number of these now, including the European Convention for the Protection of Human Rights and Fundamental Freedoms (1950),[80] the European Social Charter (1961), agreements dealing with cultural and educational questions and conventions covering patents, extradition, migration, state immunity, terrorism and others.

---

[76] See e.g. Stein and Carreau, "Law and Peaceful Change in a Subsystem: 'Withdrawal' of France from NATO", 62 *AJIL*, 1968, p.557.

[77] UK, France, West Germany, Belgium, Holland, Italy and Luxembourg.

[78] See e.g. Robertson, *The Council of Europe*, 2nd ed., 1961.

[79] As of December 1990.

[80] *Supra*, Chapter 6, p.221.

The Organisation for Economic Co-operation and Development [81]

This arose in 1960 and developed out of the European machinery created to administer the American Marshall Plan which was aimed at reviving the European economies.[82] Its membership includes the USA, Canada and Japan,[83] and it exists to maintain and encourage economic growth world-wide. Its main organ is the Council, which includes all the members of the organisation and it proceeds by way of unanimity, except in special cases. It is thus by no means a supranational body, since no state can be bound against its will. It possesses an Executive Committee and other committees and autonomous bodies aimed at encouraging co-ordination and co-operation, as well as a secretariat.

The European Communities [84]

This is undoubtedly the most important European organisation, as well as being by far the most sophisticated regional institution so far created. It consists, in fact, of three interlocking communities – the European Coal and Steel Community (created in 1951), the European Economic Community and the European Atomic Energy (Euratom) Community (both created in 1957). The basis of the Communities lies in furthering economic integration and, possibly in the longer term, political union.

The EEC aims at establishing a true, unified market with common external tariffs and the elimination of internal tariffs and quotas, and it promotes the free movement of capital and labour. There also exists a Common Agricultural Policy[85] and a

---

[81] See e.g. Bowett, *op. cit.,* p.189 *et seq.* and Miller, "The OECD", *YBWA,* 1963, p.80.

[82] This was the Organisation for European Economic Co-operation, created in 1948.

[83] By article 16 of the 1960 Treaty, membership is open to any government by unanimous invitation of the Council.

[84] See e.g. Bowett, *op. cit.,* p.199 *et seq.*; Lasok and Bridge, *Law and Institutions of the European Communities,* 4th ed., 1987; Wyatt and Dashwood, *The Substantive Law of the EEC,* 2nd ed., 1987; Parry and Hardy, *EEC Law,* 2nd ed., 1981 and Commission of the European Communities, *Thirty Years of Community Law,* 1983. See also Hartley, *The Foundations of European Community Law,* 2nd ed., 1988 and Steiner, *EEC Law,* 2nd ed., 1990.

[85] See articles 38-47 of the EEC Treaty. See also Melchior, "The Common Organisation of Agricultural Markets" in *Thirty Years of Community Law, op. cit.,* p.439 *et seq.* and Lasok and Bridge, *op. cit.,* p.375 *et seq.*

series of association agreements with Third World countries under the Yaoundé, Arusha and Lomé Conventions.[86]

The European Community, although based on the ECSC, EEC and Euratom arrangements, has a common set of institutions, which were enlarged in 1972 following the accession of the UK, Ireland and Denmark, in 1981 with Greece's entry and in 1986 with the accession of Spain and Portugal. These comprise the European Parliament, the Council of Ministers, the Commission and the Court of Justice.

The European Parliament was first created under the Treaty of Rome in 1957 and consists of at present 518 members,[87] directly elected since 1979. It holds plenary sessions about one week a month and has a variety of standing committees, studying such topics as political, legal, economic, social, agricultural and regional questions. It meets in Strasbourg or in Luxembourg. Britain, Italy, France and Western Germany have 81 seats each, Belgium and Greece 24 each, the Netherlands 25, Ireland 15, Denmark 16, Luxembourg 6 seats, Spain 60 and Portugal 24.

The powers of the Parliament are rather limited in practice. It may scrutinise the activities of the Council of Ministers and the Commission, but has no right of veto. It has the right to be consulted on community legislation and may dismiss the Commission by passing a censure motion with a two-thirds majority. It may approve, amend or reject the budget, in so far as the part dealing with the functioning of the Community's institutions is concerned,[88] but not otherwise.

The Council of Ministers consists of one representative from each of the Community states and is the guardian of national interests.[89] The question of which governmental ministers will attend the meetings depends upon the issues to be discussed. The voting procedure used by the Council is a little complex and reflects the contrary pressures to which it is subject. On the most important matters unanimity is required (which in effect gives each state a veto),

---

[86] See e.g. Flory, "Commercial Policy and Development Policy" in *Thirty Years of Community Law, op. cit.,* pp.375, 387 *et seq.*

[87] With a further 16 members to be added to represent the former German Democratic Republic, following German unification in October 1990.

[88] See e.g. Lasok and Bridge, *op. cit.,* Chapter 7. This amounts to about 25% of the total budget.

[89] *Ibid.,* Chapter 6.

while on certain other issues a majority decision upon a weighted votes calculation will be sufficient. Occasionally, a qualified majority will be necessary, otherwise a single majority will be adequate.[90]

The powers of the Council are far-reaching and amount to legislative control, although their precise extent will depend upon whether the question under discussion falls within the treaties setting up the ECSC, the EEC or Euratom.[91] The Council is the political authority of the European Community and, accordingly, the focus of ultimate power.

Subordinate to the Council, and subject to parliamentary control, is the European Commission. This currently has seventeen members chosen for their individual competence, who act independently of government control,[92] although not more than two can be from any one state. The Commission operates by majority vote and constitutes the bureaucratic machinery of the Community. It is situated at Brussels.

However, the vital point is that the Commission has certain decision-making powers, in addition to its ability to issue opinions which are solely persuasive, that are binding upon the citizens and institutions of the member-states. The Commission can, and does, make decisions which are legally binding upon the recipients, without the need for national legislation to incorporate them into domestic legal systems. This supranational characteristic is what distinguishes the Community from other regional institutions. It involves a restriction by states upon their legislative exclusivity and permits Community institutions to issue orders directly affecting Community citizens in certain cases, irrespective of national parliamentary activity.[93]

The Single European Act, signed in 1986 with the aim of eliminating the remaining impediments to the creation of a single internal market by the end of 1992, introduced several important changes. It created a new co-operation procedure whereby the

[90] *Ibid.*, p.198 *et seq.*

[91] Note, for example, that while article 145 of the EEC Treaty refers to the Council's power to take decisions, article 26 of the ECSC Treaty and article 115 of the Euratom Treaty emphasise the co-ordinating function of the Council.

[92] Article 10 of the 1965 Treaty (The Merger Treaty), which instituted a single Commission instead of the High Authority of the ECSC and the Commissions of the EEC and Euratom, and a single Council to replace the three former Councils under the three Treaties. It entered into force in 1967. See further, Lasok and Bridge, *op. cit.*, Chapter 5.

[93] *Ibid.*, Chapter 4.

Parliament is given a second opportunity to consider draft legislation. Where the Parliament objects to the proposal in question as a result of its second consideration, the Council of Ministers may only adopt it by acting unanimously and within a three months period. Where the Parliament proposes amendments, the European Commission may re-examine the proposal and if it rejects the amendments, they may only be adopted by the Council acting unanimously. The range of issues upon which the Parliament must be consulted was also greatly increased, so that the majority of measures relating to the establishment of the single internal market are included.

Under the Single European Act, the number of areas in which voting in the Council may take place by qualified majority rather than by unanimity has been extended. In fact, most of the legislation necessary to establish the internal market falls within this category. In addition, the Single European Act provides for the institutionalisation of regular meetings of Heads of State in a "European Council" covering a wide range of issues.

The Court of Justice of the European Communities[94] consists of thirteen judges,[95] appointed for a six year term each. The Court is assisted by six advocates-general, whose role is to make reasoned submissions on cases before the Court, without taking part in the judgment. It applies Community law, a composition of the relevant treaties, Commission regulations, previous case-law of the Court and general principles of member-states' municipal law, and performs various functions connected with the European Communities. The Court has a complicated jurisdiction[96] and has established the principle that EEC law prevails over national law.[97] It has so far dealt

[94] See e.g. Brown and Jacobs, *The Court of Justice of the European Communities,* 2nd ed., 1983; Lasok and Bridge, *op. cit.,* Chapter 9 and Bowett, *op. cit.,* p.303 *et seq.*

[95] I.e. in practice one judge from each of the member-states, with the thirteenth held by nationals of the four larger states (France, UK, West Germany and Italy) in rotation. See also articles 165-67 of the EEC Treaty.

[96] The Court, for example, can hear disputes between states (article 170, EEC Treaty); and between states and the Commission (article 169). It can act as an administrative tribunal hearing allegations of illegal action or inaction by Community organs (articles 173-76, 178 and 184) and as a constitutional court, deciding on the interpretation of the Treaty and Community legislation at the request of national courts (article 177).

[97] See e.g. *Costa* v. *ENEL,* [1964] ECR 858; the *Van Gend en Loos* case, [1963] ECR 1 and *Simmenthal* v. *Italian Minister of France,* [1976] ECR 187 and [1978] ECR 629. Note, in particular, the significant assertion in the *Van Gend en Loos* case that "the Community
(Footnote continued on p. 768)

primarily with issues connected with farm policy, common tariffs, monopolies, patent rights and social security rights of migrant workers.

The Single European Act provided for the creation of a new Court of First Instance in order to hear cases concerning disputes between the community and its employees, competition law issues and certain other minor matters. This Court commenced operations on 1 September 1989.

The American Continent [98]

The Organisation of American States emerged after World War II and built upon the work already done by the Pan-American Union and the various inter-American Conferences since 1890. It consists of two basic treaties: the 1947 Inter-American Treaty of Reciprocal Assistance (the Rio Treaty), which is a collective self-defence system, and the 1948 Pact of Bogatá, which is the original Charter of the OAS and which was amended in 1967 by the Buenos Aires Protocol. It is a collective security system, an attack on one being deemed an attack on all. The OAS consists of a General Assembly, which is a plenary organ with wide terms of reference; meetings of consultation of Ministers of Foreign Affairs, which exercise broad powers; a Permanent Council which performs both secretarial supervision and political functions,[99] subject to the authority of the aforementioned institutions and a number of

---

(Footnote continued from p. 767)
constitutes a new legal order of international law for the benefit of which the states have limited their sovereign rights, albeit within limited fields, and the subjects of which comprise not only member-states but also their nationals. Independently of the legislation of member-states, Community law not only imposes obligations upon individuals but is also intended to confer upon them rights which become part of their legal heritage. These rights arise not only where they are expressly granted by the Treaty, but also by reason of obligations which the Treaty imposes in a clearly defined way upon individuals as well as upon member-states and upon institutions of the Community," [1963] ECR 1, 12.

[98] See e.g. Bowett, *op. cit.*, Chapter 7; *The Organisation of American States, The Inter-American System*, 1963; Thomas and Thomas, *The Organisation of American States*, 1963; Ball, *The OAS in Transition*, 1969 and Wood, "The Organisation of American States", 33 *YBWA*, 1979, p.148.

[99] Since 1967, there have also been the Inter-American Economic and Social Council and a Council for Education, Science and Culture. The new Inter-American Committee on Peaceful Settlement is subordinate to the Permanent Council. There is also a General Secretariat, based in Washington DC, USA.

subsidiary organs. The organisation has adopted a Human Rights Convention[100] and is the most developed of the regional organisations outside Europe, but without any of the supranational powers possessed by the European Communities.[101]

The Arab League [102]

This was created in 1944 and has broad aims. It provides a useful forum for the formulation of Arab politics and encourages regional co-operation. The Council of the League is the supreme organ and performs a useful conciliatory role and various subsidiary organs dealing with economic cultural and social issues have been set up. Its headquarters are in Tunisia, having been moved there from Egypt after the Israel-Egypt Peace Treaty of 1979. There is also a permanent secretariat and a Secretary-General. The Council of the League has been involved in the peace-keeping operations, in Kuwait in 1961, where an Inter-Arab Force was established to deter Iraqi threats, and in Lebanon in 1976 as an umbrella for the operations of the Syrian troops.[103]

Africa [104]

The Organisation of African Unity was established in 1963 in Ethiopia. Its supreme organ is the Assembly of Heads of State and Government, which is a plenary body meeting annually or in extraordinary session. It has created a series of specialised commissions dealing with economic, health, defence, educational and scientific matters amongst others. There is also a Liberation Committee based in Dar es Salaam and created to assist the various

---

[100] *Supra*, Chapter 6, p.233.

[101] There exists also a number of other American organisations of limited competence, see e.g. Bowett, *op. cit.*, pp.225-29.

[102] *Ibid.*, pp.229-33 and MacDonald, *The League of Arab States*, 1965. See also Boutros-Ghali, "La Ligue des Etats Arabes", 137 *HR*, p.1. Note also the existence of the Organisation of Petroleum Exporting Countries, founded in 1960, which obtained the power to fix crude oil prices in 1973, see e.g. Seymour, *OPEC, Instrument of Change*, 1980.

[103] See e.g. Bowett, *op. cit.*, p.230 and Feuer, "Le Force Arabe de Securité au Liban", 22 *AFDI*, 1976, p.51. See also *supra*, Chapter 17, p.647.

[104] See e.g. Bowett, *op. cit.*, pp.241-44; Cervenka, *The Organisation of African Unity and Its Charter*, 1969 and *The Unfinished Quest for Unity*, 1977; Andemicael, *The OAU and the UN*, 1976, and Wolfers, *Politics in the Organisation of African Unity*, 1976. See also *supra*, Chapter 17, p.646.

liberation organisations. The Council of Ministers meets before the Assembly and prepares the way for it, while the secretariat performs the usual tasks.

A Commission of Mediation, Conciliation and Arbitration for the peaceful settlement of African disputes was set up, but has not been utilised, African states preferring to have resort to *ad hoc* mediation efforts.[105] The OAU has faced considerable problems in reconciling member-states' policies. The Western Sahara conflict is the prime example of this. That dispute provoked Morocco's withdrawal from the organisation,[106] while the OAU mediation attempts in the Chad civil war were noticeably unsuccessful.[107]

A variety of African regional economic associations exist, particularly the Economic Community of West African States.[108]

Eastern Europe

There have existed a number of important institutions in eastern Europe, such as the Warsaw Pact, which mirrored the NATO alliance, and Comecon (the Council for Mutual Economic Aid).[109] The process, however, never went as far as in western Europe and with the collapse of the Soviet system of eastern Europe, these institutions began to undergo rapid change. In particular, the Warsaw Pact military organisation began to disintegrate during 1990.[110]

Asia

In this area of the world, the development of regional institutions has been least successful of all. However, the creation in 1967 of the Association of South East Asian Nations (ASEAN) should be noted.[111] It possesses both economic and political aims and groups together Indonesia, Thailand, Malaysia, Singapore and the Philippines. It

---

[105] *Ibid.*

[106] *Ibid.*

[107] See e.g. Shaw, "Dispute-Settlement in Africa", 37 *YBWA*, 1983, pp.149, 158-60.

[108] See e.g. Bowett, *op. cit.*, pp.244-48. See also Sohn, *Documents of African Regional Organisations*, 4 vols., 1971.

[109] Bowett, *op. cit.*, pp.239-40. See also Szawlowski, *The System of International Organisations of the Communist Countries*, 1976.

[110] See e.g. *Keesing's Record of World Events*, p.37979 (1991).

[111] See e.g. Bowett, *op. cit.*, p.235. See also Allen, *The ASEAN Report*, 2 vols., 1979 and *Understanding ASEAN* (ed. Broinowski), 1982.

operates on the basis of annual ministerial meetings serviced by a Standing Committee and a series of permanent committees covering areas such as science and technology, shipping and commerce. In 1976 three agreements were signed; a Treaty of Amity and Co-operation, which reaffirmed the parties' commitment to peace and dealt with the peaceful settlement of disputes; the Declaration of ASEAN Concord, which called for increased political and economic co-ordination and co-operation, and the Agreement of Establishment of the Permanent Secretariat to co-ordinate the five national secretariats established under the 1967 ASEAN Declaration.

SOME LEGAL ASPECTS OF INTERNATIONAL ORGANISATIONS [112]

There is no doubt that the contribution to international law generally made by the increasing number and variety of international organisations is marked. In many fields, the practice of international organisations has had an important effect and one that is often not sufficiently appreciated. In addition, state practice within such organisations is an increasingly significant element within the general process of customary law formation. This is particularly true with regard to the United Nations, with its universality of membership and extensive field of activity and interest, although not all such practice will be capable of transmission into customary law, and particular care will have to be exercised with regard to the *opinio juris*, or binding criterion.[113]

As well as the impact of the practice of international organisations upon international law, it is worth noting the importance of international legal norms within the operations of such organisations. The norms in question guide the work and development of international institutions and may act to correct illegal acts.[114]

---

[112] See e.g. Bowett, *op. cit.*, Part 4; Brownlie, *Principles of Public International Law*, 4th ed., 1990, Chapter XXX and Reuter, *op. cit.*, pp.227-64. See also E. Lauterpacht, *op. cit.* and "The Legal Effects of Illegal Acts of International Organisations" in *Cambridge Essays in International Law*, 1965, p.98; Skubiszewski, "Enactment of Law by International Organisations", 4 *BYIL*, 1965-6, p.198; Whiteman, *Digest, op. cit.* vol.13, 1968; Higgins, *The Development of International Law Through the Political Organs of the United Nations*, 1963 and sources cited in footnote 1 *supra*.

[113] *Ibid.*, p.3. See also *supra*, Chapter 3, p.72.

[114] See e.g. the *Inter-Governmental Maritime Consultative Organisation* case, ICJ Reports, 1960, p.150; the *Conditions of Admission of a State to the United Nations* case, ICJ Reports, 1948, p.57 and the *Certain Expenses of the United Nations* case, ICJ Reports, 1962, p.151. See also E. Lauterpacht, *op. cit.* footnote 1, pp.388-95.

Questions dealing with the interpretation of treaties are particularly relevant in this context, since international organisations are grounded upon treaties that are also constituent instruments, but issues relating to the scope of powers and especially implied powers are also of crucial importance. Nevertheless, a two-way process of legal development is involved.

Personality [115]

The essence of the role of international organisations in the world order centres on their possession of international legal personality. Once this is established, they become subjects of international law and thus capable of enforcing rights and duties upon the international plane as distinct from operating merely within the confines of separate municipal jurisdictions. The question of personality will in the first instance depend upon the terms of the instrument establishing the organisation. If states wish the organisation to be endowed specifically with international personality, this will appear in the constituent treaty and will be determinative of the issue.[116] However, personality on the international plane may be inferred from the powers or purposes of the organisation and its practice. This is the more usual situation and one authoritatively discussed and settled (at least as far as the UN was concerned directly) by the International Court in the *Reparation for Injuries Suffered in the Service of the United Nations* case.[117]

The Court held that the UN had international legal personality because this was indispensable in order to achieve the purposes and principles specified in the Charter. In other words, it was a necessary inference from the functions and rights the organisation was exercising and enjoying. The Court emphasised that it had to be:

[115] *Supra*, Chapter 5, p.181. See also Jenks, "The Legal Personality of International Organisations", 22 *BYIL*, 1945, p.267; Rama-Montaldo, "International Legal Personality and Implied Powers of International Organisations", 44 *BYIL*, 1970, p.111; Sørensen, "Principes de Droit International Public", 101 *HR*, pp.1, 127 *et seq.*; Barberis, "Nouvelles Questions Concernant La Personalité Juridique Internationale", 179 *HR*, p.145; Seyersted, "Objective International Personality of Intergovernmental Organisations", 34 *Nordisk Tidskrift for International Ret*, 1964, p.1 and Ijalaye, *The Extension of Corporate Personality in International Law*, 1978.

[116] See e.g. article 6 of the European Coal and Steel Community Treaty, 1951, and article 210 of the EEC Treaty, 1957. See also *Costa (Flaminio)* v. *ENEL*, [1964] ECR 585.

[117] ICJ Reports, 1949, p.174; 16 *ILR*, p.318.

acknowledged that its [i.e. UN's] members, by entrusting certain functions to it, with the attendant duties and responsibilities, have clothed it with the competence required to enable those functions to be effectively discharged.[118]

The possession of international personality meant that the organisation was a subject of international law and capable of having international rights and duties and of enforcing them by bringing international claims.

In reaching this conclusion, the Court examined the United Nations Charter and subsequent relevant treaties and practice to determine the constitutional nature of the United Nations and the extent of its powers and duties. It noted the obligations of members towards the organisation, its ability to make international agreements and the provisions of the Charter contained in Articles 104 and 105, whereby the United Nations was to enjoy such legal capacity, privileges and immunities in the territory of each member-state as were necessary for the fulfilment of its purposes.

The Court emphasised that:

fifty states, representing the vast majority of the members of the international community, had the power in conformity with international law, to bring into being an entity possessing objective international personality, and not merely personality recognised by them alone.[119]

The consequences of the attribution of international legal personality, however, vary. Whereas states are recognised as possessing the widest range of rights and duties, those of international organisations are clearly circumscribed in terms of the express and implied powers laid down in the constituent instruments.[120] The twin issues of personality and powers are separate, although inevitably they intertwine. Because an organisation has personality in international law, it will thus have certain powers, but the extent of such powers is another question, even though the nature and existence of powers are crucial factors in the attribution of personality itself.

---

[118] *Ibid.*, p.179; 16 *ILR*, p.322.

[119] *Ibid.*, p.185; 16 *ILR*, p.330.

[120] The Court took particular care to emphasise that possession of international personality was far from an ascription of statehood or recognition of equal rights and duties, *ibid.*

The attribution of international personality to an organisation endows it with a separate identity, distinct from its constituent elements. It may exercise rights in its own name and be subject to duties and obligations on its own account. However, one question that has arisen is whether states or organisations that combine to create a new organisation endowed with international personality will be at all liable for the debts or wrongs attributable to that organisation. The problems faced by the International Tin Council during 1985-6 raise exactly this question.[121]

The ITC, created in 1956, conducted its activities in accordance with successive international tin agreements, which aimed to regulate the tin market by virtue of export controls and the establishment of buffer stocks of tin financed by member-states. The Sixth International Tin Agreement of 1982 brought together 23 producer and consumer states and the EEC. In October 1985, the ITC announced that it had run out of funds and credit and the London Metal Exchange suspended trading in tin. The situation had arisen basically as a result of over-production of the metal and purchasing of tin by the ITC at prices above the market level.

Since the ITC member-states refused to guarantee the debts of the organisation and since proposals to create a successor organisation to the ITC collapsed, serious questions were posed as to legal liabilities. The ITC was a corporate entity enjoying a measure of legal immunity in the UK as a result of the International Tin Council (Immunities and Privileges) Order 1972. It had immunity from the jurisdiction of the courts except in cases of enforcement of an arbitral award. The ITC Headquarters Agreement provided that contracts entered into with a person or company resident in the UK were to contain an arbitration clause. It was also the case that where a specific agreement provided for a waiver of immunity by the organisation, the courts would have jurisdiction.[122] Accordingly, the immunity from suit of the ITC was by no means unlimited.

---

[121] See e.g. The Second Report from the Trade and Industry Committee, 1985-6, HC 305-I, 1986 and *The Times*, 13 March 1986, p.21 and *ibid.*, 14 March 1986, p.17. See also Wassermann, "Tin and Other Commodities in Crisis", 20 *Journal of World Trade Law*, 1986, p.232; E. Lauterpacht, *op. cit.* footnote 1, p.412; Cheyne, "The International Tin Council", 36 *ICLQ*, 1987, p.931; *ibid.*, 38 *ICLQ*, 1989, p.417 and *ibid.*, 39 *ICLQ*, 1990, p.945.

[122] See e.g. *Standard Chartered Bank* v. *ITC*, [1986] 3 All ER 257; 77 *ILR*, p.8.

A variety of actions were commenced by the creditors, of which the most important was the direct action. Here, a number of banks and brokers proceeded directly against the Department of Trade and Industry of the British Government and other members of the ITC on the argument that they were liable on contracts concluded by the ITC.[123] The issues were argued at length in the Court of Appeal and in the House of Lords.[124] The main submission[125] for present purposes was that the members of the ITC and the organisation were liable concurrently for the debts under both English and international law. It was argued that under international law members of an international organisation bear joint and several liability for its debts unless the constituent treaty expressly excludes such liability. Although there have been hints of such an approach earlier[126] and treaty practice has been far from consistent, Lord Templeman noted that "no plausible evidence was produced of the existence of such a rule of international law"[127] and this, it is believed, correctly represents the current state of international law.[128]

The approach of the court, in effect, was founded upon the perception that without the relevant Order in Council the ITC had

---

[123] See also the attempt to have the ITC wound up under Part XXI of the Companies Act 1985, *Re International Tin Council*, [1988] 3 ALL ER 257, 361; 80 *ILR*, p.181, and the attempt to appoint a receiver by way of equitable execution over the assets of the ITC following an arbitration award against the ITC (converted into a judgment) which it was argued would enable contributions or an indemnity to be claimed from the members, *Maclaine Watson* v. *International Tin Council*, [1988] 3 WLR 1169; 80 *ILR*, p.191.

[124] *Maclaine Watson* v. *Department of Trade and Industry*, [1988] 3 WLR 1033 (Court of Appeal); 80 *ILR*, p.49 and [1989] 3 All ER 523 (House of Lords); 81 *ILR*, p.671.

[125] One submission was that the relevant International Tin Council (Immunities and Privileges) Order 1972 did not incorporate the ITC under English law but conferred upon it the capacities of a body corporate and thus the ITC did not have legal personality. This was rejected by the House of Lords, [1989] 3 All ER 523, 527-28 and 548-49; 81 *ILR*, pp.677, 703. Another submission was that the ITC was only authorised to enter into contracts as an agent for the members under the terms of the Sixth International Tin Agreement 1982. This was also dismissed, on the basis that the terms of the Order clearly authorised the ITC to enter into contracts as a principal, *ibid.*, 530 and 556-57; 81 *ILR*, pp.681, 715.

[126] See e.g. *Westland Helicopters* v. *Arab Organisation for Industrialisation*, 23 *ILM*, 1984, 1071; 80 *ILR*, p.600. See Adam, *Les Organismes Internationaux Specialisés*, 1965, vol.1, pp.129-30 and Seidl-Hohenveldern, *op. cit.*, pp.119-20.

[127] [1989] 3 All ER 523, 529; 81 *ILR*, p.680. This was the view adopted by a majority of the Court of Appeal, see Ralph Gibson LJ, [1988] 3 WLR 1033, 1149 and Kerr LJ, *ibid.*, 1088-89 (but cf. Nourse LJ, *ibid.*, 1129-31); 80 *ILR*, pp.49, 170; 101-2; 147-49.

[128] See as regards the related issues of incorporation of treaties in English law and non-justiciability *supra*, p.128.

no legal existence in the law of the UK. An international organisation had legal personality in the sphere of international law and it did not thereby automatically acquire legal personality within domestic legal systems. For that, at least in the case of the UK, specific legislation was required.

Some of the issues raised in the tin litigation re-appeared in *Arab Monetary Fund* v. *Hashim (No. 3)*.[129] This concerned the attempt by the AMF to bring an action before the English courts to recover funds allegedly embezzled. The relevant constituent treaty of 1976 between a number of Arab states gave the AMF "independent juridical personality" and a decree was adopted in Abu Dhabi giving the organisation independent legal status and the capacity to sue and be sued in United Arab Emirates law. There was, however, no Order in Council under the International Organisations Act 1968 giving the AMF legal personality within the UK. The Court of Appeal took the view that the decision of the House of Lords in *Maclaine Watson*[130] meant that the ordinary conflict of laws rules allowing recognition of an entity created under foreign law could not be applied to an organisation established under international law since this would apparently circumvent the principle arguably established in the tin cases that an international organisation with legal personality created outside the jurisdiction would not have capacity to sue in England without a relevant authorising Order in Council.[131]

The House of Lords, however, by a majority of four to one, expressed the opinion that the majority of the Court of Appeal had felt inhibited by observations made in the tin cases and that the latter cases had not affected the principles that the recognition of a foreign state was a matter for the Crown and that if a foreign sate is recognised by the Crown, the courts of the UK would recognise the corporate bodies created by that state.[132]

---

[129] [1990] 1 All ER 685 (Chancery Division), 2 All ER 769 (Court of Appeal); 83 *ILR*, pp.246, 255 and *The Times*, 22 February 1991 (House of Lords).

[130] *Supra*, footnote 124.

[131] [1990] All ER 769, 775 (Donaldson MR); 83 *ILR*, pp.259-61 and 778 (Nourse LJ); 83 *ILR*, p.264.

[132] *Supra*, footnote 129.

The Powers of International Organisations [133]

Once it is clear that an organisation has international personality, it may validly exercise certain rights and duties. The precise extent of its legal powers will depend upon the constituent document creating the organisation and the relevant circumstances. The type of legal subject with the widest recognised range of powers is, of course, the state, but there are certain powers common to most international institutions.

Apart from the grant in the appropriate constituent instrument of express powers, an international organisation may be deemed to possess a range of implied powers. [134] Such powers are those deemed necessary for fulfilment of its functions. As the International Court noted in the *Reparation* case: [135]

> [u]nder international law the organisation must be deemed to have those powers which, though not expressly provided in the charter, are conferred upon it by necessary implication as being essential to the performance of its duties.

In the *Effect of Awards of Compensation Made by the UN Administrative Tribunal* case, [136] the International Court held that the General Assembly could validly establish an administrative tribunal in the absence of an express power since the capacity to do this arose "by necessary intendment" out of the Charter. Although the functional test is determinative, it operates within the framework of those powers expressly conferred by the constitution of the organisation. [137]

---

[133] See e.g. Schneider, *Treaty-Making Power of International Organisations*, 1959 and Parry "The Treaty-Making Power of the UN", 26 *BYIL*, 1949, p.147. See also *supra*, Chapter 15, p.561, footnote 2, with regard to the Convention on the Law of Treaties between States and International Organisations. See also *Yearbook of the ILC*, 1982, vol.II, Part 2, p.9 *et seq.*

[134] See e.g. E. Lauterpacht, *op. cit.* footnote 1, pp.423-74; Rama-Montaldo, "Legal Personality and Implied Powers of International Organisations", 44 *BYIL*, 1970, p.111; Campbell, "The Limits of Powers of International Organisations", 32 *ICLQ*, 1983, p.523; Skubiszewski, "Implied Powers of International Organisations" in *International Law at a Time of Perplexity* (ed. Dinstein), 1989, p.855 and Kirgis, *op. cit.*, pp.97-109, 504-55.

[135] ICJ Reports, 1949, pp.174, 182; 16 *ILR*, pp.318, 326.

[136] ICJ Reports, 1954, pp.47, 56-57; 21 *ILR*, pp.310, 317-18.

[137] But compare the approach adopted by the International Court in the *Reparation* case, see footnote 135 above, with that adopted by Judge Hackworth in his dissenting opinion in that case, *ibid.*, pp.196-98; 16 *ILR*, pp.318, 328. See also Fitzmaurice, "The Law and Procedure of the International Court of Justice: International Organisations and Tribunals", 29 *BYIL*, 1952, p.1.

Thus any attempt to infer a power that was inconsistent with an express power would fail, although there is clearly an area of ambiguity here.[138]

Closely connected with this issue is the question of the interpretative method to be adopted with regard to constituent instruments.[139] The problems arise because of the relationship between the member-states and the organisation and between the different organs of the organisation itself, in addition to the usual difficulties associated with the interpretation of international agreements.[140] There is also the special nature of the constituent instruments as forming not only multilateral agreements but also constitutional documents subject to constant practice, and thus interpretation, both of the institution itself and of member-states and others in relation to it. This of necessity argues for a more flexible or purpose-orientated method of interpretation. However, one must be careful not to take this too far and ascribe extensive powers to international organisations upon ambiguous grounds of, for example, effectiveness, since this will inevitably lead to conflict with member-states and third parties. There is a careful balance to be maintained between inferring necessary powers for the fulfilment of the stated purposes of the organisation and assimilating organisations to states in their possession of wide powers in the context of international personality.

Of great importance is the question of the capacity of international organisations to conclude international treaties. In essence this will depend upon the constituent instrument, since the existence of legal personality is on its own probably insufficient to ground the competence to enter into international agreements.[141] Article 6 of

---

[138] See also e.g. The *International Status of South West Africa* case, ICJ Reports, 1950, pp.128, 136-38; 17 *ILR*, pp.47, 53; the *Expenses* case, ICJ Reports, 1962, pp.151, 167-68; 34 *ILR*, pp.281, 296 and the *Namibia* case, ICJ Reports, 1971, pp.16, 47-49; 49 *ILR*, pp.2, 37.

[139] See e.g. Lauterpacht, *The Development of International Law by the International Court*, 1958, pp.267-81 and E. Lauterpacht, *op. cit.* footnote 1, p.414 *et seq.*

[140] See generally *supra*, Chapter 17.

[141] See e.g. Schneider, *Treaty-Making Power of International Organisations*, 1959; Hungdah Chiu, *The Capacity of International Organisations to Conclude Treaties and the Special Legal Aspects of the Treaties So Concluded*, 1966; *Agreements of International Organisations and the Vienna Convention on the Law of Treaties* (ed. Zemanek), 1971: Nascimento e Silva, "The 1986 Vienna Convention and the Treaty-Making Power of International Organisations", 29 *German Yearbook of International Law*, 1986, p.68 and "The 1969 and 1986 Conventions on the Law of Treaties: A Comparison" in *International Law at a Time of Perplexity* (ed. Dinstein), 1989, p.461.

the Vienna Convention on the Law of Treaties between States and International Organisations 1986 provides that "[t]he capacity of an international organisation to conclude treaties is governed by the rules of that organisation". This is a wider formulation than reliance solely upon the constituent instrument and permits recourse to issues of implied powers, interpretation and subsequent practice. It was noted in the commentary of the International Law Commission that the phrase "the rules of the organisation" meant in addition to the constituent instruments, relevant decisions and resolutions and the established practice of the organisation.[142]

Privileges and Immunities [143]

In order to carry out their functions more effectively, states and their representatives benefit from a variety of privileges and immunities. Similarly, international organisations will be entitled to the grant of privileges and immunities for their assets, properties and representatives. These will arise by agreement between the organisation and the host state (or states) and not by virtue of customary international law, and their nature and extent will depend very much upon the organisation involved and its needs. The functional emphasis of such international immunities is very apparent, far more than is the case with diplomatic immunities.

As far as the UN itself is concerned, article 105 of the Charter notes that:

the Organisation shall enjoy in the territory of each of its members such privileges and immunities as are necessary for the fulfilment of its purposes

and that:

the representatives of the members of the United Nations and officials of the Organisation shall similarly enjoy such privileges and immunities

---

[142] *Yearbook of the ILC*, 1982, vol.II, part 2, p.41.

[143] See e.g. Bowett, *op. cit.*, pp.345-62; Jenks, *International Immunities*, 1961; Michaels, *International Privileges and Immunities*, 1971; the International Organisation Acts of 1968 and 1981; Kirgis, *op. cit.*, p.34 *et seq.*; *Yearbook of the ILC*, 1967, vol.II, p.154 *et seq.*; *DUSPIL*, 1978, p.90 *et seq.* and *ibid.*, 1979, p.189 *et seq.* and Morgenstern, *op. cit.*, pp.5-10.

as are necessary for the independent exercise of their functions in connection with the Organisation.

These general provisions have been supplemented by the General Convention on the Privileges and Immunities of the United Nations 1946,[144] and by the Convention on Privileges and Immunities of the Specialised Agencies 1947.[145] These general conventions, building upon provisions in the relevant constituent instruments, have themselves been supplemented by bilateral agreements, particularly the growing number of headquarters and host agreements. The UN, for example, has concluded headquarters agreements with the United States for the UN Headquarters in New York and with Switzerland for the UN Office in Geneva in 1947.[146] The International Court noted in the *Applicability of the Obligation to Arbitrate* case,[147] which concerned US anti-terrorism legislation necessitating the closure of the PLO Observer Mission to the UN in New York, that the US was obliged to respect the obligation contained in section 21 of the UN Headquarters Agreement to enter into arbitration where a dispute had arisen concerning the interpretation and application of the Agreement. This was despite the US view that it was not certain a dispute had arisen, since the existence of an international dispute was a matter for objective determination.[148] The court emphasised in particular that the provisions of a treaty prevail over the domestic law of a state party to that treaty.[149]

---

[144] This provides *inter alia* for immunity of UN property and assets from legal process unless waived; inviolability of premises and archives; certain immunities from taxes and customs duties and certain immunities with respect to the representatives of member-states at the UN and for specified UN officials. Such immunities are subject to waiver. In *Shearson Lehman* v. *Maclaine Watson* (No. 2), [1988] 1 WLR 16; 77 *ILR*, p.145 the House of Lords held that the inviolability of official documents could be lost as a result of communication to third parties.

[145] See also the Agreement on the Privileges and Immunities of the International Atomic Energy Agency, 1959.

[146] See also the agreements with Austria, 1979, regarding the UN Vienna Centre; with Japan, 1976, regarding the UN University and with Kenya, 1975, regarding the UN Environment Programme. Note also the various Status of Forces Agreements concluded by the UN with, for example, Egypt in 1957, the Congo in 1961 and Cyprus in 1964, dealing with matters such as the legal status, facilities, privileges and immunities of the UN peace-keeping forces.

[147] ICJ Reports, 1988, p.12; 82 *ILR*, p.225.

[148] *Ibid.*, pp.27-30; 82 *ILR*, p.245.

[149] *Ibid.*, pp.33-34; 82 *ILR*, p.251.

It is clearly the functional approach rather than any representational perception that forms the theoretical basis for the recognition of privileges and immunities with respect to international organisations.

The International Court has recently delivered an Advisory Opinion[150] concerning the applicability of provisions in the General Convention to special rapporteurs appointed by the Sub-Commission on the Prevention of Discrimination and the Protection of Minorities. Article VI, section 22, of the Convention provides that experts performing missions for the United Nations are to be accorded such privileges and immunities as are necessary for the independent exercise of their functions during the periods of their missions. The International Court noted that such privileges and immunities could indeed be invoked against the state of nationality or of residence[151] and that special rapporteurs for the Sub-Commission were to be regarded as experts on missions within the meaning of section 22.[152] The privileges and immunities that would apply would be those that were necessary for the exercise of their functions, and in particular for the establishment of any contacts which may be useful for the preparation, the drafting and the presentation of their reports to the Sub-Commission.[153]

As far as other international organisations are concerned, the relevant agreements have to be consulted, since there are no generalised rules but rather particular treaties. The question of states' representation to international organisations is dealt with in the 1975 Vienna Convention on the Representation of States in their Relations with International Organisations of a Universal Character, which is closely modelled on the 1961 Vienna Convention on Diplomatic Relations, although it has been criticised by a number of host states.[154]

---

[150] The *Applicability of Article VI, Section 22, of the Convention on the Privileges and Immunities of the United Nations,* ICJ Reports, 1989, p.177. This opinion was requested by the Economic and Social Council, its first request for an Advisory Opinion under article 96(2) of the UN Charter.

[151] In the absence of a reservation by the state concerned, *ibid.,* pp.195-96.

[152] This applied even though the rapporteur concerned was not, or was no longer, a member of the Sub-Commission, since such a person is entrusted by the Sub-Commission with a research mission, *ibid.,* pp.196-97.

[153] *Ibid.*

[154] *Supra,* Chapter 12, p.479. See also *DUSPIL,* 1975, p.38 *et seq.*

Responsibility [155]

Responsibility of the organisations for wrongful acts is a necessary consequence of international personality and the resulting capacity to bring claims.[156] This area of international responsibility is not, however, well developed and much will depend upon the particular circumstances. The absence of authoritative organs capable of determining conclusively whether the organisation in question has committed an illegal act is a severe problem with regard to the clear attribution of responsibility, although the Court of Justice of the European Communities does constitute an exception here.

The issue of responsibility has arisen in the context of UN peace-keeping operations and liability for the activities of the members of such forces. In such circumstances, the UN has accepted responsibility and offered compensation for wrongful acts.[157]

[155] See e.g. Bowett, *op. cit.,* pp.362-65. See also Garcia Amador, "State Responsibility: Some New Problems", 94 *HR,* p.410; Eagleton, "International Organisation and the Law of Responsibility", 76 *HR,* p.319 and Perez Gonzalez, "Les organisations Internationales et le Droit de la Responsibilité", 92 *Revue Générale de Droit International Public,* 1988, p.63. See also *supra,* Chapter 13.

[156] See the *Reparation* case, ICJ Reports, 1949, p.174; 16 *ILR,* p.318.

[157] See M v. *Organisation des Nations Unies et l'État Belge,* 45 *ILR,* p.446.

INDEX